SCRIPTING JESUS

JESUS

The Gospels in Rewrite

———⌘———

L. Michael White

HarperOne

An Imprint of HarperCollinsPublishers

HarperOne

All biblical quotations are taken from the New Revised Standard Version
unless otherwise noted.

All translations of other ancient literature are those of the
author unless otherwise noted.

All charts, diagrams, and maps were designed by the author.
Photographs are the author's unless otherwise noted.

SCRIPTING JESUS: *The Gospels in Rewrite.* Copyright © 2010 by L. Michael White.
All rights reserved. Printed in the United States of America. No part of this book
may be used or reproduced in any manner whatsoever without written permission except
in the case of brief quotations embodied in critical articles and reviews. For information
address HarperCollins Publishers, 10 East 53rd Street, New York, NY 10022.

HarperCollins books may be purchased for educational, business, or sales
promotional use. For information please write: Special Markets Department,
HarperCollins Publishers, 10 East 53rd Street, New York, NY 10022.

HarperCollins website: http://www.harpercollins.com

HarperCollins®, 📖®, and HarperOne™ are trademarks of HarperCollins Publishers

FIRST HARPERCOLLINS PAPERBACK EDITION PUBLISHED IN 2011

Library of Congress Cataloging-in-Publication Data
White, L. Michael.
Scripting Jesus : the Gospels in rewrite. / L. Michael White.
p. cm.
ISBN 978–0–06–122880–3
1. Bible. N.T. Gospels—Criticism, interpretation, etc. I. Title.
BS2555.52.W46 2010
226'.066—dc22
2009041654

11 12 13 14 15 RRD (H) 10 9 8 7 6 5 4 3 2 1

For Becki

amore eternamente, tutt'il completo

For Ron and Kay

sempre amici carissimi

CONTENTS

PREFACE

"Jesus is under fire." So says a recent book by evangelical apologists in reaction to most, if not all, forms of New Testament scholarship. At stake, they argue, are the grounds of all Christian belief, the "truth" of the Gospels. So it seems that the battle lines are clear and unmistakable: those who believe versus those who do not. Those who question historical points in the Christian Gospels or propose a different vision of what Jesus said on a particular occasion or meant on a given topic are summarily lumped together in a vast and godless army, the enemies of Christ and Christianity.

But the picture is not nearly so simple; the lines of demarcation, not nearly so neat. In fact, the "attack" comes from other angles now, as the discovery of several "new" Gospels has fueled a variety of conspiracy theories concerning the lost "truth" about Jesus that has been systematically suppressed by institutional Christianity. Inevitably, then come the sensationalist claims from works of both pseudohistory and outright fiction. One purports that Jesus was really married to Mary Magdalene, and they had children. Another recounts the private conversation between Jesus and Judas and purports to give new insights about what really led to Jesus's betrayal and crucifixion. Only partially, if at all, are these claims based on actual ancient sources, and even then scholarly study of these documents is still ongoing. Nonetheless, the fact that these new Gospels come from the early centuries of Christianity makes it hard for many people to distinguish the claims being made. It also seems natural to lump these more outlandish claims together with mainstream New Testament scholarship. After all, the discovery and decipherment of these Gospels is a legitimate field of scholarly study, and much of the scholarship starts by reading closely and raising questions.

In part the problem is media hype; inevitably these new discoveries are presented as undercutting the tradition contained in the canonical Gospels. But serious New Testament scholars and historians do not accept these so-called revelations as historical fact any more than unquestioning believers do. Yet the theories get a wide following. At least three of these new texts have been popular in recent discussions: the *Gospel of Thomas,* the *Gospel of Mary* (*Magdalene*), and the *Gospel of Judas.* Significantly all three purport to come from close followers of Jesus known from the canonical Gospels. So where did they come from, and what is their role? And do they really offer us a new "history" or an alternative portrait of Jesus?

The answer is no, and real scholarship does not read these works in quite the way suggested by either sensationalists or conservative apologists. Thus, although it is important to recognize and discuss the place of these "other" Gospels, they do not generally provide serious historical information. In fact, as we shall see later in this book, they are more like later theological explorations, each written from a distinct—some would say "heretical"—perspective. In that sense, one may call them pious fabrications from early Christianity. Studying them helps us understand the nature of storytelling as theological enterprise during the early Christian period and refocus some of the questions regarding the canonical Gospels. The fact that they were considered heretical by other early Christians and eventually excluded in the formation of the New Testament is also a part of the story that must be understood. But they were not the only pious fabrications about Jesus in antiquity; there were others that have not been treated so critically. The problem, then, is how to find our way through the maze of opinions and questions concerning Jesus and the Gospels when the ancient sources differ so dramatically.

Questioning the Gospels

Questions about Jesus and the Gospels get raised in one way or another in most forms of Christianity. They have done so for centuries, not to mention serving as the basis for key differences of belief and interpretation between denominations. Nor is it merely a case of intra-Christian dialogue and debate. Jewish tradition has a stake in the discussion too, not only because the historical Jesus himself was Jewish, but also because of the atrocities that have been perpetrated based on misreading and misinterpreting these same scriptures. One cannot respond simplistically to the Holocaust by saying, "Sorry," without also addressing the scriptural and theological assumptions—mostly mainstream Christian and ostensibly based on the New Testament—that fueled it. Ignoring such factors is tantamount to saying instead, "Sorry it went that far, *but*..." If Jesus seems to be "under fire" these days because of atrocities perpetrated in his name or suspicions that certain forms of Christianity are not willing to probe for the truth, then it is not Jesus who is to blame, or the Gospels, but rather those who have misused them.

Even so, the majority of New Testament scholars are, in fact, believing Christians. Some are more conservative, to be sure; others, more liberal. More to the point, most of the questions that scholars pose and the methods they have developed for dealing with them come from the efforts of serious believers who have discovered various difficulties through a close reading of the Gospels themselves. That's right: *through reading the Gospels closely*.

Now, all sorts of questions are raised by people, ordinary folk and scholars alike, when reading the Gospels. Why is it that the Beatitudes differ so markedly in the Gospels of Matthew and Luke? Why is it that the birth of Jesus is set in a manger (literally a "feeding trough") in Luke, but a house in Matthew? How is it that the Gospels (and other parts of the New Testament) suggest that Jesus had brothers and sisters? And there are many more.

- Why does the Gospel of John place the "cleansing of the Temple" at the beginning of Jesus's public career (2:12–22), while the Synoptics (Matthew, Mark, and Luke) place it in the last week of Jesus's life (Mark 11:15–19; Matt 21:10–17; Luke 19:45–48)?

- Why is it that the Gospels of Mark and Matthew describe an anointing of Jesus *after* the triumphal entry into Jerusalem at nearby Bethany (Mark 14:3–9; Matt 26:6–13), while the Gospel of Luke places the same event much earlier in his public career, when Jesus was still in the Galilee (7:36–50). All three of these Gospels set the story in the home of a certain Simon, described by Mark and Matthew as a leper, but by Luke as a Pharisee. In all three, the anointing is performed by an unnamed woman; only Luke calls her a "sinner." The Gospel of John has a similar episode (12:1–8) that occurs just six days before Jesus's death and at Bethany; however, it comes *before* his triumphal entry and at the house of his friends Mary, Martha, and Lazarus. Significantly, it is this Mary from Bethany who performs the anointing. (Later traditions identify her erroneously with Mary Magdalene, that is, Mary of Magdala, in the Galilee).

One can see rather quickly that such episodes in the Gospels are essentially the same, and yet they are told in different ways and occur at different points in the story of Jesus's career.

It is not my goal at this juncture to address any of these individual cases as such. Most of them will come up again in later parts of this book. For now, my first point is simply this: raising questions about the Gospels or the historical Jesus is *not* in and of itself an act of disbelief. Nor is it an *attack* on Jesus or on Christianity in general. Quite the contrary. To raise such questions is a direct result of taking the Gospels seriously and trying to study them sincerely and honestly from a historical perspective. It is one of the few ways that people from different religious and cultural backgrounds—Catholics and Protestants, Christians and Jews, conservatives and liberals, and many others—can ever come together to discuss these issues in frank and constructive ways.

The Gospel Authors as Storytellers

The main point is this: as we have seen, such questions usually arise when the story of Jesus in one of the Gospels seems to disagree with that in others. As a result, we begin to recognize that each of the Gospel authors has woven such episodes into the story in distinctive ways, changing not only the running order of the narrative, but also certain cause-and-effect relationships within each story.

For example, in the Synoptics—especially the Gospel of Mark—it is the cleansing of the Temple that serves as the immediate cause of Jesus's arrest and execution. In the Gospel of John there is no connection between these events, as the cleansing is two full years earlier. In contrast, for the Gospel of John the immediate cause of Jesus's execution is the raising of Lazarus (11:38–44), an event never discussed in the Synoptics. Thus, the story works differently in each of these versions because of basic changes in the narrative.

This is what we mean by referring to the Gospel authors as "storytellers." In my previous book, entitled *From Jesus to Christianity: How Four Generations of Visionaries and Storytellers Created the New Testament and Christian Faith,*[1] I called the process of the creation of the New Testament, and especially the Gospels, the "story of the storytellers." In other words, the story (or history) of the composition and formation of each individual Gospel can be understood by the way successive generations of these early followers of Jesus who created them attempted to tell the story about him. Each new phase of telling about Jesus reflects, not only their beliefs about him, but also new situations and conditions in the development of Christianity itself. In telling the story, they also told about themselves. In that earlier work, therefore, I focused on the historical developments and the social, cultural, and religious changes that were occurring in each successive generation. For a more general historical outline and the relative position of all the New Testament writings, readers are referred to this earlier book.

In the present study I focus instead on the stories about Jesus in the Gospels as literary and dramatic productions. Although historical and social factors inevitably come up in our discussions of the individual Gospels, our main goal will be to examine the way the stories were constructed and reconstructed and how this process conveys different images of Jesus. Within this we focus on the storytelling techniques and patterns of the Gospel writers as they reshape and recombine both old and new episodes, teachings, and characters that circulate about the central figure, Jesus. Storytelling was essentially an oral performance medium in the ancient world, even when those stories were eventually written down. Thus, any particular performance might highlight different elements in the light of the circumstances of the author and the audience.

It is similar to what happens with each new performance of a play, whether by Shakespeare or Neil Simon. Different actors, different settings, different periods of history—all of them create a different climate. Even when a script gets written down, the performances and the emphases can change or be reinterpreted. The need to "translate"—from Elizabethan English to modern diction, from script for theater to a screenplay, or from a screenplay to live, onstage performance—can change the internal dynamics of the story. In the final analysis, all of the Gospels should be understood as "faithful" retellings of the story of Jesus in a performative context. They are "performative" in that they were meant to be *heard* (not "read") in the living context of worshiping groups. In that sense, the authors were playing to an audience. They are "faithful" in that they were trying to instill and reaffirm the faith of those audiences, albeit sometimes in new and different ways. Even so, the stories are just that—*stories*—and not "histories" in any modern sense. We shall return to this point in the Prologue. So, the purpose of this book is to examine carefully all these Gospels, both those in the New Testament and those "others" that were excluded, from this performative storytelling perspective.

This book is thus a drama in three acts. Act I, "Casting Characters," begins by focusing on how the titles and attributes usually associated with Jesus would have created an image or character in light of the background to Jesus's own times. Each one has its own symbolic value and cultural background, and the Gospel writers employ them in different combinations. One of the keys that emerges is that certain of these titles, such as "messiah," are clearly more Jewish in background. They stand in marked contrast to some of the later, more Greek ideas usually associated with the portrayal of Jesus, including both "savior" and "divine man." Hence it appears that certain features of the image were developed through cultural changes over time and that the Gospels reflect changes in the culture, audience, and social setting as the Jesus movement spread to far-flung reaches of the Roman Empire.

Then in Act II, "Crafting Scenes," we examine some of the basic features or components of the Jesus tradition as found in the canonical Gospels. Here we shall examine more closely the way that key episodes or building blocks of the Gospel tradition, such as miracles, parables, the Passion, and the birth, were transmitted and retold from Gospel to Gospel. We shall also see how the various Gospel authors shaped them literarily within a narrative framework. In this way, it is possible to identify both the core components of the earliest oral traditions and how these components began to evolve and be organized into larger narrative traditions. The narrative habits of each Gospel author begin to show through and, with them, certain tendencies in their treatment of the oral tradition about Jesus. The Gospels emerge as literary products of shaping through theological reflection by the early Christians themselves.

In Act III, "Staging Gospels," we examine how each of the Gospels was composed and shaped literarily in order to understand the nature of the distinctive images presented through the story. Here we shift emphasis from the components, or "building blocks," to the "total package" as reflected in each individual Gospel. How does each Gospel author assemble an array of existing source components about Jesus (as discussed in Act II), and how are they configured through literary means into a cohesive story? In this context, it is noteworthy that the earlier Gospels come from a decidedly Jewish context in their presentation of Jesus. This fact is all the more important given the traditionally anti-Semitic and anti-Jewish uses to which these materials were later put. So too, such social tensions and contexts must be taken into account in the portrayal of Jesus. In general, however, the shape of the first Gospels (including Mark and Matthew) show the development of Jesus traditions *within* a Jewish matrix. The later Gospels of the New Testament (Luke and John) represent changing images of Jesus through the reshaping of their narratives in the context of Greco-Roman culture.

Finally, we explore how these trajectories eventuated in the production of legendary or apocryphal Gospels as well as other types of mythological traditions about Jesus (such as docetism or Gnosticism). We will define and discuss each of these key terms later. The ongoing process of composing these later Gospels may be seen in light of the development of the canonical Gospels, and how the two groups relate to one another. The book ends with a discussion of how the Gospels fit into the ancient forms of biography and history, again with a focus on the character of the storytelling involved.

Finally, a word about reading. This book is an effort to read and hear the Gospels closely and seriously. Most people, even those who believe in the New Testament Gospels very fervently, have never read all of them all the way through. Fewer still have actually tried to compare them side by side, as New Testament scholars and most ministers are trained to do. So I beg your indulgence in this book, because I will be asking you to read along carefully with me. You might even find yourself reading passages out loud just to hear how they sound as dramatic readings. Further, I invite you to have a Bible at hand, at least some of the time. Actually, any one will do. Sometimes it helps to compare different translations. I will usually be using the New Revised Standard Version (NRSV), unless otherwise noted. In some cases we will be placing comparable passages from different Gospels side by side. This is sometimes called a "harmony" or "synopsis" of the Gospels. There are several good published versions of this type of scholarly tool in English, and I encourage their use too. The main point is this: if we are going to learn to read the Gospels carefully, we must start first and always with the text itself.

Scripting Jesus

The Storyteller's Art

To be, or not to be, that is the question,
Whether tis nobler in the minde to suffer
The slings and arrows of outragious
    fortune,

And by opposing, end them, to die to sleep
No more, and by sleep to say we end
The hart-ake, and the thousand natural
    shocks
That flesh is heire to; tis a consummation
Deuoutly to be wisht to die to sleepe,
To sleepe, perchance to dreame, I there's
    the rub

Hamlet, Q2, 1710–19

To be, or not to be, that is the Question:
Whether 'tis Nobler in the minde to suffer
The Slings and Arrows of outragious
    Fortune,
Or to take Armes against a Sea of troubles,
And by opposing end them: to dye, to sleepe
No more; and by a sleepe, to say we end
The Heart-ake, and the thousand Naturall
    shockes
That Flesh is heyre too? 'Tis a consummation
Devoutly to be wish'd. To dye to sleepe,
To sleepe, perchance to Dreame; I, there's
    the rub

Hamlet, F1, 1710–19

To be, or not to be, I there's the point,
To Die, to sleepe, is that all? I all:
No, to sleepe, to dreame, I mary there it goes,
For in that dreame of death, when wee awake,
And home before an everlasting Iudge,
From whence no passenger euer retur'nd,
The undiscovered country, at whose sight
The happy smile, and the accursed damn'd.
But for this, the joyfull hope of this,
Whol'd beare the scornes and flattery of the world
Scorned by the right rich, the rich cursed of the poore?

Hamlet, Q1, 1710–25 (836–46)

Hamlet, Act 3, Scene 1, lines 55–64. This passage is one of the most famous so-liloquies in all of Shakespeare. But if you happened to go to the theater when the third script was performed, you might have been disappointed. Well, at least if you had seen it before. If not, who knows. And yet this third version, from the *First Quarto* (Q1), is the earliest of the three primary editions, dating to 1603. Shakespeare probably wrote *Hamlet* in 1600 or 1601. The *Second Quarto* (Q2) dates from 1604/5; its version looks more familiar, but is missing a famous line: "Or to take arms against a sea of troubles." It also sounds different, as it seems to deliver the famous lines "To die, to sleep . . ." as a morose statement rather than a haunting question. The other manuscript is the 1623 *First Folio* edition (F1), and it is the version of this soliloquy that most of us recognize.[1] But it was only published after Shakespeare's death in 1616.

The question is this: Which way did Shakespeare script the scene? Or which way was it originally performed? These quartos were the small-format printed texts of individual plays, the ones used by the actors for the actual stage produc-tions. The folio edition came later, after Shakespeare's death, as a large-format collection of his plays. Some Shakespeare scholars think the *First Quarto* preserves the most original version of at least parts of the play.[2]

None of these three early editions, however, preserves all of the lines or scenes usually included in the "canonical" text. First published in the early 1700s, the now standard text of *Hamlet* is a combination of the Q2 and F1 editions.[3] In other words, the text of this and many other Shakespearean plays as we now know them *never existed* in Shakespeare's own lifetime, nor for a century after his death. Moreover, there are considerable differences between the earliest versions. In the case of *Hamlet* alone, there are some 230 lines and 17 sustained passages in Q2 that are absent in the F1 version, and some 70 lines in F1 that are absent from Q2. Many notable lines change from one to the next, and the Q2 edition has a final 35-line soliloquy that is absent from the others.[4] Q1, moreover, has some of the passages in positions different from what we normally expect. At the very least, these three early versions suggest that *Hamlet* was performed in different ways in those early days.

We might call this the quest for the "historical *Hamlet*." Better yet, the quest for the "authentic Shakespeare." As we shall see, it has many similarities to the histori-cal issues we encounter in the Gospels. But then Shakespeare is not "scripture," I suppose. That is, unless you are a Shakespeare scholar or a devout thespian. Still, it is not too difficult to imagine how these scripts evolved, even within Shakespeare's own creative lifetime. Even then it depended on actors and repeated performances for how things went and what was—or was not—remembered. One might guess that changes of inflection—from a morose statement to a haunting question—might come from successive performances as the actors tried new takes on the Bard's immortal words. Well, they weren't immortal yet, were they? Flat lines with no punctuation became cadenced and inflected by dramatic delivery. In the process, the character of Hamlet also changed. In the meantime, Will was still on his way to becoming the Bard, as the 1999 film *Shakespeare in Love* so charmingly reminds us.[5] Even more to the point, it reminds us that we must allow those storytellers and performers to create and *re-create* memorable lines and stories for us. "Aye, there's the rub."

In like manner, the Gospels may be scripture now, but first they were stories—stories scripted about Jesus, stories forged out of belief, but stories nonetheless. They too changed and evolved with successive retellings. Only now we have more than one playwright to contend with and more than one lifetime. As stories, the Gospels do not merely provide raw information about Jesus. Rather, they shape our understanding of Jesus by the way they present the events of his life, career, teaching, and death. Similar questions have long been asked. Which way were those lines in the garden originally delivered? Did Jesus weep in fear and despair in Gethsemane or go to his death with confident resolve? The accounts even within the Gospels differ markedly on this point and many others. Two of the Gospels (Mark and John) give no information about the birth of Jesus. The other two (Matthew and Luke) give glaringly different accounts of the birth.

Thus, the shape of each story—what it contains, what it leaves out, and how it is arranged—creates a different picture both of what happened and how Jesus is to be imagined. In that sense, all the Gospels, even the earliest, are efforts at dramatic re-creation. They shape and reshape basic stories or key episodes in order to make a point about the Jesus who is at the center of faith for each author and audience. When the audiences or the circumstances of writing change, so do the details, and so does the picture of Jesus that emerges from the finished product. That is the storyteller's art.

From the Gospels to Jesus

This is not just another book about the historical Jesus. There are plenty of those around—some serious, some sensational, and some just plain silly—and what a baffling spectrum they present. Jesus is an apocalyptic revolutionary, a Jewish prophet, or a Cynic social critic; he is even the founder of a secret society and royal dynasty that haunt European history to this day. How can they *all* be true? Well, to put it quite simply, they cannot.

For better or worse, it has long been recognized that the Jesus of history, a first-century Palestinian Jew who roamed the hills of Galilee and who was summarily executed by a Roman governor named Pontius Pilate, is not quite the same as the figure portrayed in the Gospels. How and why that is the case is in large measure what this book is about. Or to put it another way, one often repeated in the scholarly discussions, the "Jesus of history" is not quite the same as the "Christ of faith." The Gospels are not simply an account of the events of Jesus's life; they are also proclamations about Jesus through the lens of faith. In that sense, they are "faithful."

But the "Christ of faith," as typically used in scholarly discussion, refers more to the Christ of later Christian orthodoxy and includes numerous ideas about Jesus or his identity that never came up in the time of the New Testament or, for that matter, for several centuries thereafter. Many of these later theological issues get retrojected back into the Gospels, as in the question of whether Jesus had siblings or not. In other words, by attempting to find "scriptural" proof for a particular way of viewing Jesus theologically, these efforts substitute the Gospels for the historical Jesus. But as we have already said, the Gospels themselves are part of the problem that has to be addressed.

This is a book about how to go about the process of reading and studying the Gospels as the primary sources for investigating the historical Jesus. In the end, however, I shall not try to present a reconstruction of the historical Jesus. I will leave that for readers to pursue in the light of our investigations into the background, setting, and composition of the Gospel traditions.

All too often, scholars who write reconstructions of the historical Jesus neglect to tell their audience how they reached their conclusions, assuming that the questions, issues, and methods are well known. Such issues may be well known to New Testament scholars or historians of earliest Christianity and formative Judaism. But most people do not know how to go about dealing with the questions about differing accounts of particular miracles or sayings and similar issues. Far too often, people assume that they *know* the story of Jesus, but have never actually *read* the Gospels. This is where some of the traditional tendencies toward homogenization, that is, creating one seamless story of Jesus, can be most misleading. Fewer people still actually sit down and compare details of the Gospel accounts side by side. The result is bewildering at the least.

The difficulty lies in the nature of the Gospels themselves, especially those in the New Testament canon. Nowadays, other Gospels not contained in the New Testament, the so-called apocryphal Gospels, have also been enlisted into the discussion. The two best known of late are the *Gospel of Thomas* and the *Gospel of Mary,* but there are several others that are important too. They may have a bearing on how we understand the development of the earliest Gospel tradition, or they may offer other trajectories of understanding Jesus in early Christianity. Even their rediscovery has been a result of the intensive study focused on the Jesus tradition over the past two centuries. Yet their real value for understanding the historical Jesus versus aspects of early Christian development and debate will have to be weighed carefully. In any event, we shall need to examine them along the way.

The point is this: *each Gospel, whether canonical or noncanonical, presents a rather different image of Jesus.* Some we will find traditional and familiar; others, unusual or even bizarre. What is surprising, however, is that no single Gospel incorporates all the elements that we tend to assume are part of the orthodox picture. Recognizing this fact and its implications for the approach to any study of the Gospels and of Jesus himself is more necessary than ever.

The so-called quest for the historical Jesus has been after this question for well over two centuries.[6] The problem is that we have no sources of information about Jesus from his own lifetime. Our earliest, and by far most important, sources are, indeed, the New Testament Gospels themselves; however, they come at least forty years or more after the death of Jesus. In fact, the latest of the traditional Gospels, that attributed to the apostle John, cannot be any earlier than sixty-five years after the death of Jesus; some scholars even place the span closer to ninety years. In other words, there is a significant gap between the time of Jesus and the actual writing of the Gospels.

When and how the Gospels were actually written will, of course, become an important issue in our later discussion. For now, we can summarize the matter as follows by locating them in relation to the best estimates for Jesus himself. By all accounts in the Gospels (Matt 2:1, 19–22; Luke 1:5), Jesus was born during the last years of the reign of Herod the Great, client-king of Judea. We know from the Jewish historian Josephus that Herod died in March of 4 BCE, only five days after having executed one of his own adult sons, a presumed heir.[7] This means that Jesus was born sometime before 4 BCE, but precisely how much before cannot be known with any certainty. For sake of convenience, most scholars simply place it roughly between 7 and 4 BCE, but it could be earlier still.[8]

As for his death, we have a similar problem. All the sources place his death under the governorship of the Roman procurator (or prefect) Pontius Pilate, who ruled the province of Judea from 26 to 36 CE, but precisely when during this span is hard to pin down. Traditionally, it has been common to say he died in either 30 or 33 CE, but the latter date is very doubtful. Since the Gospel of Luke says that Jesus was "about thirty years old" when he began his public ministry (3:23), that could place his death as early as 26 CE and still be during Pilate's reign. A date between 26 and 29, and certainly no later than 30 CE, seems most likely.

In virtually all New Testament scholarship, the earliest of the written Gospels is that attributed to Mark, the protégé of the disciple Peter. Ancient Christian testimonials clearly state that it was not an eyewitness account on the part of Mark.[9] Some traditional accounts sought to place the writing of Mark very early; Eusebius actually argued for a date before 40 CE, but with both Peter and Mark already in Rome. Such an early date is quite impossible, since Paul's own contemporaneous letters indicate quite clearly that Peter had not left Jerusalem for Antioch prior to the late 40s, after the so-called Jerusalem conference.[10] In turn, references in the Gospel of Mark, to be discussed later, show that Mark was written sometime near the end of the first Jewish revolt against Rome. That means sometime between roughly 70 and 75 CE, the dates used by the vast majority of New Testament scholars. The remaining New Testament Gospels come in the following decades: Matthew, ca. 80–90; Luke, ca. 90–100; John, ca. 95–120.

Although there is considerable debate by scholars about the dates within each of these ranges, the Gospels on the whole fall at least one to two generations after the death of Jesus.[11]

. . . and Back to the Gospels

The gap between the death of Jesus and the composition of the Gospels means either that the Gospels were made up out of whole cloth or that they were based on older traditions and stories that had circulated only in oral form until they began to be written down many years later. Frankly, no one today would argue that they were merely made up. Various factors support the view that a vibrant oral tradition about Jesus had already begun to circulate within a decade or so after his death. It is also possible that there were earlier written sources that are now lost. Though not likely whole "Gospels" as we think of them, they too represent stages in the development of the oral tradition from which the later Gospel writers could draw. Yet the nature and extent of this oral tradition (to be discussed in greater detail in Act II below) ensured preservation of early memories, but within fluid and malleable modes of transmission. The writers of the Gospels who used these oral traditions were also capable of combining and reshaping them to fit their own needs, or more precisely their own perceptions regarding what their audiences needed in order to believe in Jesus. They were promoting their faith by telling and retelling the story of Jesus in new and varied situations.

Even when the Gospel writers can be seen to be using earlier written Gospels, such as where Matthew or Luke is clearly following Mark, we find that they often make changes in the stories in order to fit their particular goals. Sometimes these changes are subtle; sometimes, dramatic, even to the point of reordering whole phases of Jesus's ministry or key occasions of his teaching. Rather than seeing such changes as somehow distorting or betraying the historical record, however, we inevitably come back to the goals and needs of that particular author addressing a particular audience at a particular time and place. When we analyze the Gospels closely, therefore, we can often begin to see, not only the "how" in these changes, but also the "why." That is, by virtue of patterns or themes in one Gospel's presentation over against another's, we can detect some of the issues or concerns that motivated that particular author. Ultimately this is what I mean by the term "shaping"; it refers to both the literary activities and the underlying themes and motivations of the individual Gospel authors as they told and retold these stories.

To our modern ears, this description of the process of Gospel composition does not sound much like how we would write history. Indeed, it is not. That is one of the key difficulties surrounding our perceptions of the Gospels. They are not histories or biographies in any modern sense. They are not governed by the same rules of source and evidence; nor are they concerned with an objective style of reporting that looks for neutral presentation of event sequences or cause-and-effect outcomes. The Gospels are pieces of religious literature that seek to promote a particular set of beliefs in Jesus. In that sense they are closer to what we call advertisement or propaganda, even though these terms have a far more negative connotation in our culture. For the ancient world, however, writing propagandistic "lives" of famous figures was much more the norm, and we shall examine some of these in Chapter 3 and the Epilogue.

One of these, the *Life of Moses* written by the Jewish philosopher Philo of Alexandria, a contemporary of Jesus, is worth mentioning here. It shows what kind of "biographical" presentation was possible for Jews living in the Roman world. Philo was clearly trying to promote a greater appreciation for Jews and Judaism among his Greek and Roman fellow citizens; he did so by portraying Moses as the most perfect prophet, priest, and king. Yet Moses himself was neither priest nor king. So Philo's "Life" set out to shape a portrait of Moses according to Greek ideals, while at the same time remaining "true"—at least in spirit, though not in fact—to the biblical story of Moses.

As a result of examining the process of storytelling within the Gospels, one also comes to realize that, in many ways, we never get back to Jesus himself. This is a point well made in *The Real Jesus* by Luke Timothy Johnson:

> *In sum, the character of the Gospels as narratives of faith, the differences among them, the principles of arrangement within them, and the kinds of material they contain all make extraordinarily difficult the historical analysis even within the three-year period within which Jesus's public ministry [might have] occurred.*[12]

In other words, the Gospels often tell us more about the faith of individual authors and congregations than they do about Jesus himself. The Jesus of history remains ever elusive, obscured by the passage of time as well as later efforts to portray him.

Yet this is an important result precisely because it requires us to be more careful in the use of our historical tools and more cautious about the expected results. At the same time, it shows us how and what the earliest followers of Jesus believed. Strikingly, we get different images of Jesus from Gospel to Gospel: in Mark he is the misunderstood messiah; in Matthew, the teacher of Torah; in Luke, a philosopher and martyr similar in some ways to Socrates; and in John, a heavenly man come to reveal the mysteries of God. These changing images reflect the changing situation of the Christian movement, and none of these images is in itself complete. That too is part of the story.

The "Car Wreck" Fallacy

As noted from the outset, recognition of historical questions about the Gospels is not really new. In fact, there is a rather famous, or perhaps infamous, way that people have tried to address this problem. It goes something like this. When confronted with the fact that the different Gospels sometimes tell what Jesus did or said in rather different ways, the solution is: "Well, it's just like four people on a street corner who happen to see a car wreck. Now, we all know what happens when you try to get people to tell what they've just seen, especially in startling or stressful circumstances. They all give different versions based on their particular angle of vision or how they reacted emotionally in the heat of the moment. So you get different pieces of the story from the different accounts. That's how the Gospels work too."

We may call it the "car wreck" gambit, or better yet, the "car wreck" fallacy. The underlying premise, of course, is that all of the accounts actually come from eyewitnesses of some sort. After all, they all saw *something*. Right? Even if it seems at first that their accounts do not agree, one can usually figure out what really happened by lining them up together and analyzing who saw what.

This leads us to a second basic premise of the argument: namely, that one can cross-examine the sources, very much like witnesses in a court trial, and show that they were really seeing the same thing but in different ways. The savvy sleuth or clever lawyer can always figure out how the pieces of the puzzle actually fit together to make the true story come out. It is the sort of dramatic trial scene that Perry Mason and Matlock made famous on TV, but rarely happens in real life. Nonetheless, I suspect that such a romantic ideal still lurks in the minds of many people. To be sure, courtroom metaphors and legal notions of evidence continue to be used *and misused* in current efforts to defend the Gospels.

But is that really what's going on in the case of the Gospels? For one thing, two of the four canonical Gospels, those attributed to Mark and Luke, do not claim to be by disciples of Jesus. According to tradition Mark got his information from Peter and Luke from Paul, but neither ever saw Jesus during his own lifetime. Even if Peter represents a potentially significant "eyewitness" source, he never wrote anything down. His "testimony" cannot be examined except insofar as Mark is said (by hearsay) to have preserved it. So the Gospel of Mark is at least one step removed, and perhaps more. In the case of Luke, we are at least two steps removed, since his principal informant, Paul, never saw Jesus either. Paul clearly admits that he got his information from others (1 Cor 15:3–7, to be discussed in Chapter 6). It is the case that hearsay testimony is sometimes admitted into evidence in courtroom proceedings, but only where other evidence establishes to the satisfaction of the court the trustworthiness of the hearsay.[13] Even when based on sincere belief in its own truthfulness, hearsay testimony presents problems and potential defects; however, double or triple hearsay can hardly be admitted into evidence.[14]

The prologue to the Gospel of Luke even alludes to its own layers of tradition when it talks about others who had compiled narratives of the life of Jesus and the beginnings of the movement "just as they were handed on to us by those who from the beginning were eyewitnesses and servants of the word" (1:2). Then it goes on to say: "I too decided, after investigating everything carefully for a long time, to write an orderly account" (1:3). Notice that there are actually several steps or layers supposed in this report: the eyewitnesses who handed down the tradition, presumably in oral form, then others—several, in fact—who wrote earlier narratives, and finally the author of the Gospel of Luke, who, after further reflection and research, is trying afresh to piece the story together. The term "handed on" or "delivered" (Gk. *paredosan*) in Luke 2:2 to describe the process is one of the standard technical terms for the passing on of oral tradition. We shall see it again later in Chapter 6, when we examine in greater detail the earliest accounts of the oral traditions about Jesus.

The composition and source traditions lying behind the Gospel of Mark were even discussed in early Christianity. The fourth-century church historian Eusebius records the words of the bishop Papias, writing ca. 130 CE. It is noteworthy that even here several layers of tradition are at work. Papias is reported to have said:

> And [John] the Elder used to say this: "Mark became Peter's interpreter and wrote accurately such as he remembered, not indeed, in order, of the things said or done by the Lord." For he had not heard the Lord, nor had he followed him, but later on, as I said, followed Peter, who used to give teaching as necessity demanded but not making, as it were, an arrangement of the Lord's oracles, so that Mark did not err at all in thus writing down single points as he remembered them. For to one thing he gave attention: to leave out nothing of what he had heard and to make no false statements in them.[15]

It is clear that these second-century Christian commentators are vouching for the "accuracy" of Mark's recording of what he heard from Peter, but there is nonetheless a very defensive tone. The emphasis is on the fact that Mark's record was not "in order" and was not "an arrangement"; yet Mark "did not err at all" in doing it this way. The term "arrangement" here is *syntaxis* in Greek and connotes either the appropriate composition of a narrative or the proper grammar of a sentence, as in the modern English derivative "syntax." In other words, these early Christian writers were already having to explain why the Gospel of Mark looked so different in order and details from the other Gospels.

It must also be remembered that among the vast majority of New Testament scholars the Gospel of Mark is considered to be the first of the written Gospels. Here the "car wreck" fallacy runs head-on into another roadblock. Not only are these *not* just "four guys on a street corner" who give their accounts, but it seems also now that the later-written Gospels in the New Testament, especially Matthew and Luke, actually used the Markan text as a source in their compositions. In other words, the Gospel of Mark is one of the "earlier narratives" mentioned in the prologue to Luke. But this makes the differences between Mark and the others, as noted by Papias, all the more striking. It is much like the problem of the "authentic" text of *Hamlet* discussed at the beginning of this prologue. In the case of the Gospels, this issue is now known as the Synoptic Problem.

The Synoptic Problem and
the Composition of the Gospels

It has long been recognized that the Gospel of John is rather different in outline and content from the first three Gospels, Matthew, Mark, and Luke. These three have greater similarities in outline and materials and have often been called the "Synoptics," because they may be "seen together," or side by side, and are very similar. Even so, there are some noticeable differences. We find, for example, that key events vary as we move from one Gospel to the next even among the Synoptics. Both Matthew and Luke contain a "sermon" with beatitudes (Matt 5:1–7:29; Luke 6:17–49), but they occur in different settings. Matthew's version is over three times longer (a total of 111 verses) than Luke's (a scant 32 verses), while Mark does not contain this episode at all. Then when we look at the narratives that surround these different sequences, we discover that the cause-and-effect relationships for the course of Jesus's career—particularly as they lead up to his death—vary significantly from Gospel to Gospel.

The Synoptic Problem asks the question this way: *How can it be that these three Gospels have so much material in common, even verbatim in some instances, but still have episodes moved around or new and distinctive material added?* To answer this question, we must conclude that there were some common sources lying behind the written Gospels, but that the various Gospel authors compiled their accounts with some flexibility by stitching these source materials together in different ways. There are then two key components to this process: first, the oral circulation of stories about Jesus prior to any written accounts; second, the artistry of the individual Gospel authors, each one combining and reworking older source traditions in new ways (see Appendix B).

By far the most widely accepted theory of synoptic relationships is called the "Two-Source Hypothesis." It assumes that Mark was the first of the New Testament Gospels to be written down, based on a variety of oral traditions that had been transmitted separately. Thus, Mark, written in Greek, was the first "Gospel" in the sense of an attempt to write a narrative "Life" of Jesus. Sometime later, the authors of Matthew and Luke used Mark as a source, but did so independently of one another. This fact helps account for the fact that Matthew and Luke have much of the same material, but it is repositioned within their respective narratives.

It also seems that the Matthean and Lukan authors had access to other sources, oral traditions not used by Mark. Some of these were probably unique, but others could be common to both Matthew and Luke. One of these in particular seems to be a large group of some 250 verses of Jesus's teachings. It includes such famous passages as the Beatitudes, the Lord's Prayer, and the parable of the lost sheep, none of which are found in Mark. These days, it is usually called "Q" (from German

Quelle, meaning "source") or sometimes the "Synoptic Sayings Source," and it is usually dated by scholars between 50 and 70 CE. The Two-Source Hypothesis thus proposes that Mark and Q were the two main sources used by Matthew and Luke. Both Matthew and Luke used Mark as the basic outline, but each one modified it by reordering episodes and inserting Q materials in distinctive ways. Thus, each of the three synoptic Gospels is a distinctive construction of both oral and written traditions. Each one is an expression of faith, while trying to preserve the memory and message of Jesus in new and changing circumstances.

In the final analysis all the current scholarly theories regarding the composition of the Synoptics, even the more conservative, assume four major characteristics to the development of the Gospel tradition:

1. There was a vibrant and influential oral tradition about what Jesus said and did and that the Passion narrative was its earliest core (see Chapter 6).

2. These independent oral traditions were circulated within and among individual Christian communities, where they were given context and meaning in the worship life of the community.

3. Transmission of these source traditions, whether in oral or written form, to other communities allowed for retelling and reconfiguration to fit new needs and situations.

4. The order, themes, and content of the individual Gospels reflect the local context of their respective authors and communities as an expression of their faith in Jesus in the light of their cultural background and social experience.

In other words, the Gospels as we now have them are not direct or neutral accounts of Jesus. Nor do they claim to be. They do not operate under modern conceptions of writing history, nor were there "four guys on a street corner." Instead, they are early attempts to weave the various materials, whether oral or written, into a narrative about Jesus for a particular audience in a particular context.

Each of the Gospels thus tells the story in a different way. That means more than merely rearranging certain episodes or adding new sayings here and there. The different ordering and the narrative shaping that occur in each Gospel give new shades of meaning to the teachings, interpret causes and effects in the death of Jesus, and explore themes about faith, discipleship, and community. Changing the order and wording of such episodes usually reflects a distinctive understanding of Jesus's life, teachings, and death on the part of a Gospel author, who was far more interested in the theological significance carried by the story than in historical accuracy. Dramatic scenes, pathos and irony, and even humorous interludes reflect a dynamic interaction between storyteller and audience. There were already

BOX 1.1

Jesus's Last Days: Comparing the Gospels

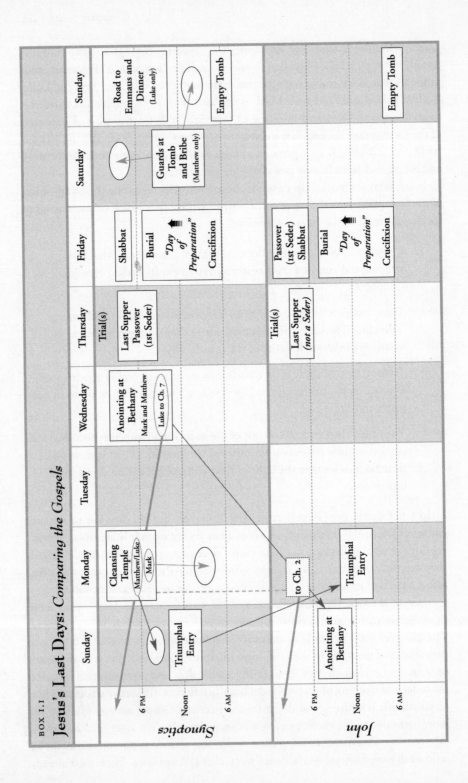

stock characters and patterns of storytelling from which they could draw, in new and changing combinations. Each Gospel thus becomes a different "script" for how the part of Jesus is to be acted and how his life is to be played out, all the while focused on exploring the changing textures of faith.

Scripting Jesus's Last Days

To see this process of storytelling at work, we may look closely at one case in point from the Gospel of John. By all traditional accounts, the Gospel of John was the latest to be written among those in the New Testament. Yet its story of Jesus is noticeably and dramatically different in many ways. Consequently, questions concerning its composition and its relationship to the three Synoptic Gospels have long been raised. We shall return to these broader compositional questions in Chapter 14. For now, however, let us focus on the way it presents a key moment in the story, specifically the last days of Jesus's life and the day on which he died.

Box 1.1 provides a graphic representation of the last week of Jesus's life comparing the three Synoptics on the top row with the Gospel of John on the bottom. The days of the week are labeled according to their traditional days in the Christian calendar, but they correspond with the basic sequence in the Gospels: the triumphal entry occurs at the beginning of the week (now Palm Sunday),[16] the Last Supper occurs on Thursday evening, and the crucifixion and burial occur during the day on Friday. It must be remembered too that in Jewish tradition, the new day begins at sundown (or roughly 6 p.m.), so that the Sabbath (Heb. *Shabbat*) commences on Friday evening. All the Gospels are explicit that Jesus was crucified during the day on Friday, prior to sundown, as they use the traditional designation "day of Preparation [for *Shabbat*]"[17] as a temporal reference (so Mark 15:42; Matt 27:62; Luke 23:54; John 19:31, 42). Within this basic sequence there are several notable differences not only between John and the Synoptics, but also among the Synoptics.

The key sequence for our present analysis revolves around the Last Supper and the Passover as articulated in the Gospel of John. Here again there is a subtle but important change from the sequence of events as it occurs in the Synoptics. In the Synoptics, the Last Supper is explicitly stated to occur on the evening of "the first day of Unleavened Bread, when the Passover lamb is sacrificed" (Mark 14:12; Matt 26:17; Luke 22:7).[18] In the Synoptics, then, the Last Supper is explicitly the first *seder* (or meal) of Passover, at which time the Passover lamb is eaten in commemoration of the Exodus from Egypt (Exod 12:1–20). In other words, the Thursday evening of the Last Supper was the 14th of Nisan according to the Jewish calendar, when the Passover was to be observed (Lev 23:5). As a result, the crucifixion, which occurred the following day (15 Nisan), was during the Passover celebration, but after the first *seder*. That it was during the day on Friday is made clear by consistent references to the "day of Preparation" in all three accounts (Mark 15:42; Luke 23:54; Matt 27:62).

In sharp contrast, the Gospel of John is equally explicit in stating that the Last Supper took place "*before* the festival of the Passover" (13:1), while the day of Jesus's trial and crucifixion is that leading up to Passover (19:14). It is also said to be the "day of Preparation [for Shabbat]" (19:42), that is, Friday evening, when the Sabbath is welcomed with a meal of consecration (*kiddus*). The Gospel of John goes so far as to clarify that it was considered a special or "great" Sabbath (19:31), precisely because the Passover meal (or first *seder*) coincided with the Sabbath meal (*kiddus*). John 18:28 confirms this point by adding the detail that when Jesus was delivered to Pilate early that morning, those who escorted him "did not enter the praetorium, so as to avoid ritual defilement and to be able to eat the Passover." Thus, in the Gospel of John, Friday was the 14th of Nisan; both Shabbat and Passover would begin that evening at sundown.

Needless to say, these are rather striking differences, and they have long been noted.[19] To put it in sharper terms, using the Jewish calendar the Synoptics would have 14 Nisan on Thursday, while John would have it on Friday. This change of the day of Passover would also have the effect of shifting all the events by at least one full year in overall chronology. Such differences have led to innumerable debates and recalculations of the precise year in which Jesus would have died, based on whether the Passover fell on Thursday or Friday.[20] In other words, these traditional debates worry about who was correct, John or the Synoptics. But efforts to resolve the dilemma by positing a different calendar (Qumran vs. Jerusalem; Samaritan vs. Judean; Roman vs. Jewish) have been unpersuasive.[21] Prominent modern New Testament scholars finally disagree over whether the Johannine or the synoptic "dating" of the Passover relative to the Last Supper and crucifixion ought to be taken as the more historical.[22]

"Lamb of God"

Where does this leave us in evaluating the Gospel accounts? Perhaps the problem is assuming that the authors were making different "historical" claims at all. Instead, we may observe that there are several ways in which the Johannine author has reworked the Passion narrative for dramatic effect by adding vignettes that nowhere appear in the Synoptics. These include the request of the Jews to remove or rephrase the inscription (19:19–22), the reference to the seamless tunic of Jesus (19:23–24), the scene of Jesus's mother and the beloved disciple at the cross (19:25–27), and the request of the Jews to break the legs and the piercing of Jesus's side (19:31–37). These added vignettes give the overall scene of the crucifixion a much more symmetrical structure and chiastic (or *abc-cba*) flow.[23] One vignette in particular helps us understand the dramatic scene being created by the Johannine author.

The key passage is John 19:31–37:

Since it was the day of Preparation, the Jews did not want the bodies left on the cross during the sabbath, especially because that sabbath was a day of great solemnity. So they asked Pilate to have the legs of the crucified men broken and the bodies removed. Then the soldiers came and broke the legs of the first and of the other who had been crucified with him. But when they came to Jesus and saw that he was already dead, they did not break his legs. Instead, one of the soldiers pierced his side with a spear, and at once blood and water came out. (He who saw this has testified so that you also may believe. His testimony is true, and he knows that he tells the truth.) These things occurred so that the scripture might be fulfilled, "None of his bones shall be broken." And again another passage of scripture says, "They will look on the one whom they have pierced."

This added Johannine vignette makes explicit what the overall reshaping of the narrative flow gives implicitly. In the Gospel of John, Jesus is depicted as hanging on the cross while the Passover lambs are being slaughtered in "preparation" for the meal that very same evening. This dramatic retelling has the effect of placing Jesus just outside the walls of Jerusalem and, as it were, just on the other side of the hill from the Temple itself, while inside the priests would have been ritually slaughtering lambs for Passover. Now the internal time sequence is made to coincide with an "event" that in turn harkens to a fulfillment of prophecy—namely, that Jesus's bones should not be broken. Yet a quick look at the "prophecy" here cited shows the inevitable connection, for it is an allusion (couched as quotation) from the regulations for preparing the Passover lamb: "You shall not break any of *its* bones" (Exod 12:46).[24] Anyone familiar with the Exodus/Passover tradition would be expected to recognize the verse and its implications. The author has thus created a scene evoking the very symbolism that is central to the overall reworking of the temporal sequence.

What, finally, does this reworking suggest? We may start by assuming with recent New Testament scholarship that the Gospel of John shows direct awareness of the Synoptics, especially Mark and/or Luke. In other words, we may also assume that the audience of the Gospel of John knew the synoptic Passion narrative in which the Last Supper was the Passover meal. Rather than an *alternative history*, however, the Gospel of John has given a creative retelling of the story that redeploys the Passover symbolism in a new way.

Symbolically at least, Jesus himself now becomes the Passover lamb. As if that were not clear enough in the Johannine retelling of the Passion narrative, the theme is made explicit at the beginning of the Gospel, when Jesus walks onstage for the first time. At the moment when he comes to John the Baptist to be baptized, John sees him and says: "Behold, the *lamb of God* who takes away the sins of the world" (1:31). This vignette likewise has a unique Johannine literary shape; this pregnant statement of John occurs in none of the other Gospels. Thus, the "lamb of God" symbolism has been "narrativized" into the story itself. That is, it has been systematically woven into both the narrative and thematic structures of the Gospel of John and brackets the entire narrative.

In the final analysis, then, we need not be concerned with whether the Johannine version is more correct at the level of "history." It is not a claim about *history* at all, but about the theological significance of the death of Jesus as understood within the Johannine community. Nor is it necessary—or even *possible*—to force the Johannine chronology to fit that of the Synoptics. To do so would destroy the entire effect of the Johannine story. In other words, unless the audience allows the Johannine author to change the story in these significant ways, the all-important Johannine message regarding Jesus's death—and the image of Jesus as Lamb of God—cannot come through.

Neither is it the case that the Johannine shift constitutes a wildly new theological idea. We have other, earlier allusions to Passover symbolism in 1 Corinthians 5:7 ("For our paschal lamb, Christ, has been sacrificed"), but with no reference to a historical event. The Johannine story has simply "narrativized" this long-standing theological interpretation by turning it into a dramatic retelling of the events surrounding the crucifixion of Jesus.

We may argue, therefore, that the author of the Gospel of John has intentionally changed the narrative flow of the story in order to achieve this symbolic or metaphorical effect. The audience, for its part, has been asked to suspend historical judgment for a moment and enter the fictive world being created by the author's new narrative. That it should agree to do so is what every audience is ultimately asked to do when hearing (or reading) this kind of highly symbolic narrative. The "truth" of the author's account lies not in the events themselves—much less in claims about history—but in the message that is being created. In that sense too it is a *faith-full* retelling, even though both author and audience know very well that the other accounts give a different picture of the events. *That is the storyteller's art.*

ACT I

Casting Characters

CHAPTER ONE

Acting the Part

Messiah

Zacchaeus was a wee little man;
a wee little man was he.
He climbed up in a sycamore tree,
for the Lord he wanted to see.

So goes a favorite children's song about a rather curious Gospel character. The Gospel of Luke is alone in telling the story of Zacchaeus, a rich tax collector who was too short to see over the crowds that lined the way as Jesus came to the town of Jericho (19:1–10). In many ways, Zacchaeus is a kind of stock character, in part because of his height. The scene is meant to be charming and somewhat humorous. Of course, the real point is that Zacchaeus is a tax collector, and this story is meant to exemplify a complaint heard frequently in the Gospels, that Jesus consorts with "tax collectors and sinners." Yet this story does not occur elsewhere, and it would seem that the Lukan author has "narrativized" this theme by creating a new vignette, as it revolves around the issue of greed and care for the poor. In fact, the author of the Gospel of Luke has quite a number of these characters who show up either as people Jesus encounters during his ministry or as figures within parables. A far less admirable "rich man" character—quite the opposite of Zacchaeus—also shows up in several Lukan vignettes (12:13–21; 16:19–31), while proper use of one's wealth to help others is described as a virtue (16:1–13). As we shall see later, some of these stories have standard counterparts in Greco-Roman literature and there too frequently provide moralizing examples. That a large number of them occur exclusively in the Gospel of Luke may say something significant about key themes in Lukan storytelling, to which we shall return later.

Stock Characters and Dramatic Scenes

The point for now is simply this: character development is an important feature of storytelling within the Gospels, and the literature of the day had a number of well-known character types. In Jewish tradition, creation of a stock character might derive from an older story in the Hebrew scriptures. In the Septuagint, the forlorn Tobit is reminiscent of Job, while the heroic Judith is based on Jael (Judg 4:17–22). The pro-Hasmonean history known as 1 Maccabees has Mattathias, the father of Judas the Maccabee, cast explicitly after the model of the ultrazealous Phinehas (Num 25:6–13).

In both Greek and Roman theater, especially comedy, there was a whole array of recognizable stock characters. The plays of Plautus (205–184 BCE), with titles such as *Miles Gloriosus* ("The Braggart Soldier") and *Pseudolus* ("The Liar Slave"), are filled with them. The movie *A Funny Thing Happened on the Way to the Forum*[1] is a musical send-up of these standard Roman scenes, set very much as a modern morality play. Interestingly, some of these same character types show up also in later Greek and Roman novels as well as in philosophical treatises and religious tracts. Nor was it only the incidental characters who were scripted this way. Classic characters such as a figure with a tragic flaw (Oedipus), a wandering hero (Odysseus), or a gluttonous tyrant (Sardanapalas) could even be used as cryptic criticisms of megalomaniacal Roman emperors.

As storytellers, the Gospel authors each spoke to specific groups of believers in whom they were trying to instill and enrich faith. Yet neither the authors nor their audiences lived in a vacuum. Rather, they lived in the rich and complex cultural mix of the Roman Empire, one of the most pluralistic environments in the ancient world. At its greatest extent, it stretched from the Persian Gulf to Spain and Britain and from northern Germany to the Sahara Desert. The administrative machinery of Roman rule, not to mention the army, spread throughout all these conquered lands, bringing Roman ideas and cultural tastes with it. Even before Rome, something similar had happened on a slightly smaller scale in the eastern Mediterranean thanks to the exploits of Alexander the Great (356–323 BCE). One important result was that Greek had become the common medium of communication and would remain so throughout the Roman period at least in the East.

The political stability of Roman rule—called the *Pax Romana* ("Roman peace")—also meant that people from all over the empire could move about with relative ease. There were Jewish enclaves in virtually all parts of the Roman world, but usually in larger cities. Like Rome itself, these cities thus became cosmopolitan mixes with many immigrant groups jostling together. They were not much different from London, New York, or Hong Kong today. Wherever people went, they carried aspects of their native culture with them—language, traditions, and religion. Hence, the vibrant social mix of Roman cities invited the interplay of these different cultures, even though Rome encouraged its subject peoples to become more "Roman" in thought and values. Cultural imperialism cuts both ways.

What this means for the Gospel authors is that they could—in fact, *had to*— address the cultural background of their respective audiences. A storyteller must speak in terms, symbols, and metaphors the audience can understand. Nor does it matter whether one is merely reflecting the views of others or attempting to change minds. The medium must be intelligible. If anything, the rhetoric of persuasion is even more dependent on knowing where your audience is coming from and using their own background to get your message across.

We can see this in Roman political propaganda when the emperor Augustus (27 BCE–14 CE) was portrayed on coins and other media of public expression in the guise of Jupiter or Poseidon.[2] Later emperors, such as Hadrian (117–38 CE) and Caracalla (197–217 CE), were portrayed as Hercules (see Box 1.2). Such expedient equations had the effect of solidifying Roman power while simultaneously co-opting older Hellenistic cultural symbols. The result was what we call the Roman imperial cult, and we shall return to it in Chapter 4. Such depictions might be communicated visually through art, but they can also be presented through verbal images that evoke the traits, personality, or exploits of a cultural icon, such as Alexander the Great or Aeneas.[3]

Something similar occurs today when a novelist creates a character using some recognizable features, such as Superman, James Bond, or the ubiquitous western hero. The intent might be serious and dramatic (like Gary Cooper in *High Noon* or John Wayne in *The Searchers*) or satirical and comic (like Mel Brooks's *Blazing Saddles* or Mike Myers's *Austin Powers*). Likewise, each new telling or performance of a traditional story will inevitably convey different perceptions of the key characters—their thoughts, motivations, and actions—and different interpretations of key events. Think of how different Hollywood westerns have depicted the famous (or infamous) event of the "gunfight at the OK Corral" and how they reflect changing American values and attitudes toward violence and gritty reality.[4]

Or consider what happens when a basic story is translated from one cultural setting to another, such as when Akira Kurosawa's *Seven Samurai* was remade into a Hollywood western, *The Magnificent Seven*.[5] Along with these cultural icons, other stock character types also come to mind; they serve as a palette of cultural images in popular media. Others still have become problematic symbols because they embody racial, ethnic, or gender stereotypes, and our cultural values have since changed. Knowing one's audience also means knowing the symbolic value of each image.

In the Gospels (written between 70 and 120 CE) something similar happens when the storyteller elects to use one or another standard image or cultural icon as a way of depicting Jesus. We have already examined one of these in the dramatic creation of the "Lamb of God" symbolism in the Gospel of John. Retelling the story results in a new narrative construction as well as new theological symbols by which the events of Jesus's life and death are interpreted. Within the Gospels, however, the more common images are Messiah, Son of God, and Savior. Each of these key titles is used of Jesus in the Gospels, but in differing combinations

BOX 1.2

Playing the Part

The emperor Caracalla (211–217 CE), depicted as Hercules. His dress, recalling the Twelve Labors or Contests, is typical of the iconography of Hercules in later art and legend. He wears the skin of the Nemean lion and carries a club in one hand; in the other hand he holds the apples of the Hesperides, symbols of immortality. Rome, Capitoline Museum.

and to differing effects. Although these images may sound familiar to us today because they are preserved in later Christian usage, they must be understood in their original historical and cultural milieu in antiquity. As we shall see in the following chapters, each of these terms has a specific cultural background and symbolic resonance.

Nor are these titles simply synonyms for one another, at least not in their original usage. With them come several related titles or images that may seem less familiar— Son of Man, Sophia's child, sage, Logos, miracle worker, divine man. They too show up prominently in the Gospels or, to be more precise, in *a* Gospel. For here too, as we shall see, the image of Jesus changes from Gospel to Gospel by virtue of the use of these standard character types and motifs. Hence, in order to catch what our ancient authors are trying to tell us through the medium of the story, we must first be able to decode the characters as they put them onstage. In the remainder of Act I, then, we shall examine some of the key titles of Jesus as reflections of character development in the light of their diverse cultural backgrounds. We begin with the oldest and in many ways most important—Messiah.

Messiah

The Gospel of Mark opens with a description of John the Baptist (1:2–8) followed immediately by the entry of Jesus onstage (1:9–11):

> *In those days Jesus came from Nazareth of Galilee and was baptized by John in the Jordan. And just as he was coming up out of the water, he saw the heavens torn apart and the Spirit descending like a dove on him. And a voice came from heaven, "You are my Son, the Beloved; with you I am well pleased."*

The scene is terse but dramatic, as Jesus's baptism ends with a heavenly announcement: "You are my Son." In the process, his character has been cast for the audience using the familiar wording of one of the royal psalms:

> *Why do the nations conspire,*
> *and the peoples plot in vain?*
> *The kings of the earth set themselves,*
> *and the rulers take counsel together,*
> *against the LORD and his anointed [messiah], saying,*
> *"Let us burst their bonds asunder,*
> *and cast their cords from us."*
>
> *He who sits in the heavens laughs;*
> *the LORD has them in derision.*
> *Then he will speak to them in his wrath,*
> *and terrify them in his fury, saying,*
> *"I have set my king on Zion, my holy hill."*

I will tell you the decree of the LORD:
He said to me, "You are my son;
today I have begotten you." (2:1–7)

No one hearing the Markan words in the ancient Jewish world could have mistaken the line or its intention.[6] The heavenly voice has affirmed Jesus as Messiah; the baptism and descent of the Spirit constitute his anointing following the messianic symbolism of the Davidic dynasty.

Between the time of David's heirs and that of Jesus, much had changed in Israel's political fortunes. The dynasty of David and an independent nation of Israel were distant memories still deeply mourned. With longing and expectation the idea of a future messiah lingered furtively in Jewish imagination—at least for some Jews. These changing fortunes and shifting expectations set the stage, not only for the climate of Jesus's own day, but also for the characterizations of him in the later Gospels.

There were also debates over meaning. Claims that Jesus was *the* messiah did not go uncontested, and the Gospels reflect these debates, such as when Jesus's messianic identity was tested by asking him to perform a miracle (Mark 8:11). The assumption behind this passage is that messiah and miracle worker were somehow equated. In Mark, at least, Jesus's reply is an emphatic denial: "Why does this generation ask for a sign? Truly I tell you, no sign will be given to this generation" (8:12). It seems that the Markan story wants to disconnect these two images. Hence much of the effort behind the storytelling centers on making Jesus "look" messianic in both bold and subtle ways. In the process it serves to reshape the definition of messiah, a way of saying, "He's not *that* kind of messiah." But why all the fuss? Was not the "character" or image of the Jewish messiah already an established idea? Didn't everyone agree on it? The answer on all points is no. Thus, the effort at casting Jesus as messiah was simultaneously harkening back to older Jewish ideas and expectations while also responding to contemporary Jewish debates, including those between the followers of Jesus and other Jews.

The Traditional Meaning of Messiah

The term *messiah* (Heb., "anointed") has a very specific background and derived meaning in formative Judaism. The noun form itself is from the common Hebrew verb *mashach,* meaning "to pour." When the Hebrew scriptures were translated into Greek (the Septuagint), the literal Greek equivalents were used for these terms: *christos* ("anointed") was taken from the standard verb *chriein* ("to pour"). In the period of the ancient Israelite monarchy this terminology came to have a specific connotation, since it was used for the coronation ritual of anointing the king. Thus, the noun form *ha-messhiach* ("the messiah") was used as a technical term to refer to the king himself, "the anointed one." The term could also be used to refer to sacred objects, such as the tabernacle or the altar (Num 7:1) or the high priest (Lev 4:3). It could also be used to designate the nation of Israel itself, in the sense of its sacred calling by God (Hab 3:13). Such wider uses are relatively rare; most often it referred to the king.

Even so, this range suggests that the underlying sense, even in the case of kingship, designated someone or something chosen, set aside, and marked for special service to God. The ritualized act of "anointing" the object or person was symbolic of this special, chosen status. Especially in Judah did this term take on an added symbolic significance related to the notion that the kings were the divinely appointed heirs of David's throne and the guardians of God's house—the Temple—on Zion.

This complex symbolism was important in the religious self-understanding of ancient Israel and was widely used in both formal and informal ways. The most formal usage is found in connection with the coronation of the Davidic kings in Judah, which had an annual renewal ceremony in conjunction with Rosh Hashanah (the fall New Year's festival). One of the ritual hymns of that ceremony is preserved in the Hebrew Bible as Psalm 2 (part of which is quoted above). In it one can see the various associated terms that were symbolic of kingship and nation. The king was viewed as God's adopted son, and the coronation ritual was the symbolic moment of his adoption signified by the act of anointing. Other passages, such as 2 Samuel 7:11–17 and Isaiah 9–11, confirm the basic connections to Israelite royal ideology. In particular, the anointing with oil as a ritual marker was taken to symbolize an outpouring of God's spirit on the king (Isa 11:2; 61:1) as both the moment and the sign of his adoption.

It was this symbolic weight placed on the image of the king as a sign of God's promise and election for the nation that also created the occasion for theological speculation. For example, the legendary warrant for the Davidic dynasty lay in the pronouncement to David by the prophet Nathan (recorded in 2 Sam 7:11–17). It too reflects the royal adoption language (7:14), but it also makes another promise to David: "Your house and your kingdom shall be made sure forever before me; your throne shall be established forever" (7:16). The royal psalms reiterate this promise (e.g., Ps 89:20–33). This expectation of a perpetual kingdom symbolized by the throne of David would prove troublesome when Judah faced repeated threats from internal corruption and external forces. Two centuries after David, it appeared the kingdom was near collapse.

That is when a prophetic figure by the name of Isaiah (ca. 740–685 BCE) stepped forward with a call for reform and with the claim that God would raise up a new and appropriate heir to fulfill the promises to David. It is from this context, near the end of the eighth century BCE, that we begin to get "messianic" predictions regarding a coming king. In their historical context, however, these prophecies of

Isaiah (especially found in Isa 7–11) pointed to an immediate successor to the current king of Judah in the form of his son Hezekiah. Indeed, the kingdom lasted for another century.

Eventually the throne of David fell to the Babylonians (586 BCE). So what about the promise of God? What about the prophecies of Isaiah? This is where reinterpretations regarding a future king began to appear. The notion of prophecy itself began to take on a more distant, future-looking sense. Thus, one will recognize the language of Psalm 2, Isaiah, and others reflected throughout the various traditions, including of course in the New Testament Gospels. Such prophetic material could be dismantled and reassembled in various configurations to give new meanings and points of reference. Through it all one finds that sense of destiny and election for the future of Israel.

So, for example, a later writer from the Babylonian period known as "Second Isaiah" saw the promises of God fulfilled in a foreign king, Cyrus the Persian, the one who allowed the exiles to return to Jerusalem.[7] Cyrus is clearly called the Lord's "messiah" (Isa 45:1), and he is viewed as a divine instrument in the return to Zion and to a new golden age (Isa 44:28). These images continued to be provocative in later periods, when new crises prompted new expectations of deliverance: "My deliverance . . . is not far off, and my salvation will not tarry; I will put salvation in Zion, for Israel my glory" (Isa 46:13). During the Maccabean revolt (167–164 BCE) the writer of Daniel took language from Jeremiah and Second Isaiah to refer to his own time. In particular Daniel 11:32–12:10 takes the "suffering servant" motif from Isaiah 52:13–53:12 and applies it to the eventual triumph of the faithful over Antiochus IV. In the Gospels the same motifs are applied to Jesus and his age.

The Rise of Apocalyptic

The mechanism behind such reinterpretation is bound up with the rise of the apocalyptic worldview. The terms "apocalyptic" and "apocalypse" come from a Greek root meaning "to uncover or reveal." From it, the noun form "apocalypse" comes to mean "a revelation." It came especially to be associated with visionary activity as part of a discrete literary genre, which we call apocalypse, and so came to signify a "divine revelation." In modern usage, however, the term has come to be transferred to some of the specific tenets of this notion of revealed knowledge, particularly expectations of the imminent end-times, but originally that was only a minor part of its meaning. For purposes of the present discussion, it will be best to think of "apocalyptic" first as an outlook or worldview and second as a literary genre (apocalypse) that embodies and conveys this worldview.

The apocalyptic worldview grew out of the new mood of crisis about the time that Judah came under Seleucid rule at the end of the second century BCE. Its first flourish then was directly related to the crisis of hellenization that produced the Maccabean revolt (167–164 BCE). Although Daniel is the best-known early reflection of this outlook, inasmuch as it was included in the biblical canon, it was neither the first nor the most influential. In part the origins of apocalyptic may be traceable to ongoing reinterpretation of earlier Israelite prophecy, in particular a later addition and reediting of Isaiah dating to the period after the Babylonian exile.[8]

The historical figure of Isaiah was active in Jerusalem ca. 740–685 BCE, during which time he served as court prophet to the kings Ahaz and his son, Hezekiah.[9] The prophetic oracles of Isaiah were collected and compiled by his disciples, but the written form of these texts dates to a time after his death. They are largely contained in Isaiah 6–35. At two later stages, the book of Isaiah was augmented with new oracles that came to be associated with his name, in large measure because they emulate themes and ideas drawn from the earlier Isaianic corpus. One of these additions, called "Second Isaiah" (chaps. 40–55) comes from the end of the Babylonian exile (ca. 539/8 BCE), when the first group of Judahites was allowed to return to Jerusalem. These oracles largely focus on the hope of that return and the expectation of reestablishing the Davidic dynasty after punishment and suffering. Hence a number of "royal" messianic themes recur in this section.

The latest addition to the work, called "Third Isaiah" (chaps. 1–5; 56–66), represents a more thorough reediting of the entire book and dates from a subsequent period of postexilic restoration in Jerusalem itself. It comes from the end of the sixth century BCE or after, perhaps as late as the time of Nehemiah and Ezra (late fifth century BCE). By this point in time efforts to reassert the David dynasty had largely failed, thereby raising new questions and expectations. It is particularly this latest addition and editing that begins to give the book of Isaiah its more future-looking tone, and it thereby sets the stage for further apocalyptic reinterpretation.[10] This expanded book of Isaiah would become a principal source for the numerous apocalyptic sects and interpretations at the time of Jesus.

The work that best characterizes the early development of apocalypticism and its abiding influence on Jewish thought is that known as *1 Enoch*. Although this work was never formally contained in the later Jewish or Christian canon, it was generally accorded scriptural status among many Jews and Christians. It was one of the most influential writings of the time and was later expanded in Christian versions.[11] The earliest portions were originally written sometime in the late third century BCE, and new sections were edited in over time.[12]

It is attributed to the ancient figure of Enoch from before the days of the flood, who "walked with God" and did not die (Gen 5:24). The core of the work (chaps. 1–36) is purportedly Enoch's own revelations from heaven in which he tells the real story of what happened before the flood by explaining how some rebellious angels challenged God and were cast from heaven. It reinterprets the brief story from Genesis 6:1–3 in the light of the Greek myth of the Titans, who rebelled against Zeus and were subsequently imprisoned in Tartarus (Hades) or, in another version, were blasted with Zeus's thunderbolt. Both elements come into the story of *1 Enoch*. In its Jewish and Christian reincarnation, it becomes the story of the "birth" of Satan, as seen in a statement attributed to Jesus in Luke 10:18. Frequent allusions to it range from the New Testament to John Milton's *Paradise Lost*.[13] *1 Enoch* is also important because it reflects a heavy dose of Hellenistic influence, even though it seeks to instill a Jewish piety in reaction against elements of Greek culture.

From this background the apocalyptic mood has been described as "a child of hope and despair: hope in the invincible power of God . . . despair of the present course of human history."[14] This sense of duality is one that pervades the tradition and is worked out through the message of apocalyptic thought and interpretation. The message of apocalyptic (i.e., what is "revealed" through the medium of the literature) varies from period to period and group to group. Yet there tend to be some typical categories.

History is seen as a linear progression defined in two great ages or epochs: the age of evil and the age of good. The present sense of despair comes from living in an evil age; the hope for good will come with divine deliverance. As in *1 Enoch*, the present evils suffered by the righteous are a direct result of those who oppose God's order and will, while any hope for deliverance comes from God's power to redeem the righteous at some future point. Hence between the two ages stands a break in time, variously referred to as "the day of the Lord" or "the last" (usually using the Gk. *eschaton*). It is from this notion of history that apocalyptic thought takes on its characteristic emphasis on "last things," "end-times," or what is regularly called *eschatology*. Thus, in Jewish apocalyptic thought there are numerous ways of understanding how this new age might come to reality. Usually the *eschaton* was thought of as an impending radical change in the present social and political order that would result in some sort of new "golden age" on earth. Although one often reads in the literature of this period phrases translated "end of time," a better rendering of the sense would be "end of the (present) age."[15]

Parallel with the dualism of ages is a notion of two powers and cosmic dualism. Indeed, the figure of Satan as an evil power in opposition to God is the invention of apocalyptic thought reinterpreting older ideas from the Hebrew scriptures. Among these was an old Near Eastern "combat myth" of creation in which the Israelite God triumphed over a sea serpent to form the earth and give it order.[16] In apocalyptic thought, the foe becomes a fallen angel who opposes God for sovereignty over the created world. Only later do the serpent/dragon and Satan become one (as in Rev 20:2).

The earliest known version of the fallen angel (called Semyaz or Azaz'el) and his conflict with God over rule of the world is that found in *1 Enoch* 1–36. Thus, apocalyptic pulls together elements from the biblical accounts of creation, the combat mythologies, and Greek thought to form a new dualistic cosmology in which the forces of God in heaven are at war with the evil power. God's final victory, as an eschatological triumph, recapitulates the primeval act of creation. Such cosmological speculation also produced the notion of a three-tiered universe (heaven, earth, hell), based in part on Greek ideas. Likewise, angels and demons proliferate and begin to take on the images that we see passed down through medieval art as the armies of good and evil. The earth is the battlefield for this cosmic struggle for supremacy, and humankind is conscripted into the fray on one side or the other. From here the cosmic dualism is correlated directly with ethical dualism—virtue and vice, good and evil, right and wrong.

Numerous dualistic symbols inculcate this outlook, including light/darkness and white/black. Such dualistic categories were apt for drawing boundaries between "us" and "them" and labeling the "other" as enemy. From here it is easy to understand how apocalyptic language and symbols were instrumental in the formation and legitimation of sectarian group consciousness.[17] In a moment we shall return to talk about one such sect, the Essenes.

New Messianic Expectations

One of the features of some, though by no means all, of the expressions of Jewish apocalyptic thought was that the "new age" as an eschatological break in time would be ushered in by some sort of figure who would deliver people from evil forces or oppression. Most of the earliest apocalyptic literature, such as *1 Enoch* or even Daniel, lacks a notion of this deliverer figure.[18] In other cases the deliverer is just a temporary agent of change, but has no clear personality or identity. In these lines of apocalyptic thought, it is really the divinely appointed destiny of Israel that is the central feature. In some cases there is no deliverer figure at all other than God.[19]

On the other hand, by the first century BCE and sporadically through the first century CE one finds apocalyptic writings that include a political deliverer who would restore the nation of Israel. Especially in those lines of interpretation that looked to the reestablishment of an idealized Davidic kingdom, this deliverer was expected to be a kingly figure. Now the deliverer becomes a new *messiah*. Other forms of apocalyptic expectation thought of the deliverer in different ways, such as a new prophetic or priestly figure. In some cases, the term *messiah* is applied to each of these. Often the precise nature of the messianic expectation was predicated on the particular crisis of the moment. One can often see a correlation between the characteristics of the messianic figure and the nature of the "enemy" to be opposed. Political domination from outside forces tended to call forth a warrior figure, like David, while internal religious dissension tended to raise the specter of a new religious leader, like Ezra or Aaron. Thus, different traits could be summoned by cobbling together various passages from scripture that seemed to speak to the present situation. Some examples from the Jewish literature of the time will help to demonstrate the diverse array of messianic expectations and the symbolism used to express them.

From the late second and early first centuries BCE, during the consolidation of the Hasmonean monarchy,[20] comes the *Testament of the Twelve Patriarchs*. On the surface, this collection of tractates (one each for the twelve sons of Jacob) does not appear to be an apocalypse in the strict sense, since it does not use the typical literary form, which features heavenly visions or dreams. Indeed, the work takes the form of ethical instruction, based on the deathbed blessings of Jacob in Genesis 49. Yet the content of these instructions bears the underlying apocalyptic worldview couched in terms of the ethical decision between "two ways"—good and evil, the way of God and the way of Beliar (or Satan):

> My grief is great, my children, on account of the licentiousness and witchcraft and idolatry that you practice contrary to the kingship. . . . In response to this the Lord will bring you famine and plague, death and the sword, punishment by siege, scattering by enemies like dogs, . . . consumption of God's sanctuary by fire, a desolate land, and yourselves enslaved by Gentiles. (T. Jud. 23)

Amid this prospect of oppression, the expectation of a coming eschatological event, when the good will triumph, is a recurring theme. The *Testament of Simeon* says:

> For the Lord will raise up from Levi someone as high priest and from Judah someone as king. He will save the Gentiles and the tribe of Israel. For this reason I command these things to you and to your children. (7:2–3)

Here notice that there are in fact two deliverer figures: one, a messianic king from Judah; the other, a priest from Levi. All Israel is told to be subject to them (cf. *T. Reu.* 6:8, 11; *T. Iss.* 5:7–8; *T. Jos.* 19:11; *T. Naph.* 5:1–5).

The royal messiah figure is accompanied by traditional Davidic imagery derived from scriptural allusions:

> And after this there shall arise for you a star from Jacob in peace: And a man shall arise from my posterity like the Sun of righteousness, walking with the sons of men in gentleness and righteousness, and in him will be found no sin. And the heavens will be opened upon him to pour out the spirit as a blessing of the Holy Father. And he will pour the spirit of grace upon you. And you shall be sons in truth, and you will walk in his first and final decrees. This is the Shoot of God Most High; this is the fountain for the life of all humanity. Then he will illumine the scepter of my kingdom, and from your root will arise the Shoot, and through it will arise the rod of righteousness for the nations, to judge and to save all that call on the Lord. (T. Jud. 24)

The allusions found here are taken primarily from the language of Isaiah 11:1–2, 10:

> *A shoot shall come out from the stump of Jesse, and a branch shall grow out of his roots. The spirit of the LORD shall rest on him. . . . On that day the root of Jesse shall stand as a signal to the peoples; the nations shall inquire of him, and his dwelling shall be glorious.*

Yet the language here also incorporates other potent Davidic symbols, such as the star and scepter from Numbers 24:17 and a patchwork of other images from Malachi 4:2 and from the peculiar wording of the Greek version of Psalm 45:4 in the Septuagint. All of these may be read as reflecting an understanding of Psalm 2 as well. Long before the writing of Mark, the *Testament of Judah* had equated the descent of God's spirit (from Isa 11:2) with the divine voice proclaiming the king's adoption (from Ps 2:7).

What is interesting is that this royal messiah is a deliverer in the sense that he will restore the nation to peace and prosperity, but he is not the ultimate victor or ruler in the cosmic struggle. It is finally the priestly figure (though not called "messiah") who is superior and who will redeem Israel from Beliar (cf. *T. Levi* 16:4–5; 18:1–12). In this case the opposing evil may well come from some of the internal political problems of the later Hasmonean period (ca. 87–63 BCE). The *Testaments of the Twelve Patriarchs* are more concerned with internal sources of corruption, including a polluted Temple and social decay.

A different picture is found in a slightly later work, called the *Psalms of Solomon,* of the Hasmonean period. One of many anonymous writings attributed to the famous king, this collection of hymns and poems most likely came from some early Pharisaic circles who opposed the Hasmonean dynasty. The work calls the Hasmonean regime an arrogant monarchy that "despoiled the throne of David" (17:6).[21] In this case the royal messianic figure is expected to be a new ruler who will forcefully purge the nation of internal corruption and foreign influences:

> *See [these evils], Lord, and raise up for them their king, the son of David, to rule over your servant Israel in the time known to you, O God. Undergird him with strength to destroy the unrighteous rulers, to purge Jerusalem from Gentiles who trample her to destruction; in wisdom and in righteousness to drive out the sinners from the inheritance; to smash the arrogance of sinners like a potter's jar. . . .*
>
> *He [the son of David] will gather a holy people whom he will lead in righteousness; and he will judge the tribes of the people that have been made holy by the Lord their God.*
>
> *He will not tolerate unrighteousness (even) to pause among them, and any person who knows wickedness shall not live with them. . . .*

And he will purge Jerusalem (and make it) holy as it was even from the be-ginning, (for) nations to come from the ends of the earth to see his glory, to bring as gifts her children who had been driven out, and to see the glory of the Lord with which God has glorified her.

And he [the son of David] will be a righteous king over them, taught by God.

There will be no unrighteousness among them in his days, for all shall be holy, and their king shall be the Lord Messiah. (17:21–23, 26, 30–32)

The tone of this work is considerably sharper than that of the *Testaments of the Twelve Patriarchs;* it suggests that the political and religious tensions in the later first century BCE had become more intense, at least for some in Jerusalem. There is no separate priestly figure, and deliverance is cast directly in political terms. In this case the militant "Lord Messiah," although clearly a human figure, is a more fearsome prospect with a "shattering rod of iron" against the nations. The picture still summons images from Psalm 2 combined with the royal victory songs, such as Psalm 110. Yet there is little tolerance for "sinners" among the chosen people; deliverance is the hope of the righteous alone. The boundaries between good and bad are thus more stringently drawn. To oppose God's messiah is to oppose God himself, an ominous prospect.

The Two Messiahs of the Essenes

The intersection of apocalyptic expectations, biblical reinterpretation, and sectarian consciousness is nowhere more evident than in the Dead Sea Scrolls and the group that produced them. First discovered in caves near the Dead Sea in 1947, the cache of scrolls and fragments appears to be an extensive library associated with the ruins of a settlement called Khirbet Qumran. Most scholars think they were produced by a sectarian group known from other references as the Essenes.[22] In their own writings, however, they tend to refer to themselves using symbolic sectarian language: "people of the covenant," "congregation of the elect," "righteous remnant," and the like. In one of the most startling of the documents, called the *War Scroll,* they call themselves the "sons of Light" who are preparing the final battle plan against the "sons of Darkness," and it is clear that other Jews are counted in the camp of the enemy.

In another text called the *Temple Scroll* there is a plan for the restoration and purification of the Temple (even though the Second Temple was still standing at that time). It seems that their self-imposed isolation was in reaction to their perceptions of the perversion of the Temple and the priestly offices at Jerusalem. For them the Temple was a flash point of piety and identity. The *Copper Scroll,* among other things, seems to include a treasure map for where various sacred goods had been hidden during the time of evil. In other words, this was a community looking forward to a new golden age for Jerusalem in which its members themselves would lead the nation in the true paths of righteousness.

The sect was apparently founded sometime near the beginning of the first century BCE by a priest who was disenfranchised from the Temple in Jerusalem at the time that the Hasmonean kings took the office of high priest. This figure, known as the "Teacher of Righteousness," seems to have suffered in some manner, perhaps as a martyr for defending the sanctity of the Zadokite priesthood. In any case, this first phase of the history of the sect seems to have come to an abrupt end during the reign of Herod, when the Qumran settlement shows signs of abandonment and severe earthquake damage. The community was then reinhabited sometime in the early first century CE and was operative up to the first Jewish revolt. It seems that the revolt was viewed as the fulfillment of the eschatological expectations, and the community took up its arms to follow the plan of the *War Scroll,* only to face defeat and destruction at the hands of the Roman forces.[23] Numerous speculations have been advanced regarding connections between the Qumran sect and Jesus or John the Baptist; however, there is no direct or substantial evidence to link them.

The key to the expectations of the Essenes is their thoroughgoing dedication to preserving and reinterpreting the scriptures. The scrolls contain virtually all of the books of the Hebrew scriptures and quite a number of the pseudepigraphical writings, including *1 Enoch, Jubilees,* and others. These are the earliest copies known for most of these biblical and extracanonical writings. But the Qumran covenanters were more than just copyists, for they also produced a number of other writings about their beliefs and rules for their community along with a body of commentaries on the scriptures that reflect these beliefs through their interpretations. Thus, a commonly found type of document among the scrolls is called a *pesher* (Heb., "explanation") on passages or whole biblical books. The prophets Isaiah, Nahum, and Habakkuk were especially popular, and through the lens of apocalyptic the *pesher* offered a "revealed" reinterpretation of the meaning of these works.

A good example of the way that various passages could be assembled and reinterpreted comes from a fragmentary treatise usually known as the *Messianic Florilegium,* a "bouquet," or arrangement, of eschatological and messianic texts. In dealing with passages from 2 Samuel it gives the following:

And concerning His [God's] words to David, "And I [will give] you [rest] from all your enemies" (2 Sam 7.11), this means that He will give them rest from the children of Satan who cause them to stumble so that they may be destroyed [by their errors]. . . .

[Explanation concerning] "The Lord declares to you that He will build you a house (2 Sam 7.11c). I will raise up your seed after you (2 Sam 7.12). I will establish the throne of his kingdom [forever] (2 Sam 7.13). I [will be] his father

and he shall be my son (2 Sam 7.14)." [This means] He is the Branch of David
(Isa 11.1) who shall arise with the interpreter of the Law [to rule] in Zion [at
the end] of time. As it is written, "I will raise up the tent of David that is fallen
(Amos 9.11)," that is to say, the fallen "tent of David" is he who shall arise to
save Israel. . . .

[Concerning "Why] do the nations [rage] and the peoples meditate [vainly;
the kings of the earth] rise up, [and the] princes take counsel together against
the Lord and against [His Messiah]? (Ps 2.1)" Interpreted, this saying concerns [the
kings of the Gentiles] who shall [rage against] the elect of Israel in the last days.
This shall be the time of trial to come [when] . . . (4QFlor 1)[24]

In these texts the *pesher,* or "explanation," moves away from the historical situation
of the original passage in the time of David or the kings to make application to
some future eschatological event.

The *pesher* on Psalm 2 is also instructive, because it indicates that the messiah
figure of the last days will rule with another figure who is called the "interpreter
of the Law." This is probably a reference to a priestly figure who plays a prominent
role in the messianic expectations at Qumran. In other texts from Qumran it is
clear that there are actually to be two messiahs and other eschatological agents who
participate in the deliverance and reign of Israel. This idea is reflected in the *Rule
of the Community,* a document that spells out not only the sectarian regulations of
admission and community life, but also the understanding of how the community
itself will come to rule the new Jerusalem in the eschatological kingdom:

As for the property of the men of holiness who walk in perfection, it shall not
be merged with that of the men of falsehood who have not purified their life by
separating themselves from [the] iniquity [of the world] and walking in the way
of perfection. They shall depart from none of the commands of the Law to walk
in the stubbornness of their hearts, but shall be ruled by the primitive precepts in
which the men of the community were first instructed [by the Teacher of Righ-
teousness?] until there shall come the Prophet and the Messiah of Aaron and the
Messiah of Israel. (1QS 9.8–11)

From the cumulative evidence of the scrolls it seems that the sectaries at Qumran looked forward to a prophetic figure who would come to announce the advent
of the *eschaton.* This figure is based on interpretations of Deuteronomy 18:15–19.
Then at the final conflict will come the royal messiah, usually called either the
messiah of Israel or of David; he will lead in the triumph over the enemies of the
sect and the nation. These enemies include both foreign oppressors of the nation
and those "worldly" Jews who do not follow the divine precepts as understood by
the community. Finally will come the priestly figure, called the messiah of Aaron,
who is analogous to the levitical figure in the *Testament of the Twelve Patriarchs.*
Given the emphasis on priestly regulations and the ideal of purifying the Temple

elsewhere in the scrolls, it seems that this Aaronic messiah is to be the ultimate ruler of the eschatological priestly state. The community itself is organized as an ideal representation of how this eschatological state should be run.

Later Messianic Ideas

It is rather easy to see how militant sectarianism and eschatological idealism such as those of the Qumran community might fuel the fervor of the first Jewish revolt. Many Jews of the day, including followers of Jesus, apparently thought that the war against Rome represented the ultimate eschatological triumph, the end of the present age. When the final defeat came and with it the devastation of Jerusalem and the Temple itself, it produced several different reactions among the population. Some at this time might have taken a decided turn against apocalyptic expectation. To be sure, later both Christianity and rabbinic Judaism would eventually alter the way the *eschaton* was conceived within each tradition. Nonetheless, this recasting of apocalyptic did not take place immediately. Indeed, it would take yet a second failed revolt in 132–35 CE before this political expectation would fall into total disrepute.

In the meantime, between 70 and 132 CE one hears of continued apocalyptic and messianic claims. Several new Jewish apocalypses are clearly intended as revealed reinterpretations that still look forward to eschatological consummation; these include 4 Ezra (or 2 Esdras), *2 Baruch, 3 Baruch,* and the *Apocalypse of Abraham,* all of which date from after the first revolt. *It must be remembered too that all of the written Gospels date from this same period, and the issue of apocalyptic reinterpretation comes up there as well* (as in Mark 13). That such messianic and political thought was continuing to ferment in Jewish expectations between the two revolts is clear from the fact that the leader of the second revolt took on a messianic title for his name, Bar Kochba; it means "son of the star," probably an allusion to the presumed messianic passage in Numbers 24:17, already used in *Testament of Judah* 24 (quoted above). He claimed to be a descendant of David. Coins struck by the revolutionaries give him kingly titles and suggest that he intended to rebuild the Temple at Jerusalem. That these views were not the isolated ramblings of a few is borne out by the fact that one of the leading members of the Pharisaic reform of that day, Rabbi Akiba, pronounced the messianic identity of Simon Bar Cosiba to be authentic.

One striking feature of most Jewish messianic symbolism in the time of Jesus is the minimal occurrence of two key titles that show up frequently in the Gospels: "Son of Man" and "Son of God." Both seem to be used regularly in reference to Jesus in his role as messiah. As a result, in later Christian theology the former has typically been thought to refer to the humanity of Jesus, while the latter refers to his divinity. Thus, in most later Christian usage, it is generally assumed that the titles "Messiah" and "Son of God" were always synonymous. Whether that is true in the earliest tradition remains to be seen.

By contrast, in Jewish expectation at the time of Jesus, there is no indication that the messiah figures were actually thought of as "sons" of God in the sense of divine beings. Where "Son of God" language is used at all, it almost always refers to the royal adoption ideology of Davidic kingship. That is to say, the messiah was still assumed to be a human "adopted" metaphorically and symbolically by God after the manner of David himself. Thus, the usage of "Son of God" in the Gospels in reference to Jesus will bear some careful discussion in later chapters. The fact that the Gospels are all later than and in large measure reacting to the Jewish revolts may help us to understand what is going on.

The title "Son of Man" represents a different problem, since it was not really a messianic title in the strict sense. The origins of this term in Jewish apocalyptic have been much debated. It has been proposed as a circumlocution for "I" (as a way of referring to oneself in the third person), but ancient examples are somewhat unclear.[25] For example, in the Synoptics, we find Jesus referring to himself as "Son of Man" in one Gospel and as "I" or "me" in the parallel passage in another Gospel (cf. Matt 10:32 with Luke 12:8; Matt 16:13 with Mark 8:27 and Luke 9:18). A far more common Semitic usage is as a circumlocution for "human" (cf. Num 23:19). It was regularly used this way in Hebrew poetry where parallel couplets demanded such word variation: "What is man that thou art mindful of him, and the son of man that thou dost care for him?" (Ps 8:4, RSV).

On the other hand, in Daniel we hear of a figure described as "one like a son of man" (7:13), but this is a heavenly, angelic figure. He is probably to be identified with the archangel Michael or Gabriel (as in Dan 10:13, 18; 12:1). In context it certainly has no "messianic" overtones. This figure has two principal roles in Daniel: first as revealer, and second as the herald of a coming eschatological break in time. Even the title probably means "one who appears like a human." In this case, however, he never actually comes to earth except as a revealer in Daniel's dreams, although he is a kind of guardian angel of the Jewish people. He is never identified with the title messiah, nor is he in any sense a deliverer figure.[26] Only much later does this title "Son of Man" become identified indirectly with a messianic expectation as seen in some late additions to the Enoch tradition (*1 En.* 37–71, also called the "Similitudes of Enoch"), where he is primarily a judge at the *eschaton*. The connection with deliverance, however, is tangential, in that the eschatological judge will ensure that the evil are punished and the suffering blessed in the new age. Even so, he is not usually depicted as an earthly messiah and never as the Davidic king.

In the Gospels more generally, "Son of Man" is taken over more directly as a messianic title.[27] In the Gospel of Mark, however, its uses are associated with two main aspects of the story: Jesus's anticipated suffering and the anticipated arrival of an eschatological judge accompanied by the angelic armies to dispense God's wrath, as in *1 Enoch*. The latter can be seen most clearly in the stark warnings of the Markan Jesus regarding the imminent *eschaton*:

> *"Those who are ashamed of me and of my words in this adulterous and sinful generation, of them the Son of Man will also be ashamed when he comes in the glory of his Father with the holy angels." And he said to them, "Truly I tell you, there are some standing here who will not taste death until they see that the kingdom of God has come with power." (8:38–9:1)*

> *"But in those days, after that suffering, the sun will be darkened, and the moon will not give its light, and the stars will be falling from heaven, and the powers in the heavens will be shaken. Then they will see 'the Son of Man coming in clouds' with great power and glory. Then he will send out the angels, and gather his elect from the four winds, from the ends of the earth to the ends of heaven." (13:24–27)*

In the second passage, the reference to the "Son of Man coming in clouds" is drawn directly from Daniel 7:13. In the Gospel of Mark the title retains its primary eschatological sense, perhaps understood as one aspect of the messiah's role as judge and deliverer. Some scholars have noted, however, that many of these sayings seem to have Jesus pointing ahead in time to a "third party" who will fulfill this role.[28] We shall return to this issue in Chapter 11 when we examine the overall shape of the story in the Gospel of Mark.

The title "Son of God" (both singular and plural) does appear, of course, in Greek renderings of the Hebrew scriptures. For example, in *1 Enoch* the expansion of the story of the "sons of God" from Genesis 6:1–3 makes it clear that they are to be understood as angels. In other cases, using passages like Hosea 11:1, it is the nation of Israel that is likened to God's "beloved child," and this idea opens up the image of God's chastisement and ultimate forgiveness of a wayward nation. But by far, the closest usage to "Son of God" language is that from the royal adoption formulation based on Psalm 2, Psalm 110, and 2 Samuel 7:14, all of which we have seen prominently in apocalyptic thought. The anointed king of Israel is God's adopted, as we saw above in both the *Testament of the Twelve Patriarchs* and the *Psalms of Solomon* and at Qumran.

Yet there is only a little evidence for the actual use of the title "Son of God" in Jewish sources prior to the first Jewish revolt, and even then it primarily reflects the royal adoption imagery.[29] In the period after the first revolt, the title does show up in some reinterpretations, notably in the later Jewish apocalypse 4 Ezra; it has God making a pronouncement regarding the four-hundred-year reign of judgment of "my son the messiah" (7:28–38). If genuine, this passage probably reflects the common use of language from Psalm 2. It has also been suggested, however, that the passage might be a Jewish reaction against Christian usage in the Gospels. Alternatively, it might reflect a later Christian reediting of the work.[30]

In its Christianized form, 4 Ezra continued to be part of the Christian canon of the Old Testament throughout the Middle Ages and was erroneously read as a "pre-Christian" prophecy of Jesus. In any case, in none of these instances, especially before the first revolt, is the messiah thought of as a heavenly figure, even when called God's "son." To understand this part of the image we must turn in the next chapter to other lines of Jewish thought, and more specifically to the Greek world, for background.

What we have seen in this survey reflects the long and complex meanderings of apocalyptic and messianic thought in formative Judaism from early in the Hellenistic period down to the period of the two revolts against Rome. There was no single line of eschatological expectation, nor was there a uniform notion of a messiah. Rather, there were variable ideas that could be reinterpreted and reconfigured owing to the social and political circumstances of each period and based on creative modes of reading and combining the scriptures. This is the kind of background one should consider when reading the Christian Gospels as well, for they are full of scenes that allude to or rely on such traditional understandings, such as in the story of Jesus's baptism discussed at the beginning of this chapter.

CHAPTER TWO

Logos and Wisdom's Child

*The Son of Man has come eating and drinking, and you say, "Look, a
glutton and a drunkard, a friend of tax collectors and sinners!" Nevertheless,
wisdom is vindicated by all her children. (Luke 7:34–35)*

In a particularly striking section from the Gospel of Luke, Jesus is found nearing
the end of his Galilean ministry (7:1–8:3). It will not be long before he "sets his
face to go to Jerusalem" (9:51) and the dramatic events that will unfold there. In
this section of Luke, Jesus is facing increasing resistance to his public activity that
will soon force him to leave his home region. At this point he draws aside to the
comfort of his disciples and a group of supporters, notably a group of prominent
women who sponsor his activity. Among them is Mary Magdalene:

> *The twelve were with him, as well as some women who had been cured of evil
> spirits and infirmities: Mary, called Magdalene, from whom seven demons had
> gone out, and Joanna, the wife of Herod's steward Chuza, and Susanna, and
> many others, who provided for them out of their resources. (8:1–3)*

This important descriptive note occurs only in the Gospel of Luke and has
fueled much later speculation about Mary Magdalene. What were her "demons"?
Is this a coded way of calling her a prostitute or a "loose woman," as later medieval
legend would have it? Or is the Lukan author just trying to give narrative background for understanding the significant role that Mary Magdalene will play later
in the story? In the earlier Gospels of Mark and Matthew, she appears only at the
very end of the story, in the crucifixion and empty-tomb scenes. The only comment given there is that she was among several women "who used to follow him

and provided for him when he was in Galilee" (Mark 15:41; cf. Matt 27:55–56). So, it appears that the Lukan author has moved this information forward in the narrative[1] to describe a scene set while Jesus is still in the Galilee. In other words, it seems at first just to be "plot exposition"[2] in anticipation of later scenes in the Passion narrative.

From a purely literary perspective one might argue that this repositioning of the little note about the ministering women is narratively more satisfying and more artistic. But is that all that's going on? Not quite. This scene is the third of three successive, but otherwise unique vignettes in the Gospel of Luke. In the first (7:24–35), Jesus speaks about John the Baptist and himself, and why they are being rejected. In the second (7:36–50), a sinful woman anoints Jesus's feet while he is at a dinner party. In the third (8:1–3), Jesus retires with his disciples and some women supporters for a respite before continuing his public teaching. This entire section of the Gospel of Luke has no direct parallel in the other Gospels, not even the anointing scene. Thus, there is more going on than just plot exposition. These unique scenes help create a dramatic statement about the character of Jesus as scripted in Luke.

Let's look more closely at what is going on. The anointing scene (7:36–50) is the key. While Jesus is at a dinner party in the home of a prominent man, an unnamed woman comes up behind him as he is reclining and begins to anoint his feet, bathe them with her tears, and dry them with her hair. When Jesus fails to rebuff her, he is criticized by the host for consorting with such people: "If this man were a prophet, he would have known who and what kind of woman this is who is touching him—that she is a sinner" (7:39). In turn, Jesus rebukes his insensitive host with a parable on the nature of forgiveness (7:40–47). He then consoles the woman with a forgiving word: "Your faith has saved you" (7:50).[3]

This scene is the Lukan equivalent to the anointing at Bethany that occurs just prior to the Last Supper in Mark 14:3–9 and Matthew 26:6–13. The Lukan version has been substantially altered, most notably in location and in the fact that the woman now anoints his feet, while in Mark and Matthew she anoints his head—a messianic symbol.[4] Such seemingly minor alterations in the action create very different dramatic effects. In addition, the Lukan repositioning here is unusual and makes it a critical intersection of several themes for the understanding of Jesus in Luke, where the emphasis on Jesus as social critic is underscored. The sinful woman is often thought to be Mary Magdalene, although nothing in the text hints at this. The proximity of the reference to Mary Magdalene in the next passage was the basis for later speculation and legendary expansion along these lines.[5]

The first of the three unique Lukan scenes now comes into sharper focus. It has Jesus speak publicly about himself and John the Baptist from this same perspective of social criticism. Here too Jesus is made to respond to external criticism that he befriends "tax collectors and sinners." At the conclusion he says:

"To what then will I compare the people of this generation, and what are they like? They are like children sitting in the marketplace and calling to one another, 'We played the flute for you, and you did not dance; we wailed, and you did not weep.' For John the Baptist has come eating no bread and drinking no wine, and you say, 'He has a demon.' The Son of Man has come eating and drinking, and you say, 'Look, a glutton and a drunkard, a friend of tax collectors and sinners!' Nevertheless, wisdom is vindicated by all her children." (7.31–35)

The final pregnant statement sets up the scene that follows, in which Jesus aligns himself with the anointing woman while at the dinner party. Hence, in the Lukan ordering of these episodes, the anointing scene is clearly meant to symbolize and narrativize his comment as he now consorts with a known sinner. The anointing scene is the centerpiece of a triptych meant to dramatize these important ideas. In Luke, therefore, it becomes clear that Jesus is referring to himself and to John the Baptist as the "children of wisdom." Jesus now seems to take the stance of the sage, not unlike Socrates or Diogenes, who stands outside of society and offers words of wisdom from on high. To understand this language and the image of Jesus that it creates, we must now look to another range of Jewish thought with important ties to the Greek tradition. Common in the first century, it is usually called the wisdom tradition.

Sophia as Divine Wisdom

As we saw in the previous chapter, although messianic expectations and apocalyptic thought were prevalent in the Jewish homeland for a century before and after Jesus, these ideas were in no way a uniform or dogmatic religious tradition. Instead, they represent a diverse spectrum of outlooks within Judaism. One of the key features in the emergence of apocalyptic thought was a kind of new cosmological speculation, stimulated in large measure by the encounter of Jews with Persian and Greek thought. Thus, when one looks at *1 Enoch,* in many respects the foundational document of the apocalyptic worldview, one notices that the biblical creation stories are being filtered through a new outlook on the nature of the world. Enoch's ostensible revelations from heaven on the order of the cosmos and the human condition are predicated on a kind of philosophical orientation toward such matters heavily informed by Persian and Greek cosmology. Among other things, it includes a gradual shift to the Greek notion of the geocentric universe, in which the earth was thought to stand at the center, while the sun, moon, and planets revolved around it. Also called the "Ptolemaic universe," it was the dominant view of planetary motion from the second century BCE until the time of Galileo and Copernicus.

Thus, apocalyptic is at least in part a product of Greek influence on the new Jewish cosmology or speculation on the nature of the world and its origins.[6] This kind of philosophical speculation is closely affiliated with the wisdom tradition. Likewise, the book of Daniel blends ethical instructions (in the form of tales of Daniel's pious perseverance) characteristic of the practical side of the wisdom tradition along with its use of visionary materials more typical of apocalyptic. In other contexts the ideal of wisdom is also tied to the prophetic tradition. Moses too could be viewed as a sage who delivers messages from on high for the proper understanding of the world and proper conduct of life in harmony with nature (as we shall see later in this chapter).

The Personification of Wisdom

The notion of wisdom (Heb. *hakmah* or *hokmah*) is associated in biblical tradition with both legal and ethical instruction. For example, it is closely linked to ethics, and hence to Torah piety, in the deathbed blessings of Jacob (Gen 49). In this story, the elderly Jacob gathers his twelve sons around him and pronounces blessings on each on in turn while simultaneously offering instruction on living virtuously. This practical instruction on virtuous living provides both commonsense morals and religious justification by linking these ethical precepts to the created order of the cosmos.[7]

By far the most prevalent form of this idea in the biblical tradition is *sapiential,* or "wisdom," literature. It includes several later works among the Hebrew scriptures, notably Proverbs, Ecclesiastes (or Qoheleth), and Job, as well as a number of other documents from the apocryphal and pseudepigraphical collections. More than any other biblical figure, it is associated with Solomon, the wise king (1 Kgs 3:10–14); his name was attached by this tradition to Proverbs and other works that were in essence collections of commonplace ethical instruction. Heroic figures like Solomon (and later Daniel and Judith) reinforce the notion that such precepts for the governance of life in society are in fact eternal truths handed down by God. Social ethics become God's precepts (Heb. *mitzvoth*) and law (*torah*).

> *Give instruction to the wise, and they will become wiser still;*
> *teach the righteous and they will gain in learning.*
> *The fear of the LORD is the beginning of wisdom,*
> *and the knowledge of the Holy One is insight. (Prov 9:9–10)*

The book of Proverbs reflects the development and transformation in Jewish thought as it moves from its earlier Near Eastern cultural context to that of the Greek world. The work is a collection of aphorisms and instructions with a timeless quality. Some sections probably come from earlier periods and reflect ancient Near Eastern influences. Other sections and the final editorial process date to the late Persian period (at the earliest), but more likely to the third century BCE.[8] Judea only came under direct Greek rule in 332 BCE, but influences from the period of Persian rule (539–332 BCE) already provided an important bridge, since there was extensive contact and cross-fertilization between Greek and Persian culture. Archaeologically, there are signs of direct trade between Judea and Greece during the Persian period.

In Proverbs 7:6–8:36, for example, the choice of two paths in life bears a striking similarity to the Greek moral tale known as the "choice of Herakles" or the Prodicus myth.[9] In it, the young Hercules (Herakles in Greek) was on a journey and came to a fork in the road. Two women then approached him. One was modestly dressed and fair, while the other was heavily made up to be alluring. The latter offered to show him a smooth and easy path to happiness, trying to lure him with promises of pleasure. The former promised only a rough and difficult road to noble deeds. Of course, the two women are personifications of Virtue and Vice. The paths likewise are metaphors: the smooth path is luxury and excess; the hard path is the virtuous life. Hercules' choice is the path to virtue.

In Proverbs, Wisdom like Virtue, personified as a woman, stands "on the heights, beside the way, at the crossroads" (8:2). She offers advice on the road to virtue and godliness. Even before the arrival of Alexander the Great (332 BCE), therefore, Jewish thought could find elements of Greek and Persian philosophy congenial. By the time of *1 Enoch* and Daniel (products of the late third and early second centuries BCE) this notion would provide the underpinnings for recasting the Jewish worldview through Greek cosmology, as noted above. Thus, we should not be too quick to draw strict boundaries between Jewish and Hellenistic cultures or traditions.

Who is this "Dame Wisdom" that we encounter in Proverbs and Luke? She is the wisdom with which God created the world, and thus she herself becomes a creative force through personification. In Proverbs 8 the personified Wisdom speaks directly to readers:

> *"The LORD created me at the beginning of his work,*
> *the first of his acts of long ago.*
> *Ages ago I was set up,*
> *at the first, before the beginning of the earth.*
> *When there were no depths I was brought forth,*
> *when there were no springs abounding with water." (8:22–24)*

The language here uses specific verbal allusions to the first verses of Genesis; it clearly identifies Wisdom as an observer of and participant in the creation story. In later Jewish tradition this tendency continued, giving rise to the idea that Wisdom was the other "person" present at creation when God said, "Let *us* make humankind in *our* image" (Gen 1:26). Moreover, since the Hebrew word for "wisdom" is feminine, the normal pronoun used was also feminine: "she" or "her" (e.g., Prov 8:1–3; 9:1–2). So too when it was rendered into Greek in the Septuagint, the equivalent feminine noun *sophia* was used. Thus, as the tradition began to develop, "she" was increasingly thought of as the feminine counterpart or consort

of the masculine God. Since Wisdom was brought forth by God before the beginning of the world, how could "she" be less than a divine persona as well?

The two writings that best illustrate this development in a Greek-speaking Jewish idiom are found in the Apocrypha; they are appropriately entitled the Wisdom
of Jesus son of Sirach (usually just called Sirach) and the Wisdom of Solomon.

Sirach

Sirach is attributed to a second-century Jewish writer of the homeland named
Jeshua ben Sirah (or Jesus son of Sirach; see Sir 50:27). It appears that he was
a professional scribe or scholar (38:24–39:11) and a member of the pious group
known as the *hasidim,* who reacted against aspects of Seleucid hellenization just
before the Maccabean revolt (ca. 180–168 BCE). But as the prologue tells us, this
work was preserved by the grandson of Jeshua; this later writer had since moved
to Alexandria and translated the work from Hebrew into Greek. It is this Greek
version (dating to roughly 132 BCE) that is now preserved in the Apocrypha.[10]

The Greek version was intended to serve as a guide for all who love learning,
including those outside Jewish tradition; yet the very process of translation shows
a progressive acculturation to its Greek environment.[11] In the Alexandrian Jewish
community, contact with Greek thought and interaction with non-Jews were of
considerable importance.[12] Thus Sirach continues the personification of Wisdom
(Sophia), drawing directly on the language of Proverbs 8:22: "Sophia was created
before all other things, and prudent understanding from eternity" (1:4). It continues: "To fear the Lord is the beginning of Sophia; she is created with the faithful
in the womb" (1:14).[13]

In a particularly provocative passage (24:3–22), Sophia sings her own praises.
It is a kind of aretalogical hymn similar to that found for the Egyptian Isis.[14] In
these aretalogies, the deity is praised for her attributes and gifts to humanity.
Thus, the Jewish Sophia is being venerated like the Egyptian Isis as a heavenly
patron. Sophia is not only the active word issuing from the mouth of God; she is
also the abiding presence of God, who dwells among his chosen people, Israel, in
the Temple at Jerusalem.[15] As God's active agent she helped create the world and
guide the patriarchs. Now she cares for the chosen people. But more than this, she
is the depth and wellspring from which flow the fountains of God's blessings and
commandments in the book of his covenant, the law of Moses (24:23). The Torah
comes from Sophia.

The Wisdom of Solomon

The Wisdom of Solomon is one of several pseudepigraphical works attributed
to the important biblical figure Solomon. It was written in Greek with at least
some vision of a non-Jewish audience. The actual author, date, and setting are

unknown, but it is usually dated on the basis of language and style to the late first century BCE or early first century CE.[16] In other words, it comes from just prior to or even during the time of Jesus. It also has direct affinities to patterns of argument and theology found in Paul's letters.[17] Because of these similarities, the work continued to be read as scripture among Christians throughout the Middle Ages as part of the Old Testament. The work includes sections on eschatology (1:1–6:11) and history (10–19), but its core is a laudatory description of the personified Sophia (6:12–9:18).

> *There is in her [Sophia] a spirit that is intelligent, holy,*
> *unique [monogenes],[18] manifold, subtle,*
> *mobile, clear, unpolluted,*
> *distinct, invulnerable, loving the good, keen,*
> *irresistible, beneficent, humane,*
> *steadfast, sure, free from anxiety,*
> *all-powerful, overseeing all,*
> *and penetrating through all spirits*
> *that are intelligent, pure, and altogether subtle.*
> *For Sophia is more mobile than any motion;*
> *because of her pureness she pervades and penetrates all things.*
> *For she is a breath of the power of God,*
> *and a pure emanation of the glory of the Almighty;*
> *therefore nothing defiled gains entrance into her.*
> *For she is a reflection of eternal light,*
> *a spotless mirror of the working of God,*
> *and an image of his goodness.*
> *Although she is but one, she can do all things,*
> *and while remaining in herself, she renews all things;*
> *in every generation she passes into holy souls*
> *and makes them friends of God, and prophets;*
> *for God loves nothing so much as the person who lives with Sophia.*
> *She is more beautiful than the sun,*
> *and excels every constellation of the stars.*
> *Compared with the [sun's] light she is found to be superior,*
> *for it is succeeded by the night,*
> *but against Sophia evil [darkness] does not prevail.*
> *She reaches mightily from one end of the earth to the other,*
> *and she orders all things well.*
> *I loved her and sought her from my youth;*
> *I desired to take her for my bride,*
> *and became enamored of her beauty.*
> *She glorifies her noble birth by living with God,*

and the Lord of all loves her.
For she is an initiate in the knowledge of God,
and an associate in his works. (7:22–8:4)

This section is cast as a fanciful expansion on Solomon's prayer for wisdom (1 Kgs 3:9), in which he sings her praises. It is also presented as Solomon's "love song" to Sophia (8:2)—with whom he had *become enamored* and whom he wanted as *his bride*—suggesting an interpretive rereading of the erotic poem called Song of Songs, better known as Song of Solomon.[19] The first and last sections of the Wisdom of Solomon deal with apocalyptic themes of judgment, in which the righteous will be exalted and the wicked punished. These sections build directly on the central portion of the work, since righteousness is defined by adherence to the teachings of Sophia through Torah. The first-century wisdom tradition was capable of considerable apocalyptic fervor. Yet the description of Sophia goes well beyond those in Sirach.

The attributes of Sophia are thoroughly attuned to a Greek world of thought and are typical of descriptions of the divine or personified Virtue among philosophers. She is God's immortal spirit (Wis 12:1), like the Stoic Worldsoul, which dwells in all things.[20] The deliverance from judgment is described as a descent and return from Hades (15:13), using the standard Greek terminology. The cure of souls comes by the word of God (15:12) that comes only through the teachings of Wisdom (7:15–22). In this text, the transcendent God has little or nothing to do with the actual lives of humans on the earth. Sophia is the active agent of creation, the divine figure who intervenes in the lives of the patriarchs in Genesis (Wis 10) and comes out in the pages of scripture. She was the one who led the people of the Lord out of Egypt through her direct guidance of Moses, the "holy prophet" (11:1). Even beyond Moses, she dwells in "holy souls" of every generation and makes them "friends of God, and prophets" (7:27). Thus, in the Gospel of Luke, Jesus's declaration about himself and John as "Sophia's children" (7:35) must be understood as linking their identity as prophets to the wisdom tradition.

In both Sirach and the Wisdom of Solomon, the Torah is the outpouring of God, but the source is Sophia herself, who gave it to Moses. To approach God one must be a lover of Sophia (in Greek the term would thus be "philosopher"); to love Sophia is to study Torah. This notion clearly reinforces traditional piety and observance of Torah, and yet the mythical dimensions of its vision of the world's origins are heavily dependent on Greek ideas. From this language it is not hard to see some of the attributes regularly associated in later Christian thought with the Holy Spirit and in Jewish tradition with the Shekinah—the source of inspiration for the prophets and Moses who dwells in the faithful. Yet other of Sophia's attributes will eventually be applied to Jesus himself, most notably in the Gospel of John.[21]

So it raises some questions about the passage in Luke 7:35, since there prophet and Son of Man are merely the children of Sophia, righteous men chosen for special deeds. Is this an older, more traditionally Jewish notion of Jesus's messiahship? It seems to be saying that he, like Moses and other prophets of old, was the "child" of Sophia as one graced with special wisdom and favor for following the will of God. Because of the fact that this passage is found only in Matthew and Luke, and hence derived from Q tradition, it may well represent a very early understanding of Jesus's identity.[22] But where does it come from? It appears that some of these disparate early elements have not yet been fully synthesized even within the mainstream of the Christian tradition. In part this was due to the wide range of uses of the wisdom material among pagans, Jews, and Christians alike.

Logos: Philo's Jewish Philosophy

Another contemporary of Jesus and Paul was Philo of Alexandria. He was a devout Jew who came from one of the wealthiest and most influential families of the chief city of the Diaspora. Alexandria was home to nearly a hundred thousand Jews; they made up nearly a third of the Greek-speaking population of the city and occupied one of the most prominent residential districts.[23] They also possessed a special status of citizenship and self-governance relative to the city and the Roman provincial administration.

Philo's family held a leading position within the Jewish community.[24] His brother Alexander was the chief financial representative (called *alabarch*) to the Roman administration on behalf of the entire Jewish population. He also donated the gold doors for Herod's rebuilt Jerusalem Temple, and there were marriage ties to the Herodian line. Still other members of the family were highly assimilated to Greek culture and active in Roman politics. Alexander's son and Philo's nephew, Tiberius Julius Alexander, apparently renounced his ancestral religion in order to enter the Roman imperial bureaucracy and seek admission to the Roman orders. He ascended to the prestigious office of prefect of Egypt during the last years of Nero's reign (67–68 CE). The timing was auspicious, since after Nero's death he would be instrumental in the accession of Vespasian, who was at that moment in command of the Roman armies in Judea during the first Jewish revolt. Prior to that the younger Alexander was stationed for a time (46–48 CE) as Roman procurator of Judea, where he dealt harshly with any potentially subversive elements among the Jewish population. Josephus records that he condemned to crucifixion James and Simon, two sons of Judas the Galilean, who were suspected of fomenting sedition.[25]

Philo, however, seems to have avoided public life in favor of his intellectual pursuits. He was born about 20 BCE and lived until the 40s CE. Still, he was drawn into the public limelight in 38–40 CE after a pogrom against the Jews of Alexandria under the governor Flaccus. Philo himself led a Jewish embassy to Rome and penned the document that was to be submitted to the emperor Gaius (Caligula). This document, known as the *Delegation to Gaius,* is an eloquent appeal for the rights of Jews as citizens of the Hellenistic-Roman city. Caligula died before resolving the case, but his successor, Claudius, was moved by Philo's arguments to compose a formal rescript to the new governor of Egypt affirming the rights of the Jewish population.

Philo also wrote an apologetic treatise against the prejudices of Flaccus and others, and he defended the intellectual respectability of Jewish tradition and thought. Above all else, he was a scholar, biblical commentator, and a philosopher in the best Greek tradition. He is perhaps the most prolific proponent of Middle Platonism still known, other than Plutarch and Clement of Alexandria. Among the many features of Philo's work, it is important to note here his ability to blend a close reading of biblical texts with his Platonic worldview. Through this means he can retain a traditional Torah-based piety, while arguing to Jews and pagans alike that the words of Moses and the scriptures are inherently consistent with the teachings of Plato.

Philo's thought and extensive writings are too complex to treat in any comprehensive way here, but two features deserve special attention. We shall see Philo again in the next chapter. The first aspect of Philo's thought is his ability to allegorize the scriptures in order to tease out of them meanings and ideas consistent with his Hellenistic cultural context. His willingness to allegorize does not mean, however, that he did not remain faithful to traditional forms of Jewish piety. For example, against some other Jews he argues that the precepts of the Decalogue (the Ten Commandments) and special laws such as circumcision must be followed literally. Yet when it comes to the stories of Genesis, which seem to be his favorite stock of material, he finds that allegorization reveals a more satisfying and abiding truth. In this way, Philo saw in the "books of Moses" a philosophical arrangement: a book on the order of society (Gk. *politeia*), like Plato's *Republic,* and a book on education (Gk. *paideia*).

Indeed, Moses, he argued, must have been the source for Plato himself. Yet his reading of Plato is typical of the middle period when it was heavily suffused with elements of Aristotelian thought and Stoicism. In this way too he follows the lead of earlier Jewish writers, such as Aristobulus and the unknown author of the Wisdom of Solomon, in speculating on the doctrine of creation from Genesis through the lens of Greek cosmology:

> His [Moses's] exordium, as I have said, is most marvelous, consisting in an account of the forming of the world [Gk. kosmos] such that the world is in harmony with the Law [of Moses] and the Law with the world, and that the man who observes the Law is immediately a citizen of the world [Gk. kosmopolites, or "cosmopolitan"], who guides his actions by the will of Nature, according to which also the entire world is governed.[26]

This same cosmology underlies Philo's affinity for Greek ideals of virtue and ethics, since the source and fountain of all virtues is "Nature's right reason."[27] The story of Abraham is the model of the "virtue-loving soul"[28] and thus becomes the basis for an elaborate allegory on the patriarch's journeys, so that Abraham, "the friend of God," represents the migration of the soul through virtue to happiness.[29] Likewise the story of Lot's narrow escape from Sodom and Gomorrah represents the virtuous soul's escape from imprisonment in sensual pleasures; thus, the five cities of the plain allegorically represent the five senses.

The ideal of virtue and reason as the goal of human endeavor brings us to the second point. Through his allegory, Philo can read the creation of humanity in a new light. Although Philo, in keeping with the wisdom tradition, uses the term *sophia* as the source of innate virtue in nature, he more typically prefers a masculine synonym favored by the Stoics—the Greek *logos* ("word" or "reason"). His interpretation of the cosmological mechanism by which *sophia/logos* encounters the world of humans, however, is predicated on a complex reading of the Genesis creation story. It starts with the assumption that the divine Logos is the source or pattern of the moral structure of the world, but that the physical creation was necessarily inferior due to its corruptible nature. Yet God brought order and harmony by making it conform to a "more excellent model," the heavenly Logos.[30] In a fuller treatment of the days of the biblical creation account, he goes on to show that God established this original order for the world through the creation of humanity. Yet there is a twist, since the human creation is likewise inferior and corruptible. Both the world and physical humans, therefore, must look to a perfect model.

Philo comes to this interpretation of Genesis by a bit of deft analysis of the biblical text. He begins by noting that there are two distinct versions of the creation of humankind as represented by terms used for the creative action of God.[31] One "man," says Philo, is that "*created* in the *image* of God" (Gen 1:26–27), while the other "man" is that "*formed* from the *dust* of the earth" (2:7). He sees these as two distinct acts of creation: the first is the creation of the heavenly Logos (or Sophia), an archetype of perfection who dwells in the realm of ideas; the second is the creation of the physical human creature of earth. It is only the first, the Logos, that Philo says is in the image of God; physical humans are patterned in the image of this image. Thus, Philo's Logos ("reason" or "word"), whom he also calls the "heavenly human,"[32] is the instrumental link between the mind of God and its expression in the order of creation.

> *There are two types of humans, the one a heavenly man, the other an earthly. The heavenly man, being made after the image of God, is completely without participation in corruptible and earthly substance; but the earthly one was compacted out of disparate matter, which he [Moses] calls clay. Wherefore, he says that the heavenly man was not molded, but was stamped with the image of God; while the earthly is a molded work [Gk. plasma] of the Craftsman, [i.e., God as creator], yet not his offspring.*[33]

Philo has taken the Genesis creation stories and read them through the model of Plato's world of forms. His view is dependent too on some later works of Plato (such as the *Timaeus*) in which Plato posits a unitary god, the source of all, whom he calls simply "the one" or just "Mind." The world of forms exists in the reason of this mind. In other words, Philo follows a Platonic cosmology in positing the existence of a realm of perfect existence in the Mind, where this Logos is created in its image as an offspring. Although the ideas have not yet been clarified, Philo has coined the terminology for the heavenly Logos as an "offspring of God." Yet it is clear that this figure cannot be part of any material creation of the earth, and Philo nowhere links it to messianic ideas. It is, rather, a further expansion of the theological speculation seen in the wisdom tradition, systematized through Philo's creative exploration of the moralist philosophers of the early Roman Empire. The point is to show the inherent ability of Jewish religion to promote the highest ideals of Greco-Roman culture, philosophy and virtue. Yet it would be wrong to suggest that Philo in any way intended for Judaism to be assimilated to "paganism"; rather, his goal was to defend and demonstrate the respectability of Judaism and Jews as citizens of the world.[34]

What the previous discussion shows is the extent to which Jews living in the Greco-Roman world could retain their traditional identity and piety while still feeling at home in the larger culture and society. To be sure there were some social differences for Jews living in the homeland, since they formed the majority of the population and viewed Jerusalem as their sacred center. Jews living in the Diaspora, in cities like Alexandria, Antioch, and Rome, were a minority culture, even when there was a sizable Jewish population. But it is inappropriate to say that one kind of Judaism was *hellenized,* while the other was not. They all were part of the larger Hellenistic-Roman culture, even in the most apocalyptic outlook.

More than anything else, the wisdom tradition reflects an abiding sense of God's presence mediated through Sophia and her gifts, including the Torah itself. The image of the prophet was also conceived as a gift of Sophia, and aspects of this rich tradition likewise flowed into the Gospels. On the one hand, it appears in the Gospel of Luke when Jesus is called "Sophia's child" as a way of understanding his prophetic inspiration and sagely wisdom. On the other hand, it enters the Gospel of John via the *logos* theology found in Philo. Only now, in a new twist, Jesus himself is that divine Logos through whose power the world itself was created:

> *In the beginning was the Word, and the Word was with God, and the Word was God. He was in the beginning with God. All things came into being through him, and without him not one thing came into being. What has come into being in him was life, and the life was the light of all people. (John 1:1–4)*

With each new application of these Hellenistic Jewish ideas, the image of Jesus is expanded and changed. In each case potent symbols script his character in new ways.

CHAPTER THREE

⁂

Divine Man

And when [Jesus] was twelve years old, they went up as usual for the festival. When the festival was ended and they started to return, the boy Jesus stayed behind in Jerusalem, but his parents did not know it. . . . After three days they found him in the temple, sitting among the teachers, listening to them and asking them questions. And all who heard him were amazed at his understanding and his answers. When his parents saw him they were astonished; and his mother said to him, "Child, why have you treated us like this? Look, your father and I have been searching for you in great anxiety." He said to them, "Why were you searching for me? Did you not know that I must be in my Father's house?" But they did not understand what he said to them. Then he went down with them and came to Nazareth, and was obedient to them. His mother treasured all these things in her heart. And Jesus increased in wisdom and in years, and in divine and human favor. (Luke 2:42–52)

They have sometimes been called the "lost years" of Jesus—the years between his birth and the beginning of his public ministry. The Gospel of Luke says that he was "about thirty years old" when he came to John to be baptized (3:23). But other than this one story, also from the Gospel of Luke, there is no other reference to Jesus's childhood, adolescence, education, or home life. This peculiar silence has long provoked questions, and numerous pop theories have floated around in recent years. In one, he went to India and there learned the teachings of the Buddha. Despite legends of medieval missionaries and Christian iconography based upon them, there is no basis for such stories. But such notions are not new; other pious legends about the boy Jesus grew up in the ancient period. One of these is called the *Infancy Gospel of Thomas,* which tells of the child Jesus between birth and age twelve. Most notably it recounts his miraculous feats and superhuman wisdom even as a child. We shall return to these later efforts to "fill in the gaps" of Jesus's life later in this book.

The interest in such stories may reflect a natural human curiosity. Such presentations of Jesus also allow Christian authors to promote certain theological tenets. Once the image of Jesus was well established in the emerging Christian culture of later antiquity, such questions became more common, and the inclination was to push aspects of Jesus's later life, as known from the canonical Gospels and developing Christian theology, back into his childhood. Highly elaborated versions of the birth narrative and legends about Jesus's parentage were also part of this tendency, as we shall see later in this book. The story from the Gospel of Luke of the precocious young Jesus at age twelve in the Temple, confounding the teachers and his parents, ends with a telling summary: "He advanced in wisdom and manhood and in favor before God and humans."[1] A precocious childhood is one of the characteristics of the "divine man" tradition, to which we shall turn in this chapter. It is part of the magical worldview at the time of Jesus and the Gospels.

Perhaps more prominent than any other aspect of Jesus's story, at least as it is commonly perceived since the Middle Ages, is the association of the title "Son of God" with his miraculous birth and his ability to perform miracles. This linkage is somewhat curious today, because claims of miracles have generally met with skepticism since the Enlightenment. The tendency has been to rationalize miracles through scientific explanation. Such scientific skepticism has led some to emphasize the teachings of Jesus to the exclusion of claims for his miraculous acts, while dismissing all other magical elements from the ancient world as superstitious mumbo jumbo. But sometimes a funny reversal sneaks in, whereby people can be skeptical of all other claims of miracles *except* those of Jesus. Why? Because he was the Son of God.

The difficulty is this. The Gospels use the miracles to prove Jesus's messianic or divine nature, as seen in the emphatic statement of the Gospel of John: "Now Jesus did many other signs in the presence of his disciples, which are not written in this book. But these are written so that you may come to believe that Jesus is the Messiah, the Son of God" (20:30–31).[2] But one cannot use the miracles to prove his identity and then turn around and use his identity to prove that his miracles, and his alone, are genuine. That is a tautology. In order to understand what was at work in the portrayal of Jesus as miracle worker, one must examine the way these miraculous elements were perceived and understood within that larger Greco-Roman culture. In this chapter we shall first examine the place of magic and miracles and then return to the divine-man tradition to see how both of these elements provide context for certain portrayals and understandings of Jesus.

The Magical Worldview

At least for the people of the first century—and for more than a thousand years on either side—there was no question: miracles really happened. Magical powers were real. But that is not to say that they were unintelligible or irrational; an explanation was forged out of the philosophic and scientific knowledge of the day. This is what we mean by the magical worldview. Miracles, properly speaking, are actions that transform the nature or circumstances of something that occurs normally in daily life. In the Greco-Roman world, however, this was only one of the magical arts. Others included divination, oracles, dream interpretation, spells, curses, and many aspects of medicine and the sciences.

Modern sociological definitions have tended to distinguish such magical practices from religion (the one superstitious, the other rational and intellectual).[3] In antiquity, however, the magical was part of the very cosmological structure that undergirded everyone's religious outlook, that of Jews as well as pagans. The extensive role of dreams, visions, angels, and demons in the apocalyptic tradition shows this magical worldview at work. It was deeply ingrained at very basic levels of popular consciousness, even among Jews. It is well exemplified by the role of angels, demons, and magic in the Jewish novelistic romance known as Tobit in the Apocrypha, which continued to be a favorite subject in medieval piety and art. In most cases, however, the assumed reality of this worldview meant that it was not debated or much discussed.

The mechanism of magic is visible whenever one encounters ancient discussions of cosmology and the created order. In *1 Enoch,* the fallen angels and their offspring, the Titans, were the source of magical practices, brought to earth from the supernatural realms. Although the assumed mechanism differed over time and from place to place, in the Roman world it involved the notion of a supernatural realm of powers existing both above and below the earth that could intrude into the physical realm, either for good or ill. The cosmos was viewed as a plasmic whole governed by a single economy of action and power to which even the gods in their realm had to respond. In Stoic philosophy this is where the notion of the Worldsoul emerges, and it gives rise to its doctrine of *sympatheia* (or "sympathy").

Thus even in the apocalyptic and wisdom traditions within Jewish thought, there is a realm of supernatural forces between the human sphere and the realm of God. Sophia and the angels move through this intermediate realm. And the cosmological structure is consistent, a notion that also underlies the practice of animal sacrifice in ancient religions. It is assumed that by doing certain acts or saying certain formulas, like elaborate alphabetical concoctions ("abracadabra"), tongue-twisting palindromes ("ablanathanalba"), or exotic foreign names and terms ("Iao Sabaoth," "Abraxas"), a person can obligate the supernatural forces, even the gods themselves, to perform in certain ways.[4]

This idea led to the production of elaborate recipe books of magical formulas, in which foreign gods appear at a premium. One of these books, now called the *Paris Magical Papyrus,* has been preserved largely intact, but there are thousands of smaller fragments of magical instruction to show how prevalent it was. Love potions, healing votives, exorcism spells, curses, and the like were commonly written on small pieces of papyrus or etched in gold or tin and worn around the neck as amulets. The secret knowledge to produce such incantations was jealously guarded. It was a power not to be taken lightly. It was also a valuable commodity. At times the authorities had to crack down on the purveyors of "black magic" for disrupting the social order.

One of the more delightful works showing this magical worldview is the novel of Apuleius of Medauros (ca. 180 CE) called the *Metamorphoses* or *The Golden Ass*. It tells the story of a traveler named Lucius, who tries to mix a magical potion in order to effect an amorous liaison. The potion goes bad, however, because Lucius does not follow the recipe precisely, and he is transformed into an ass instead. In this form he is sold, stolen, traded, and otherwise led haplessly on a number of adventures. Through it all his outward appearance affords him the opportunity to observe people unawares. Comedy, satire, and pathos ensue. The practice of magic is all around in the story, which contains witches, potions, spells, murders, sex, and fraud. In the end Lucius is miraculously transformed once again into a human, and the force behind his final salvation is no less than the goddess Isis herself, who thereby shows that she is the one deity who has power over all. In response Lucius becomes a priest of Isis and Serapis.[5] The novel ultimately reveals its underlying agenda; it is a piece of religious propaganda for the cult of Isis. It shows concern for the reality and yet randomness of magical powers, but it offers the worship of Isis as a source of control and measure of hope.

In the ancient world, it was generally assumed that special people were the guardians of this magical knowledge and were endowed with special powers. They included heroes of old like Hercules. Sometimes they were called *magi,* after the famous purveyors of secret astrological and magical powers from Persia. Even within the New Testament, *magi* appear and are portrayed both positively and negatively.[6] Significantly, among the exotic sources sought out by Greeks and Romans was a tradition of special magical powers among Jews. In particular, Moses and Solomon were reputed to know all secrets, including the magical powers associated with the Hebrew God. The exotic names of the Jewish God, like those of other deities from the eastern extremities of the empire, were thought to be especially potent in incantations. Reportedly, the Roman emperor Vespasian tried to buy some of these secret Jewish magical formulas. The wisdom tradition and the magical worldview went hand in hand.

As we shall see later (in Chapter 8) such traditions led to an extensive production of miracle stories. These stories tended to follow standard patterns that cut across pagan, Jewish, and Christian traditions. In general, the Jewish apocalyptic worldview (described in Chapter 1) easily assimilated these ideas about magic, but in keeping with its radical cosmic dualism such supernatural forces were seen in strict oppositions, either good or evil, angels or demons. Thus, magical powers were either from God or Satan in apocalyptic thought, and this is how the term "demon" (Gk. *daimon*) lost its original sense of a neutral power and came to be associated with the powers of Satan.[7] It is interesting, however, that such magical demonstrations play little part in most of the Jewish messianic expectations of the time. The miraculous tradition was later suppressed to some extent in rabbinic Judaism, in part because of these dualistic connotations and resultant medieval witchcraft charges by Christians. Still, the Mishnah preserves tales of Jewish healers and miracle workers such as Honi the Circle-drawer and the rabbi Hanina ben Dosa, who lived in the first century. We shall return to these miracle stories later.

The Miracle Worker as Divine Man

Perhaps more than any other figure of antiquity, the ability to perform miracles is most closely associated with what is usually called the *theios aner* (Gk., "divine man"). The title refers to heroes and famous figures who were known for their spectacular deeds or wisdom. Generally, their stories were told and retold as fabulous and heroic tales like the apocryphal legends of the apostles and the saints in early medieval literature. Ludwig Bieler compiled a list of these characteristics; he begins by giving the following definition:

> [The theios aner] *is a man with attributes and capabilities that exceed the human measure, darling of the gods, and a kind of mediator between the divine and mankind. At the same time he is the counselor and* kataorthotes *(powerful and successful executive) of men, and they are drawn to him from afar.*[8]

Although there was no systematic understanding or expectation of such figures among Greeks and Romans, there were nonetheless numerous characters in antiquity who were thought to possess some or all of these traits. Significantly, all were humans whose life stories were viewed, at least by some, as reflecting these attributes. Below is a list of several such figures from antiquity and the authors who wrote about them in this fashion. The list is in chronological order by the dates of the author:

Olympiodorus, *Life of Plato* (ca. 214–129 BCE)

Philo, *Life of Moses* (ca. 10–30 CE)

Philo, *On Abraham* (ca. 10–30 CE)

Suetonius, *Lives of the Caesars: Augustus* (ca. 121 CE; a fabulous account of Augustus's birth attributed to Asclepias of Mendes)

Philostratus, *Life of Apollonius of Tyana* (ca. 217–220 CE)

Iamblichus, *Life of Pythagoras* (ca. 250–325 CE)

Pseudo-Callisthenes, *The Life of Alexander the Great (of Macedon)* (ca. 300 CE; likely derives from an earlier version from the Hellenistic age)

In all these cases, the figure was a long-dead hero (Alexander the Great), ancient philosopher (Plato or Pythagoras), or national leader (Augustus, Moses) whose life was being told (and usually retold) at some later time.

After his death, Alexander the Great came to be viewed as a divine figure. Alexander himself thus became the object of much legendary heroization that enhanced the claims to divine nature. From an early stage, the story circulated that Alexander had not been born in the usual way, but was a special child born through the agency of the god Zeus-Ammon. Writing about 100 CE the Greek biographer Plutarch described it as a kind of "virgin birth," in which Alexander was conceived by Zeus-Ammon himself, in the form of a snake, while his human father, Philip, was kept from having sex with Olympias, Alexander's mother, by a divine command delivered in a dream.[9] Plutarch later refers to Alexander as a "man superior to human nature."[10]

Similar stories of miraculous birth later surrounded the emperor Augustus, as Suetonius recounts:

> When Atia [Augustus's mother] had come in the middle of the night to the solemn rite of Apollo, when her litter had been set in the temple, and while the other women went home, she slept [in the temple]. A snake slipped up to her and, after a little while, went out. When she awoke, she purified herself as if coming from her husband's bed. And immediately on her body there appeared a mark colored like a snake, and she could never get rid of it. . . . Augustus was born in the tenth month after this and because of this was considered the son of Apollo. Atia herself, before she gave birth, dreamed that her womb was carried up to the stars and spread out over all the earth and sky. Octavius, his father, dreamed [before Augustus was born] that the radiance of the sun rose from Atia's womb.[11]

The similarity of these two stories, written at about the same time, is striking. Special birth stories attended by miraculous events were typical of the divine-man tradition.

It should become apparent, then, that the divine man is more a literary tradition than a historical reality. These stories are "Lives" of renowned figures told in such a way as to portray them as divine men. Most notable among the characteristics of the divine man are unusual or magical events surrounding the birth, a precocious childhood, an ability to perform miracles (or magical events that accompany the life), demonstrations of unsurpassable wisdom (through teachings or pronouncements), and (often) unusual events surrounding the death (or disappearance). A summary of these characteristics, based on Bieler, is given in Box 3.1.

BOX 3.1

The Characteristics of a "Divine Man"
(following L. Bieler's Theios Aner)

I. Birth
   A. Special portents, in dreams and divine oracles, announce the imminent birth of a messenger of the gods.
      1. That the mother is pregnant by a divine parent is often announced.
      2. In a few cases the divine progenitor speaks directly to the mother to inform her of the special nature of the child.
   B. The actual birth is almost always marked by some unusual circumstances.
      1. It occurs on a special day (e.g., a festival of the gods).
      2. It occurs in an unusual place (e.g., a meadow, a forest, or even a foreign land while the parents are on a journey).
      3. Sometimes, especially when the father is kept out of the picture, the child is discovered as a foundling.
      4. It is accompanied by a variety of miracles, including:
         a. a pregnancy of unusual duration,
         b. unusual natural phenomena,
         c. unusual features of the delivery, or
         d. manifestations of the divine parentage.

II. Early Childhood
   A. The child's special nature begins to manifest itself almost from birth (and sometimes either at or before the birth), for example, unusual capacities of movement, speech, strength, etc.
   B. The mother, recognizing the unusual nature, determines that the child should be given special treatment or training (in some cases, also the father, who arranges for special tutors, etc.)
   C. The child is precocious and amazes all who observe him, e.g., teachers, parents, other children, visitors who come to observe because they have heard of his powers.
   D. The child excels in all aspects of growth and learning and manifests both miraculous power and innate ("divine") wisdom.

III. Adult Career
   A. Mighty deeds betray a divine providence guiding his life.
   B. Wisdom is manifested in teaching and/or decision making.

(continued)

c. He is able to perform miracles (always for noble reasons).
d. He shows strength of character in the face of trial.
e. His popularity and moral behavior are widespread (often during long journeys).
f. Unusual phenomena accompany his death or disappearance.

Apollonius of Tyana

One of the best and most complete examples of the divine-man tradition is *The Life of Apollonius of Tyana,* by Flavius Philostratus. Apollonius was a real person; he was a first-century Neopythagorean philosopher born a little later than Jesus. His home was Tyana in Cappadocia (modern Turkey), but his legend grew, as he supposedly journeyed to exotic lands, including India, and returned with mystical knowledge. During his own lifetime Apollonius came under some suspicion, as did other critical philosophers in the reigns of Nero (54–68 CE) and Domitian (81–96). According to legend, while facing trial under Domitian, he saw a vision predicting the death of the emperor and his own release. He died (or disappeared) shortly thereafter under Nerva (96–98).

There were other accounts of his life and deeds, but the only extant version is that of Flavius Philostratus (ca. 170–ca. 240 CE), an eclectic philosopher and rhetorician from Lemnos and Athens. Philostratus was a member of an elite "school" of philosophers that was sponsored by the emperor Septimius Severus (193–211) and his wife Julia Domna. In 198–99, Septimius Severus had conquered the Parthian capital of Ctesiphon (near Baghdad) and completed the annexation of Mesopotamia to the Roman Empire. After his return from the east he apparently retained a growing interest in Greek philosophy. His son Marcus Aurelius Antoninus, better known as Caracalla (emperor 198–217), is reputed to have visited Tyana, the birthplace of Apollonius, on his way to the east in 211. Caracalla's mother, Julia Domna, who was from a priestly family in Emesa, Syria, was instrumental in cultivating these interests in "Eastern religions,"[12] and she commissioned Philostratus to tell the *true* story of Apollonius. Caracalla's adopted grandson, Severus Alexander (emperor 222–235),[13] was even more exotic in his religious and philosophical tastes; he is reputed to have set up statues, in place of the traditional gods, of several foreign philosophers, including Apollonius of Tyana, Orpheus, Abraham, and Jesus.[14] Philostratus's *Life of Apollonius* was completed about 218–220 CE.[15]

Apparently, there were several competing versions of Apollonius's life circulating at the time. Some were undoubtedly flattering, but others portrayed him as a charlatan and a magician.[16] Such charges of magic—meaning malevolent use of magic—were clearly taken seriously and were hurled as slurs to impugn his character. Philostratus's goal was to refute these charges by showing Apollonius's divine inspiration as reflected in both his teaching and his miracles. *His* miracles, as we shall see, are nobler manifestations of his divine inspiration. Thus, Philostratus tells of the twofold source of Apollonius's marvelous powers: he had a special birth effected by the god Proteus, and he was an adept in the secret and mystical knowledge of the divine realm inherited from another divine man, Pythagoras.[17]

The Neopythagoreans were especially known for speculating on the occult meanings of numbers and on the magical powers associated with realms of intermediary beings that lie between the good world of the divine and the evil world of material creation. Philostratus portrays Apollonius as adopting an ascetic mode of life—unshorn, barefoot, with few possessions, and abstaining from meat, wine, and sex—after the manner of Pythagoras.[18] The point of Philostratus's portrayal is to show the coherence between his philosophy, morals, and miraculous powers. In so doing, he creates an extensive, novelistic, and anachronistic romance around the life of Apollonius, in which he weaves tales of far-flung journeys and encounters in strange lands.

Philostratus's *Life of Apollonius* is thus a propagandistic "Gospel" intended to promote a following. Two brief passages from the beginning of the story illustrate the tone:

> For quite akin to theirs [the Pythagoreans'] was the ideal which Apollonius pursued, and even more divinely than Pythagoras himself, he approached wisdom [Gk. sophia] and excelled above kings. . . . Nor does the fact that Apollonius foresaw and foreknew so many things disqualify us in the least from imputing to him this very same wisdom [as attributed to Plato and others], or we shall have to impute such ills to Socrates also, on account of his well-known daimon, and likewise Anaxagoras on account of the things which he foretold. (1.2)

Apollonius's powers were not mere wizardry or "black magic"; they were, in fact, a by-product of his philosophic wisdom, just like those of Pythagoras, Plato, and Socrates. Though clearly still a human, he was above other mortals, as evidenced by the strange circumstances that surrounded his birth:

> There came to his mother, while still pregnant with him, an apparition of an Egyptian demon—Proteus, who according to Homer changes his form thus. Not being frightened at all, she asked him what sort of child she would bear. And he replied, "Me." "But who are you?" she asked. He said, "I am Proteus , the Egyptian god.". . . Now [Apollonius] is said to have been born in a meadow, near where there is now a temple erected to him, nor should we ignore the manner of his birth. For just as the hour of his birth was approaching, his mother was warned in a dream to walk out into the meadow to pick some flowers. When she arrived, of course, her maids looked to the flowers and spread out through the

meadow, but she fell asleep reclining in the grass. Whereupon some swans, who were accustomed to feed in the meadow, took the stance of a chorus around her while she slept, and raising their wings, as is their custom, they cried out together all at once, for there was some sort of breeze that blew in the meadow. And then at the sound of their song, she jumped up and gave birth, for such a sudden fright is sufficient to become an untimely midwife. Yet, the residents of that district say that just at the moment of the birth, a thunderbolt seemed about to strike the earth and then rose on high and disappeared aloft. Thus, I think, the gods demonstrated and foretold his fame, how he would transcend the terrestrial to approach the gods, and what sort of man he would become. (1.5)

Apollonius is credited with a divine gift. When we return later (Chapter 8) to discuss how miracle stories were told in antiquity, we shall look again at some of the tales of Apollonius.

The rest of the extensive story, which fills eight books, covers his precocious youth, his travels to India, where he cultivated his mystical insights, and his teachings and miracles in Rome and throughout the empire. Finally, he disappeared magically, according to Philostratus, to escape the tyrannical Domitian.

What is difficult to assess from this third-century example is the degree to which the divine-man tradition was directly operative in the days of Jesus. In some ways, the *Life of Apollonius* exaggerates every aspect of the divine-man tradition and may even be seen to compete with images of Jesus in the Gospels. Some New Testament scholars have even questioned whether the divine-man tradition was so well codified or widely understood.[19] The attributes of the figures often called divine men varied from period to period. In Greco-Roman usage the title "divine man" was not the same as "god man" in later Christian theology. Nor was the title "Son of God" associated with this tradition in typical Greek usage. Only in Philostratus do they all seem to come together to fit Bieler's paradigm perfectly.

So it has been asked: Is this really an appropriate way to understand Jesus or his portrayal in the Gospels? Indeed, most of these earlier figures are not called "gods" in the strict sense, even though they are thought of as somehow superhuman. In general, however, it only meant they were assumed to possess some sort of special divine nature that afforded them divine inspiration, wisdom, and powers.[20] Of these, Apollonius of Tyana seems to be the lone exception, although it must be noted that even the language of Philostratus is somewhat guarded, as it were, making Apollonius a man who became divine due to his saintly life. One wonders here too whether competition with later, third-century, claims about Jesus and the apostles had further shifted the tradition of the divine man beyond what it earlier had been.

On the other hand, it has now been shown that the Greek world before and during the time of Jesus *did* have a concept of human figures that possessed a special "godlike" or "divine" nature that afforded them superhuman insights and magical powers.[21] Other scholars have suggested the term "holy man" to convey the same idea in Greco-Roman as well as Jewish and Christian tradition.[22] "Holy men" included poets and lawgivers of old as well as healers like Hippocrates and philosophers such as Pythagoras. Another is the figure of Moses, whom the Jewish historian Josephus even calls by the Greek term *"anēr theios"* ("divine man").[23]

On the other hand, it must be noted that the title "Son of God" is not generally applied to these "divine men" in any strict way. In other words, the two terms had not yet merged in common Greek usage any more than "messiah" and "Son of God" had merged in Jewish usage (as discussed in Chapter 1). Nor should we assume that all the Gospels portray Jesus in this way just because of his miraculous powers. In the final analysis, we should keep two caveats in mind: first, that the divine-man tradition is primarily a Greco-Roman literary device for interpretation and image construction; and, second, that only some of the Christian Gospels seem to employ this tradition. Specifically, we may see it in the Gospel of Luke and in the apocryphal *Infancy Gospel of Thomas*. In later discussions we shall deal with these cases more directly.

A Jewish Counterpart: Philo's *Life of Moses*

Does our discussion suggest that Jesus was just another one of these divine-men characters? Or that he thought of himself in these terms? No, of course not. Neither did the historical Apollonius of Tyana. The point is, rather, that such depictions reflect later efforts to popularize and heroize certain individuals using this particular character type from Greco-Roman culture. It would be like transforming the image of Jesus into that of Superman or Batman.[24] In fact, such elements seem quite alien to the world of Jewish messianic expectations of that day. Consequently, when we observe such shifts in the characterization of Jesus, we are also watching a change in cultural paradigms.

One key point of intersection may lie in the Jewish wisdom tradition, since we have already seen it in the underpinnings of apocalyptic cosmology as well as the magical worldview; it also made possible significant assimilation of Jewish ideas to the Greek cultural idiom. The prophet figure, Moses in particular, also stands as the child of wisdom (as in Wis 11.1), from whom he receives divine inspiration. Philo describes Moses in very much this same way.[25] Well before Philostratus and the Gospels, Moses was already being portrayed with some of the divine-man attributes. Writing at the end of the first century in Rome, Josephus reflects this tradition, but it was already at work in Philo at the beginning of the first century.[26] It has also been suggested that this tradition of Moses as divine man was known and used in Pauline churches in the middle of the century, before the Gospels were written, and that it was already having an impact on the portrayal of Jesus and his followers.[27]

Moses had already become a figure of renown in Greek circles since the later Hellenistic age, in part by the diffusion of the Jewish population to major cities such as Alexandria. His legend as lawgiver, national leader, and miracle worker attracted attention, sometimes admiring but often spiteful, from pagan writers.[28] Like Apollonius and (as we shall see) Jesus, Moses was slandered by some as a mere magician, a charlatan who only employed sorcery to create a following among the dispossessed rabble he led out of Egypt.[29] Yet such slanders did not sway the production of numerous magical texts and collections as well as apocalyptic writings in the name of Moses. The basis for this tradition is twofold, and both derive from renderings of the Exodus narrative. The first comes from tales of Moses's ability to perform magic, notably in confronting the priests of Pharaoh (Exod 7:8–24). This story was later elaborated into the apocryphal tale of Jannes and Jambres (cf. 2 Tim 3:8). The second comes from Moses as the recipient of divine revelations in the desert and on the thunder-shrouded mountain, places known for their supernatural powers. Most of all, Moses was given the secret name of God and thus was entrusted with the secret "mysteries."

Philo's version of the *Life of Moses* seems primarily to have an apologetic purpose, similar to that of Philostratus nearly two hundred years later. In the light of mixed claims regarding Moses, Philo portrayed him as a recognizable type, the divine man, in order to show that his accomplishments and laws were essentially good and respectable for Jews and non-Jews alike. In the final analysis, he argues that Plato actually got his philosophy from Moses, thus reinforcing his own allegorical interpretations of Genesis.

In Philo, then, Moses becomes the ideal philosopher-king with special divine powers. Although his birth was not special, his infancy was guided by miracles and divine providence, for his parents had put him out by the river to die as a result of the royal decree. He was found in an unusual way, in the marshes, as the king's daughter took an unaccustomed stroll down to the river (the functional analog to Apollonius's birth in a field). He possessed surpassing beauty, so that she could not resist claiming him as her own. It is his precocious childhood that sets him apart as a divine man:

> As he began to grow and increase steadily, he was weaned quicker than they had reckoned. . . . He was noble and pleasing to look at. . . . So he received as his right the nurture and service due to a prince. Yet he did not bear himself like the mere infant that he was, nor delight in fun and laughter and sport, though those who had charge of him did not grudge him relaxation or treat him severely. But rather with modest and serious bearing he applied himself to hearing and seeing what was sure to profit the soul. Teachers soon arrived from diverse regions, some unbidden from the neighboring countries and the nomes of Egypt, while others were summoned from Greece with promises of great rewards. But in short time he advanced beyond their capacities; his gifted nature anticipated their

attempts to lead him, so that it seemed to be a recollection (for him) rather than a learning. And indeed he confounded them with unsolvable theorems. For great natures produce many innovations in knowledge.

As he was already passing the boundaries of childhood, he excelled in judgment. He did not allow adolescent lusts to go unchecked, as some do, even though there were a myriad of provocations through the abundance that the royal palace provided. But by self-control and patience he restrained them, as reins to pull back their headlong force. . . . In general he watched the first directions and impulses of the soul as one would a restive horse, lest it should run away with the reasoning part of the soul [Gk. logismos] that ought to rein it in, and thus bring complete chaos. For these passions are the causes of things both good and evil: good when they are obedient to the hegemony of reason [Gk. logos], but the opposite when they depart from accustomed ways into anarchy.[30]

In the case of Philo the portrayal goes well beyond the traditional accounts of Moses's life and teachings. The arrival of Greek teachers of philosophy and mathematics is clearly an anachronism. Nonetheless, it provides the mechanism for claiming that Moses taught the Greek forebears of Socrates and Plato. Thus, he is no longer just the founder of an eccentric cult followed by a self-absorbed ethnic group; he is the ultimate source of Greek law and philosophy. According to another Jewish legend, the Greeks had revered Moses as lawgiver, but erroneously assumed he was the messenger-god they called Hermes.[31] But even more striking is the degree to which the surpassing excellence of the young Moses is cast in terms of the ideals of Greek culture. As a divine man and ideal philosopher-king he becomes a cultural paradigm for a certain kind of virtue. The tone and wording of the description of the exceptional darling ought to remind one of the precocious Jesus at age twelve (Luke 2:41–52).

The career of Moses then bears out this auspicious beginning by showing him to possess unique and mysterious knowledge of things divine. From these he gave laws to the nation and organized government. One of the most significant scenes is the giving of the law from Sinai, where Moses appears transfigured in a divine way because he was inspired by God:

He descended with countenance far more beautiful than when he ascended, so that those who saw him were filled with awe and amazement; nor even could their eyes continue to stand the dazzling brightness that flashed from him like the rays of the sun.[32]

Philo's elaboration applies to the end of the tale as well, for Moses does not just die (as in Deut 34:5–6). Instead, Philo's account concludes with Moses being taken away by God into heaven. The language of the account shows it to function as a completion of the transformation begun in the "transfiguration" episode on Sinai. Philo says:

After much time, when he was about to be sent to a colony in heaven and, aban-doning mortal life, to become immortal, he was called back by his Father, who harmonized his dual nature of body and soul into a single elemental nature, transforming his whole being into mind as brilliant as the sun.

Now indeed we find him possessed by the spirit, no longer uttering general truths to the whole nation, but to each tribe in particular foretelling the things which were to be and hereafter must come to pass. Some of these have already taken place, others are still looked for, since confidence in the future is assured by fulfillment in the past.[33]

This tradition was widely taken up and is seen in a separate pseudepigraphical legend known as the *Assumption* or *Testament of Moses;* Philo's account seems to reflect a knowledge of this apocalyptic version. This is the view of Moses that had become popular in Jewish tradition by the time of Jesus. It lies behind Moses's return with Elijah to converse with Jesus in another transfiguration story (Mark 9:2–8: Matt 17:1–9; Luke 9:26–36). It is also reflected in other early Christian references (cf. Jude 9).

A Case of Fraud: Lucian's *Alexander*

As seen already in some of the slanders against Apollonius and Moses, the ability to perform miracles was not by itself sufficient to claim divine powers. Charges of "sorcery and magic" were taken seriously and caused some to react against the magical tradition. Nonetheless, this reaction likewise demonstrates the broad cultural acceptance of the magical worldview and the divine-man figure within it. A sure sign of its status as a cultural commonplace is the fact that it also shows up in parodies and satire. One of these is the delightful satire by Lucian of Samosata (ca. 180 CE) of a well-known figure of the day, Alexander of Aboneuteichos, the prophet of the oracle cult of Glykon. In a kind of parody of the genre of "life of a divine man," Lucian's exposé, known by the title *Alexander, the False Prophet,* unmasks him as the consummate charlatan (Gk. *goēs*).[34]

Although in his youth Alexander was extremely handsome and intelligent, his true character comes through as we are shown his chicanery and his less than noble motivations for performing magical feats. He concocts elaborate illusions that trick people into thinking he can perform miracles and is the direct spokesman for the god Glykon. The oracle, we are told, speaks in an unintelligible divine gibberish that only Alexander can translate. The oracle cult of Glykon becomes large and famous, but it is really a cover for the greed of Alexander and his followers. Worst of all, he seduces the innocent with his religious charade in order to satisfy his own insatiable lusts. Money and sexual perversions, Lucian wants us to see, are his real gods.

At the end, Alexander predicted that he would depart earth in a lightning bolt after a hundred and fifty years. But Lucian says he really died before age seventy of an excruciating gangrene in his leg. Bald, feeble, and "seething with worms," he died a miserable death.[35] His corrupt oracle cult devolved into an immodest power struggle among Alexander's followers. What's interesting in Lucian's satire is that he only partially discredits Alexander's ability to perform magic by showing how some illusions were performed. Yet his ultimate charge against Alexander is that his morals do not match his miraculous powers; therefore, he is not a genuine divine man, but a sham. Both the typical features of the divine-man tradition and this exaggerated lampoon of them would lead to the production of a fairly standard type of miracle-story form. We shall see this form again when we turn to the Gospels in Act II.

By way of conclusion, it is worth noting that the ancients also saw similarities between Apollonius and Jesus. They were recognized as contemporaries, and their later followers were often in conversation or competition. Philostratus and the Christian philosopher Origen were precise contemporaries, a century or more later. The fact that Alexander Severus is reputed to have been a devotee simultaneously of Jesus and Apollonius further shows the similarities, at least in the public eye. By the end of the third century, Hierocles, a provincial governor under Diocletian, wrote a treatise called *The Lover of Truth* in which he made explicit the comparison. Just on the eve of the great persecution, he attempted to show that Apollonius was superior to Jesus by arguing, in effect, that Jesus was a feeble imitation. But the key is the realization of so basic a similarity.

In response, Eusebius of Caesarea, the bishop and first great church historian, wrote a treatise against the *Life of Apollonius* by Philostratus. Rather than attacking the notion that Jesus and Apollonius were similar, however, Eusebius attacked the miraculous claims made about Apollonius. Instead of possessing divine powers, he argued, those claims were attributable to Apollonius's natural gifts or to cunning and fraud. In other words, Apollonius was the imitation; Jesus, the real thing, the son of God. Eusebius thus levels the same charges brought by Lucian against Alexander.

What this shows is that the divine-man paradigm had become a fixture in dealing with the persona of the miracle worker and sage. Yet it shows that in the Greek context, at least, the title "Son of God," as it had begun to evolve in Christian usage, came closest to the connotation of a divine man, that is, a human who somehow possessed divine attributes and achieved a degree of divinity at the end of his life. After all, to both Jews and Greeks the idea of the divine actually becoming a human was unthinkable, although very special humans might on occasion be elevated to the status of gods, as we shall see more in the next chapter.

CHAPTER FOUR

Savior

As they were watching, he was lifted up, and a cloud took him out of their sight.
While he was going and they were gazing up toward heaven, suddenly two men in
white robes stood by them. They said, "Men of Galilee, why do you stand looking
up toward heaven? This Jesus, who has been taken from you into heaven, will come
in the same way as you saw him go into heaven." (Acts 1:9–11)

The scene in Acts 1:9–11 is the lone depiction in the New Testament of Jesus's ascension into heaven after his resurrection.[1] Despite the lack of other early accounts, the idea behind the ascension—that after his death Jesus had been exalted to heaven, where he waits to return—is one of the most common beliefs among early Christians.[2] It was taken, of course, as a proof of their claims about the identity of Jesus. On the other hand, it often comes as a surprise to modern folk to learn that such an idea was not all that uncommon in that day.

Nor is it clear in the earliest stages what it was meant to demonstrate in regard to Jesus's person or nature. Was he—like Enoch, Moses, and Elijah—a mortal who had achieved such spiritual insight and moral goodness that God had taken him away and granted him immortality? Or was he a god, come to earth in some manner, who was just returning home? We shall see both ideas operating in the New Testament era. Both figures could bear the title "Son of God" in the Greek and Roman world, and therein lay the beginnings of a debate that would last centuries. In this chapter we shall survey some of the issues surrounding notions of divinity and of the so-called savior-gods among the Greeks and Romans.

Becoming a God

Pagans looking at early Christianity were often amused by the stories about the resurrection and ascension of Jesus. After all, pagans knew of many such stories in their own tradition. Christians knew them too. Writing about 150 CE, the Christian philosopher and apologist Justin Martyr used this same observation to defend Christians facing persecution. He said:

> *In asserting that the Logos, Jesus Christ our teacher, who is the first born of God, was born without sexual intercourse, and that he was crucified and died and rising again ascended into heaven, we present nothing new compared to those whom you call sons of Zeus. You know how many sons of Zeus the historians revered by you claim—Hermes, the hermeneutic Logos and teacher of all; Asclepius, who was also a healer and after being struck by lightning ascended into heaven, as did Dionysius, who was torn in pieces; Herakles, who to escape his torments threw himself into the fire; the Dioscuri born of Leda; and Perseus [born of] of Danaë; and Bellerophon who, though of human parentage, rode the [divine] horse Pegasus [to the heavens]. Why don't we talk about Ariadne and those who, like her, are said to have been placed among the stars? And what about your deceased emperors, whom you regularly think worthy of being deified, summoning as witness one who swears to have seen the cremated Caesar ascending into heaven from the funeral pyre? And what sort of deeds are narrated about each of these who are called sons of Zeus? It is not necessary to say more to you who already know, except that these things have been written for the benefit and exhortation of schoolboys. For everyone considers imitating the Gods to be good. . . . Now we have been taught that only those who live near God in holiness and virtue are deified. . . . But the son of God who is called Jesus, even if only an ordinary human, is worthy to be called son of God because of his wisdom, for all [your] historians call God the father of men as well as gods. And if we also say, as we said before, that he [Jesus], in an unusual way compared to an ordinary birth, was born from God as the Logos of God, it should be ordinary to you, since you call Hermes the premonitory Logos that proceeds from God. . . . And if we also present him as being born through a virgin, it should be as ordinary to you as that pertaining to Perseus. Or if we add that he brought healing to the lame, paralytics, and those blind from birth, and that he caused the dead to rise, we would just seem to assert things similar to that reportedly done by Asclepius.*[3]

For Justin the legends of Greek and Roman mythology were proof that the stories about Jesus should be taken seriously, that such things really could happen through the power of the divine. Justin adopts the more traditional Greek notion of "son of God" in his definition in this passage and seems to concede that Jesus was just an ordinary human. Moreover, by identifying Jesus as Logos with Hermes as the "premonitory Logos," Justin is employing a common philosophical explanation, found in Stoicism as well as Philo, for divine inspiration through the mechanism of nature, since the Logos ("reason/word") pervades all things. Ultimately, Justin wants to show that Christian claims about Jesus are perfectly ordinary and therefore reasonable. For pagans, however, it was neither the miraculousness nor the preposterousness of the Christian stories that bewildered them; it was when Christians tried to argue that they were somehow unique.

About the year 180 CE, a Greek philosopher named Celsus took exception to the exclusiveness of Christians' claims about Jesus. So he turned Justin's argument back against them:

> If you Christians believe the stories of Jesus's miracles, if you believe the story of Jesus's miraculous birth, if you believe the story that Jesus was raised from the dead and ascended into heaven, and so on, why do you refuse to believe precisely the same stories when they are told of the other savior gods: Herakles, Asklepios, the Dioscuri, Dionysios, and a dozen others I could name?[4]

Celsus had a point, for clearly the same stories of humans who became gods or gods who intervened in human affairs were widely known. They were part and parcel of the magical worldview that dominated the cultures of the ancient Mediterranean (see Chapter 3). The tacit acknowledgment that such things could happen was at the root of Jewish and Christian belief as well, so much so that Christian writers from the beginning used allusions to the pagan myths and legends to support and explain the stories about Jesus. They range from comparing Jesus's death to that of Socrates[5] to comparing his resurrection to that of the phoenix, the legendary bird that every five hundred years dies and rises from his own ashes.[6]

Despite these similarities, there was one key sticking point for Celsus. It was perfectly reasonable to claim that Jesus, like Hercules or Asclepius, was a mortal who was transformed into a god. As we shall see, that sort of thing happened all the time with heroes and emperors. But to Celsus's dismay, some Christians were saying that Jesus was in fact a god who came to earth as a mortal and then became a god again:

> But what kind of God is it who "comes down" to earth and brings fire along with him? As Plato has taught, God is that which is beautiful and happy and exists within himself in the most perfect of all conceivable states. This means that God is changeless. A god who comes down to humans undergoes a change—a change from good to bad, from beautiful to shameful, from happiness to misfortune, from what is perfect to what is base. Now what sort of a god would choose a change like that? Is it not rather the nature of a mortal to undergo change and remolding, and the nature of an immortal to remain the same without alteration? Accordingly, it cannot be the case that God came down to earth, since in so doing he would have undergone an alteration of his nature. To be blunt: Either God really does change, as they suggest, into a human (and this, as said before, is an impossibility), or else he does not change, but rather makes those who see him merely think that he is mortal, and so deceives them and tells lies—which it is not the nature of a god to do.[7]

This way of thinking about Jesus would eventually (by the early fourth century) become the norm for Christianity, but to Celsus it was just silly—contrary to rational thinking. Not that a god is incapable of doing such a thing, but why would any god choose to do so? It was an ungodly thing to do. Still, the critique of Celsus shows us some of the developments taking place in early Christian thinking about Jesus, and also some of the difficulties. Some Christians of the time agreed with Celsus; they believed that Jesus merely *appeared* to be human, and his "death" was only an illusion. As we shall see, they also wrote Gospels from this novel theological perspective.[8] Other Christians argued that, on the contrary, Jesus had first been an ordinary human and only later, after his death and resurrection, was made divine. Other new Gospels were written from this theological perspective too.[9] Of course, this idea accorded better with both pagan and Jewish tradition and may be reflected in some of the earliest Gospel traditions. Yet both of these views, and the various Gospels associated with them, would eventually be deemed heretical. We shall return to them in later chapters.

The Deification of Kings and Emperors

For most inhabitants of the Roman world, the scene of Jesus's ascension, as depicted in Acts, more than anything else would have called to mind what happened when Roman emperors died. They became gods and were taken away to the realm of immortals in a process usually called *apotheosis* (from a verb meaning "to deify" or, more literally, "to god away").[10] One scene from Roman art is typical; it depicts the apotheosis of the empress Sabina, wife of Hadrian (117–38 CE) (see Box 4.1). Hadrian is shown looking on as she ascends above her own funeral pyre, borne away from earth on the back of a winged Victory. In another, the emperor Antoninus Pius (138–60 CE) and his wife, Faustina, are shown ascending together on the back of an almost angelic, winged male figure resembling Icarus.[11]

As a contemporary of these events in Rome, Justin Martyr[12] undoubtedly knew such scenes, as is shown in his comments (quoted above). There he cites what is probably the prototype for all these later imperial depictions, the apotheosis of Augustus; however, Justin has apparently conflated it with the apotheosis of Julius Caesar. Here are the two stories as told by the imperial biographer Suetonius:

> He [Julius Caesar] died at fifty-six years of age, and was numbered among the gods, not only by a formal decree, but also in the conviction of the common people. For at the first games which his heir Augustus gave in honor of his **apotheosis**,[13] a comet shone for seven successive days, rising about the eleventh hour, and was believed to be the soul of Caesar which had been taken to heaven; and this is why a star is set upon the crown of his head in his statue.[14]

> He [Augustus] was carried on the shoulders of senators to the Campus Martius and there cremated. There was even an ex-praetor who swore an oath that he

had seen the form [lit., effigy] of the Emperor, after he had been cremated, going to heaven.[15]

Perhaps Justin reflects prevailing popular misperceptions of the day. Being "placed among the stars" seems to reflect the story of Julius Caesar, while witnessing the deceased "ascending into heaven from the funeral pyre" comes from

BOX 4.1

Apotheosis of an Empress

Relief showing the Empress Sabina, wife of Hadrian, being carried away from her funeral pyre to Heaven by an angelic figure. Hadrian sits at the right looking on. Rome, 136 CE. Capitoline Museum.

the story of Augustus. At the same time, it shows how such stories circulated and gave rise to new legends. Indeed, they were taken quite seriously by emperors and populace alike.

For example, in the year 130 CE Hadrian deified his favorite companion and lover, the slave Antinous, who had recently died in Egypt, and dedicated a new worship cult to him. The historian Cassius Dio describes it this way:

> *Thus he [Hadrian] gave divine honors to Antinous, either because he loved him or because he died voluntarily (it apparently being necessary for a life to be freely offered to accomplish what Hadrian wanted). [Hadrian] built a city near the place where he died and he named it after him. He erected statues, actually sacred images, of him almost all over the world. Finally, Hadrian said he had seen a certain star, which, it seemed to him, was that of Antinous, and he welcomed the fanciful stories of his friends, namely, that the star was created from the soul of Antinous and had only just appeared. He was ridiculed on account of these things and also because, when his sister Paulina died, he did not at once pay her any divine honors.*[16]

A commonplace deification may have been, but it was still subject to imperial caprice, as reflected in Cassius Dio's tone. Similarly, Justin Martyr denigrated the forced worship of Antinous, but this shows up even more clearly the respect with which he treated the traditional accounts of apotheosis.[17]

Divine Kingship

The tradition of according some sort of divine status to kings has a long history in the Mediterranean world. The kings of ancient Mesopotamia, like those of Greece, usually had their patron deity who accorded the king a special place above the rest of his subjects. Coronation ceremonies did double duty, since they functioned as New Year's celebrations in which creation stories were also recited or re-enacted. Thus, kingship, creation, and national or civic identity were often bound up together in a single religious festival. Something like this was even operative in ancient Israel's kingship ideology as reflected in the so-called royal psalms of the Davidic monarchy. As in Psalm 2, the king, through the ritual of anointing, is adopted annually to be God's son as a symbol of the special relationship between God and nation.[18] In this sense the origins of "messianic" language in Israelite and Jewish tradition stem from a broader pattern of ancient Near Eastern divine kingship ideology. It is often referred to as divine investiture or royal adoption; that is, the king is thought of as specially designated and overseen by the gods, though not divine himself.

A different view of kingship grew up in ancient Egyptian culture, and this too had a profound influence on Hellenistic and Roman views. Beginning at least with the New Kingdom period in Egypt (ca. 1465–1165 BCE), it was normal to consider the pharaoh a god. In the New Kingdom coronation ritual, the old pharaoh was symbolized as Osiris, god of the dead; his successor was Horus, the son of Osiris and Isis. The elaborate coronation ritual reenacted the myth of Isis and Osiris at the great temples of Luxor and Thebes. It reflected both the special status accorded to the pharaoh and the sense of order in the world. In Theban cosmology, that order was governed by the powers of Isis and Osiris as the offspring of the creator gods of the Egyptian pantheon. This view of divine kingship was much more literal; the pharaoh and his family were thought of as really divine, set apart from the rest of humanity in status as well as nature.

This view of kingship enters our story at a key juncture in history. In 332 BCE, after Alexander the Great had conquered the Persians, he took control of their provinces in Palestine and Judea and finally marched into Egypt. In Egypt Alexander was crowned, not only as a conquering king, but as a new pharaoh, as a god. He was hailed as Ammon himself. A decade later, after the death of Alexander, this acclamation of his divinity would become the germ of a new Hellenistic notion of kingship. Alexander himself thus became the object of much legendary heroization that enhanced these claims to divine nature. This tradition may well be one of the seeds of the divine-man tradition discussed in Chapter 3. From an early stage, the story circulated that Alexander had not been born in the usual way, but was a special child born through the agency of the gods, or more particularly the god Zeus-Ammon. Similar stories of miraculous birth later surrounded the emperor Augustus as recounted by Suetonius.[19]

Such stories of miraculous birth link the divine-man tradition to the rise of the Roman imperial cult. Thus, there were several lines of thought on the divine man converging in the Roman period, and they took on even greater colorations of divinity from the legends of Alexander. Throughout the Roman period shrines and cults of the deified Alexander continued to be popular, especially in the eastern Mediterranean. So too when Hadrian proclaimed the deity of Antinous, he did so by declaring that he was "Osiris Antinous the Holy."[20]

Needless to say, such deification of the king became very popular among Alexander's successors, especially the Ptolemies and Seleucids, who ruled Egypt and Syria-Palestine, respectively. The impact can be seen most clearly when we remember that Antiochus IV, the Seleucid monarch who prompted the Maccabean revolt, was called Epiphanes, meaning "god manifest." The book of Daniel, written during the Maccabean revolt (167–164 BCE), includes a number of thinly veiled attacks against this notion of honoring or worshiping the Seleucid king as divine (see esp. Dan 3; 6; 11:29–45). From its conservative Jewish perspective, such a view was tantamount to idolatry. The kingship ideology of the Hellenistic monarchies had not been shy in according such titles. If anything the Ptolemies were even more blatant in their divine claims and global aspirations than were the Seleucids. Here is the list of titles accorded to Ptolemy V Epiphanes (210–180) at his twelfth birthday, as set down in three languages on the famous Rosetta Stone:

In the reign of the young king by the inheritance from his father, Lord of the Diadems, great in glory, pacifier of Egypt and pious toward all the gods, superior over his adversaries, restorer of the life of man . . . king like the sun. Great King of the Upper and Lower Lands, child of the gods through the love of the father [Ammon or Osiris] . . . living image of Zeus, son of the sun [Ammon-Ra], Ptolemy the immortal . . . priest of the divine Alexander and the savior gods and the benefactor gods and the gods of the love of the father, the god manifest, for whom thanks be given.[21]

In addition to the cult of the deified Alexander, the Ptolemies promoted the cult of Isis and Osiris, the latter called by the hellenized name Sarapis, as part of their dynastic claims. These ideas began to filter into the rest of the Hellenistic world through Ptolemaic trade and influence, and (as we shall see later in this chapter) the cult of Isis and Sarapis later became one of the most popular in the Greco-Roman world. Kingship ideology also came down to the Romans, who took over Egypt in the time of Cleopatra VII, the lover of Julius Caesar and Mark Antony. She was the last Ptolemaic monarch of Egypt.

Cult and "Gospel" of the Roman Emperors

After Octavian defeated the forces of Antony and Cleopatra at Actium in 31 BCE, he became Rome's first emperor. In 27 BCE, the senate conferred on him the title Augustus—a Latin word meaning "hallowed" or "revered." The title eventually became a part of the imperial nomenclature and was inherited by all later emperors. Throughout his reign there were times when he was suspected of harboring divine aspirations, but the exorbitant claims of Antony and Cleopatra called for caution. The worship of the emperor as divine did not sit quite so well with the old Roman aristocracy as it might have with Greek provincials.

For example, the first imperial cult temple in Asia was established at Pergamon in the year 29 BCE; it was dedicated to Roma (i.e., the personification of the city of Rome) and Augustus. Similarly, in 9 BCE Herod the Great dedicated a golden-roofed temple to Roma and Augustus overlooking his newly created harbor, which he named Caesarea Sebaste in honor of the emperor. The temple contained colossal statues of Augustus and Roma said to rival the ancient statue of Zeus at Olympia.[22] A proclamation of the same year from the important province of Asia reflects the typical "eastern" language of divine honors:

*Whereas Providence, which divinely ordered our lives, created with zeal and munificence the most perfect good for our lives by producing Augustus and filling him with virtue for the benefaction of humankind, sending us and our descendants a savior to put an end to war . . . , and Whereas when Caesar [Augustus] appeared, he exceeded the hopes of all who had anticipated his **good tidings***

[Gk. euangelion*] . . . , and Whereas the birthday of the god [Augustus] marked*
for the world the beginning of said good tidings through his coming . . .[23]

With this decree, the provincial assembly also proposed to change the calendar
to make Augustus's birthday the beginning of the New Year. He is hailed as the
"savior" of humanity who brings peace. Moreover, the term here translated "good
tidings" is actually the Greek *euangelion,* or "gospel," a term used frequently in
Augustan propaganda. Of course, it is the same term used in the New Testament.
Another proclamation from the region is even more blunt in its divine honors by
beginning: "Since Emperor Caesar, son of god, [himself] the god Sebastos, has by
his benefactions to all humans outdone even the Olympian gods . . ."[24] Augustus
here is hailed as the god Sebastos (the usual Greek rendering of the name/title
Augustus), and the son of god, meaning the deified Julius Caesar.

Although Augustus was regularly accorded divine honors during his lifetime in
the eastern provinces, he seems to have been more cautious about such titles at Rome
itself. He could still be called *divi filius* ("son of god"), since Julius Caesar had been
divinized at death; however, Augustus regularly deflected direct use of divine titles
for himself. Later emperors of the first century, notably Caligula and Domitian, did
not always exercise such self-restraint. The imperial cult and its trappings would become more of a test of faith as well as a cause for debate among later Christian writers. The view of 1 Peter 2:13–17, which calls on Christians to "honor the emperor"
as ordained by God,[25] stands in sharp contrast to that of the Revelation to John,
which identifies the emperor as the satanic beast, whose henchmen force the world
to worship his statue (13:1–18; 17:8–14).[26] These two works reflect the situation in
Asia Minor in the last decade of the first century, at just about the same time that
the Gospels of Luke and John were being written. In other words, the language of
the Gospels themselves, and even the very title "gospel" ("good news," *euangelion*),
reverberate with the contemporary language and resonance of the imperial cult and
the deification of emperors. Some mortals did become gods.

What to Do with Poor Claudius?

Although the cult of the Roman emperors was growing in popularity, both
east and west, throughout the first century CE, not all the emperors received equal
treatment. Domitian (81–96) himself, the "evil force" targeted in the Revelation
to John, was eventually "damned from memory" by the Roman senate after his
death, because of his excesses and demagoguery. His colossal statue at Ephesus
was thrown down, and his temple renamed in honor of his father, Vespasian.
Domitian was no longer a god.

A different fate was reserved for the emperor Claudius (41–54 CE). True to
form, when he died he was proclaimed *divus,* a god, by the Roman senate, and a
monumental tomb and temple were built in his name at Rome, near the grounds of

Nero's palace. But Claudius was not quite as much a darling of the Roman people as other emperors before or after, in part because of his birth defects—a clubfoot, a misshapen head that twitched uncontrollably, hunched shoulders, and a speech impediment, or what might well now be diagnosed as cerebral palsy. Indeed, many people thought that when the praetorian guard placed the poor, cowering Claudius on the throne, immediately after they had assassinated his nephew and predecessor, Gaius Caligula, it had all just been a big joke. Yet Claudius proved to be fully competent and a capable administrator, even though his marriage and private life continued to be a source of ruthless gossip and personal embarrassment at Rome.[27] Nonetheless, at death he was deified, and one of the first major imperial cult facilities in the West was dedicated in his honor at Colchester in Roman Britain.

The tittering and gossip, however, did not die with Claudius, and his adopted son and successor, Nero (54–68 CE), seems to have relished heaping additional insults on Claudius in order to feed his own megalomania. He cleverly punned that Claudius "no longer played the fool" among the living, suggesting perhaps that he was still doing so elsewhere. In another pun Nero called mushrooms the "food of the gods," because his mother, Julia Agrippina (whom he later killed), reputedly poisoned Claudius in this way.[28] In other words, she had helped turn Claudius into a god by killing him. Thus, though Nero publicly honored Claudius at his funeral,[29] privately he scorned him in death. Eventually Nero revoked the deification of Claudius, but it was later restored by Vespasian.[30]

Nero's puns also suggest another line of amusement among his courtiers, as they speculated how the bumbling, foolish Claudius might fare among the gods. It became the basis for a biting satire. Nero's accomplice in this task seems to have been his court philosopher and political adviser, L. Annaeus Seneca, the most famous Latin Stoic philosopher of the century.[31] Seneca had been exiled for a time under Claudius for criticisms of his rule, and so it is often suggested that he took out his revenge on Claudius after death in an uproarious lampoon entitled *The Apocolocyntosis of the Divine Claudius*. The title clearly apes the term *apotheosis* or its synonym *apathanatisis* (meaning "to deify" or "to make immortal"), the ascension of the emperor into heaven. But it is a concocted Greek compound from the word *kolokynthe*, meaning a gourd or squash. Thus, the lampooning title is usually translated *The Pumpkinification of the Divine Claudius*. I prefer to call it *The Zucchinification of the Divine Claudius*.[32]

Seneca begins by reporting the usual events on earth attesting to Claudius's apotheosis at his death, those same reports used to authenticate the divine status of other emperors. But then, as a kind of exposé, he tells what happened when poor stumbling, bumbling Claudius got to heaven. There he encounters the other mortals who have been elevated to divine status. First he meets Hercules, who thinks that Claudius is some sort of strange denizen of the deep sent as another adversary to test his heroic stamina once again.[33] After a long debate over whether

Claudius should be admitted, Hercules is persuaded, apparently because Claudius is kin to Augustus, who is there in heaven too. So, next, Augustus himself steps forward in the heavenly council to disavow Claudius, saying, "Is this why I became a god? Is this why I conquered land and sea?" The council of the gods then votes to kick Claudius out of heaven, and he is summarily escorted to the regions of Hades. The final barb for Seneca is portraying the poor Claudius in Hades; Claudius is shown to be enjoying himself there. The jest is complete for author and audience: What kind of a fool must Claudius have been? No matter what the senate may decree, the gods will have the last word.

As with other satirical literature, Seneca's treatment tells far more than just how Claudius was regarded. As with Lucian's satirical exposé *Alexander, the False Prophet* (see Chapter 3), the work presupposes that the audience will recognize both the genre of writing and the type of character it is portraying. In this case Seneca must presuppose that people know and really accept the stories of apotheosis of the emperors and their families. Satire and parody play off of the accepted and the real. Seneca also shows clear awareness of the traditional stories about what happened at the apotheosis of Augustus and others. So the comical scene in heaven in which Hercules, Augustus, and other deified mortals debate Claudius's future presupposes that they have all now entered the divine realm and live on the same level as the other gods. The deification of Claudius may be treated with disdain, but deification of mortals through the process of apotheosis is nonetheless an assumed reality in that world.

The So-called Dying and Rising Gods

What the previous discussion shows is that the notions of "going away to heaven" and "becoming immortal" meant becoming a god. It was not for ordinary humans, not even for the emperor Claudius, at least in the eyes of some. Hence, these notions were not about what people normally think of as "salvation." In fact, the epithet "savior" was most often applied to Hellenistic kings and Roman emperors, sometimes to city founders and benefactors, and somewhat less often to the traditional gods.[34] The hero-god Asclepius, one of those mentioned by Justin and Celsus, was commonly called "savior," but the sense of the term is also the common one. To be "saved" here means to be "healed" from illness or disease.[35]

On the other hand, there were a number of relatively new cults in the Hellenistic and Roman period that did use the term "savior" for their gods in the sense of some special benefit for ordinary humans. These are what we now call "mystery cults," and one of their characteristic features is that they often celebrate the stories of gods or mortals who—like Jesus, in the eyes of some—had died and come back to life. They have sometimes been called the "dying and rising gods." Such stories of death and regeneration—although not the same as resurrection among

Jews or apotheosis among the Romans—were a common mythic tradition in the Hellenistic-Roman world.

The Greek "Mysteries"

The term "mystery" (Gk. *mysterion*) comes from the Greek verb *myein,* meaning "to close" the eyes or lips. It is sometimes taken to mean that the knowledge of the rites is unutterable. But the verb *myein* is often used in later contexts where the connotation is clearly "to initiate," perhaps in the sense of an "eye-opening" ritual.[36] In any case, though the origins of the terminology and the underlying phenomenon are debatable, these mysteries all seem to have had some regular ritual of initiation associated with a peculiar (often local) mythic cycle.

For example, in the case of the Zeus of Panamara, there were four large golden statues of feet, said to commemorate the epiphanies of the god there. These epiphanies were thought to be especially beneficial for both the city and individuals. An annual festival lasting ten days was celebrated, during which those who joined in the great procession from Panamara to Stratonicea and back were given special treats. Those who did so were the *mystai,* the initiates in the mysteries. It is not clear what other, if any, "spiritual blessings" might have ensued, but the statues of the gods were supposed to have had special healing powers, particularly during the festivals.

The cult established by Alexander of Aboneuteichos to Glykon in the second century CE, which Lucian satirized in his *Alexander, the False Prophet,* was also called a mystery. Lucian says that he promised direct benefits of healing and oracles to followers; however, in this case it would seem that Alexander's claims were intentionally aping those of the famous Eleusinian mysteries.

The Eleusinian Mysteries

The most famous cult in all antiquity, and the one that probably influenced many of the new Hellenistic and Roman mysteries that proliferated later, was that at Eleusis, near Athens. The foundation of the local cult probably goes back to the Archaic period (ca. eighth century BCE). By the early classical period (seventh to sixth centuries BCE) it had already developed a panhellenic reputation. Sanctuaries to Demeter and her festival, the Thesmophoria, were found in most Greek cities, but Eleusis was special. In the founding legend, known to us from the Homeric *Hymn to Demeter,* Eleusis was the home of the king Keleos, with whom the goddess Demeter found hospitality while on her search for her long-lost daughter, Persephone. It was there that she finally got Persephone back.

The sanctuary at Eleusis preserves some of these legendary elements. Situated on a promontory overlooking the bay of Eleusis, the great hall, called the Telesterion (from *telete,* "initiation"), supposedly stands where the palace hall of the king, Keleos, once stood. Nearby, at the entrance to the sanctuary, is a grotto, a cavern thought to lead to the underworld. According to the legends, it was through it that Persephone returned annually. Temples to Demeter and Persephone (Kore) stand in prominent spots throughout the complex. By the classical and Hellenistic periods it had grown into one of the most revered sanctuaries in all of Greece. Throughout the Roman period it continued to grow and became a tourist destination for philosophers and emperors, for any and all who could afford to make the trip and pay the fees.

The Story of Demeter and Persephone

What lies behind this fame is the myth itself. The story, which circulated in several forms in antiquity, is best known from the *Hymn to Demeter*. It surrounds the abduction of Persephone (or Kore), the daughter of Demeter, the goddess of grain. Demeter searched for her everywhere, but found nothing. When she entreated the other Olympian deities to help her, she got no reply. Finally, she came in desperation to seek the help and hospitality of humans, and so she arrived at the palace of Keleos, but in the guise of a haggard old woman. The daughters and wife of Keleos took the old woman in and offered her hospitality. Eventually she was taken into their household service as nurse for the king's baby son, Demophon.

Under Demeter's care, Demophon grew "like a god."[37] Unbeknownst to his mother, Metaneira, it was not because of ordinary food. Rather, the disguised Demeter was feeding him on the favorite food of the gods, ambrosia, and each night she would dangle the child over the hearth, "hiding him like a firebrand within the might of the flame."[38] Delighted, his parents still could not understand why the child was so precocious and why his appearance was so godlike. So one night Metaneira slipped in to watch and, understandably, she shrieked when Demeter placed the child over the fire. Interrupted, Demeter revealed her true identity, sloughing off her haggard human disguise and growing immediately into the giant stature and radiant beauty of a goddess. Yet her plans for Demophon—to transform him from a human into a god as some sort of replacement for her lost child—had been thwarted. Meanwhile, Metaneira and her daughters supplicated and appeased Demeter. Keleos ordered that a new temple be built for her there on his property at Eleusis. So the goddess came to reside there, but still she was desolate and angry.

Next, Demeter began to oppress the human realm by withholding the growth of crops, her special domain. So meager were the crops that humans could offer none of their regular harvest sacrifices to the Olympian gods. Zeus and the other gods began to wonder what had gone wrong. They liked their ambrosia made from the harvest offerings, but there was none to be had. Finally Zeus sent out messengers to find out what was wrong and to discover where Persephone had been taken. When he found out, he summoned Demeter to Mt. Olympus. She came, but refused to submit to his demands that she restore the crops to earth.

At last Zeus gave in and dispatched Hermes to broker a deal with Hades, the god of the underworld, who had taken the fair Persephone to his realm to be his mistress. At last Persephone was to return to her mother in the realm of the living. But there was still another catch, for by tricking Persephone into eating a pomegranate Hades forced her to spend a third (or a half, in some versions) of the year with him in the underworld. The deal was finally struck and ratified by Zeus. In response Demeter returned the crops to the land during those months when Persephone was with her, but made them wither with heat during that time when Persephone went to live with Hades. In thanks to Keleos and Metaneira, Demeter showered gifts on them and blessed the nearly divinized child, Demophon, with special attributes as a hero.

At its root, this myth is clearly an archaic Greek etiological legend to explain the seasons and the crop cycle. Such seasonal or vegetative myths are, in fact, common to most of the ancient cultures of the Mediterranean, and all are climate specific to their own regions. In Greece, the scorching hot summer months are the time of no crops; the fall is the planting season; and harvest is in the spring. The *Hymn to Demeter* also serves as a foundation myth for the particular sanctuary at Eleusis. But in their evolved form, the Eleusinian mysteries ultimately came to have another significance for individuals who were initiated there. Persephone, like the grain, was reborn each year, but her rebirth also came to symbolize a quest for immortality among mortal humans.

Like the hope for an afterlife in ancient Egyptian culture, belief in the immortality of the soul came to prominence in Greek religion and philosophy. Persephone's rebirth was the constant symbol of that possibility, over against the inherent mortality and finitude of human existence. Also, in the central vignette of the myth, the taste of full immortality, or divine nature, that Demeter offers to the child Demophon, although never fully realized, is the symbol of the divine spark of immortality that the Eleusinian mysteries offer the initiate. The story finally says, in effect, that Demeter offers this to all who come to her at Eleusis. This is what transforms it into a special cult, a *mystery*, where the reenacting of the myth through procession and the rituals of initiation causes the symbolic religious play of faith and reality for the adherent.

By the late sixth century BCE, Eleusis had been incorporated into the civic territory of Athens, and the Eleusinian festivals were integrated into the Athenian civic cult. Each year in the fall, the Athenians made ritual preparations and marched in solemn procession to Eleusis, some thirteen miles away. After fasting and other rituals, they spent the night in the Telesterion. During the night each in turn was taken into the sacred chamber and shown the secrets of Demeter. The ritual moment was called the *epopteia* ("unveiling" or "inspection"). Some have suggested the holy object was a stalk of wheat as symbol of the reborn Persephone. But what was actually revealed no one knows; it has been kept the secret of the *mysteries*.

The fall rituals were known as the Great Mysteries. The Lesser Mysteries were celebrated in the spring, near the time of the annual festivals of flowers and the dead (the Anthesteria) at another Demeter sanctuary in Athens itself. After completion of the full cycle, worshipers were considered full initiates into the cult. These rituals of initiation effectively reenacted the mythic stories in the experience of the participants. Recitations of the basic myth in hymnic refrains and staged theatrical performances of the main scenes were part of the Great Mysteries at Eleusis.

New Mysteries and Other Gods

The Eleusinian mysteries were by far the most famous in the ancient world. After the Mediterranean was unified under Rome, people would come from far and wide to be initiated into the rites of Demeter. Even emperors, including Augustus and Hadrian, and divine men, such as Apollonius of Tyana, were said to have made the pilgrimage to Athens to participate in the sacred procession to the sanctuary at Eleusis. It was the same route that St. Paul would travel from Athens to Corinth. The sanctuary remained in operation for nearly a thousand years before Christian emperors finally shut it down at the end of the fourth century CE. Still, the Eleusinian mysteries mark a more traditionally Greek form of cult, a cult attached by legend and lore to a particular place. The prospective worshipers had to come there to be initiated and thus to receive the benefits afforded by the story of Persephone's return from death.

At the same time, the type of cult seen at Eleusis sparked new mysteries that came into the Greek and Roman religious orbit from the ancient cultures that had been conquered—from Egypt, Mesopotamia, and Anatolia. One of the earliest such cults, in fact, belongs to the classical Greek period and revolves around Bacchus or Dionysus, the god of the vine. In one particular form of the myth, known as the Orphic tradition,[39] Dionysus himself was a dying-and-rising god.[40] Eventually, Dionysiac elements were appropriated into the Eleusinian mysteries. In turn, these earlier Greek cults had a profound influence on the notions of immortality of the soul and afterlife as found in Plato and other philosophers of the later classical and Hellenistic periods.

The initial catalyst for other new mysteries to emerge had come with the conquests of Alexander the Great and the subsequent hellenization of the Near Eastern world. Next, Rome took over the legacy of these Hellenistic kingdoms and the varied cultural and religious traditions that came from them. As people began to move to and fro in the Roman Empire, they carried their local gods and religious traditions with them. Nonetheless, the vernacular of the entire eastern Mediterranean was Greek, and these local traditions were easily translated and syncretized into new forms.

The Mysteries of Isis and Sarapis

A good example is the development of the ancient Egyptian myth of Isis and Osiris, which had been at the center of the pharaonic kingship ideology and ritual in the New Kingdom period (as discussed above). The conquest of Alexander brought the New Kingdom to an end and gave birth to a new syncretistic dynasty known as the Ptolemies. Macedonian Greeks, the Ptolemies nonetheless invested themselves with the trappings of Egyptian divine kingship, as we saw above in the citation from the Rosetta Stone. Their patron deities were Zeus-Ammon and Sarapis, the latter being the hellenized form of Osiris (contracted with the god Apis). But this Sarapis also took on the attributes of Zeus. The hyphenation of names and blending of attributes reflects the syncretism of Egyptian and Greek cultural elements. The political overtones of the Egyptian myth supported the dynastic claims of the Ptolemies in the same way it had for the New Kingdom pharaohs for over a thousand years.

In time the myth of Isis and Sarapis also took on the characteristics of a mystery cult and spread out into the Greek world, in part under the influence of the Eleusinian tradition. Egyptian cults are known from the Greek islands as early as the latter part of the third century BCE and from Athens itself by the second century BCE. By the end of the Hellenistic period, when Augustus finally made Egypt a Roman province, the Egyptian mysteries were rapidly becoming among the most prominent in the Mediterranean world. While clearly trading upon its ties to mysterious Egypt—thus with connotations of the secrets of mummification and expectations of afterlife—the cult of Isis and Sarapis offered a new degree of portability. A person did not have to go to Egypt to be initiated. A new phenomenon was being born—mystery cults that spread by translocal conventicles.

The analogies to the Eleusinian tradition are readily discernible. In its earliest form, the myth of Isis and Osiris (Sarapis) was an etiological agrarian myth that explained the crop cycle of life and death within the Nile region. Osiris was the god of the Nile and also of grain, who died and was reborn with the seasons. His sister/consort, Isis, now plays the role of Demeter in bringing him back to life. By extension, then, this agrarian myth came to be associated with a personal benefit for humans, in the form of some guarantee of blessings or security in the afterlife.

These similarities to the Eleusinian myth were recognized by the ancients. For example, the Greek philosopher-biographer Plutarch wrote a treatise, *On Isis and Osiris,* in which he makes the ties even more explicit. In one scene, Isis, who has been wandering the world looking for her dead consort, pauses to dwell with a local king, but she disguises herself as a nurse for their child. At night she secretly braises away the child's mortality over a hearth until being discovered by the horrified mother. Plutarch even admits that these are borrowings from the Eleusinian myth of Demeter and Persephone. This section of the myth of Isis and Osiris does not seem to occur in the older Egyptian forms of the story, only in the hellenized form in which it is serving very clearly as a mystery in which initiation provides the adherent with the same benefits of immortality. Plutarch even speculates on the allegorical and metaphorical aspects of this myth. Other myths, such as that of Io, were also woven into the Isis cycle.[41] At the same time, this case shows how the basic myth could be changed and adapted to fit its new cultural context and ritual function.

The popularity of the Isis cult can also be seen in the propagandistic novel of Apuleius, *The Golden Ass,* and in the number of Isis-Sarapis sanctuaries spread throughout the Greek and Roman world. One of the special traits of the Egyptian cults was the emphasis on a communal meal at which the god Sarapis was thought to be present. Still, it was Isis, the nurturer, the life-giver, who stood at the center of the cult. One of the best-known iconographic representations of the myth portrays her nursing the infant Horus, symbolic of the rebirth of Sarapis. It is the iconography later taken over for the Madonna and child in Christian art.

Myth, Ritual, and Gospel

In this chapter we have surveyed a number of aspects of Greek and Roman religion that bear striking similarities to elements of the Jesus tradition. Yet many of these elements—for example, celebrating Jesus's birth on December 25, the same day as that of Mithras—are clearly much later appropriations. There is no hint of them in the earliest Gospel tradition. Nor does any one of these religious phenomena explain all the features that would eventually make up the rich texture of Christian tradition. Divine men, emperors who ascend to heaven, and gods who die and rise again are, in fact, quite different streams within the Greek and Roman world of thought and religion. There seems to be a lot of picking and choosing, just as there was within the Jewish tradition to forge a unique understanding of Jesus's messianic identity out of the larger apocalyptic worldview. Yet it is noteworthy that the term "gospel" (or "good news") itself comes specifically from one of these religious contexts.

There are, therefore, three key aspects to the Greco-Roman religious environment as it relates to the development of the Jesus tradition. The first is to recognize that terms like "messiah," "savior," and "son of god" are not merely interchangeable concepts. Rather, they come from different cultural backgrounds and religious ideas. Depending on the context or the combination of concepts, they might have entirely different meanings or inspire entirely different theological expectations.

Second, it is important to recognize how powerful were the stories of ancient holy men and gods who interceded in the human realm. "Myths" we often call them—at least when they are about other religions. But these stories reflect deep-seated symbols and expectations about how the world works, about the finitude of human nature and how it might be transcended, at least within the framework of Greek and Roman culture. They are very important in forming cultural and communal identities, but they must be understood in their cultural context. So too the creation of new episodes or scenes is an important exercise in cultural change. We shall turn in Act II to deal more directly with how such scenes are scripted.

Finally, we should note how myth and ritual work together in these ancient religious traditions. The rituals regularly involve performative reenactments of the basic myths or key episodes, and they are then simultaneously explicated for religious meaning. Thus, ritual and performative storytelling go hand in hand. Here, the mystery cults are an especially important development, since they take over traditional, and in many cases quite archaic, myths and infuse them with entirely new realms of meaning. Myth and religion change with time and culture. So too the mysteries mark a particular type of appropriation of myths to a new sense of personal benefit. The reformulation of the legend itself is key to the new meaning, which is seen in the interaction between myth and ritual. Whether it is Demeter and Persephone or Isis and Osiris, telling and retelling the story becomes a reenactment of its mythic symbols and powers, which in turn are appropriated by human worshipers by means of a ritual act that employs similar symbols. By participating in the ritual, worshipers both ratify and participate in its reality and power. Again, the key to understanding is the context and combination of stories, ritual actions, and symbolic elements employed. Thus, shaping and reshaping of individual scenes and whole cycles will become an important process in scripting Jesus.

ACT II

Crafting Scenes

CHAPTER FIVE

Orality, Memory,
and Performance

When you come together, each one has a hymn, a lesson,
a revelation, a tongue, or an interpretation. Let all things be done
for building up. (1 Corinthians 14:26)

In the previous section we saw how various features of the portrayal of Jesus as reflected in the Gospels relate to common elements from the larger cultural environment, both Jewish and Greco-Roman. Titles, traditions, and character types—whether Jewish or Greco-Roman—convey certain images. Naturally, one begins to wonder how there could be so many different images and how they came to be woven together in the Gospel tradition. Why are there such different perceptions of Jesus in that time? Why does one Gospel seem to come closer to Jewish apocalyptic ideas and another to Greek notions of the divine man? The answer lies in the development of the earliest traditions about Jesus, for Jesus did not write anything himself. Nor are there any written accounts that come from his lifetime or for a full generation after his death. The Gospels of the New Testament are all much later; even the earliest is at least forty years or more after the death of Jesus. This fact is very important to understanding both how the various portrayals of Jesus came about and how we must proceed in recovering the historical features of Jesus's life, teachings, and death.

The crucial fact is, quite simply, that there is a gap between the time of Jesus and the time of the Gospels (as discussed in the Prologue). How big that gap is and how the tradition bridged it are questions we must consider in this chapter. We may begin by giving a rough timetable, even though it must be quickly noted that the dates used here are themselves the result of historical analysis. How these dates are determined is also one of the issues in later chapters of this study. Nonetheless, the timetable in Box 5.1 will demonstrate the nature of the problem.

The gap now looms large, since Jesus died ca. 27–29 CE, but what we now think was the first Gospel, namely Mark, was not written until after 70 CE.[1] Its composition falls in the tumultuous aftermath of the first Jewish revolt against Rome. The other Gospels of the Christian New Testament come later still. What this means overall is that the New Testament Gospels—the earliest narrative accounts of the life and death of Jesus—are anywhere from forty to nearly a hundred years after his death.

So how does the story of Jesus get passed on, told and retold, during these early years of the movement? The answer is by word of mouth, that is, through traditional forms of oral storytelling or what has usually been called the "oral tradition." Such oral forms are common to most ancient societies and offer significant parallels to the type of material we find preserved in the Gospels. It may also say something about the nature of the Gospels themselves as performative scripts.

BOX 5.1

From Jesus to the Gospels: *A Timetable*

Dates	Events	Christian Writings	Non-Christian Writings
Before 4 BCE	Birth of Jesus		
ca. 27–29 CE	Death of Jesus		
ca. 50–60 CE		Letters of Paul	
ca. 60–64 CE	Deaths of James, Peter, and Paul		
64 CE	Great fire in Rome		
66–74 CE	First Jewish revolt vs. Rome		
ca. 70–75 CE		Gospel of Mark	
ca. 80–90 CE		Gospel of Matthew	Josephus, *Jewish War*
ca. 90–100 CE		Gospel of Luke, Acts	
ca. 95 CE	Death of John		Josephus, *Antiquities*
ca. 95–120 CE		Gospel of John	
ca. 117 CE			Tacitus, *Annals*

We may have a glimpse of the process from a very early stage in the letters of Paul. In describing various "spiritual gifts" that were exhibited in worship, Paul says:

When you come together [as a church], each one has a hymn, a lesson, a revelation, a tongue, or an interpretation. Let all things be done for building up [the congregation]. (1 Cor 14:26)[2]

As we shall see in the next chapter, Paul clearly recites one such hymn about Jesus in Philippians 2:6–11. A key observation in recent studies is the fact that much of the oral tradition was still being composed, or at least modified, in Paul's own day.[3] Here we may also compare a similar practice in Jewish worship as described by Philo:

Next, the one standing [the president of the assembly] sings a hymn composed to God, either a new one of his own composition or an old one by the ancient poets—for they too have left behind many measures and melodies of verse, hexameters and iambics, lyrics suitable for processions or in libations and at the altars, or for the chorus while standing or dancing, all carefully measured out. After him all the others take their turn in order as befits decorum, while all the rest listen quietly except when they have to chant the chorus and refrain; then they all, both men and women, sound forth.[4]

Prior to this the group had been listening to an oral exposition of the scriptures by one of the members, who "lingers and slows his speech, with repetitions in different words, imprinting his thoughts on the souls of his hearers."[5] Following the succession of individual performances of hymns, they share a sacred communal meal.[6]

This rather surprising description comes from Philo's account of the so-called Therapeutae, Jewish ascetic philosophers sometimes thought to be similar to the Essenes. To be sure, it is a heavily idealized description reflecting Greek influence, but that is not the point here. Rather, it is the idea of carefully delivered oral expositions and newly composed hymns being performed alongside the traditional psalms in the assembly. The paintings from the Dura-Europos synagogue (ca. 244–56 CE) show such a scene (see Box 5.2), where the figure of Moses reading from the law mirrors the public "reader" in worship. Also noteworthy is the responsive participation of the audience. One central genre of literature among the Dead Sea Scrolls is that of "Hymns" (Heb. *hodayot*) composed by a prophetic teacher. We have other examples of such compositions from the early Jewish writer known as Ezekiel the Tragedian, who composed a version of the Exodus story in the form of Greek dramatic poetry.[7]

Some two centuries after Philo, the Christian apologist Tertullian made a similar observation about the practice of individually composed hymns at Christian gatherings, where worship was conducted at the evening meal, just as in Paul's day:

Reading Orally in Ancient Times

Dura–Europos, the Later Synagogue (ca. 244–56 CE). "Moses" reads orally from a scroll of the Law. Yale University Art Gallery.

We do not recline at dinner until first we sample an oration [or prayer] to God. . . . After [eating] comes water for washing the hands and lights, so that anyone who has ability—either from the holy scriptures or from his own talent—is called to the middle to sing to God. Hence he proves how much he has imbibed. In like manner also, prayer ends the banquet.[8]

In some cases Tertullian uses the verb "to sing" (Lat. *canere*)—which literally means "to hymn or chant poetically"—to describe "prophesying" in the sense of oral exposition from the prophets and psalms. For this reason, the phenomenon of ongoing prophetic activity within early Christianity has sometimes been called "charismatic exegesis."[9] Surviving collections of such early Christian hymns are relatively rare precisely because most of them were never recorded in writing. At least one may be seen in the so-called *Odes of Solomon,* a compilation of forty-two hymns dating to the early second century CE.[10] Many of them are about Jesus in the voices of the prophetic hymnists, but some portray Jesus speaking about himself. He both speaks through their mouths and hears their voices.[11] The hymns from the *Odes of Solomon* have a dynamic oral quality. They were meant to be performed aloud and to be heard. They also bear striking similarities to the "I am" discourses in the Gospel of John.

Oral Tradition and the Gospels

The notion that the earliest layers of the Gospel story were spread by oral tradition has been a fixture in New Testament scholarship since the late nineteenth century. In much of this earlier work, the goal was to be able to identify earlier oral strands that lie behind the Gospels as a way of pushing backward in time toward the historical Jesus. It posited the existence of several independent lines or components of oral tradition that come into the different Gospels as well as the existence of a discrete source of Jesus's sayings that can be seen in the Gospels of Matthew and Luke. This is what we call the Q source.[12] Some scholars have tried recently to argue that Q—or, to be more precise, an early layer within Q—is our best glimpse of the words of Jesus himself.[13] Other scholars question whether such "positivist" historical claims can be made on the basis of Q, when it too had already gone well beyond the historical and social context of Jesus himself.[14] Whether Q was only oral or had been written down also remains a matter of some debate among New Testament scholars.[15] We shall return to these issues in Chapter 12.

As important as it may be, this debate about Q in many ways obscures the real issue. In the minds of many scholars, the oral tradition ceases when it comes to be written down and thus "crystallized."[16] The assumption is that it is then fixed or ossified into a literary form. In this view, the technology and media of writing are so fundamentally different from oral communication that they even restructure how people think, leading to a "literate" mind-set in contrast to an "oral" mind-set.[17]

In reality, however, much of the recent discussion of orality is more concerned with the nature of Q and its sociopolitical location, rather than with the process of oral transmission as such.[18] The move from the broader stream of oral traditions about Jesus, including Q, to the written Gospels is too often assumed to remove the tradition—and story forms in which it was carried—from the dynamics of orality. The view taken in this book is that oral or performative storytelling was still the ordinary medium of *literary* production in the Greco-Roman world. It was an "oral culture." Written texts thus served first as scripts *of* and *for* oral presentations. Writing down such stories or traditions did not necessarily fix them any more than did repeating them orally or translating them to new contexts.

Oral performance of these stories also involved compositional activity that set the stage for and continued into the narrative form of the written Gospels. Indeed, the patterns of storytelling we shall examine in this section continue to operate by norms of oral performance even when they were written or rewritten from one Gospel to the next. By the same token, if the shape and style of one particular Gospel betrays more formal literary or textual features, that too says something about the social situation and outlook of storyteller and audience. Nor does the fact that we must employ modes of literary analysis diminish their applicability to oral storytelling. In the final analysis, both improvisational oral storytelling and literary shaping contributed to the process of scripting the stories of Jesus.

An Oral Culture

For the majority of people growing up in contemporary Western culture, it is very difficult to imagine the oral culture that predominated in the Roman world and for a millennium on either side. This problem is caused in large measure by the prevalence of written or print media in our systems of communication, record keeping, and entertainment. Such a "writing culture" also assumes a generally high level of literacy, higher than in many other parts of the world. Both of these tendencies have their roots in the privileged place of the Christian Bible in the formation of Western culture. The text of the Bible as "sacred scripture," where scripture means "writings," gives it an iconic place in our thought world. This idea can also be seen in many of the medieval illustrations of the Gospel authors closed up in cells and writing. Of course this way of imagining them more resembles the monastic transmitters, the medieval scribes who copied the scriptures, than the real practice of the Gospel authors themselves.

Thus, in our culture, we tend to see the fundamental dynamic of communication as the interplay between writer (or text) and reader, rather than between speaker and hearer. Even in the visual and performance media, such as movies, television, or theater, the author and the written script occupy a special position alongside the actors and those who direct the performance. Yet what we may properly recognize as artistic creativity is present in all three dramatic crafts.

Such was also the case in the ancient world that gave birth to the biblical "texts." Traditional stories, successive performances, and written scripts all contributed to the evolving shape of the Gospel narratives. It was an oral culture first, and writing, where it emerges at all, remains secondary. Even in highly literary activity, such as that of classical Greece or the Roman Empire, the written text was usually the companion piece of an oral performance, whether in the theater, the courts, or religious rites. We need only think of the poems of Pindar, most of which were songs performed publicly for victorious athletes in the Panhellenic games. Or the great plays of Sophocles, Euripides, and Menander, with their setting in Athenian theatrical performance and political life. Or the speeches of Demosthenes or Lysias, which come from Athenian law courts. Of course, the best known of these are the Homeric epics, the *Iliad* and *Odyssey,* which arose out of oral, bardic performance of legends from a distant, and largely forgotten, past. The fact that we now have so much of this literature preserved is, to be sure, a result of its having been written down and transmitted to later generations. Nonetheless, we must start with the realization that the primary locus of this "literary" activity was in oral performance.

Once we come to the early Roman period, however, literature was typically produced in written form. By the late first century CE, we have evidence of a growing book trade, at least among Greek and Roman aristocrats and intellectuals.[19] The papyri from Egypt have preserved a number of copies of earlier classical authors, including Homer, Sappho, Alcman, Baccylides, and others—including a number of works thought to be entirely lost—all dating to the second and third centuries CE. It is worth noting also that the early third century CE is when we start to see a significant increase in copies of early Christian books, including the first Gospel collections.[20] Even so, this evidence may be somewhat misleading, if we infer from it that the Roman Empire had thus become predominantly a "reading and writing culture" rather than "oral culture." Most of these works were still meant to be read aloud. At the same time, the notion of a "sacred text," whether from the Jewish scriptures or the Sibylline books, occupied a special place in the culture in that the physical object was itself also important as a symbol.[21]

Most private reading of written texts was done aloud, in part because the aural quality of the words was meant to be heard. Very often, a trained slave read orally from the text while the master or mistress listened; hearing was the medium by which the text entered mind and soul to cultivate knowledge, provide entertainment, or evoke pathos. Also, since the vast majority of ancient manuscripts, including literary and philosophical works, were written in all capitals with no breaks between words or sentences and little or no punctuation, sounding out the words and voicing the inflections were essential to understanding. Some works clearly presuppose a small audience, perhaps a literary circle, in which poems might be performed, even if they were later "published" in a broader sense.[22] Pliny the Younger invited his closest friends to dinner parties or his bedroom for oral readings of his Catullan poetry, but he was not terribly pleased on those occasions when he received criticism.[23] Recitations of poets, philosophers, or satirists were often the featured entertainment at lavish Roman dinner parties.

It would be better to think of much of this literature as a "script" for what was intended as an oral presentation, as in the case of both Cicero and Julius Caesar.[24] In some cases, however, the "script," or written form, seems to have come after the actual performance. Among the famous rhetoricians of the Second Sophistic period (late first–early third century CE), it was considered inappropriate to read from a prepared text in making a speech. They were supposed to compose extemporaneously.[25] Now in reality they may well have planned out their speeches rather carefully in their minds or made notes on a wax tablet, but it appears that the written versions that come down to us were often transcribed later. They sometimes preserve what must have been gestures or visual gags that interrupt the grammatical structure in the place of spoken words.[26] One may also wonder whether the written versions were in any way polished or corrected by the author from their actual oral form. Alas, we may never know for sure.

Finally, we know that much of the literary composition, especially in longer prose works, was done by dictation. The author stood and expounded orally while a scribe copied down what was being said. We have such a description of the literary process from Pliny the Younger (d. 113 CE):

> [On rising] if I have anything on hand, I work it out in my head, choosing and correcting the wording, and the amount I achieve depends upon the ease or difficulty with which my thoughts can be marshaled and kept in my head. Then I call my secretary, the shutters are opened, and I dictate what I have put into shape; he goes out, is recalled, and again dismissed. Three or four hours after I first wake, I betake myself according to the weather either to the terrace or to the covered arcade, work out the rest of my subject, and proceed to dictate it.[27]

The church historian Eusebius reports that Origen, the third-century Christian philosopher from Alexandria, would compose several works at once by walking around the room dictating to different scribes in succession.[28] We also have evidence of earlier and later drafts of some works, suggesting that scribes or the author later edited the text into a finished form. But the key point is that they were first delivered orally, and they were meant to be heard as such by "readers," whether privately or in public recitations.

Orality and Literacy

A related issue is the level of literacy in the ancient world. Here too we must be careful, as "literacy" too easily becomes a cipher for "civilization" or "social class." Until recent decades, it was common to assume that Greece and Rome were highly literate cultures in the modern sense.[29] Recent studies have shown, instead, that in Greece the ability to read and write was rare and limited to certain classes or segments of society. In other words, it was an elite and predominantly male preserve. Nor did all the citizens of Athens, meaning the freeborn male landholders, take advantage of the educational opportunities to achieve literacy.

Even more has been made of literacy rates in the Roman Empire, because of the high degree to which written documents were used as a vehicle for political administration, especially as seen in the extensive evidence of the papyri from

Roman Egypt. William Harris summarizes the problem this way: "The classical world, even at its most advanced, was so lacking in the characteristics which produce extensive literacy that we must suppose that the majority of people were always illiterate."[30] Thus, although levels of literacy surely increased in Hellenistic and, especially, in Roman times, they were never as high as often assumed by modern standards. Harris estimates that perhaps only 10 percent of the total population of the Roman world could read and even fewer could write.[31] Scholarly estimates for the level of literacy in Roman Palestine vary from as little as 3 to just over 10 percent, with the numbers decreasing in more recent work.[32]

Even so, some challenges have been offered toward this more pessimistic assessment. First, we should differentiate between the basic skills of reading and writing, where writing means the careful scribal scripts or formal conventions used for legal documents or literary composition.[33] In other words, in these ancient cultures where "universal education" was unheard of, it is quite common to find people who could read a written sign or document, but who were unable to write.

Second, there is the matter of the diverse native languages of the far-flung Roman provinces. *Literacy* often refers to Greek or Latin alone. The term *idiōtēs* (meaning "private or common," but by derivation "uneducated") appears quite frequently in the papyri to denote a person not literate *in Greek,* the administrative language of Roman Egypt and most of the East. At least one important papyrus, the record of the confiscation of a Christian church building in the year 304 CE, says that the "reader" of the church who made the declaration of the property to the magistrates was illiterate.[34] The "reader" was a common church office in antiquity—now often called the "lector"—the person who read the scriptures in worship. Here we have a case of someone trained to read written texts orally in public, but who is unlettered in writing. It may well mean that he was illiterate in Greek; thus, his church was a local Coptic-speaking congregation. But it is also possible that he had not been trained to write in any formal sense, even to sign his own name.[35]

Third, we should draw a more careful distinction between "functional literacy," the ability to read and write at a basic level for social and economic reasons, and "higher literacy," the ability to read or compose in a more formal or literary sense.[36] As Rosalind Thomas puts it, simply calculating statistical rates of literacy may be misleading:

All we can really say with plausibility is that more people could read than write; the ability to read or write very simple messages, often in capitals, was probably not rare; and in cities like Athens, where there was a profusion of democratic documents, most citizens had some basic ability and perhaps "phonetic literacy" was pretty widespread; but that the written texts of poetry and literary prose had a reading audience confined to the highly educated and wealthy elite, and their secretaries.[37]

We should not conclude from this survey that the masses of the population, though perhaps less literate in the higher sense, were any less sophisticated in their ability to access and understand ancient literature. Most ancient literature was meant to be heard orally or performed in public, even when it was written down. Even Paul's letters to his churches, the earliest writings in the New Testament, attest to this basic feature of written communication. The letters were meant to be read aloud in the churches to which they were sent. One of Paul's co-workers (such as Timothy or Titus) was entrusted with both carrying the letter and reading it.

In the case of the massive Roman letter, Paul himself incorporates a letter of introduction for Phoebe, his house-church patroness from Cenchreae (16:1–2); he then sends greetings to the various house churches in Rome (16:3–16). We must guess, then, that Phoebe herself was expected to carry the letter to these various congregations and read it aloud to them. She was thus entrusted with the task of presenting the letter orally so as to convey Paul's message as he intended.[38] We also know from his letters that Paul used trained scribes. One of these, Tertius, shows up in the final greetings of the Roman letter (16:22). In other words, Paul usually dictated the letter aloud to the scribe, who transcribed it. Careful study of the style of Paul's letters reveals a high degree of artistry in the rhetorical and aural qualities of these letters. In the final analysis, these letters were meant to be *heard,* not just *read* in our modern sense.

That having been said, we should not assume too much of a gulf between "orality" and the emerging "textuality" of the Roman world. It must be remembered that many "texts" were publicly displayed in the form of inscriptions; they include not only imperial proclamations or public honors, but also letters and literature. The *Res Gestae,* Augustus's account of his accomplishments, was set up as propagandistic "billboards" across the empire. Horace's *Carmen Seculares* (or *Secular Songs*) were commissioned by Augustus for public performance at the Secular Games of 26 BCE; they were then posted in the Roman forum.[39] A speech of the emperor Claudius delivered before the Roman senate in 46 CE was put up on bronze tablets at Lyons (in France) as well as copied into the text of Tacitus's *Annals.*[40]

So there was a sense of the text as written text, even if the entire populace could not read it. In some ways, this notion of text is itself a kind of symbol or icon of culture. After all, certain writings were by then thought of as of special importance, such as the Homeric epics and the books of the Sibylline oracle. So too in Jewish tradition, the text of the scriptures already held a special place, as we see especially in the Dead Sea Scrolls, where the name of God is often written in a distinct, archaic script. The text of the *Copper Scroll* was actually incised into copper to preserve it. Finally, one should note that the genre of apocalypse often carries a strong sense of "textuality," either because the work is fictively conceived as an ancient source or because writing was one of the media in which a revelation might be delivered. So it would not appear that religious and political dissenters were automatically opposed to written texts simply because writing might be associated with the dominant power structure of Jerusalem or Rome.

Oral Performance

Homer—meaning the Homeric epics, the *Iliad* and *Odyssey*—has often been called "the Bible of the ancient world," because of its status in Greek and Roman culture.[41] It was used as a primer in education and as a dominant allusion in much of the later Greek and Latin literature. It was copied and transmitted as text throughout the Roman period. It could also be rendered artistically, such as in the elaborate Roman frieze depicting each of the twenty-four books of the *Odyssey*. Even Christian scribes continued to copy and comment upon it into the Byzantine period and Middle Ages. But originally it was an oral poem performed by bards. It continued to be read orally and performed throughout classical antiquity.

New studies of orality in Greek literature, specifically of Homer, have revolutionized our understanding of how this foundational work was produced and transmitted through the centuries. Unfortunately, this new work has been more influential in the field of classics, and fewer New Testament scholars have taken serious note of it, in part because it came out before much of the recent interest in orality.[42] As a result, some of the studies of orality in connection with Q and the Gospels sometimes draw a sharper divide between orality and writing than is appropriate.

Two classicists, Milman Parry and Albert Lord, observed how illiterate Yugoslav poets performed extremely lengthy epic poems through improvisational formulas in retelling traditional stories from long-past periods of history.[43] The oral poet composed while performing by "using a traditional stock of set pieces, [metrical] formulae, and set themes to help him compose as he sang."[44] They concluded that the Homeric epics were the product of centuries of oral performance by generations of mostly illiterate, traditional bards instead of the single, compositional act of one poetic genius named Homer. Since these early studies, the "Parry-Lord theory"—as it is sometimes called—has been applied to other archaic traditions of poetic epic, such as Old Norse, Anglo-Saxon, and African.

Since these formative studies, more recent work on Homeric style and diction has raised questions and offered refinements of the basic model.[45] It has also raised the question of how these poems came to be transcribed as written text. Gregory Nagy, for example, has suggested that the poems were not written down until the sixth century BCE and that further revisions were still being incorporated into the written text into the fifth century. He then argues that the text was still being "standardized" in the fourth century and that a "fixed" text was only achieved in the second century BCE.[46] Following Nagy, Erwin Cook has argued further that these ongoing changes were more or less conscious adaptations of the story to an explicitly Panhellenic Athenian political agenda, even as the epic continued to be performed in public.[47] We also know that several different texts of Homer circulated in antiquity. Some versions had additional scenes not contained in the others. The three main lines are associated with later schools of literary study at Athens, Pergamon, and Alexandria. By the third and second centuries BCE, ancient Greek scholars had begun to notice and discuss these disparities, not unlike what happened to the Christian Gospels in the second and third centuries CE.

Although not all Homer scholars have accepted such a late date for the establishment of a fixed Homeric text,[48] these models of orality and performance are important for several reasons. Nagy and others have stressed the fact that the text of the poems was never static; it changed with each performer, even when it was becoming more or less standardized.[49] Even so, we must guess that these performers learned from each other and carried on certain traditions in the performance, while improvising others out of their own circumstances. The bard did not memorize the whole poem as such. Key formulas, characters, events, and phrases were enough to provide the basic episodic structure around which he then composed as he performed. Perhaps there were cues, such as the "story stick" used by some African tribal groups; carvings and symbols on the stick provide a rough outline, or sequence of episodes, which the tribal shaman or storyteller then retells orally using both older versions and his own improvisations.

One younger scholar has likened it to the performance of jazz, where traditional tunes and standard riffs evoke infinite variations through improvisational performance and constant refinement.[50] We must imagine the storyteller too like a stage performer today, trying new lines, intonations, or adaptations of basic episodes, all the while listening for the right combination and looking to the audience for responses. The ones that work—that strike the right notes and evoke response—are kept; older variations eventually disappear. We saw this at work earlier in the Prologue with the changing form of Shakespeare's "To be or not to be" soliloquy from *Hamlet*. Authors and actors create new variations over time through the oral performance medium.[51]

The audience also played a key role by means of the interaction between the poet and the audience in the moment of performance. It was "the principal means for putting the here and now of one's existence into some larger [historical] context."[52] The key point here is that such performance is, not only reinterpretive of the "ancient traditions" being rehearsed, but also constitutive or integrative for the communal identity of the audience, who now are able to see themselves in line with the narrative tradition. Storytelling is, therefore, a mechanism of cultural identity and group formation. To achieve that end it may retell older tales, but it also operates with typical characters and plotlines drawn from the cultural landscape of the tellers and audience, as discussed in Act I.[53]

This process suggests that transcribing the poem into a written form does not necessarily "crystallize" it. Further adaptations and modifications are still made over time. In that sense too each new reading of the text, especially in a public or communal context, becomes a new moment of performance, a new situation or context in which the audience might interact in new and different ways, and thereby an opportunity for further revisions and reinterpretations. The resultant tradition is thus the cumulative effect of all these performances and the rich blending, revising, and sorting that comes down in a later form. Of course, this also means that some of the earliest layers and older forms will inevitably be lost along the way.

Orality, Memory, and Jesus Stories

These models for describing the production of ancient literature through oral performance provide important insights for dealing with the relationship between the Gospels and their antecedent oral traditions. A key point has to do with memory. The Parry-Lord model argued that the early Greek bards did not memorize as such, but rather composed in performance. Critics of this view have shown, however, that there must have been some form of memorization taking place.[54] So the more recent versions of this theory stress the ability of the poet to create afresh in performance while working with set pieces, stock characters, formulaic metrical lines, and even memorized sections. Nagy argues that the oral performance medium ensured both preservation and change, since performance is composition and composition is performance.[55] He thus argues that there are always three aspects of this kind of oral tradition: composition, performance, and diffusion.[56] The writing down of a text served initially as a script for performance and diffusion, but writing did not halt the process of performative explorations in new settings.[57]

In this context, we must surmise that memory is important, for both the storyteller *and* the audience, in the sense that they both had expectations of how the story should go. One of our difficulties in imagining this ancient world of oral performance is the fact that such stories were told over and over again. Even written books were not just read and then discarded or traded in at the local half-price bookstore, as they so often are today. Thus, in antiquity the oral rehearsal of a story presupposed that both teller and audience knew the basics, while improvisations and variations were expected in each new performance setting. The question, then, is how fixed or rigid is this memory?

Here we must address some recent discussions of the early oral traditions about Jesus, chiefly that of James D. G. Dunn in *Jesus Remembered*.[58] Dunn's model of oral remembering employs the notion of an "informal, controlled oral tradition."[59] Crucial to Dunn's premise is the idea that variations in the wording of Jesus's sayings, among the Synoptics in particular, may be explained by oral storytelling techniques in the preliterary stage of the sayings tradition and were not part of the writing or redactional stage of the Gospels per se. Here Dunn uses "oral performance" as the key term for this preliterary stage and its resultant variations. But they are still "authentic memories" of Jesus, as Dunn says:

> *The variations between the different versions of the same story in the tradition do not indicate a cavalier attitude or lack of historical interest in the events narrated. In almost every case . . . it is the same story which is being retold. Rather the variations exemplify the character of oral retelling. In such oral transmission* the *concern to remember Jesus is clear from* the key elements *which give the story its identity, just as the* vitality of the tradition is indicated by the performance variants.[60]

Thus, the concern of the tradents—those who carry on the tradition—to "remember" is understood to mean retaining some authentic element of the teaching. "There was no concern to recall all the exact words of Jesus," says Dunn; nevertheless, the oral tradition was free from "creative invention" or "subverted [of] their original impact."[61] Much of this view coheres well with the new ideas of oral performance discussed above. The key issue, however, is the role of memory containing "controlled" units of oral tradition. The question is: How much variation does this notion of control allow before it is no longer the same "memory"?

Dunn's imaginative picture of how these memories were first generated and transmitted reminds us of telling stories around a campfire.[62] Perhaps that is even suitable for some of the initial stages, but it does not quite fit the circumstances once we go beyond the original circle of Jesus's followers in the days immediately following his death. There were groups in Jerusalem, but other groups seem to have originated in the Galilee.[63] As we shall see in the next chapter, Paul certainly heard various forms of the same basic oral tradition, but from different sources, probably in different localities, and all at least one or two steps removed from the actual events.

In part, the problem here is the term "memory." For many people working in the area of Gospel studies, it is taken to imply an "authentic kernel of teaching or a historical episode" that is preserved more or less without variation in later oral reports. But is that really what is reflected in studies of oral tradition? Even Kenneth Bailey's work, which served as the basis for Dunn's model, suggests a rather different notion of memory.[64] Bailey focused on the fact that, in the regular storytelling gatherings of modern Middle Eastern villages, many of which are Christian minorities, long-term records show the same stories being passed down over time.[65] This process is what results in his notion of an "informal, *controlled* oral tradition." The sense of "control" implies for Bailey that the story remains relatively constant through repetition over long periods of time. Here "informal" means that the stories were not strictly memorized or controlled in some authoritative way, but were changed very little over time.

On the other hand, closer examination of Bailey's own sources shows that many of these stories as preserved are far removed from early authentic accounts of what really happened.[66] Instead, they were often episodes or stories that were shaped through the later experience of those village communities and then passed down in this later, evolved form. In one case, the story discussed by Bailey even reflects a conscious and collective effort of villagers to concoct a fictional account to cover up an accidental death.[67] In another, the original episode was fancifully embellished into a story of a Christian preacher's nighttime encounter with a band of robbers, who then converted to Christianity. Such elements never appear in the earliest version, yet it is this fanciful version that is "remembered" in later storytelling.[68] In a third, a traditional Bedouin folk tale was intentionally altered in oral presentation by one respected village elder in order to make a new didactic point; meanwhile the villagers knew quite well what he was doing. Yet both the original version and the altered one were preserved in later storytelling.[69]

This last case is analogous to what we saw happening in the Johannine variation of the Last Supper, as discussed in the Prologue. What this all means is that, although stories were indeed preserved and passed on in the life of these villages, they usually represent some sort of "constructed memory" that reinforces the identity and self-consciousness of the community, not just "what really happened." Subsequently Dunn has also clarified his view, maintaining that the stories changed dramatically in the early stages of the transmission, and it is these versions that are often preserved in the ongoing oral tradition.[70]

This same idea is what some scholars now call "cultural memory" or "social memory."[71] Alain Gowing also calls it "mnemohistory."[72] In applying the concept to the way Roman imperial historians "remembered" the late Republic, Gowing says:

> It is the capacity of texts to create or establish memory—or if you prefer, to fictionalize—that renders them somewhat problematic as sources of historical information. But the Roman view of historia and memoria inevitably leads to a refashioning of the meaning of the past, requiring authors to give it meaning in the present and decide not only what to remember but how it should be remembered. This is why from one regime to the next the use of Republican history varies significantly.[73]

The point is that the "memory" here is both constructed and maintained, usually by ruling elites.[74] Susan Alcock has also applied it to archaeology and material remains; monuments of the past may also be used to construct and reconstruct "social memory."[75] We too often forget that a "monument" by definition is "something that reminds."[76] Alcock specifically cites the Christian "construction" of the "Holy Land," with all of its human-made monuments to commemorate the stories of Jesus.[77] The symbolism of Masada, the famed "last stand" of the first Jewish revolt, is an equally powerful monument in modern Israeli social memory. Yet even these memories are not uncontested.[78] For many Americans, Plymouth

Rock is the same sort of *monument,* whether or not it ever served as the landing place for the Mayflower pilgrims. Needless to say, however, it does not have the same symbolic value for every American.

This notion of socially constructed memories stands in marked contrast to earlier efforts to argue that the transmission of those early memories about Jesus was rigidly controlled, following patterns within the early rabbinic tradition in Palestine. Birger Gerhardsson proposed that the tradition originated from Jesus himself and that it was transmitted carefully, in a controlled manner.[79] In attempting to show a relatively stable process of transmission, he hypothesized that followers systematically memorized and passed down Jesus's teachings. Gerhardsson further suggested parallels to the rabbis, based on technical terms used for rabbinic transmission also found in the New Testament.[80] Using these, he stressed the role of memorization in a disciple's learning his teacher's words by heart. He even argued that Jesus must have required his disciples to memorize in this fashion during his ministry and that the later Gospel writers were thus using fixed, reliable teachings directly from Jesus himself.[81]

Some features of Gerhardsson's model of oral tradition units fit well with our general view that they should be formulaic, pithy, with a "punch-line" quality, and portable, so that they can easily be inserted into new situations or compositions.[82] On the other hand, his fundamental claim that it follows known rabbinic patterns of memorization and controlled oral transmission has been decisively refuted by rabbinic scholars, who showed that in its early decades this tradition was much less concerned with historicity than Gerhardsson claimed.[83] Indeed, such a "controlled" rabbinic transmission was not really happening in Palestine prior to 70 CE and thus the comparison is anachronistic, at the very least, for the time of Jesus. More to the point, later rabbinic traditions regarding the pre-70 period were necessarily working from less-controlled oral tradition. They too were "constructed memories." Recent studies of rabbinic *midrash* (commentary) have also shown that the rabbis were often self-consciously fictionalizing stories in order to make their didactic or theological point.[84]

Finally, the notion of "memory" or "remembering" as used in early Christianity, and especially in conjunction with the story of Jesus's death, is perhaps better understood as "commemoration," that is, a communal act whereby storytelling and reflection interact interpretively, just as in the Exodus story as retold annually at Passover.[85] It clearly presupposes the effort to recall past events, but it lacks a strict notion of memorization in fixed or controlled terms. Nor would anyone claim that the Haggadah, the ritualized story that is enacted communally at the Passover meal, in all its various modern forms, is exactly the same as "what really happened" at the Exodus.[86] The Hebrew word *haggadah* (also *aggadah*) literally means "to announce or tell" and is thus the functional equivalent of *kerygma* (as "core story") in Greek (to be discussed in the next chapter). In traditional Jewish (and specifically rabbinic) usage, it gives the sense of "story," but with a much more "imaginative, freewheeling, and varied" form.[87] At the same time, it looks forward to the continued life of the community that is given identity through the story, especially in the light of more recent historical events and most significantly the Holocaust. As it were, they too have now been woven into the Exodus story. As a result, such constructed memories function as "master stories," that is, collective reconstructions of our shared past that "not only *inform* us, but more crucially, *form* us."[88] Master stories create "both a model for understanding the world and a guide for acting in it." Oral tradition is thus not only "conservative," in keeping these older stories alive, but it is also "malleable" in allowing them to be adapted within the life of the particular communities for whom these stories mean something. That is in part the point: the stories must mean something to the community that retells them. At the same time, each new performance brings the story into closer conformity with the ideals and values of the community itself, in some cases quite far removed from the original context or events.[89]

Improvising Jesus: A Test Case in Oral Adaptation

As a test case we may take the conjecture of Richard Bauckham that the Letter of James in the New Testament contains numerous authentic sayings of Jesus "remembered and transcribed" by his brother James.[90] None of these sayings are directly attributed to Jesus himself within the letter, nor do they match up identically with any particular sayings in the Gospels.[91] As a way of explaining this lack of explicit citation or quotation of Jesus, Bauckham looks to Sirach and the wisdom tradition. He argues that the author of Sirach, writing in his own name, regularly *emulates* rather than quotes passages from the Septuagint, presumably working in part from memory. Bauckham then describes the author of the Letter of James similarly as "re-expressing the insight learned from Jesus's teaching."[92] Ironically, Bauckham argues that this very *freedom of expression* in reformulating the sayings is "proof" that it was written by Jesus's own brother at a stage before the Gospels existed. What would this do to Gerhardsson's view of "memorization" or of Bailey's theory of a "controlled" oral tradition?

Bauckham's work has been critically reviewed by John Kloppenborg.[93] Though Kloppenborg rightly rejects Bauckham's logical jump regarding the authorship, he does see merit in the model of verbal adaptation undertaken self-consciously by the author. Kloppenborg then goes on to look for evidence of this practice and criteria for this kind of *expressive adaptation*. What he documents is an extensive practice in the Greek philosophical tradition of the *progymnasmata*, the handbooks used in rhetorical education. In these handbooks, students of rhetoric were trained to restate or paraphrase *chreiai*, aphorisms or wisdom sayings, "while supplying rationale, and offering arguments from the contrary, analogies, examples, and other proofs."[94] He cites the definition of the rhetorical teacher Aelius Theon, under the term *appangelia*—meaning "recitation" or "restatement," a cognate of *euangelia* ("gospel")—which "allowed for the reporting (or 'interpreting') of a saying or *chreia* 'very clearly in the same words or in others as well.' "[95] As we shall see in Chapter 9, the *chreia* will become an important component in the presentation of Jesus's sayings in the Gospels.

This kind of paraphrase is called *aemulatio,* or "emulation." Kloppenborg then cites some examples from the schoolbooks in which students were asked to adapt well-known sayings of the philosophers (or *chreiai*). Thus, the received *chreia* of Isocrates that says, "Isocrates the Orator said that the student with natural ability was a child of the gods" becomes "The saying has become memorable that Isocrates the Orator said that the student . . ." Or one might take the standard formula of attribution, "Diogenes the Cynic said," and reformulate it to make it more lively or more realistic to a putative real-life situation: "To Diogenes the Cynic philosopher, on seeing a rich youth who was uneducated, it seemed right to say, 'He is dirt plated with silver.' "[96] The grammatical structure of the frame remains consistent, but the narrative contents may change.[97] Yet in the end this would yield what might look like an entirely new saying derived from a different life situation. As we shall see, the same sorts of changes occur in the Gospels.

Finally, Kloppenborg goes on to test this model against the Letter of James and some of its putative Jesus sayings by comparing them to material from various Gospels. He concludes that the Letter of James was indeed dependent on Q-type sayings, but with discernible leanings toward the Matthean version; however, it was *not* derived from the oral tradition at a stage before Q and possibly not even before the Matthean line of Q. In other words, the author of the letter was actually working from *written* sources about the words of Jesus. Even so, the writer felt free to adapt, paraphrase, combine, and transform through this typical rhetorical practice of *aemulatio,* while assuming that the audience would recognize the intertextual play. Says Kloppenborg, the author of the letter thus simultaneously aligns with the *ethos* of the source tradition, but also mediates it to the new rhetorical situation of the audience.[98] In other words, he was creating a new oral performance.

The point for our purposes is that the exercise of writing down such originally oral materials—no matter whether the initial transcription or a subsequent revision—does not depart significantly from the pattern of oral storytelling itself. Helmut Koester offers the fruitful insight that the Jesus tradition existed in oral streams long after the Gospels were written, even into the second century.[99] These patterns continue to inform both the interactions within the canonical Gospels and the scripting of new Gospels. Following this same line, Moody Smith concludes that the process of narrative development one finds in the Gospel of John in its relationship to the Synoptics—such as we have seen in the "Lamb of God" vignette (in the Prologue)—is a more dynamic process. He concludes:

One must say simply that what was true of the relationship of the so-called apoc-
ryphal gospels to the Synoptics, and to the canonical four, even in the mid-second
century, would have been all the more true to the relationship of John to the
Synoptics at the end of the first century and the very beginning of the second.[100]

Here oral tradition, written texts, and new performance settings yield new and
strikingly different stories of Jesus. In the next chapters, we shall focus on the
canonical Gospels and how they tell and retell, shape and reshape, key types of
stories within the Jesus tradition. As we shall see, instead of "crystallizing" or
"killing" the dynamic oral tradition, these Gospels carried storytelling into written forms, probably first and foremost as oral scripts to be performed in assembly
and worship. We shall begin with the earliest oral traditions of Jesus's Passion.

CHAPTER SIX

‒‒‒‒‒‒‒

Heralding the Crucifixion

When I came to you, brothers and sisters, I did not come proclaiming the mystery of God to you in lofty words or wisdom. For I decided to know nothing among you except Jesus Christ, and him crucified. (1 Corinthians 2:1–2)

You foolish Galatians! Who has bewitched you? It was before your eyes that Jesus Christ was publicly exhibited as crucified! (Galatians 3:1)

Long before there were written Gospels, there were stories about Jesus that circulated orally. They were passed on by word of mouth, and they were "performed" in worship. Yet the Jesus story does not begin where most people might expect—at Bethlehem. The birth narrative, as we shall see, came later. At the center of the early oral tradition was the story of Jesus's death, burial, and resurrection—what we now call the Passion narrative. It is sometimes called the *kerygma*, from a Greek word meaning "proclamation" or "heralded announcement."[1] It was the core of oral preaching about Jesus.[2]

Most scholars think that the story of the crucifixion was the real beginning point of storytelling about Jesus. The earliest Gospel, Mark, for example, has often been called "a Passion narrative with an extended introduction."[3] There are two main reasons for this view. First, the final third of the story (Mark 11–16) narrates the last week of Jesus's life, corresponding to Holy Week in the Christian liturgical calendar. It begins with the triumphal entry into Jerusalem (11:1–10, "Palm Sunday") and ends with the empty tomb (16:1–8, "Easter Sunday").

Second, much of the first two-thirds of the Markan story anticipates the fact of Jesus's death. The story telegraphs the ending not only by having Jesus predict it on three occasions (8:30–31; 9:30–32; 10:33–34), but also by means of various allusions to the crucifixion throughout the story. Some are subtle; others are not. One of these is the transfiguration (9:2–8), which is often described as a preview of the resurrection. We shall return to it in the next chapter. In another of these, Jesus says: "If any want to become my followers, let them deny themselves and take up their cross and follow me" (8:34). But imagine for a moment how those hearing Jesus during his lifetime would have reacted to "take up their cross and follow me." It makes no sense unless one already knows how the story will turn out.

Narratively within Mark, this episode is sandwiched between Jesus's first prediction of his Passion and the transfiguration; however, it is long before the disciples know by what means Jesus will actually die. In fact, in the preceding scene Peter rebukes Jesus for even hinting that he might die (8:32). Nor do Peter, James, and John really understand what the transfiguration signaled (9:10). Here we begin to see a clue to the storytelling art of the Gospel of Mark: the disciples, as characters *within* the story, cannot possibly comprehend what the audience of the Gospel is expected to understand. In other words, there is an inner, fictive world within the story that is made to interact dramatically and ironically with the audience. This odd saying, then, like many others in the Gospels, is a later Christian retrospection about the death of Jesus woven back into the narrative of his life. We shall return to Markan storytelling in a later chapter, but for now we can see how the Passion narrative was the core around which everything else was assembled. Or to put it another way, the storyteller started with the Passion and added episodes from Jesus's life and teachings as narrative preface and explanation, all the while hinting at the drama of the final scenes.

We can already see this basic idea when we look at the earliest writings in the New Testament, the letters of Paul. They were written between 50 and 60 CE and thus precede Mark by as much as twenty-five years. But Paul never saw or heard Jesus. Where did he get his information? Most likely it was from other disciples, such as Peter and James, who were closer to the events. Glimpses of Paul's early statements regarding Jesus in his letters are our best sources for traceable elements of the oral tradition at a point midway between the death of Jesus and the first written Gospel.

That being said, however, the fact still remains that Paul leaves out much that we would tend to think central to the Jesus story.[4] Paul never mentions any of Jesus's miracles. Nor does he seem to know a birth narrative; his lone comment is that Jesus was "born of a woman" (Gal 4:4), meaning that he was human. With but a few exceptions Paul only gives vague hints of recognizable sayings of Jesus.[5] In that sense the word "gospel" (*euangelia*) for Paul has not yet come to mean a narrative of Jesus's life. It refers instead to some "good news" that has been announced, just as it does in Roman imperial propaganda.[6] For Paul, the "good news" is clear and unmistakable: "Jesus Christ, and him crucified" (1 Cor 2:2). Paul thought of himself as bringing the story of Jesus's death to some kind of visual reality for his audience. In Galatians he refers to the death of Christ as "publicly exhibited before your eyes" (3:1). This latter statement must refer to Paul's own oral proclamation about Jesus and suggests that he employed his rhetorical powers to make the scenes palpably real and evocative. Paul's handling of these oral stories becomes an important starting point for the eventual narrative development of the Passion story.

The Earliest Oral Traditions

There are numerous passing references to the story of Jesus's death in Paul, such as the two quoted at the beginning of this chapter. Because he uses technical terms, such as *stauros* ("pale" or "cross") and *stauroun* ("to impale" or "crucify") some seventeen times in his letters, there is little doubt that he understood the Roman practice of crucifixion as the manner in which Jesus was executed.[7] Even so, he never gives an actual description of the event, nor does he seem to know an oral account with that level of detail. As we shall see in the next chapter, neither do the Gospels. Instead, there are two principal passages in which he clearly cites specific points within the Passion tradition in such ways as to indicate a direct dependence on an earlier oral story. The first is 1 Corinthians 11:23–26, in which Paul rehearses the oral tradition of Jesus's "Last Supper"; the second is 1 Corinthians 15:3–8, in which Paul recounts the death, burial, and resurrection sequence. They are shown in Box 6.1.

That both passages come from 1 Corinthians gives us a discernible time frame for Paul's statements, because we know that this letter was written around 53–54 CE from Ephesus—about twenty-five years after the events.[8] We are further able to recognize the oral-tradition quality of this material from the way Paul introduces it. He uses a formula: "I received . . . what I also I handed on to you, that . . ." Paul uses the same formula in reverse order in 1 Corinthians 15:3. The first part of this formula—"I received and handed on"—was regularly used for passing on oral tradition and is also found in rabbinic sources.[9] It is sometimes called the "tradition summary formula."[10] The word "that" functions in Greek like quotation marks, to signal direct discourse or quoted material. Hence, the formula tells us that the words immediately following "that" are part of the oral tradition being recited. By laying it out graphically (as in Box 6.1) we can see the oral units more clearly.

In both passages Paul appeals to the oral traditions in order to validate a point he wants to make in the letter. Hence, he assumes that the recipients at Corinth had heard them before, most likely from Paul's own preaching. As a result, we may deduce that Paul must have heard these same traditions sometime earlier, perhaps when he visited with Peter and James in Jerusalem in the late 30s or late 40s CE.[11] Thus, we are much closer to the time of Jesus and within the first decade or so of the movement. We may guess that these are the same types of oral sources behind the Gospels. It also shows us something about the nature of oral tradition itself. On the one hand, there is certainly a reverence for the tradition and the way

BOX 6.1

Paul's Oral Tradition of the Passion

1 Corinthians 11:23–26

For *I received* from the Lord *what I also handed on to you, that . . .*

the Lord Jesus on the night in which he was delivered up, took a loaf of bread, and when he had given thanks, he broke it and said, "This is my body that is for you. Do this in remembrance of me."

In the same way, after the dinner, he took the cup also, saying, "This cup is the new covenant in my blood. Do this, as often as you drink it, in remembrance of me."

For as often as you eat this bread and drink this cup, you proclaim the Lord's death until he comes.

---

1 Corinthians 15:3–7

For *I handed on to you* as of first importance *what I in turn had received,*

that . . .	(1) **Christ died** *{for our sins}*
	in accordance with the scriptures
and *that . . .*	(2) **he was buried,**
and *that . . .*	(3) **he was raised on the third day**
	in accordance with the scriptures
and *that . . .*	(4) (a) **he appeared to Cephas, then to the twelve;**
next	(b) **he appeared to more than 500 brethren at one time**
	{most of whom are still alive, though some have died};
next	(c) **he appeared to James, then to all the apostles.**

KEY: **Bold** = units of oral tradition
Regular type = Paul's framing elements
Italics = tradition summary formula
{small italics} = Paul's editorial comments

NOTE: In both cases I have tried to stay as close to the NRSV version as possible, but some changes have been made to capture the Greek phrasing more literally. Significant changes are treated in the accompanying discussion.

it continues in the life of the early churches. On the other hand, there are some noticeable differences from the later versions of these same events as portrayed in the Gospels.

The Death and Resurrection Tradition
(1 Corinthians 15:3–7)

The key passage is 1 Corinthians 15:3–7, because it gives us the basic outline of the story with a relative sequence of events. At the same time we are struck by how stark an account it is: "He died, he was buried, he was raised, and he appeared." Each step or moment in the action is reduced to a single verb with a kind of staccato parallelism in the Greek. Each one is introduced by its own quotation marker ("that"), suggesting that they might be somewhat separable. The longest section is the list of appearances in section 4. That this rehearsal of "what happened" is so brief is characteristic of oral tradition, but it leaves much of the story hanging. Another, even briefer, version may be seen in 1 Thessalonians 4:14: "For since we believe that Jesus died and rose again . . ." The introductory formula "we believe" suggests an early kind of creedal affirmation, while the double predicate "died and rose again" replicates the basic nodes of the oral tradition.[12] A reverberation of public proclamation of such summaries may be seen in 1 Corinthians 15:12: "Now if Christ is *proclaimed* as raised from the dead . . ." The word "proclaimed" (*kērussein*) here clearly assumes oral forms of preaching or, more properly, storytelling.[13]

Within the terse summary of 1 Corinthians 15:3–7, we also find additional editorial comments using phrases such as "for our sins" and "in accordance with the scriptures." Here "the scriptures" refers to the Jewish scriptures, for Paul typically in the Greek of the Septuagint. Although it is possible that these interpretive comments were already part of the oral tradition, it is just as likely that they could have been added by Paul himself. Such editorial elaborations are one of the ways that oral stories are shaped and reshaped over time. What may start as an interpretive gloss can later become a narrative component.

Perhaps the strongest indication that the phrase "in accordance with the scriptures" in this recitation had already become part of the oral tradition before Paul is that its wording in Greek is distinctive and quite different from Paul's usual scripture citation formula, "as it is written."[14] Here it is used twice, and in the second case it explicitly supports the temporal statement "on the third day." Notice also that it is "on the third day" and *not* "after three days," as found in some of the later Gospels.[15] At least one of the later accounts, that of Luke-Acts (Acts 2:25–31), attributes this three-day time frame directly to an interpretation of scripture by linking Jesus's resurrection to the promise: "nor let your holy one experience corruption" (quoting from Ps 16[15]:10, LXX).[16] The phrase "on the third day" implies that Jesus was raised from the dead before physical decomposition could set in, at least as understood by ancient medicine.

Paul's summary of the oral tradition must presuppose a similar explanation based on an interpretation of older Jewish scriptures. This way of understanding the burial-and-resurrection sequence supports a physical or bodily resurrection of Jesus. In the following passage (1 Cor 15:12–57), Paul discusses resurrection of the body by playing on precisely the same notion of "corruption" and decay.[17] It must be noted, however, that this interpretation depends on the peculiar wording of Psalm 16[15] in the Greek rather than the Hebrew.[18] The Septuagint version of Hosea 6:2 has also been suggested as a possible source for the actual wording "on the third day," which is identical in Greek to the phrase found in 1 Corinthians 15:4. Here are the two texts as they appear in the Septuagint version:

On account of this, my heart is gladdened and my tongue rejoices. Even now my flesh rests in hope, because you will not leave my soul in Hades, nor give your holy one to see corruption. (Ps 15:9–10, LXX)

He will restore us to health after two days, and on the third day he will raise us up and we shall live before him. (Hos 6:2, LXX)[19]

It seems, then, that an intertextual play between these two passages to form a scripture-fulfillment interpretation—and thus a way of explaining what had happened to Jesus—lies behind the oral tradition preserved by Paul.[20] Similarly, his earlier reference to the fact that the death was "for our sins in accordance with the scriptures" (1 Cor 15:3) may also be an allusion to Isaiah 53:4–6.[21] Precisely when these ideas were introduced into the oral tradition is uncertain; however, one clue comes from the fact that they rely almost entirely on the Greek version of scriptures.[22] One must guess that it reflects further elaborations beyond what Paul might have heard in Jerusalem when he met Peter and James (Gal 1:18–19; 2:9). There one would have expected Aramaic traditions to dominate.[23] We may thus have additional clues to the way that the oral tradition had already started evolving by the time it was being received by Paul. The oral tradition continued to be fluid and interactive as it moved into Greek-speaking Jewish areas such as Antioch.

A careful look at the appearances of the risen Jesus (section 4 in Box 6.1) also reveals a degree of fluidity in the tradition: two of those reported by Paul—(4b) to "five hundred brothers and sisters," and (4c) to "James and all the apostles"—do not occur in the Gospels. Nor do they reappear in any later Christian sources. They seem to have disappeared from the oral tradition.[24] Even the appearance "to Cephas (Peter) and the twelve" is not without problems relative to the later Gospel accounts, where Jesus never appears to more than eleven disciples.[25] The appearance stories in the Gospels presuppose the story of Judas and his subsequent death, which, in turn, gets elaborated in different ways within the Gospels.[26]

The James mentioned here must be the brother of Jesus. Neither Acts nor the Gospels reports an appearance of the risen Jesus to this James; however, Paul clearly knew him as an early leader of the Jerusalem church alongside Peter and John (see Gal 1:19; 2:9). Paul's knowledge of an appearance to James would accord well with his status as a leader of the church in Jerusalem, especially since the formulation puts him with "all the apostles." In Acts, by contrast, James only rises to prominence after the departure of Peter and the death of other original disciples (12:17; 15:13; 21:18).[27] A careful look at the wording of Paul's summary also shows that there is a strong parallelism between the report about "Cephas and then the twelve" and the one about "James and then all the apostles." It may suggest that these were originally two distinct but similar accounts that had already been rendered into a formulaic oral tradition. Perhaps Paul heard one from Peter and one from James, with each one placing himself in the pivotal role. The appearance to the "five hundred" may well come from an entirely different source, because Paul's editorial comment ("some of whom are still alive . . .") suggests that he had actually met some of them or heard statements to this effect.

Another feature of Paul's summary is the repetition of the identical word "appeared" (Gk. ōphthē) three times in conjunction with the three epiphanies, to Peter, "the five hundred," and James. Patterns of repetition, especially in threes, is another typical feature of oral traditions; we have the three verbs "died," "was buried," and "was raised" in the first part of the tradition. Though the Greek word ōphthē is commonplace, it is regularly used of divine epiphanies; here it must refer to a visionary appearance of Jesus alive. It may or may not connote an actual face-to-face encounter with the physical Jesus. The word by itself does not provide that degree of specificity, nor does Paul give clarification. This question will only become significant by the time that the Gospels were being composed.

Perhaps the most striking feature of Paul's account is that some of these earliest oral traditions about Jesus's death and resurrection should have been lost in later oral tradition. It shows that oral transmission may well preserve certain features, but others are more fragile or malleable. James and the "five hundred" get dropped from the story; later stories about Judas alter the number of disciples who see the risen Jesus. In this light too we must take careful note of what is not mentioned here by Paul. Specifically, there is no reference to anyone witnessing the actual resurrection itself or to the women finding the tomb empty (Mark 16:1–8: Matt 28:1–8; Luke 24:1–12), and there is no reference to Jesus's ascension to heaven (Luke 24:50–53; Acts 1:9–11). As we shall see, each of these episodes, like the Judas character, is a later addition to the story.

The Last Supper Tradition
(1 Corinthians 11:23–26)

Equally important is Paul's recounting of the oral tradition of the "Last Supper," which depends on the same tradition summary formula. Here we have an important additional component, namely, words spoken by Jesus himself in instituting dining as a commemorative practice. Hence telling the story is given both a social and liturgical anchor within early worship. It was a natural locus for repeating and elaborating the oral tradition.[28] Paul begins with an important temporal marker: "on the night in which he was delivered up." The word here translated "delivered up" (Gk. *paradidonai*) in this context properly means "delivered up to death" or "handed over for execution."[29] This is our first clue that there is sequence of events that connects this episode with that of the death-and-resurrection tradition recounted in 1 Corinthians 15:3–7. It may imply that Jesus was "arrested" and then "handed over" for execution, but an "arrest" remains only an implication. Nonetheless, the Gospels will incorporate an "arrest scene" after the Last Supper, at which time Judas "hands Jesus over" to the authorities.

On the other hand, there is no mention of Passover at all in connection with the supper, or for that matter with any of the events in Paul's account. The closest we get is a symbolic allusion, when Paul says elsewhere "for Christ, our *pascha,* has been sacrificed" (1 Cor 5:7). The same word, *pascha,* in the Septuagint can mean either the Passover meal (Exod 12:48)[30] or the Passover lamb (Exod 12:12); however, the reference to "sacrifice" rather clearly makes this an allusion to Christ as the Passover lamb. Hence we are left with a basic question: Does this suggest that the version of the Gospel of John or that of the Synoptics is more likely correct in the staging of the Last Supper scene (see the Prologue)? Or could this same interpretive comment be the basis for both versions, each one taking the symbolism in a different way as a means of fleshing out the narrative? In Paul it had been only a secondary comment on the meaning of Jesus's death. There is no indication that he understood it as the actual time. Each of the later Gospel versions would then represent alternative efforts to narrativize this Passover symbolism into the story.

Another question arises with the verb *paradidonai* ("to deliver up"), because it is regularly translated as "betrayed" in this passage. This mistranslation results from the fact that in the later Gospels, in the context of the Supper and arrest scenes, Judas is described as the one who will "hand him over" to the authorities, using this same verb.[31] In virtually all of these instances the word is translated "betray." In fact, it is the story of Judas in the Gospels that gives it a sense of "betrayal"; the Greek tradition does not use the word in this way. As we saw above in discussing the appearances in 1 Corinthians 15:5–7, Paul does not seem to know anything about the role of Judas. His reference to an appearance "to Cephas and the twelve" (1 Cor 15:5) ought to include Judas. At least, it does not suggest that Paul knew of a tradition in which one of the "twelve" was complicit in Jesus's execution.[32]

More to the point, Paul regularly uses the word *paradidonai* ("to deliver up") in reference to the death of Jesus; it never refers to an arrest scene or a "betrayal" by one of his own, but rather to the actual death itself. In one of these key references, it is God who delivers Jesus up (Rom 8:32); in another, it is Jesus himself who does it (Gal 2:20). No one could imagine translating Roman 8:32 as: "He who did not withhold his own Son, but *betrayed* him for all of us." Thus, Paul's oral tradition of the Last Supper and the Passion does not include the "betrayal" scene as such. On the other hand, it shows an important link between the Last Supper and the death-and-resurrection sequence.

Excavating the Layers of Oral Tradition

One issue emerges from the preceding discussion of Paul's oral tradition of the Passion. We need to be cautious about our assumptions of what was actually contained in these earliest versions of the story. Our tendency is to read later episodes or theological ideas back into Paul's day, because we "know" these later versions and how they have all been made to fit together narratively. In that sense we have to "excavate" the story archaeologically to discern earlier and later layers of the tradition. It is like walking through Rome or Athens and trying to imagine what the ancient city would have looked like by mentally "removing" all the modern buildings.[33]

But imagine taking it a step further by trying to remove other, older buildings that had been added later in antiquity, so that we might compare the Rome of Augustus's day with that of Constantine, some three hundred years later. Or the Athens of Plato's day compared to that of Paul, nearly four hundred years later. Now we have to be more careful and precise; we need more subtle archaeological clues to discern earlier from later phases of construction. At the same time, such an approach can help us understand how these ancient cities grew organically and changed over time. So also with our ancient stories about Jesus. We can see such evolution of the dramatic tradition in several of the later versions of episodes from the Passion narrative, especially in the scene of Jesus's Last Supper.

The Words of Jesus at the Last Supper

The words of Jesus at the Last Supper as quoted by Paul are by far the earliest we possess. Yet they too show that the oral tradition was still evolving. Box 6.2 shows the Pauline account (in Column 4) in comparison with those of the three synoptic Gospels.[34] A characteristic of the Pauline version is the formulaic quality and close parallelism of the two sayings: "This is . . . Do this . . . in remembrance of me." This kind of repetition is not only consistent with oral tradition, but also with ritual patterns. What becomes rather clear is that the basic scheme is quite consistent. It uses the meal elements of bread and wine to commemorate the death of Jesus, and these symbols are linked by Jesus's words authorizing the commemoration. In particular the cup/blood element also employs covenant language in all the accounts. We may thus be confident that each of these traditions originated from some common source.

Although there are some notable variations in the actual words attributed to Jesus, most are minor and could easily be explained by natural changes in the

BOX 6.2

The Words of Jesus at the Last Supper

Matthew 26:26–29	Mark 14:22–25	Luke 22:15–20	1 Corinthians 11:23–25
[26] While they were eating, Jesus	[22] While they were eating, he	He said to them, "I have eagerly desired to eat this Passover with you before I suffer; [16] for I tell you, I will not eat it until it is fulfilled in the kingdom of God."	[23] The Lord Jesus . . .
		[17] Then he took a cup, and after giving thanks he said, "Take this and divide it among yourselves; [18] for I tell you that from now on I will not drink of the fruit of the vine until the kingdom of God comes."	
took a loaf of bread, and after *blessing* it he broke it,	took a loaf of bread, and after *blessing* it he broke it,	[19] Then he took a loaf of bread, and when he had *given thanks,* he broke it and gave it to them, saying,	took a loaf of bread, [24] and when he had *given thanks,* he broke it
gave it to the disciples, and said,	gave it to them, and said,		and said,
"Take, *eat*; this is my body."	"Take; this is my body."	"This is my body, ‡ *which is given for you. Do this in remembrance of me.*"	"This is my body *that is for you. Do this in remembrance of me.*"
[27] Then he took a cup, and after giving thanks he gave it to them, saying,	[23] Then he took a cup, and after giving thanks he gave it to them,	[20] And he did the same with the cup *after supper,* saying,	[25] In the same way he took the cup also, *after supper,* saying,
"Drink from it, all of you;	and all of them drank from it.		*(continued)*

Matthew 26:26–29	Mark 14:22–25	Luke 22:15–20	1 Corinthians 11:23–25
28 for this is my blood of the covenant, which is poured out for many for the forgiveness of sins.	24 He said to them, "This is my blood of the covenant, which is poured out for many.	*"This cup that is poured out for you is the new covenant in my blood."* ‡	*"This cup is the new covenant in my blood. Do this, as often as you drink it, in remembrance of me."*
29 I tell you, I will never again drink of this fruit of the vine until that day when I drink it new with you in my Father's kingdom."	25 Truly I tell you, I will never again drink of the fruit of the vine until that day when I drink it new in the kingdom of God."	*[cf. v. 18 above]*	

KEY: *Italics* = core elements that should be compared closely

transmission of the oral tradition. Still the patterns of change are worth noting. For example, the versions in Mark and Matthew use the word "bless" for the bread rather than "give thanks," as in Paul and Luke. The former is a more typically Jewish meal blessing, while the latter is more Greek.[35] It may well be that the move to Greek-speaking areas influenced this change, but it is also possible that evolving patterns of Christian worship were at work.[36] We notice that the actual words of Jesus's "grace" or prayer over the food are never mentioned, only the formula "to bless" or "give thanks." In traditional Jewish meal blessings (*berakoth*), however, there was a specific content that began "Blessed be thou, O Lord, who bringest forth bread from the earth" and "who createst the fruit of the vine."[37] Presumably, in the historical situation of a Jewish meal, Jesus would have uttered these words; however, in the later tradition, they have disappeared in favor of the words regarding the bread and cup that establish the later memorial actions.

The word "give thanks" in Greek is *eucharistein,* from which we get the liturgical designation "Eucharist"; it is more characteristic in the later Greek ecclesiastical tradition. "Thanksgiving prayers" (*hodayot*) do occur in Jewish tradition, but they were not typically over food or wine.[38] The mixture of blessing (bread) and giving thanks (wine) found in Mark and Matthew would be quite strange in Jewish tradition. The Pauline tradition, followed in the Gospel of Luke, at least makes a consistent shift in the wording. Even so, there seems to be an awareness of both formulas in Paul.[39]

In a clear allusion to the Lord's Supper, but used in a broader discussion of dining, Paul says:

The cup of blessing that we bless, is it not a sharing in the blood of Christ? The bread that we break, is it not a sharing in the body of Christ? (1 Cor 10:16)

Each of Paul's rhetorical questions emulates the formulas from the words of institution, but here Paul substitutes "bless" for "give thanks." Similarly, both terms occur in Mark and more generally in the synoptic tradition in eucharistic allusions.[40] It would appear, therefore, that the two formulas "bless" and "give thanks" were used somewhat interchangeably, and both were attributed directly to Jesus in the words spoken at the Last Supper.

Finally, in Mark 14:13 we have the purely descriptive phrase "and they all drank from it," not found in Paul. It presupposes a narrative depiction of the actual supper. In Matthew 26:27, however, this phrase has been transformed into actual words spoken by Jesus: "Drink from it, all of you." In Luke and in Paul, however, there is nothing analogous to this moment in the text. So it looks as though a purely descriptive comment of the Markan author has been used to narrativize the earlier oral tradition, but then Matthew has further transformed it into putative words of Jesus in the Last Supper scene. In other words, the Markan author has introduced more narrative action to the story, and the Matthean author has woven this new component into the script for the character of Jesus to make the scene even more dramatic.

"In Memory of Me"

Other changes are even more striking. For example, the key commemorative terminology in the Pauline version, "Do this in remembrance of me," is totally missing in both Matthew and Mark. The Gospel of Luke retains this familiar pronouncement, likely taking it from the Pauline tradition (discussed further below). Its omission in the other two may be an additional clue that the oral tradition of the Supper behind the Synoptics, as coming through Mark, had a different configuration at several key points. On the other hand, there are indicators elsewhere in Mark and Matthew that seem to suggest an awareness of this important symbolic language. One comes in the scene of the "anointing at Bethany," in Mark and Matthew at least, where Jesus is at dinner with his disciples on one of the evenings immediately preceding the Last Supper.[41] After the woman anoints Jesus's feet and Jesus defends her against criticism for doing so, he concludes with a final pronouncement about the significance of her action:

"She has done what she could; she has anointed my body beforehand for its burial. Truly I tell you, wherever the good news is proclaimed in the whole world, what she has done will be told in remembrance of her." (Mark 14:8–9; cf. Matt 26:12–13)

Though the "remembrance" phrasing is not identical to that in Paul's version of the Last Supper,[42] for some scholars it is close enough to suggest a conscious allusion on the part of the Markan author.[43] If so, then the omission of this phrase in the actual Last Supper scene in both Mark and Matthew is even more indicative of subtle manipulation of the oral tradition. It has also been suggested that the addition of this scene in Mark, with its clear reference to an anointing "for burial," was intended to fill a gap in the story of Jesus's burial (15:42–47) and set the stage for the women to return later to "anoint him" (16:1–2), at which time they find the tomb empty.[44]

Two Cups?

In this vein, the most notable change is seen in the preliminary words of Jesus and the extra cup at the beginning of the Lukan version. Some aspects of this added section in Luke replicate the last section in Mark (14:25; cf. Matt 26:29), especially in the language associated with the cup. The order in Luke is noticeably different, however. More significant, perhaps, is the fact that in Luke there are now two cups, one before the bread and one after. It has been argued that this change might have been made to make the supper look more like a traditional Passover meal, in which the cup comes first.[45] But that still leaves the problem of what to do with the "second cup," not to mention the substantial difference in what Jesus says. In some ancient manuscripts, the Lukan text stops immediately after "This is my body" in verse 19 (as marked with ‡ in Box 6.2); the remainder of verse 19 and verse 20 are omitted. In other words, the second cup has been removed, and the Lukan order is merely reversed from that in the other Synoptics and in Paul. Yet it is the second cup in Luke that is more similar to the tradition preserved by Paul.

Some scholars have suggested that the second cup was added later by Christian scribes to make the Lukan Last Supper look more like that in Mark by having a cup after the bread; the language for this addition was taken from Paul. Other scholars have argued, instead, that the Lukan author is the one who originated this two-cup sequence because of the differences between the synoptic tradition and Paul, and also to make it more like a real Passover meal. The latter view is likely correct.[46] It means that the Lukan version was consciously constructed by taking elements from the synoptic tradition (specifically from Mark) and combining them with elements from Paul. It was the Lukan author who attempted to mediate the discernible differences between two streams of oral tradition (represented by Mark and Paul), while also making the Last Supper conform to a Passover meal. Once again, the script is changing with each new rendition of the story.

Another implication now arises from the fact that we have two basic versions of the Last Supper—one from Paul and one from Mark. Paul's version is the earlier in time; however, some features of that in Mark seem older in oral form. For example, the Markan version contains less parallelism in the two elements. As a result, we must try to account for the different wording found in Mark and later reflected in Matthew and Luke. One possibility is that the oral tradition of the Last

Supper had split into these two distinct streams with somewhat different wording at some point before being passed down to Paul or Mark. One stressed the *cultic* dimensions, associated with later liturgical repetition, while the other stressed the *testamentary* dimensions associated with Jesus's legacy to his followers.[47]

A second possibility is that the Markan version retains elements of an older Jewish (perhaps Aramaic) form that diverges from the Greek tradition known by Paul. Even so, it is also likely that the author of Mark was intentionally changing the wording of the oral tradition to emphasize sacrificial imagery.[48] In any case, the actual phrasing of Jesus's prayers had already disappeared from the oral tradition. Thus, changes seem to be happening at several stages in the transmission. At the same time, Paul may well be elaborating the tradition for his own purposes by adding the phrase "after supper," thus forcing the bread and cup to bracket the entire meal.[49] Either way, we see that the oral tradition remained malleable, and the Gospel authors seemed to continue this process, just as the author of Luke later recombined the two versions in a somewhat awkward way.

Exaltation and Ascension

We see other developments in later stories about Jesus's appearances after the resurrection. Notably, in the oral tradition cited by Paul, there is no qualitative distinction between the appearance to himself (1 Cor 15:8) and those to the first three groups (vv. 5–7); he uses exactly the same verb (*ōphthē*) in all four instances. In later tradition, as reflected in Acts, it became common to draw a sharper distinction between those appearances of Jesus after his resurrection but *before* his ascension and any other appearances *after* his ascension. The former were physical encounters with a living Jesus, while the latter were merely visions, typically from heaven.[50] The vision of Paul on the Damascus road, as described in Acts 9:1–9, conforms to this later distinction.[51] That Paul himself does not hint at such a distinction may be taken to suggest that he—or the earlier oral tradition—was not using the word "appeared" in this more subtle way. Or it may be taken to suggest that the oral tradition heard by Paul did not yet have an "ascension" event separate from the resurrection proper.[52] In other words, it seems that Jesus's being "raised" from the dead was considered simultaneous with his being "raised up" to heaven.[53]

Other passages may reflect oral tradition materials used by Paul for another component to the story—namely, Jesus's ascent to heaven. Only Luke-Acts, as noted earlier, actually describes an "ascension scene" as such (Luke 24:50–53; Acts 1:9–11). Yet we know that there was an early belief that after his resurrection Jesus was taken away to heaven. Paul clearly shows a knowledge of this oral tradition in two key passages. The first of these is from Paul's earliest letter, 1 Thessalonians, which dates to about 51 CE:[54]

For the people of those regions report about us what kind of welcome
    we had among you, and how
you turned to God from idols,
to serve a living and true God,
and to wait for his Son from heaven,
whom he raised from the dead—
Jesus, who rescues us from the coming wrath. (1:9–10)[55]

Based on the way it opens, this passage is regularly suggested to be a kind of shorthand of Paul's preaching to his new converts.[56] It contains three statements about Jesus—that God raised him from the dead, that he is currently in heaven and waiting to return, and that his return will be part of the eschatological deliverance. Notably, it is in his present "heavenly" condition that Paul refers to him as "[God's] son."[57] We may compare Romans 1:4, which equates the resurrection with his being "designated God's son."[58] So one notable feature of this unit is that it assumes a sequence that runs from the death (implied), to having been raised (past tense), presently being in heaven, and awaiting a return (soon). That Paul has such an expectation of Jesus's return is clearly spelled out in 1 Thessalonians 4:16: "For the Lord himself, with a cry of command, with the archangel's call and with the sound of God's trumpet, will descend from heaven."[59] Some scholars have also suggested that this is a pre-Pauline formulation as such; however, others think it is more of a summary statement.[60]

The second is the so-called Christ hymn of Philippians 2:

[Christ Jesus,]
who, being in form of God,
did not reckon equality with God
as something to be exploited (or robbed),
but emptied himself,
taking form of a slave;
[and who] being in likeness of humans
and in shape being found as human,
humbled himself,
being obedient to the point of death
—even death on a cross.
Wherefore God also highly exalted him
and graced to him the name
that is above every name,
so that at the name of Jesus
every knee should bend,
in heaven and on earth and under the earth,
and every tongue should confess that

Jesus Christ is Lord,
  to the glory of God the Father. *(2:6–11)*[61]

Although scholars debate the precise arrangement of the "stanzas," the fact that it is a hymn is widely assumed, even though questions have been raised.[62] The key is how the whole hymn—or perhaps a chanted confession—is attached grammatically to the name "Christ Jesus" in the preceding verse as its antecedent. The basic structure as reflected here is the parallelism of repeating words or phrases (underlined) at the beginning and end of the first two stanzas with a key verb (double underlined) in the middle to anchor the action. Hence the basic action of the hymn follows the path of the four main verbs: Jesus "emptied" himself and "humbled" himself unto death whereupon God "exalted" him to heaven and "graced" him with the title "Lord." Phrases in roman type are regularly assumed to be elaborations or editorial comments by Paul himself.

Some scholars have argued that calling Jesus "Lord" here in the hymn as a reference to his exalted heavenly status was itself a Pauline adaptation based on another allusion to scripture, specifically Isaiah 45:23, as paraphrased in the last stanza of the hymn.[63] The term also shows up in Paul's version of the Last Supper tradition (1 Cor 11:23, twice), and he even calls the commemorative meal as practiced in his churches "the Lord's supper" (1 Cor 11:20).[64] The usage of "Lord" in the hymn also suggests that it had already become a confessional slogan repeated by Paul's converts.[65]

It is now widely thought that the basic hymn perhaps had antecedents in Jewish wisdom speculation or in the suffering servant songs of Isaiah; however, in its present form it has become an evocation of Jesus as the Messiah with more Hellenistic overtones.[66] Paul seems to have taken it over and used it as a kind of core formulation, but it was also likely used in worship.[67] It has also been suggested that it represents a substantial shift in social location and theology from the oral tradition in 1 Corinthians 15:3–7.[68]

For our purposes at this moment, the key points of the hymn as elaborated by Paul are as follows: that Jesus, in his role as Messiah, humbled himself and died "on the cross" as "slave" in service to God, and that, as a reward for or vindication of this service, God exalted him to a superior position (in heaven) and gave him the confessional title "Lord."[69] In other words, what this early hymn yields—or at least Paul's exegesis of it—is the explanatory mechanism of what happened to Jesus after his death that "proved" to Paul that he was indeed the Jewish messiah.[70] It was his exaltation to heaven in conjunction with his resurrection from death.

As a hymn it may well have originated in worship, in part from scriptural allusions to Psalm 110:1 and Isaiah 45:23.[71] It also reflects an anticipation of Jesus's imminent return as expressed in worship, such as we see in 1 Corinthians 16:22 with the term *marana tha,* meaning "Our Lord, come."[72] What is not spelled out by Paul is whether and how an exaltation or elevation into heaven is related to the resurrection proper. That is to ask, "Are they the same 'moment' or two entirely separate events?" Though the Gospel of Luke later addresses this issue more directly, the answer for Paul remains unclear. But there would be nothing inconsistent with Paul's theology in collapsing these two events—at least as they are understood in later tradition—into one basic moment, assumed by Paul to be accomplished at the resurrection.

A Summary of the Pauline Passion Tradition

What we have begun to see is that these oldest units of oral tradition are clearly being preserved and passed down to later generations; however, deletions, additions, and other modifications are being incorporated even as early as Paul's own time and continuing into the writing of the different Gospels. Yet the raw outline is still very spare, a kind of bare-bones skeleton of the Passion story and hardly a full narrative. Its components as seen in the oral traditions cited by Paul may be schematized as follows:

> *"on the night"* (an evening meal, 1 Cor 11:23)
>
> 1. **"took bread/cup"** (commemorative meal, 1 Cor 11:23–25)
>
> 2. **"delivered up" to death** (same night, 1 Cor 11:23)
>
> 3. **"died"** (1 Cor 15:3; 1 Thess 4:14)
>
> *"even death on a cross"* (Phil 2:8; 1 Cor 2:2)
>
> 4. **"buried"** (1 Cor 15:4)
>
> 5. **"raised"** (1 Cor 15:4; 1 Thess 1:10; 4.14)
>
> *"on the third day"* (1 Cor 15:4)
>
> 6. **"appeared to"**
>
> "Cephas and the twelve" (1 Cor 15:5)
>
> *"more than five hundred"* (1 Cor 15:6)
>
> "James and all the apostles" (1 Cor 15:7)
>
> *"Paul"* (1 Cor 15:8); (untimely; cf. Gal 1:16)
>
> 7. **"exalted"** to heaven (Phil 2:9–11; 1 Thess 1:10–11)
>
> 8. waiting to **"return"** (1 Thess 1:10; 4:15–16)

This list is more of an outline than a narrative, although it contains the rudiments of narrative features, such as "on the night" and "on the third day." The individual nodes of the tradition function as moments or episodes, but their interconnections are at best loose. Paul uses them in his letters in bits and pieces. They do not yet have cohesive dramatic flow. They have not yet been expanded or explicated in narrative terms. In the next chapter we shall follow this process as it moves into the period of the Gospels. There we shall see how the process of "searching" the Jewish scriptures, already at work in Paul's day, as we have just seen, provided the basis for further narrativization of the story through individual scenes and episodes.

During the forty or so years prior to the composition of the first Gospel (Mark), the oral tradition of the death of Jesus clearly played a central role in the communal life of Jesus's followers. More than likely, these episodes were already being told and retold in various ways from community to community. As we have seen, the movement into a Greek-speaking context seems to have prompted some important changes, as did growing ritual elements in worship associated with the Lord's Supper as a commemoration of Jesus's death. Confession and proclamation went together, hand in hand, to reinforce the beliefs and identity of these early communities.

On the other hand, by the time of Paul, in the 50s CE, there does not yet seem to be a cohesive narrative or a unified dramatic telling of the story of Jesus's death. A full "life" of Jesus does not yet exist. In the letters of Paul we never hear of a birth narrative, Galilean ministry, or extensive teachings of Jesus. As yet, there are no parables, no miracle stories, no Judas, no triumphal entry, no Gethsemane, no betrayal, no trials, and no Mary Magdalene. All these elements, so familiar from later tradition, would have to wait for further developments to occur, as we shall see in the next chapter. In the meantime, the dynamics of oral storytelling in living contexts continued to promote the diverse traditions about Jesus and to propel their further elaboration into performative scripts.

CHAPTER SEVEN

Marking the Passion

*When they heard it, they raised their voices together to God and said, "Sovereign Lord, **who made the heaven and the earth, the sea, and everything in them,** it is you who said by the Holy Spirit through our ancestor David, your servant:*

> *'Why did the Gentiles rage,*
> *and the peoples imagine vain things?*
> *The kings of the earth took their stand,*
> *and the rulers have gathered together*
> *against the Lord and against his Messiah.'*

For in this city, in fact, both Herod and Pontius Pilate, with the Gentiles and the peoples of Israel, gathered together against your holy servant Jesus, whom you anointed, to do whatever your hand and your plan had predestined to take place.[1]
(Acts 4:24–28)

As we have seen, the earliest oral traditions about Jesus were brief, schematic statements about the Last Supper and his death, burial, resurrection, and appearances. What we typically call the Passion narrative was an outgrowth of those earliest traditions. So what happens from here? How do we get from loosely connected story "moments" to a flowing narrative? This is where the storyteller's art comes into play to weave them all together. In the process, new questions arise, and they necessitate other changes in the script. We have already seen glimpses of this process at work in the move from Paul to the Gospels. New components, such as the Judas story or the "ascension" scene, fill "gaps" in the story or resolve differences between earlier versions of the oral tradition. In other instances, looking to the Jewish scriptures offers a means of fleshing out the narrative while also lending a sense of divine guidance to the events. Then there are apologetic agendas that spin the narrative in certain directions. In each case, there is also a domino effect, as any particular change requires other adjustments or elaborations to smooth out the story line or propel the drama.

One such elaboration may be seen in the Gospel of Luke, which has an additional trial before Herod Antipas (23:6–16). It occurs as an interlude in the trial of Jesus before Pilate: upon hearing that Jesus is a Galilean (23:5), Pilate seeks to avoid dealing with the case by sending Jesus off to Antipas, son of Herod the Great and tetrarch of the Galilee:

> *When Pilate heard this, he asked whether the man was a Galilean. And when he learned that he was under Herod's jurisdiction, he sent him off to Herod, who was himself in Jerusalem at that time. (23:6–7)*

After the hearing, at which Jesus is further mocked and abused, Antipas sends him back and leaves Jesus's fate to Pilate.

This additional trial before Antipas does not occur in any of the other canonical Gospels. In some ways it is analogous to Matthew's distinctive addition of the death of Judas (27:3–10) and the guards at the tomb (27:62–66; 28:11–15, to be discussed below). These scenes serve as glosses on the basic narrative found in Mark as new questions have come to bear. In contrast to those in Matthew, however, the Lukan addition is made to fit seamlessly into the narrative.[2] It is used by the author[3] to emphasize that Pilate did not think Jesus was guilty of any crime punishable by death. By virtue of other changes, the order of the Lukan trial better fits formal Roman judicial procedure, even though Pilate, as a provincial procurator, was not bound by such legalities in judging criminal cases involving non-Romans. It is also the case that in Luke, in marked contrast to all the other Gospels, Pilate never has Jesus flogged.[4] The Lukan author also adds the comment that after this exchange Pilate and Antipas became friends (23:12).

Where does this additional scene come from? Did the Lukan author have access to another oral tradition of Jesus's trials not known by the other Gospel authors? Not necessarily. In large measure, the scene depends on an allusion to yet another of the Psalms in order to assert "messianic" imagery in and around Jesus's trials. The interpretive link is provided in the companion volume to the Gospel of Luke, the book of Acts. Both volumes were written by the same author as part of a continuous narrative running from the birth of Jesus to Paul's final sojourn in Rome at the end of his life.[5] The key passage is Acts 4:24–28 (quoted at the beginning of this chapter). This particular scene is set in the early days of the church in Jerusalem. Here the *two trials*—before Pilate and Antipas—are mentioned again and said to fulfill the "prophetic" words of Psalm 2:1–2, as quoted verbatim from the Septuagint in Acts 4:25–26:

Why did the Gentiles rage and the people threaten worthlessness? The kings of the earth stood by and the rulers came together as one, against the Lord and against his Christ (or anointed).[6]

Of course, this is the opening of the all-important royal psalm that provides so much background for Jewish messianic understanding (see Chapter 1). Each part of the psalm quotation now is given a direct correspondence in the story of Jesus's trial and death, at least as found in the augmented version of the Lukan author. Antipas is the king; Pilate, governor of Judea, is the ruler; their burgeoning friendship and the crucifixion itself represent the collusion of the Gentiles with the "people" who "threaten worthlessness" (Ps 2:2). The wording in the Greek version of this psalm reflects some differences from the Hebrew—primarily by changing all the verbs from present to past tense—that allows for this interpretation. The Lukan author can thus interpret them as pointing to the past event of Jesus's death instead of a current event, as in the Hebrew. At the same time this interpretation depends on reducing the plural nouns ("kings" and "rulers") to single individuals. Ironically, the interpretation given in Acts transforms the scheming "peoples" into a shorthand for "the people of Israel" (explicitly stated in Acts 4:27), whereas in the original form of Psalm 2 they are clearly "foreign nations" who conspire against Israel and its king. This narrative adaptation by the Lukan author depends on reinterpretation both of Psalm 2 and of the sequence of events surrounding Jesus's death.

The story of the trial before Herod Antipas is clearly a later addition in the Lukan Passion narrative. It appears in none of the other canonical Gospels, written before or after. So where did it come from? The author of Luke-Acts gives us a clue to the process in which passages from the Jewish scriptures, such as Psalm 2, might provide the occasion for these new script elements. It comes in the follow-up story in Acts 4, where the early followers of Jesus in Jerusalem are shown reflecting communally on the death of Jesus. This episode is the narrative parallel in Acts for the trial scenes in Luke; together they form an integrated doublet to facilitate the author's interpretive innovations. The story in Acts 4:13–22 says that Peter and John were imprisoned by Jewish authorities. When they were released, they were ordered to cease proclaiming the story of Jesus. When they returned to the other followers of Jesus (4:23–30), the entire gathering spontaneously broke into prayer to God, in which they unanimously offered this particular interpretation of how the "words of David" had been fulfilled in the person of Jesus as the Messiah (Christ).

Interestingly, the key "proof text" comes from Psalm 2, while the rather formal address to God (also in boldface above) is a pastiche from several biblical doxologies, or hymnic praises of God, typical from the Psalms and Jewish liturgical texts.[7] Both of them follow the Greek, of course, and depict the early followers in Jerusalem bursting spontaneously and uniformly into psalmic poetry. At this point the story begins to seem rather far-fetched on a purely historical level; however, this use of the scriptures gives the whole scene a strong "promise fulfillment" tone rather typical of the Lukan author.[8] In other words, this vignette was designed intentionally as a mirror scene or literary doublet to explain the events already depicted in the Lukan Passion narrative by the addition of the trial before Herod Antipas. On the other hand, it seems that the Lukan author was continuing the kind of "mining" of language from the Psalms to elaborate the story, just as we saw happening earlier on in Paul's day.

Thus, the Lukan narrative exhibits an ongoing process of reflection within the later churches through these dramatic innovations. It shows how the Psalms and other scriptures were first understood to explain what had happened to Jesus and why. Then later the same components were narrativized into the Gospel story as a way of fleshing out the scenes dramatically. In this particular case, however, it is substantially a Lukan creation.[9] In other words, it shows the author of the Gospel of Luke continuing patterns of oral adaptation at a much later stage in the dramatic evolution of the narrative as new episodes are woven into the story. Now they begin to create literary interconnections and new cause-and-effect relationships within the plotline of Jesus's life and death. In the process, the drama of the Passion grows and changes.

From Nodes to Narrative

In many ways, this type of use of the Psalms and other supposedly "prophetic" passages seems very much like "proof texting." By "proof texting" we mean the practice of selecting passages from the Jewish scriptures, usually in Greek, to shore up a particular story or interpretation of Jesus, even when the passage did not have that meaning or implication in its original context. From the perspective of dramatic storytelling, the main question is whether the Jewish scriptures are in some way "scripting" the depiction of what happened or whether new versions of the story allowed other scriptures to be insinuated narratively as "proof texts." In reality, it is probably some of both. Stories or wording from the Jewish scriptures, whether or not in keeping with their original intent, might be taken to provide new details to help flesh out the narrative; at the same time, they could also serve as validations for new ways of telling the story. We see both moves at work in the Gospel narratives.

As we saw in the case of the "Lamb of God" symbolism in the Gospel of John (see the Prologue), scriptural allusions could facilitate basic narrative changes by the later Gospel authors, even when they surely knew the earlier versions. It can also be seen in the case of the two bandits crucified with Jesus in the Lukan version. In both Mark and Matthew the two bandits mock Jesus. In Luke—but only in Luke—the first bandit mocks him, while the other, after affirming Jesus's innocence and asking to be remembered, ultimately receives a blessing.[10] Although

Matthew and Luke basically follow the same outline of episodes found in Mark, there are notable changes in each one that fit the distinctive narrative needs and theological ends of each author. In Matthew, we have the unique addition of Pilate "washing his hands" to symbolize his uncertainty. The Lukan change regarding the two criminals reflects this Gospel's peculiar theme of having other characters pronounce the innocence of Jesus even more directly.[11] Such subtle narrative changes, when noted consistently through each Gospel, can show key differences of tone and intent. A synopsis of these basic narrative changes for the Passion

---

BOX 7.1

The Development of the Passion Narrative

Story Nodes in Paul	Elaborations →	Later Gospel Scenes (*individual variants in parenthesis*)
1. "took bread/cup" "dinner/evening" (1 Cor 11:23–25)	*Passover* "*paschal lamb*" (1 Cor 5:7)	**Last Supper** Passover Meal (*Synoptics only*) Farewell dinner (*John only*)
2. "delivered up" to death (same night) (1 Cor 11:23)	*arrest*	**Conspiracy Judas Betrayal and Arrest scenes**
	trial (?)	Trial—Sanhedrin
	trial (?)	Trial—Pilate Trial—Herod (*Luke only*) Presentation (*John only*)
3. "died" (1 Cor 15.3) "crucified" "even death on a cross" (cf. 1 Thess 4:14; Phil 2:8; 1 Cor 2:2; Gal 3:1)	"*according to the scriptures*"	Crucifixion and Brigands Final Words Centurion (*Synoptics only*) John and Mary at cross (*John only*) Break legs / pierce side (*John only*)
4. "buried" (1 Cor 15:4)	*tomb*	Preparations for burial Women observe tomb (*Mark only*) Guards at tomb (*Matt only*)
5. "raised" "*on the third day*" (1 Cor 15:4) (1 Thess 1:10; 4:14)	"*according to the scriptures*"	Women come to tomb Empty tomb "tell disciples" Peter at tomb (*Luke only*) Peter and John at tomb (*John only*) Guards (*Matt only*)

episodes from the Last Supper to the death of Jesus as we move from Paul to the Gospels can be seen in Box 7.1.

The Changing Character of Judas

Another good example is the Judas story, which does not show up in the Pauline tradition at all (as discussed in Chapter 6). The basic story that Judas was the one who turned Jesus over to the authorities appears in all four Gospels, but with

Story Nodes in Paul	Elaborations →	Later Gospel Scenes *(individual variants in parenthesis)*
6. "appeared to"	*where?* *when?*	to Mary Magdalene (*John only*) —in the Galilee (*Mark/Matt*)
"Cephas and the Twelve" (1 Cor 15:5)	*no more than 11 !*	Suicide of Judas (*Matt only*) Death of Judas (*Acts only*) Peter and 11 in the Galilee (*Matt/John*) Road to Emmaus (*Luke only*) Peter and 11—Jerusalem (*Luke-Acts/John*)
"more than five hundred" (1 Cor 15:6)		(omitted)
"to James and all the apostles"(1 Cor 15:7)		(omitted)
7. "exalted" to heaven (Phil 2:9–11; 1 Thess 1:10–11)		Ascension—Jerusalem (*Luke-Acts only*)
8. waiting to "return" (1 Thess 1:10; 4:15–16; "*marana tha,*" 1 Cor 16:22)		(cf. Mark 13:24–32 / Matt 24:29–36)

some key differences from one to the next. The two most important variations are Judas's motivation and what happened to him afterward. In Mark, Judas seems to approach the priests of his own volition, but with no expectation of a reward. Only then did they offer him money (14:10–11). Some scholars would argue that Judas's motivation as depicted in Mark was to force Jesus to show his hand as the Messiah.[12] Rather than a "betrayer," he was an overly zealous disciple with revolutionary leanings who really believed that Jesus was about to usher in a new kingdom. Other than a cryptic comment at the Last Supper (14:21), the Markan author makes no mention of what happened to Judas.

We may contrast the two accounts of Judas in Matthew and Luke-Acts. In the Gospel of Matthew, Judas asks for money at the outset, and this scene now begins with a direct question by Judas: "What will you give me if I hand him over to you?" (26:15). The addition of this putative quotation serves not only to liven up the narrative, but also to paint a darker profile; Judas is no longer a misguided idealist, as in Mark, but a disloyal and greedy friend.[13] Now the notion of "betrayal" begins to loom larger. Even so, after the crucifixion, the remorseful Judas throws the blood money back at the priests and commits suicide (27:3–10).[14]

The structure of the Matthean narrative also is balanced: the two scenes involving Judas (26:14–16; 27:3–10) flank the central events of the Last Supper and the arrest. The added scene of Judas's death interrupts the flow of the narrative, as seen in Mark, at the juncture where Jesus is taken before Pilate.[15] It also reflects later events than the surrounding narrative, including the purchase of a field with the blood money, where Judas was buried. An editorial comment by the author also betrays a later perspective from which the story is being told: "For this reason that field has been called the Field of Blood to this day" (27:8). The story thus reflects later developments in the tradition. We shall return to another such editorial comment regarding later-day developments in Matthew at the end of this chapter.

Finally, the story ends with another fulfillment of prophecy quotation (27:9–10), this time attributed to Jeremiah. In reality, however, this ostensible quotation loosely pieces together three different passages from Zechariah and Jeremiah to assemble all the narrative components.[16] Though not seamless within the narrative, the story of Judas's death fills a basic gap in the story and is narratively satisfying, at least within Matthew.

The Lukan author fills out the story of Judas in an entirely different way. It begins with an even more diabolical motivation when "Satan entered into Judas" to prompt his action (22:3). At the arrest scene, the Lukan Jesus is made to comment in direct discourse on the fact that Judas was there to identify him to the authorities with, of all things, a kiss (22:48). Now, the kiss occurs in Mark and Matthew as well. That is not the key change. Instead, in Mark and Matthew, the intent to identify Jesus with a kiss is described as a plan by Judas himself, who speaks in direct dialogue. In the garden he is then described as approaching and actually kissing Jesus.

By contrast, in Luke, Judas's earlier plan is entirely missing. Instead, when Judas approaches Jesus with the intent of kissing him, Jesus preempts him by asking him the question, "Judas, is it with a kiss that you are betraying the Son of Man?" Again the action shifts with the dialogue, but now it is Jesus who speaks. Consequently, Jesus is now portrayed as already knowing what Judas had conspired to do, but then the actual kiss does not happen. The overall mood of the scene has changed dramatically. Jesus is now shown to be divinely prescient and far more serene. Judas becomes far more malevolent. A kiss should be a sign of love and friendly affection. The sense of irony and betrayal now seems to grow stronger. The Lukan arrest scene also ends with a telling addition, as Jesus's final words to the arresting authorities now come out as, "But this is your hour, and the power of darkness" (22:53). Thus, both Judas himself (22:3, as noted above) and the Jewish authorities are now portrayed as operating under the direct influence of Satan.

This change in tone and character further sets up a distinctive ending to the Judas saga as described by the Lukan author. In contrast to Matthew, where the subsequent death and burial of Judas interrupt the sequence of the Passion narrative, the Lukan version leaves the description of Judas's death until after Jesus's resurrection and ascension. The story is told in Acts 1:15–20, as part of Peter's decision to seek a replacement for him. Then we get an editorial aside from the narrator explaining what had happened to him. But it is a different story. Now Judas himself keeps the blood money, instead of hurling it back at the authorities (as in Matt 27:5). He actually uses it to buy a field, and while he was apparently out surveying his new property, he was killed *accidentally:* "And falling headlong, he burst open in the middle and all his bowels gushed out" (Acts 1:18). The Judas of Luke remains unrepentant to the end. In keeping with the Satanic influence seen earlier in Luke, the author now concludes the story by quoting passages from two entirely different psalms that better suit this portrayal of Judas's fate and his eventual replacement among the twelve.[17] There's more than a little hint of divine retribution here, a theme that continues in Luke-Acts.[18] The Lukan Judas is a far cry from the pitiful character described in Matthew.

Finally, in the Gospel of John, Judas becomes the treasurer among the disciples, who has been pilfering all along (12:1–8), another clue to his negative character. He has no direct conversation or interaction with Jesus at the arrest because of his thoroughly demonic persona (18:1–11; cf. 17:12). His character is sealed, although Jesus is ultimately in charge. Here again there is a quotation from scripture, but it is yet a different "prophecy" (Isa 40:3) that is said to be fulfilled in John (13:18). The fate of Judas is never described in the Gospel of John, although something like the Lukan version may well stand in the background.

The progression goes like this. The role of Judas is introduced at a later stage of the evolution of the story to account for Jesus's arrest on the same night as the Last Supper.[19] Then, in later Gospel versions his character changes from misguided idealist (Mark), to disloyal friend (Matthew), to diabolical schemer (Luke), and finally to demonic antagonist (John). The play of each scene varies with the depiction to create the characterization and provide a fitting end. In each one a different set of texts is marshaled to show how scripture was being "fulfilled."[20] A key dramatic technique of storytelling involves transforming an action or gesture into direct discourse in the form of dialogue ostensibly spoken by the character. Dialogue not only makes the story more lively and dramatic, it also helps to foster a particular impression of the character by conveying subtle elements of tone or intent. It is often difficult to discern when these are real quotations and when they are narrative devices. In subsequent chapters we shall take up later efforts to expand on the character of Judas, as seen in the gnostic *Gospel of Judas*.

"In Accordance with the Scriptures"

One feature of the process of creating such flowing narratives, as seen in the case of Judas and the trial before Antipas, involved using passages from the Psalms and other scriptures to explicate or flesh out a particular episode.[21] It was already at work in the oral tradition summaries used by Paul, as we saw above in conjunction with the temporal marker "on the third day" (1 Cor 15:4). The story was refracted through the Jewish scriptures; ancient heroes provide both potent images and narrative details, as Moses, David, Elijah, Elisha, and others served as models of faithfulness in the face of trial. We already see this in Jewish tradition in the chronicles of the Maccabean revolt when Judas's father, Mattathias, is likened to Phinehas, the exceedingly zealous grandson of Aaron (1 Macc 1:26, alluding to Num 25:7–8). Is it possible that the Markan Judas was meant to evoke a failed Mattathias?

The process of scripture allusion is nowhere clearer than in the crucifixion scene itself. Although all the sources—already evidenced in Paul—are agreed that Jesus was executed by means of crucifixion, none of them give any details of the actual procedure or the specific sequence of actions in placing Jesus on the cross. Paul says only that Jesus was "crucified" or died "on the cross" with no further information.[22] Likewise, the Gospels simply say: "they crucified him" without further elaboration.[23]

What is striking is the lack of any details regarding the actual process of Jesus's crucifixion in physical terms. In fact, we have very few actual descriptions of crucifixion from ancient authors, whether pagan, Jewish, or Christian. Most of our knowledge of the details comes by way of allusion instead, such as the practice of having the condemned "carry his own cross."[24] Yet even here there are differences among the Gospels; all three of the Synoptics say that a passerby, Simon of Cyrene, was compelled to carry Jesus's cross; only the Gospel of John depicts Jesus doing so himself.[25]

Sometimes the criminal was nailed both hand and foot; other times, the hands were merely tied with ropes. The earliest representations of the crucifixion of

BOX 7.2

The Earliest Images of the Crucifixion of Jesus

A. THE PALATINE GRAFITTO, ROME, THIRD CENTURY CE

The crudely carved grafitto on plaster shows a man (left) bowing before a donkey-headed man on a cross, toward whom he makes a gesture of veneration with his left hand. The man tied to the T-shaped cross has his feet and hips resting on crossbars. The Greek text reads: "Alexamenos worships his god." Because it clearly represents an unsympathetic view of Christian belief, the depiction reflects common assumptions of the day regarding the Roman practice of crucifixion. Rome, Museo Nazionale delle Terme. *Used by permission, Alinari/Art Resource, NY.*

B. CARVED GEMSTONE AMULET, SYRIA (?), THIRD CENTURY CE

This bloodstone intaglio is probably the oldest extant depiction of the crucifixion of Jesus. He is shown bearded and tied to a T-shaped cross, with feet spread wide as though standing on a bar. The first three lines of the Greek text are an invocation: "Son, Father, Jesus Christ . . ." The text uses several magical words and formulas, showing that the gem was to be worn as a magical amulet, presumably by a Christian. It is noteworthy that both depictions clearly show the victim's hands tied rather than nailed to the crossbar of a T-shaped cross. *Used by permission, Trustees of the British Museum, London (1986.0501.1).*

Jesus show the practice of using ropes alone for the arms; only much later did the traditional portrayals emerge in Christian art (see Box 7.2). The earlier Synoptics (Mark and Matthew) make no comment. The traditional understanding depends on the later stories found in Luke and John. In the Gospel of John, "doubting Thomas" insists on seeing and touching "the mark of the nails in his hands" (20:25). Only here there is no mention of nailing the feet. In the Gospel of Luke

Jesus himself says, "Look at my hands and my feet" (24:39), but without further explanation. Not until recent decades has clear archaeological evidence from first-century Jerusalem been discovered that shows the precise way that it was done; here too there are sharp contrasts to most later Christian iconography (see Box 7.3).

In keeping with ancient sensibilities, the "gory details" of such executions were left to the imagination. It was up to the storyteller to evoke the hearers' (i.e., readers') visualization through words. Even Paul suggests that he did just this to bring the story to life using his rhetorical powers (Gal 3:1, see Chapter 6). We can see this also in the Gospels, as the spare form of the crucifixion scene is elaborated by allusions to Psalms, specifically Psalms 22 and 69, which reflect the experience of the righteous person who suffers. Key elements in the crucifixion scene are thus

---

BOX 7.3

Archaeological Evidence for Crucifixion

A tomb discovered in 1968 at Giv'at ha-Mivtar, a suburb north of the Old City of Jerusalem, contained several ossuary burials. The burials date to the mid-first century CE. One of the ossuaries contained the bones of a man in his twenties who had been crucified. The inscription on the ossuary identifies the man as "Jehohanan, son of HGQWL" (the father's name is uncertain). The main piece of evidence comes from the fact that the man's right heel bone (*calcaneum*) is pierced from the side by an iron nail, measuring 11.5 cm (5 1/8 in.). Because the point of the nail had been bent when driven into the upright of the cross, it made removal impossible without causing severe damage. As a result, the nail was left, thus providing us with the only known piece of physical evidence for the practice of crucifixion in Roman Judea at the time of Jesus. The position of the nail shows that it was common to nail the feet and ankles from the side to the upright of the cross. A small plaque of olive wood was placed on the outside of the foot to keep the man from being able to tear free of the nail. Driving a nail through the calcaneum in this manner must have caused excruciating pain, and could have only been done once the man had been hoisted onto the cross, probably already tied to the crossbar. There is some evidence from artistic depictions (see Box 7.2), that the man might have been made to stand first on a crossbar, but the nailing of the feet would have represented the final blow. The arm bones of the man show no signs of scarring from nails in the hands or above the wrists. It would appear, therefore, that the man was tied to the crossbar rather than nailed. The T-shaped cross, shown here, was likely the most common form in Roman practice, because it would have allowed the crossbar to be hoisted on top of the upright that was already mounted in the ground.

taken from these psalms; they include offering Jesus something to drink, dividing his clothes, and mocking by onlookers.[26] Even the nailing of Jesus's "hands and feet" may well come from the language of Psalm 22:16 (21:17, LXX), where the distinctive wording of the Greek says: "My hands and feet have they *gouged*."[27] The most important, however, comes in Jesus's words uttered from the cross: "My God, My God, why have you forsaken me?" (Mark 15:34), which is a direct quotation of Psalm 22:1. In Mark it is a sign of Jesus's abject desperation at the moment of death, and he looks all the more human for it.[28] Left as it is, the Markan scene ends on a curious note, which, as we shall see later, depends on the author's use of dramatic irony to set up the empty-tomb scene in a peculiar way (to be discussed in Chapter 11). Some of the later Gospel authors must have found the Markan

Heel bone with nail (*left*) and reconstructed model of the man's right foot (*right*). Photo and reconstruction by Joe Zias, Jerusalem. *Used by permission.*

Diagram of the practice of nailing the feet to the upright of the cross. Drawing by Eytan Zias. *Used by permission.* The footrest has been added by the author.

FURTHER READING

Hengel, M. *Crucifixion*. Philadelphia: Fortress, 1989.

Tzaferis, V. "Jewish Tombs at and near Giv'at ha-Mivtar," *Israel Exploration Journal* 20 (1970) 18–32. [original discovery]

Zias, J. "Crucifixion: The Anthropological Evidence." http://joezias.com/CrucifixionAntiquity.html.

Zias, J., and E. Sekeles. "The Crucified Man from Giv'at ha-Mivtar: A Reappraisal," *Israel Exploration Journal* 35 (1985): 22–27.

BOX 7.4

Psalms and the Crucifixion Scene in Mark 15:22–32

²² Then they brought Jesus to the place called Golgotha (which means the place of a skull).

Ps. 69:21 — They gave me poison for food, and for my thirst they gave me vinegar to drink.

²³ **And they offered him wine mixed with myrrh;** *but he did not take it.*

²⁴ And they crucified him, *and* **divided his clothes among them,** casting lots *to decide what each should take.*

Ps. 22:15 — my mouth is dried up like a potsherd, (see Mark 15:36)

²⁵ It was nine o'clock in the morning when they crucified him.

Ps. 22:18 — They divide my clothes among themselves, and for my clothing they cast lots.

²⁶ The inscription of the charge against him read, "The King of the Jews."

²⁷ *And with him they crucified two bandits,* **one on his right and one on his left.**

Ps. 22:16 — For dogs are all around me; a company of evildoers encircles me. My hands and feet have shriveled (LXX: they have been gouged).

[²⁸ *This verse omitted in most mss.*]

²⁹ **Those who passed by derided him, shaking their heads** and saying, *"Aha! You who would destroy the temple and build it in three days,*

³⁰ *save yourself, and come down from the cross!"*

Ps. 22:7–8 — All who see me mock at me; they make mouths at me, they shake their heads; "Commit your cause to the LORD; let him deliver—let him rescue the one in whom he delights!"

³¹ *In the same way the chief priests, along with the scribes, were also mocking him among themselves and saying,* "He saved others; he cannot save himself.

³² *Let the Messiah, the King of Israel, come down from the cross now, so that we may see and believe."*

Ps. 22:17 — I can count all my bones. They stare and gloat over me.

Those who were crucified with him also taunted him.

Ps. 22:1 — My God, my God, why have you forsaken me? (see Mark 15:34)

KEY: Regular type = the core narrative (possibly pre-Markan)
    Italics = Markan editing to create the narrative flow
    Bold = features taken from the "suffering psalms"
    (esp. Pss 22; 69)

irony perplexing, for these particular words of Jesus have been removed in both Luke and John.

Box 7.4 shows how these passages from two psalms are woven around the core narrative, which in turn was further smoothed out by the Markan author. Both Matthew and Luke follow this basic outline, while the Gospel of John, once again, elaborates further, including details such as the untorn tunic and the breaking of the legs (19:23–24, 31–37).[29] In both cases, these new details in the story come from the continuing effort to weave elements from the scriptures into the narrative in order to force a correspondence.

The "seamless tunic" comes from a misreading of the parallelism in Psalm 22:18 [21:19, LXX], where two words for "garment" are used. Whereas there is only one garment mentioned in the Synoptics, the Gospel of John now has two. Because it is seamless, the second is not torn apart and divided; the soldiers cast lots for it instead. This unique Johannine symbolism may be an allusion to the seamless robe of the high priest that was worn when he performed important sacrifices. The "unbroken legs" is said explicitly to fulfill "prophecy," but specifically an element drawn from the preparation of the Passover lamb (as discussed in the Prologue). Even the crucifixion of two other bandits (or "brigands") with Jesus seems to stem from the language of the Psalms; yet this part of the story too changes from Gospel to Gospel, as we have already seen.[30]

When we set aside all the elements in the Markan crucifixion scene drawn from other scriptures, the core narrative boils down to the following:

> *Then they brought Jesus to the place called Golgotha (which means the place of a skull). . . . And they crucified him. . . . It was nine o'clock in the morning when they crucified him. The inscription of the charge against him read, "The King of the Jews." (15:22–26)*

It is significant that this Markan core adds two key elements to the story not found in the earlier Pauline tradition: the time and the inscription bearing the charge. Some scholars think that the latter, at least, is solid historical evidence retained through the Markan stream of the oral tradition, but even this point is debated.[31] The location, because of its symbolic name, may also be part of a later oral tradition. The Gospel of John further modifies and elaborates both points by changing the time and having the inscription disputed.[32]

Box 7.5 provides a full comparison of all the scenes from the Last Supper to the crucifixion in all four Gospels to highlight where there are key differences and significant elaborations from one Gospel to the next. In general, the later Synoptics (Matthew and Luke) follow the outline of the Passion narrative provided by the Gospel of Mark. The number of key variants is rather small. Even the Gospel of John seems to be somewhat dependent on the basic Markan outline, even though it makes more substantial changes. Whether the Gospel of John is dependent directly on Mark or through an intermediate source is a question to be addressed later.

BOX 7.5
A Comparison of the Trials and Execution of Jesus

Matthew	Mark	Luke	John
Supper (26:26–29) [= 1st Seder of Passover]	Supper (14:22–25) [= 1st Seder of Passover]	Supper (22:14–20) [= 1st Seder of Passover]	Supper (13:1–15) [not Passover]
Gethsemane/prayer (26:36–46)	Gethsemane/prayer (14:32–42)	Mt. of Olives/prayer (22:40–46)	*Discourse with disciples* (14:1–17:26)
Arrest (26:47–56)	Arrest (14:43–52)	Arrest (22:47–52)	Garden/Arrest (18:1–11)
Trial 1: Caiaphas (26:57–68) *(at night)*	Trial 1: high priest (14:53–65a) *(at night)* Beating by guards (14:56)	To high priest's house (22:54) Peter's denial (22:55–62) Mocking and beating (14:63–65) *(through night)*	Trial 1: Annas (18:12–14) Peter denies [1/0] (18:15–18) Trial 1b: Annas (18:19–23) Trial 2: Caiaphas (18:24)
Peter's denial [3/1] (26:69–75)	Peter's denial [3/2] (14:66–72)		Peter denies [2/1] (18:25–27)
		(next morning) Trial 1: Chief Priests (22:66–71)	
(next morning) Taken to Pilate (27:1–2)	*(next morning)* Taken to Pilate (15:1)		*(early in morning)* Taken to Praetorium and Pilate comes out (18:28–30) Pilate appeals 1 (18:31–32)

Matthew	Mark	Luke	John
Death of Judas (27:3–10)	—	*(contrast Acts 1:18–19)*	—
Pilate hearing 1 (27:11–14)	Pilate hearing 1 (15:2–5)	**Taken to Pilate** (23:1) Accusations by priests (23:2) Pilate hearing 1 (23:3) Pilate refuses 1 (23:4–5)	**Pilate summons Jesus into Praetorium** (18:33–38a) Pilate appeals 2 (18:38b) Release of Barabbas (18:39–40)
		Trial before Herod Antipas (23:6–11a) Sent back to Pilate (23:11b)	
Pilate refuses 1 (27:15–16) Calls for Barabbas (27:17–21) Pilate's wife (27:19) Calls to crucify Jesus (27:22–23) Pilate washes hands (27:24) Crowd replies (27:25) Release of Barabbas and Has Jesus flogged (27:26a) Hands Jesus over (27:26b)	Pilate refuses 1 (15:6–7) Calls for Barabbas (15:8–11) Calls to crucify Jesus (15:12–14) Release of Barabbas and Has Jesus flogged (15:15a) Hands Jesus over for crucifixion (15:15b)	**Pilate hearing 2** (23:13) Pilate refuses 2 (23:14–16) Crowd calls for Barabbas (23:18–19) Pilate refuses 3 (23:20) Calls to crucify Jesus (23:21) Pilate refuses 4 (23:22) Calls continue (23:23) No Flogging	Pilate has Jesus flogged (19:1)
Mocking by soldiers Crown of thorns, etc. (27:27–31a)	Mocking by soldiers Crown of thorns, etc. (15:16–20a)		Mocking by soldiers Crown of thorns (19:2–3)

Matthew	Mark	Luke	John
			Pilate appeals 3 (19:4–5)
			Calls to crucify Jesus (19:6a)
			Pilate appeals 4 (19:6b)
			Crowd answers (19:7)
			Pilate addresses Jesus (19:8–11)
			Pilate appeals 5 (19:12a)
			Crowd responds (19:12b)
			Brings Jesus out and asks again (19:13–15a)
			Priests answer (19:15b)
			Pilate hands Jesus over for crucifixion (19:16)
Soldiers lead Jesus away (27:31b) Compel Simon to carry cross (27:32)	Soldiers lead Jesus away (15:20b) Compel Simon to carry cross (15:21)	Soldiers lead Jesus away (23:26a) Compel Simon to carry cross (23:26b)	Jesus led away, carrying own cross (19:17a)
		Women along the way, Jesus speaks (23:27–31)	
		Two *criminals* sent for crucifixion (23:32)	
Arrival at Golgotha, offer Jesus drink (27:33–34)	Arrival at Golgotha, offer Jesus drink (15:22–23)	Arrival at place (23:33)	Arrival at Golgotha (19:17b)

Matthew	Mark	Luke	John
"When they had crucified him" (27:35a) Soldiers divide clothes (27:35b) and keep watch (27:36)	"And they crucified him" (15:24a) Soldiers divide clothes (15:24b)	"They crucified Jesus there with the *criminals*" (23:33) *Jesus speaks* (23:34a) Soldiers divide clothes (23:34b)	"They crucified him, and with him two others" (19:18)
			Pilate and priests argue over the plaque (19:19–22)
The plaque (27:37)	The inscription (15:26)		Soldiers divide clothes (19:23–24)
Two bandits crucified (27:38)	Two bandits crucified (15:27)		
Bystanders mock Jesus (27:39–40) Priests mock Jesus (27:41–43) ⸺ Both bandits mock (27:44)	Bystanders mock Jesus (15:28–30) Priests mock Jesus (15:31–32a) ⸺ Both bandits mock (15:32b)	⸺ Priests mock (23:35) Soldiers mock (23:36–37) *The inscription* (23:38) **One criminal mocks but other defends; Jesus blesses (23:39–43)**	
			Jesus speaks to Mary, John, and disciples (19:25–27)
Jesus's final cries and death (27:45–50)	Jesus's final cries and death (15:33–37)	Jesus cries out and dies (23:44–48)	Jesus dies (19:28–30)

KEY: **Bold** = indicates key differences in each Gospel

The Empty Tomb

So far, we have several different motivations and mechanisms for transforming and elaborating the narrative from the skeletal nodes of the earlier oral tradition. Ultimately, they reflect the faith of those believers who told and heard these stories, whether or not they were based on historical details. This theological dimension of the storytelling process is best seen in the development of the empty-tomb story. Many people assume it was the original core of the proclamation, but it too was a later elaboration that went through several modifications over time within the Gospels.

We must start this discussion of the empty tomb by recognizing the fundamental proclamation at its base. As we saw in the previous chapter, the story begins with the oral tradition in Paul, which states categorically that Jesus was first buried and then raised from the dead (1 Cor 15:4; cf. 1 Cor 15:12; 1 Thess 1:10; 4:14). Paul never mentions the tomb itself or anyone finding it empty. The tomb as such is merely an inference occasioned by the reference to a burial and being raised "on the third day." Yet it remains absolutely clear that Paul fully believed Jesus had been resurrected bodily. For Paul, however, the proof was not the tomb, but the appearances of Jesus to Peter, James, "the five hundred," and, most important, to himself (1 Cor 15:5–8; cf. Gal 1:16). What led to further development is likely a combination of several factors, not least of which were the challenges of skeptics. Paul may even allude to such when he says "but we proclaim Christ crucified, a stumbling block to Jews and foolishness to Gentiles" (1 Cor 1:23).

Christian claims about the resurrection and ascension of Jesus were still being debated by pagan detractors throughout the second century (see Chapter 4). We already have a glimpse of these debates lying behind the narrative formation of the tomb scene in the Gospel of Matthew. It comes at the end of the scene in the story of the bribing of the guards.

> *While they [the women at the tomb] were going, some of the guard went into the city and told the chief priests everything that had happened. After the priests had assembled with the elders, they devised a plan to give a large sum of money to the soldiers, telling them, "You must say, 'His disciples came by night and stole him away while we were asleep.' If this comes to the governor's ears, we will satisfy him and keep you out of trouble." So they took the money and did as they were directed. <u>And this story is still told among the Jews to this day.</u> (28:11–25)*

Here once again we catch the perspective of the Matthean author, in this case referring to a rumor that the disciples had stolen Jesus's body. The most telling feature is the final clause "to this day," an unmistakable allusion to some later perspective. This rumor is attributed to Jews, presumably some Jews in conflict with the Matthean community near the time the Gospel was being written, probably sometime in the 80s CE. It was meant to show that the resurrection of Jesus was all a hoax perpetrated by his followers. In turn, by telling the story of "what really happened" with the guards, the Matthean author has debunked the rumor, thus showing that the story of Jesus's resurrection must be true.

In a later chapter we shall return to discuss other internal references to this tension between the Matthean community and its Jewish neighbors. Such internecine Jewish polemics clearly had an impact on the shape of the Gospel of Matthew and the image of Jesus portrayed there. For now, however, we focus instead on how this later debate has reshaped the story of the empty tomb. The story of guards at the tomb is, in fact, entirely a Matthean addition to the Passion narrative.[33] We can begin to see the impact at the level of the narrative when we compare the two versions in Matthew and Mark. The texts are shown in parallel in Box 7.6. The Gospel of Luke closely follows the text in Mark and shows no awareness of the changes in the Matthean version.

BOX 7.6

The Empty-Tomb Scene in Matthew and Mark

A. The Burial of Jesus (ending verse)

Matthew 27:61	Mark 15:47
Mary Magdalene and the other Mary were there, sitting opposite the tomb.	Mary Magdalene and Mary the mother of Joses saw where the body was laid.

B. The Guards at the Tomb (Matthew 27:62–66 only)

The next day, that is, after the day of Preparation, the chief priests and the Pharisees gathered before Pilate and said, "Sir, we remember what that impostor said while he was still alive, 'After three days I will rise again.' Therefore command the tomb to be made secure until the third day; otherwise his disciples may go and steal him away, and tell the people, 'He has been raised from the dead,' and the last deception would be worse than the first." Pilate said to them, "You have a guard of soldiers; go, make it as secure as you can." So they went with the guard and made the tomb secure by sealing the stone.

C. The Empty Tomb

Matthew 28:1–10	Mark 16:1–8
After the sabbath, as the first day of the week was dawning, Mary Magdalene and the other Mary *went to see the tomb.*	When the sabbath was over, Mary Magdalene, and Mary the mother of James, and Salome bought spices, <u>so that they might go and anoint him.</u>
And suddenly there was a great earthquake; for an *angel* of the Lord, *descending from heaven, came and rolled back the stone and sat on it.* His appearance	And very early on the first day of the week, when the sun had risen, <u>they went to the tomb.</u> *(continued)*

Matthew 28:1–10	Mark 16:1–8
was like lightning, and his clothing white as snow. *For fear of him the guards shook and became like dead men.*	<u>They had been saying to one another, "Who will roll away the stone for us from the entrance to the tomb?"</u>
But *the angel* said to the women, "Do not be afraid; I know that you are looking for Jesus who was crucified. He is not here; for he has been raised, as he said. *Come, see the place where he lay.*	<u>When they looked up, they saw that the stone, which was very large, had already been rolled back.</u>
Then go quickly and tell his disciples, 'He has been raised from the dead, and indeed he is going ahead of you to Galilee; there you will see him.' **This is my message for you."**	<u>As they entered the tomb, they saw a young man, dressed in a white robe, sitting on the right side; and they were alarmed.</u>
So they left the tomb quickly with fear and great joy, *and ran to tell his disciples.*	But <u>he</u> said to them, "Do not be alarmed; you are looking for Jesus of Nazareth, who was crucified. He has been raised; he is not here. Look, there is the place they laid him.
Suddenly Jesus met them and said, "Greetings!" And they came to him, took hold of his feet, and worshiped him.	But go, tell his disciples and Peter that he is going ahead of you to Galilee; there you will see him, just as he told you."
Then Jesus said to them, "Do not be afraid; go and tell my brothers to go to Galilee; there they will see me."	So they went out and fled from the tomb, for terror and amazement had seized them; <u>and they said nothing to anyone, for they were afraid.</u> [The End of Mark]

D. Bribing the Guards (Matthew 28:11–15 only)

While they were going, some of the guard went into the city and told the chief priests everything that had happened.

After the priests had assembled with the elders, they devised a plan to give a large sum of money to the soldiers, telling them, "You must say, 'His disciples came by night and stole him away while we were asleep.' If this comes to the governor's ears, we will satisfy him and keep you out of trouble." So they took the money and did as they were directed.

And this story is still told among the Jews to this day.

E. Jesus Appears to the Disciples (Matthew 28:16–17 only)

Now the *eleven disciples went to Galilee, to the mountain to which Jesus had directed them. When they saw him, they worshiped him; but some doubted.*

KEY: <u>Underlined</u> = parts of Mark significantly altered in Matthew
     Bold = parts of the story unique to Matthew
     Italics = keys to changes in the narrative structure in Matthew

We begin by observing that in Matthew the two scenes concerning the guards immediately flank the empty-tomb scene. As a narrative technique, this is similar to what the Matthean author did with the two scenes concerning Judas (discussed above), where we also have another retrospective comment using the phrase "to this day" (27:8). It should also be noted that the guard story is already scripted to set up its required ending (from the Matthean perspective) by having the Jewish authorities petition Pilate to place guards at the tomb out of fear that his disciples might try to steal the body (27:63–64). Afterward, they bribe the guards to say that this is just what happened. We can also see how the story of the guards has caused the internal narrative of the empty-tomb story to be reworked in several ways.

First, there is an actual reference to the guards within the empty-tomb scene, as they are dumbfounded by the appearance of the angel who rolls away the stone (28:4). Such a reference would not make sense in Mark. In effect the guards are actual witnesses to the moment, just as are the women. The "real" story of what they told the priests who bribed them, as explained by the Matthean author, is further "proof" that the resurrection was true.

Second, a major change in the narrative occurs with the initial arrival of the women and with their intentions in coming to the tomb. Mark clearly says that they had bought spices the night before (Saturday evening, after the Sabbath had ended), intending to go and anoint the body of Jesus the next morning. Accordingly, while they are on their way to the tomb, they ask one another, "Who will roll away the stone?" (16:1–3). In other words, these women, who had seen Jesus buried two nights earlier (15:47), were planning to go into the tomb and anoint Jesus. Their only concern was the stone; the idea of guards preventing them access plays no part in the narrative flow of the Markan version. Narratively, it would be completely incomprehensible.[34]

Now when we turn to the Matthean version, we see that the setup for the women has changed dramatically. Now the women only intend to go and "see the tomb" (28:1). There is no longer any reference to their having bought spices for the purpose of anointing him. There is no hint of a plan to go inside the tomb; nor are they worried about the stone. Why? Because the guards have come onstage in the plot. Next, this allows the Matthean author to change their actual arrival at the tomb, as now they witness an angel sitting on the stone that had been rolled away while the guards are terrified. Notice that in Matthew the angel meets and addresses them outside the tomb (28:5); only after he speaks to them does he invite them inside to see where the body had been (28:6).

In Mark, on the contrary, the women had found the tomb already open (16:4); they did not witness the rolling back of the stone, as Matthew suggests (28:2–5); and they went in (Mark 16:5). Inside, they see a "young man, dressed in a white robe," sitting on the right side of the slab. Only then does the "young man" address them. It is clear that the words spoken by the man/angel are essentially the same in both versions, but the narrative structure and flow of the scene has changed radically. One (Matthew) takes place outside the tomb in the midst of miraculous events; in effect, the women nearly see the resurrection moment as the tomb is opened. The other (Mark) takes place inside the tomb, but the women only see the aftermath of the resurrection in the emptiness of the tomb.

Finally, both Mark and Matthew have the man/angel instruct the women to tell the disciples to go to Galilee, where they will see Jesus (Mark 16:7; Matt 28:7).[35] In Matthew, the women depart joyfully, eager to tell the disciples (28:8). While on their way Jesus appears to them directly, and they touch him, further "proof" of the resurrection (28:9–10). After this we get the report about the bribing of the guards (28:11–15), and then the appearance of Jesus on a mountain in Galilee (28:16–20). And here the Gospel of Matthew ends.

It is at this point that we also see the only real changes in the Lukan version. Once again, there is no mention of the guards at the tomb. Now there are two angels who meet the women when they go inside the tomb (24:4). Their instructions differ only in that they do not tell the disciples to go to Galilee, where they will see Jesus (24:5–7). This change is important to the Lukan narrative, as all of the postresurrection appearances occur in and around Jerusalem, and the disciples are told not to depart from the city (Luke 24:47; Acts 1:4). Of course, this change in Luke also sets up the ascension scene, which takes place just outside Jerusalem (Acts 1:9–11; cf. Luke 24:50–53) after Jesus had remained with the disciples in the city for forty more days (Acts 1:3–4). It also sets up the subsequent events located in Jerusalem with the initial founding of the church (Acts 2–7). Also after the women go and report to the disciples, Peter runs to the tomb and sees it empty for himself (Luke 24:10–12).[36]

In Mark, as the women leave the tomb, they are terror stricken, and "they said nothing to anyone, for they were afraid" (16:8). And this is the abrupt and dramatic ending of the Gospel of Mark. Neither the women nor the disciples ever actually see Jesus. Although longer endings were later added to Mark to provide postresurrection appearances like those in the other Gospels and in Paul, it is very likely that this was the original ending of the Gospel of Mark.[37] But as we shall see, the real "ending" of the resurrection story occurs elsewhere in Mark.

We may now see the overall impact of the Matthean reshaping of the narrative with the story of the guards flanking the empty-tomb scene. It was clearly created to rebut the charges of the Jewish rumor.[38] In that sense it is a secondary reaction and hence a later addition, as the comparison with Mark also shows on the narrative level. It works by reversing the guard's purported "lie" about the body being stolen and narrativizing it into the text itself. As a result, it requires changes in the narrative running order and internal details of the story. There is little doubt that it depends on a prior knowledge of the Markan version, and yet the Matthean author felt free to make these changes in retelling the story. In this case, the addition of the two vignettes concerning the guards, flanking the empty-tomb scene itself, serves primarily to disprove the Jewish "rumor" that the body was merely stolen. The need to defend belief in the resurrection of Jesus was greater than the need to just tell what happened.

We may also begin to see what led to the new Matthean version by looking at the earlier stages in the transmission of the story. The very existence of a Jewish "rumor" (as described in Matthew) about the body being stolen presupposes that there was an earlier version of a story about the empty tomb being told by followers of Jesus. The "rumor" was invented to rebut this earlier tomb story. We may also deduce that this earlier tomb story simply described finding the tomb empty, but had no other witnesses or "proofs" per se. In other words, it is very likely that the "rumor" was a secondary reaction to the Markan empty-tomb scene, or something very much like it. We now have three distinct layers or stages in the development of the empty-tomb narrative as reflected in Mark and Matthew: first came the Markan version of finding the tomb empty; next, the "Jewish rumor" to debunk it; and last, the Matthean version of the tomb story with the addition of the guards to rebut the "rumor."

In this same vein, we may guess that the Markan empty tomb also developed, at least in part, out of a similar need to answer challenges or rebuttals that had already arisen in reaction to claims about Jesus's resurrection. The fact that Mark ends with the women telling no one also hints at this issue, because it allows for the fact that no one else but the women saw the tomb empty.[39] It is as if to say, "We only heard about the tomb later." Remember that the earliest version of the oral tradition says only that he was raised from the dead and "appeared to us." The postresurrection *appearances* to Peter and the twelve, "the five hundred," James and the apostles, and Paul were the first and most important witnesses to the resurrection story. Limiting the story to this simple form in no way diminishes the belief of the first followers of Jesus. Yet the logical response of skeptics might be, "You only saw a ghost!"

This same charge seems to be a concern in both Luke and John, where disciples are told to touch him, and Jesus eats food (Luke 24:36–43; John 20:24–29). The Lukan version of the appearance to the disciples makes this earlier charge more explicit, as Jesus says, "Look at my hands and my feet; see that it is I myself. Touch me and see; for a ghost does not have flesh and bones as you see that I have" (24:39). A story about finding the tomb empty is both a natural way of responding and a logical inference to the fact that he was buried and was raised. It is only a short step in the development of the story tradition, as the tomb scene leads narratively to the postresurrection appearances, as seen in the later Gospels. But assuming that Mark 16:8 is the original ending, the Gospel of Mark has no postresurrection appearances. Did the Markan version merely assume them based on the oral tradition? Such appearances are anticipated in the instructions to the disciples to go to Galilee, "There you will see him, just as he told you" (Mark 16:7), which alludes to a statement in the Last Supper scene (14:28). As we shall see, the Gospel of Mark not only presupposes such an appearance scene, but presents one—but not at the end of the Gospel. We shall return to it in the concluding section of this chapter.

At this point we are probably looking at the moment of transition between the earlier oral tradition as preserved in Paul and the beginnings of a new narrative tradition that would eventuate in the Gospel of Mark. We may think of it in archaeological terms as a stratigraphy of the story: the top layers are later; the farther down one digs, the earlier the layers are. Each new layer builds on and is shaped by the previous layers (see Box 7.7). The empty-tomb story evolved out of basic nodes in the earlier oral tradition ("was buried"; "was raised on the third day") to answer new questions and respond to continuing debates in subsequent decades and generations.

That crucifixions, mourning women, and empty tombs were by no means unusual elements of storytelling in the Roman world is further shown by a passage from Petronius's *Satyricon,* a spicy fiction with biting social satire from the mid-first century. Because this text is earlier than any of the written Gospels, it shows what kinds of elements might have been considered ordinary in crucifixion stories. It is also significant for its depiction of how the characters within the narrative—itself a work of total fiction—tell tales for the purposes of entertainment in a social setting. For sake of comparison, the full text of this episode is given in Box 7.8.

BOX 7.7

"Stratigraphy" of the Empty-Tomb Scene

Stratigraphy is the term used in archaeology and geology to refer to deposits or layers of soil that accrue upward over time. By excavating downward through these layers, using careful controls, one can analyze the patterns of deposition vertically. On analogy, one can do the same with stories by evaluating how successive layers of storytelling—and in this case counterstories as well—evolved over time. "Dig" from the top down; "read" from the bottom up. Arrows represent reaction vectors—solid are known; dashed, conjectured.

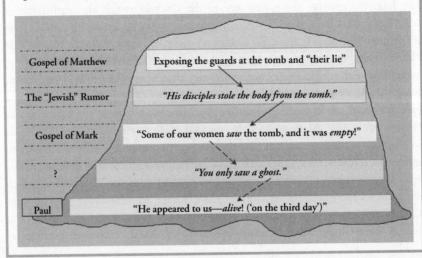

Gospel of Matthew	Exposing the guards at the tomb and "their lie"
The "Jewish" Rumor	*"His disciples stole the body from the tomb."*
Gospel of Mark	"Some of our women *saw* the tomb, and it was *empty!*"
?	*"You only saw a ghost."*
Paul	"He appeared to us—*alive*! ('on the third day')"

BOX 7.8

Another Crucifixion Story, Another Empty Tomb

The following story is told as a ribald tale by one of the characters in Petronius's *Satyricon*. If the author, Petronius Arbiter, is the same as the senator and courtier of Nero described by Tacitus (*Annals* 16.17–18), he was forced to commit suicide in 66 CE. Although the precise identity of the author is debated, the work seems clearly to be from no later than the Neronian period (54–68 CE). The section given here follows the "dinner of Trimalchio," when the main characters are relaxing with drinks and conversation late of an evening. A bout of storytelling ensues to liven up the evening. The Latin text is a prosimetric satire; the translation is that of the author, adapted from M. Heseltine (and E. H. Warmington), Petronius, rev. ed., Loeb Classical Library (Cambridge, MA: Harvard University Press, 1969).

Satyricon 110–113

110 . . . Then Eumolpus, both our advocate in peril and author of our present concord, lest our joy be silenced for lack of rousing stories, began to hurl many taunts at the fickleness of women: how easily they fall in love, how quickly they forgot even their children, how no woman was so chaste that she could not be led away into utter madness by a passion for a stranger. He was not referring to ancient tragedies or notorious names from history, but to an affair which happened in his lifetime, which he would tell us, if we wanted to hear it. So all eyes and ears were turned upon him, and he began as follows:

111 "There was a matron in Ephesus who was so renowned for modesty that she drew women even from the neighboring clans to gaze upon her. Therefore when she had buried her husband, the common fashion of following the procession with loose hair, and beating the naked breast in front of the crowd, did not satisfy her. She followed the dead man even into his resting place, and began to watch and weep all night and day over the body, which was placed in an underground vault (*hypogeum*) in the Greek fashion. Neither her parents nor her relations could divert her from this torturing herself, and courting death by starvation; the officials were at last rebuffed and departed; and she was mourned by all as a woman of unique character, and she was now passing her fifth day without food. A very loyal servant girl sat by the failing woman, shed ample tears in sympathy with her woes, and at the same time filled up the lamp, which was placed in the tomb, whenever it waned. So there was but one opinion throughout the whole city, every class of person admitting this was the one true and brilliant example of modesty and love.   *(continued)*

At that very moment the governor of the province gave orders that some robbers should be crucified close behind the small chamber in which the lady was mourning over her recently deceased [husband]. So on the next night, when the soldier who was guarding the crosses—lest someone should remove one of the bodies for burial—observed a light shining plainly among the tombs and heard a mourner's groans, a very human weakness made him desire to know who it was and what he was doing. So he went down into the vault, and on seeing a very beautiful woman, at first halted in confusion, as if he had seen a portent or some ghost from the world beneath. But afterwards noticing the dead man lying there, and looking at the woman's tears and the marks of her nails on her face, he came to the correct conclusion, that she found her regret for the lost one unendurable. He therefore brought his supper into the tomb, and proceeded to urge the mourner not to persist in useless grief, and break her heart with unprofitable sobs; for all men made the same end and found the same resting-place, and so on with the other platitudes which restore wounded spirits to health. But ignoring his consolation, she beat and tore her breast more violently than ever, tearing out her hair, and laying it on the dead body.

Still the soldier did not yield, but tried to give the poor woman food with similar encouragement, until the slave girl, who was—I am certain—seduced by the smell of his wine, first gave in herself, and put out her hand at his kindly invitation, and then, refreshed with food and drink, began to assail her mistress's obstinacy saying, 'What will you gain by all this, if you faint away with hunger, if you bury yourself alive, if you breathe out your undoomed soul before Fate calls for it?

'Do you believe that the ashes or the spirit of the buried dead can feel thy woe? Will you not begin life afresh? Will you not shake off this womanly failing, and enjoy the blessings of the light so long as you are allowed? Your poor husband's body itself here ought to persuade you to keep alive.'

People are always ready to listen when they are urged to take food in order to keep alive. So the matron, being thirsty after several days' abstinence, allowed her resolution to be broken down, and filled herself with food as greedily as her servant who had been the first to yield.

[112] Well you know what temptation generally assails a man of a full stomach. The soldier used the same insinuating phrases which had persuaded the

matron to consent to live, to conduct an assault upon her virtue. Her modest eye saw in him a young man, handsome and eloquent. Her servant begged her to be gracious, and then said, 'Wilt thou fight love even when love pleases thee? [Or don't you remember in whose lands you now rest?]'

I need hide the fact no longer. The woman did not hold back even this part [of her body—*perhaps petting Tryphaena lasciviously*], and the conquering hero won her over on both counts. So they passed not only their "wedding night" together, but the next and a third, of course shutting the door of the vault, so that any friend or stranger who came to the tomb would imagine that a most virtuous lady had breathed her last over her husband's body.

Well, the soldier was delighted with the woman's beauty, and his stolen pleasure; he bought up all the fine things his means permitted, and carried them to the tomb the moment darkness fell. So the parents of one of the crucified, seeing that the watch was ill-kept, took their man down in the dark and administered the last rite to him. The soldier was eluded while he was off duty, and next day, seeing one of the crosses without its corpse, he was in terror of punishment, and explained to the lady what had happened. He declared that he would not wait for a court-martial, but would punish his own neglect with a thrust of his sword. So she had better get ready a place for a dying man, and make one gloomy vault for both her husband and her lover. The lady's heart was tender as well as pure. 'Heaven forbid,' she replied, 'that I should look at the same moment on the dead bodies of two men whom I love. No, I would rather make a dead man useful, than send a live man to death.'

After this speech she ordered her husband's body to be taken out of the coffin and affixed to the empty cross. The soldier availed himself of this very prudent woman's cleverness, and the people wondered the next day by what means the dead had ascended the cross."

[113] The sailors received this tale with a laugh; Tryphaena blushed deeply, and laid her face caressingly on Giton's neck. But there was no laugh from Lichas; he shook his head angrily and said: "If the governor of the province had been a just man, he should have put the dead husband back in the tomb, and hung the woman on the cross."

Was There a Pre-Markan Tomb Narrative?

One way of possibly responding to this kind of evolving story tradition might be to ask this question: "Since the early followers of Jesus clearly believed that Jesus was raised from the dead, why didn't they just go and check his tomb, even if it was sometime later?" Of course, such a question assumes that they knew and remembered the site of his tomb. There is no evidence for commemoration of such a place for centuries after the death of Jesus.[40] Although this may seem logical from a modern perspective, the practice of burial in first-century Judea was rather different.

Most tombs of the sort in which Jesus was buried—at least as described in the Gospels—were only used temporarily, until the body had fully decomposed. This took roughly one year. Then the bones were bundled up and reburied in small ossuaries (lit., "bone boxes") that were typically housed in collective or "family" tombs.[41] A number of these family tombs and ossuaries have been found around Jerusalem and have been the subject of both recent archaeological interest and not a few scandals.[42] What this means, however, is that tombs of the first type, where the body was laid out for decomposition, were emptied out on a regular basis and reused. They might or might not be associated with a particular family tomb.[43] Both types could easily be created out of natural caves. Mortuary rituals, reburial, and multigenerational use mean that both types of tombs needed to have easy access. Tombs were rarely, if ever, sealed permanently, and "roll-away" doors or the like were commonplace. Or to say it another way, at any given moment, there might have been many such empty tombs; they were "a dime a dozen." While not in use (or "occupied"), a tomb of the first type might easily—or preferably—be left open and visible. Yet this fact may also say something about the evolution of the story of Jesus.

It has often been suggested that the Markan Passion narrative was based on an older form of the story that circulated independently from that in Paul and from other components of the Gospel tradition. The empty-tomb scene is often assumed to be part of this pre-Markan tradition, even though it does not appear in the Pauline oral tradition. A putative "oral source" for the empty tomb is mediated primarily through the Markan tradition. In more recent scholarship, however, the basic structure of the Markan Passion and a growing number of episodes within it have been attributed more directly to the creative efforts of the Markan author.

For example, it is clear that the author knows and uses basic elements from the older tradition as seen in Paul. One of these is "the third day" for Jesus's being raised. The Markan author has carefully crafted the narrative around this sequence, as seen in the description of the women buying the spices later in the evening on Saturday ("when the sabbath was over"), intending to visit the tomb on Sunday morning (16:1–2). A hiatus in the action between the burial on Friday, the "day of Preparation" for the Sabbath (15:42–47), when the woman looked on, and the women buying the spices on Saturday evening is thus accounted for narratively by the timing of the Sabbath. The idea of plotting the story against the days of the week, so that the triumphal entry occurs on the Sunday prior to the empty tomb, is likely the creative effort of the Markan author.[44] The several episodes concerning the Temple (triumphal entry, cleansing, and the apocalyptic discourse) have also been shown to fit Markan thematic interests and compositional design.[45] We shall return to these elements in Chapter 11.

The Markan narrative, taken as a whole, has an integral generic character, based in part on older Jewish stories of the suffering and vindication of the righteous person.[46] Joseph (Genesis), Mordecai (Esther), Daniel and his three friends, and Judith all reflect this tradition.[47] Several other examples occur in literature even closer to the time of Jesus. In 2 Maccabees 6–7 there are two stories—of Eleazar and the mother and seven sons—who willingly face martyrdom by Antiochus IV rather than transgress kosher laws.[48] These stories are repeated and further elaborated in 4 Maccabees.[49] At the end the martyred mother and sons are depicted as vindicated, having been "gathered together into the chorus of the fathers and [having] received pure and immortal souls from God" (4 Macc 18:23). Vindication of the righteous person who suffers and dies is also seen in Wisdom of Solomon 2, 4, and 5.

These tales are heavily laced with allusions to the "suffering servant" of Second Isaiah, and particularly the passage in Isaiah 52:13–53:12, which also becomes so influential in the development of the Passion tradition.[50] We should also note that the word "to suffer" in Greek (*paschein*) is homonymic with the Greek form of the word for Passover (*pascha*). This wordplay may have helped forge new narrative ties between such tales of the suffering righteous and the Passover/Passion tradition in the Gospels. Such a tie is already fully developed in the Gospel of Mark.[51]

What this suggests is that the author of Mark both knew and used the earlier oral tradition, as seen in Paul, as the outline for a more fully developed Passion narrative. Many of the individual scenes and elaborations can be accounted for on the basis of older Jewish models, allusions to scriptures, or key Markan themes. They are woven together to help stitch the individual nodes of the earlier oral tradition into a flowing narrative framework. Far from "fictionalizing" the narrative, however, the goal of the author was to bring it to life for the audience. They assumed that the story was "true" in its basics, but giving it a narrative quality required texture and detail that the older oral tradition simply did not provide. The interaction of the author and audience—storyteller and hearers—was a driving mechanism in composing the story.

This perspective leads to the question of whether the Markan author used or incorporated other oral traditions about Jesus's death and resurrection that predated the narrative in Mark. From a formalistic perspective, being able to demonstrate such elements might push other components of the story to an earlier stage in the history, even to the point of approaching the earlier days of Paul or other first-generation followers of Jesus. At least some scholars have argued that such a source—perhaps even a written "Passion Gospel"—existed and was used as a base text by the author of Mark.[52] The principal candidate suggested for such a source comes from a later text known as the *Gospel of Peter,* because it contains a unique "resurrection" scene with strong similarities to the Markan transfiguration story (Mark 9:2–8)[53] (see Appendix C).

Transfiguration or Resurrection?

The transfiguration story, in which Jesus is met by two heavenly figures, Elijah and Moses, and is physically transformed into a shining brightness, occurs in all three synoptic Gospels, but Mark is our earliest version:

> *Six days later, Jesus took with him Peter and James and John, and led them up a high mountain apart, by themselves. And he was transfigured before them, and his clothes became dazzling white, such as no one on earth could bleach them. And there appeared to them Elijah with Moses, who were talking with Jesus. Then Peter said to Jesus, "Rabbi, it is good for us to be here; let us make three dwellings, one for you, one for Moses, and one for Elijah." He did not know what to say, for they were terrified. Then a cloud overshadowed them, and from the cloud there came a voice, "This is my Son, the Beloved; listen to him!" Suddenly when they looked around, they saw no one with them any more, but only Jesus. (9:2–8)*

Within the plot of Mark the transfiguration story is not part of the Passion narrative as such, as it occurs before Jesus departs the Galilee for Jerusalem. Yet many of its features clearly anticipate the Passion narrative. In recent New Testament scholarship the Markan transfiguration has often been called a "displaced" appearance story, one that should have come after Jesus's resurrection.[54] In part, this idea comes from the realization that the oldest manuscripts of the Gospel of Mark end at 16:8, when the women flee in fear from the empty tomb (see the discussion in Chapter 11). Noticeably missing are the all-important "appearances" of the risen Jesus that so dominated the earliest oral traditions, as we saw in 1 Corinthians 15:3–8. The older understanding is reflected in the term "displaced." This view typically assumed that its position within the Gospel of Mark was somehow a mistake or happenstance and thus led to the later confusion. This view has been challenged and largely dismissed.[55]

Others have assumed that the transfiguration must depend on some early oral tradition, but admit that it has been reshaped by the Markan author into a "preview" of the empty tomb.[56] More recent discussions follow a different line, as we shall see.[57] In this view, the position of the transfiguration in the Gospel of Mark is an intentional move on the part of the storyteller, and the audience was expected to catch what was going on narratively and dramatically.

Several features of the transfiguration story clearly anticipate the empty-tomb scene. First, it occurs on a mountain in Galilee[58] "after six days." The only other occurrence of this kind of temporal notation in Mark is that concerning the Last Supper and, more important, the resurrection—"after three days"—and thus suggests a deliberate narrative cue to elements in the Passion sequence.[59] Another is the fear of the onlookers. Both expressions are very similar: Mark 9:6 says of Peter, "He did not know what to say, *for they were terrified*" (*ekphoboi gar egeneto*); Mark 16:8 says of the women, "And they said nothing to anyone, *for they were afraid*" (*ekphobounto gar*).

As has also been noted, the Markan transfiguration has notable similarities to the resurrection/ascension scene in the *Gospel of Peter*. Here is the key passage:

> *Now in the night in which the Lord's Day dawned, when the soldiers were keeping guard, two by two in every watch, a loud voice rang out in heaven. And they saw the heavens opened and two men full of great brightness came down from there and drew near the tomb. But that stone which had been laid against the entrance to the tomb, having rolled by itself, moved a distance off to the side. And the tomb opened and both the young men entered.*
>
> *When the soldiers [on watch] saw this, they awakened the centurion and the elders—for they were present also guarding [the tomb]. And while they were relating what they had seen, they then saw three men exit the tomb, two supported the one, and a cross followed them. The heads of the two reached to heaven, but the one whom they supported with their hands stretched beyond the heavens. And they heard a voice from the heavens which said, "Have you proclaimed to those who are asleep?" And they heard an answer from the cross, "Yes." (Gos. Pet. 9.35–10.42)[60]*

Among the components in common between them are the dazzling white clothes, the two men who come down from heaven, and the voice from heaven (see Appendix C). These same features also occur in the ascension scene in the *Apocalypse of Peter*, another second-century text found in the same codex with the *Gospel of Peter*. Understanding the transfiguration as a resurrection/ascension is reflected further in late "Petrine" tradition in which Jesus is said to have "received honor and glory" from the divine "voice" that pronounced: "This is my beloved Son, with whom I am well pleased" (2 Pet 1:17)[61] This seems to be a secondary witness to the transfiguration story, but understood as the moment when Jesus was given his heavenly "glory," which would normally be associated with his resurrection or ascension.

It should also be noted that the "two men in dazzling clothes" occur in both the Lukan and Johannine empty-tomb scenes (Luke 24:4; John 20:12) and the ascension scene (Acts 1:10).[62] Because these are the only versions of the empty tomb to mention "two men," it has been suggested that they (or at least the one in Luke) knew of the story in *Gospel of Peter* and adjusted the story accordingly, correlated with the ascension scene.

The "two men" in the *Gospel of Peter* who carry Jesus out of the tomb, as noted earlier, are clearly not the same as the two men/angels in Luke-Acts. The Lukan author has made a secondary adaptation to match the traditions. In the *Gospel of Peter* they are more like the figures of Elijah and Moses in the Markan transfiguration. It should be noted that the naming of such figures (as seen in Mark and followed by Matthew and Luke) is often a secondary elaboration. In other words, the version in the *Gospel of Peter* looks more archaic on this point. *Gospel of Peter* 10.40 says only that their heads "reached to heaven," which reinforces their heavenly character. So why might the Markan author have thought of Elijah and Moses? Because by this time both of them were known as prophets who had not died, but had been transported directly to heaven.[63] Elijah's return was already associated with apocalyptic expectations.[64] Likewise, the "assumption" (meaning "ascension") of Moses, as described in several ancient traditions, included a dazzling transformation of his physical body in preparation for being taken away to heaven. Philo's *Life of Moses* describes it as follows:

> [Moses] . . . having been summoned [to heaven] by the Father, who dissolved his duality of body and soul into a unity, transforming his whole nature throughout into mind bright as the brightest sun.[65]

Who better, then, to come and escort the risen Jesus to heaven than those who had gone before?

The *Apocalypse of Peter* makes exactly the same move with its modified version of the transfiguration story for Jesus's final ascension:

> And, behold, there came suddenly a <u>voice from heaven</u> saying, <u>"This is my Son, whom I love and in whom I have pleasure,</u> and my commandments.". . . And there came a great and <u>exceedingly white</u> cloud over our heads and <u>bore away our Lord and Moses and Elias.</u> And I trembled and was afraid, and we looked up and the heaven opened and we saw men in the flesh, and they came and greeted our Lord and Moses and Elias, and went into the second heaven. (17)[66]

In the opening of the *Apocalypse of Peter*, Jesus and the disciples are sitting on the Mount of Olives, where Peter asks Jesus to explain about the fig tree (cf. Mark 11:20–25). It is a composite of the cursing of the fig tree and cleansing of the Temple from Mark 11 with the setting of the apocalyptic discourse from Mark 13:1–5. The passage above comes near the end, after Peter offers to build "three tabernacles" for Jesus, Moses, and Elijah, clearly a component taken from the Markan transfiguration scene (cf. Mark 9:5).

What is significant here is that this is not an empty-tomb scene. It is an ascension scene based on the imagery of the dazzling bodily transformation similar to that in Philo's *Life of Moses*. In its present form, it too seems to be a combination of several canonical traditions; however, it again reminds us that these early writers clearly associated the "transfiguration" scene with Jesus's resurrection and ascension. So also the scene in the *Gospel of Peter* in which Jesus is carried from the tomb by "two men" reflects a resurrection/ascension story, after which Jesus returns to present himself to the disciples.

Marking the Layers

Some features of the Markan transfiguration scene bear clear marks of secondary compositional activity to make it fit into its present narrative frame (9:2–8). They include the following elements: (1) "after six days"; (2) location on a mountain (in Galilee); (3) the presence of Peter, James, and John; (4) the identification of Elijah and Moses; (5) Elijah and Moses "appear" (*ōphthē*);[67] (6) the words spoken by the voice from heaven (from Ps 2); and (7) the "fear" of the onlookers.

All of these serve in one way or another to link this scene narratively and dramatically into the Markan presentation in several important ways. The location in Galilee, the presence of the disciples (especially Peter), and the use of *ōphthē* give it an anticipatory function in place of the missing postresurrection appearances at the end of Mark, which are to take place in Galilee (16:7; 14:28). The fear of the onlookers anticipates the pregnant final verse in Mark 16:8. The naming of "Elijah *with* Moses"[68] further anchors the place of the transfiguration scene within the surrounding section of the Markan narrative, beginning at 6:14–16 (where Jesus is first suggested to be "Elijah or one of the prophets") and resumed more emphatically in Peter's "confession" at Caesarea Philippi (8:27–21) only six verses before the transfiguration. The theme is then resolved in Mark 9:9–13, the Elijah discourse immediately following the transfiguration.

As seen in each of these passages, the Elijah theme in Mark is also bound up with notions of misunderstanding Jesus's true messianic identity. Significantly, it is Peter himself who serves as the spokesman and narrative foil for this misunderstanding in both the "confession" scene (8:32–33) and the transfiguration (9:5–6).[69] In the former, Peter rebukes Jesus for saying that he would die. In the latter, it is Peter who speaks up for the three bewildered disciples, "for they were terrified" (9:6). The misunderstanding of Peter and the disciples becomes a major plot device in Mark (to be discussed later in Chapter 11). At the same time, the words spoken by the voice from heaven (as modified from Ps 2) clearly project backward to the baptism by John (1:9–11), and John the Baptist themes also play into the Elijah-misunderstanding motif in 6:14–16 and 8:27–33.[70] But here too the voice anticipates the resurrection and exaltation of Jesus after his death. So we begin to see that the transfiguration story in its present position in Mark is one of the key ingredients in creating the anticipation of the death and resurrection throughout the preceding narrative, and especially in the immediate chapters leading up to it. It can hardly be called "misplaced."

Once these secondary features of Markan adaptation have been isolated, what are we left with? Two heavenly men, bright shining clothes, Jesus's transformed appearance, and the voice. These core elements form the basic story. Yet they are essentially the same as the resurrection scene in *Gospel of Peter* 10.38–42. More to the point, for the transfiguration story to serve its proper narrative function in Mark, we must assume—as did the Markan author—that the audience already knows these elements as a resurrection/ascension event and recognizes the dramatic play that is being created. As a result, we may guess that something very much like the resurrection scene in *Gospel of Peter,* but in an earlier form *without* any reference to the guards at the tomb, was the source tradition already known to the Markan audience. This leaves only one other question: Was this an earlier source used by the Markan author or was it a literary creation of his own? If we assume the latter, we must also assume that it had already been used in earlier versions of the developing Markan story prior to its reworking in the present position as the transfiguration story.

At least three features of this base resurrection story cohere with elements of the earlier oral tradition as seen in Paul: it lacks the figure of Judas; it assumes an appearance to "Peter and the twelve";[71] and it keeps the resurrection and exaltation/ascension as one event. At this point, we should perhaps return to our earlier discussion of the "stratigraphy" of the tomb story (see Box 7.7), for now we have added one more layer to the picture as an intermediate step between Paul (with putative criticisms of "ghost stories") and Mark. The development of a resurrection scene—with Jesus exiting the tomb and being taken away to heaven—is logically prior to and sets the stage for the further Markan elaboration to create the empty-tomb scene in Mark 16.[72] Both narratively and dramatically, as the finale of the story, it holds the place for the repositioned resurrection story, now adapted as the Markan transfiguration scene in 9:2–8. For these reasons I am inclined to think that this basic form of resurrection scene is pre-Markan; however, certainty is impossible. On the other hand, the present shape of the transfiguration and empty tomb are thoroughly Markan adaptations and point us to the essence of Markan storytelling, where the whole Gospel anticipates the Passion narrative.

We may conclude with three final points regarding these early developments in the Passion narrative. First, in its present form, the *Gospel of Peter* represents a conscious reworking of the narrative at some later point in time by drawing from Matthew and the other canonical Gospels, creating new theological interpretations, and giving considerable priority to the Gospel of Mark, presumably understood as "Peter's" tradition. Even so, it may also depend on earlier traditions, and specifically on a resurrection/ascension scene.

Second, the Gospel of Mark in its present or "final" form probably represents several stages of editing and reworking of the story. As such the Markan author (or authors) is the major architect of the Passion narrative as we have come to know it by virtue of its continued use and adaptation in the other canonical Gospels, all of which use either the transfiguration scene or the empty tomb or both.

Third, the recurring "Elijah motif" in Mark is one of the clearest signals of the Markan author weaving all these scenes together narratively and dramatically. It can also be seen in the pregnant final mention of Elijah while Jesus is on the cross:

> *At three o'clock Jesus cried out with a loud voice, "Eloi, Eloi, lema sabachthani?" which means, "My God, my God, why have you forsaken me?" When some of the bystanders heard it, they said, "Listen, he is calling for Elijah." And someone ran, filled a sponge with sour wine, put it on a stick, and gave it to him to drink, saying, "Wait, let us see whether Elijah will come to take him down." Then Jesus gave a loud cry and breathed his last. And the curtain of the temple was torn in two, from top to bottom. Now when the centurion, who stood facing him, saw that in this way he breathed his last, he said, "Truly this man was God's Son!" (15:34–39)*

The scene drips with drama and irony, as the same themes and components reflected in the Markan transfiguration resurface. Jesus addresses God, but the onlookers misunderstand. They think he's talking about Elijah. They say, "Wait, let us see whether Elijah will come to *take him down*." But because of the way the Markan story has been set up already, in large measure because of the transfiguration scene, the audience knows what is really going on and what will take place. "No," they might have said, "Elijah will come to *take him up!*"[73] And just then a voice comes through from the centurion—a most unlikely and equally ironic source in Mark—saying, "Truly, this man was God's Son!"

We may suggest the following process for the composition of the Markan scenes. The Markan author, as we shall see later, has intentionally reconfigured a number of traditional scenes in the life of Jesus, knowing full well that the audience will recognize the narrative artistry and artifice. The key scene that is distinctive from any other known form of the pre-Gospel oral tradition is the resurrection/ascension itself—similar to that in *Gospel of Peter* 10.37–42, but without the guards—recast and repositioned in Mark to become the transfiguration. It serves as a dramatic foretaste of the actual resurrection of Jesus, which the disciples, including Peter, fail to understand. Next the Markan author has created the empty-tomb scene as the culmination of the narrative to fill the position of the resurrection and to flag both the disciples' and the audience's expectations. It also serves as a response to earlier challenges that the appearances, as seen in the Pauline oral tradition, were merely "ghost" stories. Whereas the disciples and the women (as characters within the narrative) are left stunned and frightened, the audience knows the "real" story and can say, "We believe." We shall return to the drama of Mark's Gospel, taken as a whole, in Chapter 11.

BOX 8.1
Jesus the Magician in Catacomb Art

These two scenes from the Via Latina Catacomb in Rome reflect the standard iconography of depicting miracles, especially in the use of the staff or wand, which was often associated with miraculous powers. Note the similarity of the depictions of Jesus and Moses, on which see also Box 8.2. See Box 8.3 for another scene from the same catacomb.

Above: Jesus raises Lazarus, using his wand. Fresco. Rome, Via Latina Catacomb, mid–fourth century. *Below:* Moses closes the Red Sea onto the pursuing Egyptians, using his wand. Fresco. Rome, Via Latina Catacomb, mid–fourth century. *Used by permission, Scala/Art Resource, NY.*

CHAPTER EIGHT

Casting Spells

Then he came again to Cana in Galilee where he had changed the water into wine. Now there was a royal official whose son lay ill in Capernaum. When he heard that Jesus had come from Judea to Galilee, he went and begged him to come down and heal his son, for he was at the point of death. Then Jesus said to him, "Unless you see signs and wonders you will not believe." The official said to him, "Sir, come down before my little boy dies." Jesus said to him, "Go; your son will live." The man believed the word that Jesus spoke to him and started on his way. As he was going down, his slaves met him and told him that his child was alive. So he asked them the hour when he began to recover, and they said to him, "Yesterday at one in the afternoon the fever left him." The father realized that this was the hour when Jesus had said to him, "Your son will live." So he himself believed, along with his whole household. Now this was the second sign that Jesus did after coming from Judea to Galilee. (John 4:46–54)

Apart from the Passion narrative, one of the earliest facets of Jesus's public career to receive notoriety was the fact that he was a miracle worker. Even so, it must be noted that miracles were not a part of the oral tradition of Jesus reported by Paul. So it would appear that initially, at least, different types of stories about Jesus were collected and transmitted by genre. That is, miracle stories formed but one component of the later tradition about Jesus, and they were first transmitted orally as collections of miracles separate from the Passion narrative. Only later were they woven together into the larger narrative framework of the Gospels as we now know them.

One clue that miracles and other components of the Jesus tradition traveled separately comes from the way that they are sometimes listed within the Gospels.

For example, the healing of the official's son at Cana in John 4:46–54 (quoted at the beginning of this chapter) closes with an editorial comment: "Now this was the *second sign* that Jesus did after coming from Judea to Galilee" (4:54). The "first sign," the changing of water to wine at Cana, is also enumerated in a similar fashion: "Jesus did this, *the first of his signs,* in Cana of Galilee" (2:11). Then there is a kind of summary statement regarding Jesus's miracles at the end of John:

> *Now Jesus did many other signs in the presence of his disciples, which are not written in this book. But these are written so that you may come to believe that Jesus is the Messiah, the Son of God, and that through believing you may have life in his name. (20:30–31)*

Taken together, these comments in the Gospel of John indicate that we have an enumeration of miracles stories as "first, second, . . . many others." This type of enumeration suggests that these particular stories already existed in a set order. Their treatment in the Gospel of John is dependent upon this existing order as derived from the earlier oral tradition.

At the same time, there is further adaptation of these same miracles within the Johannine narrative. The concluding statement in John 4:54 says that *both* miracles took place "*after* coming from Judea to Galilee." Yet that is not the narrative sequence of events in the Gospel of John. According to this Gospel, Jesus originally travels from Judea to Galilee sometime after his baptism (1:43). Three days later comes the wedding feast at Cana (2:1–11). Afterward Jesus travels back to Jerusalem for Passover (2:13), where he cleanses the Temple, and then goes back again to Galilee (4:45) before coming to Cana for the "second" miracle (4:46–54). Hence the Johannine narrative has woven these two miracles into the story in a slightly different way than was previously the case. Notably, the Temple cleansing (2:13–22), the discourse with Nicodemus (3:1–15), and the encounter with the Samaritan woman (4:1–42) now occur between the first and second miracles in Cana.

It should be remembered, moreover, that the Temple cleansing in this position represents a significant narrative reconfiguration from its placement in the Synoptics, where it occurs during the last week of Jesus's life.[1] It is also worth noting that the wedding at Cana and the healing of the official's son do not appear anywhere else in the canonical Gospels. Hence, it looks as though the Gospel of John may have a separate "signs source," or collection of miracle stories drawn from earlier tradition, that was used as a source in compiling the Gospel in its present form.[2] The author of the Gospel of John has apparently separated them when they were interspersed within the narrative, even though the traditional enumeration and putative situation were retained. Or it is possible that the two miracles were originally closer together in the narrative and, at a later stage of editing, the intervening trip to Jerusalem was inserted. In either case, it would appear that the Johannine author has manipulated these source materials in creating the story in its present form.

Other features of miracle stories within the Gospels also suggest that they tended to cluster together by type and circulate in small oral collections. Perhaps this came about because certain types of miracles, such as healings and exorcisms, were similar to one another. It may well be another storytelling dynamic of the oral tradition. A good example is the fact that several miracles in the Gospel of Mark seem to be near duplicates of one another, and they run in similar order as two strands within the Gospel.

The most obvious case in point is the two feeding miracles in Mark 6:30–44 and 8:1–10. In both cases, Jesus is shown magically providing food for great crowds (five thousand and four thousand, respectively) from only a small serving of bread and fish at the beginning and with baskets to spare at the end. Even Jesus's key actions are nearly identical.[3] Similarly, there are the two storm miracles found in Mark 4:35–41 and 6:45–52. In both cases, the disciples go out on the Sea of Galilee at night planning to cross to the other side. A storm comes up, and they cower in fear. Jesus then stills the storm with a mere word or action, and they are astounded. The remaining doublets may be listed as follows:

MARK 4–6	MARK 6–8
Stilling the storm (4:35–41)	Storm, walking on water (6:45–52)
Exorcism: Gerasene demoniac (5:1–20)	Exorcism: Daughter of Syrophoenician woman (7:24–30)
Healing: Woman with hemorrhage (5:25–34)	Healing: Deaf-mute (7:31–37)
Raising of Jairus's daughter (5:21–24, 35–43)	Healing: Blind man at Bethsaida (8:22–26)[4]
Feeding of five thousand (6:30–44)	Feeding of four thousand (8:1–10)

It has been suggested, therefore, that the Gospel of Mark was dependent on two distinct strands or clusters of oral tradition that recounted a similar series of miracles, each of which was woven into the structure of the narrative.[5] Of course, the other possibility is that the Markan author has intentionally replicated certain stories for some narrative or thematic purpose. After all, doesn't it seem strange that the disciples are still surprised the *second time* that Jesus is able to feed the multitudes or still the storm? Yet that is their reaction in both cases, at least in the Markan drama (cf. 8:4). In the case of the second storm miracle, the narrator's voice even signals a connection between these elements in the story by calling attention to the feeding miracle:

> *Then he got into the boat with them and the wind ceased. And they were utterly astounded, <u>for they did not understand about the loaves,</u> but their hearts were hardened. (6:51–52)*[6]

Once again, we have evidence of both older oral traditions and manipulation by the Gospel author in construction of the narrative.[7] We shall return to this point later in this chapter.

It is also worth noting that the Gospel of Matthew retains all of these doublets, although they are somewhat reorganized and augmented. For example, Matthew 14:22–33 expands the story of Jesus's walking on water (Mark 6:45–52) to include Peter getting out of the boat and having to be rescued by Jesus. The Gospel of Luke, on the other hand, seems to be alarmed by the duplication in Mark and deletes each of the miracles in the right-hand column above.[8]

Only two miracles in the Gospel of John clearly replicate any of those found in the Synoptics: the feeding of the five thousand (6:1–13) and the walking on the water (6:16–21). It is worth noting that they are both found in the double strand of miracles in Mark—the same as the last in the left column and first in the right column, and they are in the same order. In other words, it seems that the author of the Gospel of John also knows both of these miracle collections. Either that, or the Gospel of John used the Markan Gospel as a source.[9] That these two miracles come from a different source than the two miracles at Cana discussed above (John 2:1–11; 4:46–54) is indicated by the fact they do not carry an enumeration consistent with the distinctive Johannine "signs source."[10]

Other miracles in John bear similarities to those in the Synoptics, but are not the same stories as such. At the same time, the Gospel of John contains only seven actual miracle episodes, while the Synoptics contain thirty-two.[11] Exorcisms (casting out demons) are the most frequently mentioned miracles in the Synoptics, and especially in Mark.[12] There are a total of eleven distinct exorcism episodes in the Synoptics, of which nine occur first in Mark; Mark contains four full exorcism stories.[13] In contrast, the Gospel of John contains not a single miracle dealing with demon possession.

So there are clearly some differences of emphasis and approach in the treatment of miracles among the Gospels. One must suspect that these differences are due in part to the variable nature of the oral tradition, but it is also likely that the storytelling tastes and thematic interests of the individual authors are also at work. By looking more closely at how the individual authors shape and reshape these same basic stories, we get a better clue to what those tastes and interests might be.

How Ancient Miracle Stories Were Cast

As we saw in Chapter 3, belief in miracles and miracle workers was widespread in the ancient world. Not all miracle workers were thought of as divine men, and not all divine men were primarily miracle workers. But the belief in miracles was predicated on the magical worldview that dominated ancient cultures. Hence, the miracle worker, or magician, was the one who knew how to harness supernatural powers, usually by means of special knowledge of incantations, spells, and rituals. Having special knowledge of secret formulas and special magical words or phrases was commonplace. Even prayer was viewed as operating by these magical mechanisms, and prayer forms commonly appear within magical spells.[14]

As we shall see, the miracles of Jesus as presented in the Gospels are patterned after standard types of miracle stories in both Jewish and Greco-Roman tradition. Thus, the common currency of the miracle worker is further reflected in depictions of Jesus in early Christian art. For example, in Christian catacomb paintings that illustrate miracles of both Jesus and Moses we see a standard iconography of the miracle worker with his staff or "magic wand" (see Box 8.1). Through the early centuries, the depictions of Jesus's miracles remained very consistent in retaining these basic features from the culture (see Box 8.2).

Miracles of various types were usually presented as positive or beneficial (hence "miracles"), but they could also be treated as negative or malevolent ("magic"), in the form of curses.[15] This way of distinguishing "miracles" from "magic" was sometimes used in antiquity, even though it recognized that they were operating by the same mechanism. But as such stories go, one person's curse may be another person's miracle.[16] Other expressions within the Gospels reflect the wide currency of magical terminology and assumptions. For example, the power to "bind and loose," which appears at first to be primarily juridical language, is also the language of curse spells, or *defixiones*.[17] In the two cases where this phrase is used in the Gospels (only in Matt 16:19; 18:18), it is said to have an efficacy in heaven as well as on earth, further equating the action with the assumptions of magical power.

The miracle story as a kind of testimonial took on a life of its own in relation to the larger magical tradition. In Jewish tradition it may be traced to the stories of Moses or the miracle-working prophets Elijah and Elisha. Some of the stories of Jesus in the Gospels seem to be close replicas. The story of Jesus's raising the son of a widow at Nain (Luke 7:11–17) bears strong similarities to Elisha's raising the son of a Shunammite woman (2 Kgs 4:18–37), which in turn has a close parallel in Elijah's raising of a widow's son at Zarephath (1 Kgs 17:17–24). One might say that this particular miracle seems to function as a kind of job description for a Jewish prophet, at least as reflected in the Gospel of Luke.

These "classic" stories from the Hebrew scriptures continued to be used and retold in Jewish tradition. For example, a famous miracle of Elisha that dealt with a local legend regarding a spring (or oasis) near Jericho continued to be associated

BOX 8.2

Miracles of Jesus in Early Christian Art

The Raising of Lazarus. Fresco. Rome, Catacomb of the Giordani. Late third century. *Used by permission, Scala/Art Resource, NY.*

By the end of the third century CE, artistic representations of key episodes from Jesus's life were beginning to become a commonplace. While based generally on familiar stories from the Gospels, certain themes gained greater popularity. For example, representations of the crucifixion were relatively rare prior to the fifth century. By contrast, certain miracles of Jesus were widely used. One of the favorites was the raising of Lazarus, which is found only in the Gospel of John (11:38–44).

Among all the resuscitation miracles in the Gospels, this one is the most frequently depicted in early Christian art, especially in the catacombs at Rome. There are several reasons why. First, the story's narrative lends itself to dramatic presentation, as Jesus weeps and then stands before the tomb calling Lazarus to life. Second, the story's structure already has resonances to the resurrection of Jesus himself, and so evokes key theological ideas, especially in a setting for Christian burial. In the middle of this miracle story, Jesus says, *"I am the resurrection and the life"* (John 11:25). But there is one more key factor. As with most of the early Christian art, the emerging iconography took over stock scenes and themes from existing Greek and Roman art, elements that were woven together and quickly became standardized. A comparison of the two versions of this miracle shown above and in Box 8.1 show these typical features. Lazarus is depicted as a mummified corpse standing inside a small "house tomb," rather than the "cave" clearly described in the text of John. More to the point for our discussion, however, is the depiction of Jesus himself. He wears a Roman toga and stands in a patterned pose as he reaches out toward the tomb with a wand in his right hand. These features, the wand in particular, are part of the standard portrayal of miracle workers, and especially healers of the day. So, too, compare the depiction of Moses in Box 8.1. Thus, the iconography, like the Gospel stories themselves, was drawn from their surrounding culture (see also Box 8.3).

with the same village for many centuries. The story was still being told during the time of Josephus, who lived ca. 37–105 CE. Here is the story as reported in 2 Kings:

> *Now the people of the city said to Elisha, "The location of this city is good, as my lord sees; but the water is bad, and the land is unfruitful." He said, "Bring me a new bowl, and put salt in it." So they brought it to him. Then he went to the spring of water and threw the salt into it, and said, "Thus says the* LORD, *I have made this water wholesome; from now on neither death nor miscarriage shall come from it." So the water has been wholesome to this day, according to the word that Elisha spoke. (2:19–22)*[18]

Here is Josephus's retelling of the same story:

> *Now nearby Jericho is a copious spring of excellent value for irrigation. . . . Tradition holds that this spring not only blighted the earth and the fruits of trees, but it also caused women to miscarry, and that to everything it brought disease and corruption, until it was transformed and became the opposite—most healthful as well as fertile—by a certain prophet Elisha, who was the disciple and successor of Elijah. Having been the guest of the people of Jericho and having been treated by them with great hospitality, he gave a great favor for all time to them and to their region. For he went out to this spring and cast into it a ceramic bowl full of salt; then, <u>raising his just right hand to heaven and pouring propitiatory libations upon the ground, he called on the earth</u> to mollify the stream and open sweeter channels, and <u>he called on heaven</u> to temper its waters with more fertile breezes, and at the same time to give the inhabitants an abundance of fruits, a succession of children, and an unfailing supply of water conducive to such procreation. . . . <u>By these prayers, having performed many rituals out of his scientific skill,</u> he changed the nature of the spring, and the water—which had previously been a source of childlessness and famine for them—henceforth became a source of fecundity and plenty.*[19]

We notice how Josephus has reworked the story in important ways to make it fit the form and style of miraculous activities from the Greco-Roman world. Specifically, Josephus has added narrative descriptions (underlined) of Elisha's ritual actions accompanying his invocations to heaven and earth, presented as Elisha's words in indirect discourse. Here too we see that prayer is not differentiated from these magical rituals. Yet none of these narrative elements, not even prayer, appear in the original version. In effect, Josephus is recasting the story, so that Elisha is more like the magical practitioners of the Roman world, where knowledge of special spells and rituals was viewed as an important mechanism (see Chapter 3).

Types of Miracle Stories

Several terms were used in antiquity to refer to miracles or miracle stories. The Latin term "miracle" (*miraculum*), equivalent to "wonder" (*thauma*) in Greek, has been used to cover all of them, often without more subtle distinctions.[20] The other most common terms are "marvels," "powers," and "signs," all of which occur in the New Testament.[21] Although the wide use of miracle stories within the Gospels depends on the larger magical tradition, we should not confuse them with magical spells as such. The miracle story might be used as testimony to the powers of a particular god, healer, magician, or spell, but it is not the same as the spell itself. Often times, special events or special status, such as the birth of a future emperor or the calling of a Jewish prophet, were thought to be signaled by divine signs or miraculous powers. Because miracle stories were commonplace, the genre was already well established in both Jewish and Greco-Roman tradition.[22]

Nature Miracles

Despite some differences in terminology, miracle stories generally follow very similar patterns by type. The water miracle of Elisha just discussed falls into one of these standard types. It may be called a "nature miracle," because it involves transforming the state of something occurring in nature. Typical nature miracles also include stilling a storm, making crops sprout or die, causing miraculous yields of crops or fish, and the like. Each of these types is found in the Gospels, as we have already seen in the two miracle cycles of Mark (both multiplication of food and stilling a storm occur twice). We shall discuss the storm miracles later in this chapter. The Gospels of Luke and John each have a miraculous catch of fish, but at two different points in Jesus's career (Luke 5:4–11; John 21:4–8).

The basic types of nature miracles were also common Greco-Roman culture. Here, for example, is a wine miracle, analogous in some respects to the one performed by Jesus at Cana (John 2:1–12, the "first" miracle).

> *[At Elis] there is an ancient theater between the agora and the Menius and also a shrine of Dionysus. The statue [of Dionysus] is a work of Praxiteles. Of all the gods, the Eleans especially worship Dionysus, and they say the god consistently visits them at the annual festival of the Thyion. Outside the city by eight stadia is the place where they hold the festival, called the Thyia. [On the evening before,] the priests carry three kettles into the sanctuary and set them down empty, while both citizens of the town and even strangers are present, as many as happen to be there. Both the citizens and the priests, and whoever may wish to do so, put seals on the doors of the sanctuary. In the morning they come to read the signs for themselves, and when they go into the building they find the kettles filled with wine. These things the most trustworthy men of Elis, and even strangers, swear it*

to be just as I have described. The Andrians also say that every other year, at the Feast of Dionysus, wine flows of its own accord from their temple.[23]

In this case, the "miracle" serves as a kind of testimonial to the favored status of the local cult of Dionysus in Elis. Such local cult sanctuaries liked to use this sort of story to attract pilgrims to their annual festivals—an ancient equivalent of the tourist industry.[24]

Health or Healing Miracles

The other main type of miracle story involves healing. Such "healing miracles" fall into several different subcategories by they type of malady being treated. They include:

Healings of general maladies or even chronic diseases, e.g., fevers, blindness, deafness, "palsy" (neuromuscular disorders), and leprosy;

Exorcisms, in which the malady is possession by a demon or evil spirit;

Resuscitations, in which the malady is the ultimate human "disease," namely, death.

Because of developments in Greek medicine, in which biological causation and natural remedies were studied, "healing miracles" also follow some specific patterns for each main type of malady.

Healings

Here is an example of a common "healing" story by the legendary Jewish miracle worker Hanina ben Dosa, who lived in the mid-first century CE. He was a close contemporary of Jesus and is the most frequently mentioned miracle worker in the Mishnah and Talmud.

Once upon a time Rabban Gamaliel's son got sick. He sent two men of learning to Rabbi Hanina ben Dosa to beg him mercy from God for the boy. [Rabbi Hanina] saw them coming and went to a room upstairs and asked mercy from God concerning him. When he had come back down he said to them, "Go, the fever has left him." They said to him, "What? Are you a prophet?" He said, "I am not a prophet, nor the son of a prophet. But this I have received from tradition: if my prayer of intercession flows unhesitatingly from my mouth, I know it will be answered, and if not, I know it will be rejected." They sat down and wrote and determined exactly the moment he said this, and when they came back to Rabban Gamaliel, he said to them, "By the Temple! You are neither too early nor too late but this is what happened: in that very moment the fever left him and he asked for water!" (b. Ber. 34b)

Several features of this story are particularly noteworthy. One is that the "marvel" of the episode is expressed in noting that the fever left the boy at exactly the same time as Rabbi Hanina's pronouncement, even though the characters were in different cities. Exactly the same motif is found in Jesus's healing of the official's son in John 4:43–54 (quoted at the beginning of this chapter), which also involved the cure of a fever. This common feature of "fever" stories may have arisen from the unpredictability of fevers; it serves to "prove" that the cure was not simply by chance.

Next we note that the miraculous mechanism in this story is explicitly prayer; however, that makes it no less a miracle, at least by ancient standards, as both this story and the one in John 4 clearly demonstrate. Finally, there is a "sign" in the story that the miracle has indeed worked. They can see that the fever has left the boy because he asks for water. As we shall see, ancient miracle stories take on recognizable patterns like these.

Exorcisms

Similarly, exorcisms have their own peculiar characteristics due to the particular nature of the problem. Demons were the "germs" of the ancient world; they were assumed to infest the body and cause a myriad of ills. To bring about a cure, the demon must be expelled. Consequently, exorcism stories employ the technical terminology of "demon spells" from the magical papyri. In fact, the term "exorcism" comes from the Greek magical term *exorkizein,* meaning "to conjure out"; it is the key formula used to expel demons.[25] One of the distinctive features of demon-possession stories is that one must know which demon to address; consequently these "conjure" formulas often seek to know the name of the demon, as a way of placing it under control. Other possession spells circumvent this need for a specific name by invoking general formulas, such as, "I conjure you, whichever demon you may be . . ."

One particular example from the Gospels shows how exorcism stories follow these mechanisms drawn from ancient magical theory and practice:

> *They came to the other side of the sea, to the country of the Gerasenes. And when he had stepped out of the boat, immediately a man out of the tombs with an unclean spirit met him. He lived among the tombs; and no one could restrain him any more, even with a chain; for he had often been restrained with shackles and chains, but the chains he wrenched apart, and the shackles he broke in pieces; and no one had the strength to subdue him. Night and day among the tombs and on the mountains he was always howling and bruising himself with stones. When he saw Jesus from a distance, he ran and bowed down before him; and he shouted at the top of his voice, "What have you to do with me, Jesus, Son of the Most High God? I adjure you by God, do not torment me." For he had said to him, "Come out of the man, you unclean spirit!" Then Jesus asked him, "What is your name?" He replied, "My name is Legion; for we are many." He begged*

him earnestly not to send them out of the country. Now there on the hillside a great herd of swine was feeding; and the unclean spirits begged him, "Send us into the swine; let us enter them." So he gave them permission. And the unclean spirits came out and entered the swine; and the herd, numbering about two thousand, rushed down the steep bank into the sea, and were drowned in the sea. (Mark 5:1–13)

This story of the Gerasene demoniac is one in the double cycle of miracle stories used in Mark, as discussed above. In some ways it is an unusual miracle story, in part because of its length and complexity; however, it is a typical miracle story nonetheless.

Now let's look more closely at the way the Markan scene is played out. What is particularly distinctive is the initial interaction of Jesus and the demon-possessed man (5:6–10). First, it is the demon who is actually speaking and who shouts at Jesus. Then the demon actually tries to *exorcize Jesus* by saying, "I adjure you by God, do not torment me" (5:7). The word usually translated "adjure" here is the Greek *orkizein* ("conjure"), just as was used in demon spells. Ironically, it is the demon who uses a standard magical formula and who calls on the power of God to ward off Jesus's power: "I conjure you by God. Do not torture [or cross-examine] me." The Greek word *basanizein*, usually translated "torment" in this passage, actually means "to examine or cross-examine" in the legal sense, that is, to put the witness to the test of proof. It gets its sense of "torture" from the notion of cross-examination under torture to ensure that the witness is telling the truth. Hence, in the humorous byplay of this Markan miracle, the demon knows he is about to be forced under oath to disclose his true identity as a prelude to the exorcism. Thus, all the features of this tale rely on the audience's familiarity with recognizable features of demon spells. The audience, like the demon, can already see what is coming.

Next, Jesus begins to address the demon and asks its name. Unable to resist, the demon tells it: "My name is Legion; for we are many." The demon is about to be controlled; its efforts to ward off Jesus's power have failed. Now the stage is set for Jesus to command the demon to leave. So this story not only employs the standard language of exorcism spells; it uses it in quite humorous ways to make the story more compelling. Even the name of the demon (Legion) is likely to have symbolic significance for the audience, given its rather obvious Roman military connotations. Most of these features reflect the Markan author's intentional elaborations on a basic story outline. All of these details have been removed in the abbreviated Matthean version, while the Lukan version retains only the naming component (cf. Matt 8:28–34; Luke 8:26–39). Thus, expansion or contraction of such details casts a rather different shape *and* meaning for the entire scene. We too have to watch these cues.

Exorcism stories like this one were widely known. In a parody of a Palestinian exorcist, the satirist Lucian employed elements very similar to those in Mark, especially the naming element in the Gerasene demoniac story and the epileptic symptoms of the demoniac boy of Mark 9:14–29.[26] That miracle stories were told with such humor, while still carrying religious meaning, is also shown by another one about Hanina ben Dosa. This one, having to do with a deadly snake, has some similarity to an exorcism:

> Once upon a time, a poisonous snake was injuring people. They went and made it known to Rabbi Hanina ben Dosa. He said to them, "Show me its burrow." They showed him its burrow and he placed his heel upon the mouth of the hole. It came forth and bit him—and it died. He put the snake on his shoulders, went to the House of Study, and said to them, "See my sons, it is not the snake that kills, but sin." Then they said, **"Woe to the man a snake attacks, but woe to the snake that Rabbi Hanina ben Dosa attacks."** (b. Ber. 33a)

Snakes were, of course, powerful symbols in antiquity. They were associated with immortality, the hearth, evil, and healing. The symbolic play of this story seems to rely on the passage from Genesis 3:15—God's curse on the snake in the garden: "I will put enmity between you and the woman, and between your offspring and hers; he will strike your head, and you will strike his heel." Symbolically, then, Rabbi Hanina is the "offspring" of Eve who conquers the snake of Eden. This underlying play is supported by the moral lesson about the deadliness of sin, and the snake becomes its symbol. So we see that miracle stories may also be transformed into moralizing lessons with subtle religious meaning, while also serving as charming tales.

Resuscitations

Resuscitation stories likewise have their own peculiar elements owing to the fact and fear of death as well as to ancient customs surrounding burial and commemoration. One concern sometimes expressed in ancient medical discussions is how to be certain the person is really dead. The fear of being accidentally buried or, worse yet, cremated alive must have been widespread. So also was the idea that death marks a boundary from which there is no return. We see these ideas showing up in a number of resuscitation stories, both in the Gospels and more generally. Here is one told by the second-century philosopher and novelist Apuleius, author of *The Golden Ass*, who was quite fascinated with the miraculous:

> One day, when Asclepiades returned from his country house to the city, he noticed in the suburb the preparations for an enormous funeral procession, with a great many people, a huge crowd standing around to pay their respects, all of them looking very sad and wearing their oldest clothes. [Asclepiades] came closer to find out—he was human, after all—who it was. . . . In any case, it was destiny that brought him to the person who lay there, stretched out and practically buried already. The poor creature's whole body had already been sprinkled with aromatic essences, the face already covered with a fragrant cream, and he had

already been arrayed [in the customary way] for his funeral and prepared for the funeral pyre. Asclepiades examined him very carefully, noted certain symptoms, palpated the body again and again, and discovered in him a hidden vein of life. At once he cried, "This man is alive. Throw away your torches!". . . With great difficulty and extreme effort Asclepiades obtained a brief respite for the dead man, rescued him from the hands of the undertakers, brought him back to his own house, and, if I may say so, reclaimed him from the underworld. There he quickly revived his breath and with certain drugs immediately stimulated the life force that had been languishing in the recesses of his body.[27]

One could ask whether this story is really a miracle, since the man was not actually dead. But that question misses the point of these ancient story forms. Had not the healer Asclepiades come along, the man surely would have died, either from cremation or from sheer proximity to the moment of death, since he had already stopped breathing. The miraculous element lies in the special insight of Asclepiades to see "a hidden vein of life" and his medical skill to "stimulate the life force that had been languishing in the recesses of his body." For this reason, Apuleius and others considered Asclepiades a potent magician and healer.

As we shall see in the Gospels, in some resuscitation stories characters teeter at the edge of death; other stories make the point more clear. One of the miracles of Apollonius of Tyana shows how resuscitations tend to follow these basic elements:

Here also is a wonder (thauma) of Apollonius. A maiden seemed to have died in the very hour of her marriage and the bridegroom was following the bier, weeping over his unfulfilled marriage. Rome also mourned together with him, for it happened that the maiden belonged to a consular family. Now happening upon their suffering, Apollonius said, "Put down the bier, for I myself will stop you from weeping for this maiden." And then he asked, "What might her name be?" The crowd thought he was going to deliver an oration of the sort given at burials which also increase the mourning. But he did not. Instead, touching her and addressing her quietly, he awakened the girl who seemed dead. And the girl let out a cry and returned to her father's house, just like Alcestis who was brought back to life by Herakles. But when the relatives of the maiden wanted to give him 150,000 pieces of silver as a reward, he replied that he would make it a gift to the girl for her dowry.

Now whether he detected some spark of life within her, which had escaped the notice of those treating her—for it is said that, although it was misting, a vapor arose from her face—or whether her life being already extinguished, she grew warm again and received it back [from his touch], a proper grasp of what happened has become a mystery not only to me but also to those who were present.[28]

This resuscitation miracle is very similar to that of Jesus's raising the daughter of Jairus (Mark 5:21–24, 35–43), although the latter has some distinctly Markan

BOX 8.3
Hercules Raises Alcestis from the Dead

Hercules escorts Alcestis from Hades, as they pass by Cerberus. To the right sits Admetus, in whose place she offered to die. This scene expresses a complex mixture of belief in miracles and the afterlife. Most of the paintings in this catacomb are of an explicitly Christian nature. Rome, Via Latina Catacomb, mid–fourth century. *Used by permission, Scala/Art Resource, NY.* See also Box 8.1.

touches, to be discussed below. Internally, however, it draws direct comparison to a story of Hercules, which already had a wide currency in antiquity (see Box 8.3). Like the story of Asclepiades in Apuleius, it shows that the miraculous power over life is thought of as a mysterious combination of special medical insight and magical powers. Here too we notice how the chance circumstances whereby Apollonius happened upon the funeral procession are meant to demonstrate his humanitarian interests. Even when he was offered a reward, he refused to take the money. The author, Philostratus, wants it to be clear that Apollonius was a true miracle worker, not just some charlatan or trickster.

Form and Function in Telling Miracle Stories

As we see in these previous examples, most ancient miracle stories, whether pagan, Jewish, or Christian, followed a basic narrative pattern with some key variations according to type. The basic pattern or form goes something like this:

*On a certain occasion . . . our hero was going along and he/she came upon X,
and it was very bad, so that . . . Then, recognizing what the problem was, he/she
did Y and . . . Now the situation was corrected, and the problem disappeared, as
shown by how . . . And all who saw it marveled at his/her power.*

Of course, at each point, the details of the story must be supplied, and this is
where the storyteller's artistry comes in. If we reduce these narrative features to an
outline, it would look like this:[29]

1. Description of the situation
   a. narrative opening
   b. type of malady or danger
   c. demonstration of the dreaded effects (demons), dangers (nature),
      duration, or expectation (diseases and death)
2. Action by the miracle worker
   a. usually arrives on the scene by accident or invitation
   b. recognizes the situation/problem
   c. takes action (the miraculous intervention—usually by touch
      and/or special "words")
   d. cure or change completed
   e. demonstration that the cure or change has been effective (usually
      mirrors description of the malady or danger)
3. Response of onlookers: "amazement" or other testimonials

As such, miracle stories can be brief and formulaic or complex and elaborate depending on the aims or thematic interests of the storyteller. We have already seen
such thematic shaping of the story in the case of the Elisha miracle of Josephus and
the Markan version of the Gerasene demoniac.

Here, for example, are two other Markan miracles that reflect shorter and
longer versions of the basic narrative pattern of healings:

*As soon as they left the synagogue, they entered the house of Simon and Andrew,
with James and John. Now Simon's mother-in-law was in bed with a fever, and
they told him about her at once. He came and took her by the hand and lifted
her up. Then the fever left her, and she began to serve them. (1:29–31)*

*Then he returned from the region of Tyre, and went by way of Sidon towards
the Sea of Galilee, in the region of the Decapolis. They brought to him a deaf
man who had an impediment in his speech; and they begged him to lay his hand
on him. He took him aside in private, away from the crowd, and put his fingers
into his ears, and he spat and touched his tongue. Then looking up to heaven, he
sighed and said to him, "Ephphatha," that is, "Be opened." And immediately his
ears were opened, his tongue was released, and he spoke plainly. Then Jesus ordered them to tell no one; but the more he ordered them, the more zealously they*

proclaimed it. They were astounded beyond measure, saying, "He has done everything well; he even makes the deaf to hear and the mute to speak." (7:31–37)

The first of these, the healing of Peter's mother-in-law, is very brief. Each component of the outline is reduced to a simple statement:

Jesus goes to Peter's house (1.a/2.a).

Peter's mother-in-law is in bed with a fever (1.b).

Jesus is told of her condition (2.a).

Jesus goes to her (2.b), takes her by the hand, and lifts her up (2.c).

She is cured (the fever leaves her, 2.d).

She demonstrates how well she feels by making Jesus, Peter, and their friends something to eat (2.e).

The story is basically complete. It has all the components of the typical outline, although the degree of danger of the malady (1.c) has been glossed over. Only the "response" of the onlookers (3) has been omitted entirely.

In the second case, we see a more elaborate story as a man is brought to Jesus with a request for healing (1.a/2.a). The man has a double malady (1.b)—both deafness and a speech impediment—suggesting how serious is his condition (1.c).[30] Correspondingly, Jesus takes him aside in private (2.b) and performs two ritual actions—putting his fingers into his ears and spitting, then touching his tongue—accompanied by a magical invocation (2.c). The invocation is an Aramaic word, *ephphatha*. To an ancient Greek audience it would have sounded very much like the mysterious words (such as *ablanathanalba* and the like) that one finds regularly in magical spells. This use of Aramaic words in Jesus's healings is a distinctive feature of the Gospel of Mark. The cure is effected by the "unlocking" of his tongue and ears (2.d), and he demonstrates it by speaking plainly (2.e). Finally, we have a typical "response" (3)—"they were astounded beyond measure"— made more dramatic by the addition of a statement attributed to the crowd in direct discourse to illustrate how they spread the news of his power despite Jesus's effort to keep it quiet.

This emphasis on Jesus's wish to suppress public knowledge of his miraculous powers is a recurring refrain in the Gospel of Mark and represents one distinct line of thematic shaping by the Markan author.[31] This theme, sometimes called the "secrecy motif," relies on the fact that the audience can see what is happening, while the characters within the story regularly miss the point. Thus, the author and audience are *interacting* in the staging of the drama just as much as the characters themselves, who *act* it out. In the next section, we will watch this process at work.

Thematic Shaping of Miracle Stories

A good example of how the basic form of a miracle may be elaborated to serve a particular thematic and theological function may be seen in another case from the Talmud. It is a nature miracle, in which a young Jewish boy calms a storm at sea:

(1) Rabbi Tanchuma said, "Once upon a time a certain cargo ship belonging to goyim *(Gentiles) was crossing the Great Sea; in it there was a certain Jewish boy. A great tempest rose up upon the seas, and every single one amongst them arose and bowed down, taking his idol in his hand and crying out in prayer, but to no avail.*

(2) Then, when they saw it was no use, they said to the Jewish boy, "Come, my son. Call on your God; he will hear us. For he responds to you when you complain to him, and he is strong." So the boy got up and begged with all his heart, and God received his prayer and quieted the sea.

(3) Then as they came to the shore, they all went down to buy things they needed. They said to the little [Jewish] boy, "Is there not anything that you want to buy for yourself?" He said to them, "Why do you ask this of me, a poor foreigner?" They said to him, "You, a poor foreigner? No, we are the poor foreigners! For some are here and their idols are back in Babylon; others are here but their idols are in Rome; and others are here who have their idols with them, but none of them is any help to anyone. But you know every place where you go that your God is with you, as it is written: 'What great nation is there that has a God so near to them as our God is whenever we call to him? (Deut 4:7)'" (y. Ber. 9:1)[32]

The first thing to observe is that the three parts of the story as shown here (by paragraphs) correspond to the three main parts of the miracle-story outline discussed above. Only now the response of the onlookers (par. 3) has been expanded, so that it is nearly as long as the other two parts combined. Next we can see that the basic story, whatever its original source and form, has very little in the way of historical reality behind it. From the outset the story is told from a decidedly Jewish perspective regarding ancient religious sensibilities. After all, when confronted with a deadly storm, the sailors and passengers on the ship all take their "idols" and pray to them. Ordinary "pagans" would never call their gods "idols." It even says that the boat belonged to *goyim* (Gentiles). Thus, the dramatic play of the story is set up by the fact that all the Gentiles aboard the ship find themselves in dire straights in the storm, and all pray to their respective gods, but "to no avail." The role of prayer in Jewish theology is an important theme.

Now the little Jewish boy comes onstage, quite unexpectedly, and the others turn to him and implore him also to pray to his God: "For he responds to you whenever you complain to him, and he is strong." Here is our second clue to the storyteller's agenda: the Gentiles in the story tell us about what Jews should believe. So the boy prays, and the storm ceases to rage. Interestingly, the miraculous action of the little boy is minimal at best, even though it clearly occupies the requisite position within the story. Then we come to the lengthy "response" section, as the narrative leaps ahead and the ship reaches harbor. Now the passengers and crew all go down to buy provisions and ask the Jewish boy if he wants to go buy things as well, to which the boy replies, "Why do you ask this of me, a poor foreigner?" The rest of story is told as a "choral reply" of the passengers, as they all extol the boy and the greatness of his God, the one who had saved them. None of our "idols" is of any help to anyone, they say, "but you know every place where you go that your God is with you." It even ends with these Gentiles quoting scripture (from Deut 4:7) to the Jewish boy as a proof text of a Jewish theological axiom: wherever we go our God is with us through prayer. Ironically, it is the Gentiles who wind up educating the little Jewish boy about his faith.

In the final analysis, this charming little story has very little air of reality about it, even though it has all the components of a basic miracle story. In fact, it sounds much more like a moralizing tale to be told to "little Jewish boys" in order to inculcate faith and an understanding of the importance of prayer. Theologically, it contains an explicit repudiation of idolatry. It may also reflect an implicit repudiation of Christian miracle stories. It is as if to say, who needs a famous miracle worker—like Jesus—when any little Jewish boy can work the same type of miracles through prayer? By virtue of their basic form and careful reshaping, miracle stories can become vehicles for powerful as well as charming tales of faith.

As we have already seen, the miracle stories within the Gospels may be expanded or contracted to meet the narrative goals of the author. Within the Synoptic Gospels, it is possible to detect certain stylistic tendencies and thematic interests of each author by the way the same basic miracle is manipulated. For example, a number of miracles in the Gospel of Mark are extremely long and complex. They include double healings and other slightly odd elements that seem to point to the thematic concerns of the Markan author. The miracles in Mark often possess a mysterious quality to them, in part because they portray Jesus as ordering people not to tell what he has done and the disciples as often missing the point. By contrast, the Gospel of Matthew tends to have much briefer versions of most of these same miracles; in some cases they are only a third to a half as long. Often they become lessons about faith rather than just miracles in themselves. Thus, the same basic miracle may be serving a different dramatic or didactic function in each retelling. The subtle spin comes in the details or what is included and excluded. Here we may examine some specific examples from the Gospels.

The Blind Man at Bethsaida

A good example of distinctively Markan treatment of miracles is the healing of the blind man of Bethsaida.

They came to Bethsaida. Some people brought a blind man to him and begged him to touch him. He took the blind man by the hand and led him out of the village; and when he had put saliva on his eyes and laid his hands on him, he asked him, "Can you see anything?" And the man looked up and said, "I can see people, but they look like trees, walking." Then Jesus laid his hands on his eyes again; and he looked intently and his sight was restored, and he saw everything clearly. Then he sent him away to his home, saying, "Do not even go into the village." (8:22–26)

Although possessing the typical form of a healing, this story is odd because Jesus is not able to heal the man fully the first time. He has to make a second try to get it right. On the surface, it does not seem like the kind of story that would inspire confidence in Jesus's miraculous powers. But perhaps that is not the point, for this story may involve an allegorical meaning built around the idea of seeing things clearly (to be discussed further in Chapter 11). Either way, it would appear that the Gospels of Matthew and Luke found this miracle to be less than satisfactory as a depiction of Jesus's miraculous powers, as it was removed in both. The Gospel of Luke seems to have deleted it outright, along with all the other doublets in this section of Mark; the Gospel of Matthew seems to have dealt with the problem a different way.

In what appears to be the Matthean version of this same story, Jesus now heals two blind men at once. It occurs along with a variant form of the deaf-mute in Matthew 9:27–31, in a cluster of miracle stories found in different parts of Mark. These two miracles do not occur in this form in either Mark or Luke, yet it seems that they represent the Matthean analogues reworked to fit a different set of narrative and thematic interests. If so, then the Matthean reshaping of this basic story from the Gospel of Mark shows the extent to which manipulation of the narrative might go. On the other hand, this strange miracle plays a very important role in Mark, as we shall see Chapter 11.

Two Storm Miracles

An example of the distinctive aspects of Matthean reshaping of Markan stories can be seen in the two storm miracles. In the first case (Mark 4:35–41; Matt 8:18–27), whereas the Markan version runs as a continuous story, the Matthean author has inserted a Q saying about "following" Jesus (cf. Luke 9:57–60) into the story as Jesus is on his way to the boat (see Box 8.4). The story is also changed internally by adding that disciples "followed" Jesus into the boat, and yet the faith of the disciples wavers in the face of the storm. We can also see how the Matthean author has changed the way Jesus responds to them by altering the Markan question, "Have you still no faith?" to the recurring Matthean epithet "You of little faith."[33]

BOX 8.4

A Storm Miracle: *Stilling the Storm*

Matthew 8:18–27	Mark 4:35–41

Matthew 8:18–27

¹⁸ Now when Jesus saw great crowds around him, he gave orders to go over to the other side.

¹⁹ A scribe then approached and said, "Teacher, I will <u>follow</u> you wherever you go." ²⁰ And Jesus said to him, "Foxes have holes, and birds of the air have nests; but the Son of Man has nowhere to lay his head."

²¹ Another of his disciples said to him, "Lord, first let me go and bury my father." ²² But Jesus said to him, "<u>**Follow**</u> me, and let the dead bury their own dead."

²³ **<u>And when he got into the boat, his disciples followed him.</u>**

²⁴ A windstorm arose on the sea, so <u>great</u> that the boat was being swamped <u>by the waves</u>; but he was asleep. ²⁵ And they <u>went and</u> woke him up, saying, "<u>Lord, save us!</u> We are perishing!" ²⁶ And he said to them, "Why are you afraid, <u>you of little faith?</u>" Then he got up and rebuked the winds and the sea; and there was a dead calm.

²⁷ They were amazed, saying, "What sort of man is this, that even the winds and the sea obey him?"

Mark 4:35–41

³⁵ On that day, when evening had come, he said to them, "Let us go across to the other side."

And leaving the crowd, behind,

<u>they took him with them in the boat, just as he was. Other boats were with him.</u>

³⁷ A <u>great</u> windstorm arose, <u>and the waves beat into the boat,</u> so that the boat was already being swamped.

³⁸ But he was <u>in the stern,</u> asleep <u>on the cushion</u>; and they woke him up and said to him, "<u>Teacher, do you not care that</u> we are perishing?" ³⁹ He woke up and rebuked the wind, and said to the sea, "<u>Peace! Be still!</u>" <u>Then the wind ceased</u>, and there was a dead calm. ⁴⁰ <u>He said to them, "Why are you afraid? Have you still no faith?</u>" ⁴¹ And they were filled with great awe and said to one another, "Who then is this, that even the wind and the sea obey him?"

KEY: <u>Underlined</u> = points to compare
<u><u>Double underlined</u></u> = key differences in the narrative
Bold = Matthean theme

BOX 8.5

Another Storm Miracle: *Jesus Walks on Water*

Matthew 14:22–23

Mark 6:45–52

²² Immediately he made the disciples get into the boat and go on ahead to the other side, while he dismissed the crowds.

⁴⁵ Immediately he made his disciples get into the boat and go on ahead to the other side, to Bethsaida, while he dismissed the crowd.

²³ And after he had dismissed the crowds, he went up the mountain by himself to pray.

⁴⁶ After saying farewell to them, he went up on the mountain to pray.

When evening came, he was there alone, ²⁴ but by this time the boat, <u>battered by the waves,</u> was far from the land, for the wind was against them.

⁴⁷ When evening came, the boat was out on the sea, and he was alone on the land.

²⁵ And early in the morning he came walking toward them on the sea.

⁴⁸ When he saw that they were straining at the oars against an adverse wind, he came towards them early in the morning, walking on the sea.

²⁶ But when the disciples saw him walking on the sea, they were terrified, saying, "It is a ghost!" And they cried out in fear. ²⁷ But immediately Jesus spoke to them and said, "Take heart, it is I; do not be afraid."

<u>He intended to pass them by.</u>

²⁸ <u>Peter answered him, "Lord, if it is you, command me to come to you on the water." ²⁹ He said, "Come." So Peter got out of the boat, started walking on the water, and came toward Jesus. ³⁰ But when he noticed the strong wind, he became frightened, and beginning to sink, he cried out, "Lord, save me!" ³¹ Jesus immediately reached out his hand and caught him, saying to him, "*You of little faith*, why did you doubt?"</u>

⁴⁹ But when they saw him walking on the sea, they thought it was a ghost and cried out; ⁵⁰ for they all saw him and were terrified. But immediately he spoke to them and said, "Take heart, it is I; do not be afraid."

³² When they got into the boat, the wind ceased. ³³ <u>And those in the boat worshiped him, saying, "Truly you are the Son of God."</u>

⁵¹ Then he got into the boat with them and the wind ceased. And they were utterly astounded, ⁵² <u>for they did not understand about the loaves, but their hearts were hardened.</u>

KEY: <u>Underlined</u> = points to compare
<u>Double underlined</u> = key differences in the narrative
Italics = characteristic Matthean phrase

In the second storm miracle, the Matthean author has expanded the Markan miracle by adding an extra vignette to the story, in which Peter walks on the water with Jesus and then begins to sink (see Box 8.5). This added section has distinctively Matthean "fingerprints" as Jesus once again calls Peter "You of little faith." We can also see more clearly the distinctively Markan cast on miracles as the disciples still fail to understand about Jesus even after witnessing this miracle. By contrast, the disciples in Matthew worship him as the Son of God. So, although this is clearly the same basic miracle story, it is shaped in very different ways by these two Gospels, while the Gospel of Luke deletes the story entirely.

The Matthean author tends to shorten the miracle stories and turn them into lessons about faith, often by adding a saying or short discourse of Jesus to make the lesson clear. Usually, the disciples are portrayed as getting the lesson and believing in Jesus, even if they waver at times. By contrast the Markan author tends to have lengthy and complex miracle stories that leave the disciples baffled and confused. Rather than producing belief, the miracles highlight their lack of understanding about Jesus's true identity and mission. These differences can be traced in a number of other cases where Mark and Matthew have the same parallel story.

A Boy with a Demon

Another good example is the demon-possessed (or epileptic) boy (Mark 9:14–29; Matt 17:14–21; Luke 9:37–43). The Matthean and Lukan versions of this miracle are roughly half the length of that in Mark, and yet it is clear that each one takes the basic story from Mark. Each one preserves elements in Mark that the other one omits, such as the description of the dreaded effects of the demon.[34]

Only the Matthean version identifies the boy's problem as epilepsy; however, it is no less explicit in attributing the disease to a demon (17:18). The entire miracle in Matthew is reduced to two sentences (17:14–17, 18). What makes the Matthean version even more distinctive is the addition at the end of a discourse between Jesus and the disciples in which he explains why they could not cast out this demon. After calling them, once again, "little faiths," the Matthean Jesus instructs them, "If you have faith the size of a mustard seed, you will say to this mountain, 'Move from here to there,' and it will move; and nothing will be impossible for you" (17:20). This final saying is not found anywhere in Mark. It is drawn from Q material and appears elsewhere in Luke 17:8, but in a different context. In the Matthean version, this final discourse is as long as the rest of the miracle. By adding it to the miracle story, the Matthean author has effectively transformed the miracle into a lesson on faith.

The Lukan version is also abbreviated and ends very much as a straightforward miracle, by emphasizing the amazement of the crowd. There is no separate discourse with the disciples. The lengthy Markan version contains an added miraculous element as the boy apparently dies when the demon is expelled and

Jesus is forced to resuscitate him. It ends, once again, with the disciples confused at an enigmatic statement of Jesus.

A Double Miracle: Jairus's Daughter and the Hemorrhaging Woman

A final example that shows these characteristic trends of each Gospel writer comes from the double miracle of Jairus's daughter and the woman with the hemorrhage (Mark 5:21–43; Matt 9:18–26; Luke 8:40–56). They too derive from the Markan "double cycle" of oral tradition discussed at the beginning of this chapter. In effect, they were originally two separate miracles that came to be *intercalated,* or interwoven, probably by the Markan author. As the Markan story goes, Jesus was asked to come and heal the daughter of Jairus, but while on his way he encountered the woman with the hemorrhage. After she was cured, he then proceeded to the house of Jairus, but the girl had already died. Jesus then raised her from the dead (see Box 8.6). In other words, the story about the woman with the hemorrhage has been "sandwiched" between the two halves of the story of raising Jairus's daughter. This intercalation has the effect of forcing the two stories to play off one another. By looking at this interplay we are better able to detect the thematic interests of the author.

Here is how it works. A number of features in the story point to the fact of Markan adaptation to weave the two together in this manner. The young girl is twelve years old; the woman had suffered from a menstrual disorder for twelve years. These conditions also set the two characters at opposite ends of a social spectrum, because menstruation was subject to an important set of purity regulations in Jewish tradition. By virtue of her condition, the woman would have been ritually impure for twelve years; the girl is premenstrual and pure. The woman represents a marginal figure in ancient society, since she would have been restricted from attending the Temple or even public events. She should not even be out in public and touching other people, especially a man. By contrast, the girl's father, Jairus, is described as a "leader of the synagogue." In the resuscitation Jesus again uses an Aramaic phrase (here "*Talitha cum*"), as he did in the Markan story of the deaf-mute (7:31–37). That the resuscitation miracle of a young girl might easily stand alone is shown by the very similar miracle of Apollonius of Tyana, discussed above.

The dramatic play of this Markan composition creates a subtle dynamic by juxtaposing the reactions of the different characters within the story to Jesus. The woman with the hemorrhage is nameless and marginal and yet she is the one who shows the greatest understanding of who Jesus really is and what it means to have faith in him. She goes so far as to risk public ridicule and disgrace merely to touch his garments. When she does so, she is healed immediately (5:29). In effect, by virtue of her act of faith, she has healed herself. The Markan version makes this

BOX 8.6

A Double Miracle
Jairus's Daughter and the Hemorrhaging Woman

Matthew 9:18–26	Mark 5:21–43 (cf. Luke 8:40–56)
[18] While he was saying these things to them, suddenly a leader of the synagogue came in and knelt before him, saying, "<u>My daughter has just died</u>; but come and lay your hand on her, and she will live." [19] And Jesus got up and followed him, with his disciples.	[21] When Jesus had crossed again in the boat to the other side, a great crowd gathered around him; and he was by the sea. [22] Then one of the leaders of the synagogue named Jairus came and, when he saw him, fell at his feet [23] and begged him repeatedly, "My little daughter is at the point of death. Come and lay your hands on her, so that she may be made well, and live." [24] So he went with him.
[20] Then suddenly a woman who had been suffering from hemorrhages for twelve years came up behind him and touched the fringe of his cloak, [21] for she said to herself, "If I only touch his cloak, I will be made well." [22] Jesus turned, and seeing her he said, "Take heart, daughter; your faith has made you well." <u>And instantly the woman was made well.</u>	And a large crowd followed him and pressed in on him. [25] Now there was a woman who had been suffering from hemorrhages for twelve years. [26] She had endured much under many physicians, and had spent all that she had; and she was no better, but rather grew worse. [27] She had heard about Jesus, and came up behind him in the crowd and touched his cloak, [28] for she said, "If I but touch his clothes, I will be made well." [29] <u>Immediately her hemorrhage stopped; and she felt in her body that she was healed of her disease.</u> [30] Immediately <u>aware that power had gone forth from him, Jesus turned about in the crowd and said, "Who touched my clothes?"</u>

point quite explicit, for Jesus does not even know she is there until he feels that "power had gone forth from him" at the moment she touched him (5:30). Only then does Jesus turn to face her and acknowledge her. But the miracle had already been performed without his prior knowledge or direct action.

By contrast, Jairus has asked Jesus to heal his daughter, who is "at the point of death" (5:23). As part of the drama of the story, it is Jesus's encounter with the woman that keeps him from arriving before the little girl dies. But the real point comes when those who inform Jairus of her death then say, "Why trouble the

Matthew 9:18–26	Mark 5:21–43 (cf. Luke 8:40–56)
	31 And his disciples said to him, "You see the crowd pressing in on you; how can you say, 'Who touched me?'" 32 He looked all around to see who had done it. 33 But the woman, knowing what had happened to her, came in fear and trembling, fell down before him, and told him the whole truth. 34 He said to her, "Daughter, your faith has made you well; go in peace, and be healed of your disease."
23 When Jesus came to the leader's house and saw the <u>flute players and the crowd making a commotion</u>, 24 he said, "Go away; for the girl is not dead but sleeping." And they laughed at him. 25 But when the crowd had been put outside, he went in and took her by the hand, and the girl got up. 26 And the report of this spread throughout that district.	35 While he was still speaking, some people came from the leader's house to say, <u>"Your daughter is dead. Why trouble the teacher any further?"</u> 36 But overhearing what they said, Jesus said to the leader of the synagogue, "Do not fear, only believe." 37 He allowed no one to follow him except Peter, James, and John, the brother of James. 38 When they came to the house of the leader of the synagogue, <u>he saw a commotion, people weeping and wailing loudly</u>. 39 When he had entered, he said to them, "Why do you make a commotion and weep? The child is not dead but sleeping." 40 And they laughed at him. Then he put them all outside, and took the child's father and mother and those who were with him, and went in where the child was. 41 He took her by the hand and said to her, "Talitha cum," which means, "Little girl, get up!" 42 And immediately the girl got up and began to walk about (she was twelve years of age). At this they were overcome with amazement. 43 He strictly ordered them that no one should know this, and told them to give her something to eat.

KEY: <u>Underlined</u> = key points where story is different

teacher any further?" (5:35). In other words, Jairus and his household believed that Jesus might be able to heal the girl so long as she was still alive, but they did not believe that he had the power to bring her back to life once dead. Thus, all the main dramatic points of these miracles rely on reading the two stories together and having them interact narratively.

Although both Matthew and Luke follow Mark in retaining the basic intercalation, only Luke keeps most of these dramatic elements intact. The young girl is alive at the beginning and dies while Jesus is en route (Luke 8:42, 49). The woman touches Jesus and is healed immediately before Jesus feels his power drained and turns to acknowledge her (8:44, 46–48). The Lukan version is only slightly shorter than that of Mark, mostly due to condensed phrasing at some key points.

The Matthean version shows the greatest changes. First, this version is much shorter than that in Mark, just a little over one-third the length of the Markan

---

BOX 8.7
Jesus Heals the Hemorrhaging Woman

The scene depicts the moment when the woman touches Jesus's cloak and he turns to face her. The depiction seems to be closer to the Matthean rather than the Markan version of the story, as it compresses her touch and his turning to face her into a single narrative moment. Fresco. Rome, Catacomb of SS. Peter and Marcellinus. Late third century. *Used by permission, Scala/ Art Resource, NY.*

version. Next, we note that Jairus's daughter is already *dead* at the beginning, and Jesus is asked *to raise her* (9:18). Now there are no retainers of Jairus who come to tell him of her death, and when Jesus arrives at his house a funeral procession has already begun (9:23). The characteristically Markan motif of having Jesus order people not to tell about what he has done is entirely omitted in Matthew. The Matthean version thus produces a simpler version of the resuscitation with no ironic elements about Jairus's social standing or his failure to understand Jesus properly, both of which are at the center of the drama in Mark (and Luke).

Even more striking is what happens in the Matthean version of Jesus's encounter with the hemorrhaging woman (see Box 8.7). For now the entire vignette has been altered by deleting all the play about her touching his garment and being healed instantly. Instead, when she tugs on his cloak, he turns and speaks to her. Only after he pronounces her well is she healed. Once again, the Matthean version has removed the odd and ironic elements found in the Markan drama to create a more straightforward and simpler portrayal of Jesus as miracle worker. The focus now shifts away from the characters and their reaction to Jesus and toward Jesus and his miraculous powers in a traditional sense. In every respect, the Markan version is more subtle and complex on the narrative level and more powerful as a theological statement about Jesus. Here, once again, we see the storyteller's artistry at work.

Although the Gospel of Matthew undoubtedly used the Gospel of Mark as the main source for this story, its storytelling technique and thematic interests are quite different. These distinctive features of how each Gospel author tends to handle miracle stories will gain further relevance for understanding their respective portrayals of Jesus and the disciples once we examine how other components of Jesus's teachings are treated. As we shall see, the two types of stories are paired thematically in the different Gospels, but for different purposes and with different effects. Dramatic shaping is a package deal.

CHAPTER NINE

⁓⁓⁓

Spinning Parables

He also said, "The kingdom of God is as if someone would scatter seed on the ground, and would sleep and rise night and day, and the seed would sprout and grow, he does not know how. The earth produces of itself, first the stalk, then the head, then the full grain in the head. But when the grain is ripe, at once he goes in with his sickle, because the harvest has come."

He also said, "With what can we compare the kingdom of God, or what parable will we use for it? It is like a mustard seed, which, when sown upon the ground, is the smallest of all the seeds on earth; yet when it is sown it grows up and becomes the greatest of all shrubs, and puts forth large branches, so that the birds of the air can make nests in its shade."

With many such parables he spoke the word to them, as they were able to hear it; he did not speak to them except in parables, but he explained everything in private to his disciples. (Mark 4:26–34)

As with miracle stories, it appears that the teachings of Jesus—or what we may call "sayings stories"—developed and circulated separately prior to the writing of the Gospels. Chapter 4 of the Gospel of Mark contains a string of four loosely connected parables (4:1–9, 13–20; 4:21–25; 4:26–29; 4:30–32) plus two enigmatic statements about Jesus's use of parables (4:10–12; 4:33–34). The rather simple and formulaic quality of the collection may be seen in the passage quoted at the beginning of this chapter, which shows how two of the several short parables with a similar theme about seeds are strung together by nothing more than the terse narrative opening, "He also said." It has long been argued that the three seed parables derive from an older oral tradition where they had already been collected together, but they have been interspersed with additional dialogue added by the

Markan author. Of these, the parable of the mustard seed (4:30–32) is thought by some scholars to be authentic to Jesus;[1] however, it is generally agreed that the concluding "summary" (4:33–34) and other portions of the chapter are part of the framework created by the Markan author rather than deriving from the pre-Markan oral tradition.[2]

The parallel section in the Gospel of Matthew (13:1–52) contains all but one of the same parables found in Mark 4, but then supplements the collection by adding six more. A possible oral source for these added parables is difficult to pin down, because only one of them comes from the Q tradition (Matt 13:33; Luke 13:20–21). The remainder are unique to the Matthean story, and at least one of them—the parable of the weeds (13:24–30, 36–43)—seems to be an allegorical elaboration and reinterpretation of the simpler "seed parable" of Mark 4:26–29. Both Gospel authors show the tendency to group parables together after the pattern of oral collections.

Similarly, the bulk of the Q material is in fact sayings of Jesus with little or no connective narrative. It contains fourteen parables or "parabolic words" that seem largely to be clustered together in a single block, albeit interspersed with other sayings.[3] What narrative does appear in the Q material usually functions to ground the teaching in a putative life situation that helps to clarify the point of the saying.[4] These small sayings units and clusters appear to be somewhat portable and can be reassembled in various configurations. That collections of Jesus's teachings circulated in this form in both oral and written versions is further evidenced by the noncanonical *Gospel of Thomas*, which contains a serial listing of 114 sayings without any clear ordering principle. Most of them are introduced by a simple connective formula, such as "And he said," or by a question posed to Jesus by the disciples.

Hence it appears that collections of "sayings" or "sayings stories" developed and circulated separately from other components of the Gospel tradition. Within these collections, certain types of sayings also tended to cluster together. The parables of Jesus and the Golden Rule are perhaps two of the most familiar types in the Gospels. We will discuss both at greater length below.

Teacher, Prophet, and Sage

A passage called the "Song of the Vineyard" comes from the prophet Isaiah (ca. 740–685 BCE):

Let me sing for my beloved
my love-song concerning his vineyard:
My beloved had a vineyard
on a very fertile hill.
He dug it and cleared it of stones,

and planted it with choice vines;
he built a watchtower in the midst of it,
and hewed out a wine vat in it;
he expected it to yield grapes,
but it yielded wild grapes. (5:1–2)

It is a parable or allegory about the people of Israel's failure to live up to the moral demands of their God. Here God is the "lover" who plants and tends the vineyard, Israel.[5] Teachers, prophets, and parables—in Jewish tradition they go together.

In the Synoptics, Jesus is shown telling the parable of the wicked tenants (Mark 12:1–12; Matt 21:33–46; Luke 20:9–19), which is clearly based on this same metaphor from Isaiah:

A man planted a vineyard, put a fence around it, dug a pit for the wine press, and built a watchtower; then he leased it to tenants and went to another country. When the season came, he sent a slave to the tenants to collect from them his share of the produce of the vineyard. (Mark 12:1–2)

By showing Jesus teaching in parables, he too was being cast in the role of the prophets of old. Some of them, like Elijah and Elisha, performed miracles as well. Others, like Isaiah or Jeremiah, are better known for their biting criticism of Israelite society. Their teachings, as preserved by later scribes, became a central part of the Jewish scriptures.

On the other hand, Greek philosophers and moralists, like Aesop, also used metaphors and fables. Hence, the image of Jesus as teacher—as well as the preservation of his teachings and sayings stories—was strongly influenced by two cultural traditions, one more Jewish, the other more Greco-Roman. It is another way in which his character is shaped in the development of the Gospel tradition (see Chapter 1). As we shall see later, the Gospel of Matthew focuses more on the prophetic image, while the Gospel of Luke leans more toward the philosophical.

Certain patterns of speech associated with Jesus's teaching in the Gospels were derived from the style of Israelite prophetic oracles. These include introductory formulas, such as, "Thus says the Lord" (Matt 11:20), and admonitory formulas, such as, "He who has ears, let him hear" (Mark 8:38).[6] Certain metaphors were commonly used by the prophets as ways of dramatizing the "word of the Lord" delivered by the prophet. One is the metaphor of Israel as God's lover or bride. In turn, it led also to the metaphor of an unfaithful wife or "playing the harlot" as a symbol of apostasy. It was used extensively as a call to repentance by Hosea in the late eighth century (Hos 2:2–12) and by both Jeremiah and Ezekiel in the sixth century (Jer 3:1–10; Ezek 16:30–35).

On a few occasions we hear of parables, though surprisingly they are more rare. After King David had the husband of Bathsheba killed, the prophet Nathan is reported to have confronted him by telling him a parable about a poor man with one lamb (2 Sam 12:1–7). On the whole, however, parables only became more common in Jewish usage closer to the time of Jesus and especially in the later rabbinic tradition, where a strong tie to the tradition of the sages is also seen.

From the Jewish side, then, the teacher as religious or social critic derived from this prophetic tradition, which had so profoundly reformed Israelite theology in the periods just before and after the Babylonian exile (586–538 BCE).[7] In turn, these prophetic writings were further reinterpreted through the rise of the apocalyptic worldview, which has been called the "child of prophecy in a new idiom."[8] What this means is that apocalyptic, while often confused with or called "prophecy," is actually a new medium of interpretation.[9] It assumes that works or episodes of divinely generated "revelation" continue and have relevance for new situations. In addition, it is facilitated by transforming the prophetic oracles of earlier figures, such as Isaiah or Jeremiah, which were always addressed to their own day, into future predictions regarding an eschatological age. In Chapter 1 we saw this practice at work in the Dead Sea Scrolls and more generally in the diverse forms of Jewish apocalyptic literature. Among these common ideas was the expectation of a new religious leader for Israel, a "prophet" like Moses (Deut 18:15) or a latter-day Elijah (Mal 3:1–4; 4:4–5). These images were applied explicitly to Jesus and John the Baptist in the Gospels (cf. Matt 11:13; 17:9–13; Mark 6:14; Luke 1:17).

The analogue in Greco-Roman culture was the sage or philosopher, after the model of Socrates, Pythagoras, or Diogenes.[10] Like the prophet in ancient Israel, the philosopher was often a critic of social ills, announced new ideas, or called for reform. In some cases, philosophers too were persecuted or killed for challenging prevailing norms of belief or practice.[11] In contrast to the prophets, however, the sage stood for the betterment of individuals and of the society as a whole, no matter what the personal cost. Yet it was also assumed that not everyone could become a sage. Consequently, the philosophical schools that followed these sages constituted something of an esoteric tradition, not unlike the diverse sects within Judaism. Indeed, the term "sect" (Gk. *hairesis*) was used of these philosophical schools. In turn, Josephus described the various sects of Judaism as "schools" or "philosophies," in imitation of the Greek model.[12]

The image of the sage permeated both Greco-Roman and Jewish cultures, in part through the development of the wisdom tradition (see Chapter 2).[13] The sage, or wise man, was often depicted as traveling around and examining others in order to criticize and bring them improvement. Pythagoras was thought to have a special mystical insight, later attributed to his status as a divine man. Socrates was understood to have been driven by a divine force—also called his *daimon* or *genius*—to instruct and criticize others. In Plato's account of the trial, calling it his "service to God," Socrates himself is made to describe it as a kind of divine commission:

If you should let me go on this condition, as I have stated [i.e., no longer practicing philosophy], then I would say to you, "Men of Athens, I salute you and love *you, **but I shall obey God rather than you,** and so long as I may live and am able, I will in no way take my leave from philosophizing or from exhorting you and showing the truth to anyone I happen to meet. . . . For know well that **God commands** me to do this, and I think that no greater good has ever come about in this city than **my service to God.**"*[14]

Of course, personal criticism was not always welcome, and this stance often set the sage at odds with others. He also taught by means of aphorisms and metaphors that were meant to inculcate basic morals and philosophical ideals, confronting the status quo in an indirect or surreptitious way.

At the same time, the key ideas or teachings of the sage became watchwords for others. Socrates was known for the slogan, "Know yourself"; Pythagoras, for his "golden verses."[15] The phrase that often accompanied such characteristic teachings was *ipse dixit* ("He himself said it"), as a kind of personal testimonial to the authority of the sage behind it.[16] On the other hand, such truisms or aphorisms were easily appropriated by others. In later rhetorical handbooks, students were even encouraged to reformulate these sayings of the sages to make them more lively and "real" or to make them fit better into a new rhetorical framework of the student's composition. The practice was called "emulation" (*aemulatio*), but they did not worry about reshaping the basic story or scene in substantial ways (see Chapter 5). We shall return to this point below in discussing certain types of sayings material.

Formal Classification of Sayings Stories

Analysis of the basic types of stories within the Gospels and their formal characteristics has a long tradition in New Testament study; however, many of the assumptions and emphases have changed in more recent scholarship. In earlier work, identifying the rudimentary form of a particular story, as we have seen in the case of miracles, operated as a starting point for assessing whether the story itself might go back to an earlier stage in the oral tradition and potentially all the way back to the historical Jesus.[17] Further elaboration or shaping of the story reflected how the author—often called the *redactor* (or editor)—of a particular Gospel wove these individual story units into a larger fabric of narrative. These types of analysis came to be called *form* and *redaction criticism*.[18] The goal, then, was to isolate the later elaboration from the "original" form or core, with an eye for what might be authentic to Jesus himself.[19]

In more recent scholarship on the whole, there has been less concern to find the putative historical core of each story or story form. Determining which sayings actually go back to Jesus himself and in what precise form or wording is different from examining how they are recast in each particular Gospel.[20] The emphasis has shifted to literary aspects, and specifically how the story units have been adapted or shaped to fit into the narrative as evidence for both the stylistic and thematic (or rhetorical) concerns of the particular Gospel author.[21] One key element in this shift is the recognition that the Gospel authors are just that, *authors,* who create new and cohesive stories. They are not, as once assumed, merely "editors" with scissors and paste who piece together otherwise unretouched bits of oral tradition. Hence there is a renewed appreciation for the creative process of storytelling at work in each new Gospel.

In addition, this approach has brought a much greater awareness of the interaction between author and audience, as both a historical factor in the development of individual Gospels and a literary dimension. In this way, we may now be more attuned to the narrator's voice in the story and the dynamics of how the characters interact with the readers, who stand outside the narrative world of the story. All of these issues will become important when we turn to the Gospels themselves.

As a result, other modes of literary criticism may shed new light on the narrative construction or rhetorical design of individual scenes as well as whole Gospels.[22] As we have seen, although at least some of the miracles clearly go back to earlier stages of the oral tradition about Jesus, their "original form" may tell us little beyond what was typical in telling miracle stories of each type. On the other hand, their adaptation within each Gospel may be much more significant for understanding how Jesus was viewed and presented through the literary shaping of these traditional stories. Something analogous is at work in the numerous stories about Jesus as teacher and his key sayings. In this section, therefore, we will focus on the characteristic features of different types of sayings and then look at how they have been adapted or reshaped by the individual Gospel authors.

With both Jewish and Greco-Roman models in mind, it is possible to classify the main types of sayings materials found in the Gospels into four basic types by their genre or form.[23] They are:

- Wisdom Sayings (proverbs and aphorisms)

- Apocalyptic Sayings

- Pronouncement Stories (*chreiai*)

- Similitudes and Parables

A full catalogue of these four types and their subcategories, with examples from the Gospels, is shown in Box 9.1. We shall examine the characteristic features of each type in greater detail below. As we shall see, each type has its own formal characteristics based on content, grammar, or structure. Certain types of sayings are associated with particular images or traditions. For example, proverbs and aphorisms are commonly associated with the sage in many different cultures, while *chreiai* are frequently found in the Greek philosophical tradition. Both apocalyptic sayings (especially judgment oracles) and parables are associated with

BOX 9.1

Types of Sayings Material

Wisdom Sayings (proverbs and aphorisms)

1. Declarative	Matt 12:34; 6:34; Luke 10:7
2. Interrogative	Matt 6:27; Mark 2:19
3. Imperative or hortatory	Luke 4:23; Matt 8:22

Apocalyptic Sayings (future-looking announcements with conditions or warnings)

1. Prophetic oracles (often conditional formulations)	Mark 9:35; 10:31, 43; Matt 23:11; Luke 14:11
2. Blessings and woes	Matt 5:1–11; Luke 6:20–26
3. Judgment oracles ("if-then" form; parallel structure)	Mark 8:38; Matt 6:14; 10:32/Luke 12:8–9; Luke 11:30
4. I-sayings ("I tell you"; may be added to any of above)	Mark 9:1, 15; Matt 5:17; 17:20; 18:3; Luke 12:8

Pronouncement Stories (chreiai)

1. Simple chreiai (biographical apothegms)	Mark 9:33–35; Matt 8:19–22
2. School or controversy sayings	Mark 8:11–13, 14–21; Luke 14:1–6
3. Complex pronouncement stories (stitching other types of sayings material onto basic chreia openings)	Matt 5–7; Luke 6:20–49

Similitudes and Parables

1. Simple similitudes (figures of speech, similes, metaphors)	Matt 5:13–14; 9:14–17; 15:14; Luke 14:34–35
2. Extended similitudes or parables ("X is like Y" with one main point)	Matt 13:33; 13:44–45; 13:52; Mark 4:26–29; 4:30–32
3. Allegories (elaborated parables with built-in point for point comparisons)	Mark 4:1–9 + 4:13–20; Matt 13:2–30 + 13:36–43; Matt 22:1–14; Luke 14:16–24

the Jewish prophetic tradition; similitudes and fables were widely used in Greek philosophy and more generally in wisdom literature. Thus, each type of saying tends to connote a specific background; however, by combining and reshaping them in different ways, they can take on new meaning.

Wisdom Sayings (Proverbs and Aphorisms)

Proverbs and aphorisms represent one of the commonest forms of teachings in the ancient world, in keeping with the idea, noted above, of the "truisms" taught by sages. Usually, they deal with aspects of everyday life or how to live nobly and ethically in the world. Some scholars draw a subtle distinction between proverbs and aphorisms. *Proverbs* are generic truisms that anyone might say, while *aphorisms* are attributed to a particular sage.[24] In practice, however, the lines sometimes get blurred, as many of these ideas—and very often the same basic sayings—are found in different cultures, reattributed to their own sagely figure, for example, Solomon in Jewish tradition, Ahikar in Babylonian and Persian traditions,[25] or Socrates and Pythagoras in Greek tradition. The same phenomenon occurs in other world cultures, such as the wise sayings of Confucius in Chinese culture or Benjamin Franklin in American.

In ancient Near Eastern cultures, the basic form of such sayings evolved from the idea of patriarchal blessings and instruction, as the wise father instructed his children. This idea is seen in the farewell blessings of Jacob to his twelve sons (Gen 49:1–28), which in turn was the source for the extended apocalyptic reinterpretation in the *Testament of the Twelve Patriarchs* (see Chapter 2). The book of Proverbs, though anonymous, is attributed to Solomon. It opens with the following admonition: "Hear, my child [lit., son], your father's instruction, and do not reject your mother's teaching" (1:8; cf. 4:1). The opening address, "my child (son)," prefaces many of the individual sections of the work.[26] Although the form is generally patriarchal in nature (i.e., framed as fathers speaking to sons), there are maternal instructions that use the same form. One of these occurs in the last chapter of Proverbs (31:1–31), which is a self-contained set of instructions said to be given to King Lemuel by his mother (31:1).

The Wisdom of Sirach (discussed in Chapter 2) is similar, containing the proverbs of the elder Jesus son of Sirach preserved by his grandson.[27] The Hellenistic Jewish romance known as Tobit employs the same motif in an extensive set of instructions from Tobit to his son Tobias, but also hints that this wisdom comes from the sage Ahikar, now claimed as a relative (1:21).[28] Such cross-cultural borrowing of basic ideas occurs frequently. In the case of Sirach, for example, the work is also dependent on both Hellenistic and Egyptian wisdom traditions.[29] As a result, many of the same proverbs occur in different works; however, they are sometimes modified or used in different configurations within each text.

The basic form of these aphorisms is a brief, usually pithy, statement of self-affirming truth, such as, "Train children in the right way, and when old, they will not stray" (Prov 22:6); and, "A child who gathers in summer is prudent, but a child who sleeps in harvest brings shame" (Prov 10:5). Notice how both preserve the ideal of parental wisdom for children. A variant form of the latter is found in Proverbs 6:6–8: "Go to the ant, you lazybones; consider its ways and be wise. . . . It prepares its food in summer, and gathers its sustenance in harvest." The same basic idea was also rendered into a charming parable or fable of an ant and a grasshopper by the Greek sage Aesop. Other parallels with Greek tradition may also be seen in the famous passage from Proverbs 7 regarding the lures of the wanton woman. It has strong similarities to the so-called Prodicus myth, preserved by Xenophon among the memoirs of Socrates; the latter recounts a story about the youthful Hercules, who had to make a choice between two women—personifications of virtue and vice—standing at a crossroads.[30]

Perhaps the most famous aphorism of Jesus within the Gospels is what most people call the Golden Rule: "Do to others as you would have them do to you" (Luke 6:31); "In everything do to others as you would have them do to you; for this is the law and the prophets" (Matt 7:12). It is now recognized that this same maxim was used a century or more earlier in the *Epistle of Aristeas* 207, and a negative formulation occurs in Tobit 4:15: "And what you hate, do not do to anyone."[31] It also appears in *2 Enoch* 61:1 (late first century BCE) and among the teachings of Hillel, an older contemporary of Jesus and one of the most revered figures among the Pharisees.[32] Hillel's version is worth recounting in detail, for both its formulation and the circumstances out of which it came:

> *On another occasion it happened that a certain heathen came before Shammai and said to him, "[You can] Make me a proselyte, on one condition, that you teach me the whole Torah while I stand on one foot." Thereupon he repulsed him with a builder's cubit which was in his hand. When he [the heathen] went before Hillel, he [Hillel] said to him, "What is hateful to you, do not to your neighbor; that is the whole Torah, while the rest is commentary thereof. Go and learn it. (* b. Sabb. 31a)*[33]

In addition to Hillel, the later rabbinic tradition preserved it as a saying of both Rabbi Eleazar and Rabbi Akiba,[34] typically in this "negative" form following Hillel, while in the teachings of Jesus (from Q) it is reformulated as a positive statement.[35] In its Q form (as preserved in both Matthew and Luke), the saying is set in the context of showing mercy to others, either out of need or demand. Several aspects of the Hillel story are also similar to the "great commandment" episode (Matt 22:39–40; Mark 12:31).[36]

Such sayings tended to travel independently as isolated units or small clusters by theme or type. For example, another variant of the idea behind the Golden Rule also appears in a separate saying from the Q tradition, in Luke 6:38 and

Matthew 7:2: "For the measure you give will be the measure you get"; it is set in the context of a teaching on judging and forgiveness. The same saying, presumably from a different oral tradition, also occurs in Mark 4:24–25, where it is set in the context of heeding the teachings of Jesus: "And he said to them, 'Pay attention to what you hear; the measure you give will be the measure you get, and still more will be given you. For to those who have, more will be given; and from those who have nothing, even what they have will be taken away.'"

As with the Golden Rule, we notice how the basic meaning of the aphorism shifts depending on the context in which it is set. In the case of the Gospel of Mark, it has been combined with another saying about giving and receiving that contains a more ominous warning. This last saying occurs separately elsewhere in a parable from the Q tradition (Matt 25:29; Luke 19:26), suggesting that it too at first traveled independently and was only combined with the "measure for measure" saying by the Markan author. The ominous tone of this last saying also points us to the next category: apocalyptic sayings.

With many of these common aphorisms, it is difficult to know whether and precisely how it might have been used by Jesus, for, as we have seen, they can easily be modified in grammatical form and combined with other sayings of different type to create new meanings. It was also common for such aphorisms to gravitate in later tradition toward Jesus or other sages. A good example is a saying attributed to Socrates by the first-century-CE Stoic Musonius Rufus, a contemporary of Paul. In a treatise on food and diet he says:

> *Therefore, it is fitting for us to eat that we may live, not for pleasure, if indeed we wish to stay in line with the excellent advice in the saying of Socrates, who said that <u>the majority of people live in order to eat, but that he ate in order to live.</u>*[37]

The source of Musonius's attribution is unknown; however, in about the year 200 CE the Christian philosopher Clement of Alexandria attributes this same saying to Jesus:

> *Whereas some people <u>live in order to eat,</u> as though [they were] indeed irrational creatures, "for whom nothing but the belly is life," the Paedagogue [Jesus] instructs us, <u>to eat that we may live.</u>*[38]

In this case, we know that Clement actually read and quoted extensively from Musonius, and he felt free to reappropriate this common aphorism of Socrates and work it into a saying of Jesus, even though it never appears within the Gospels.[39]

Something similar happens in other early Christian writings, including the Gospels and Acts. In a speech reported in Acts, Paul says:

> *In all this I have given you an example that by such work we must support the weak, remembering the words of the Lord Jesus, for he himself said, "<u>It is more blessed to give than to receive.</u>" (20:35)*

Again, this saying never appears within the Gospels, although a similar idea occurs in Sirach 4:31. The closest parallel for this precise saying, however, comes from the Greek historian Thucydides, who attributes it to the Persian kings, who say "It is better to give than to receive."[40] The Greek moralist Plutarch, who lived at the end of the first century CE contemporaneous with the composition of Luke-Acts, also cites it as a maxim of the Persian king Artaxerxes.[41] The only difference is that the version in Acts has been turned into a kind of beatitude by the addition of "it is more blessed (*makarion*)," and this change may account for its attribution to Jesus.[42] Hence, aphorisms, like the other kinds of sayings material, are highly malleable in form and content, and their meaning can change by virtue of the literary context in which they are set.

Apocalyptic Sayings

- Prophetic oracles

- Blessings and woes

- Judgment oracles

- I-sayings

As already noted, the categories of wisdom and apocalyptic sayings at times overlap. Their common ground lies in syntactic similarities, as both incorporate instructional and hortatory expressions. Likewise, they share a common background in the Jewish prophetic tradition. In recent New Testament scholarship, the interconnection between wisdom literature and apocalyptic has been increasingly accepted and explored.[43] While recognizing that some overlap exists, it is nonetheless possible to draw basic distinctions for charting these categories as sayings traditions within the Gospels. Here we are not dealing with separate genres of literature per se. Rather, we are dealing with small sayings units that evoke the cultural and theological resonances of these other genres while being imbedded in stories about Jesus's life and teachings. To be sure, the Jewish culture in which Jesus lived was heavily laced with both wisdom and apocalyptic traditions.

Whereas wisdom sayings focus on general truisms for a moral life, apocalyptic sayings often contain a more ominous or judgmental tone, based on the idea of what might happen if one fails to follow certain prescripts. A good example of this shift occurs in the Matthean Sermon on the Mount:

> *You will know them by their fruits. Are grapes gathered from thorns, or figs from thistles? In the same way, every good tree bears good fruit, but the bad tree bears bad fruit. A good tree cannot bear bad fruit, nor can a bad tree bear good fruit. Every tree that does not bear good fruit is cut down and thrown into the fire. Thus you will know them by their fruits. (7:16–20)*

The opening and closing lines of this little Matthean speech are the same. They represent the Matthean frame, which is based on the aphorism "Each tree is known by its fruit," which is how it is given in both Luke 6:44 and Matthew 12:33. Then we get three variations on the same idea to make it more explicit. Only now it has been transformed into "good and bad" fruit, likened to the contrast between "figs and thistles," rather than a simpler notion of apples versus oranges. Next comes the more pointed statement, "Every tree that does not bear good fruit is cut down and thrown into the fire." Now the same idea has been rendered into an apocalyptic saying, with a threat of punishment for those who do not "bear good fruit." When we get to the closing frame, the whole meaning of the basic aphorism has been transformed by this apocalyptic tone.

Apocalyptic sayings characteristically contain this kind of future-looking perspective, either as promise of reward or threat of punishment. In this sense they are fully consistent with the dualistic quality of apocalyptic worldview, with its stress on the present evil age and a coming transformation. They often possess an eschatological dimension that is generally lacking from the more common forms of proverbial wisdom. Their dualistic ethic also evinces prophetic overtones of calls to reform and rigorous adherence to more sectarian forms of piety and observance. As a result, they were often used and expanded by the followers of Jesus after his death to reinforce sectarian group boundaries. Hence, even these very basic sayings units were subject to adaptation and change. The "bear good fruit" string discussed above, with its concentrated apocalyptic tone, occurs only in the Gospel of Matthew.[44]

Prophetic Oracles

The basic features of apocalyptic sayings are reflected in a common two-part structure—representing present and future—that often characterizes the simpler form of such sayings.[45] It also has a conditional tone, like an "if-then" sentence, which may be explicit or implicit. For example, within the Gospels Jesus is reported to say, "Whoever wants to be first must be last of all and servant of all" (Mark 9:35). This type of saying may be called a *prophetic oracle*. It appears in several variations in the Gospels:

Whoever wishes to become great among you must be your servant, and whoever wishes to be first among you must be a slave of all. (Mark 10:43–44; Matt 20:26–27; Luke 22:26)

But many who are first will be last, and the last will be first. (Mark 10:31; Matt 19:30; 20:16; Luke 13:30)

All who exalt themselves will be humbled, and all who humble themselves will be exalted. (Matt 23:12; Luke 14:11; 18:14)

This kind of status-reversal formulation implies future rewards for those who adhere to the teachings. Here the conditional quality is implied. Whereas the first two versions derive from Markan tradition, the last derives from Q, and thus may represent a subtle shift in the way oral tradition preserved what is basically the same saying.

Similar types of two-part sayings occur frequently in the Gospels:

> For those who want to save their life will lose it, and those who lose their life for my sake . . . will save it. (Mark 8:35; Matt 16:25; Luke 9:24; cf. Matt 10:39; John 12:25)

> Whoever does not receive the kingdom as a little child will never enter it. (Mark 10:15; Luke 18:17; cf. Matt 18:3–4)

Blessings and Woes

Closely akin to this simpler form of apocalyptic saying are *blessings and woes*. They convey a similar type of dualistic message, but expressed more bluntly, either as a positive reward or as a threat of punishment in eschatological terms. Here too there is often a status-reversal element. Although this type of saying is not as common in the Gospels, it is among the most famous, especially in the Matthean form of the Beatitudes:

> Blessed are the poor in spirit, for theirs is the kingdom of heaven.
> Blessed are those who mourn, for they will be comforted.
> Blessed are the meek, for they will inherit the earth.
> Blessed are those who hunger and thirst for righteousness, for they will be filled.
>   (5:3–6)

They are sometimes called makarisms, from the Greek word *makarismos* (here translated "blessed") at the beginning of each statement; the Latin equivalent is *beati,* from which we get the term "beatitude."[46] In part because they are only formulated as positive statements, they are often assumed to refer primarily to one's spiritual life; however, a social dimension is also present.

These sayings occur in slightly different form in the Gospels of Matthew and Luke and thus derive from Q tradition. Their formulation in the Lukan version, while structurally similar, conveys a much sharper tone:

> Blessed are you who are poor, for yours is the kingdom of God.
> Blessed are you who are hungry now, for you will be filled.
> Blessed are you who weep now, for you will laugh. (6:20–23)

The Lukan version has a much stronger sense of status reversal between the now and the future, but couched in explicitly socioeconomic terms. Poverty, hunger, and sorrow here are real social ills. This social aspect of the Lukan version .

comes through especially in the following verses, where—in sharp contrast to the Matthean version—the "blessings" are paralleled by corresponding "woes":

> *But woe to you who are rich, for you have received your consolation.*
> *Woe to you who are full now, for you will be hungry.*
> *Woe to you who are laughing now, for you will mourn and weep. (6:24–26)*

Hence, even though the Matthean and Lukan versions of these sayings clearly seem to derive from a common oral tradition, their tone and meaning change dramatically based on different subtle shifts in wording by each of these two Gospel authors. Both versions are based in apocalyptic ideas, but the one in Matthew has been taken in the direction of moral guidelines that are understood to govern one's whole life. The Lukan version seems to be more about correcting particular ills of society. Which of the two versions is more likely to have come from Jesus himself is thus a matter of some debate, but most scholars tend to view the Lukan form as the more original. The Matthean form has been adapted to a new social and literary context.

Judgment Oracles

Included in apocalyptic sayings is a more elaborate form called *judgment oracles.* The more complex structure involves parallel first and second clauses, with a judgment or reversal stated. In these sayings, the "if-then" conditional quality is usually explicit:

> *If anyone is ashamed of me and of my words in this adulterous and sinful generation, of that one will the Son of Man also be ashamed when he comes in the glory of his Father with the holy angels. (Mark 8:38)*

> *And I tell you, whoever acknowledges me before others, the Son of Man also will acknowledge before the angels of God; but the one who denies me before others will be denied before the angels of God. (Luke 12:8–9; Matt 10:32)*

Here again we see slight variations of wording and tone between the Markan tradition and that derived from Q. In both cases, I have given a more literal translation to show the explicit "if-then" syntax of the Greek. The parallelism is seen in the repetition of the key verbs, either "to be ashamed" or "to acknowledge/ deny." The sense of judgment and future reward or punishment is made even more explicit. This particular type of saying is sometimes called a "holy (or sacral) law pronouncement." It typically uses the pregnant eschatological title "Son of Man" as the warrantor of the judgments.[47]

A similar type of elaborated apocalyptic saying is sometimes called a "legal admonition." It too has an explicit "if-then" structure and promise of future reward or punishment, but it lacks the stronger parallelism of the "sacral law pronouncement." A good example comes at the end of the Matthean version of the Lord's

Prayer. In this case it is a double saying, one part stated positively and the other negatively:

> For if you forgive others their trespasses, your heavenly Father will also forgive you; but if you do not forgive others, neither will your Father forgive your trespasses. (6:14)

Interestingly, this saying does not occur at all in the Lukan version of the Lord's Prayer (11:2–4). Instead, it appears to be a Matthean addition to the prayer based on a separate saying found in Mark 11:25, where it serves as commentary on bearing proper fruit. The Markan version only contains the positive form of the condition, while the Matthean version adds the negative, making it even stronger. The Matthean author seems to have appended it to the end of the prayer as an expansion and reinforcement for the simple supplication: "Forgive us our debts, as we also have forgiven our debtors" (6:12). With its new context and expanded form, it establishes a legal injunction that sets the conditions upon which eschatological forgiveness may be expected.

I-sayings

Finally, some scholars have identified a separate type of apocalyptic saying called an *I-saying;* it always opens with "I say unto you" or just "I tell you" (Mark 9:1; Matt 5:17; 17:20). Sometimes, in the synoptic Gospels the form is augmented with the Aramaic word *amen* ("truly" or "verily"); the Gospel of John is unique in strengthening it further with *amen, amen.*[48] Although it evokes personal authority for the speaker, it was not as common in ordinary Greek usage; nor was it used in the earlier Hebrew prophets as a "messenger formula."

Nonetheless, it had come into use in various Jewish contexts prior to the time of Jesus, where it assumes the social hierarchy of a superior addressing inferior(s). It was also widely used in later rabbinic literature. In fact, this phrase may be added to almost any kind of saying, but is especially apposite to apocalyptic pronouncements and legal admonitions when delivered in direct speech. It is possible that the phrase was used by Jesus himself, but it was not a distinctive feature or a marker of authenticity, as has sometimes been assumed.[49] In the Gospels it generally serves as a literary device to emphasize Jesus's authority and/or to punctuate and enliven dialogue sections of direct discourse.[50]

Pronouncement Stories (*Chreiai*)

- Simple *chreiai* (biographical apothegms)

- School or controversy sayings

- Complex pronouncement stories

Whereas apocalyptic sayings evoke the Jewish prophetic tradition, pronouncement stories (or *chreiai*) were especially prominent in the Greco-Roman philosophical and rhetorical traditions. Schoolboys were often taught their first lessons in philosophy by learning these characteristic sayings or maxims, and they were widely quoted in many arenas of society.[51] *Simple pronouncement stories (chreiai)* are similar to aphorisms, but their characteristic feature is that they use a brief narrative about a particular sage to set the stage for a specific saying associated with that sage.

The Greek word *chreia* (pl. *chreiai*) literally means "need" or "use," but in a derived sense can mean "usual" or "familiar." It also conveys the sense of something "useful." In ancient rhetorical handbooks, the term was then used to refer to the familiar or characteristic maxims of particular philosophers that were considered useful for living.[52] They are not as generic as aphorisms, but they are typically brief anecdotes that make a moral point.

At a formal level, the key is that the brief narrative opening about the circumstances should provide just enough detail or action to help make the point of the saying that follows.[53] As a shorthand, we may describe it as a narrative opening plus a punch line; it takes both components to constitute a *chreia*.[54] *Chreiai* are also called pronouncement stories, because the "story," or narrative component, sets up the "pronouncement," or saying component.[55] The simpler *chreiai* in the Gospels have often been called biographical apothegms, because the occasion for the saying (apothegm) carries some putative biographical information.

A good example comes from the founder of the Cynics, Diogenes, who was a contemporary of both Aristotle and Alexander the Great.[56] He earned his nickname, "the Dog," from his irascible and often uncouth behavior in public, often for the purpose of making a philosophical or moral point. He was especially known as a proponent of simple living and a harsh critic of wealth and luxury. Many of his characteristic sayings convey these ideas. The following examples are typical *chreiai* of Diogenes:

> *Diogenes the philosopher, on being asked by someone how he might become famous, responded: "By worrying as little as possible about fame."*[57]

> *Diogenes, the Cynic philosopher, on seeing a rich man who was uneducated, said: "This man is silver-plated filth."*[58]

As we see here, some *chreiai* may be delivered as a response to a question, while others are in the form of piqued observations. In some cases, the response may be delivered by an action instead of a saying, but the point is the same.

> *Diogenes, on seeing a boy who was a gourmand, struck [the boy's] paedagogus [tutor] with his staff.*[59]

An example of a more elaborate description shows how the interactions in the story might be used to set up the punch line:

When Alexander [of Macedon] stood opposite him and asked: "Are you afraid of me?" [Diogenes] said: "Why, what are you, a good thing or a bad?" When Alexander replied, "A good thing," Diogenes said: "Who then is afraid of the good?"[60]

Because Diogenes did not produce written philosophical treatises, most of his ideas are preserved in the form of brief *chreiai* with little or no systematic framework. Only later did other Cynics and philosophical handbooks attempt to codify his ideas. The *chreiai* then serve also as quasi-biographical reminiscences of his life and words. In this way, he is similar to both Socrates and Jesus.

The ancient *chreiai* also show a good deal of wit and invention. For example, here is one attributed to the mother of Alexander the Great:

Olympias, on hearing that her son Alexander was proclaiming himself the offspring of Zeus, said: "Won't this fellow stop slandering me to Hera?"[61]

Needless to say, this saying is not likely historical since it reflects legends and attitudes toward Alexander from later periods, including the story of his miraculous birth. Nonetheless, it shows the ability to play on the traditions through the medium of *chreiai*. In other cases, we see familiar types of *chreiai* spun off in duplicate forms. For example, here are four more about Diogenes that are clearly variants of the same "action *chreia*" discussed above:

Diogenes, the Cynic philosopher, when he noticed some well-born boys attacking their food in an ill-mannered way, struck their paedagogus with a staff.[62]

Diogenes, on seeing a youth misbehaving, beat the paedagogus.[63]

Diogenes, on seeing a youth misbehaving, beat the paedagogus and said, "Why were you teaching such things?"[64]

A paedagogus was in the company of a boy, but the boy was not maintaining the proper decorum. To Diogenes his behavior seemed to need correction. What then does he do? He ignores the young man and goes after the one in charge, inflicts many blows on his back, and adds to the blows the remark that such a man should certainly not be a teacher.[65]

In this case we see how a basic *chreia* might be passed down in variant forms, including an expanded narrative. The basic structure of the story remains essentially the same, even though the details of the episode on which it relies change with each variation. Yet the point of each one becomes a different vice to be corrected, ranging from bad table manners to gluttony to misbehaving in public. They surely are not all historical.

Aelius Theon, an Alexandrian sophist and author of a collection of preliminary exercises for the training of orators, also discusses classroom exercises for the students of rhetoric in which they might alter *chreiai* to fit new grammatical frames or new literary compositions or to give them more dramatic wording.[66] In some cases, they might even be formulated as objections, or they might be condensed or expanded to elaborate the main point. Aelius Theon says:

> *We expand the chreiai whenever we enlarge upon the questions and responses to it, and upon whatever act or experience is in it. We condense by doing the opposite. For example, a concise chreia: Epameinondas, as he was dying childless, said to his friends: "I have left two daughters—the victory at Leuctra and the one at Mantineia." Now, let us expand like this: Epameinondas, the Theban general, was of course a good man in time of peace, and when war against the Lacedaemonians came to his country, he displayed many outstanding deeds of great courage. As a Boeotarch at Leuctra, he triumphed over the enemy, and while campaigning and fighting for his country, he died at Mantineia. While he was dying of his wounds and his friends were lamenting, among other things, that he was dying childless, he smiled and said: "Stop weeping, friends, for I have left two immortal daughters—our country's two victories over the Lacedaemonians, the one at Leuctra, who is the older, and the younger, at Mantineia, who is just now being born."* [67]

Thus, while the *chreiai* were considered reminiscences of the sage or hero, they were nonetheless susceptible to shaping and manipulation for rhetorical effect, and this process was taught regularly in the rhetorical schools.[68]

When we turn to the Gospels, we find similar forms and treatment. Many of the *chreiai* in the Gospels have been expanded to create continuity and flow within the narrative. They also allow for the stitching together of more than one independent saying. They often take the form of Jesus in discussion with his disciples or Jesus being confronted by outsiders or opponents. For this reason, the expanded *chreiai* in the Gospels are often referred to as either *school sayings* (when teaching the disciples) or *controversy sayings* (when responding to critics or opponents). One of the latter:

> *Then they sent to him some Pharisees and some Herodians to trap him in what he said. And they came and said to him, "Teacher, we know that you are sincere, and show deference to no one; for you do not regard people with partiality, but teach the way of God in accordance with truth. Is it lawful to pay taxes to the emperor, or not? Should we pay them, or should we not?" But knowing their hypocrisy, he said to them, "Why are you putting me to the test? Bring me a denarius and let me see it." And they brought one. Then he said to them, "Whose head is this, and whose title?" They answered, "The emperor's." Jesus said to them, "Give to the emperor the things that are the emperor's, and to God the things that are God's." And they were utterly amazed at him. (Mark 12:13–17)*

In this case the action has been expanded to dramatize the final saying and to emphasize the opposition to Jesus.

Others are transformed by repositioning them, so that the context alters the import of the saying:

Now when Jesus saw great crowds around him, he gave orders to go over to the other side. A scribe then approached and said, "Teacher, I will follow you wherever you go." And Jesus said to him, "Foxes have holes, and birds of the air have nests; but the Son of Man has nowhere to lay his head." (Matt 8:18–20)

Whereas the Gospel of Luke gives this Q saying in the context of Jesus's travels from city to city (9:57–58), the Matthean version (8:18–20) has been inserted before the miracle of stilling the storm (discussed in Chapter 8 and Box 8.4), in which the disciples had "followed Jesus," but then cowered in the face of the storm (8:23–27). Among the Synoptics, only the Gospel of Matthew configures these two episodes in this particular way.

Another example also shows how a basic *chreia* might be manipulated further within the narrative of one particular Gospel:

As Jesus passed along the Sea of Galilee, he saw Simon and his brother Andrew casting a net into the sea—for they were fishermen. And Jesus said to them, "Follow me and I will make you fish for people." (Mark 1:16–17).

The Gospel of Matthew (4:18–20) replicates the Markan form and placement of this *chreia*, whereas the Lukan version of the story is both repositioned within the narrative and shows significant reshaping and elaboration:

Once while Jesus was standing beside the lake of Gennesaret, and the crowd was pressing in on him to hear the word of God, he saw two boats there at the shore of the lake; the fishermen had gone out of them and were washing their nets. He got into one of the boats, the one belonging to Simon, and asked him to put out a little way from the shore. Then he sat down and taught the crowds from the boat. When he had finished speaking, he said to Simon, "Put out into the deep water and let down your nets for a catch." Simon answered, "Master, we have worked all night long but have caught nothing. Yet if you say so, I will let down the nets." When they had done this, they caught so many fish that their nets were beginning to break. So they signaled their partners in the other boat to come and help them. And they came and filled both boats, so that they began to sink. But when Simon Peter saw it, he fell down at Jesus's knees, saying, "Go away from me, Lord, for I am a sinful man!" For he and all who were with him were amazed at the catch of fish that they had taken; and so also were James and John, sons of Zebedee, who were partners with Simon. Then Jesus said to Simon, "Do not be afraid; from now on you will be catching people." When they had brought their boats to shore, they left everything and followed him. (5:1–11)

The final saying shows that this is still the same basic *chreia*. The Lukan version is more dramatic, with additional action, including a miraculous catch of fish, and more direct dialogue between the characters. It may be called a *complex pronouncement story*. It may be argued, therefore, that the *chreia* is one of the most basic building blocks of the Gospel narrative, because its basic story frame allows for other materials to be stitched onto it as a way of creating narrative flow and continuity.

One of the distinctive features of the Gospel of John is a series of lengthy discourses attributed to Jesus that have no basic parallel in the other Gospels. They are usually called the "I am" discourses, and they are built on simple metaphors, which will be discussed in the next section. These discourses are also built on the model of the *chreia,* as Jesus makes a symbolic gesture and then delivers one of the "I am" sayings as a punch line, but the process is elaborated narratively. A good example is the first one, in which Jesus discusses "bread from heaven" (6:22–34) on the day after his miracle of feeding the five thousand (6:1–15). The discourse then expands on the theme of bread, as Jesus says, "I am the bread of life" (6:35); it continues through John 6:59. Although this type of discourse goes well beyond the *chreia* in form, it is based on the same premise of a narrative episode and correlative saying. In the Johannine Gospel Jesus gives seven of these discourses either as an instruction to his disciples or as a response to opponents.

Similitudes and Parables

- Simple similitudes (figures of speech, similes, metaphors)

- Extended similitudes or parables

- Allegories

The term "parable" is often used erroneously in contemporary parlance to refer to almost any "saying of Jesus" found in the Gospels. As we shall see, however, a true parable is an extended simile couched in a small story narrative. Hence, the larger category of sayings stories under discussion here is called "parabolic speech" or "similitudes"; they are sayings that deliver information about one thing by "likening," or comparing, it to another. This category includes simpler and more complex forms, ranging from simple metaphors and similes to parables and complex allegories.[69] Each one has distinct features and contexts for usage. That the more elaborate parables and allegories found in the Gospels constitute short narratives—that is, stories—to convey religious meaning will become important to understanding the signal place of parables in both the teachings of Jesus and the development of the Gospel tradition.

As noted earlier, metaphors were commonly employed in the earlier prophetic tradition of ancient Israel, but true parables were more rare.[70] The word *mashal* in Hebrew comes from a root meaning "to be like," but was used broadly to refer to various kinds of proverbial statements, including such diverse forms as riddles, taunts, and proverbs, sometimes with allegorical elements.[71] The word *mashal* takes on more of its characteristic meaning as "similitude" in wisdom literature, which often inculcates its proverbs (*mashalim*) in simple comparisons.[72] In Proverbs 10–28, for example, there are some seventy sapiential statements built on simple metaphors or similes.[73] Here are just a few examples:

> *Like vinegar to the teeth, and smoke to the eyes, so are the lazy to their employers.* *(10:26)*

> *The way of the LORD is a stronghold for the upright. (10:29)*

> *Rash words are like sword thrusts, but the tongue of the wise brings healing.* *(12:18)*

> *The teaching of the wise is a fountain of life, so that one may avoid the snares of death. (13:14)*

The full development of these simpler similitudes into the more characteristic parables and allegories familiar from Gospels reached its zenith in the later rabbinic tradition. That Jesus is depicted as using forms very similar to post-70 CE rabbinic literature puts him squarely in the lines of the early development of the Pharisaic tradition.[74]

The Greek word used in the Gospels and early Christian tradition to render *mashal* in all of its senses is *parabolē,* from a verb meaning to "to cast beside, put before, or place alongside." The Latin equivalent is *parabola,* from which we get "parable." The noun form can thus mean a parable in the traditional sense, but also an illustration or simple comparison (Luke 5:36), a symbol or lesson (Mark 13:28), a proverb or maxim (Luke 4:23), or a riddle (Mark 3:23; 7:17). It should be noted that some of these uses carry an enigmatic sense. In marked contrast to most assumptions regarding the parables of Jesus, rather than conveying a simple message in metaphoric terms, they are sometimes meant to confound or seem strange while causing hearers to ponder possible meanings.[75] In particular, the Gospel of Mark emphasizes the fact that Jesus intentionally used parables to prevent his message from being understood by the masses (4:10–12); instead, he explained things privately to his disciples (4:33–34). As we shall see, this is another feature of the "messianic secret" motif that we observed in the Markan miracle stories. We shall return to it again in Chapter 11.

The way in which parables convey meaning is heavily dependent on literary context and internal shaping, by which any one parable may take on vastly different meanings. Consequently, the parables vary significantly from Gospel to Gospel in both their literary presentation and their meaning. The Gospel of Luke contains eleven parables that do not appear in any of the other Gospels, including some of the most famous, such as the good Samaritan (10:29–37), the prodigal son (15:11–32), and the rich man and Lazarus (16:19–31). All eleven occur in what is often called "Luke's special section" (9:51–18:4), and most of them reflect either composition or substantial reworking by the Lukan author. A number of these uniquely Lukan parables also have strong similarities to fables and exemplary tales found in the Hellenistic moralists and novels.[76]

By contrast, the Gospel of John contains no parables; nor is the word "parable" (Gk. *parabolē*) ever used. Only in John 10:1–6 do we find something similar, an adage about a shepherd and the sheepfold. It does not contain a short narrative or story as such, but is framed as a kind of hypothetical situation. In Greek this little discourse is referred to as a *paroimia* in John 10:6, which is now usually translated as "figure" (RSV) or "figure of speech" (NRSV).[77] Thus, if one were to rely on the Gospel of John for a picture of how and what Jesus taught, the traditional notion of the parables of Jesus would be lost entirely, as to both form and content. On the other hand, the Gospel of John uses simple metaphors—such as "I am the bread of life" (6:35), "I am the gate" (10:7), and "I am the vine, you are the branches" (15:5)—as the basis for constructing the signal "I am" discourses that dominate the teachings of Jesus in the Johannine version.

Simple Similitudes

We may begin to understand the mechanisms of parabolic speech by examining the rudimentary forms, which we call *simple similitudes*. They include figures of speech (or word pictures) as well as simple metaphors and similes, such as the ones seen earlier from Proverbs. A number of these appear in the Q tradition, which also seems to have strong affinities for wisdom literature in its presentation of the teachings of Jesus:

You brood of vipers. (Matt 3:7; Luke 3:7)

A reed shaken by the wind. (Matt 11:7; Luke 7:24)

You are like whitewashed tombs. (Matt 23:27)

You are like unmarked graves. (Luke 11:44)

In general, such statements tend to be very brief and imply simple comparisons.

These rudimentary forms may then be combined and elaborated to form more complex ideas. In the Gospel of Matthew, for example, a cluster of otherwise independent metaphors and word pictures have been woven together in order to create a small discourse unit. First, we have two simple metaphors, "You are the salt of the earth" (5:13) and "You are the light of the world" (5:14). The first basic statement seems to be based on a simple saying about the value of salt found in Mark 9:50 and Luke 14:34–35, but it has been transformed in the Matthean version to serve as a metaphor for discipleship. Then comes a simple word picture, "A city built on a hill cannot be hid" (Matt 5:14). Another independent word picture then follows: "No one after lighting a lamp puts it under the bushel basket" (5:15), which is found used in other contexts in Mark 4:21 and Luke 11:33–36. In the former it is used as a comment about the value of parables. In the latter it is used to inform an entirely different metaphor: "Your eye is the lamp of your body."

Taken individually, these word pictures are rather transparent and uncontroversial. Together, however, they take on new meaning depending on the context in which they are used. In the Matthean version, they set up a final exhortation: "Let your light shine before others" (5:16), which ultimately informs the initial metaphor regarding the nature of discipleship.

Extended Similitudes or Parables

In turn, simple similitudes may be expanded to make more concrete comparisons by describing everyday situations. In the narrowest sense, this is what we properly call a *parable*. It works by sketching a brief narrative describing an ordinary but fictional situation. Some feature of the characters or action described within the narrative then stands as the basis of comparison, usually for a significant symbol, such as the kingdom of God.[78] In their simpler form they usually contain only one sentence and one main action, as in the following examples:[79]

> *Therefore every scribe who has been trained for the kingdom of heaven is like the master of a household who brings out of his treasure what is new and what is old. (Matt 13:52)*

> *But to what will I compare this generation? It is like children sitting in the marketplaces and calling to one another, "We played the flute for you, and you did not dance; we wailed, and you did not mourn." (Matt 11:16–17; Luke 7:31–32)*

> *To what should I compare the kingdom of God? It is like yeast that a woman took and mixed in with three measures of flour until all of it was leavened. (Luke 13:20–21)*

> *The kingdom of heaven is like treasure hidden in a field, which someone found and hid; then in his joy he goes and sells all that he has and buys that field. (Matt 13:44)*

> *Again, the kingdom of heaven is like a merchant in search of fine pearls; on finding one pearl of great value, he went and sold all that he had and bought it. (Matt 13:45–46)*

Parables may be further extended and elaborated by making the narrative more detailed; this can be done by adding other characters and/or by making the action more complex. Each added element of description then offers further points of comparison, both with other features within the narrative and with the main symbol that is the object of comparison. We may schematize the parable form as follows:

X *is like* Y, *where* Y = *a story in several steps:*

a _____

b _____

(c _____)

(d _____)

The narrative may be longer or shorter, but one reads through the narrative in a linear way to derive the moral or lesson, which usually has one main point.

A good example of an extended parable is that of the laborers in the vineyard (Matt 20:1–16). It tells the story of a landowner who early in the morning hires day laborers from the marketplace to work in his vineyard. The action is embellished when the owner returns four more times during the day to hire other workers, the last group coming at five o'clock in the evening. Then at the end of the day it comes time to pay all the hired help, which occurs in reverse order, but each one receives the usual daily wage. Then when those hired first are paid and also receive the same wage, they are outraged, to which the owner responds:

> *"Friend, I am doing you no wrong; did you not agree with me for the usual daily wage? Take what belongs to you and go; I choose to give to this last the same as I give to you. Am I not allowed to do what I choose with what belongs to me? Or are you envious because I am generous?" So the last will be first, and the first will be last. (Matt 20:13–16)*

The last line of the passage is that familiar apocalyptic saying: "So the last will be first, and the first will be last" (Matt 20:16). This is a true parable in that there is no other comparison to be found except in the owner's actions and his response to the outrage of those who had worked longest and hardest. The point, at least internally within the parable, is that because of God's beneficence,[80] those who come into the kingdom, whether early or late, will all receive the same reward. The parable then functions as a narrative illustration of the two "first-last" sayings that frame it in a carefully crafted chiastic structure that emulates the reversal within the parable itself.[81] The whole thing is a distinctively Matthean construction.

Here is how it works. This parable is unique to the Gospel of Matthew and appears to be an expansion on the preceding scene, in which Jesus is discussing the rewards that the disciples can expect for having left everything to follow him (19:25–29). It occurs immediately following Jesus's encounter with a rich young man who cannot bring himself to abandon his possessions in order to follow Jesus (19:16–24). The whole passage ends with another version of the status-reversal saying: "But many who are first will be last, and the last will be first" (19:30). It is worth noting that the parallel versions of the rich young man story found in

Mark 10:17–31 and Luke 18:18–30 lack the parable of the laborers. So it appears that the Matthean author has created this new parable to illustrate and explain the final apocalyptic saying.

In this case, however, not only is the narrative expanded, but the climax is a series of sayings by the fictional landowner. Thus, this new sayings unit (parable) becomes a kind of paradigm for Jesus in the Gospel of Matthew, as it contains a narrative and a set of final sayings about just desserts and beneficence, which are exemplary of the kingdom. Though it is not an allegory in any overt way, it is moving in that direction, as the interplay between the two passages invites readers or hearers to equate characters within the parable with other figures, including God, Jesus, and the disciples. In general, as parables get longer and more detailed in any of the Gospels, they tend to become more allegorical in character, and such allegorizations are usually a product of that Gospel author's theological or rhetorical agenda.

Allegory

This brings us to the final form of similitude, the *allegory*. Parable and allegory are very similar in that both contain narratives that describe actions that then serve as comparisons for some larger symbolic meaning. In the Gospels, the term "parable" is also used for allegories; therefore, understanding the formal distinction is very important. The key difference is that embedded within the allegory is another set of equations for the identity or significance of the key characters and actions. If we use the same type of schematic as above, we could sketch the allegory as follows:

X *is like* Y, *where* Y = *a story in several steps*:

$$a \ \underline{\hspace{3cm}}$$
$$b \ \underline{\hspace{3cm}}$$
$$c \ \underline{\hspace{3cm}}$$
$$d \ \underline{\hspace{3cm}}$$

but where each element in the story has its own separate equation with something else:

$$a \ = \ w \ \underline{\hspace{3cm}}$$
$$b \ = \ x \ \underline{\hspace{3cm}}$$
$$c \ = \ y \ \underline{\hspace{3cm}}$$
$$d \ = \ z \ \underline{\hspace{3cm}}$$

One then must read across the narrative from the actual element to the implied equivalents before deriving the point of the story. The allegorical equations may either be given explicitly within the allegory or through a separate explanation. They may also be given implicitly through other mechanisms to be discussed below. The most familiar allegory in the Gospels is the parable of the sower (Mark 4:1–8; Matt 13:1–9; Luke 8:4–8). The allegorical explanation is given in a separate passage (Mark 4:13–20; Matt 13:18–23; Luke 8:11–15), where each of the elements is given its full equation.

What really differentiates allegories from parables is the implied system of interpretation that underlies the allegorical equations. In the Gospels, these allegorical equations almost always presuppose elements that come from the social and cultural situation of the author and audience of one particular Gospel, rather than from the world of Jesus. Allegories may thus be efforts of the Gospel authors, and of the early Christians more generally, to resolve the enigmatic quality of Jesus's teachings in ways that made sense to them. Allegories in the Gospels are generally later reinterpretations, and each one has a different meaning based on the literary and social context of a particular Gospel.[82]

A good example of the mechanism of allegory is Augustine's reading of the parable of the good Samaritan (Luke 10:29–37), as quoted by C. H. Dodd:

> A certain man went down from Jerusalem to Jericho: *Adam himself is meant;* Jerusalem *is the heavenly city of peace, from whose blessedness Adam fell;* Jericho *means the moon, and signifies our mortality, because it is born, waxes, wanes, and dies.* Thieves *are the devil and his angels.* Who stripped him, *namely, of his immortality;* and beat him, *by persuading him to sin;* and left him half-dead, *because insofar as man can understand and know God, he lives, but insofar as he is wasted and oppressed by sin, he is dead; he is therefore called* half-dead. The priest *and* Levite *who saw him and passed by signify the priesthood and ministry of the Old Testament, which could profit nothing for salvation.* Samaritan *means Guardian, and therefore the Lord Himself is signified by this name.* The binding of the wounds *is the restraint of sin.* Oil *is the comfort of good hope;* wine, *the exhortation to work with fervent spirit.* The beast *is the flesh in which He [Jesus] deigned to come to us.* The being set upon the beast *is belief in the incarnation of Christ.* The inn *is the Church, where travelers are refreshed on their return from pilgrimage to their heavenly country.* The morrow *is after the resurrection of the Lord.* The two pence *are either the two precepts of love, or the promise of this life and that which is to come.* The innkeeper *is the Apostle (Paul).* The supererogatory payment *is either his counsel of celibacy, or the fact that he worked with his own hands lest he should be a burden to any of the weaker brethren when the Gospel was new, though it was lawful for him "to live by the Gospel."*[83]

In this passage, the items in roman type represent words or phrases from the actual parable as found in Luke. The italicized portions represent Augustine's allegorical interpretation. Even at first glance, one must be struck by what Augustine supposes to be the meaning and intent of the parable as attributed to Jesus. What we have here is clearly not a theological outlook consistent with homeland Jewish culture during the lifetime of Jesus. Nor is it characteristic of an early Christian outlook from the time of the Gospels, the first century CE. Rather, it is a fully developed Christian theology characteristic of Augustine's own day, at the end of the fourth century CE. In effect, this is the difference between a parable and an allegory in the Gospels as well, for these allegories encode a system of meaning that betrays the later situations, perspectives, and cultural resonances of the particular Gospel in which it appears.[84] To say it another way, allegorization of parables, whether implicit or explicit, inevitably reflects the dramatic and thematic reshaping of that particular Gospel author.

From Parable to Allegory as Storytelling Technique

In each Gospel there are certain themes and motifs that tend to show up in more than one parable, reflecting the manipulation of the story materials by that particular Gospel author. Inevitably, the same root parable, when allegorized by different Gospel authors, becomes something entirely different in each case.

Allegorizing the Parables of the Weeds and the Net

A good example of thematic shaping for allegorical effect may be in seen two of the added "parables" in Matthew 13. As noted at the beginning of this chapter, the author of the Gospel of Matthew has supplemented the collection of three "seed parables" found in Mark 4 by adding six other parables.[85] The theme of "seeds" serves as an important link in this process. Immediately following the interpretation of the parable of the sower (Matt 13:18–23; Mark 4:13–20), the Matthean passage now continues as follows:

Parable of the weeds (13:24–30)

Parable of the mustard seed (13:31–32; taken from Mark 4:30–32)

Parable of the yeast (13:33; taken from Q; cf. Luke 13:20–21)

On the use of parables (13:34–35, taken from Mark 4:33–34, but augmented)

Allegorical interpretation of the weeds (13:36–43)

Parable of the hidden treasure (13:44)

Parable of the pearl (13:45–46)

Parable of the net (13:47–50)

Parable of old and new treasures (13:51–52)

We shall be focusing on the parable of the weeds (and its allegorical interpretation) and the parable of the net (see Box 9.2 for the text). Both parables have a very similar structure. In one a farmer sows a field with good seed, but weeds grow up as well. His servants ask whether they should go through and pull the weeds, but the farmer says no, for fear of losing some of his crop. Instead, he tells them to wait until the harvest and then separate the good from the bad plants. In the other, fishermen cast a net into the sea, and it comes up with all kinds of fish, some good and some bad. When they pull it on shore, they separate them into baskets and throw out the bad. In both cases, the theme of good and bad is taken in the direction of an eschatological metaphor, similar to what we saw earlier in the Matthean reworking of the "good fruit/bad fruit" aphorism (Matt 7:16–20). By means of allegorization the author makes this point even more explicit.

The first thing to note about this section in the Gospel of Matthew is that the author has done more than just add several more parables after those taken from the Gospel of Mark. A more subtle process of literary reconfiguration has taken place. First, immediately following the allegorical interpretation of the parable of the sower (Mark 4:13–20; Matt 13:18–23), the author of Matthew deleted two passages: a section on the purpose of parables (Mark 4:21–25)[86] and the parable of the seed growing secretly (Mark 4:26–29). Next, the parable of the weeds (Matt 13:24–30) was added in place of the seed growing secretly and before the parable of the mustard seed, which derives from Mark (Mark 4:30–32; Matt 13:31–32). Then, comes the parable of the yeast (13:33), derived from Q. It is followed by the concluding summary on parables (13:34–35), which is derived from Mark (4:33–34), but it has been augmented by the Matthean author with a modified quotation from Psalm 78:2 (77:2, LXX). Whereas the Markan version of the story ends here, the Matthean version continues, and this added quotation from the psalm anticipates this continuation. It is followed by an allegorical interpretation of the parable of the weeds (13:36–43).

The other additional parables (Matt 13:44–52) are strung along after this reprise on the parable of the weeds. Even here we see subtle intertextual elements tying one passage to the next. For example, the Matthean quotation (13.35) from Psalm 78 (77):2 substitutes the phrase "I will proclaim what has been hidden (*kekrymmena*)" for the phrase "I will utter questions or problems (*problēmata*)" as found in the Septuagint. Instead of carrying an enigmatic sense, as seen in both the Markan parallel and the original text of the psalm (in both Hebrew and Greek), this summary on parables now seems to promise new revelations.[87] The same word, "hidden" (*kekrymmenō*), then appears in the parable of the hidden treasure (13:44). Next, the word "treasure" in this same parable (13:44) is repeated again in the final parable about old and new treasures (13:52). The overall effect is a more careful reworking of the Markan section with the addition of new themes and intertextual connections. Rather than a loose collection of otherwise

BOX 9.2

The "Parables" of the Weeds and the Net

The Parable of the Weeds

Mark 4:26–29	Matthew 13:24–30

26 He also said, "The kingdom of God is as if someone would scatter seed on the ground, 27 and would sleep and rise night and day, and the seed would sprout and grow, he does not know how. 28 The earth produces of itself, first the stalk, then the head, then the full grain in the head. 29 But when the grain is ripe, at once he goes in with his sickle, because the harvest has come."

24 He put before them another parable: "The kingdom of heaven may be compared to someone who sowed good seed in his field; 25 but while everybody was asleep, an enemy came and sowed weeds among the wheat, and then went away. 26 So when the plants came up and bore grain, then the weeds appeared as well. 27 And the slaves of the householder came and said to him, 'Master, did you not sow good seed in your field? Where, then, did these weeds come from?' 28 He answered, 'An enemy has done this.' The slaves said to him, 'Then do you want us to go and gather them?' 29 But he replied, 'No; for in gathering the weeds you would uproot the wheat along with them. 30 Let both of them grow together until the harvest; and at harvest time I will tell the reapers, Collect the weeds first and bind them in bundles to be burned, but gather the wheat into my barn.' "

The Interpretation of the Parable of the Weeds (Matthew 13:36–43)

36 Then he left the crowds and went into the house. And his disciples approached him, saying, "Explain to us the parable of the weeds of the field." 37 He answered, "The one who sows the good seed is the Son of Man; 38 the field is the world, and the good seed are the children of the kingdom; the weeds are the children of the evil one, 39 and the enemy who sowed them is the devil; the harvest is the end of the age, and the reapers are angels. 40 Just as the weeds are collected and burned up with fire, so will it be at the end of the age. 41 The Son of Man will send his angels, and they will collect out of his kingdom all causes of sin and all evildoers, 42 and they will throw them into the furnace of fire, where there will be weeping and gnashing of teeth. 43 Then the righteous will shine like the sun in the kingdom of their Father. Let anyone with ears listen!

The Parable of the Net (Matthew 13:47–50)

47 "Again, the kingdom of heaven is like a net that was thrown into the sea and caught fish of every kind; 48 when it was full, they drew it ashore, sat down, and put the good into baskets but threw out the bad. 49 So it will be at the end of the age. The angels will come out and separate the evil from the righteous 50 and throw them into the furnace of fire, where there will be weeping and gnashing of teeth.

independent seed parables (as in Mark), the whole literary ensemble begins to take on a more coherent message.

Central to this new message is the parable of the weeds and its allegorical interpretation. As already noted, the parable of the weeds has been substituted by the Matthean author for the simpler parable of the seed growing secretly (Mark 4:26–29). Several features of the two parables are similar in language (see Box 9.2), and it appears that the Matthean author has used the Markan passage as a base and expanded it into this much more elaborate allegory. For example, the following elements—the "scattering" or "sowing" of the "seed";[88] the farmer (in the Greek called "a man or person" in both) who "sows" and then "sleeps"; the "plants sprout and bear fruit"; and finally the coming of the "harvest"—all retain identical or very similar wording in the Greek, even though the story has been changed dramatically in the Matthean version. It is also the case that the earlier Markan parable has eschatological overtones, for which the word "harvest" (*therismos*) is the key thematic signal.

The Matthean version then has expanded and strengthened this eschatological theme by using the same Greek word group ("harvest" and "reapers/harvesters") a total of five times in the two passages.[89] The result is a much more dramatic eschatological theme. The further elaboration of each point within the story line already implies an allegorical interpretation; however, the Matthean author has made it explicit by providing the equation for each element in the second passage (13:36–43). This allegory reveals a major new theme emerging in the Matthean interpretation of the teachings of Jesus, namely, that the *eschaton* ("the end of the age," 13:40) will be a time when the good and the bad of the present age are separated, but that the kingdom has in some sense already been inaugurated. Angels will then "collect out of his [the Son of Man's] kingdom . . . all evildoers, and they will throw them into the furnace of fire, where there will be weeping and gnashing of teeth" (13:41–42).

The parable of the net (Matt 13:47–50) delivers essentially the same allegorical message, but in this case the allegorical equations are left implicit. They are nonetheless transparent to readers/hearers, because the parable of the weeds has already provided the interpretative paradigm. Now the fishermen, rather than the harvesters, play the role of the eschatological angels. It may well be that this second parable, which is briefer and more to the point, was the real source behind the Matthean reworking of the parable of the weeds by changing the metaphor from a catch of fish to a harvest of grain. But why the change of metaphor? Because of the theme of seeds that already served as the thematic linkage found in the Gospel of Mark. The parable of the weeds now follows directly on the interpretation of the parable of the sower and just before the parable of the mustard seed. Having done so, however, the author now forces all these parables to be read together, and they mutually allegorize one another. The parable of the net now sums up the new message, as the Matthean author makes the point emphatic by explicating the allegorical point of the story in now familiar language:

> *So it will be at the end of the age. The angels will come out and separate the evil from the righteous and throw them into the furnace of fire, where there will be weeping and gnashing of teeth. (13:49–50)*

The wording here is almost identical to that at the end of the interpretation of the parable of the weeds (13:40–42), thus creating the intertextual allegorization between the two passages. The parable of the weeds and the parable of the net, with their powerful allegorical message, now dominate the entire "sermon" of parables running throughout Matthew 13:1–52. The allegory calls for the members of the Matthean community to assess their own place within this eschatological drama.

That this ominous eschatological warning represents uniquely Matthean language and themes becomes even clearer when we realize that this same phrase, "there will be weeping and gnashing of teeth," occurs six times in the Gospel of Matthew alone, and its theme of the final judgment is reprised powerfully with several more allegories in Matthew 24:37–25:46 as the culmination of the Matthean version of the apocalyptic discourse (24:1–36).[90] In sharp contrast, the phrase "weeping and gnashing of teeth" occurs only once in all of the other canonical Gospels (Luke 13:28), and that in a passage of Q material with similarly strong apocalyptic overtones. This same Q material occurs in Matthew 8:12, as the first of the six times that the phrase is used in this Gospel. So it would appear that the Matthean author has taken this kernel of Q material and used it as a thematic filter through which to rework several key parables taken from the Gospel of Mark and to weave them together intertextually through the story. The phrase "weeping and gnashing of teeth" now looms large under the microscope like fingerprints of the Matthean author on the surface of the narrative.

Allegorizing the Parable of the Great Banquet

We may see the same process of allegorical reinterpretation in the treatment of another parable from the Q tradition that is taken in rather different directions by the authors of Matthew and Luke. It is called the parable of the great banquet (Luke 14:16–24) or the parable of the wedding banquet (Matt 22:1–14). It also occurs in the *Gospel of Thomas* 64. The text of all three versions is given in Box 9.3, which highlights the common elements and distinctive features in each version. That this is essentially the same parable can be seen from the basic story line and nearly identical wording at key points: a person gives a banquet and invites certain guests; when the time comes the invited guests each make excuses; the host then becomes angry and sends his servants out to bring people off the street to enjoy the banquet. In its original Q form, the parable probably reflects the experience of

BOX 9.3

A Parable from Q
The Great Banquet

Matthew 22:1–10, 11–14	Luke 14:13–15, 16–24	Gospel of Thomas 64

[Parable of the Wicked Tenants 21:33–46]
 	
¹ Once more Jesus **spoke to them in parables, saying:** ² *"The kingdom of heaven may be compared* to a person, *a king, who* **gave** *a wedding banquet for his son.* ³ **He sent his slaves to call those who had been invited to the** *wedding banquet,* **but they would not come.** ⁴ **Again he sent other slaves, saying, 'Tell those who have been invited: Look, I have prepared** my dinner, my oxen and my fat calves have been slaughtered, and **everything is ready;** *come to the wedding banquet.'* ⁵ But they made light of it and went away, **one to his farm, another to his business,** ⁶ *while the rest seized his slaves, mistreated them, and killed them.* ⁷ *The king* **became angry. He** *sent his troops, destroyed those murderers, and burned their city.* ⁸ **Then he said to his slaves,** *'The wedding banquet* **is ready, but those** invited *were not worthy.* ⁹ **Go therefore into the main streets, and invite everyone you find to** *the wedding banquet.'* ¹⁰ Those
	¹³ *But when you give a banquet, invite the poor, the crippled, the lame, and the blind.* ¹⁴ *And you will be blessed, because they cannot repay you, for you will be repaid at the resurrection of the righteous.*
	
	    ¹⁵ *One of the dinner guests, on hearing this, said to him, "Blessed is anyone who will eat bread in the kingdom of God!"*
	
	¹⁶ Then he said to him, "A person gave a great dinner and invited many. ¹⁷ At the time for the dinner he sent his slave to say to those who had been invited, 'Come; for everything is ready now.' ¹⁸ But they all alike began to make excuses. The first said to him, 'I have bought a farm, and I must go out and see it; please excuse me.' ¹⁹ Another said, 'I have bought five yoke of oxen, and I am going to try them out; please excuse me.' ²⁰ Another said, 'I have just been married, and therefore I cannot come.' ²¹ So the slave returned and reported this to his master.
	    Then the owner of the house *became angry and said to his slave, 'Go out at*
		Jesus said, "A person was receiving guests. When he had readied the dinner, he sent a servant to invite the guests. The servant went to the first and said to that one, 'My lord invites you.' The guest said, *'Some merchants owe me money, and they are coming to me tonight.* Please excuse me from the dinner.' The servant went to another and said to that one, 'My lord invites you.' The guest said to the servant, 'I have bought a house, and I have been called away for a day. I shall have no time.' The servant went to another and said to that one, 'My lord invites you.' The guest said to the servant, 'My friend is to be married, and I am to arrange the [wedding] dinner. I shall not be able to come. Please excuse me from the dinner.' The servant went to another and said to that one, 'My lord invites you.' The guest said to the servant, 'I have bought an estate, and I am going to collect the rent. I shall not be able to come. Please excuse me.'
		
		The servant returned and said to the lord, 'Those

Matthew 22:1–10, 11–14	Luke 14:13–15, 16–24	*Gospel of Thomas 64*
slaves went out into the streets and gathered all whom they found, *both good and bad; so the wedding hall* was filled *with guests.* *11 But when the king came in to see the guests, he noticed a man there who was not wearing a wedding robe, 12 and he said to him, 'Friend, how did you get in here without a wedding robe?' And he was speechless. 13 Then the king said to the attendants, 'Bind him hand and foot, and throw him into the outer darkness, where there will be weeping and gnashing of teeth.' 14 For many are called, but few are chosen."*	*once into the streets and alleys of the town and bring in the poor, the crippled, the blind, and the lame. 22 And the slave said, 'Sir, what you ordered has been done, and there is still room.'* 23 Then the master said to the slave, 'Go out into the roads *and lanes*, and compel people to come in, so that my house may be filled.' *24 For I tell you, none of those who were invited will taste my dinner."*	whom you invited to dinner have asked to be excused.' The lord said to his servant, 'Go out on the streets, and bring back whomever you find to have dinner.' *For buyers and merchants [shall] not enter the places of my Father."*

KEY: **Bold** = similar wording in all three versions that probably reflects the original form of the parable
Regular type = each Gospel author's editorial work in smoothing the narrative
Italics = framing elements and interpretive changes by each Gospel author

early followers of the Jesus movement who are meeting resistance to their message about Jesus and beginning to turn to others.[91] Yet each of the three Gospels alters the parable in significant ways.

For example, the Gospel of Matthew compresses the excuses into a generic statement, rather than having each one given in turn. That they are based on the same source, however, can still be seen in the fact that the reasons for the excuses are the same: "one to his farm, another to his business" (22:5). The three excuses in Luke are a farm, buying oxen, and a marriage. In contrast, the version in the *Gospel of Thomas* focuses on the excuses in order to shape its message. Thus, the excuses are modified slightly to emphasize "buying" things (a farm, a house) and expanded by adding one more—collecting from merchants who owe money. These subtle changes produce a new thematic slant, as seen in the closing summation: "For buyers and merchants [shall] not enter the places of my Father."

In many ways the version in the Gospel of Luke seems to be closest to the original; however, there is a key change, a second invitation for new guests. The Lukan author has chosen to elaborate the final portion of the parable in order to create a new emphasis. The technique is straightforward. All three versions have new guests brought from the streets. Consequently, the second invitation in Luke is closest to the original form. The added element, then, is the first invitation, to the "poor, the crippled, the blind and the lame," which has been inserted as a doublet (14:21b–22). Because these new invitees replicate the same terms in the preceding passage (14:13–14), which is uniquely Lukan material, this addition represents an intentional intertextual allusion on the part of the author and not part of the original Q parable. As a technique, we should note that a small internal change in the parable is used to stitch it into a new literary context, for the Lukan author has positioned the banquet parable within a larger section of stories about dinners, hosts, and guests told in a banquet setting (14:1–24). One of these is also called a "parable" about wedding banquets (14:7–11). As a result of these intertextual elements, the Lukan version begins to take on allegorical meaning as a reference to the gentile mission, a prominent theme in Luke-Acts.[92] It also then anticipates the complex set of three parables that follow in the next chapter, the lost sheep (15:1–7), lost coin (15:8–10), and lost or prodigal son (15:11–32).

The most dramatic alteration can be seen in the Gospel of Matthew, which transforms the parable into an allegory about a wedding banquet, a prominent eschatological metaphor in other Jewish apocalyptic.[93] In the *Rule of the Community* from Qumran, the communal meal of the Essene sect emulates the messianic banquet.[94] The eschatological overtones of this basic metaphor are reflected both in Markan tradition (2:19–20) and in Q (Luke 13:28–29; Matt 8:11–12). In order to make this transformation, the Matthean author has combined the great banquet parable with a separate parable about a man who attends a wedding without the proper clothes. We may call this the parable of the wedding garment (22:11–14). The Matthean version thus uses the setting of a wedding banquet given by a king for his son as the occasion for telling the two parables together. At the same time, the theme of the son and several other features within the parable serve as intertextual links to the preceding passage in Matthew, the parable of the wicked tenants (21:33–46), which in turn is derived from Mark (12:1–12).

The Matthean author has used these internal changes to stitch the combined parable/allegory into this new story frame. As we have already seen, when parables and allegories follow one after another in the Gospels, they tend to create even more complex intertextual allegorizations. In this case, the basic banquet parable has been modified so that the excuses have been compressed into a single generic statement, while the role of the servants who summon the guests has been expanded. Now some of the invited guests not only refuse to come to the banquet, but also seize the slaves, mistreat them, and kill them (22:6). This new element serves as an intertextual allusion to the parable of the wicked tenants, where the tenants seize the slaves of the landowner and even kill his son (21:35–36, 39).

Similarly, the enraged king's response ("he sent his troops, destroyed those murderers, and burned their city," 22:7) harks back to the wicked tenants (21:41); the burning of "their city" is an allusion to the destruction of Jerusalem in 70 CE. This is our first clue that these complex Matthean allegories are elaborate reflections on the death of Jesus in the light of the destruction of Jerusalem. Already in Q tradition, such stories refer to the killing of the prophets in ancient Israel turned as eschatological judgments against "this generation" (Matt 23:37–39/ Luke 13:34–35; Matt 23:29–31, 34–36/Luke 11:47–52).[95] This same theme continues in the next chapter of Matthew in the woes against the Pharisees (23:1–36), where most of these Q materials about "killing the prophets" are clustered in the Matthean version. Consequently, through these intertextual allegorizations the parables of the wicked tenants and the wedding banquet anticipate and prepare for this polemic.

The second part of the parable, the wedding garment, also has distinctive Matthean touches. Now the wedding hall has been filled, with "both good and bad." The most obvious is the ending, where the king now tells his servants to take the man without proper wedding clothes and "bind him hand and foot, and throw him into the outer darkness, where there will be weeping and gnashing of teeth" (22:13). Here again we see the Matthean fingerprints on the narrative; however, the seam appears at first to be rougher than in other places. After all, according to the first part of the parable, these newly invited guests have been brought in off the streets to fill the wedding hall. How could they be expected to have the proper garments? It is at this point that we see the sharper lines of yet a different parable with eschatological themes. The best example of this garment parable comes from rabbinic tradition, where it is attributed to Rabbi Johanan ben Zakkai, a disciple of Hillel who led the reconstruction after 70 CE.[96]

> R. Eleazer said: "Repent one day before your death."[97] His disciples asked him, "Does then one know on what day he will die?" "Then all the more reason that he repents today," he replied, "lest he die tomorrow, and thus his whole life is spent in repentance."
>
> And Solomon too said in his Wisdom, "Let thy garments be always white, and let not thy head lack ointment."[98]
>
> R. Johanan b. Zakkai said: "This may be compared to a king who summoned his servants to a banquet without appointing a time. The wise ones adorned themselves and sat at the door of the palace, [for] they said, 'Is anything lacking in a royal palace?' The fools went about their work, saying, 'Can there be a banquet without preparations?' Suddenly the king summoned his servants. The wise entered adorned [for the banquet], while the fools entered soiled. The king rejoiced at the wise but was angry with the fools. 'Those who adorned themselves

for the banquet,' he ordered, 'let them sit, eat, and drink. But those who did not adorn themselves for the banquet, let them stand and watch.'" (b. Sabb. *153a)*[99]

This Jewish parallel suggests that the so-called wedding garment is not meant to be a special set of clothes worn only at weddings, but clothes properly cleaned in honor of the festive occasion. It is the ancillary motifs of expectancy and preparation that give it eschatological dimensions.

Two other passages from the Gospels seem to reflect this same motif of preparedness for the wedding banquet. One is the familiar parable of the ten bridesmaids, which occurs only in the Gospel of Matthew (25:1–13).[100] Instead of having proper garments, however, their preparations involve having adequate oil for their lamps to await the bridegroom's delayed arrival. This parable has allegorical elements derived from the preceding apocalyptic discourse (24:36–44), and it follows immediately after another parable that ends with the uniquely Matthean "weeping and gnashing of teeth" (24:45–51).

Another version of the garment metaphor occurs in Luke:

Be dressed for action and have your lamps lit; be like those who are waiting for their master to return from the wedding banquet, so that they may open the door for him as soon as he comes and knocks. Blessed are those slaves whom the master finds alert when he comes; truly I tell you, he will fasten his belt and have them sit down to eat, and he will come and serve them. If he comes during the middle of the night, or near dawn, and finds them so, blessed are those slaves. (12:35–38)

Although this passage has no direct parallel in Matthew, it may well be derived from Q.[101] The following section of Luke (12:39–46) is clearly derived from Q and appears in Matthew in the two passages that precede the parable of the ten bridesmaids (24:43–51). So it is worth noting that this Lukan version explicitly mentions a "wedding banquet" and opens with an exhortation, "Be *dressed* for action and have your *lamps lit*" (12:35).

On this basis, we may surmise that the parable of the ten bridesmaids represents one of two Matthean allegorizations of this apocalyptic exhortation transposed to follow rather than precede the parallel warnings from Q. The emphasis on the lamps is more suited to the theme of the bridegroom's delayed arrival.[102] If so, then the simpler Lukan passage probably represents something close to the Q version of this saying.

Similarly, the Matthean author has created a second elaboration of this same apocalyptic exhortation by focusing on the dress or garment. It has been used to create both the beginning and the ending of the combined parable of the wedding banquet (22:2, 11–14). As a result of these intertextual allusions, the Matthean parable of the wedding banquet (22:1–14) serves as a major allegorical crux for the last of Jesus's "sermons" in that it anticipates both the woes against the Pharisees

(23:1–36) and the ending of the eschatological discourse followed by the parable of the ten bridesmaids (24:36–25:13). The whole section (23:1–25:13) then culminates with two other eschatological allegories, the parable of the talents (25:14–30), a combination of Markan and Q elements, and the allegory of the sheep and goats or last judgment (25:31–46), which is unique to Matthew.

As a result, the Matthean reshaping of the parables/allegories begun in chapter 13 (as a "sermon" of parables) establishes themes that run through the rest of the Gospel and build to this climactic ending in chapter 25, just prior to the beginning of the Matthean Passion narrative (26:1). The two parables, wicked tenants and wedding banquet (21:33–22:14), have been allegorized intertextually to set the stage for both. We shall return to this feature of the Matthean story of Jesus in Chapter 12.

A Matter of Style?

By way of conclusion, although miracle stories and sayings stories represent very different cultural backgrounds and story forms, their treatment in the Gospels has certain features in common. Each Gospel writer has certain patterns or tendencies in handling key types of material, and these tendencies allow the author to reshape the older oral traditions into new dramatic scenes. Above we called them the author's "fingerprints" on the narrative. If they were modern playwrights, they would be as distinctive as Tennessee Williams, Neil Simon, and Alan Bennett. Legendary film directors, like John Ford, Martin Scorsese, or Oliver Stone, each have certain favorite themes and subjects as well as characteristic ways of staging scenes. It is like the "palette" of an artist or the signature themes of a composer. Think of Van Gogh's "blue period" or Chagall's stained-glass effect. The movie scores of Elmer Bernstein or John Williams, even when they work in very different film genres, have their own distinctive qualities that show through. It is hard to miss the hand of John Barry, whether it's *Midnight Cowboy* (1969), *Moonraker* (1979), *Out of Africa* (1985), or *Dances with Wolves* (1990), and with directors as different as Sidney Pollack and Kevin Costner. Such signature features can also be used intentionally for effect, as when Elmer Bernstein reprises a variation of his *Magnificent Seven* theme (1960) in *Stripes* (1981). In other words, they each have something we obliquely call a "style," and the audience knows and recognizes it over time.

As we noted at the end of the last chapter, the particular treatment of miracles and sayings is often a package deal within each respective Gospel. For example, the Gospel of Mark stresses the complex and enigmatic quality of Jesus's miracles, but the parables, likewise, are intentionally enigmatic (4:10–12), and his teachings, like his miracles, are regularly misunderstood (8:14–21). In sharp contrast, the Gospel of Matthew tends to abbreviate the miracles found in Mark, but then adds in more elements about faith (14:22–33). In some cases, the miracles in Matthew become little more than the narrative setup for a saying about faith (17:14–21). In that sense, the Matthean miracle stories are really functioning as *chreiai* and emphasize Jesus as teacher.

Even the disciples look much smarter in Matthew than they do in Mark. In the case of the sayings, the Matthean author has typically expanded the Markan material by adding both Q sayings and a large number of uniquely Matthean sayings. As we saw in the case of the parable string in Matthew 13, the new shape given to these sayings takes them in a rather different direction than one finds in the briefer version in Mark 4. Certain themes—good and bad, apocalyptic judgment, "weeping and gnashing of teeth"—now dominate the message of the Matthean Jesus.

Thus, with both miracles and sayings, the distinctive reshaping by each author gives new meaning to these traditional materials. In each case, the audience is supposed to understand what is happening and get the message. At the same time, the reworkings each create a new image of Jesus. By watching the cues to how these scenes are shaped we are better able to understand what is going on in each Gospel on its own terms. In Act III we shall do just that. But before we do, there is one more component of distinctive—and very dramatic—storytelling that needs to be discussed. It is the story of Jesus's birth, which only occurs in the Gospels of Matthew and Luke. The two versions will also tell us something about the tastes, interests, and style of each author.

CHAPTER TEN

Plotting the Nativity

Now after they [the wise men] had left, an angel of the Lord appeared to Joseph in a dream and said, "Get up, take the child and his mother, and flee to Egypt, and remain there until I tell you; for Herod is about to search for the child, to destroy him." Then Joseph got up, took the child and his mother by night, and went to Egypt, and remained there until the death of Herod. This was to fulfill what had been spoken by the Lord through the prophet, "Out of Egypt I have called my son."

. . . When Herod died, an angel of the Lord suddenly appeared in a dream to Joseph in Egypt and said, "Get up, take the child and his mother, and go to the land of Israel, for those who were seeking the child's life are dead." Then Joseph got up, took the child and his mother, and went to the land of Israel. But when he heard that Archelaus was ruling over Judea in place of his father Herod, he was afraid to go there. And after being warned in a dream, he went away to the district of Galilee. There he made his home in a town called Nazareth, so that what had been spoken through the prophets might be fulfilled, "He will be called a Nazorean." (Matthew 2:13–15, 19–23)

In those days a decree went out from Emperor Augustus that all the world should be registered. This was the first registration and was taken while Quirinius was governor of Syria. All went to their own towns to be registered. Joseph also went from the town of Nazareth in Galilee to Judea, to the city of David called Bethlehem, because he was descended from the house and family of David. He went to be registered with Mary, to whom he was engaged and who was expecting a child. While they were there, the time came for her to deliver her child. And she gave birth to her firstborn son and wrapped him in bands of cloth, and laid him in a manger, because there was no place for them in the inn.

After eight days had passed, it was time to circumcise the child; and he was called Jesus, the name given by the angel before he was conceived in the womb. When the time came for their purification according to the law of Moses, they brought him up to Jerusalem to present him to the Lord. (Luke 2:1–7, 21–22)

All of the canonical Gospels contain a Passion narrative, miracles, and sayings stories, but only two of them, Matthew and Luke, contain birth narratives. Neither Mark nor John, the earliest and the latest of the four, mention anything about the nativity of Jesus. This omission perhaps seems odd to modern sensibilities, where such stories are more commonplace in biography; however, the Gospels do not belong to the modern genre of "biography."[1] In ancient "Lives," birth narratives— when they occur at all—tend to be added later and embellished over time, especially as famous figures, such as Alexander the Great or the emperor Augustus, grew to mythic stature. Some, but not all, might develop along the lines of the divine-man literature discussed in Chapter 3. Despite the relative sophistication of Greek and Roman medicine, in such literary treatments the details of childbirth were either left obscure or glossed by means of stereotyped scenes.[2] As birth stories developed, more emphasis was attached to surrounding events, such as dreams, portents, and astrological signs, that might be used as symbols or prognostications of the famous life ahead. In that way, birth narratives were typically written in retrospect and shaped thematically to anticipate known events or character traits from the person's later life and career.

In marked contrast to other elements of the Gospel stories, there is no underlying "oral tradition" for the nativity stories as such. It has been argued that earlier versions or traditions lie behind certain elements in the respective Matthean and Lukan birth narratives; however, each set is functionally specific to that Gospel alone (to be discussed below). In other words, they do not constitute a common ground of oral tradition from which the later Gospels then drew. Nor are there hints of extensive birth traditions to be seen in Paul or the Gospel of Mark.

For example, only two comments in the Pauline letters have significance for the later birth narratives. The first has to do with Jesus's Davidic lineage: "concerning his Son, who was descended from David according to the flesh and [who] was declared to be Son of God with power according to the spirit of holiness by resurrection from the dead, Jesus Christ our Lord" (Rom 1:3–4).[3] This formulation may have pre-Pauline roots, but it has at least been adapted by Paul, predicated on the "Son of God" title characteristic of Jewish messianic traditions (as discussed in Chapter 1).[4] More to the point, both of these phrases are dependant on the preceding statement about the "the gospel of God, which he promised beforehand through his prophets in the holy scriptures" (Rom 1:1–2).[5] As we saw in Chapter 6, the Jewish scriptures were a wellspring for the creation of later traditions.

The second is really a statement about Jesus's Jewishness: "But when the fullness of time had come, God sent his Son, born of a woman, born under the law, in order to redeem those who were under the law" (Gal 4:4–5). As most commentators agree, the phrase "born of a woman" was a common way of referring to humans in the Jewish scriptures. The comment says nothing about a preexisting state or about Jesus's mother.[6] As Raymond Brown says:

There is not the slightest hint here that Jesus was her "first born" (see Luke 2:7) or that she was a virgin. Paul simply does not mention the virginal conception, and there is no reason to think that he knew of it.[7]

It is not even clear that Paul knew much if anything about Jesus's mother, although he knew "James the Lord's brother" personally (Gal 1:19; 2:9). We must surmise, therefore, that interest in Jesus's birth, childhood, and family had not yet become a topic of interest, much less a story, among the early followers of Jesus for twenty to thirty years after his death.[8]

This fact is further attested in the slim treatment afforded Jesus's mother and family in the Gospel of Mark, written nearly twenty years after Paul. The mother and siblings of Jesus are mentioned three times, but his father is not mentioned at all. In the first two cases, Jesus's mother and siblings are not called by name, and they stand in opposition to Jesus and his ministry. In fact, they think Jesus is insane:

Then he went home; and the crowd came together again, so that they could not even eat. When his family heard it, they went out to restrain him, for people were saying, "He has gone out of his mind." (3:19–21)

On the whole, the Markan picture of Jesus's mother is generally more negative. A similarly negative statement regarding his family is found in John 7:5: "For not even his brothers believed in him."

These portrayals stand in sharp contrast to the pious and thoughtful Mary of the Lukan birth narrative, who accepted her role (1:38), extolled God (1:46–56), and "treasured all these words and pondered them in her heart" (2:19; cf. 2:52). Moreover, the Lukan narrative (at 11:14–16) deletes the "insanity" passage found in Mark 3:19–21 (quoted above) and removes all mention of his family in its heavily reworked version of the rejection at Nazareth episode (4:16–31). These narrative changes help support the more positive picture being generated by the Lukan birth narrative. In all probability, both pictures are later creations of the respective Gospel authors.

Missing Elements

Another striking feature of the birth narratives is what is not said. For most people today, familiarity with the nativity story comes from church traditions or popular expressions around the Christmas season—such as a crèche or a Christmas play, where the magi and shepherds typically stand side by side in front of a stable.[9] As a result, people are generally unaware that the two versions in Matthew and Luke are thoroughly different and mutually contradictory. For example, there are *no shepherds, manger, census,* or *travel to Bethlehem* in the Gospel of Matthew. In the Gospel of Luke there are *no magi, star, killing of babies,* or *flight to Egypt.* Some of these differences are reflected in the two passages quoted at the beginning of the chapter, and they will be discussed further in the next section. The popularized version is actually an interweaving of the two as a way of smoothing over the contradictions.

Numerous other elements now assumed to be central to the story are also missing. We hear nothing about the age of Mary or Joseph and nothing about their home life or family background. We are never told a date or time of year. We are not told how soon the magi arrived or how many magi (three or four?) there were. They are never identified as "kings," nor are they named. Many of these elements are legendary accretions that were superimposed on the Gospels in later centuries and proliferated through medieval Christian art and literature.[10]

Other characters, such as midwives or St. Catherine of Alexandria also enter the nativity scene. Many of them derive from later apocryphal Gospels, which will be discussed later. Then there are hymns and popular songs, coming down even to recent times, that continue to add new characters or other elements, such as the "little drummer boy."[11] But that is in part how the Gospels themselves began. Many such elements were born of popular piety and imagination in an early stage of the development of the story. Some arose out of efforts to harmonize the disparities between Matthew and Luke. Others grew up around the liturgical calendar and the cycles of worship for major holy days, especially during Advent and the Christmas season.

"The Ox and Ass Kept Time, pa-rum-pa-pum-pumm . . ."

A good example of added elements is the stable and animals, which arose as overlays on the Lukan narrative. An actual "stable" (whether a cave or building) is never mentioned in Luke. The word translated "manger" (2:7) literally means a crib or feed trough for animals, into which Jesus was laid. The "stable" as an enclosure for animals is thus an inference and may rely on the wording of Isaiah 1:3: "The ox knows its owner, and the donkey its master's crib; but Israel does not know, my people do not understand" (see below). The idea that it was a cave used as a sheep pen grew up around the legends associated with the Church of the Nativity built at Bethlehem by Helena Augusta, the mother of the emperor Constantine, in 324 CE. In turn, the cave goes back to Justin Martyr (mid-second century CE) based on using Isaiah 33:16 (in the Greek) as a messianic prophecy: "He will live in the heights; his stronghold, in a cave of rock. His bread will be provided for him, and his water shall be constant (or faithful)." The word "cave" only comes into this verse in the Septuagint.[12]

In the later Western tradition, however, the cave disappears because the word does not occur in the Latin of the Vulgate in Isaiah 33:16, which in turn is based more directly on the Hebrew. For this reason, the iconographic tradition of the West tends to portray the "manger" as a stable rather than a cave. Some later Greek traditions combine a cave and a stable, as seen in the apocryphal *Protevangelium of James* 22:1, where the holy family moves from the cave to a stable a few days after Jesus's birth to hide from Herod's assassins. (This Gospel will be discussed at length in Chapter 15.)

The animals first appear in early Christian art in the fourth century. They are usually an ox and ass, and sometimes sheep. The sheep are inferred from the shepherds mentioned in Luke, facilitated by a further imaginative supposition about the "stable." In particular it was suggested to be the stable belonging to these same shepherds, who just happened to be away "in the field" (Luke 2:8) at that time of year. The ox and the ass (or any other animals) are likewise unmentioned in the Lukan narrative. They apparently came from later efforts by patristic commentators, including Origen and Augustine, to use Isaiah 1:3 (quoted above) as a messianic prediction.

How was such a connection made? In the Septuagint the wording of the Isaiah passage may be read as "the ass knows its Lord's manger"; it uses the same Greek word for "crib" or "manger" as in Luke 2:7 and plays on the ambiguity of the word "lord/master."[13] Once again, we see the continuing use of the Jewish scriptures as a rich source for creating "prophetic" links (or proof texts) to the story. Eventually, these new elements come to be read back into story: the pregnant Mary must have ridden the ass to Bethlehem and later on to Egypt.[14]

"'Tis the Season . . ."

As is well known, there is no reference to a specific date for Jesus's birth in the canonical narratives. The usual date is now typically placed between 7 and 4 BCE. This conclusion is based on the fact that the Gospels of Matthew (2:1) and Luke (1:5, 26) both place the birth of Jesus during the reign of Herod the Great, who died in March of 4 BCE. Despite numerous efforts to narrow down this date based on astronomical phenomena—by way of using the "star" associated with the visit of the magi (Matt 2:2–10)—no satisfactory solutions have appeared.[15] In addition, the Matthean story of the return from Egypt (2:19–22) leaves the impression that the birth occurred some time—perhaps a few years—before Herod's death. In the Gospel of Mathew, Joseph and Mary are reported to have taken the infant Jesus away to Egypt, only to return after Herod's death, during the reign of his son Archelaus. Archelaus ruled Judea from 4 BCE to 6 CE. This information would place their return to Judea and eventual settlement in Galilee sometime before 6 CE, when Archelaus was deposed. From a historical perspective, that is about as close as we can come.

As for the time of the year, the shepherds out "in the field" in Luke (2:8) would suggest a date in the spring or early fall, but nothing more precise. In the early centuries speculation ranged from March 28 to January 6 and December 25. Epiphany, as it is called in the Greek Orthodox tradition (January 5–6), originally celebrated Jesus's birth and baptism.[16] In Roman churches December 25 was eventually chosen to celebrate Jesus's birth, while Epiphany (January 6) was used to commemorate the visit of the magi, again helping to interweave the two narratives. December 25 was the winter solstice according to the Roman calendar and also the birthday of Mithras. The date stuck in part because it helped "Christianize" the Roman cycle of seasonal festivals, and in part because it was based on a calculation of nine months from the annunciation to Mary, by then celebrated on March 25.[17] In the Roman calendar, March 25 marked the spring equinox and one of the Roman celebrations of the new year. This new Western Christian calendar of holy days was in place at Rome before the year 354 CE.[18]

Comparing the Plotlines

The first thing to note when comparing the birth narratives in Matthew and Luke is the massive disparity in length (see Box 10.1). The Matthean narrative is only 31 verses in total, and the portion describing the annunciation and birth proper takes only 8 verses (less than a third). By contrast, the Lukan narrative is 150 verses, over half of which (84 verses) are devoted to the annunciation and birth. In part this disparity is due to the fact that the Lukan narrative also incorporates the annunciation and birth of John the Baptist as a parallel narrative. Even so, the Lukan account of the annunciation and birth of Jesus alone is still twice as long as the entire Matthean story from beginning to end. The Lukan version is much more elaborate and dramatic at every turn, with more dialogue and long soliloquies by key characters (Zechariah, Mary, and Elizabeth) to punctuate the extensive narration. In sharp contrast, the Matthean account has very little direct dialogue, and none by the characters themselves. Even without these soliloquies, the Lukan narrative is still much longer than the Matthean, and the narrative style is built around the dialogic encounters.

Some scholars[19] have claimed that at least part of the additional material in Luke was based on a separate source about John; however, the parallelisms in the two narratives point to extensive Lukan compositional activity. The Lukan author effectively makes John and Jesus cousins, since their mothers, Elizabeth and Mary, are kin (1:36). This fact also seems to make Mary (like Elizabeth, 1:5) a descendant of Aaron and thus of the tribe of Levi (and not of Davidic descent).[20] There is no reference to such a relationship in the other canonical Gospels, and especially not in Matthew.[21] The Gospel of John (1:33) emphasizes the fact that John did not know Jesus until the baptism. Kinship between the two had no currency among other early Christians. This idea appears to be a Lukan creation, and with it the birth narrative immediately takes on a new shape, to which we shall return.

Next we note that the Matthean narrative focuses all the action on Joseph, while Mary is hardly mentioned (1:20–21; 2:11). She has no active role in the drama (cf. 2:14, 19). By contrast, Joseph has only a minor role in the Lukan narrative (2:4–5), and the bulk of the action is focused on Mary (cf. 2:48–49). The

BOX 10.1
Comparing the Birth Narratives

Matthew		Luke		
1:1–17	"Book of Generations" Genealogy		1:1–4	Formal Prologue no genealogy—see 3:23–38
1:18–25	Annunciation and Birth	A1	1:5–25	Annunciation of John the Baptist's birth
		B1	1:26–38	Annunciation of Jesus's birth (Nazareth)
		C1	1:39–56	Mary visits Elizabeth (*the Magnificat*)
		A2	1:57–80	Birth and circumcision of John
		A3		(*the Benedictus*)
		B2	2:1–8	Birth of Jesus *Census and Journey to Bethlehem*
			2:9–20	Angelic announcement to shepherds and their visit
2:1–12	Visit of wise men *NB: 2.11: "on entering the house"*	B3	2:21–38	Jesus circumcised (8th day); taken to Jerusalem; presentation at the Temple (*the Nunc Dimittis*)
2:13–18	Slaughter of Children and the flight to Egypt	B4	2:39–40	Return to Nazareth
			2:41–52	Jesus at the Temple at age twelve
2:19–23	Return to Judea, but settle in Nazareth because a son of Herod is on the throne	A4	3:1–20	John's ministry and death
		C2	3:21–22	Baptism of Jesus
			3:23–38	Genealogy (*Beginning of ministry*)

Matthean narrative operates through a series of brief statements about dreams in which Joseph is instructed by angels what to do at each turn. In each case, the result is then interpreted (by the narrator) as a fulfillment of prophecy. The Lukan account has direct visitations by the angel Gabriel, who converses at length with both Zechariah (1:10–20) and Mary (1:26–38). In both episodes, the angel's speech is liberally sprinkled with phrases taken from the Jewish scriptures, but in Greek, and these serve as "prophetic" indicators for what will take place. In the Gospel of Luke, therefore, it is the role of characters within the story, notably the angel Gabriel, to deliver most of the interpretation drawn from the scriptures. By contrast, in the Gospel of Matthew such uses of "prophecy and fulfillment" are delivered by the narrator instead, and with a fixed formula. Each Gospel is thus distinctive in both its narrative strategy and its use of a narrator to convey information. To answer why this is the case, we must examine the way each story is told.

In addition to these distinctive characteristics, there are key moments in each story that are contradictory at the narrative level. We may list the major points of disagreement as follows:

1. There are key differences in the two genealogies: the Matthean genealogy comes at the very beginning of the narrative (1:1–17) and contains forty-two generations from Abraham to Jesus, all using the formula "*A* was the father of *B*." These forty-two generations are then divided into three equal groups of fourteen each (1:17). The Lukan genealogy comes after the baptism by John (3:23–38) and serves as a break between the birth narrative and the beginning of Jesus's ministry. It reads in reverse order, from Jesus back to Adam, using the formula "*Y* was the son of *X*." It contains seventy-seven generations, fifty-six of which are in the same period covered by the Matthean genealogy; many of the names in this section do not match. More to the point, the name of Joseph's father (Jesus's "grandfather") is given as Jacob in Matthew (1:16), but Eli in Luke (3:23).[22]

2. The visit of the wise men (or magi) and the star are unique to Matthew, while the angelic chorus and the visit of the shepherds are unique to Luke. The magi in Matthew play a significant role in the drama surrounding Herod and the slaughter of the children. This threat leads to the flight to Egypt (2:13–23). In Luke there is no reference to a threat from Herod, and shortly after Jesus's birth and circumcision, his parents take him to the Temple in Jerusalem (2:21–38). Such an action would make no sense in the Matthean narrative and seems to be a distinctive Lukan invention.[23]

3. In Matthew the *magi* arrive at Bethlehem and find Jesus and Mary "on entering the house" (Matt 2:11). The Gospel of Luke clearly has Mary and

Joseph travel from Nazareth to Bethlehem for the census. Because there is no room for them in the local inn when the birth took place, Mary placed the child in the "manger" or feed crib (2:4–7). There is no reference to a house in the Lukan narrative, nor would it fit the narrative.[24]

4. In Matthew, Joseph and Mary are residents of Bethlehem and only move to Nazareth after returning from Egypt, as instructed in a dream. This move takes place after the death of Herod, but while his son Archelaus is king of Judea (2:19–23). As already noted above, the Gospel of Luke has Mary and Joseph living in Nazareth and only traveling to Bethlehem because of the census (2:4–5). They return "to their own town of Nazareth" (2:39) immediately after going to Jerusalem.

We may now analyze the literary and historical implications of these differences in greater detail.

"On Entering the House" (Matthew 2:11)

Several aspects of the two narratives are not merely different; they are mutually exclusive. That is to say, one set of actions makes the other set impossible to fit into a single narrative or historical framework. A good example of the problem is the "house" mentioned in Matthew 2:11 versus the inn and manger in Luke 2:7. Most traditional crèche scenes show the magi at the stable. But Matthew 2:11 clearly says that when the magi arrived they "entered the house." Whose house was it? When did they go there? Various explanations and fictions have been concocted over the centuries in an effort to harmonize these divergent stories.

One of the more common, as often reflected in art, is that Joseph and Mary arrived in Bethlehem after traveling from Nazareth, found no room in the inn, and the baby was born in a local stable, where the shepherds visited. Then sometime later, the magi arrived, but by then someone had felt sorry for the couple and had invited them into their house. The visit of the magi took place at this house. But with each effort to harmonize the two accounts, further problems arise. How much later did they move to this house? Was the visit of the magi before or after Jesus was circumcised (Luke 2:21)? And what does this do to the timing of Herod's order to kill the children?[25] This scenario would seem to take too long when compared with the narrow window of time afforded by the Lukan Gospel (less than forty days) before Joseph and Mary take Jesus to Jerusalem and then back to Nazareth.[26] How can we then accommodate the Matthean elements of the slaughter of the children and the flight to Egypt?

As the only reference to a physical location for the birth in the Matthean narrative, the house (2:11) is most naturally understood as the family home of Joseph (and his wife) in Bethlehem.[27] It supports the Matthean claim about Joseph's Davidic lineage. It is narratively consistent with the previous statement that

Joseph did as he was instructed in a dream, taking Mary as his wife even though she was pregnant (1:20). This statement presumes the prior condition of Matthew 1:18, which states that Mary was discovered to be pregnant "before they lived [or had come] together." The resolution of this plot movement comes in Matthew 1:24; "he took her as his wife" means he took her *to his home* in accordance with Judean marriage practice.[28] The continuation of this same sentence makes the point clearer still by affirming that she was now living with him in marital fashion, "but [he] had no marital [i.e., sexual] relations with her until she had borne a son" (1:25).[29] That their home was in Bethlehem is also consistent with the narrative of their return from Egypt, for they clearly intend to return to Judea, and specifically to their home in Bethlehem. They do not do so only because they hear that Archelaus, son of Herod, is ruling Judea, and they are instructed in a dream to go to Galilee instead. The Matthean narrative confirms this understanding by virtue of its sequence of steps; it says:

> But when he [Joseph] heard that Archelaus was ruling over Judea in place of his father Herod, he was afraid to go there. And after being warned in a dream, he went away to the district of Galilee. There he made his home in a town called Nazareth, so that what had been spoken through the prophets might be fulfilled. (2:22–23)[30]

In other words, the Matthean narrative makes it explicit that Nazareth did not become their home until after they returned from Egypt. But this moment in the story shows a great deal about the assumptions of the Matthean author in creating the geographic flow of the narrative. It moves from Bethlehem to Egypt, then back to Judea and then to Nazareth. By contrast, the geographic flow of the Lukan narrative is from Nazareth to Bethlehem to Jerusalem and back to Nazareth, and all within a very tight time frame. The Lukan itinerary does not allow for the visit of the magi, the slaughter of the children, or the flight to Egypt. The Matthean itinerary does not allow for the census, the journey to Bethlehem, or the birth in a manger.

The Census of Quirinius (Luke 2:1–5)

The census presents another well-known problem. Our major source for this period is the Jewish historian Josephus, who tells us that Archelaus, who succeeded his father, Herod, as ruler of Judea, was ultimately deposed in 6 CE. Judea was then annexed to the province of Syria.[31] Syria was at that point being governed by the proconsul P. Sulpicius Quirinius, the person mentioned in Luke 2:2. According to Josephus, Quirinius was ordered by the emperor to assess and liquidate the estates of Archelaus and to census the people of Judea for tax purposes (see Box 10.2). Then a lower-ranking procurator, Coponius, was sent to manage Judea while answering directly to Quirinius. Direct Roman rule had come to Judea for the first time.[32]

The Census of Quirinius

P. Sulpicius Quirinius

Publius Sulpicius Quirinius was from a less than noble family, but rose to the ranks of the Roman Senate due to his character, military career, and loyal service to the emperors Augustus and Tiberius. From the perspective of the Roman historian Tacitus, he was a model of duty and honor (Annals 3.22–23; 3.48). He was born in the 50s BCE and died ca. 22 CE. Aspects of his career are also recorded by the historians Suetonius (*Tiberius* 49) and Strabo (*Geography* 12.6.5).

He seems to have first come to the attention of Augustus and other leaders due to his military skills, having risen to the rank of praetor by ca. 15 BCE. At this point he embarked on the public career of a senator and was sent to govern the province of Crete-Cyrene, where there were local uprisings. By 12 BCE he was named consul of Rome. From 6 to 1 BCE he was governor of the province of Pamphylia-Galatia. He led a successful campaign against the Homanadenses, a tribe from upper Armenia allied with the Parthians, and received a "triumph" at Rome. In 2 CE he was named chief adviser to Augustus's grandson Gaius, who had been appointed commander of the East and governor of Syria.

In 6 CE he was appointed proconsul and legate of Syria and was delegated by Augustus to liquidate the estates of the deposed Archelaus, son of Herod, and census Judea. Judea was annexed to Syria as a second-order province. An equestrian procurator by the name of Coponius was sent to manage Judea, reporting to Quirinius. After his year of service, he retired to Rome, where he continued to be a favorite of the emperor Tiberius. The account of the census at this time is described explicitly by Josephus in *The Jewish War* 2.117–118 and *Antiquities* 17.355; 18.1–4, 23–26; 20.97, 102.

Josephus's Account of the Census in 6 CE

> *Now Quirinius, a man of Senatorial rank, when he had progressed through the other magistracies to the consulship, and who was extremely distinguished in other respects, arrived in Syria, dispatched by Caesar to dispense justice to the nation (i.e., govern) and to make a valuation of their property. And Coponius, a man of equestrian rank, was sent along with him to govern the Jews with all authority. Quirinius also came to Judaea, which had been annexed to Syria, to make a census (valuation) of their property and to liquidate the estate of Archelaus. (Antiquities 18.1–2)*

In *Antiquities* 18.26, Josephus says further that this occurred in "the 37th year after Caesar [Augustus] defeated Antony at Actium." The Battle of Actium took place in 31 BCE. Both Quirinius and the census are mentioned in the epitaph of one of his officers, Q. Aemilius Secundus, who died ca. 14 CE (*ILS* 2683):

> *Quintus Aemilius Secundus, son of Quintus, of the tribe Palatina, in the military contingent of the Divine Augustus under P. Sulpicius Quirinius, legate of Caesar for Syria, decorated with honors, Prefect of the First Augustan Cohort and Prefect of the Second Naval Cohort, by order of the same Quirinius I took a census of the city of Apamea, a city of 117,000 citizens. By the same Quirinius I was sent to fight the Ituraeans in the Libanus Mountains, and I captured their citadel. Before military service I was praefect of builders under two consuls, assigned to the treasury, and in the colony (of Venatus?) [I served] as quaestor, aedile, twice, duovir, and pontifex.*
>
> *Here are buried Quintus Aemilius Secundus, son of Quintus, of the tribe Palatina, and Aemilia Chia, his freedwoman [wife]. This tomb shall not succeed to any others but heirs.*

Quirinius's governorship in Syria in 6–7 CE is also documented by coins and other inscriptions.

The Governors of Syria

It has sometimes been argued that there was an earlier census of Judea or that Quirinius might have served as governor of Syria more than once. Neither of these claims has any historical merit. On the first, there was no need for a census of Judea so long as Herod or one of his sons was on the throne. Augustus's census edict only applied to provinces governed directly by Rome, not client-kingdoms. On the second, the names of the governors of Roman Syria are now nearly complete between the years 23 BCE and 17 CE. They are as follows:

23–13 BCE	M. Agrippa
13–11 BCE	?
ca. 10 BCE	M. Titius
9–6 BCE	S. Sentius Saturninus
6–4 BCE (? later)	P. Quintilius Varus
4–2 BCE	?
2/1 BCE –4 CE	Gaius Caesar
4–5 CE	L. Volusius Saturninus
6/7 CE	P. Sulpicius Quirinius
12–17 CE	Q. Caecilius Creticus Silanus

(continued)

During this entire period of forty years, the name of the governor is not known in only two intervals totaling four years, as shown above. In both cases, however, it is impossible for Quirinius to have been the "unnamed" governor, since his appointments and whereabouts are known to be elsewhere. In the period 13–11 BCE, he was serving as consul in Rome, and in the period 4–2 BCE, he was serving as governor of Pamphylia-Galatia and leading the campaign against the Homanadenses, for which he won a "triumph" in Rome. Thus, Quirinius cannot have held an earlier governorship in Syria.

FURTHER READING

Brown, R. E. *The Birth of the Messiah.* Garden City, NY: Doubleday, 1977. 547–56 (app. vii).

Fitzmyer, J. *The Gospel According to Luke.* 2 vols. Anchor Bible 28. Garden City, NY: Doubleday, 1981. 1:399–405.

Levick, B. *Roman Colonies in Southern Asia Minor.* Oxford: Clarendon, 1967. 203–14 (app. V).

Moehring, H. R. "The Census in Luke as an Apologetic Device." In D. E. Aune, ed., *Studies in the New Testament and Early Christian Literature.* Leiden: Brill, 1972. 144–60.

Potter, D. S. "Quirinius." *Anchor Bible Dictionary.* New York: Doubleday, 1981. 5:588–89.

Schmitz, P. C. "Census, Roman." *Anchor Bible Dictionary.* 1:883–85.

Sherwin-White, A. N. *Roman Law and Roman Society in the New Testament.* Oxford: Clarendon, 1963. 162–71.

Syme, R. "The Titulus Tiburtinus." In *Vestigia: Akten des VI Internationalen Kongresses für Griechische und Lateinische Epigraphik,* 1972. Munich: Beck, 1973. 585–601.

Roman coins and historical records confirm the fact that the Quirinius mentioned in Luke was the provincial legate of Syria in 6–7 CE. Inscriptions from Syria confirm the fact that he ordered a census at this time. Josephus tells us further that this census was the spark that set off the first wave of anti-Roman rebellion, led by a famous local chieftain named Judas the Galilean:

> *Now when the region of Archelaus was delimited to a province, a procurator of the equestrian order, Coponius, was soon sent by the Romans, having received full authority by Caesar, even for capital punishment. Under him a certain man, a Galilean named Judas, led the people of his region into rebellion.*[33]

The rebellion led by this Judas the Galilean "in the days of the census" is also mentioned in Acts 5:37. The author of Luke-Acts thus clearly knows the connection between the census and the rebellion of Judas, both of which took place in 6 CE. Yet the same author also places the birth of Jesus at the time of the census of Quirinius (Luke 2:1–5), and thus a full decade *after* the death of Herod.

On the other hand, a census in 6 CE is clearly at odds with the Matthean version of the birth of Jesus and produces several historical problems for the story in Luke:

> As long as Herod or one of his heirs was on the throne of Judea as client-king appointed by the emperor, there was no reason to conduct a census.[34]

The king alone was responsible for the taxes owed to Rome; how they were collected did not concern the emperor.

In 6 CE, after the removal of Archelaus, Quirinius would have only been commissioned to census Judea (not the Galilee), since only Judea had been brought under his jurisdiction. The Galilee remained a Jewish client-kingdom under Herod Antipas, another son of Herod the Great, until 37 CE.[35]

Antipas is the other "Herod" mentioned in the Gospels, who was responsible for the death of John the Baptist, and before whom Jesus was also tried, at least according to Luke. In this last incident (Luke 23:6), the Lukan author shows a clear awareness of jurisdictional prerogatives of the Herodian client-king of the Galilee over against the Roman governor of Judea.[36]

There is no evidence from other Roman provinces to suggest that residents of one area would be required to return to their native home in another province in order to register for a tax census.[37]

The census would place the birth of Jesus well after the death of Herod the Great.[38] Yet there is no evidence for an earlier census in Judea or for an earlier governorship of Quirinius in Syria[39] (see Box 10.2).

Taken together, these facts show that the census was a new imposition in 6 CE and only in the region of Judea. It did not affect the Galilee, where the Lukan author says Joseph and Mary were living at the time. In the end, it does not fit the historical circumstances for the birth of Jesus, nor does it fit with the Lukan claim that the birth took place during the lifetime of Herod the Great (Luke 1:5, 26).

Despite efforts of some scholars to account for some sort of "confusion" on the part of the Lukan author, the story seems, rather, to be a conscious Lukan invention. But why? Raymond Brown offers the following explanation:

> *Even if Luke was inaccurate on the dating of the census of Quirinius and mistakenly thought that it could have been associated with the birth of Jesus, we must recognize that the association enabled Luke to explain why Joseph and Mary were in Bethlehem when the child was born. It also served admirably the interests of Lukan theology, giving the nativity a backdrop of world and Israelite history.*[40]

In other words, the story of the census is primarily a literary and theological device for the Lukan author. It serves as an explanation of how Jesus could have been born in Bethlehem but "came" from Nazareth.

The Slaughter of the Children (Matthew 2:13–23)

A similar conclusion emerges from the story of the slaughter of the children and the resultant flight to Egypt, both of which are unique to the Gospel of Matthew.

The first point to note is that the slaughter of the children is suspect on historical grounds. Other than this passage in the Gospel of Matthew, there is no other historical record that such an event occurred at any time during the reign of Herod or his sons. Josephus carefully documents the final, rather tragic years of Herod's life, especially his ruthless treatment of his own sons. Several of them were killed or executed publicly due to Herod's paranoia about plots to overthrow him. In each case, however, the son was already an adult. Josephus never mentions a massacre of other children, and especially not a conscious campaign to target "children [lit., boys] age two and under in and around Bethlehem"[41] (Matt 2:16). One would think that such an unusual and horrifying event would have left some historical traces.[42] As a result, Raymond Brown, among many others, considers this story to be a Matthean creation, a case of literary *verisimilitude:*

> *And so once more we are led to verisimilitude. There are serious reasons for thinking that the flight to Egypt and the massacre at Bethlehem may not be historical. Yet, at the same time, if one can trace the basic story to another origin, there are good clues to why it has been cast in its present form.*[43]

By verisimilitude Brown means a story that gives the appearance of being real when it is not, and more specifically one that creates its aura of "factuality" by being based on some other, usually well-known, legend or event. In fact, both elements come from the Moses tradition. Brown argues that Matthew's version is modeled directly on the story of Moses's birth and the pharaoh's attempt to kill all the male children of the Israelites age two and under (Exod 1:22–2:4). Thus, the age of the male children comes from the Moses tradition and serves as a literary allusion rather than as a temporal framework for the Matthean narrative.[44] Most scholars would agree.[45]

The prophecy-fulfillment quotations so characteristic of the Matthean birth narrative also point to the Moses-Joshua (or Egypt-Exodus) tradition as background for the story. These motifs can be seen clearly in the slaughter of the children and flight to Egypt sequence:

> *This was to fulfill what had been spoken by the Lord through the prophet, "Out of Egypt have I called my son." (Matt 2:15)*

This quotation is taken from Hosea, where it is clearly a reference to the Exodus; the "son" or "child" mentioned there is explicitly Israel itself: "When Israel was a child I loved him, and out of Egypt I called my son" (11:1). This retrospective statement of Hosea is thus transformed by the Matthean author into a "prophecy" to predict the movements of Joseph, Mary, and Jesus at the level of the narrative. The return from Egypt and detour to Nazareth is similarly cited as a fulfillment of scripture: "He will be called a Nazorean" (Matt 2:23). It is based loosely on the wording of Isaiah 11:1, likewise taken out of context: "A shoot shall come from the stump of Jesse, and a branch shall grow out of his roots."[46]

Bethlehem and Nazareth

It appears, then, that both the Lukan and Matthean authors have freely created scenes that propel the geographical flow of the narrative and the travel of the characters within the story. At the same time, the resultant plotline in Matthew is radically different from that in Luke. They are, in fact, narratively incompatible. In Matthew Herod's slaughter of the children drives Joseph to take Mary and the infant Jesus from their home in Bethlehem to Egypt. Later they return to Judea, intending to move back to Bethlehem, but they settle in Nazareth instead on hearing that Herod's son is the ruler of Judea. By contrast, in Luke the census drives Joseph to take the pregnant Mary from their home in Nazareth to Bethlehem, where the birth of Jesus occurs in some sort of stable. Then in forty days or less they return home to Nazareth by way of Jerusalem.

The only common element is that both authors seem intent on having Jesus born in Bethlehem, in order to affirm his Davidic lineage, while having him grow up and come from Nazareth when he embarks on his ministry. As we noted earlier, Davidic lineage is one of the few elements of earlier oral tradition about Jesus's origins to be seen in Paul. Davidic lineage was widely assumed as a feature of Jewish messianic expectation.[47] Hence the two accounts of how the birth occurred in Bethlehem, combined with the respective genealogies, reflect distinct mechanisms for narrativizing the idea of Jesus's descent from David.

At the same time, the fact that Jesus was known to be a Galilean from Nazareth is central to all the Gospel narratives, especially the Passion tradition. This fact would seem to be incontrovertible on historical grounds.[48] Thus, the two localities, Bethlehem and Nazareth, geographically anchor the story of Jesus's birth. Yet each author has chosen to create his "dual citizenship" by different, and even contradictory, narrative devices.[49] Within each Gospel the continuity of the story and the itinerary is rather seamless, as the remainder of the narrative is adjusted accordingly. In each case, the narrative supports the themes and theological motifs of that particular author. The problem arises only when one compares the two accounts both at the level of narrative and in the light of known historical facts. Having done so, we may now turn to examine the main lines of the story in each birth narrative by focusing on their distinct literary designs.

The Matthean Story

The genealogy (Matt 1:1–17) serves as the introduction to the Matthean birth narrative. It opens with an allusion to the genealogical formula ("an account of the genealogy [or generations]") characteristic of Genesis.[50] It concludes with Joseph, the father of Jesus. Following the genealogy, the literary structure of the Matthean birth narrative is built around three occasions on which Joseph is instructed in a dream what he should do next. The structure and phrasing of the three scenes are very similar. In each case he is told to "take Mary" or "take the child and his mother" and do something. Then the event is interpreted by the narrator as a fulfillment of prophecy. These Joseph scenes are then interwoven with the stories of the magi and the slaughter of the children, both of which use Herod as their dramatic foil. The birth narrative may thus be divided into six key scenes as follows:[51]

A.	1:	1:18–25	First angelic dream, instructing Joseph to take Mary as his wife even though she was pregnant; annunciation.
	2:	2:1–6	Herod and the magi (the star); birth of Jesus.
	3:	2:7–12	The magi visit Bethlehem (the star) and venerate Jesus, but are warned in a dream not to return to Herod.
B.	1:	2:13–15	Second angelic dream, instructing Joseph to take Mary and the baby to Egypt because of Herod.
	2:	2:16–18	Herod orders the slaughter of children.
	3:	2:19–23	Third and fourth angelic dreams, instructing Joseph to return to Judea, and then to go away to Galilee instead.

Although unequal in length, these six scenes fall into two "acts" of three scenes each. The first three (A) deal with the birth of Jesus and adoration of the magi; the second three (B) deal with the flight to Egypt, slaughter of the children, and relocation to Nazareth. In this sense, the two acts deal with two different questions: the first (A) with "who and where" Jesus is at birth; the second (B) with "who and where" Jesus will be as he grows up to begin his ministry in chapter 3.[52]

Was There a "Pre-Matthean" Birth Story?

Raymond Brown and others have argued that underlying this Matthean composition lies an earlier oral tradition regarding Jesus's birth.[53] His reconstruction of this "pre-Matthean" tradition involves five scenes built around dreams:

a. Joseph's dream regarding Mary and the birth

b. Herod's dream regarding the birth of the Messiah at Bethlehem

c. Joseph's dream telling him to flee (to Egypt?)

d.   Herod's dream telling him to kill the children

e.   Joseph's dream telling him to return to Israel

Notably, this supposedly earlier tradition does *not* contain the story of the magi and the star. Instead, the dreams alternate in parallel between Joseph and Herod. Brown himself argues that the story of the magi was added by the Matthean author based on the Balaam story in Numbers 24 (to be discussed below).[54] He argues that the prophecy and fulfillment citations, now so prominent in the Matthean plot, were likewise later additions by the Matthean author rather that deriving from a "pre-Matthean" tradition.[55] Yet he concedes that *"Any pre-Matthean material has been edited so thoroughly that we cannot get behind the Matthean wording."*[56] In other words, this reconstruction of a "pre-Matthean" core is, as he admits, "partial and approximate" at best.[57]

Other scholars would go farther in identifying components that might or might not derive from a "pre-Matthean" source. In the final analysis, it must be concluded that even if some of these elements are "pre-Matthean" in relation to the present form of the Gospel, they probably belong to an earlier stage of the evolution of the Matthean tradition itself. In turn, it has been subsequently revised and modified to bring out key literary and theological ideas. In the end, we should not call it a "pre-Matthean" birth narrative at all. As we have it, then, the birth narrative is a thoroughly Matthean composition, although likely in several stages.

Literary Patterns in the Matthean Script

From this perspective, several literary patterns may be identified as part of the Matthean composition. Here we are working with the outline of the six scenes sketched above as we now have them in their fully developed form.

- The three scenes involving Joseph serve to open and close the birth narrative (A.1 and B.3) as well as to open the second act (B.1). Each of these scenes involves a dream, and the structure and phrasing of the three scenes are very similar.[58]

- Inserted between these are the two scenes involving Herod (A.2, B.2), each of which stands at the center of its act and serves to drive the action narratively. These two scenes involving Herod are also tied to one another by virtue of the prophetic elements that announce the birth of a new king (A.2), followed by Herod's efforts to kill the newborn king (B.2).

- Also, each act is framed by two scenes with dreams, especially the angelic dreams to Joseph (in A.1, B.1, and B.3). One is a small note (at the end of A.3) to indicate that the magi were "warned in a dream not to return to Herod" (2:12), which is very similar to the last one to Joseph in B.3 (2:22).

Consequently, the angelic dreams serve as a second major force driving the action.

- Finally, each of these six scenes is punctuated by some sort of prophecy-fulfillment statement. Five of them (A.1, A.2, B.1, B.2, B.3) employ some form of the citation formula "this took place to fulfill what was spoken/written by the prophet." Three of them occur in the Joseph dream scenes (A.1, B.1, B.3), while two occur in the scenes involving Herod (A.2, B.2).

Although only one scene—the star and the magi (A.3)—does not contain the explicit prophecy-fulfillment formula, it does contain important prophetic elements. In effect, this particular scene stands at the center of the entire birth narrative and serves as the major symbolic statement of the Matthean author regarding the identity of Jesus as the long-awaited Jewish messiah. We shall return to this central scene at the end of this section.

The Matthean Theme of Prophecy and Fulfillment

Before turning to an analysis of the important central scene, a brief comment is in order regarding the scriptures used in the Matthean prophecy-fulfillment citations. As has already been noted, in their original form none of these scriptures refer directly to Jesus or aspects of his birth. The flight to Egypt (2:15) is derived from Hosea 11:1, where it was originally a reference to the Exodus itself. The Matthean appropriation requires Hosea's retrospection on Israel's past to become a future prediction; the "son" shifts from Israel itself to the future messiah. The move to Nazareth (2:23) is derived from Isaiah 11:1, where it is originally a reference to the Davidic line in the days of Hezekiah. The Matthean appropriation relies on a wordplay, as the word "root" (*nezer*) in the original Hebrew is transformed into "Nazorean" (*nozri*).

The virginal conception (1:23) is derived from Isaiah 7:14, where it was originally a statement about a contemporaneous event in Isaiah's own time, probably the birth of the future king Hezekiah himself. As is widely known, the original wording of Isaiah 7:14 in the Hebrew reads: "a *young woman is* pregnant and will bear a son." The shift to the word "virgin" and the change of tenses (from present to future) both depend on the Septuagint, but have been further modified to fit into the Matthean structure.[59]

This pattern of formulaic citation of scriptures appears throughout the Gospel of Matthew. Consequently, all of the prophecy-fulfillment citations in Matthew are part of the Matthean design and composition of the narrative. They are almost all based on the Greek of the Septuagint, albeit with modifications of the wording in some cases. In each instance they are carefully selected and adapted to give the actions described an aura of verisimilitude. Yet the Matthean technique of using scriptures is not unusual; it was common in other forms of Jewish writing at the time, including the Dead Sea Scrolls. Consequently, the pattern of reinterpreting scriptures to signify a new meaning, especially through apocalyptic expectations, had already been established.[60] The prophecy-fulfillment citations reflect a major component of the Matthean theological agenda in shaping the image of Jesus. Within in the birth narrative, at least, they also establish an important structuring element to the narrative. Most of them revolve around traditions associated with David or Moses, while one (Hos 11:1, as used in Matt 2:15) clearly evokes the Exodus story.

Enter the Magi: The Central Scene

We may now turn to the underlying features of the scene featuring the magi and the star to show how two important Jewish traditions—Moses and the messiah—are being woven together in a unique way by the Matthean author. It is worth noting that the actual birth of Jesus is not described at all; it is only mentioned in passing as the occasion for the appearance of the "wise men," or magi. The magi themselves represent foreign astrologers "from the East" (2:1), probably meaning Babylonia/Persia or Arabia.[61] The word *magus* means "magician" and could be used positively or negatively in antiquity. The use of astrological phenomena as portents or predictions was commonplace in the Greco-Roman world, but Babylonian and later Persian astrologers were renowned.

The magi are fitted into the narrative in order to bring the star into the story, which they then interpret as a messianic portent. Because they are not Jewish, their subsequent actions in venerating Jesus are meant to show that they take this indicator of his identity seriously. At the same time, their main function within the narrative is to hark back to older Jewish traditions, and thus they are another, more subtle form of prophecy fulfillment.

For example, the actions they perform when they come to venerate Jesus in Bethlehem, already confirmed as the proper birthplace for the messiah (2:5–6), include "kneeling down to worship him" and "offering gifts of gold, frankincense, and myrrh" (2:11). These two gestures function as unmarked scriptural allusions, especially when we look at the Septuagint version of each passage. One comes from Psalm 72(71):10–11:

> *The kings of Tarshish and the isles shall <u>bring forth gifts;</u> the kings of Arabia and Saba shall offer <u>gifts.</u> All kings shall <u>kneel down before him;</u> all nations shall serve him.*[62]

This passage was clearly understood in later centuries as background to the magi story and probably is the source for the later tradition of calling them "kings."

The second comes from Isaiah 60:6, also from the Septuagint:

Herds of camels shall cover you; the camels of Midian and Gapha. All those from Saba [Sheba?] shall come <u>bearing gold, and frankincense shall they bring</u>. They shall <u>tell the good news</u> of the Lord's salvation.

This passage probably helped put the camels into the traditional iconography of the magi. In this case the phrasing in Greek has elements that differ markedly from the Hebrew, notably the last phrase. It uses the pregnant Greek word "to tell the good news" (*euangelizein*), which becomes a code word in Christian usage for the "gospel" of Jesus. Taken together with the other allusions (kneeling and offering gifts), it frames the event of the *magi's* visit so as to signal the momentous import of Jesus's birth as the "beginning of the gospel" (see Matt 2:2; cf. Mark 1:1).

"We Observed His Star at Its Rising" (Matthew 2:2)

The astrological sign of the star turns out to be the key component—but not in the way most people assume. It is not an actual astronomical event; rather, it comes from literary verisimilitude.[63] It is based upon yet another scriptural allusion that has been narrativized into the story. This time it is Numbers 24:15–17, again from the Greek version of the Septuagint:[64]

> *And when he [Balaam] had received his proverb, he spoke: "Says Balaam son of Beor, says the man who sees truly—the one who hears the <u>oracle</u> of the Lord, the one who knows the knowledge of the Most High, the one who sees the vision of the Lord in dreams, the one whose eyes are opened by revelation: 'I will show him, but not now; I bless him, and he is not near; <u>a star shall rise out of Jacob and a man out of Israel shall be raised up.</u>'"*

The oracle of Balaam was a famous story from the wilderness wanderings after the Exodus from Egypt. It is part of the Moses/Exodus tradition. Balaam was a foreign diviner who was called out to curse Israel, but he received an oracle from the God of Israel and blessed it instead. The passage above is part of this blessing oracle. This is where the star becomes important, for the text of Matthew twice refers to the magi seeing the "star at its rising" (2:2; 2:9). This phrase in Matthew (*astēr en tē anatolē*) implies rising "in the East" and uses a form of the same Greek word found in the Septuagint of the Balaam oracle for the "rising" of the star out of Jacob (*anatelei astrōn ex Jakob*).

Once again, the Septuagint version changes the text in significant ways from that of the Hebrew and thus sets the stage for the Matthean appropriation. Notably, in the Hebrew, the last phrase reads "a scepter shall rise in Israel." The Hebrew word "scepter" (or "rod") here is the same found in Psalm 2:9 (the royal coronation psalm) as a prominent symbol of the Davidic king (cf. Isa 11:4).[65] In the Greek this phrase has been replaced by "*a man* out of Israel *shall be raised up.*"[66] Whereas in the original Hebrew it functioned as a sign of the coming Davidic dynasty retrojected as a "prophecy" from the Exodus, in the Greek it could be taken as a later man of Israel being "raised up" *as king,* thus pointing to the future messiah.[67]

That it was read this way through the lens of apocalyptic is exemplified by its use in coining Bar Kochba's messianic name, "Son of the Star."[68] More important, apocalyptic reinterpretation of the Balaam oracle as "messianic prediction" was already at work long before the time of Jesus. It occurs, for example, in the *Testament of the Twelve Patriarchs* (first century BCE):

> *And after this there shall arise for you a Star from Jacob in peace: And a man shall arise from my posterity like the Sun of righteousness, walking with the sons of men in gentleness and righteousness, and in him will be found no sin. And the heavens will be opened upon him to pour out the spirit as a blessing of the Holy Father. And he will pour the spirit of grace upon you. And you shall be sons in truth, and you will walk in his first and final decrees. This is the Shoot of God Most High; this is the fountain for the life of all humanity. Then he will illumine the scepter of my kingdom, and from your root will arise the Shoot, and through it will arise the rod of righteousness for the nations, to judge and to save all that call on the Lord. (T. Jud. 24)*

The underlined portions of the text reflect quotations or paraphrases of either lines from Numbers 24 (in the first sentence) or typical "messianic" phrases from Psalm 2 or Isaiah 7–11.[69] This cluster of messianic symbols, signaled by the star, will resound through the rest of the Matthean story as well. In other words, reading the Balaam oracle in this manner was already an established Jewish tradition long before Jesus. The author of the Gospel of Matthew has merely adapted the same allusions to fit more precisely to the story of Jesus. Or to put it another way, the story of the magi has been crafted narratively by the Matthean author to create the sense that Jesus's birth fulfills this particular "prophecy."

At the same time, the phrase "man shall be raised up" as rendered in the Septuagint might be understood as a man from Israel being "raised up" *from the dead.* The word "to raise up" (*anastēnai*) used here in the Septuagint is the same word used by Paul and the Gospel of Mark to refer to the resurrection of Jesus.[70] The double entendre was not likely overlooked by the early Christians. Thus, the "star at its rising" could be taken as a symbolic allusion to this passage now understood as a "prophecy" of *both* Jesus's birth *and* his death.

By way of conclusion, it is worth noting that in his *Life of Moses* Philo explicitly calls Balaam both a *mantic* (i.e., oracle) and a *magus* (using the same Greek word as Matthew) who came from Mesopotamia (i.e., Babylonia)—"a far journey from the East."[71] Thus, the magi of Matthew strongly resemble Balaam, an oracular prophet who travels "from the East" to announce a blessing on Israel. While this text carries connotations of the Davidic dynasty consistent with other elements in the Matthean motifs of Bethlehem and the prophecy-fulfillment citations, it adds a new dimension by bringing in the Moses and Exodus traditions. The Moses and Exodus traditions are clearly signaled in the following Matthean scenes of the slaughter of the children and the flight to Egypt. Here it must also be remembered that it was another Joseph, the son of Jacob, who went down into Egypt and was the forebear of Moses.[72]

The Matthean Jesus: Davidic and Mosaic

The conscious blending of these two motifs—David/Messiah and Moses/Exodus —now signals something more subtle and more powerful about the Matthean construction of the birth of Jesus: he is not only from the lineage of David, as both the genealogy and his birth in Bethlehem had already affirmed, but he is also from the legacy of Moses and the Exodus. This messiah, it wants to say, is more than just a Davidic king; he is the "prophet like Moses" whom God will raise up in later days (Deut 18:15).[73] Of course, the text of Deuteronomy originally pointed to Joshua as Moses's immediate successor, but it had already been taken over in some forms of Jewish apocalyptic expectation. For the Matthean audience, however, the verse must also have been taken as pregnant with symbolism, for the name Jesus (*Iēsous*) is the standard Greek form in the Septuagint for the traditional Jewish name Joshua (Heb. *Jehoshua*, later *Jeshua*). By weaving these elements together, the Matthean author has created a more complex set of expectations about the character of Jesus that will be played out in the rest of the Gospel. He will be both the awaited Davidic messiah *and* the anticipated "prophet like Moses."[74] We shall return to this double image of Jesus in Chapter 12.

The Lukan Story

The Gospel of Luke opens with a formal prologue (1:1–4) that announces the literary aspirations of the author. It leads directly into the birth narrative beginning at 1:5. On a formal level, at least, the birth narrative continues through to the baptism of Jesus (3:21–22), which is followed by the Lukan genealogy (3:23–38).[75] The genealogy then serves as a break between this "extended birth narrative" and the beginning of Jesus's public ministry, commencing with the temptation story (4:1–13). Both the style and structure of the Lukan nativity are more polished and florid as narrative prose. The description of scenes and actions is nothing like the terse, formulaic style of Matthew. Instead, it is flowing and dramatic, punctuated by long sections of direct dialogue. Three of these—traditionally known as the *Magnificat* (1:46–55), the *Benedictus* (1:67–79), and the *Nunc Dimittis* (2:29–32)—are virtually operatic in tone and function as hymnic interludes in the narrative. Even relatively minor characters who never appear in the other Gospels, such as the old man Simeon and the prophet Anna (2:25–38), are given detailed treatment. Simeon delivers one of the key hymnic soliloquies (the *Nunc Dimittis*) that serve as defining moments in the story.

A Double Birth Narrative

Adding to the highly stylized character of the prose is the complex plotline that interweaves the birth stories of Jesus and John the Baptist (see Box 10.1). The two stories are told in tandem: the annunciation of John's birth followed by the annunciation of Jesus's birth; the birth and circumcision of John followed by the birth and circumcision of Jesus. In both cases the mother's pregnancy is unexpected; the birth, a cause célèbre and the occasion for prophetic revelations. The Jerusalem Temple serves as the primary stage for principal scenes dealing with John (1:5–25) and Jesus (2:22–38; 2:41–52), respectively, thereby framing the birth narrative proper and anticipating key events at the end of the Gospel (24:53) and the beginning of Acts (2:46). The main scenes may thus be outlined as follows:

Act 1: The Annunciations
    a. Annunciation of John's birth (1:5–25)
    b. Annunciation of Jesus's birth (1:26–38)
    c. Mary visits Elizabeth (1:39–56)

Act 2: The Births
    a. Birth of John (1:57–80)
    b. Birth of Jesus (2:1–20)
    c. Circumcision, visit to the Temple, and return to Nazareth (2:21–40)

Act 3: The Preparatory Years
    a. Jesus in the Temple at age twelve (2:41–52)
    b. John's ministry begins (3:1–20)
    c. Jesus comes to John to be baptized (3:21–22)

The two birth stories are not only made to parallel one another, but also to intersect at two key moments in the story: the visit of the pregnant Mary to John's mother, Elizabeth (1.c, 1:39–56), and the visit of Jesus to John at his baptism (3.c, 3:21–22). Meanwhile, the whole story is set on a grander stage, as Roman imperial notices twice mark the birth narrative with reference to Jesus and John, respectively (2:1–2; 3:1–3). The Lukan birth narrative is thus a complex and highly crafted literary effort.

It has sometimes been proposed that the double birth narrative reflects two distinct source traditions that have been woven together by the Lukan author.[76] One of these putative sources is a tradition about John the Baptist, sometimes suggested to come from followers of John. The other putative source concerns the birth of Jesus alone; it supposedly came from Mary herself, or so it has been claimed.[77] But the dramatic parallels between the two stories and the way the poetic or hymnic materials, largely based on septuagintal language, are woven into both narratives argue against fully developed sources materials, let alone "eyewitness" traditions from Mary or anyone else. Although there may be some pre-Lukan traditions, such as the names of John's parents, the stories themselves are largely Lukan compositions.

Brown argues further that there were two distinct stages in the Lukan composition: first, a basic narrative, and later, an overlay of florid additions.[78] In this view, the basic narrative includes the interwoven parallel annunciations and births of John and Jesus. The structure is a series of diptychs, or "paired facing scenes": the annunciation of John's birth (1:5–25) paired with that of Jesus (1:26–45, 56); the birth, circumcision, and naming of John (1:57–66, 80) paired with those of Jesus (2:1–27, 34–40). The second stage includes all the hymns or canticles and much of the two Temple scenes.[79] Brown's argument is based on the fact that the inclusion of the *Magnificat* (1:46–55) "unbalances" the neat diptych structure and makes Mary's visit to Elizabeth into a separate scene. He argues further that these later additions might derive from other pre-Lukan sources that originally had no connection to the birth narrative proper.[80]

In my view, the scene of Mary's visit to Elizabeth is the central scene of the entire story and anticipates the visit of Jesus to John at the baptism. In that way, it is the real key to the symmetrical Lukan structure, which is more of a triptych of scenes within three succeeding acts (as outlined above).[81]

The Symmetry and Unity of the Lukan Narrative

A principal argument against Brown's view of two stages arises from analysis of the basic motifs surrounding the double-birth narrative as a Lukan creation. Central to both stories is the fact that the mother either could not or should not be pregnant. In this sense, the stories emulate two key traditions from the Hebrew scriptures about special births, namely, Sarah and the birth of Isaac (Gen 18:1–15) and Hannah and the birth of Samuel (1 Sam 1:1–2:10). Certain motifs are drawn from each. For example, Zechariah and Elizabeth's advanced age, Zechariah's skepticism, and Mary's surprise bear resonances to the Abraham-Sarah story (compare Gen 18:12–15).[82] A further allusion to the story of the birth of Isaac and the promise to Abraham may be seen in the closing lines of the Magnificat:

> *He has helped his servant Israel, in remembrance of his mercy, according to the promise he made to our ancestors, to Abraham and to his descendants forever. (Luke 1:54–55)*

Even so, the dramatic and powerful story of Hannah is surely the more influential on the shape of the Lukan narrative. The Samuel narrative contains a Temple scene, the barren Hannah's petition to God, a blessing by the priest Eli, and Hannah's hymnic prayer in thanks to God. Thus, we see the basic thread of both Lukan birth stories. Yet the influence continues into the canticles, as seen especially in the *Magnificat,* which is modeled directly on the prayer of Hannah (1 Sam 2:1–10). The wording of the opening line is very similar in Greek:

> *My heart exults in the LORD;*
> *my strength is exalted in my God.*
> *My mouth derides my enemies,*
> *because I rejoice in my victory.*
> *There is no Holy One like the LORD,*
> *no one besides you;*
> *there is no Rock like our God. (1 Sam 2:1–2)*

> *My soul magnifies the Lord,*
> *and my spirit rejoices in God my Savior,*
> *for he has looked with favor on the lowliness of his servant.*
> *Surely, from now on all generations will call me blessed;*
> *for the Mighty One has done great things for me,*
> *and holy is his name. (Luke 1:46–49)*

Though the wording is by no means identical, there are clear borrowings. In 1:48, for example, the Lukan author has supplemented Hannah's hymn with a phrase from her petitions in 1 Sam 1:11 (LXX): "O LORD of hosts, if only *you will look with favor on the lowliness of your servant,* and remember me, and not forget your servant." The wording of the first part (in italics) is nearly identical in the Greek of the Septuagint. Earlier in the story, the angel's announcement, "Do not be afraid, Mary, for you have *found favor* with God" (1:30), and Mary's response, "Behold, the servant of the Lord; let it be with me according to your word" (1:38), are both modeled after Hannah's response to the pronouncement of Eli: "Let your *servant find favor* in your sight" (1 Sam 1:18, LXX). As a result, we find that, as with the Abraham-Sarah story, the Samuel narrative—and explicitly the words of Hannah—are used in both the main narrative and the canticle. Consequently, Brown's division into an earlier and later stage of composition for these two components (i.e., the base narrative and the canticle) is unworkable.

Something similar occurs with the annunciation of John's birth, where the angelic pronouncement that "he must never drink wine or strong drink" (Luke 1:15) is modeled after the vow of Hannah regarding Samuel: "I will set him before you as a nazirite until the day of his death. *He shall drink neither wine nor intoxicants,* and no razor shall touch his head" (1 Sam 1:11). Again, the wording is similar in the Greek, although it is also informed by blending in the wording of the nazirite laws in the Septuagint (Num 6:3; Lev 10:9). Finally, in the *Benedictus* of Zechariah we find yet another resonance of Hannah's prayer, which ends with these words: "And he shall give strength to our king and he shall exalt the power [lit., horn] of his anointed [christ]" (1 Sam 2:10, LXX). This verse in turn reprises the second line of Hannah's prayer: "My power [lit., horn] is exalted in my God" (1 Sam 2:1, LXX). After the birth of John, Zechariah says: "He has raised up the power [lit., horn] of salvation in the house of his servant David" (Luke 1:69). I have intentionally given a rather literal translation of the Greek in each case, so the similarities of wording are more visible. The Greek word *keras* ("horn"), with its derived sense of "power," acts as a verbal cue. So, though the bulk of the *Benedictus* is modeled on passages from the Psalms, it picks up this important bit of Davidic symbolism from Hannah's prayer, as John is now made to point the way toward Jesus as the Davidic messiah. This too was a theme of the angelic annunciation of John in Luke 1:17, with its allusion to Elijah symbolism drawn from Malachi 4:5–6 (3:24, MT, LXX).

In the final analysis, then, it is very difficult to separate the Lukan narrative into neat layers, as it is skillfully and seamlessly woven around septuagintal language at every turn. Even the "addition"—as Brown thought—of Jesus's visit to the Temple at age twelve (2:41–47) has been shown to be distinctively Lukan in style and vocabulary, as is the birth narrative as a whole.[83] A close reading of each of the angelic announcements and each of the canticles shows that they were composed by masterful blending of passages from the Septuagint. None is merely a direct quotation; however, the result is that the whole narrative is imbued with septuagintal language and tone.[84] Moreover, the story of Hannah and the birth of Samuel, with its important connections to the David narrative, creates another backdrop for literary verisimilitude, now carried farther by the dramatic skill of the Lukan author. It is no mere accident, then, that the aged prophet who sees the infant Jesus at the Temple is named Anna, which in Greek is the same as Hannah.[85]

Mary Takes Center Stage

Having seen the basic triptych structure and septuagintal resonance of the parallel Lukan birth stories, we may now turn to the central scene. Contrary to traditional assumptions, as reflected in later Christian art and Marian piety, it is not the annunciation to Mary (1:26–38) that stands at the center. Rather, it is the following scene, the visit of Mary to Elizabeth (1:39–56), which, as Brown thought, breaks the neat diptych structure and stands on its own.[86] But this too was a conscious Lukan design, as it consciously weaves themes and language from the two annunciation stories into a single moment of realization, for both the characters in the story and the audience.[87]

In order to set the stage, we must first note some features of the annunciation scene itself. It opens (1:26) with a temporal marker setting the visit of Gabriel to Mary in the sixth month of Elizabeth's pregnancy. The scene closes with a reprise of this marker, only now it is given on the lips of the angel (1:36–37). With this fact we see that the basic story line and the direct discourse of the angelic voice are synchronized at the narrative level. Next, we note Mary's surprise (1:34) at the announcement that she will conceive and bear a son of the lineage and kingship of David (1:32–33). The angelic voice here is built around passages from 2 Samuel 7:10–16 and Isaiah 9:6–7. In reply to Mary's query, the angel then speaks again with phrases drawn from Isaiah 11:1–2; 4:2–3. The scene then ends with Mary's Hannah-like acquiescence, "Here am I, the servant of the Lord; let it be with me according to your word," and the angel's departure (1:38).

At this point in the story, Mary has received the astonishing announcement, but has no idea what to make of it. It is not at all clear from the narrative that at that moment she knew she was pregnant.[88] Rather, at the level of the narrative it is the fundamental implausibility of the miraculous event described by the angel that raises the question. Nor is it resolved by her psychological state, as is sometimes assumed.[89] But the angelic announcement adds one more element by reporting that her kinswoman Elizabeth, now old and barren, is already six months pregnant. Contrary to Mary's own uncertainty, here is a sign of the miraculous power of God (1:36–37). It is this move, finally, that sets up the next scene, for Mary, still uncertain what is happening, now goes to visit Elizabeth to see if what the angel said is true.

The change of venue in the story seems immediate at first, but there is a temporal gap as Mary must travel from Nazareth to the "hill country of Judea," where Zechariah and Elizabeth live (1:39). As Mary now enters the house of Elizabeth and greets her, the fetus in Elizabeth's womb leaps at the sound of Mary's voice (1:40–41). At this moment Elizabeth is filled with the Holy Spirit and offers a benediction: "Blessed are you among women and blessed is the fruit of your womb. And why has this happened to me that the mother of my Lord comes to me?" (1:42–43). The theme of Mary's "blessedness" will be reprised shortly in the Magnificat (1:48).

But notice, the child (fetal John) had leaped in Elizabeth's womb before she was filled with the Spirit to offer her benediction and prophetic reference to Mary as "mother of my Lord." In other words it is fetal John who has signaled the prophetic realization that Mary is now pregnant, even before Elizabeth or Mary herself knew. In fact, this scene encapsulates and foreshadows John's role as prophetic forerunner to Jesus (1:17; cf. 3:15–18), but in a new way, even before he was born. And yet this motif too was already spelled out earlier by the same angel, Gabriel, in the annunciation of John's birth: "Even before his birth he will be filled with the Holy Spirit" (1:15). Thus, the Lukan author has already anticipated the scene of Mary's visit to Elizabeth in the annunciation of John's birth. They cannot be from two separated sources. In the same way, the scene of Mary's visit and John's prophetic leap anticipates the final encounter between Jesus and John, at the baptism (3:21–22).

It is this central scene, where fetal John has just given a prophetic leap in the presence of fetal Jesus, that finally lets Mary know—along with Elizabeth *and*

the audience—that Mary is now pregnant. Elizabeth's pregnant statement—
"Blessed is she who believed that there would be fulfillment of what was spoken
to her by the Lord" (1:45)—then sets the stage for Mary's *Magnificat* at the realization of her pregnancy and the fulfillment of the angelic announcement. In
the Lukan construction, it is this moment when the two stories of John and Jesus
come together that the real drama and power of the Lukan birth narrative come
to the fore.

We see too that there is a much higher degree of literary integration in the story,
as details and motifs work both forward and backward in the narrative, making
it a much more cohesive story than Matthew's choppy, episodic tale. From here
the rest of the birth narrative is set in motion, as the momentous events surrounding the birth of Jesus as the long-awaited messiah of Israel transpire. The same
themes come to a culmination in Luke 3:21–22, when Jesus again meets John,
at his baptism. One may thus view the entire birth narrative as a Lukan effort to
anticipate and explain the voice from heaven at Jesus's baptism: "You are my son,
the Beloved, with you I am well pleased" (3:22). In turn, it sets the stage for the
beginning of Jesus's ministry in his sermon at Nazareth, when he reads the words
of the prophet Isaiah: "The Spirit of the Lord is upon me, because he has anointed
me to bring good news to the poor . . ." (4:18).

Weaving the Scenes Together

Seen from this perspective, what do we make finally of the Lukan birth narrative?
Its elegant and grandiose tone elevates the story to a new level. Of course, the
"second" encounter between Jesus and John, at the baptism, was already part of
the story in the Gospel of Mark. The Gospel of Matthew incorporates it too. But
in neither case is it directly connected to the birth narrative. After all, there is no
birth narrative in the Markan Gospel. The Gospel of Luke now gives us a new
take on the backstory, filling in the gaps and explaining the relationships in narrative fashion. Like the Matthean birth narrative in some respects, it emphasizes
angelic direction and miraculous events, but to a different end. In the Gospel of
Matthew, however, there is little about the baby or his mother, as most of the emphasis is on the events and portents surrounding his birth.

Not so for the Lukan story. The baby is already more special and, accordingly,
the birth is more spectacular also. Events surrounding the birth that draw Mary
and Joseph to Bethlehem now take on global dimensions, as the "whole world"
(lit., *oikoumenē*, the "managed realm" or "empire") is under Augustan aegis (2:1).
But God is at work above the world stage, as the angelic announcements have
already shown. Other characters in the story react to the child, both before birth
(John and Elizabeth) and after (Simeon and Anna). At this key moment comes
the narrator's summary: "The child grew and became strong, filled with wisdom;
and the favor of God was upon him" (2:40). From the start the infant Jesus stands

out more in the Lukan narrative, and this suggests a different intent and background for the Lukan narrative. Unlike the Matthean narrative, where it is all about external signs and angelic warnings, in Luke the infant himself is already special from the moment of birth. In his presence priests and prophetesses burst into songs and benedictions. But it began even before his birth, with the prophetic leap of fetal John in the presence of fetal Jesus (1:41–43). The stage is now set for this special child to grow up.

The Lukan Jesus: A Divine Man?

The Lukan birth narrative, in the more limited sense, draws to a close with the distinctively Lukan scene of Jesus visiting the Temple at age twelve (2:41–51). As scholars have shown, this scene uses characteristically Lukan style and vocabulary throughout.[90] It thus should not be treated merely as a separate narrative inserted "awkwardly" by Luke, as suggested by some. Rather, it is the culmination of a peculiarly Lukan theme regarding the special child. His special wisdom and maturity have begun to show. While his worried parents think he is lost, Jesus is in the Temple amazing the teachers with his questions and answers. When confronted by them, he responds: "Why are you searching for me? Did you not know that I must be in my Father's house?" (2:49). The phrasing in Greek is characteristically Lukan. The point is Lukan too: Jesus understands what his parents *and others* do not.[91] It occurs in the Temple, where the birth narrative had begun (1:8–23). Thus, the episode ends with a reprise of 2:40: "And Jesus increased in wisdom and in years, and in divine and human favor" (2:52). At this juncture the stage is set for the arrival of Jesus as an adult. After his final encounter with John, at his baptism (3:21–22), Jesus will take center stage alone in his ministry. This depiction is what we call the precocious-childhood motif. It was a characteristic element in divine-man biographies, as we saw in the case of both Philo's *Life of Moses* and Philostratus's *Life of Apollonius* in Chapter 3.

In contrast to some older theories of the Gospels as divine-man biographies, I would argue that the Gospel of Matthew has little or nothing that evokes this Greco-Roman literary tradition (see Chapter 3). Even with miraculous elements and angelic intervention, such is not the point of the Matthean birth narrative, because the precocious child—who will become the divinely gifted adult—is not a feature of the Matthean story.

The Gospel of Luke, on the other hand, I would argue, contains much more of the divine-man element throughout. This element is set in motion precisely in the birth narrative and continues right through to the Passion narrative and into Acts. In fact, it is part and parcel of the Lukan theology of "salvation history." A number of key features cohere with this tradition. One is the depiction of events surrounding the birth proper. They have not merely been predicted or prophesied, but divinely orchestrated. In the case of the Lukan narrative this feature applies even to the census order given by the emperor Augustus (2:1), which in turn drives the geographical progression of the story as it moves from Nazareth to Bethlehem to Jerusalem and back to Nazareth. It is but a small step to make the theological claim that it was the same God who made Augustus ruler of the world in the first place. In this way, the Lukan narrative may well be playing directly off Roman imperial propaganda associated with the divine-man portrayal of Augustus's own birth and epic traditions from Vergil's *Aeneid*.[92]

Next, the awe-inspiring infant and the precocious child set the stage for a rather different kind of Jesus to come forward in his ministry. The themes of divine guidance, and eschatological fulfillment are intertwined through the role of the Holy Spirit.[93] In the end, Jesus shows a clear awareness of a divine compulsion not unlike that of Socrates (as discussed in Chapter 9). The Lukan Jesus now goes through his ministry with a different character and attitude, as may be seen in the distinctive Lukan introduction of prefacing statements about his suffering and death with "I must" or "It is necessary."[94] In Chapter 13 we shall return to look at how the entire story of Jesus correlates with these key Lukan themes and images already set in motion through this artfully constructed birth narrative.

ACT III

Staging Gospels

CHAPTER ELEVEN

The Misunderstood Messiah

The Gospel of Mark

Whenever the unclean spirits saw him, they fell down before him and shouted, "You are the Son of God!" But he sternly ordered them not to make him known. (Mark 3:11–12)

When he [Jesus] was alone, those who were around him along with the twelve asked him about the parables. And he said to them, "To you has been given the secret of the kingdom of God, but for those outside, everything comes in parables; in order that 'they may indeed look, but not perceive, and may indeed listen, but not understand; so that they may not turn again and be forgiven.'" (Mark 4:10–12)

But when they saw him walking on the sea, they thought it was a ghost and cried out; for they all saw him and were terrified. But immediately he spoke to them and said, "Take heart, it is I; do not be afraid." Then he got into the boat with them and the wind ceased. And they were utterly astounded, for they did not understand about the loaves, but their hearts were hardened. (Mark 6:49–52)

"Do you not yet understand?" Jesus rails at his disciples in a moment of frustration (Mark 8:22). It is but one of several times he chastises them for their lack of understanding (cf. Mark 6:49–52, quoted above). This portrayal of the disciples as rather dense and "hardheaded" (for that is what "their hearts were hardened" really means) is one of the distinctive features of the Gospel of Mark. In sharp contrast, the parallel passages in Matthew (such as 16:12) explicitly alter the story

line in order to show them understanding and even confessing him to be the "Son of God" (14:32–33; 16:16). But in the Gospel of Mark none of the twelve disciples—*not even Peter*—ever confesses that Jesus is the "Son of God" (cf. Mark 8:29; Matt 16:16). At Jesus's arrest they all flee out of fear; nor do they return to witness the crucifixion (14:50; cf. 14:27).[1]

In fact, the last moment at which any of the male disciples is present in the Markan story is the pathetic scene of Peter's denial (14:54, 66–72). Significantly, the women in Mark are a different matter, as we shall see. Given that the "twelve" do not show up again in the narrative, even Peter's denial ends on a rather strange note, as he weeps when he remembers Jesus's prediction of his desertion (14:72; cf. 14:28–31). At the dramatic level of the narrative, then, one is left wondering about Peter's understanding even at that moment. Of course, the later Gospels "correct" this perception in various ways to show Peter's repentance and faith. Before those other Gospels entered the picture, however, the Markan story left the question open. Yet this aspect too is part of the Markan design.

That is the point. All the Gospels have a dramatic narrative design. Although there are key similarities and differences among the various Gospels, canonical and noncanonical alike, both features derive from the fact that basic episodes and components were passed on through oral tradition and constantly reshaped and reconfigured through storytelling. New contexts bring new issues and concerns that must be worked out through recasting the narrative. That is, as we have seen, the storyteller's art. Each storyteller develops certain themes and ideas that are carried through the plot and the dramatic structuring of the action. Character, scenes, narration, and dialogue change from one to the next.

In Act III we shall now look at the way the different Gospels have been put together by combining and reshaping the various story components that we saw at work in Act II. In this process, we will be looking for literary characteristics, stylistic trends, and themes at work in each particular Gospel as a reflection of the author, audience, and situation. Because of their dramatic power and evocative force, these Gospels eventually became scriptures for the emerging Christian groups. But before they were scripture, they were stories told and retold in the living context of a worshiping community. We begin with the Gospel of Mark, by most accounts the first of the Gospels to be written down. In turn, it served as the base for later efforts to retell the story. In this way we must try to hear it on its own terms, both to understand its image of Jesus and to see how it will change. In order to do so, we shall focus first on this curious matter of misunderstanding that is so distinctive to the Markan Gospel.

Missing the Mark

The theme of misunderstanding runs throughout the Markan story. It may be seen in the surprising portrayal of Jesus's mother and siblings (3:19–21, 31–33), who clearly think Jesus is insane. Once again, the later Gospels delete this component.[2] Others also misunderstand: local authorities are perplexed at his powers and think he is demon-possessed (3:22); his hometown folks reject him (6:1–6); Herod Antipas thinks he is John the Baptist come back to life (6:14–16); the Pharisees test him (8:11–13; cf. 3:6) and then try to entrap him (12:13–17); and especially the Temple leadership views him as a threat, ultimately plotting to kill him (11:18, 27–33; 12:1–12; 14:1–2, 10, 43, 55; 15:11).

But how could these people understand? After all, as the Markan author tells the story, Jesus consistently tried to conceal his identity and his message. For example, he frequently orders those whom he heals not to tell anyone (1:44; 5:43; 7:36; 8:26), and he silences the demons who call him "Son of God" (3:11–12, quoted above; cf. 1:32–34; 5:7–9). In addition, when Jesus begins to teach, he does so only in parables, and then explains things privately to his disciples (4:34). They are likewise instructed not to tell what he says (8:30; 9:9, 30–31).

The purpose of the parables in Mark is not to clarify Jesus's message, but rather to conceal it, so that people *will not understand and will not repent*:

> *When he was alone, those who were around him along with the twelve asked him about the parables. And he said to them, "To you has been given the secret of the kingdom of God, but for those outside, everything comes in parables; in order that* **'they may indeed look, but not perceive, and may indeed listen, but not understand; so that they may not turn again and be forgiven.'"** *(4:10–12)*

No wonder they cannot understand; it's a "secret" that Jesus apparently is trying to conceal. As the story goes along, even the disciples are increasingly left in the dark, as Jesus shows the secret only to an inner circle consisting of Peter, James, John, and occasionally Andrew (9:2–6; 13:1–4; 14:33–42).[3]

The first of these occasions is the transfiguration; the last, in Gethsemane just prior to his arrest. These disciples, in turn, prove to be "hardheaded" too. Peter complains about what they have given up (10:28), while James and John beg for seats of honor in Jesus's kingdom (10:35–45), apparently thinking that he will bring a political revolution. In Gethsemane (14:37–42) they all three fall asleep, three times over, leaving Jesus angry and frustrated at them and dreading his arrest that follows. Then they flee with the rest of the disciples (14:50). Above all, Peter fails miserably (14:37). After Jesus's arrest, he follows at a distance, but ultimately deserts like the rest (14:54, 66–72). At this moment, we see how two key themes—secrecy and misunderstanding—are skillfully woven together throughout the Markan narrative and are drawn together in a dramatic climax through the Passion narrative. On the one hand, Jesus suppresses and conceals his true message from all but his closest disciples; they, on the other, repeatedly fail to understand what he is showing and telling them. The drama of the Passion narrative reaches its climax when they all flee, leaving Jesus to suffer and die alone.

At the center of the story stands Mark 9:9, where Jesus tells the same three disciples, Peter, James, and John, not to tell anyone, including the other disciples, what they had just seen and heard at the transfiguration (9:2–8) until "after the Son of Man had risen from the dead." Their response, once again, is telling: "So they kept the matter to themselves, questioning what this *rising from the dead* could mean" (9:9–10). The themes of secrecy and misunderstanding, now punctuated with scenes of Jesus's self-revelation, point directly to the Passion and resurrection narrative. But as we have already seen (Chapter 7), the transfiguration story itself may well represent an early form of the resurrection narrative. If so, then the author has intentionally repositioned and reshaped it in keeping with the secrecy motif in the narrative. The audience, on the other hand, is expected to recognize it for what it is. What might this tell us about the narrative structure and intent of the Gospel of Mark? And what might this say about the purpose of the author and the response of the audience? What kind of story of faith is this?

The First Gospel:
Why Was It Produced?

The challenge for modern readers of the Gospels, and especially Mark, is to approach the story on its own terms. That means taking it from the historical perspective of the Markan audience and without the overlay of changes and additions from the later Gospels or from later Christian theology and doctrine. Since the middle of the nineteenth century, it has become increasingly apparent within New Testament scholarship that the Gospel of Mark was the first of our "written" Gospels. The Gospels of Matthew and Luke, and perhaps even John, used it as a source. This discovery of the primacy of Mark initially led scholars to assume that it was a reliable "historical" source for the life of Jesus. Both its brevity and crude Greek style were taken as signs of its "primitive" character as a "historical document . . . in touch with the facts."[4] Specifically, they took key themes, such as Jesus's silencing of the demons, as an indication of his growing messianic consciousness during the course of his ministry. In other words, literary motifs were taken as historical facts and indications of Jesus's own thought.

This picture was soon to change, however, with the realization that the entire Markan narrative was structured to set up the story of Jesus's death and resurrection. In Mark the last week of Jesus's life, beginning with the triumphal entry (11:1–10), makes up one-third of the entire story. This view is characterized nowadays by the often repeated shorthand that Mark is "a passion narrative with an extended introduction."[5] What this means is that themes and motifs from the Passion are woven into the structure of the preceding narrative, as discussed above in Chapter 7.

That such structuring devices represent early theological reflections rather than just historical facts was first suggested by Wilhelm Wrede in his study of the "messianic secret" in Mark.[6] He showed that the secrecy motif was not a historical reminiscence of Jesus's own time, but was a later retrospection from the perspective of the disciples who had failed to understand what was happening until after the resurrection. In other words, Wrede argued that it was, instead, a historical feature of the disciples' later reflections pushed back onto the story of Jesus.[7] Though his main insight remains an important starting point in Markan scholarship, his further assumption regarding the disciples has not. It is now widely recognized that the secrecy motif was a literary invention of the Markan author. With it came several other key themes and motifs within the Markan story, including the misunderstanding of the disciples. In the remainder of this chapter, we will explore both the setting and the construction of the secrecy motif and related themes of the Gospel of Mark. Along the way we will discover how it delivers a unique message about the identity of Jesus.

Although the Gospel of Mark, as we now know it, is the earliest of the written Gospels, it is by no means a primitive or simplistic telling of the story of Jesus. Far from it. In recent studies, then, the role of the author as narrator and oral storyteller has come increasingly to the fore. At the same time, the role of the audience as participants in shaping and reacting to the narrative dramatically has been more widely recognized.[8] Above all, it must be remembered that the Gospel was meant to be performed, to be heard as interaction between author/narrator and audience in a communal setting.[9]

The Historical Setting

Discovering the situation and purpose of the Gospel is more difficult. An early tradition attributed to Papias (ca. 130 CE) holds that the Gospel of Mark came from John Mark, who traveled with Peter to Rome and there wrote down his *reminiscences* of Peter's "gospel":

> [Papias said:] *"And the Presbyter [John of Ephesus] used to say this: 'Mark became Peter's interpreter and wrote accurately all that he remembered, although not in order, of the things said and done by the Lord.' For he had not heard the Lord, nor had he followed him, but later on, as I said, followed Peter, who used to give instruction as needed but did not make an arrangement, as it were, of the Lord's oracles. So Mark did nothing wrong in thus writing down single items, as he remembered them. For to one thing he gave attention: to leave out nothing of what he had heard and to make no false statements in them."* These words, then, were narrated by Papias about Mark.[10]

This tradition would seem to place the writing of Mark sometime around 64 CE, the legendary date of Peter's death. Yet even this assumption is clouded by several pieces of evidence. First, the Christian historian Eusebius of Caesarea, who is our only source for the Papias tradition, also says that Mark had left Rome for Alexandria by 40 CE carrying the completed Gospel with him[11] The difficulty is that Paul's Galatian letter (2:1–14), which dates to the mid-50s CE, clearly places Peter still in Jerusalem and Antioch through the late 40s.[12] Second, it must be recognized that the early "testimony" attributed to Papias is heavily laced with editorial comments, either from Papias or from Eusebius himself, all of which show an awareness of the differences between Mark and the other Gospels. Effectively, they are an effort to explain them away by saying that Mark's reminiscences are "accurate," but "not in order" or not "an arrangement."

Internal evidence from the Gospel itself gives a different picture. Many of the materials in the story seem to depend on earlier oral traditions, some of which might have already been written down, and these were then reshaped by the author/storyteller. Whether this was actually the person named Mark cannot be affirmed, since the author is nowhere identified within the text. On the other hand, it does appear that the Gospel was written for a Greek-speaking audience that had little or no knowledge of Judean culture and language. By contrast, there seems to be an awareness of official Roman terminology and practices.[13] Consequently, a setting in Rome, as several early legends report,[14] is a distinct possibility, but the putative connection to Peter raises some doubts.

In general now, the Gospel of Mark is understood to have been prompted in some measure by the first Jewish revolt against Rome, which began in 66 CE. Military actions continued to 74 CE with the eventual capture of Masada, but the critical blow came with the storming of Jerusalem and the destruction of the Temple in August and September of 70 CE. It was a devastating blow for Jews everywhere, including those who had come to follow Jesus. For this reason, some have wanted to see the triumphal procession of Titus in 71 CE, when he returned to Rome with the spoils of the Temple, as a possible motivation for the writing. This procession is depicted dramatically on the inner panel of the Arch of Titus at the eastern entrance to the Roman Forum.[15] Consequently, Rome is at least a possibility for the location where this Gospel was produced.

On the other hand, Antioch might provide an equally likely setting for the writing, since it had an established community of the Jesus movement, and the supposed author, John Mark, is last reported in Acts as based there (15:36–39). Antioch also had a clear view of the war, and there were threatened reprisals against Jews in Antioch afterward. Moreover, after completing the sack of Jerusalem, Titus passed through Caesarea Philippi, Berytus, and Antioch with the Temple spoils and prisoners in tow on his way back to Rome.[16] All these factors suggest that Antioch or somewhere near there is the more probable location.[17] But certainty is impossible. Alexandria has also been suggested, since another later legend places Mark there, and Vespasian had spent the last year of the war there. With its large Jewish community and close ties to Jerusalem, one could imagine that the course of the war was watched with considerable interest in Alexandria.[18]

Clues from Mark 13

Although we cannot be sure where the Gospel was produced, the situation is rather clearly dependent on the Jewish war.[19] The main question debated by scholars is whether it was written just prior to the destruction of Jerusalem or sometime afterward. Arguments based on internal evidence of the Gospel can be mounted on both sides, but tend to favor a date of writing after the destruction had taken place, hence sometime between 70 and 75 CE. In large measure, the dating depends on how one understands references and images in chapters 11–13 in relation to the destruction of Jerusalem.

The key to understanding the historical situation of the Gospel is the apocalyptic discourse, sometimes called "The Little Apocalypse" (13:1–37), which occurs narratively during the last week of Jesus's life. It begins with Jesus and the disciples leaving the Temple for the day and heading back to Bethany, where they were staying. That would take them across the Mount of Olives, and as they go one of the disciples comments on the architectural grandeur of the Temple (13:1), to which Jesus replies: "Not one stone will be left here upon another; all will be thrown down" (13:2). Clearly this is a reference to the destruction of the Temple in 70.

Next, Peter, James, John, and Andrew, the inner circle, privately ask Jesus, "When will this be?" (13:4), and that prompts the rest of the discourse, given as an instruction to them alone (13:5–37). Following a warning about some signs that will foreshadow the events, including false messiahs, famine, and war (13:5–7), comes that powerful apocalyptic image of expectant Jerusalem: "This is but the beginning of the birth pangs" (13:8).

Next comes a warning about persecution for those who proclaim the gospel (13:9–13). Here we see a reference to the experiences of the later followers of the Markan community. Then come the real "signs" of the destruction:

> "But when you see the <u>desolating sacrilege</u> set up where it ought not to be (<u>let the reader understand</u>), then those in Judea must flee to the mountains. . . . Woe to those who are pregnant and to those who are nursing infants in those days! Pray that it may not be in winter. For in those days there will be suffering, such as has not been from the beginning of the creation that God created until now, no, and never will be. And if the Lord had not cut short those days, no one would be saved; but for the sake of the elect, whom he chose, he has cut short those days. And if anyone says to you at that time, 'Look! Here is the Messiah!' or 'Look! There he is!'—do not believe it. False messiahs and false prophets will appear and produce signs and omens, to lead astray, if possible, the elect. But be alert; I have already told you everything." (13:14–23)

Here we see the author of Mark step out from behind the character of Jesus and speak directly to the audience: "let the reader understand" (13:14). The phrase "desolating sacrilege" is one used in writings of the Maccabean revolt period to refer to the desecration of the Temple by Antiochus Epiphanes (1 Macc 1:54; Dan 9:27; 11:31; 12:11). Here it may refer to one of several threats to the Temple during the course of the war: the confiscation of the Temple treasury and ensuing carnage that sparked the revolt (66 CE);[20] the occupation of the Temple by the Zealots (67/68);[21] the cessation of the daily sacrifices in the last months of the siege (August 70);[22] or the final burning of the Temple edifice followed by a Roman sacrifice within the Temple courts and a slaughter of priests (September 70).[23] Each of these has been argued as the "event" signaled in Mark 13:14 as a further clue to the precise date of the composition.[24] At the very least, the "desecration" is a sign that destruction is nigh, if not a fait accompli.[25] Then the passage warns against false messiahs who will arise in conjunction with these events.

It is significant, therefore, that the discourse is framed as a private instruction to the inner circle of Jesus's disciples, since it then becomes part of the secrecy/misunderstanding motif. It seems to be an effort to correct a misunderstanding on the part of at least some in the Markan community who had thought that the war really was to be the eschatological return of Jesus, presumably when he would establish a new earthly kingdom. Instead, the Markan author has Jesus "predict" these events, including the war and the destruction, as a way of correcting the apocalyptic expectations by using an apocalyptic mode of discourse to deliver the reinterpretation.

The point is twofold. First, the destruction of the Temple was—like the cursing of the fig tree (11:12–25; cf. 13:28–29)—a punishment, because the Temple had not been pure. This perspective on the events is very much in line with other Jewish views of the day. To it the Markan author adds another dimension by linking the putative role of the "chief priests" in the plot to kill Jesus with the impurity of the Temple. In effect, the destruction of the Temple is being interpreted, at least in part, as a punishment for killing Jesus.[26] Second, the author makes the destruction of the Temple not the eschatological event itself, but merely the "birth pangs" for the *eschaton*. In other words, the Markan audience was being told that the traumatic events that had so recently transpired in Jerusalem were—like the onset of labor—the signal that the eschatological age was now about to dawn, in fact within the lifetime of that very generation (13:24–32). Despite their previous misunderstanding, Jesus would return soon.

Thus, by portraying the various *misunderstandings* of characters within the story—friend and foe alike—the Markan narrative thereby gives shape to *proper understanding* of Jesus's messianic identity and eschatological expectations for its own audience decades later. In other words, the theme of misunderstanding, and its attendant motifs of secrecy and privacy, is primarily a vehicle for reinterpretation through storytelling, and all in the light of the tragic aftermath of the war.

Organizing the Markan Narrative

We may now turn to several features in the composition and literary construction of the narrative. The basic outline of Mark is shown in Box 11.1. Though it is clear that the Gospel of Mark is dependent on older units of oral tradition, they have been thoroughly reworked and integrated into the narrative framework of the story. One such unit was the Passion narrative itself, probably including the transfiguration story as a resurrection scene (see Chapter 7). It has also been argued that the double cycle of similar miracles in Mark 4–8 reflects two distinct *catenae,* or oral collections, of miracles that were incorporated by the author.[27] Even so, it must be recognized that most of the narrative is the composition of the Markan author and these older traditions have been heavily reworked for thematic and dramatic effect. This fact may be observed literarily by a number of patterned structural features that stretch across the narrative (see Box 11.2). One of these is the geographical ordering of the story in three major sections: in Galilee and on the sea (1:14–6:6a), beyond Galilee and turning toward Jerusalem (6:6b–10:52), and in Jerusalem (11:1–16:8).[28]

Markan Fingerprints

Other "fingerprints" of the Markan author include the use of the word *euangelion* ("gospel"), which occurs in the narrator's prologue, but is also placed by the author on the lips of Jesus. Also, nine generalizing summaries punctuate the first six chapters; they bear a remarkable consistency in wording and consciously interlink key episodes running forward and backward in the narrative. A good example is the last one (6:53–56), which describes crowds of sick people begging "that they might touch even the fringe of his cloak." Here is an allusion back to the healing of the hemorrhaging woman (5:25–34, esp. v. 27). In turn, an earlier summary in Mark 3:7–11 anticipates this same miracle by referring to a boat at the seaside "so that they [the crowd] would not crush him" and mentioning that "all who had diseases pressed upon him to touch him" (3:9).

In addition, the last part of this summary continues: "Whenever the unclean spirits saw him, they fell down before him and shouted, 'You are the Son of God!'" (3:11). It thereby anticipates the Gerasene demoniac story (5:1–20, esp. vv. 6–7), which immediately precedes the miracle of the woman with the hemorrhage. Thus, the stories are linked by verbal allusion through the narrative, with the cluster of three consecutive and lengthy miracles in Mark 4–5 as a kind of centerpiece. At the same time, one of these three miracles, the Gerasene demoniac together with its anticipation in Mark 3:11, is central to the secrecy motif. In both cases, Jesus silences the demons so that they cannot say who he is. Thus there is more artistry to the Markan narrative than is often recognized.

BOX 11.1

The Gospel of Mark

DATE: ca. 70–75 CE

AUTHOR: Unknown

SETTING: Rome, Antioch, or Alexandria?

ATTRIBUTION: John Mark, disciple of Peter

AUDIENCE AND OCCASION: Greek-speaking followers of the Jesus movement in the period following the first revolt. Concerns over how to understand the messiahship and teachings of Jesus in light of the failure of the revolt and the disconfirmation of widely held apocalyptic expectations regarding the war.

OUTLINE

  I. Apocalyptic Announcements: "The Beginning of the gospel" (1:1–13)

 II. Jesus's Ministry in Galilee (1:14–6:6a)
   A. Authority displayed in word and deed (1:14–3:19a)
   B. Jesus's teachings misunderstood (3:19b–4:34)
   C. Jesus's miracles misunderstood—rejection at Nazareth (4:35–6:6a)

III. The Ministry Beyond Galilee (6:6b–10:52)
   A. Mission of the Twelve (6:6b–29)
   B. Miracles misunderstood by the disciples and others (6:30–8:26)

Finally, a number of the episodes, and especially miracles, in the Markan narrative seem eerily familiar. It is a result of intentional patterns of repetition and includes the miracle doublets in Mark 4–8 (see Box 11.2). In each case, the second version of the miracle intensifies some aspect of the first, usually dealing with the theme of misunderstanding. For example, the second storm miracle (walking on water, 6:45–52) concludes with this comment by the narrator: "Then he got into the boat with them and the wind ceased. And they were utterly astounded, for they did not understand about the loaves, but their hearts were hardened" (6:51–52). Narratively, the point of this doublet is that even after seeing Jesus calm a storm once before (4:35–41), the disciples fail to understand. At the same time, this ending harks to the feeding of the five thousand (6:30–44), which, in turn, is intensified later by the feeding of the four thousand (8:1–10). All four miracles are then woven together by a third tense scene in a boat (8:14–21), where Jesus

C. Confession and first Passion prediction (8:27–9:1)

D. Transfiguration and second Passion prediction—misunderstood by disciples (9:2–50)

E. Journey toward Jerusalem and third Passion prediction (10:1–52)

IV. The Ministry in Jerusalem and the Passion Narrative (11:1–16:8)

A. Triumphal entry (11:4–10)

B. Cleansing the Temple, cursing the fig tree (11:11–26)

C. Teaching and controversy in the Temple (11:27–12:44)

D. Apocalyptic discourse regarding the destruction of the Temple (13:1–37)

E. The Passion narrative (14:1–15:47)

1. Conspiracy (14:1–2, 10–11)

2. Anointing at Bethany (14:3–9)

3. Last Supper (14:12–25)

4. Mount of Olives, betrayal, and arrest (14:26–52)

5. Trial before Sanhedrin, Peter's denial (14:53–72)

6. Trial before Pilate (15:1–20)

7. Crucifixion and death (15:21–41)

8. Burial (15:42–47)

F. The empty tomb (16:1–8)

chastises them for not understanding about bread. Consequently, even if some of these miracle doublets were earlier oral traditions, they have been thematically intertextualized by the author through the structure of the narrative.

Other significant literary patterns confirm these intentional intertextual connections. There are, for example, a number of triplets, such as Jesus's three predictions of the Passion or the three boat scenes (mentioned above), where, once again, subsequent episodes serve to intensify and interconnect themes (see Box 11.2). Another method of intensification is intercalation, whereby the author intentionally "sandwiches" one key story in the middle of a continuing theme or story. It thus forces the audience to read one episode in the light of the other.[29]

A good example of this motif is the sandwiching of a scene in which Jesus is charged with having a demon (3:22–30) between two scenes about Jesus's family and their misunderstanding (3:19–21, 31–35). Later two scenes in which

BOX 11.2

Markan Fingerprints
Structuring Elements in the Gospel

1. The Geographical Outline

1:1–6:6a	In Galilee (beside sea)
6:6b–10:52	Galilee and beyond, toward Jerusalem
11:1–16:8	In Jerusalem: triumphal entry, Passion, Resurrection

2. Cycles of "Word and Deed"

1:16–3:6   3:7–6:6   6:30–8:26

3. The "Generalizing Summaries" in Mark 1–6

1:14–15	Summary of initiation of ministry in Galilee
1:21–22	Summary of teaching, miracles in Capernaum
1:39	Teaching, miracles in Galilean synagogues
2:13	Teachings, miracles by the sea
3:7–10 + 13–15	The Crowds and Appointing the Twelve
4:33–34	Teaching in parables
6:7 + 12–13	Mission of the Twelve
6:30	Return of the Twelve
6:53–56	Summary of healings

4. The Word "Gospel" (euangelion): Characteristic of the Author

1:1; 1:14–15; 8:35; 10:29; 13:10; 14:9

5. Miracle Doublets

Mark 4–6	Mark 6–8
Stilling the storm (4:35–41)	Walking on water (6:45–52)
Exorcism: Gerasene demoniac (5:1–20)	Exorcism: Daughter of Syrophoenician woman (7:24–30)
Healing: Woman with hemorrhage (5:25–34)	Healing: Deaf-mute (7:31–37)
Raising: Jairus's daughter (5:21–24, 35–43)	Healing: Blind man at Bethsaida (8:22–26)
Feeding of 5000 (6:30–44)	Feeding of 4000 (8:1–10)

6. Triplets

Cycles of "word and deed" (see item 2 above)
Parables about seeds (4:3–9, 26–29, 30–32)
Stories in a boat (4:35–41; 6:45–52; 8:14–21)
Opinions about John the Baptist (6:14)

Opinions about Jesus (8:22–28)
Jesus predicts his Passion and resurrection (8:31–32; 9:30–32; 10:32–34)
Nameless women (5:25–34; 7:24–30; 14:3–9)
The "inner circle" [Peter, James, John] instructed privately (9:2; 13:3; 14:33)
The "inner circle" falls asleep in Gethsemane (14:37–42)
Denials of Peter (14:66–72)
Pilate calls Jesus "King of the Jews" (15:2, 9, 12)
Three women at the cross (15:40) and the tomb (16:1)
The "voice" proclaiming Jesus as "Son [of God]" (1:10; 9:8; 15:39)

7. Intercalations

Family, opponents (3:21–35)
Raising dead, healing (5:22–42)
Sending disciples, disciples and death of John (6:7–30)
Elijah figure, transfiguration (9:1–13)
Disciples have left everything, Third Passion prediction (10:28–45)
Temple, fig tree (11:11–25)

Peter, James, and John seek assurances and protest that they have left everything (10:28–31, 35–45) flank the poignant scene of Jesus's third prediction of his Passion (10:32–34). Here again the apparent misunderstanding of the inner circle is heightened, while in the two flanking scenes Jesus responds with a very similar status reversal saying: "The first shall be last" (10:31, 44–45). In addition there are allusions back to, among other scenes, the parable of the sower (10:30; cf. 4:3–9). Two important miracles likewise achieve their narrative impact through this literary device of intercalation; they are Jairus's daughter and the hemorrhaging woman (5:21–43) and the cleansing of the Temple and the cursing of the fig tree (11:12–25). The former was discussed above and earlier in Chapter 9; we shall discuss the latter in greater detail below.

The Ending of Mark

One feature of the Markan narrative that has often stumped readers is the ending. As most critical English versions of the text now show, the oldest manuscripts end at Mark 16:8, when the women leave the empty tomb:

> But he said to them, "Do not be alarmed; you are looking for Jesus of Nazareth, who was crucified. He has been raised; he is not here. Look, there is the place they laid him. But go, tell his disciples and Peter that he is going ahead of you to Galilee; there you will see him, just as he told you." So they went out and fled from the tomb, for terror and amazement had seized them; and they said nothing to anyone, for they were afraid. (16:6–8)

Verses 9–20 are widely recognized to be a later addition in an effort to make the ending of Mark more closely resemble those of the later Gospels.[30] Noticeably lacking here are the postresurrection appearances of Jesus, which (as we saw in Chapters 6 and 7) were an important component of the earliest oral tradition in Paul. It has long been recognized, however, that the "Longer Ending" (16:9–20) sounds very much like a pastiche of elements drawn from Matthew, Luke-Acts, and even John in an effort to smooth over the differences. Hence an increasing number of scholars now agree that the stark ending at verse 8 was the original as intended by the author.[31] In this view, there is no need to supply some "lost ending" (as has sometimes been proposed),[32] because the tone of the ending is perfectly compatible with the thematic shaping of the Gospel, and specifically with the theme of misunderstanding.

On the narrative and dramatic level, this view is further substantiated if we recognize that the transfiguration story (9:2–8), as discussed in Chapter 7, is in reality a repositioned resurrection scene that the (original) audience is expected to recognize. Notably, the transfiguration likewise ends with the themes of fear and misunderstanding (9:6, 10), and there the disciples are further told to tell no one (9:9). In other words, the Markan transfiguration story fully anticipates the ending of the Gospel at the narrative level. As we shall see below, this ironic scene, where Peter once again speaks out but fails to fully grasp what he sees, is emblematic of the entire Markan narrative. The ending at Mark 16:8 continues this theme and, once again, shows the intentional literary structures and dramatic motifs that were shared by the author and audience of the Gospel of Mark.[33]

Hearing the Markan Story

The Gospel of Mark presents a version of the Jesus story that few people recognize today, because it is so far removed from normal expectations. The story is actually rather short and moves quite briskly as narrative. Yet it is often choppy and episodic. Quite a few scenes seem at first crudely stitched together by little more than a change of location, with no other apparent plotline. A large number of scenes in the second phase of the Galilean section (3:13–6:6) as well as in the pregnant middle section (6:6–10:52) take place merely by having Jesus "cross again in a boat to the other side of the sea [of Galilee]" or some variation of this narrative device (5:21; cf. 4:35–36; 5:1; 6:45; 8:13).

Something similar happens in the last section of the Gospel as Jesus goes back and forth between Jerusalem and Bethany (11:1, 11, 15, 20, 27; 13:1–4; 14:3, 12); the first of these is the triumphal entry, and the last of these is the preparation for the Last Supper. When they go out afterward to Gethsemane (14:32), it will result in his arrest and eventual crucifixion. In addition, much of the Gospel's dramatic play comes from irony and indirection. Jesus tries desperately to conceal his identity from all but a few. Virtually everyone misunderstands him, but especially that chosen few. Dominant male characters, including Peter, typically fail to understand Jesus fully. Marginal, nameless female characters do far better, at least until the very end. So how was the audience supposed to hear this story of Jesus?

Miracle Stories as Allegories on the Drama

One narrative device in the Markan Gospel that speaks directly to the audience, but without a narrator's aside or editorial comment, comes by allowing the stories *within the narrative* to serve as *commentary on the narrative,* or more precisely on characters and events within the narrative. At this moment, the narrator and audience are engaged in a performative act of storytelling that also stands outside the story in a conscious way by dramatizing things in certain ways. In fact, a number of the miracle stories in Mark do just this; Box 11.3 shows the miracles in their narrative order and context. In particular the miracle doublets (discussed above and in Box 11.2), and especially the three central miracles in 4:35–5:43, characterize this dynamic of the story looking inward at itself.

For example, the double miracle of Jairus's daughter and the hemorrhaging woman (5:21–43) clearly intertexts these two stories by virtue of intercalation as well as the girl's age and the duration of the woman's ailment (twelve years). These two characters are thereby set in dramatic opposition to one another: one is the "pure," virginal daughter of a synagogue official; the other, an "impure" woman with a menstrual disorder. Even more to the point, however, is the action of the respective characters within the story as they react to Jesus. The impure woman *believes* in Jesus and thus touches him, even when it is unthinkable to do so. She is healed instantly through her own faith and initiative even before Jesus takes any miraculous action.[34] The synagogue official and his household *believe* in Jesus initially, so long as his daughter is still alive, but then consider him powerless after she dies. Jesus raises her from the dead anyway, despite their lack of proper faith. *As we see, this juxtaposition of faith is precisely where the theme of misunderstanding shows through most clearly.* The characters in the story are thus *caricatures* from the perspective of the audience, but also serve as exemplars. That one is a nameless and impure woman, and thus a marginal character from social perspective, while the other is a named and socially prominent man, further heightens the polarities associated with proper belief and understanding. Another miracle serves as a doublet on this same motif. Similarly, the exorcism of the daughter of the Syrophoenician woman (7:24–30) uses a nameless woman, and here even more marginal since she is a Gentile, to exemplify a belief in Jesus going well beyond even that of the male disciples. We shall here take two additional examples of how miracles serve as allegories on the narrative.

BOX 11.3
The Miracles in the Markan Narrative Framework

The Markan miracle stories in order, organized according to the Geographical Outline; see Box 11.1.

I. Prologue: "The Beginning of the Gospel" (1:1–13)

II. A. Ministry in the Galilee: Cycle of Words and Deeds, Phase I
(1:14–3:19a)

Narrative Frame: 1:14–20   Call of First Disciples
(the "inner circle"—Peter, Andrew, James, and John)

1:21–28	Teaches in synagogue, heals demoniac
1:29–31	Healing of Peter's mother-in-law
1:32–34	Sick healed at evening
1:39–45	Healing of a leper
2:1–12	Healing of the paralytic
3:1–6	Healing of a man with withered hand
3:7–12	Healing multitudes and demons

Narrative Frame: 3:13–19a   Call of the Twelve

II. B. Ministry in the Galilee: Cycle of Words and Deeds, Phase II
(3:19b–6:6a)

Narrative Frame: 3:19b–30   Accusations Against Jesus
(*"He has a demon"*)

4:35–41	Stilling of the storm
5:1–20	Gerasene demoniac
5:21–43	Jairus's daughter and the hemorrhaging woman

Narrative Frame: 6:1–6a   Rejection at Nazareth, Cannot Perform Miracles

III. Ministry Beyond the Galilee (6:6b–10:52)

Narrative Frame: 6:6b–13   Sending Out the Twelve with Power to Cast Out Demons

6:30–44	Return of the Twelve, Feeding of 5000
6:45–52	Walking on the water
6:53–56	Healings at Gennesaret
7:24–30	Exorcism of daughter of Syrophoenician woman

7:31–37	Healing of a deaf-mute
8:1–10	Feeding of 4000
8:22–26	The blind man at Bethsaida
9:2–8	The transfiguration
9:14–29	The boy with the spirit
10:46–52	The blind man Bartimaeus

Narrative Frame: 11:1–10   Approach to Jerusalem, Triumphal Entry

IV.   11:1–16:8   Ministry in Jerusalem and Passion Narrative

Narrative Frame: 11:11   Jesus Enters Temple and Then Leaves

11:12–25   Cursing of the fig tree, cleansing of the Temple

Narrative Frame: 11:27–33   The Chief Priests Question Jesus's Authority (in the Temple)

Cleansing of the Temple, Cursing of the Fig Tree (Mark 11:11–25)

A famous episode in all the Gospels is when Jesus casts the money changers out of the Temple. In the Gospel of Mark—in stark contrast to the other Gospels—this episode plays an especially important role, because it is the act that ultimately gets Jesus killed (11:18). The scene is also presented in Mark in an unusual way, since Jesus's actions in the Temple are spliced together with an odd miracle story in which Jesus curses a fig tree. This literary construction, known as intercalation[35] (see Box 11.2), is diagrammed in Box 11.4.

The scene follows directly on the triumphal entry (A), but whereas Matthew and Luke have Jesus cleanse the Temple immediately, Mark only has Jesus enter the Temple and leave (B¹). Then on the way to the Temple the next day Jesus first curses the fig tree (C¹) and then cleanses the Temple (B²). Mark then says explicitly that his action caused the "chief priests and scribes" to plot his death, and through the remainder of Mark's Passion narrative they, and they alone, are responsible. Finally, the sequence ends with another trip past the fig tree, now withered. By sandwiching the Temple cleansing in between the two encounters with the fig tree, it forces readers to look at one in the light of the other. In other words, the fig tree becomes an allegorical symbol for the Temple, so that the cleansing is actually a cursing. The withered fig tree represents the destruction of the Temple.

BOX 11.4

The Markan Temple Cleansing Scene (11:11–24)

A *Triumphal Entry*	(Mark 11:1–10)
B¹ *In the Temple*	¹¹ Then he entered Jerusalem and went into the temple; and when he had looked around at everything, as it was already late, he went out to Bethany with the twelve.
C¹ *Curses Fig Tree*	¹² On the following day, when they came from Bethany, he was hungry. ¹³ Seeing in the distance a fig tree in leaf, he went to see whether perhaps he would find anything on it. When he came to it, he found nothing but leaves, for it was not the season for figs. ¹⁴ He said to it, "May no one ever eat fruit from you again." And his disciples heard it.
B² *Cleanses Temple*	¹⁵ Then they came to Jerusalem. And he entered the temple and began to drive out those who were selling and those who were buying in the temple, and he overturned the tables of the money changers and the seats of those who sold doves; ¹⁶ and he would not allow anyone to carry anything through the temple. ¹⁷ He was teaching and saying, "Is it not written, 'My house shall be called a house of prayer for all the nations'? But you have made it a den of robbers."
B³ *The Conspiracy*	¹⁸ And when the chief priests and the scribes heard it, they kept looking for a way to kill him; for they were afraid of him, because the whole crowd was spellbound by his teaching. ¹⁹ And when evening came, Jesus and his disciples went out of the city.
C² *Lesson of Fig Tree*	²⁰ In the morning as they passed by, they saw the fig tree withered away to its roots. ²¹ Then Peter remembered and said to him, "Rabbi, look! The fig tree that you cursed has withered." ²² Jesus answered them, "Have faith in God. ²³ Truly I tell you, if you say to this mountain, 'Be taken up and thrown into the sea,' and if you do not doubt in your heart, but believe that what you say will come to pass, it will be done for you. ²⁴ So I tell you, whatever you ask for in prayer, believe that you have received it, and it will be yours."

But why a fig tree? The story is odd in another way, since it says that the tree was in leaf, but it was not the season for figs. So why should Jesus curse it for not having any? Another clue to the dramatic play of the story comes when the fig tree shows up again in the apocalyptic discourse of chapter 13:

> *From the fig tree learn its lesson: as soon as its branch becomes tender and puts forth its leaves, you know that summer is near. So also, when you see these things taking place, you know that he is near, at the very gates.* **Truly I tell you, this generation will not pass away until all these things have taken place.** *(13:28–30)*

Now the fig tree *in leaf* (cf. 11:13) becomes a symbol of the approaching *eschaton;* therefore, the destruction of the Temple is presented by the Markan author as a sign that the *eschaton* would arrive during that very generation. We shall return to this motif in the final section of this chapter in discussing Jesus's eschatological title as "Son of Man."

The Blind Man at Bethsaida (Mark 8:14–21)

A second example shows how the miracle stories play within the secrecy and mis-understanding motif. It is the story of Jesus's healing the blind man at Bethsaida (8:22–26). We noted it briefly above in Chapter 8 as an example of a peculiarly Markan miracle story that the other Gospels choose to omit. The reason seems to be its curious suggestion that Jesus was unable to perform the miracle correctly the first time. In the light of other elements of Markan shaping of the story, we may now take another look at what is going on in this particular story in the narrative of Mark.

The scene is set up with now familiar Markan literary touches. It opens as Jesus and the disciples are crossing by boat from the other side of the Sea of Galilee. It will close with Jesus saying, in effect, "Don't tell!"

> *They came to Bethsaida. Some people brought a blind man to him and begged him to touch him. He took the blind man by the hand and led him out of the village; and when he had put saliva on his eyes and laid his hands on him, he asked him, "Can you see anything?" And the man looked up and said, "I can see people, but they look like trees, walking." Then Jesus laid his hands on his eyes again; and he looked intently and his sight was restored, and he saw everything clearly. Then he sent him away to his home, saying, "Do not even go into the village." (8:22–26).*

Structurally we must observe that this miracle occurs immediately after the third boat scene in which Jesus chastises the disciples for their lack of under-standing about the "bread" in light of the misunderstandings (the "yeast") of the Pharisees and Herod (8:14–21). On the one hand, it is a reprise of the two storm miracles (4:35–41; 6:45–52). On the other, it harks back to the two feeding miracles (6:30–44; 8:1–10). Both feeding miracles consciously anticipate features of the Last Supper (14:22–25), specifically emulating Jesus's actions in the words of institutions ("take," "bless/give thanks," "break," and "give"). Consequently, the narrative frame of this brief little scene is pregnant with numerous thematic resonances that move both forward and backward in the story.

Next, it is important to see that this strange miracle of the blind man occurs immediately before the all-important scene of Peter's confession at Caesarea Philippi (8:27–30), which in turn sets up the first prediction of the Passion (8:31–33) and the transfiguration (9:2–8). Both scenes end with Jesus instructing the disciples not to tell what they have heard and seen (8:30; 9:9). The miracle of the blind man now sets up the dramatic play of Peter's confession, as an intercalation between the two scenes of Jesus instructing his disciples. In response to Jesus's question, "Who do people say that I am?" Peter replies poignantly, "You are the Messiah" (8:29). So it would seem that Peter understands Jesus's true identity. At least that is how Matthew will understand the story (Matt 16:13–19). But the Markan narrative has a different dynamic, for when Jesus then begins to tell them he must die, Peter immediately rebukes Jesus for saying this. In turn Jesus then rebukes Peter for his failure to understand what is about to happen. In other words, Peter's understanding, while meaningful, is only partial, just like the blind man's sight after the first attempt.

The miracle of the blind man at Bethsaida is really an allegory about the disciples' understanding of Jesus's messianic identity in his role as suffering savior. Blindness and blurred vision are metaphors for ignorance and misunderstanding. Miracle stories in the Gospel of Mark are thus designed to provide the audience with commentary via allegory on issues of understanding and interpretation of Jesus's messianic identity. Precisely at those moments where the disciples fail to understand, the narrator and the narrative provide the audience with a cue about what should be understood.[36]

Misunderstanding the Messiah

So what is it that Peter *fails to understand* when he confesses that Jesus is the *Messiah*? What is it the audience is supposed to get at the same moment? The simple answer is that, because he believed Jesus to be the Messiah, Peter did not understand that Jesus must die. This line is continued through the remaining narrative right up to the point of Peter's ultimate denial (14:66–72). It means that Peter, like Judas and most other characters in the story, assumes that the messiah is primarily a Davidic royal figure who will bring a new kingdom. Although it has been shown that suffering and even death were already associated with some forms of Jewish messianic expectation, the dominant view—here being parodied as a misunderstanding—assumed a connection with some form of political eschatology. In Chapter 1 we saw just this type of messianic expectation at work among the Essenes, who also viewed the Jewish war as an eschatological event. So there is more to Peter's misunderstanding. It reflects a problem with the title "Messiah" as applied to Jesus by later believers within the Markan community. They too, like most other Jews, assumed a political messiah. It seems they were now wondering about their failed political expectations in the light of the war and the destruction of Jerusalem.

Immediately following the first Passion prediction (as discussed above) is a scene of Jesus's instructing the disciples on eschatological expectations and the coming of the Son of Man (8:34–9:1). It is followed immediately by the transfiguration (9:2–8), after which Jesus again tells the inner circle not to tell anyone, even the other disciples. But they again fail to understand:

> *As they were coming down the mountain, he ordered them to tell no one about what they had seen, until after the Son of Man had risen from the dead. So they kept the matter to themselves, questioning what this rising from the dead could mean. (9:9–10)*

So we begin to notice yet another subtle narrative pattern, in that Jesus does not refer to himself as the Messiah, as the disciples do; rather, he seems to refer to himself as the "Son of Man," even when predicting his own death and resurrection. On the surface of the narrative, then, it would appear that this shift in titles for Jesus is a kind of symbolic flag in service to the secrecy/misunderstanding motif. Or, to put it another way, at the level of the narrative, the disciples are unable to catch what Jesus means, because he uses a title they do not fully comprehend. After all, in ordinary biblical usage "son of man" was typically another way of saying "human." This ambiguity seems now to be an intentional play within the story. What should the audience think?

Juggling the Titles of Jesus

Now we may carefully examine the use of these key Christological titles: *Messiah* (or *Christ*), *Son of Man,* and *Son of God.* Later Gospels use them in combination, and thus more or less interchangeably (contrast Mark 8:29 with Matt 16:16), but the Gospel of Mark emphatically does not. Like other literary devices of the Markan author, the deployment of these titles within the narrative is a conscious decision. In this case it is effected by restricting the use of each title to certain characters within the story. This pattern of usage is shown in Box 11.5 in narrative order. It may be summarized briefly as follows:

- Within Mark, only Jesus refers to himself by the title "Son of Man"; no other character in the story ever uses this title.

BOX 11.5

Who Says It? *The Use of Christological Titles in the Gospel of Mark*

References are listed by verse number in sections of the narrative (according to the outline in Box 11.1); they show which character utters the term in the story as well as an indication of the way it is used (including the secrecy/misunderstanding motif). In addition, Column 1 shows the occurrence of the word "gospel" (*euangelion*) in relation to these key Christological titles; those in **bold**, are also uttered by Jesus in the story.

"Gospel"	"Messiah" (Christos)	"Son of Man"	"Son" / "Son of God"
I			
1:1	1:1 author: prologue (about Jesus)		1:1 author: prologue (about Jesus)
			1:11 heavenly voice at baptism 15 (*"my Son"*)
1:14,15 (2x)			
II			
		2:10 Jesus: about miracles (authority/eschatological)	
		2:28 Jesus: about the sabbath (authority/eschatological)	
			3:11 demons ("summary") (secrecy)
			5:7 demon (exorcism story) (secrecy)
	8:29 Peter: "confession" about Jesus (misunderstanding)	8:31 Jesus: Passion prediction 1 (*"Son of Man must suffer"*)	
		8:38 Jesus: about the eschaton (*"Son of Man with angels"*)	
III			
8:35		9:9, 12 Jesus: *"after resurrection"* (2x) (secrecy/misunderstanding)	9:7 heavenly voice at transfiguration (*"my Son"*) (misunderstanding)

"Gospel"	"Messiah" (Christos)	"Son of Man"	"Son" / "Son of God"
	9:41 Jesus: *"bear the name of Christ"* (indirect)	9:31 Jesus: Passion prediction 2	
10:29		10:33 Jesus: Passion prediction 3	
		10:45 Jesus: *"give his life as a ransom"* (misunderstanding)	
	12:35 Jesus: *"How can the Christ be the son of David?"* (indirect)		
13:10 ==	13:21 Jesus: apocalyptic discourse, *"Look, here is the Christ"* (indirect) ==	13:26 Jesus: apocalyptic discourse (Son of Man at *eschaton*) ==	
IV		14:21 Jesus: about arrest (2x)	
14:9		14:41 Jesus: in Gethsemane	
	14:61 high priest: at trial (to Jesus) ==	14:62 Jesus: at trial, response to high priest (*"Son of Man at right hand . . . with clouds"*—eschatological) ==	14:61 high priest: at trial (to Jesus) ==
	15:32 bystanders at the cross (mocking Jesus)		15:39 centurion at the cross (mocking/ironic?)

KEY: == indicates parts of the same passage
Italics = dialogue of Jesus

- By contrast, the disciples, as represented by Peter, only use the title "Messiah" to refer to Jesus (8:29), as do the derisive high priest and the mocking bystanders at the cross. It and other messianic phrases, such as "Son of David" (10:47–48; 12:35), are used in such a way as to suggest that this was also the popular understanding of Jesus, particularly at the triumphal entry (11:1–10), which intentionally emulates a royal procession.[37]

- Closely associated with "Messiah" is the phrase "King of the Jews," which is only used of Jesus by Pilate and other "Roman" characters during the trial and crucifixion scenes (15:2, 9, 12, 18, 26). It may be taken as a parody of the title "Messiah" and more generally of the political aspects of Jewish expectation, as denigrated by non-Jews.

- Finally, the title "Son of God" is only used by the demons, the high priest (derisively), the centurion at the cross (mockingly), and, most important, the voice from heaven at the baptism and the transfiguration. Its use by the demons is clearly meant to be dramatic irony, played off against that by the priest and centurion. Ironically, neither Jesus nor any disciple ever utters the title in the Gospel of Mark.

That these titles carry symbolic weight in the structure of the story is shown by the fact that the prologue of the Gospel opens with these words: "The beginning of the good news [or gospel, *euangelion*] of Jesus Christ, the Son of God" (1:1). Here we see three of the key terms that are characteristic of the Markan author and his effort to depict the "true" understanding of Jesus as the Messiah.

"Messiah"

The title "Messiah" as used within the Markan narrative represents a *misunderstanding* of Jesus. It is the title used by Peter in the confession at Caesarea Philippi, but Peter fails to understand that Jesus must die (8:29, discussed above). It assumes the widespread messianic expectations of an earthly king from the Davidic line that would have been popular before and during the war. It assumes also that many of the followers of Jesus had gone into the war with this same basic notion of Jesus. That is precisely the problem that the author of Mark is trying to correct. The Markan author does this by recasting the meaning of "Messiah" through two dramatic mechanisms in the narrative: first, by characterizing the traditional messianic ideas as a "misunderstanding"; and, second, by reconfiguring it in terms of the other two titles—"Son of Man" and "Son of God"—to give it a new sense.

"Son of Man"

By virtue of their restrictive usage, the two key titles in Mark are "Son of Man" and "Son of God." As noted in Chapter 1, the title "Son of God" was not frequently used in earlier Jewish messianic expectation. When it was used, however, it was typically understood in traditional Davidic terms. That is, it was used of the symbolic anointing of the Davidic king as God's "adopted" son. As we shall see, it retains this basic sense in Mark, but with a bit of a twist.

The title "Son of Man," however, was not typically a messianic title. In earlier Jewish usage, and especially in the Hebrew poetry of the Psalms and prophets, it is just another way of referring to a human being. The classic example is Psalm 8:4: "What is *man* that thou art mindful of him, and the *son of man* that thou dost care for him?"[38] The title is found in the New Testament as a title of Jesus only in the Gospels and then principally from Mark and Q materials. The type of usage seen in these cases had taken on new meaning in Jewish apocalyptic context.[39] Ultimately, the title derives from Daniel 7:13, whence it came to be associated in later apocalyptic literature with an angelic figure who would come as eschatological judge of Israel's righteous remnant.[40] In the Gospel of Mark it continues to be used in this way, and a number of Jesus's own references to the "Son of Man" could be taken on the surface as references to this "other" eschatological figure (8:38; 13:26; cf. 2:10, 28).[41] Here is a good example:

> *"Those who are ashamed of me and of my words in this adulterous and sinful generation, of them the Son of Man will also be ashamed when he comes in the glory of his Father with the holy angels." And he said to them, "Truly I tell you, there are some standing here who will not taste death until they see that the kingdom of God has come with power." (8:38–9:1)*

In other passages, however, the Markan usage clearly makes the term self-referential of Jesus, usually in anticipation of his death and resurrection in the three Passion predictions (8:31; 9:31; 10:33; cf. 9:9, 12; 10:45). Thus, notice that this key term is also given added emphasis within the narrative by the Markan thematic device of triplets.

In only one instance do these two meanings of "Son of Man"—as suffering human and eschatological judge—seem to come together. Significantly, it occurs at Jesus's trial, when the high priest derisively asks Jesus if he is the "Messiah" and then "Son of the Blessed One [God]" (14:61). It is also the only time that all three titles are used in the same episode. For the Markan audience this dramatic convergence has to be a clear signal. To the high priest's question Jesus responds affirmatively, "I am," at last dropping his secretive stance, but ironically in a context where no one will listen. Then he adds, "And 'you will see the Son of Man seated at the right hand of the Power,' and 'coming with the clouds of heaven'" (14:62).

The first part of this response alludes to Psalm 110(109):1, which we discussed (Chapter 7) as a principal text for the development of the Passion and resurrection tradition. It was taken as a scriptural "proof text" for the exaltation of Jesus to heaven. We shall return to it below. The second is a direct reference to Daniel 7:13 and the eschatological figure. It also picks up the earlier usage in Mark 8:38 and 13:26 (see Box 11.5). Thus, the distinctive feature of the Markan use of the title

"Son of Man" is that it serves to link his suffering and death with his return as eschatological figure.[42] In part, then, the "Son of Man" title fundamentally alters the meaning of the title "Messiah," at least as it was understood by the disciples and other characters within the story. It is as if to say that Jesus as Messiah would *not* bring an earthly messianic kingdom, at least *not yet*.

"Son of God"

With this shift of meaning we come to the most important title of all: "Son of God." It now stands in between the other two, to explain how Jesus as "Messiah" becomes the eschatological "Son of Man."[43] To do so, we must first notice the opening of Mark, which includes the author's prologue containing three key terms: "gospel," "Messiah," and "Son of God" (1:1). Then, after a very brief summary of John's preaching, we get the arrival of Jesus at his baptism. There, as the heavens "split open," he is "anointed" with the Spirit, and a voice announces, "You are my Son, the Beloved; with you I am well pleased" (1:11). This scene already anticipates the crucifixion, where the curtain of the Temple will be "split in two" *using the same Greek word,* after which the centurion will call Jesus "Son of God" (15:38–39).

Because the Gospel of Mark contains no prior story of Jesus's birth or background, he steps onstage at his baptism as an ordinary mortal. The descent of the Spirit alludes to royal messianic themes from Isaiah 11:1–2 and 61:1–2, and the words of the voice from heaven are a paraphrase of Psalm 2:7 and Isaiah 42:1, referring to the chosen servant (see Chapter 1).[44] Only at his baptism is Jesus tapped to be God's Son, very much like the coronation of the Davidic king. But it also seems that only he sees the "dove" and hears the voice. *His new messianic identity is still a secret.*

Next, we must once again return to that crucial sequence of scenes in the middle section of the Gospel, now with an eye to how the key titles are deployed (see Box 11.5). It opens with the allegorical story of the blind man at Bethsaida (Mark 8:22–26) followed immediately by Peter's "blurred" confession that Jesus is the "Messiah" (8:27–29). The confession is then followed by a suffering "Son of Man" saying (8:31) and then an eschatological "Son of Man" saying (8:38). Then comes the transfiguration, where the voice from heaven identifies Jesus as "my Son, the Beloved" (9:7), followed by two more suffering "Son of Man" sayings (9:9, 12). The staccato succession of these scenes is probably the most dramatic, poignant, and pregnant moment in the Gospel of Mark other than the crucifixion itself. It is marked by themes of misunderstanding four times (8:25–26; 8:32; 9:6; 9:10) and then followed by the allegorical exorcism of the boy with a demon (9:14–29) and concluding with the second Passion prediction, where once again the disciples fail to understand (9:30–32).[45] It is also worth noting that the distinctively Markan term "gospel" also shows up in this same sequence (8:35).

All of this allows the Markan audience to see these key titles in a new light, in fact from the omniscient perspective of the narrator. The voice from heaven at the transfiguration, as a resurrection "preview," is ultimately the cue: the Messiah must indeed suffer and die so that he can come back as eschatological "Son of Man." The title "Son of God" thus refers, in the first instance, to his "royal adoption" at baptism to assume his role as Messiah. In the second instance, it refers to his exaltation—*or* rather "adoption"—into heaven at his resurrection, so that he can assume his heavenly seat until his eschatological return (see Chapter 7). That the disciples fail to comprehend helps to drive the story to its inevitable conclusion. But the audience knows what is coming, even though the characters within the story do not.[46]

The Riddle of the Psalms

What may be underpinning this "double adoption" idea is yet another case of using the Psalms to interpret and narrativize the story of Jesus's death and resurrection. Psalm 2, of course, is the principal source for the traditional messianic language and especially the "royal adoption" ideology associated with the Davidic line: "You are my son; today have I begotten you" (2:7). It clearly stands behind the voice from heaven at both the baptism and the transfiguration. But as early as Paul, another Psalm, 110 (109 in the Septuagint), had already become central to the understanding of Jesus's resurrection and exaltation. In these earlier traditions, its first verse is the key:

> *A Psalm by David. The Lord said to my Lord, "Sit at my right hand, until I shall place your enemies as a footstool for your feet." (109:1, LXX)*

We note, then, that this psalm, traditionally assumed to have been authored by David himself, has him referring to an enthronement of his "Lord" *at the right hand* of God.[47]

In early Christian interpretation, this "Lord" was of course taken to be Jesus.[48] This is precisely how it was interpreted in the earliest oral tradition as a way of validating the resurrection of Jesus. We see it clearly in Paul:

> *Who is to condemn? It is Christ Jesus, who died, yes, who was raised, <u>who is at the right hand of God</u>, who indeed intercedes for us. (Rom 8:34)*

In this case, an allusion to the psalm stands as a synonym for Jesus's resurrection and his present exalted position in heaven at the right hand of God.

An even more telling line of interpretation comes in Paul's discussion of the resurrection of the dead at the *eschaton*. It comes in the section following his all-important rehearsal of the oral tradition of Jesus's death, burial, and resurrection in 1 Corinthians 15:3–8:

For as all die in Adam, so all will be made alive in Christ. But each in his own order: Christ the first fruits, then at his coming those who belong to Christ. Then comes the end, when he hands over the kingdom to God the Father, after he has destroyed every ruler and every authority and power. For he must reign until <u>he has put all his enemies under his feet.</u> The last enemy to be destroyed is death. For <u>"God has put all things in subjection under his feet."</u> But when it says, <u>"All things are put in subjection,"</u> it is plain that this does not include the one who put all things in subjection under him. (1 Cor 15:22–27)

The first of the allusions (here underlined) is clearly to Psalm 110(109):1. The second is a quotation of Psalm 8:6 (v. 7 in the LXX), which is being treated as a version of the same idea based on the nearly identical wording "under your/his feet" in both psalms. Psalm 8 was originally about the status of humans as "a little lower than God," but it must be remembered that this is the same psalm that uses "son of man" to refer to humanity in this way. This further intertextual clue may say something about how the "Son of Man" title originally came into the picture as an interpretation of these two psalms.[49] Clearly, Paul understands Psalms 8 and 110 here to refer to Christ's heavenly status pursuant to his resurrection, whence he will return to resurrect the righteous. Then, it says, Christ will "hand over the kingdom to God." Thus, once again we have the royal messianic ideology behind the titles; only now it is a cosmic drama being carried out in heaven *after* Jesus's resurrection.[50]

It seems, then, that this second step in the "Davidic drama," if we may call it that, may be behind the "double adoption" in Mark: as Messiah Jesus can be exalted to heaven as "Son of God" at his resurrection, where he will wait to return as "Son of Man" at the *eschaton*.[51] Significantly, the Gospel of Mark has Jesus himself twice quote Psalm 110(109):1. The first occurs in Mark 12:36, just prior to the apocalyptic discourse of Mark 13. In this case, Jesus is shown teaching in the Temple. He quotes the psalm (in the Greek, of course), but then poses a riddle about its meaning: How can David call the Messiah "my Lord," since the Messiah is supposed to be David's son? In other words, this Markan scene is playing precisely with the same questions. The Markan Passion drama will provide the answers. The Messiah is no longer just David's son; he is God's Son in heaven.

Here is how it does so. The second Markan quotation of Psalm 110 occurs, as noted earlier, in the trial scene, when the high priest derisively asks Jesus if he is the Messiah:

Again the high priest asked him, "Are you the Messiah, the Son of the Blessed One?" Jesus said, "I am; and 'you will see the <u>Son of Man seated at the right hand of the Power,</u>' and 'coming with the clouds of heaven.'" (14:62)

This is the one place in all of Mark where all three key titles come together. In fact, the refrain of the Son of Man "coming with the clouds" is found in both Mark 8:38 and 13:26, the other two uses of the title with this eschatological sense (see

Box 11.5). But now it adds Psalm 110 (underlined) to identify the heavenly position of the "Son of Man" prior to his eschatological return. At the same time, it has Jesus affirm his identity *for the first time* as both Messiah and "Son of the Blessed One," that is, "Son of God." It thus blends the royal adoption language of Psalm 2 with the heavenly exaltation language of Psalm 110. By narrativizing the psalms in this way, the Markan author thus preserves the traditional apocalyptic elements of messianic expectation while systematically reinterpreting them for their application to Jesus's identity in the aftermath of the war.

Bit Parts with Big Impact in the Markan Drama

By way of conclusion, we may touch on three other characterizations that finally fall into place in the light of this narrative sequence and the use of dramatic irony. The first is Judas.

Judas

As we noted in Chapter 7, the character of Judas changes drastically in the later Gospels. By contrast, in the earliest oral tradition (Paul), he plays no role at all. The first "appearance" of Judas onstage in the Gospel tradition thus comes in the Gospel of Mark. I would argue that it is part of the Markan plot design. There Judas appears to be an overly zealous disciple who fully and ardently believes that Jesus is the Messiah, but only a Davidic political deliverer. His actions in turning Jesus over to the authorities seem designed to force his hand in showing his real identity. So Judas, like Peter, actually understands, at least partly. It may thus be argued that the role of Judas in the Gospel of Mark is largely a development of the author for two key purposes: first, as a way to narrativize the sequence from Last Supper to the crucifixion and, second, to serve as counterpoint to Peter. Both Judas and Peter fail to understand, but Judas's misunderstanding is worse, because it pushes the revolutionary assumptions that led to the failed revolt. Jesus is always depicted in Mark as resisting these revolutionary ideas (see esp. 12:13–17). In the end Peter's denial leaves him wondering and thus opens the door for reinterpretation. This characterization of Judas is more plastic and brittle. He has fallen into the apocalyptic trap that takes messianic language solely in political and revolutionary terms.

The Woman Who Anoints Jesus

Next, there is the woman who anoints Jesus's head at Bethany (14:3–9) just prior to the Last Supper. She is the last of three nameless, marginal women who show the proper understanding of Jesus's true identity.[52] Three statements of Jesus in this very brief scene mark her as exemplary. First, she stands in opposition to the male onlookers (presumably including some of the disciples), who criticize her waste of the oil. In response Jesus says, "She has anointed my body beforehand for its burial" (14:8). This statement anticipates the arrival of the women at the tomb (16:1), but also serves as Jesus's final messianic anointing in preparation for his death and resurrection.[53]

Second, Jesus says, "Wherever the *good news* [or *gospel*] is proclaimed in the whole world" (14:9), another case of the author's compositional perspective.[54] Third, Jesus's statement continues, "what she has done will be told in remembrance of her" (14:9). This comment serves as an allusion to the commemorative language ("Do this in remembrance of me") in the Last Supper tradition (1 Cor 11:24–25), but which is noticeably absent in the Markan Last Supper scene (14:22–25). The statement ("will be told") also reverses Jesus's usual command in Mark not to tell. Here, of course, it refers to "performing" the Gospel itself, just as the Markan author has done. Ultimately, though marginal and scandalous, she is the model disciple and the model of proper faith in Jesus for the Markan audience.[55]

The Centurion at the Cross

Last, there is the centurion at the cross (15:39). Despite being a male, he too is a marginal character: nameless, a Gentile, and a Roman "oppressor." Yet at the moment of Jesus's death, he utters the fateful words, "Truly this man was God's Son." It is the final occurrence of this all-important title in the Gospel of Mark. Later tradition, beginning with the Gospel of Matthew, will take this scene as a sign that the centurion saw the truth and became a follower of Jesus. In apocryphal legends he would even be given a name, Longinus, and eventually considered a saint.[56]

Although many scholars continue to take this scene in a serious way, or at least in the vein of later martyr tales, others have argued that it is to be read as dramatic irony.[57] Rather than confessional, the centurion's response may be taken as mockery, but, ironically, he was speaking the truth.[58] In contrast to the Matthean version, where the moment of Jesus's death is accompanied by miraculous events (Matt 27:51–55) that are witnessed by the centurion, in Mark he sees only that Jesus "breathed his last," or more literally in Greek, "expired." In other words, he has watched Jesus physically exhale his final breath, undoubtedly accompanied by the "death rattle." So rather than taking a heroic reading of the centurion's response, it seems as though we should see it as mockery: *O sure, this was God's son.* Yet at this dramatic moment, the audience knows something more. Jesus's death is what will finally and fully make him "God's Son." Perhaps we should imagine the audience of Mark's Gospel chuckling at the centurion's unwitting "confession." Although the character in the story fails to understand, the audience knows.

To glimpse the audience's role in the dramatic interplay of the Gospel we need only back up just a few verses before the scene with the centurion, when the bystanders at the cross think Jesus is calling for Elijah: "Eloi, eloi, lema sabachthani" (15:34–35). Clearly, they also misunderstand both Jesus and his words. The characters in the story say, "Let's wait and see if Elijah comes and *takes him down*" (15:36). As we saw in Chapter 7, the transfiguration story is a "preview" of Jesus's resurrection. In it Elijah and Moses come down and stand with Jesus, while he is physically transformed or "glorified," as in his ultimate heavenly form. So, in response to the characters at the cross, the audience might be expected to say, "No, Elijah will come and *take him up*"—to heaven. At that moment, the audience has uttered the very confession that makes Jesus's story real for them.

Even so, it appears that the Markan Christology is still at an early stage of development and still in line with a traditionally Jewish messianic model of a royal adoption, being worked out dramatically through oral performance. That is the Markan drama. It is an act of faith for its own time and place.

CHAPTER TWELVE

The Righteous
Teacher of Torah

The Gospel of Matthew

When Jesus saw the crowds, he went up the mountain; and after he sat down, his disciples came to him. Then he began to speak, and taught them, saying:

"Blessed are the poor in spirit, for theirs is the kingdom of heaven.

"Blessed are those who mourn, for they will be comforted.

"Blessed are the meek, for they will inherit the earth.

"Blessed are those who hunger and thirst for righteousness, for they will be filled. . . .

"Do not think that I have come to abolish the law or the prophets; I have come not to abolish but to fulfill. For truly I tell you, until heaven and earth pass away, not one letter, not one stroke of a letter, will pass from the law until all is accomplished. Therefore, whoever breaks one of the least of these commandments, and teaches others to do the same, will be called least in the kingdom of heaven; but whoever does them and teaches them will be called great in the kingdom of heaven. For I tell you, unless your righteousness exceeds that of the scribes and Pharisees, you will never enter the kingdom of heaven." (Matthew 5:1–6, 17–20)

To describe the composition of the Gospel of Matthew we might start with a take-off on an old saying: "Something old, something new, something borrowed, and something Q." Yet, the Gospel of Matthew, as we shall see, is more than a mere interfolding of elements *borrowed* from Mark and Q. It is a thorough reworking of both through the lens of the Matthean author and audience. We can see it in the passage quoted above. It shows something that never occurs in the Gospel of Mark, namely, a picture of Jesus teaching crowds of people through extended discourses or "sermons." More to the point, in the Gospel of Matthew Jesus delivers five such sermons that are intended to explicate his message publicly. We shall discuss them later in this chapter.

We begin with what is perhaps the most famous sermon of Jesus known from the Gospels—the Sermon on the Mount. In setting, construction, and content, however, it is unique to the Gospel of Matthew: it is set on a mountain in Galilee and runs to III verses—three full chapters (Matt 5–7). A similar collection of sayings appears in the Gospel of Luke (6:20–49). This Lukan episode, however, is called the Sermon on the Plain, because it was delivered instead on a "level place" beside the Sea of Galilee (6:17). It contains a scant 29 verses, including a series of blessings, or what we usually call the Beatitudes, and woes:

> *Then he looked up at his disciples and said:*
> *"Blessed are you who are poor, for yours is the kingdom of God.*
> *"Blessed are you who are hungry now, for you will be filled.*
> *"Blessed are you who weep now, for you will laugh. . . .*
> *"But woe to you who are rich, for you have received your consolation.*
> *"Woe to you who are full now, for you will be hungry.*
> *"Woe to you who are laughing now, for you will mourn and weep."*
> *(Luke 6:20–21; 24–25)*

Although these two sermons clearly depend on some of the same basic sayings of Jesus, there are subtle but important differences in the wording. The versions in Matthew seem to be more about spiritual matters and righteousness. Those in Luke reflect a biting social criticism. Many scholars would suggest that they go back to Jesus himself; however, which form is the more original (that in Matthew or Luke) is debated by scholars. But the vast majority of scholars would argue that these sayings, and the very idea of a sermon of Jesus, comes from a separate oral tradition of Jesus's teachings, what we typically call Q.

Different as these sayings may be, such images of Jesus as teacher stand in sharp contrast to the secretive Jesus of the Markan Gospel, where only the disciples are given his real message, and even they misunderstand it. When Jesus speaks publicly in Mark, it is usually limited to brief, cryptic statements. In these later Gospels, however, the teachings of Jesus now rise to a new level of importance. Even so, there are significant differences between the Gospels of Matthew and Luke in how they depict both the image of Jesus as teacher and the nature or content of his teachings. At the same time, it is clear that the Matthean and Lukan Gospels used the Gospel of Mark as a source and yet modified it to suit their own ends. Consequently, each author has reshaped older sources, introduced new material, and interwoven them through creative retelling of the story.

In order to understand how the Gospels of Matthew and Luke have reshaped the older traditions about Jesus, we must first give some attention to the content and shape of the material drawn from Q. Then we will examine the way that the Matthean author has integrated it into the Markan outline. We shall return to the Gospel of Luke in the next chapter.

Jesus as Teacher in the Q Tradition

As discussed earlier, "Q" is the scholarly shorthand for the *other* source, besides Mark, that was used by the authors of Matthew and Luke. It probably dates from the period just before the first Jewish revolt (ca. 60–66 CE) and represents, at least in part, an oral tradition of Jesus sayings that had circulated since the early days, most likely in the Galilee.[1]

Yet Q is not a narrative Gospel in the same sense as Mark and the others. It was a collection of sayings of Jesus assembled in a loosely ordered manner. Many of these sayings are in the form of brief *chreiai,* or "pronouncement stories" (see Chapter 9), that contain little in the way of quasi-biographical situations. They resemble brief dialogues that set up a key saying or punch line.[2] There is almost no discernible sequence of Jesus's life and career; nor are there any miracle stories, as we shall see below. Most important, there seems to be no Passion narrative as such. The sayings of Jesus stand as independent units or short clusters grouped by theme and woven into small performative vignettes[3] (see Box 12.1). There are more than 250 verses of this common material and approximately 70 distinct sayings or sayings clusters.[4] (For a reconstruction of the "text" of Q, see Appendix D.)

At center stage stands Jesus as teacher, but a teacher with a special image and authority as Wisdom's child:

> *For John the Baptist has come eating no bread and drinking no wine, and you say, "He has a demon." The Son of Man has come eating and drinking, and you say, "Look, a glutton and a drunkard, a friend of tax collectors and sinners!" Nevertheless, Wisdom (Sophia) is vindicated by all her children." (Q20 = Luke 7:33–35; Matt 11:16–19)*

In this saying we clearly see an appeal to the authority of Sophia, Woman Wisdom, who is depicted as the parent of Jesus and John. To be called the child of Sophia was a typical way of referring to the prophets of old or just to the righteous person in the Jewish wisdom literature (cf. Chapter 2).[5] It seems that Q fits into the Jewish wisdom tradition and follows the genre of wisdom instruction as a way of presenting the teachings of Jesus.[6]

Some scholars have argued that the Q material preserved in the Gospels of Matthew and Luke reflects a later stage of transmission of its oral tradition of

BOX 12.1

The Content of Q
The Synoptic Sayings Source

Since it is typical in scholarship to record the Q material using the verse numbering in the Gospel of Luke, we follow this convention (Column 1); the Q ordinals in Column 1 follow Kloppenborg, as do the topical headings (with some modification). Items in brackets [ ] are debated; items marked with double asterisk** also have Markan variants (see final section). Column 2 gives the Matthew parallel; Column 3 gives parallels in Paul; and Column 4 gives the parallels in the *Gospel of Thomas*, cited by logion number (following Koester). Sources: J. S. Kloppenborg, *Q Parallels* (Sonoma, CA: Polebridge, 1988), xxxi–xxxiii; H. Koester, *Ancient Christian Gospels* (Philadelphia: Trinity Press International, 1990) 53, 87–89. For the text of Q, following this reconstruction, see Appendix D.

Q / Luke	Matthew	Paul	*Gospel of Thomas*
The Preaching of John			
Q3 3:7–9	3:7–10	1 Thess 1:10	
Q4 3:16b–17	3:11–12		
The Temptation			
Q6 4:2–13	4:2–11		
A Sermon			
Q7 6:20a	5:1–2		
Q8 6:20b–23	5:3–12		54; 68; 69
Q9 6:27–35	5:38–47; 7:12	Rom 12:14, 17 1 Thess 5:15	95; 6b
Q10 6:36–38	5:48; 7:1–2	Rom 14:10	
Q11 6:39b–40	15:13–14; 10:24–25		34
Q12 6:41–42	7:3–5		26
Q13 6:43–45	7:15–20; 12:33–35		43; 45
Q14 6:46–49	7:21–27		
John and Jesus vs. Their Generation			
Q15 7:1b–10	8:5–13		
Q16 7:18–20, 22–23	11:2–6		
Q17 7:24–28	11:7–11		78; 46
Q18 16:16	11:12–15		
Q20 7:31–35	11:16–19		*(continued)*

Q / Luke		Matthew	Paul	*Gospel of Thomas*
Q21	9:57–60	8:18–22		86
Q22	10:2–12	9:36–38; 10:1–16	1 Cor 9:14	72; 14b
Q23	10:13–15	11:20–24		
Q24	10:16	10:40		
Q25	10:21–22	11:25–27		61b
Q26	10:23b–24	13:16–17		17
Q27	11:2–4	6:7–13		
Q28	11:9–13	7:7–11		92, 94
Q29	11:14–18a, 19–23	12:22–30; 9:32–34		
Q30	11:24–26	12:43–45		
[Q31	11:27–28] ?	–		79a
Q32	11:16, 29–32	12:38–42		
Q33	11:33–36; cf. 8:16	5:14–16 6:22–23		33b; 24
Q34	11:39b–44,**			
	46–52; 13:34–35	23:1–39; 13:34–35		89
On Anxiety *or* The Fate of God's Messengers				
Q35	12:2–3**	10:26–27		5; 6; 33a
Q36	12:4–7	10:28–31		
Q37	12:8–9**	10:32–33		
Q38	12:10	12:31–32		44
Q39	12:11–12	10:17–20, 23		
[Q40	12:13–14, 16–21] ?	–		73; 63
Q41	12:22–31	6:25–34		36
Q42	12:33–34	6:19–21		76
On Judgment				
Q43	12:35–38**	22:11–14; 25:1–13**		21c; 75
Q44	12:39–40	24:42–44	1 Thess 5:2	21b; 103
Q45	12:42b–46	24:45–51		
Q46	12:[49] 51–53	10:34–36		10; 16
Q47	12:54–56	16:2–3		91
Q48	12:58–59	5:25–26		
Parables of Growth				
Q49	13:18–21	13:31–33		20; 96
The Two Ways				
Q50	13:24–27	7:13–14, 22–23		
Q51	13:28–30	8:11–12; 20:16		
Q52	13:34–35	23:37–39		
Q54	14:11; cf. 18:14b	23:6–12		
Q55	14:16–24	22:1–10		64

Q / Luke		Matthew	Paul	Gospel of Thomas
Q56	14:26–27; 17:33	10:37–39		55; 101
Q57	14:34–35	5:13		
Miscellaneous Sayings				
Q58	15:4–7	18:12–14		107
[Q59	15:8–10] ?	—		
Q60	16:13	6:24		47
Q61	16:16–18	11:12–13; 5:18, 32		
Q62	17:1b–2	18:6–7		
Q63	17:3b–4	18:15–17, 21–22		
Q64	17:6b**	17:19–20	1 Cor 13:2	48
Eschatological Sayings				
[Q65	17:20b–21] ?	—		113
Q66	17:23–29, 30, 34–35, 37b	24:23–28, 37–42		61a (cf. 3; 51)
Q67	19:12–13, 15b–24, 26	25:14–30		41
Q68	22:28, 30	19:27–29		
Q69	15:11[28–32]	21:28–32		

Q Sayings** with Markan variants		Matthew	Markan Parallel	Paul	Gospel of Thomas
Q34c	11:43	23:6	12:38–39		
Q35a	12:2	10:26	4:22		
Q37	12:8–9	10:32–33	8:38		
Q43	12:35–38; 9:26	22:11–14; 25:1–13		13:35–36	21c; 75
Q64	17:6b	17:19–20	11:23	1 Cor 13:2	48

Jesus's sayings.[7] They point to the rather disparate and inconsistent quality of the sayings in Q and argue further that the *earlier* wisdom tradition has been overlaid or interspersed with *later* and rather alien apocalyptic elements. They also argue that, by removing these "later" elements, one can then isolate the earliest layer(s) of Q that go back nearer to the time of Jesus. Although other scholars would agree that there are different types of material woven together in Q, some would not agree that these represent layers or strata of composition that can be separated chronologically.[8] Likewise, they have questioned the supposed discrepancy between the wisdom and apocalyptic traditions.[9] Many of these same scholars have seriously questioned the efforts of some to separate Q into distinct chronological layers merely by selecting certain sayings.[10] Q is not a cohesive narrative, but it does have an integral literary structure that reflects a later stage of development in the oral tradition.[11] Even the linking of Jesus's and John's careers through the image of "Sophia's children" reflects a later stage of reflection.[12]

Setting and Audience of Q

The use of the Jewish wisdom tradition for presenting the teachings of Jesus in Q suggests a setting in the Jewish homeland amid a predominantly (though not exclusively) Jewish population. The fact that several Galilean towns are named, often in a negative light, may well suggest the early Q collection originated in the Galilee.[13] Notice Q23:

> "Woe to you, Chorazin! Woe to you, Bethsaida! For if the deeds of power done in you had been done in Tyre and Sidon, they would have repented long ago, sitting in sackcloth and ashes. But at the judgment it will be more tolerable for Tyre and Sidon than for you. And you, Capernaum, will you be exalted to heaven? No, you will be brought down to Hades." (Luke 10:13–15; cf. Matt 11:23–24)

The point of this saying is that Chorazin, Bethsaida, and Capernaum have rejected Jesus and his teachings; therefore, they will be rejected at the "judgment." So we see some key apocalyptic elements emerging within Q.

But this saying goes farther, because it contrasts the towns of Chorazin, Bethsaida, and Capernaum with Tyre and Sidon. These first three are part of the "lower Galilee," where Jesus's ministry originated. But the remainder of the saying may suggest that the movement had subsequently moved farther to the north, into the "upper Galilee," near the Syrian border regions and Hellenistic cities such as Tyre and Sidon. So it would seem that the area of the Galilee would seem to fit well with Q's social location.[14] Based on wording and the use of quotations from the Septuagint, it had already moved into a Greek-speaking orbit, where contact with Gentiles was a cultural reality. As a result of growing tensions and growing interaction, the followers of Jesus were beginning to broaden their cultural horizons.[15] Again, these elements fit the region of the Galilee, especially in the period just prior to and after the first revolt. On the other hand, the fact that prominent lower Galilean cities, such as Tiberias and Sepphoris (only three miles from Nazareth), are not mentioned suggests a semirural rather than urban background for the early Jesus movement out of which Q evolved. As we shall see, its continuing development is shown by the fact that many of the prophetic sayings attributed to Jesus in Q show secondary elaboration to meet the needs of the author and audience.[16]

From Q to Matthew

The Gospel of Matthew probably comes from a later phase of this same trajectory, still in the predominantly Jewish regions of the upper Galilee or lower Syria some two to three decades later.[17] A good example of the link may be seen in the healing story of the centurion's servant (Luke 7:1–10; Matt 8:5–13). Here is the Matthean version:

> When he entered Capernaum, a centurion came to him, appealing to him and saying, "Lord, my servant is lying at home paralyzed, in terrible distress." And he said to him, "I will come and cure him." The centurion answered, "Lord, I am not worthy to have you come under my roof; but only speak the word, and my servant will be healed. For I also am a man under authority, with soldiers under me; and I say to one, 'Go,' and he goes, and to another, 'Come,' and he comes, and to my slave, 'Do this,' and the slave does it." When Jesus heard him, he was amazed and said to those who followed him, "Truly I tell you, in no one in Israel have I found such faith. _I tell you, many will come from east and west and will eat with Abraham and Isaac and Jacob in the kingdom of heaven, while the heirs of the kingdom will be thrown into the outer darkness, where there will be weeping and gnashing of teeth._" And to the centurion Jesus said, "Go; let it be done for you according to your faith." And the servant was healed in that hour.[18]

At base this episode appears to be a miracle story; however, many of the typical features of miracle stories (discussed in Chapter 8) have been truncated or deleted. There is no healing action, nor is the cure demonstrated. Instead, the miracle story serves primarily as a narrative episode that sets up a dialogue between Jesus and the centurion (Matthew) or his friends (Luke). In effect, the miracle story has been transformed into a *chreia*, that is, a sayings story used to set up the punch line about the faith of the centurion, a Gentile. Notably, the story takes place at Capernaum. It thus continues the Q theme of rejection by these Galilean cities, as noted above.[19] In this case, it appears that the Matthean version is closer to the original, at least for the central portion of the dialogue. The Lukan version shows other secondary changes and stresses the centurion's piety as a "God-fearer" who helped build the local synagogue.[20]

This episode is one of only two references to miracles in the entire Q collection; however, even it had already been transformed into a sayings story instead.[21] The Matthean version of this episode has been elaborated further by adding in a second, independent saying also drawn from Q (Q51, underlined above). This point is indicated by the fact that it is found in an entirely different location in Luke (13:28–29) and has no intrinsic connection to the centurion story.

By combining these two units of Q material, this new version emphasizes what will become a key theme and literary device in the Gospel of Matthew: transforming miracles into sayings stories. Hence, there are two stages to be seen here in reshaping the story. First, its dramatic transformation from a simple miracle into a *chreia* about faith and rejection comes from the Q stage of transmission prior to the Gospel of Matthew. This point is demonstrated by the fact that the traditional miraculous elements are missing in both Matthew and Luke. Second, its combining of several independent Q units to extend this vignette into a more elaborate saying comes from the Matthean author.

Two final points may be noted here regarding the Matthean use of this Q material. First, the tendency to transform miracle stories into teaching episodes, as seen here already in Q, will serve as a model for the Matthean author's handling of other miracles drawn from Mark.[22] In general, the Markan miracles will be abbreviated and slanted in the direction of teachings about faith. In several cases they are augmented by adding Q sayings to serve as punch lines, as seen in the Matthean version of stilling the storm (8:18–27; cf. Mark 4:35–41) and the exorcism of the epileptic boy (17:14–21; Mark 9:14–29).

Second, the end of the added saying from Q51 ("thrown into the outer darkness, where there will be weeping and gnashing of teeth") will also be taken over as a Matthean fingerprint. It is replicated five more times, and in each case inserted into a Matthean parable.[23] We discussed the allegorical impact of this type of Matthean reshaping in the parables of the weeds and the net in Chapter 9. In other words, the portrayal of Jesus's teachings that had already evolved through elaboration in the Q tradition provides a direct influence on the narrative shaping of the Matthean portrait of Jesus. Several key themes of rejection, sectarian tension, and apocalyptic judgment will come directly from the Q tradition into the Gospel of Matthew.[24] The path that led from Q to Matthew will be discussed further below.

The Narrative World of the Matthean Drama

The narrative outline of Matthew basically follows that of the Markan Gospel, and the Passion narrative is particularly close to Mark until near the end (see Chapter 7). Even so, there are significant changes in the Matthean outline (see Box 12.2). This Matthean reshaping can be seen in several ways.

The Geographical Outline of the Narrative

First, whereas the geographical outline of Mark is divided into three roughly equal parts (Galilee, beyond Galilee, and Jerusalem), in the Gospel of Matthew the Galilee section alone comprises almost half of the narrative. Thus, the rejection at Nazareth occurs in Mark at 6:1–6, but in Matthew at 13:53–58, relatively much

BOX 12.2

Comparison of the Outlines of Matthew and Mark

Matthew	Mark
[Birth Narrative–*added*]	
Jesus and John the Baptist (3:1–4:11)	Jesus and John the Baptist (1:1–13)
Baptism	Baptism
Temptation	Temptation
Ministry Phase I:	Ministry Phase I: Galilee (1:14–6:6)
Galilee (4:12–13:58)	
Call of First Disciples (4:18–22)	First Miracles (1:29–34, 40–45; 2:1–12)
I. Sermon on Mount (5:1–7:28)	Parables (4:1–34)
First Miracles (8:1–9:34)	Three Miracles (4:35–5:43)
	Rejection at Nazareth (6:1–6) *first third*
II. Mission Sermon (9:35–10:42)	*second third*
III. Parables Sermon (13:1–52)	Ministry Phase II: Beyond Galilee (6:7–10:52)
Rejection at Nazareth (13:53–58) *first half*	Mission of the Twelve (6:7–13)
second half	Feeding of 5000 (6:30–44)
Ministry Phase II:	Confession and Prediction[1] (8:27–33)
Beyond Galilee (14:1–18:35)	Transfiguration (9:2–8)
Feeding of 5000 (14:13–21)	Passion Prediction[2] (9:31)
Confession and Passion Prediction[1] (16:13–23)	Journey to Judea (10:1–52)
Transfiguration (17:1–8)	Passion Prediction[3] (10:32–34)
Passion Prediction[2] (17:21)	*last third*
IV. Sermon on Discipline (18:1–35)	Ministry Phase III: Jerusalem (11:1–13:37)
Ministry Phase III:	Triumphal Entry (11:1–10)
Judea (19:1–20:16)	Cleansing of Temple / Cursing of Fig Tree (11:11–25)
Passion Prediction[3] (20:17–19)	The Conspiracy[1] (11:18)
Preaching in Jerusalem (21:1–25:46)	Teachings in Temple (11:27–12:44)
Triumphal Entry (21:1–9)	Discourse on the Destruction of Temple and Eschaton (13:1–37)
Cleansing of Temple (21:10–22)	
IV. Sermon[a] vs. Pharisees (23:1–36)	The Passion Narrative (14:1–16:8)
Sermon[b] on Destruction (24:1–51)	The Conspiracy[2] (14:1–2)
Sermon[c] on Judgment (25:1–46)	Anointing at Bethany (14:3–9)
	Betrayal Arranged (14:10–11)
The Passion Narrative (26:1–28:20)	Last Supper (14:17–31)
	Prayer and Arrest (14:32–52)
	Trial before Sanhedrin (14:53–72)
	Trial before Pilate (15:1–21)
	Crucifixion and Death (15:22–41)
	Burial (15:42–47)
	Empty Tomb (16:1–8)

later in the narrative. The Galilee section has been expanded significantly and given a new prominence in the Matthean story. As we saw in the case of the Q tradition, this narrative restructuring to emphasize the Galilee as the center of Jesus's ministry probably says something about where the Gospel was written. We shall return to this point below.

Repositioning Key Episodes in Jesus's Career

The Matthean expansion of the Galilee section is accomplished in part by repositioning some key episodes within the Gospel (see Box 12.2). For example, the mission of the Twelve, in which Jesus sends out his core group of disciples to spread his message, has been moved earlier, from the second geographical section in Mark (6:6–13, 30) into the Galilee section of Matthew (9:35–10:1). The Matthean version has also been expanded into one of the five key sermons of Jesus to be discussed below. Conversely, there is a cluster of miracle stories found in Mark shortly after the beginning of Jesus's ministry (Mark 1:21–34, 40–45; 2:1–12). They include the healing of a demoniac, Peter's mother-in-law, a leper, and various others.[25] In the Gospel of Matthew all of these are repositioned much later in the Galilee section. Instead of falling in Matthew 4—their relative position to Mark 1—they are in Matthew 7:28–9:34. They all occur *after* the Sermon on the Mount, where they have been interspersed with the three large miracles drawn from Mark 4:35–5:43: the Gerasene demoniac, the stilling of the storm, and the double miracle of Jairus's daughter and the hemorrhaging woman. The Matthean version of the centurion's servant, discussed above, is inserted into this newly constructed miracle cluster.

This repositioning of the miracles has an additional impact on the dynamics of the Matthean drama. In Mark the three large miracles of 4:35–5:43 directly follow the parables of the kingdom (4:1–34) and immediately precede the rejection at Nazareth (6:1–6). In effect, these miracles, by virtue of the misunderstanding and scandal they engender, are the proximate cause of his rejection, at least in the Markan version.[26] They epitomize key elements of the Markan theme of secrecy and misunderstanding, as discussed in the previous chapter. In Matthew, however, these same three miracles have been abbreviated and minimized by interspersing them with a number of smaller miracles drawn from Mark. They have nothing to do with the rejection at Nazareth.

The entire cluster (Matt 8:1–9:34) now contains a total of ten miracles in a row. They all follow just after the Sermon on the Mount and serve to dramatize Jesus's power as a teacher sent from God. In the middle of this section comes the story of the calling of Matthew, the authorial namesake of the Gospel, to become a follower of Jesus (9:9–13), to be discussed further below. What follows immediately after this cluster of miracles is the naming of the twelve disciples and their mission instructions (9:35–10:42), already mentioned above. This section becomes a tightly constructed Matthean drama, where themes of following and discipleship now come to the fore, replacing the Markan themes of secrecy and misunderstanding.

Finally, the parables (Mark 4:1–34) that occur just before the three large Markan miracles have been moved much later in Matthew (13:1–52). They too have been expanded into a sermon. Now, these parables become the principal cause of the rejection, which follows immediately (13:53–58). The Matthean author has not only given new emphasis to the teachings of Jesus, but has also made his teachings the center of the growing controversy that surrounds him.

What does all of this repositioning of Markan episodes add up to? To put it succinctly, it changes the running order of episodes and drives the drama of Jesus's life in a new way. The critical shift can be seen in the relative position of four key episodes. Whereas the original Markan order is *parables, three large miracles, rejection, mission* (or *a-b-c-d*), the order in Matthew is *ten miracles, mission, parables, rejection* (or *b-d-a-c*). Even this simplified picture does not do justice to the complex Matthean reworking of the narrative. We can see the contrast this way; the Markan order of narrative episodes runs:

1. Call of first disciples

2. First miracles and controversies

3. Call/naming of the Twelve

4. Three seed/*kingdom parables*

5. *Three miracles*

6. *Rejection at Nazareth*

7. *Mission of the Twelve*

8. Return of the Twelve and the feeding of the five thousand

The Matthean order runs:

1. Call of first disciples

2. Sermon on Mount

3. *Ten miracles,* call of Matthew

4. Appointing the Twelve and *Mission Discourse* (sermon)

5. Controversies

6. Nine *kingdom parables* (sermon)

7. *Rejection at Nazareth*

8. Feeding of the five thousand

Over all, then, the narrative order of the Galilee section in Matthew is significantly expanded and rather different than in Mark. It creates a distinctive story line of cause-and-effect relationships in Jesus's ministry. The rejection at Nazareth still marks a decisive shift in the geographical outline (the end of the Galilee ministry), but most of the drama in the narrative now occurs before it rather than after. It is also noteworthy that three of the distinctive Matthean sermons, none of which appear in Mark, occur within this Galilee section alone.

The Galilean Ministry of Jesus Becomes Central to the Drama

The "beyond Galilee" section basically follows Mark, with only a few notable additions. The Markan material in this section is usually abbreviated; therefore, the relative or proportional significance of this section is reduced. Even so, it contains three key scenes: the confession at Caesarea Philippi (Matt 16:13–23), the transfiguration (17:1–8), and the fourth Matthean sermon, on disciplining others (18:1–35). In this section Peter now plays a major role, usually serving as spokesman for the disciples. The story of Peter walking on the water (14:22–33) and the blessing of Peter after his "confession" (16:17–19) are both Matthean additions and reflect a more positive portrayal of the disciples generally and especially of Peter. If the "Galilee" section establishes the demands of discipleship through the first three sermons of Jesus, this section establishes the special relationship between Jesus and the twelve disciples as exemplifying this call to discipleship.

Abbreviating Markan Stories and Adding Q

Although Matthew is approximately one-third longer than Mark, much of the Markan material is abbreviated or compressed in its Matthean version. The overall lengthening of Matthew is thus a result of the addition of the Q material as well as a significant amount of peculiarly Matthean elaboration. The bulk of the Q sayings occur in the first half (the Galilee section) of the Matthean outline. Though the teachings of Jesus have been expanded, most of the Matthean miracle stories are much shorter than their Markan counterparts.

For example, in the "beyond Galilee" section the miracle of the boy with the epileptic demon (Matt 17:14–20) is less than half as long as the version in Mark (9:14–29). Even this raw statistic is somewhat misleading, because the Matthean version has also added a Q saying at the end (Matt 17:20; Luke 17:6) that accounts for an additional thirty-two words (in Greek) and makes up nearly one-fourth of the total episode in Matthew.[27] It is another case where the miracle has been transformed into a setup for a saying, in other words, into a teaching about faith. Also, the Gospel of Matthew adds several unique episodes, such as the Temple tax (Matt 17:24–27), Peter walking on the water with Jesus (14:28–31), and the blessing of Peter (16:16–30), all in the "beyond Galilee" section.[28] By far, however, the most significant Matthean additions occur in the sermons of Jesus, where the Q material is largely incorporated along with other Matthean elaborations. To say it another way, the basic geographical scheme of Mark is retained in Matthew, but it has been restructured narratively and supplemented by the insertion of the Q material to form the sermons. The dominant organizing principle is now provided by the sermons themselves.

Jesus as Teacher: The Matthean Sermons

By far and away, the most distinctive feature of the Matthean drama is the picture of Jesus delivering sermons. There are five of them in all, and all are in some way unique to Matthew in their internal construction and their placement within the narrative. Even the Gospel of Luke, which contains most of the same Q material, does not have a single sermon that matches any of those in Matthew. In each case, the Matthean sermon presents a key theme regarding Jesus and his message, which is further developed or worked out in the surrounding episodes. In turn, the sermons build thematically on one another. Some scholars have suggested that the five sermons represent an allusion to the Torah, or "five books" of Moses (see Box 12.3).

The Shape of the Matthean Sermons

As we have already seen, Moses imagery is very prominent in the Matthean birth narrative (see Chapter 10). The level of intentional authorial activity in creating these five sermons may be seen in several ways, not the least of which is the framing narrative that opens and closes each of them. Each of them opens with a short narrative situation in the form of a single *chreia*. Each one closes with nearly identical wording, variations on that found at the end of the Sermon on the Mount: "Now it came to pass when Jesus had finished these sayings . . ." (7:28; cf. 11:1; 13:53; 19:1; 26:1).[29] The phrase is probably derived from the Q version of the healing of the centurion's servant (as in Luke 7:1); however, the Matthean author has transformed it verbally into a careful, formulaic narrative device. In each case, this statement, delivered by the narrator's voice, serves as a dramatic cue to wrap up the sermon and transition to the next section of narrative. In effect, it brings down the curtain for a change of scenes. At 11:1 it introduces a series of controversies over Jesus teachings that will come to a head in the sermon of parables (13:1–52). At 13:53 it sets up the rejection at Nazareth; at 19:1 it introduces the move to Judea; and at 26:1 it opens the Passion narrative proper. Thus, each sermon effectively becomes a soliloquy of Jesus and serves as capstone to a major act of the Matthean drama.

BOX 12.3
The Gospel of Matthew

DATE: ca. 80–90 CE

AUTHOR: Unknown

SETTING: The village culture of the Upper Galilee or lower Syria

ATTRIBUTION: Matthew, the tax collector, one of Jesus's disciples

AUDIENCE AND OCCASION: A predominantly Greek-speaking Jewish community of the Jesus movement in a dominantly Jewish cultural context. In the period after the first revolt, the community is being faced with new pressures from the emergence of the Pharisaic movement in the Galilean region, with the result that many Jews are now beginning to side with the Pharisees and the followers of Jesus are being marginalized.

OUTLINE

　I.　The Book of Generations and the Birth of the Messiah (1:1–2:23)

　II.　Book 1 (Galilee): Call of First Disciples and First Sermon (3:1–7:29)
　　　Sermon on the Mount (5:1–7:27)

　III.　Book 2 (Galilee): First Miracles and Mission of the Twelve Disciples (8:1–10:42)
　　　Sermon: Mission discourse (10:5–42)

　IV.　Book 3 (Galilee): Controversies and Rejection at Nazareth (11:1–13:58)
　　　Sermon: Parables on the kingdom (13:1–52)

　V.　Book 4 (Beyond Galilee): Death of John; Jesus Predicts His Own Death (14:1–18:35)
　　　Sermon: Repentance and forgiveness in the church (18:1–35)

　VI.　Book 5 (Judea): Triumphal Entry and Conflict with Pharisees (19:1–25:46)
　　　Sermon on Judgment, in three parts:
　　　　A.　Woes vs. Pharisees (23:1–36)
　　　　B.　Apocalyptic discourse (24:1–51)
　　　　C.　Eschatological judgment (25:1–46)

　VII.　The Passion Narrative (26:1–28:20)

Sermons and sayings are clearly central to the Matthean portrait of Jesus as teacher. The author sometimes inserts isolated Q sayings into various types of episodes, including miracles, as in 8:18–22 (stilling the storm) and 17:20 (the boy with a demon/epilepsy; see Chapter 8). As noted earlier, in both cases, the miracle becomes more of a lesson on faith for the disciples, by having the miracle serve as the narrative to set up some key saying. In this way, the Matthean miracles generally function more like *chreiai* as occasions for teaching rather than sheer demonstrations of miraculous power. They have thus been reshaped to support the creation of the sermons that dominate the narrative structure of the Gospel of Matthew.

For the most part, the Matthean author has chosen to integrate the Q sayings into the Markan framework by clustering them into one of the five large sermon blocks.[30] At the same time, the sermons offer the best glimpse of the author's own distinctive compositions and theological concerns.

Crafting the Dialogue

The first, and most famous, of the Matthean sermons is the Sermon on the Mount (5:1–7:27). In relative terms, it is inserted into the Markan narrative order immediately after Mark 1:39 combined with a reference to Jesus's growing popularity with the multitudes taken from Mark 3:7–8, 10. The sermon itself has virtually no correspondence to Markan materials. It is based on the "covenant renewal sermon" of Q7–14, corresponding to the Lukan "Sermon on the Plain" (Luke 6:20–49).[31] The Matthean version has been expanded significantly, so that the resulting sermon is more than three times as long as the Lukan counterpart. Just over 44 percent of the sermon is comprised of uniquely Matthean material.[32] A good example is the added statement about "the law and the prophets," which is inserted immediately after the Beatitudes (Matt 5:17–20, quoted at the beginning of this chapter). In other words, although the Sermon on the Mount derives largely from Q sayings, in its present form it is a thoroughly Matthean creation (see Box 12.4).

A close look at the composition of the Sermon on the Mount shows that many of the Q sayings have been augmented or expanded by the Matthean author in order to work them into a more systematic framework. Q's "covenant renewal sermon" (Q7–14) forms the core in both content and general order. Other Q sayings found scattered through Luke are assembled together in Matthew to develop key thematic sections of the sermon. In turn, many of the individual sayings have been expanded or revised by the Matthean author. The well-known differences between the Matthean and Lukan versions of the Beatitudes (Matt 5:3–12; Luke 6:20–23) and the Lord's Prayer (Matt 6:9–15; Luke 11:2–4) are good examples of the Matthean tendency to expand and change the content.

BOX 12.4
The Formation of the Sermon on the Mount

Matthew	Mark	Luke
5:1–2 Opening Frame (*chreia*)	*(cf. 1:39 + 3:7–8)*	*(cf. 6:17–19 + 6:12–16 [call of disciples])*
5:3–12 Beatitudes	—	❖ 6:20–23 (Q7)
5:13–16 Salt and Light	9:50	14:34–35 (Q57)
5:17–20 Law and Prophets	—	❖ 16:17 (Q61.17)
5:21–26 On Murder	—	❖ 12:57–59 (Q48)
5:27–30 On Adultery	—	—
5:31–32 On Divorce	❖ 10:11–12	16:18 (Q61.18)
5:33–37 On Swearing	—	—
5:38–42 On Retaliation	—	❖ 6:29–30 (Q9.29–30)
5:43–48 Love of Enemies	—	❖ 6:27–28 (Q9.27–28) ❖ 6:32–36 (Q9.32–35; Q10.36)
6:1–4 On Righteousness	—	—
6:5–8 On Prayer	—	—
6:9–15 Lord's Prayer	❖ cf. 11:25–26 (*forgiveness*)	❖ 11:2–4 (Q27)
6:16–18 On Fasting	—	—

The third sermon in Matthew, the Parables on the Kingdom (13:1–52), reflects a similar pattern of literary expansion and shaping. It is based largely on the seed parables of Mark 4:1–34, but it has been significantly expanded (see Box 12.5). In this case, however, there is very little added from Q material (Matt 13:2–21, Q49). The bulk comes from uniquely Matthean materials, *including five new parables*. The Matthean reshaping is discussed in detail in Chapter 9. Most noteworthy is the allegorical program of intertextual readings among the parables, which

Matthew	Mark	Luke
6:19–21 On Treasures	—	❖ 12:33–34 (Q42)
6:22–23 The Sound Eye	—	11:34–36 (Q33.34–36)
6:24 On Two Masters	—	16:13 (Q60)
6:25–34 On Anxiety	—	12:22–31 (Q41)
7:1–5 On Judging	—	6:37–38 (Q10.37–38) 6:41–42 (Q12)
7:6 Pearls to Swine	—	—
7:7–11 Prayers Answered	—	11:9–13 (Q28)
7:12 Golden Rule	—	6:31 (Q9.31)
7:13–14 Narrow Gate	—	❖ 13:24 (Q50)
7:15 False Prophets	—	—
7:16–20 By Their Fruits	—	❖ 6:43–45 (Q13)
7:21–23 On Self-deception	—	❖ 6:46 (Q14.46)
7:24–27 Hearers and Doers	—	❖ 13:27 (Q50.27)
7:28–29 Closing Frame		6:47–49 (Q14.47–49)

KEY: **Bold** = the "sermon" from Q7–14
Regular type = nearly verbatim material, usually in another location (Mark or Luke/Q)
❖ = only partial parallel to material in Matthew
Italics = similar material in another location
( ) = Q references

establishes the key Matthean themes of discipleship and judgment within the kingdom. In this case we see the characteristic apocalyptic warning about being "cast into the furnace of fire where there is weeping and gnashing of teeth" (13:42, 50). Although drawn from a single Q saying (Q51, Luke 13:28), it has been transformed into a Matthean fingerprint that will be carried forward into the parable/allegory of the wedding banquet (22:1–14) and the final sermon of Matthew 23–25.

BOX 12.5
A Sermon of Parables on the Kingdom (Matthew 13:1–52)

Matthew		Mark	Luke
13:1–2	Opening Frame (*chreia*)	4:1–2	8:4
13:3–9	Parable of Sower	4:3–9	8:5–8
13:10–13	Why Parables?	4:10–12	8:9–10
13:14–15	Isaiah's Prophecy	—	—
13:16–17	Discipleship	—	10:23–24
13:18–23	Parable of Sower Allegorized	4:13–20	8:11–15
—		(4:21–25)	(8:16–18)
—		(4:26–29)	—
13:24–30	Parable of Weeds	—	—
13:31–32	Parable of Mustard Seed	4:30–32	13:18–19
13:33	Parable of Yeast	—	13:20–21 (Q49)
13:34–35	Use of Parables	4:33–34	—
13:36–43	Parable of Weeds Allegorized	—	—
13:44	Parable of Treasure	—	—
13:45–46	Parable of Pearl	—	—
13:47–50	Parable of Net	—	—
13:51–52	Parable of Old and New	—	—
13:53	Closing Frame	—	—
13:54–58	Rejection at Nazareth	6:1–6	4:16–30

The Sermon on the Mount

Each of the sermons thus reflects a carefully crafted internal order and shaping that creates thematic links running throughout the Gospel of Matthew. Here we may turn again to the Sermon on the Mount. Following the Beatitudes, which introduce the sermon, it breaks into three sections. The first section concerns Torah (5:17–48). Several of the Q sayings in the first section are introduced by uniquely Matthean additions. They are set up by the formula: "You have heard it said to those of ancient times, 'You shall not . . . ,' but I say to you . . ." (5:21–22, 27–28, 31, 33–34, 38–39, 43–44). Three (5:31, 38–39, 43–44) combine Matthean sayings with Q material. The other three, however, comprising more than half of this section, have no corresponding Q saying and are uniquely Matthean insertions. The introductory formula itself is a Matthean "fingerprint." Overall, the theme of this first section may be summarized as follows: *the law (Torah) defines moral obligations, but the demands of the kingdom require stringent observance.*

In the second part of the sermon (6:1–34), a number of other key passages are entirely Matthean additions dealing with alms (6:2–4), prayer (6:5–8), and fasting (6:16–18). They are introduced with another uniquely Matthean thematic statement: "Beware of practicing your piety [lit., righteousness] before others in order to be seen by him; for then you have no reward from your Father in heaven" (6:1). The Lord's Prayer (Q27, Luke 11:2–4) and a Markan saying on forgiveness (11:25–26) have been inserted into this section on proper forms of observance. It would seem that this section of the sermon has its own internal unity built around issues of Jewish "piety" or observance, which the Greek actually calls "righteousness" (6:1). The same term is also central in Pharisaic discussions of Torah observance and charity, where it generally carries a sense of one's standing before God.[33] The term "righteousness" also shows up prominently in the uniquely Matthean unit (5:17–20) that introduces the sayings on Torah in the first section of the sermon. The last section of the Sermon on the Mount (7:1–27) centers around judgment and discernment in the kingdom as the natural outgrowth of this emphasis on Torah and righteousness. The remaining sermons of Matthew will build on these same themes.[34]

Key Matthean Themes in the Sermons

As we have seen, the *Sermon on the Mount* focuses on Torah observance and piety as the proper path to righteousness. It stands as a call to discipleship under the guidelines of Torah.

The second sermon, the *Mission Discourse* (10:5–42), focuses on the demands of discipleship in the face of growing persecution and sectarian tension. It reflects the later experiences of the followers of Jesus after the first Jewish revolt, at a time when they are increasingly being marginalized within Jewish society. At the same time, it maintains its original identity as a Jewish sect: "Go nowhere among the Gentiles . . . but go rather to the lost sheep of the house of Israel" (Matt 10:5).

The third sermon is the expanded *Parables of the Kingdom* (13:1–52). It focuses on the nature of the kingdom and the urgency of the proper choice for those who would be disciples. Now themes of apocalyptic judgment between "good and bad," as the penalty for those who do not choose well, begin to come to the fore: "So it will be at the end of the age. The angels will come out and separate the evil from the righteous and throw them into the furnace of fire, where there will be weeping and gnashing of teeth" (13:49–50).

The fourth sermon, *On Discipline and Forgiveness* (18:1–35), focuses on division and discipline within the "church," that is, within the Matthean community. It continues to stress the sense of Jewishness and a desire for unity, even though it projects new sectarian boundaries: "If the member refuses to listen to them, tell it to the church; and if the offender refuses to listen even to the church, let such a one be to you as a Gentile and a tax collector" (18:17). We shall return to this sermon in the next section. As we shall see, more than any of the others, this sermon speaks directly to members of the Matthean community and their current experience.

Finally, the fifth sermon, *On Judgment* (23:1–25:46), combines the apocalyptic discourse drawn from Mark with a series of "woes" against the Pharisees drawn from Q. From the Sermon on the Mount it stresses proper observance of Torah as the basis for righteousness as opposed to hypocrisy (23:2). From the Mission Discourse it emphasizes coming persecutions and the need for continued watchfulness and faith (24:9–14).[35] It concludes with several powerful parables about the final judgment, when the good will be separated from the bad, as in the Sermon of Parables, specifically those of the weeds and the net. The fifth sermon thus recapitulates key themes from each of the previous sermons as the culmination of Jesus's teachings as presented in the Matthean Gospel. It also sets the stage for the transition to the Passion narrative proper. A number of these individual themes and their narrative interconnections will be discussed further in the final section of this chapter.

Author and Audience

Unlike Mark, the Gospel of Matthew was attributed to one of the actual disciples of Jesus. With its stress on Torah and observance, it is by far the most Jewish of the Gospels. Most of the ancient legends about the Gospel of Matthew, including those of Papias and Irenaeus, seem to reflect this fact: "Matthew also issued a written Gospel among the Hebrews in their own dialect."[36] It was revered as the "only" Gospel among later forms of Jewish Christianity continuing into the fourth and fifth centuries CE.[37] Even the early legend of Papias (ca. 130 CE) raises other questions: "Matthew collected the sayings [of the Lord] in Hebraic dialect, and each one interpreted them as he was able."[38] The problem is that such statements do not fit the New Testament Gospel of Matthew very well, since it is far more than a collection of sayings, and it was composed in Greek instead of Hebrew. There is no lost "Hebrew original" of Matthew.[39]

The Figure of Matthew

Where might Papias have gotten this notion that the Gospel of Matthew was a collection of Jesus's "oracles"? It has been proposed that what we now call the Q source was this earlier "Matthew gospel" noted by Papias. But this does not fit either, because the Q tradition as we know it comes down to us only in Greek. Some scholars would argue that the author of Matthew had a distinctive written version of Q (sometimes called Q[Matt]) that served as a core source even though it was substantially rearranged.[40]

As we have seen, there are a number of ways that the Q tradition has influenced the shape and tone of the Gospel of Matthew. Central to it are the image of Jesus as teacher and the five sermons as the core of his message. In turn, the Gospel of Matthew probably represents a later stage in the development of the same Galilean trajectory of the Jesus movement that had originally produced and used the Q tradition.[41] To be sure, there are some important shifts in setting and outlook by the time we get to the Matthean Gospel, at least as we now know it. Even so, it is at least feasible that the author and audience of this Gospel—or what we may call the Matthean community—associated the Q tradition with the figure of Matthew as a symbolic founder of the community.[42]

The figure of Matthew, as the authorial namesake, is also now woven into the drama in a new way. The key scene is Matthew 9:9–13. It occurs in the middle of the cluster of ten miracles that follow the Sermon on the Mount. The disciple Matthew is described as a Jewish tax collector who first encountered Jesus in Capernaum. This Matthean story is a reworking of the Markan episode of the call of a tax collector named Levi son of Alphaeus (Mark 2:13–17), but the name has been changed. Since there is also a disciple named James son of Alphaeus in all the lists of disciples (including Matt 10:3), it would appear that the story in Mark refers to this person rather than Matthew.[43] Only the Matthean list of the disciples adds the "fact" that Matthew was a tax collector (10:3). Later traditions would attempt to smooth over the problem by naming him Levi-Matthew.

The call episode of Matthew 9:9–13 is thus a creation of the Matthean author by reworking the Markan story of the call of Levi. It clearly seeks to establish the identity of the authorial namesake for the Matthean community and to use him as an example of discipleship. The marginal status of tax collectors in the pre- and postwar Judean political economy also seems to be a thematic interest of the Matthean author. We shall return to say more about the community, its social matrix, and theological concerns in the final section of this chapter.

Where and When Was It Produced?

A number of different localities have been proposed for the composition of the Gospel of Matthew, ranging from Alexandria to Judea or Caesarea Maritima to the interior regions of northern Syria or the area around Edessa. None of these seems very likely. By far the most common view for many years was that it came from Antioch, the capital of Roman Syria, where there was both a large Jewish community and early Jewish cells of the Jesus movement on the margins of a gentile environment. Some scholars who locate it in Antioch would also argue that the author was a gentile convert rather than a Jewish follower of the Jesus movement.[44]

On the contrary, recent archaeological work has shown that the Upper Galilee remained a predominantly Jewish village culture, but was somewhat isolated from the Lower Galilee. It was more culturally mixed and had strong commercial ties to the large Hellenistic-Roman cities of the Tyre, Sidon, and Caesarea Philippi.[45] As a result, a growing number of New Testament scholars would now locate the Matthean community somewhere in or near this Upper Galilean village culture on the border of Roman Syria.

Although the author and the audience admit gentile converts into their fellowship, their primary social location and self-understanding remains thoroughly Jewish. Even its polemics against the Pharisees (Matt 23) arise in this Jewish matrix. They may be understood in the light of the gradual demographic shift to the Galilee in the period after the first revolt, where the Pharisaic movement would emerge as the new religious leadership, or what we come to know as rabbinic Judaism.[46] Thus, it is quite feasible to see the author of Matthew as a Jewish follower of the Jesus movement whose community is facing conflict with other Jews, and especially the emergent rabbinic movement of the postwar period. We may thus think of it as "sibling rivalry" in which the followers of Jesus, after being in the region for many years, are now feeling marginalized by their Jewish neighbors.[47] The depiction of Jesus and his teachings on Torah are thus a means of defining and defending their place within Jewish tradition. The Gospel of Matthew, as we now have it, was likely composed between 80 and 90 CE, but probably toward the end of this span or even a few years later.[48] It was a critical period of transition for Jews, both politically and religiously. The followers of Jesus felt it too.

The Image of Jesus in the Gospel of Matthew

Three key symbols help to define the complex image of Jesus in Matthew. He is the Davidic Messiah, emphasized primarily in the birth narrative. He resembles Moses, in both the birth narrative and his teachings on Torah, especially in the Sermon on the Mount. And he stands over against other Jewish "teachers" or "rabbis" of the day, as reflected especially in the "woes" against the Pharisees (Matt

23). His Davidic descent is stressed, but it does not seem to be the real problem or concern of the Gospel, except insofar as other Jews would deny that he was really the Messiah after all, as shown by the Matthean addition of the guards at the tomb (27:62–66; 28:11–15; discussed in Chapter 7). Yet messianic identity is straightforwardly affirmed, by means of the miraculous elements and prophecy-fulfillment citations of the narrative.[49]

If there is an issue relating to Jesus's messianic identity for the Gospel of Matthew, it has more to do with his continuing messianic or eschatological role in the time that the Gospel was written, well after the destruction of Jerusalem, and in light of new social and religious tensions. Hence, the other two symbols—Moses and teacher—are more at the heart of the Matthean portrayal of Jesus. Naturally, the sermons of Matthew play a major role in this image.

As seen in a key passage from the Sermon on the Mount, the Matthean Jesus's attitude toward the Torah is overwhelmingly positive:

> *Do not think that I have come to abolish the law or the prophets; I have come not to abolish but to fulfill. For truly I tell you, until heaven and earth pass away, not one letter, not one stroke of a letter, will pass from the law until all is accomplished. Therefore, whoever breaks one of the least of these commandments, and teaches others to do the same, will be called least in the kingdom of heaven; but whoever does them and teaches them will be called great in the kingdom of heaven. For I tell you, unless your righteousness exceeds that of the scribes and Pharisees, you will never enter the kingdom of heaven. (5:17–20)*

Though this passage reflects Matthew's tensions with Pharisees, it is important to note that referring to the scriptures as "the law and the prophets" is a decidedly Pharisaic way of talking. The key is the observance of Torah as the grounds of righteousness. The Pharisees would have agreed. So also, later in the Sermon on the Mount, the term "righteousness"—understood as acts of piety, alms, prayer, and fasting (6:1–8, 16–18)—reappears to mark the battleground between proper observance of Torah and hypocritical observance. Both passages are unique to the Gospel of Matthew. Yet both are placed on the lips of Jesus as his own teaching. There is no sense of abrogation of Torah or the ritual laws in either of these passages. Instead, Jesus is presented as a rigorous proponent of strict Torah observance, even to the point of intensifying the personal demands of the Jewish law.

The same point comes through later in the "woes" against the Pharisees, where Jesus is presented as saying:

> "The scribes and the Pharisees sit on Moses' seat; therefore, do whatever they teach you and follow it; <u>but do not do as they do, for they do not practice what they teach.</u> They tie up heavy burdens, hard to bear, and lay them on the shoulders of others; but they themselves are unwilling to lift a finger to move them. They do all their deeds to be seen by others; for they make their phylacteries

broad and their fringes long. They love to have the place of honor at banquets and the best seats in the synagogues, and to be greeted with respect in the marketplaces, and to have people call them rabbi. <u>But you are not to be called rabbi, for you have one teacher, and you are all students.</u> And call no one your father on earth, for you have one Father—the one in heaven. Nor are you to be called instructors, for you have one instructor, the Messiah. The greatest among you will be your servant. All who exalt themselves will be humbled, and all who humble themselves will be exalted." (23:2–12)

This passage is actually the opening of the fifth and last sermon in the Gospel of Matthew, which will effectively carry through in three parts to the end of Matthew 25. This first section is built around Q material, but its driving theme is framed by this uniquely Matthean passage with which it opens. So it should be noticed that the Matthean Jesus in no way disavows the teachings of the scribes and Pharisees. Instead, he says, "Do whatever they teach and follow it" (23:3). Rather, the tension comes in the next thought, as he accuses them of hypocrisy, "But do not do as they do, for they do not practice what they teach." The theme of hypocrisy will carry through the rest of Matthew 23. It is essentially the same idea as seen in the Sermon on the Mount (6:1–8), but here stated negatively.

We may notice also that this later passage shows a tension over the terms "rabbi" and "instructor" (or "leader"), where the line is drawn between others who may use these titles and the Messiah, who is the only real "teacher" and "leader" (23:8–10). So though the Gospel of Matthew clearly shows animosity toward the Pharisees, it is not based on *what* they teach, only on how they follow these teachings. At base, Jesus and the Pharisees are depicted as operating from the same religious tradition of Torah observance. At the same time a line is being drawn. The opposition of the Pharisees to Jesus is also heightened in the Matthean telling of the story.

Many of the thematic features of the Gospel of Matthew reflect a tension with its Jewish culture. On the one hand, Jesus is a Jewish teacher of disciples and interpreter of Torah, very much like the Pharisees. In the mission instructions he explicitly tells the disciples: "Go nowhere among the Gentiles, and enter no town of the Samaritans, but go rather to the lost sheep of the house of Israel" (10:5–6). These tensions ultimately say more about the experience of the Matthean community in the period after the first revolt than they do about the days of Jesus. The Matthean narrative has some subtle changes of language that reflect sectarian tensions, such as the association of the Pharisees with *"their* synagogues."[50] The refrain of persecution in *"their* synagogues," as a reflection of post-70 tensions, may be seen in several key warnings attributed to Jesus (10:17; 23:40). On the other hand, it does not mean that the community has entirely broken away from Judaism. Quite the contrary. The problem is one of marginalization, sectarian identity, and community boundaries.

Standing over against "their synagogues" is "the church" as the marker of the Matthean sect. Matthew is alone among the Gospels in using this term (once in 16:18 and twice in 18:17), and only in uniquely Matthean additions to the dialogue of Jesus. The second of these passages is very telling, as it comes from Jesus's fourth sermon and concerns discipline and forgiveness within "the church."[51] Jesus is speaking:

> *"If another member [lit., brother] sins against you, go and point out the fault when the two of you are alone. If the member listens to you, you have regained that one. But if you are not listened to, take one or two others along with you, so that every word may be confirmed by the evidence of two or three witnesses. If the member refuses to listen to them, **tell it to the church**; and if the offender refuses to listen even **to the church**, let such a one be to you as a Gentile and a tax collector." (18:15–17)*

Here we have disciplinary regulations for a sectarian community that are closely paralleled by those in the *Rule of the Community* from the Dead Sea Scrolls. The sectarian group is thus called the "church," that is, "congregation," as in traditional Jewish usage synonymous to "synagogue." But now these two terms for the congregation stand in some opposition to one another: *our congregation* ("church") vs. *your congregation* ("synagogue"). On the other hand, they do not yet represent "Christianity" over against "Judaism." This fact is shown by the striking language used to describe the excommunication or "othering" of an offender within the congregation: he is to be shunned as "a Gentile and a tax collector." If being removed from the Matthean community's fellowship causes the offender to be labeled a "Gentile," then being *in* the community can only be understood as being Jewish. Consequently, although the Matthean "church" is clearly at odds with neighboring Pharisaic "synagogues," it still thinks of itself very much as a Jewish sect.

Another clue to the social as well as geographical location of the Matthean community comes from the episode that immediately precedes and introduces the fourth sermon (18:1–35). It is called the Temple tax scene (17:24–27). It is not contained in any of the other Gospels and thus reflects some distinctive experience of the Matthean community. It concerns a question about Jesus posed to Peter: "Does your teacher not pay the temple tax?" Peter's answer is, "Yes, he does" (17:24–25). What follows then is a putative discussion between Peter and Jesus on this matter. Jesus first asks a riddle whose point is that the children of the king should *not* have to pay tribute, that is, they really should not have to pay such a tax. But then Jesus tells Peter: "However, so that we do not give offense to them, go to the sea and cast a hook; take the first fish that comes up; and when you open its mouth, you will find a coin [shekel]; take that and give it to them for you and for me" (17:27).

This seemingly minor episode is quite telling, for the half-shekel "temple tax" was what was appropriated by the Romans after the revolt as the *fiscus Iudaicus* ("Jewish tax") to pay war reparations to Rome. In addition to being a punishment for the war, it was also quite literally a per capita tax on being Jewish. Only Jews had to pay it, and its collection was diligently monitored in postwar Judea as a sign of submission to Rome. Thus, for Jesus to say "pay the tax" *in order not to offend* is the same as admitting to being Jewish too. It also points strongly at a location in or very near the homeland. On the other hand, the little riddle does hint at a growing rupture. Perhaps those gentile converts in the Matthean community, even if they had been circumcised and were Torah observant, were now beginning to question whether maintaining Jewish identity was really necessary or worth the trouble. The author's answer, now spoken by Jesus, is a solid yes. Despite the tensions with other Jews, they were nonetheless still a Jewish sect.

In the final analysis, then, the Jesus of the Gospel of Matthew is understood as the apocalyptic Messiah from the line of David. Even the title "Son of God" still functions in traditional Jewish ways to affirm the peculiar relation between the Messiah and God.[52] Notably, now Peter articulates both titles together in his "confession" at Caesarea Philippi (16:16), and for his understanding Peter is given a unique blessing (16:17–19). As a result the title "Son of God" has lost its peculiar dramatic function seen in Mark. The miraculous elements of the birth narrative do not attribute divinity to Jesus in the strict sense; rather, they affirm his genealogical lineage as "son of David." Many of the episodes in Jesus's career, especially the exorcisms, function to defend this premise.[53] As Davidic Messiah, he was chosen or "anointed" by God to redeem Israel by calling it to a proper observance of God's law.

At the same time, the Matthean Jesus is the new "prophet like Moses" based on Deuteronomy 18:15. As Moses was both leader and lawgiver, so also is the Messiah. As Moses's successor in Deuteronomy was named Joshua, so also is the Messiah, Jesus.[54] The wisdom traditions drawn from Q also legitimate this prophetic role, as he now stands as Messiah/Teacher of Torah for an abiding community of followers. But their Jewish observance has been called into question, in part perhaps because they welcome Gentiles into their fellowship, but even more because they follow Jesus. In sharp contrast to the portrayal in Mark, the disciples in Matthew are shown in a much more positive light and serve as models of discipleship, as they come to understand the proper way to "follow" Jesus.

The portrayal of Jesus in the Gospel of Matthew is thus both a defense of his messiahship and an apologetic for the community and their mode of Jewish piety. His sermons and miracles summon hearers to decision and observance by following Jesus. Yet the message has a cutting edge, as there are fateful warnings for those who do not follow properly, whether inside or outside the community. The recurrent Matthean theme of "weeping and gnashing of teeth," with its traditional apocalyptic tone, ultimately refocuses on judgment within the community (22:13–14; 25:30, 45–46).

One more shift of emphasis occurs in Matthew as a different title for Jesus—"Son of Man"—rises above the others in finally establishing his identity.[55] Because of its apocalyptic associations as eschatological judge, seen also in Q,[56] the impending return of Jesus as Son of Man now serves as warning and warrant for the proper understanding of Torah and observance. This proper understanding is what the Matthean author characterizes by the theme of discipleship that pervades the Gospel, for the Son of Man will ultimately be the judge (25:31–46). Jesus's return will ultimately vindicate the community members' discipleship and piety, for they will be judged righteous, and sooner than expected (24:34–25:13).[57] The Gospel of Matthew dramatizes Jesus as a teacher of Torah in a strident call to discipleship for a community increasingly on the margins of Jewish society.

CHAPTER THIRTEEN

The Martyred Sage

The Gospel of Luke

He unrolled the scroll and found the place where it was written: "The Spirit of the Lord is upon me, because he has anointed me to bring good news to the poor. He has sent me to proclaim release to the captives and recovery of sight to the blind, to let the oppressed go free, to proclaim the year of the Lord's favor." And he rolled up the scroll, gave it back to the attendant, and sat down. The eyes of all in the synagogue were fixed on him. Then he began to say to them, "Today this scripture has been fulfilled in your hearing."

All spoke well of him and were amazed at the gracious words that came from his mouth. They said, "Is not this Joseph's son?" He said to them, "Doubtless you will quote to me this proverb, 'Doctor, cure yourself!' And you will say, 'Do here also in your hometown the things that we have heard you did at Capernaum.'" And he said, "Truly I tell you, no prophet is accepted in the prophet's hometown. But the truth is, there were many widows in Israel in the time of Elijah, when the heaven was shut up three years and six months, and there was a severe famine over all the land; yet Elijah was sent to none of them except to a widow at Zarephath in Sidon. There were also many lepers in Israel in the time of the prophet Elisha, and none of them was cleansed except Naaman the Syrian." When they heard this, all in the synagogue were filled with rage. (Luke 4:17–28)

If the Jesus of Matthew speaks primarily to Jewish identity, the Jesus of Luke-Acts offers a wider outlook, with a view toward the Greco-Roman world. Several features of its narrative construction help to make this point. Its reordering of material and reshaping of key episodes help to give a new depiction to the character of Jesus and the disciples. Like the author of Matthew, the author of Luke restructures the Markan outline and inserts Q materials along with a significant proportion of uniquely Lukan material. As a result, the Gospel of Luke is the longest of the three Synoptics by far. Yet only about half of its content comes from Mark, and less than a quarter from Q. As we shall see, there is much new in the Gospel of Luke. The Lukan rearrangement of Mark differs in significant ways from the Matthean and thus suggests an entirely independent reworking of the Markan outline.

The Lukan Restructuring of the Narrative

The author of Luke reorders and expands the threefold Markan geographic outline (Galilee, beyond Galilee, Jerusalem) in four main ways: by expanding the Galilee section, including Q material, constructing a travel narrative, and repositioning the rejection at Nazareth. The Q material and significant Lukan additions are woven into this new structure through careful reshaping of the story. Read on its own terms, it is a stylish and flowing narrative. Only when examined carefully for its narrative changes does the real artistry of the Lukan author show through. We will look at each of the four changes in order. Box 13.1 shows graphically the resulting effects in comparison with Mark.

Expanding the Galilee Section (Luke 4:14–9:50)

The Galilee section is expanded by taking over material from Mark 6–8, the first half of the "beyond Galilee" section. The Lukan Galilee section now runs from 4:14 to 9:50. In order to do this the Lukan author had to delete or reformulate those episodes in Mark 6–8 that were set beyond Galilee. This change is most notable in the central Markan scene of the confession at Caesarea Philippi (Mark 8:27–33), in which Peter affirms that Jesus is the Messiah. It occurs in roughly the same relative position in the Lukan outline (9:18–22); however, all references to the location have been removed. Why? Because the location in Mark, Caesarea Philippi, would put it well outside the Galilee region.[1] Now the prior section of Luke (8:40–9:17) is all set in the Galilee and forces the confession to be located there as well. Specifically, the preceding episode in Luke now explicitly relocates the feeding of the five thousand to Bethsaida at the north end of the Sea of Galilee (9:10–11).[2] By contrast, in Matthew it took place on the west side of the Sea of Galilee, nearer Capernaum.[3] The result in Luke is that the confession of Peter also takes place at Bethsaida, immediately after the feeding of the five thousand, and both are taken to be part of the Galilee. (See Appendix E.)

This change in the Lukan order and geography is also created narratively by deleting six intervening episodes found in the Gospel of Mark (6:45–8:26). They include several important Markan scenes and several key miracles, all removed by

BOX 13.1

Comparison of the Outlines of Mark and Luke

Mark	Luke
Jesus and John the Baptist (1.1–13)	<<Birth Narrative (1:1–2:52)>>
Baptism of Jesus (1:9–11)	
Temptation (1:12–13)	Jesus and John (3:1–20)
	Baptism (3:21–22)
Phase I: Galilee (1.14–6.6)	<<Genealogy (3:23–38)>>
	Temptation (4:1–13)
First Miracles (1:29–2:12)	
Controversies (2:18–3:35)	I. Ministry in Galilee (4:14–9:50)
Parables (4:1–34)	
Three Miracles (4:35–5:48)	<<Rejection at Nazareth (4:16–30)>>
Rejection at Nazareth (6.1–6)	First Miracles (4:31–5:11)
	Controversies (5:33–6:18)
Phase II: Beyond Galilee (6.7–10:52)	<Sermon on the Plain: Q (6:20–49)>
	<Special Episodes: Q + L (7:1–8:3)>
Mission of the Twelve (6.7–13)	<Anointing in Galilee (7:36–50) >
Confession at Caesarea Philippi	Parables (8:4–18)
(8.27–33)	<True Relatives (8:19–21)>
Transfiguration (9.2–8)	Three Miracles (8:22–56)
Passion Predictions[1, 2] (8.31; 9.31)	Mission of the Twelve (9:1–6)
Turns Toward Judea (10.1–31)	Confession [at Bethsaida] (9:18–22)
Passion Prediction[3] (10.32–34)	Transfiguration (9.28–36)
Heals Bartimaeus (10:46–52)	Passion Predictions[1, 2] (9:21; 9.43)
Phase III: Jerusalem (11:1–16:8)	II. Journey to Jerusalem (9:51–19:27)
Preaching in Jerusalem (11.1–13.37)	<"Luke's Special Section">
Triumphal Entry (11.1–10)	<Beelzebul controversy (11:14–23)>
Cleansing of Temple, Cursing	<Teachings at Dinners (14:1–18:14)>
of Fig Tree (11.11–25)	Passion Prediction[3] (18:31–34)
The Conspiracy[1] (11.18)	Heals Bartimaeus (18:35–43)
Teachings in Temple (11.27–12.44)	< Zacchaeus (19:1–10)>
Discourse on the Destruction of	
Temple and Eschaton (13.1–37)	III. The Arrival and Preaching
The Passion Narrative (14.1–16.8)	at Jerusalem (19:28–21:38)
The Conspiracy[2] (14.1–2)	
Anointing at Bethany (14.3–9)	Triumphal Entry (19:28–38)
Betrayal Arranged (14.10–11)	Predicts Destruction (19:39–44)
Last Supper (14.17–31)	Cleansing of Temple [no Fig Tree]
Prayer and Arrest (14.32–52)	(19:45–48)
Trial before Sanhedrin (14.53–72)	Teachings in Temple (20:1–21:4)
Trial before Pilate (15.1–21)	Discourse on Destruction (21:5–36)
Crucifixion and Death (15.22–41)	IV. The Passion Narrative (22:1–24:53)
Burial (15.42–47)	
Empty Tomb (16.1–8)	The Conspiracy (21:1–2)
	<Added Trial before Antipas (23:6–16)>
	<Added Postresurrection scenes at
	Jerusalem (24.1–53 + Acts 1)>

the Lukan author: the walking on water; healings at Gennesaret; the Syrophoeni-cian woman's daughter; the healing of many sick at Tyre; the feeding of the four thousand, and the blind man at Bethsaida.[4] Of these changes, the omission of the blind man at Bethsaida is perhaps the most significant for understanding what the Lukan author is up to in creating this new drama. Though this scene disappears in Luke, the setting in Bethsaida remains.[5] But a setting in Bethsaida can only have come from the Markan narrative.[6] The author of Luke has brought these episodes narratively into the Galilee section and then telescopes the action directly from the feeding of the five thousand to the confession.[7] All of this says something about the geographical framework and narrative world being created consciously in the Lukan drama.

Integrating Q Material:
The Sermon on the Plain (Luke 6:20–49)

Next, the Lukan author inserts the first major block of Q material into the Galilee section at 6:20, comparable to Mark 3:19.[8] For the sake of comparison, remember that the Gospel of Matthew had inserted this same Q material (the "covenant renewal sermon," Q7–14) at roughly Mark 1:39 and then expanded it to become the lengthy Sermon on the Mount.[9] The Lukan version is shorter, relatively later, and is now cast as the Sermon on the Plain (6:20–49). It is followed immediately by the Q miracle/saying of the centurion's servant (7:1–10) and a uniquely Lukan miracle story, the raising of the widow's son at Nain (7:11–17). We shall return to these two miracles in the next section. These insertions culminate with a short section drawn from Q (7:18–35),[10] followed by the Lukan repositioning of the anointing woman (7:36–50).[11] The section ends with a unique Lukan scene of Jesus and his entourage traveling around the Galilean villages. It adds that there are several women of means, including Mary Magdalene, who support Jesus and the disciples (8:1–3).[12]

The remainder of the Lukan Galilee section follows Mark for the most part (from Luke 8:4–56) and comes to a close with the material drawn from the Markan beyond Galilee section discussed above. It covers Luke 9:1–50 and includes the mission of the Twelve, their return, and the feeding of the five thousand (9:1–17).[13] It then jumps immediately to the confession, now at Bethsaida (Luke 9:18–22), the transfiguration (9:28–36), the miracle of the boy with the spirit (9:37–43), the second Passion prediction (9:43–45), and the dispute about greatness (9:46–48). The final portions of this Lukan section closely follow the Markan order, but much has been omitted and the tone has changed considerably, in part by inser-tion of the Q material. The Lukan author adds subtle comments and alterations of both the Markan and Q material. They help draw out the narrative thread and highlight certain thematic features. We shall return to them in the next section.

Creating the Travel Narrative (Luke 9:51–19:27)

The next major restructuring of the Lukan narrative also follows from this re-working of the Galilee section. Now the turn toward Jerusalem in Mark 10:1–52 is significantly expanded to take on a major role as a separate section in the Lukan narrative. Running from Luke 9:51 to 19:27, the journey of Jesus and the disciples from Galilee to Jerusalem is regularly called the "Lukan travel narrative"[14] (see Box 13.2). In my view, the Lukan author continues the travel narrative through their stay in Jericho, after which they enter Jerusalem.[15] The basic Markan episodes have been supplemented by the addition of one uniquely Lukan scene, Jesus's en-counter with Zacchaeus (19:1–10), and one Q passage, the parable of the pounds/talents (19:11–27), both set at Jericho. Following this, Jesus and his now growing entourage march from Jericho to Jerusalem, culminating at the triumphal entry (19:28–38).[16] From a literary perspective, this last part of the travel narrative thus parallels in form the Lukan framework at the end of the Galilee section. It does so by concluding with a series of episodes that return the narrative to the basic Markan outline as it then transitions to the Jerusalem section and Passion narra-tive that follows.

The Lukan travel narrative is unlike any section of any of the other Gospels. As stated above, it is comprised almost entirely of Q material or uniquely Lukan epi-sodes, except at the very end.[17] The bulk of the Q material (more than two-thirds) is located within this section of Luke. It also contains some of the best-known parables in all the Gospels, including the good Samaritan (10:29–37), the rich fool (12:13–21), the prodigal son (15:11–32), and the rich man and Lazarus (16:19–31), all of which are uniquely Lukan compositions. Altogether, this section of Luke contains thirteen new parables and three new miracles that have no correspon-dence in the other Gospels.[18] This unique composition is expanded to nearly ten full chapters, the largest narrative unit in the Gospel of Luke. It is roughly double the length of either of the sections (Galilee and Jerusalem) that flank it. Its central placement and distinctive story line develop some of the most important themes in the Lukan portrayal of Jesus. We shall return in a later part of this chapter to discuss its significance for understanding the Lukan image of Jesus.

Repositioning the Rejection at Nazareth (Luke 4:16–30)

The last, and in some ways most telling, Lukan restructuring device involves a dramatic repositioning and expansion of the rejection at Nazareth episode (4:16–30, quoted at the beginning of this chapter). In the Gospel of Luke, this episode opens the Galilee section of the narrative. In effect, it is the first scene in Jesus's public ministry. By contrast, in the Gospel of Mark (6:1–6), this same episode comes at the end of the Galilee section and marks the transition to the beyond Galilee section. Relatively speaking, it should occur between Luke 8:56 and 9:1.

BOX 13.2

The Lukan Travel Narrative (9:51–19:27)

Lukan Passage	Scene	Parallels[1]	Source[2]
9:51–56	Departure for Jerusalem, passing through Samaritan villages	[cf. Mark 10:1–12 **and Matt 19:1–12**]	L
9:57-62	Potential Followers of Jesus	*Matt 8:19–22*	Q21 + L
10:1–(16)	Sending out of the Seventy	—	L
10:2–16	Instructions to the Seventy	*Matt 9:37–38 + 10:7–16; 10:40*	Q22–24
10:17–20	Return of the Seventy	—	L
10:21–22	Prayer of Thanks	Matt 11:26–27	Q25
10:23–24	Blessing of Disciples	Matt 13:16–17	Q26
10:25–28	The Great Commandment	*Mark 12:26–31 / Matt 22:34–40*	L (*from* Mᴋ)
10:29–37	Parable of Good Samaritan	—	L
10:38–42	Visiting Martha **and** Mary	[cf. John 11:1–4]	L
11:1–4	The Lord's Prayer	Matt 6:9–13	Q27 + L
11:5–8	Parable of the Friend at Midnight	—	L
11:9–13	Answers to Prayer	Matt 7:7–11	Q28
11:14–23	The Beelzebul Controversy	*Mark 3:22–27; 9:40 Matt 12:22–30; 9:32–34*	Mᴋ + Q29 + L
11:24–26	Return of an Unclean Spirit	Matt 11:24–26	Q30
11:27–28	Hearing and Obedience	—	L
11:29–32	The Sign of Jonah	*Mark 9:11–13 Matt 12:38–42*	Mᴋ + Q32 + L
11:33–36	A Light Metaphor	*Matt 5:15*	Q33 + L
11:37–52	Discourse at Dinner: *Against Pharisees*	*Matt 23:25–26, 23, 6–7, 27, 4, 29–31, 34–36 Mark 12:38–39*	Q34 + Mᴋ + L
11:53–12:1	Anger of the Scribes and Pharisees	(Mark 8:15)	L
12:2–12	Exhortation to Fearless Confession	*Matt 10:26–33;* (Mark 8:38)	Q35–39 + L

Lukan Passage	Scene	Parallels[1]	Source[2]
12:13–21	Parable of the Rich Fool	—	L
12:22–34	On Anxiety	Matt 6:25–33; 19–21	Q41–42
12:35–46	Watchfulness	[cf. Matt 25:1–13] Matt 24:43–51	Q43–45 + L
12:47–48	Parable of Slave's Wages 1 (cf. 17:7–10)	—	L
12:49–56	On Division Within Households	Matt 10:34–36; 16:2–3	Q46–47 + L
12:57–59	Settling Disputes	Matt 5:25–26	Q48 + L
13:1–5	On Repentance	—	L
13:6–9	Parable of a Fig Tree	(Mark 11:12–14, 20–25)	L
13:10–17	Healing a Crippled Woman	—	L
13:18–21	Parable of the Mustard Seed, Parable of the Yeast	Mark 4:30–32; Matt 13:31–33	MK + Q49 + L
13:22–30	The Narrow Door	Matt 7:13–14; 7:22–23; 8:11–12; 20:16	Q50–51 + L
13:31–33	Warning and Turn to Jerusalem	—	L
13:34–35	Lament over Jerusalem	Matt 23:37–39	Q52 + L
14:1–6	Healing of a Boy	—	L
14:7–14	Discourse at Dinner: Parable on Humility	(Matt 18:4)	L (+ Q54)
14:15–24	Parable of Great Banquet	Matt 22:1–10	Q55
14:25–35	The Cost of Discipleship	Matt 10:37–38; 5:13 (Mark 9:50)	L + Q56–57
15:1–7	Parable of Lost Sheep	Matt 18:12–14	Q58 + L
15:8–10	Parable of Lost Coin	—	L
15:11–32	Parable of the Lost ("Prodigal") Son and His Brother	[cf. Matt 21:28–32]	L (from Q?)
16:1–13	Parable of the Unjust Manager	(Matt 6:24)	L (+ Q60)
16:14–15	On Hypocrisy	—	L

Lukan Passage	Scene	Parallels[1]	Source[2]
16:16–18	About the Law	*Matt 11:12–13; 5:18; 5:32*	Q61
16:19–31	Parable of the Rich Man and Lazarus	—	L
17:1–2	On Cause of Stumbling	*Mark 9:42; Matt 18:7*	Mᴋ + Q62 + L
17:3–4	On Forgiveness	*Matt 18:15, 21–22*	Q63
17:5–6	On Faith	*Matt 17:20; Mark 11:22–23*	Q64
17:7–10	Parable of Slave's Wages 2 (cf. 12:47–48)	—	L
17:11–19	Healing of Ten Lepers	—	L
17:20–21	On the Kingdom	[cf. Mark 13:21]	L
17:22–37	The Day of the Son of Man	*Matt 24:26–28, 37–39; 40–41*	Q66 + L
18:1–8	Parable of the Unjust Judge	—	L
18:9–14	Parable of the Pharisee and Tax Collector	—	L
18:15–17	Jesus Blesses the Children	**Mark 10:13–16**	Mᴋ
18:18–30	The Rich Young Man	**Mark 10:17–31**	Mᴋ
18:31–34	Third Passion Prediction	**Mark 10:32–34***	Mᴋ + L
18:35–43	Healing of Bartimaeus	**Mark 10:46–52*** **(omission, cf. Luke 22:24–27)*	Mᴋ + L
19:1–10	Zacchaeus	—	L
19:11–27	Parable of the Talents	*Matt 25:14–30*	Q67 + L
	End of the Travel Narrative		
19:28–38	Triumphal Entry into Jerusalem	**Mark 11:1–10**	Mᴋ

[1] **Bold:** nearly complete verbal parallel in Mark or Matthew; *Italics:* Partial verbal parallel; (Parentheses): indirect parallel, i.e., a different story or scene; [cf.] = contrasting story in another Gospel.

[2] The sources are: Q (by saying number; see **Box 12.1**); Mᴋ = Gospel of Mark; L = The Lukan author (by addition of new material and/or by reworking source material in observable ways).

As we have already seen, the Lukan author has effectively collapsed these two sections of Mark into an exclusively Galilee section running from 4:14 to 9:50.

Consequently, the rejection episode no longer fits narratively into the story in the same way. Similarly, the Lukan travel narrative (9:51–19:27) now takes the place of the beyond Galilee section. The rejection episode, as framed by Mark, might have been placed at this point (roughly Luke 9:50), but the Lukan author chose not to do so. Instead, the storyteller has repositioned it to the beginning of Jesus's Galilean ministry. Relatively, it is the equivalent position to Mark 1:14–15, and even these opening verses have been reworked by the Lukan author (4:14–15) to smooth the transition to the new episode that follows.

The rejection episode has also been expanded by the author to contain Jesus's first "sermonette," at least in Luke, delivered in the synagogue of his hometown, Nazareth. Gone from the story are key Markan themes associated with the secrecy and misunderstanding motifs. The Lukan author has removed all traces of the doubts about Jesus by his mother and siblings (see the discussion in Chapter 10). As a result, the rejection episode no longer functions as it does in Mark, primarily as a widening of Jesus's horizons due to misunderstanding and increased local resistance. Instead, the repositioning and reshaping of the passage have the effect of making a wider audience the focus of Jesus's messianic calling from the very beginning.

The Narrative Artistry of the Lukan Storyteller

The extensive reworking of the rejection episode results in the creation of a distinctive Lukan thematic. It also shows the unity and artistry of the narrative. It can be seen in the construction of the sermonette, in which Jesus reads from the book of Isaiah and then comments on it (4:16–21). This setup for the episode is missing entirely from the Markan and Matthean versions, as are the extended discourse of Jesus and the reaction of the enraged Nazarenes. In its present form it is a thoroughly Lukan creation.[19] Let's take a closer look at how it works and its impact on the rest of the narrative.

The Sermon at Nazareth

The reshaped Galilee section opens with a brief summary about the beginning of Jesus's ministry after his return to the Galilee following his baptism (Luke 4:14–15). Gone now is the call of the first disciples (Mark 1:16–20), which has been repositioned to Luke 5:1–11. Instead, Jesus then goes to his hometown and visits the local synagogue on the Sabbath (4:16).[20] He steps forward to read from the scriptures, and the attendant hands him the scroll for that day. As the story is set up, by custom the scroll would have already been in use on the prior Sabbaths and would have been left rolled up, but at the place for the next reading. It just *happens* to be the scroll of Isaiah and a passage pregnant with messianic language.

Although some scholars have downplayed these happenstance elements, I would argue that they are part of the dramatic artistry and verisimilitude of the scene.[21] Whether it accurately depicts a practice of reading from the Prophets (in addition to the Torah) in synagogues of the period before the Jewish revolt remains questionable on historical grounds.[22] The scene is consciously constructed around the text of Isaiah. It thus carries a kind of prophetic significance, and the scripture now serves as a programmatic statement for Jesus's messianic mission as conceived by the Lukan author:

> *And having opened the scroll, he found the place where it was written: "The Spirit of the Lord is upon me, because he has anointed me to bring good news to the poor. He has sent me to proclaim release to the captives and recovery of sight to the blind, <u>to let the oppressed go free,</u> to proclaim the year of the Lord's favor." And he rolled up the scroll, gave it back to the attendant, and sat down. The eyes of all in the synagogue were fixed on him. Then he began to say to them, "Today this scripture has been fulfilled in your hearing." (4:17–21)*[23]

The scripture here "read" by Jesus is actually a composite of two different passages from the Septuagint: Isaiah 61:1–2 and 58:6. In fact, the phrase from Isaiah 58:6 (underlined above) is inserted between Isaiah 61:1 and 2. Because these passages are so far apart in the actual text of Isaiah, there is no way a person could see or read both of them at the same time if holding a scroll.[24] In addition, a portion of Isaiah 61:1 has been omitted, as has the latter part of verse 2, while the phrase "recovery of sight to the blind" occurs only in the Greek version of the Septuagint.[25]

So what kind of "reading" is this that skips some phrases and adds in others? Does it really mean that Jesus was reading a Greek scroll in a Galilean village synagogue some forty years before the Jewish war? That is verisimilitude. It may be plausible on the narrative level, but it is historically impossible. It reflects a reshaping of the scripture to fit the author's intent. In other words, the Lukan author has carefully crafted the scene so that *by chance* Jesus is given this precisely phrased text to read, and as a prophetic sign it applies to him. Of course, the audience cannot see the text to realize how it is being manipulated. Jesus's messianic anointing now marks him as the one who will bring comfort and release to the poor, the captives, the blind, and the oppressed. Drawn from the apocalyptic section of the "Third Isaiah," this statement is a vision for Zion (Jerusalem) in the eschatological age, when even some Gentiles will turn to God.[26]

Isaiah "Prophecies" and the Gentile Mission in Luke-Acts

The scene in Luke 4:16–30 stands in sharp contrast to Jesus's instructions in Matthew 10:5–6: "Go nowhere among the Gentiles, and enter no town of the Samaritans, but go rather to the lost sheep of the house of Israel." Now the Lukan presentation asserts that, from the very beginning, Jesus intended to welcome Gentiles. This theme is largely drawn from Paul's thought, and its full lines are finally developed in the second volume of the Lukan work, the Acts of the Apostles.[27] But the motif of Jesus welcoming Gentiles is woven into the Lukan Gospel from the beginning. The pregnant language of Isaiah 49:5–6, now referring to Jesus as "light to the Gentiles,"[28] is already present in the Lukan birth narrative. Specifically, it occurs in the scene of Simeon's blessing of the baby when he was taken to the Temple for the rites of purification (2:28–32; see Chapter 10 for fuller discussion). On seeing the child, the old priest burst spontaneously into another distinctively Lukan prophetic song:

> *Master, now you are dismissing your servant in peace, according to your word;*
> *for my eyes have seen your salvation, which you have prepared in the presence*
> *of all peoples, <u>a light for revelation to the Gentiles</u> and for glory to your people*
> *Israel. (2:29–32)*

Known as the *Nunc Dimittis,* from its first words in the later Latin version, it signals what will become a key theme in Luke and Acts—the mission to the Gentiles. As we noted in the Lukan birth narrative, the author/narrator does not usually tell the audience directly that something is a fulfillment of prophecy in the way that the Matthean author does. Rather, the "prophecy" is voiced by characters in the story, just as here, usually as paraphrases or allusions to the passages from the Jewish scriptures, but in Greek of course. Hence, key Lukan themes now begin to project through the story as a way of narrativizing other prophecies as being fulfilled in the career of Jesus.

After Nazareth: The Lukan Saga Continues

The theme of the gentile mission is further developed in two new miracles inserted into the Galilee section. The first is the Lukan version of the centurion's servant (7:1–10), in which Jesus heals the slave of a Roman officer and comments on his exemplary faith. The story is drawn from Q15,[29] but it has been reworked to stress the gentile centurion's devotion to Judaism and the respect he receives for it. The second new miracle is the widow's son at Nain (Luke 7:11–17), in which Jesus raises the dead son of a poor widow. It is modeled on famous miracles of Elijah and Elisha that involve marginal women in ancient Israel.[30]

This is where the narrative artistry of the Lukan author can really be seen, for it should be noted that these same two miracles are already prefigured in Jesus's response to the crowd during the rejection at Nazareth story in Luke 4, just after he reads from the scroll of Isaiah. There Jesus refers precisely to the stories of Elijah and Elisha having ministered miraculously to Gentiles:

And he said, "Truly I tell you, no prophet is accepted in the prophet's hometown. But the truth is, there were many widows in Israel in the time of Elijah, when the heaven was shut up three years and six months, and there was a severe famine over all the land; yet Elijah was sent to none of them except to a widow at Zarephath in Sidon. There were also many lepers in Israel in the time of the prophet Elisha, and none of them was cleansed except Naaman the Syrian." (4:24–27)

This entire passage has been added to the Lukan story of the rejection, and it is explicitly this statement regarding Gentiles that is said to have enraged the Nazarenes to expel Jesus and try to kill him (4:28–30). Thus, in the Lukan construction, the centurion's servant now corresponds to the story of Naaman, and the widow of Nain now corresponds to the widow of Zarephath.[31]

A glimpse at the integrated quality of the story line is shown by the episode that follows immediately after these two miracles in the Lukan narrative, for this is where the second block of Q material is inserted into the Galilee section (7:18–35). It involves three units of Q material (Q16, 17, 20) that deal with John the Baptist. The result, once again, is a thoroughly Lukan construction with a high degree of narrative continuity.

The episode opens with John the Baptist hearing about Jesus's miracles and sending messengers to ask Jesus if this means that he is "the coming one" (7:18–19). The Lukan positioning of this episode is relatively early, just prior to the parables.[32] John's question reflects the original wording of Q, as shown by the characteristic title "the coming one." The Lukan author adds the middle portion of this episode with John's messengers witnessing more of the same types of miracles about which they have heard (7:20–21). It is Jesus's reply that now draws the Lukan themes into sharper focus:

And he answered them, "Go and tell John what you have seen and heard: the blind receive their sight, the lame walk, the lepers are cleansed, the deaf hear, the dead are raised, the poor have good news brought to them. And blessed is anyone who takes no offense at me." (7:22–23)

This statement is also drawn from Q16 (cf. Matt 11:4–6) and shows that several similar passages from Isaiah (61:1–2; 35:5–6; 29:18) had already been woven together as a sign of Jesus's prophetic identity in the Q tradition. The remainder of the story uses two more passages based on Q (Luke 7:24–35 = Q17, 20) about John as messenger and Jesus as prophet.

What we now see is that Jesus's response in 7:22–23, taken over from Q16, was the basis for the overall narrative scheme behind the Lukan reworking of the rejection story. In other words, the Lukan author has narrativized this saying using verisimilitude by creating the rejection story to open the Galilee section. The plotline of the rejection story, as discussed above, now weaves as a thematic thread through the Galilee section to the miracles of 7:1–17 (centurion's servant and widow of Nain) and the discourses about John in 7:18–35. It is punctuated by the passages from Q16 ("the blind receive their sight, the lame walk, the lepers are cleansed, the deaf hear, the dead are raised, the poor have good news brought to them") and Q20 ("Wisdom is vindicated by all her children").

This complex, running theme is then capped off narratively when the Lukan author next moves the story of the woman who anoints Jesus's feet from the Markan Passion story (Mark 14:3–9) to Luke 7:36–50. While Jesus is at a dinner hosted by a prominent Pharisee named Simon, a woman comes behind him as he is reclining on the dining couch and begins to anoint his feet and wipe them with her hair. In this version, it is the host who sneers at the woman and Jesus, saying, "If this man were a prophet, he would have known who and what kind of woman this is who is touching him—that she is a sinner." The Lukan author then further elaborates the story by having Jesus turn on his host, Simon, and tell him a parable about two men who owe debts (7:40–43), to which he then likens Simon and the woman. It concludes with poignant statement about forgiveness, and more, about acceptance:

> Then turning toward the woman, he said to Simon, "Do you see this woman? I entered your house; you gave me no water for my feet, but she has bathed my feet with her tears and dried them with her hair. You gave me no kiss, but from the time I came in she has not stopped kissing my feet. You did not anoint my head with oil, but she has anointed my feet with ointment. Therefore, I tell you, her sins, which were many, have been forgiven; hence she has shown great love. But the one to whom little is forgiven, loves little." (7:44–47)

In effect, this story now serves as a narrativized version of the Q sayings about Jesus consorting with "tax collectors and sinners" (Luke 7:34–35 = Q20). A key summary statement regarding the wealthy women who travel with Jesus and support him then concludes this Lukan vignette:

> Soon afterwards he went on through cities and villages, proclaiming and bringing the good news of the kingdom of God. The twelve were with him, as well as some women who had been cured of evil spirits and infirmities: Mary, called Magdalene, from whom seven demons had gone out, and Joanna, the wife of Herod's steward Chuza, and Susanna, and many others, who provided for them out of their resources. (8:1–3)

It too continues the themes initiated in the sermon at Nazareth, but, as we shall see, it also points ahead to dining as another important feature of the Lukan story. All in all, then, it seems that a ring composition has thus been used to create the thematic spine for reworking the Galilee section of the Lukan narrative.

It is thus a remarkable weaving of the Q material into the Markan outline and nothing like the Matthean counterpart discussed in the previous chapter. In other words, it is very difficult to imagine how any of this could have been based on Matthew. The Lukan author must have been working out this new story independently from the earlier sources, Mark and Q. In the end, all of this earlier material has been strategically reworked and woven into the Lukan outline to stress four main points: (1) Jesus is the prophet-messiah, "the coming one" of the Q tradition; (2) his message, framed in apocalyptic language from Isaiah, stresses relief to the poor, healing of the sick, and "freedom" for the oppressed; (3) these gifts are open to all who turn to the Lord, Gentiles as well as Jews; and (4) the "year of the Lord's favor," understood eschatologically, has now been inaugurated by the event of Jesus's messianic anointing.[33]

Widening Horizons in the Travel Narrative

These same motifs continue in the travel narrative. Jesus's encounter with the rich tax collector Zacchaeus (19:1–10), which is unique to Luke, and the parable of the talents (19:11–27), drawn from Q67, hold a parallel position at the end of the travel narrative and reflect the same themes seen in 7:36–8:3. Such parallel scenes and themes stretching across Luke and Acts are a signal feature, a fingerprint, of the Lukan author and point to the overall narrative unity of the work.[34]

The travel narrative opens with another uniquely Lukan episode, the mission of the seventy (10:1–20; see Box 13.2). Even though the episode is built around the "mission instructions" of Q22–24, there are three key shifts from their deployment in the Matthean mission sermon.[35] This second mission of Luke now involves seventy other disciples who are commissioned to spread the word as Jesus approaches:

> *After this the Lord appointed seventy others and sent them on ahead of him in pairs to every town and place where he himself intended to go. He said to them, "The harvest is plentiful, but the laborers are few; therefore ask the Lord of the harvest to send out laborers into his harvest. Go on your way." (10:1–3)*

This new mission occurs after Jesus and his growing entourage pass into Samaria (9:51–56). It is framed by two uniquely Lukan units (10:1, 17–20) that help turn the instructions to a broader audience.[36]

Next, the Lukan reworking of these mission instructions from Q sets the stage for the parable of the good Samaritan (10:29–37). The occasion for this parable is further set up through another key Lukan revision of the Markan narrative, by moving the discussion of the great commandment from the Jerusalem section (at Mark 12:28–34) into the travel narrative. In contrast to the Markan story, where the scribe who asks the question is said to be "not far from the kingdom" (Mark 12:34), the Lukan version is openly adversarial. Now, a "lawyer" asks a question about the kingdom "to test Jesus" (Luke 10:25) and, after Jesus's reply, seeks to justify himself by asking sarcastically, "And who is my neighbor?" (10:29). The familiar parable delivers a poignant message through the concluding question posed by the Lukan Jesus: "Which of these three [priest, Levite, or Samaritan] do you think was a neighbor to the man who fell into the hands of robbers?" Given the uniquely Lukan elements of the lawyer's challenge and the parable itself, it can only offer a distinctively Lukan vision that Samaritans and Gentiles can also properly follow the commandments and thus gain eternal life (10:25–27).[37]

BOX 13.3

The Book of Luke-Acts

DATE: ca. 90–100

AUTHOR: Uncertain

ATTRIBUTION: Luke, the physician, a traveling companion of Paul

SETTING: Ephesus, Corinth (or Antioch?)

AUDIENCE AND OCCASION: A predominantly gentile audience in the tradition of the churches of Paul from the Aegean region. As a late expression of the second generation, the work begins to reflect on the history of the movement and how far it has come since the days when the church was founded. This reflection allows for a further apologetic interest in promoting tolerance for the Christians in the larger Roman political arena and a concomitant distancing from Jews.

OUTLINE

Part I: The Gospel of Luke

A. Prologue (1:1–4)

B. Birth Narrative and Ministry of John (1:5–3:22)
   <Interlude: Genealogy (3:23–38)>

C. The Ministry of Jesus in the Galilee (4:1–9:50)
   1. Temptation (4:1–13)
   2. Rejection at Nazareth (4:14–30)
   3. Wider Galilean ministry (4:31–9:16)
   4. Confession and Passion predictions (9:17–50)

D. The Travel Narrative (to Jerusalem; 9:51–19:27)
   1. Samaria and the mission of the seventy (9:51–10:20)
   2. Instructions to the disciples (10:21–13:35)

This view is underscored by several other episodes in the travel narrative, including the parable of the great banquet (14:15–24) and the parable of the prodigal son (15:11–32). The latter is a uniquely Lukan parable in which the prodigal (or "lost") son and the elder brother stand as allegories for Gentiles and Jews, respectively. This parable may also depend on a Q original, if one takes the parable of two sons from Matthew 21:28–32 as its counterpart.[38] In this case, the Matthean version is closer to the Q original. The elaboration of the story of the prodigal and his plight and the allegorization about Gentiles are part of a thoroughly Lukan reworking, set in the framework of two other parables about God's rejoicing over the "lost" (15:1–10).

The parable of the great banquet clearly derives from Q, but has been given a distinctively Lukan theme by supplying an additional invitation to "outsiders":

> *"Then the owner of the house became angry and said to his slave, 'Go out at once into the streets and lanes of the town and bring in the poor, the crippled, the blind, and the lame.' And the slave said, 'Sir, what you ordered has been done, and there is still room.' Then the master said to the slave, 'Go out into the roads and lanes, and compel people to come in, so that my house may be filled. For I tell you, none of those who were invited will taste my dinner.'" (14:21–24)*

Comparison of the other versions of this parable in the Gospels of Matthew and *Thomas* show that the second invitation here reflects the Q original (see Chapter 9 and Box 9.3). The first invitation (as underlined) has been added by the Lukan author. The same four terms, "poor, crippled, blind, and lame," occur in combination in 14:13, within the uniquely Lukan passage (14:7–14) that immediately precedes the parable of the great banquet. It too is set at a dinner, and Jesus instructs his host to welcome and accept the underprivileged.

These scenes of dining, with their theme of hosting the poor and sick, now show as a Lukan fingerprint on the narrative. It forces us to think back to the dinner scene of the anointing woman (7:36–50) and ahead to the dinner with Zacchaeus (19:1–10), but with a new wrinkle. If the first invitation in this new Lukan version of the banquet parable is to the marginal people within that society, then who are the others brought in from the "roads and lanes" to fill the eschatological banquet? Ultimately, the great banquet and prodigal son parables have now been transformed into allegories about welcoming Gentiles into the community of faith. At the same time, the picture of Jesus teaching at dinners and dinners as occasions for social integration are powerful symbols within Greco-Roman culture. Dinner scenes also punctuate the Passion narrative (22:15–30; 24:28–35) and the story in Acts (2:46; 5:42; 20:7). These distinctive Lukan features present not only a different image of Jesus and his message, but also a different sense of the audience for which Luke-Acts was written.

Author and Audience

The traditional author of both the Gospel of Luke and Acts is Luke, the "physician," a co-worker of Paul[39] (see Box 13.3). That these works come from a follower of the Pauline tradition, and probably a gentile convert, is not disputed. Since all references to "Luke" in the Pauline corpus occur in so-called prison letters, the legend grew up that he had accompanied Paul to Rome and there wrote down his account of Paul's career sometime just before or after Paul's death in 64 CE.[40] There are several points in Acts where the narrative shifts from third to first person, and these "we passages" are assumed by some to reflect the work of an actual traveling companion of Paul.[41] Yet close comparison with Paul's letters reveals some notable differences in the account of Paul's life.[42]

There are also problems of dating in the light of current theories of Gospel relations, since the Gospel of Luke must be later than both Mark and Matthew, and thus no earlier than 80–85 CE. An earlier generation of scholars argued that Luke-Acts might have been written as late as the mid-second century or after, but this opposite extreme is no more attractive on historical grounds. In current New Testament scholarship, the dates given for Luke-Acts are usually 80–90. Even at this later date, some scholars still assume that the "historical" Luke was the author, but most do not.[43] A recent trend among scholars has seen the date slide slightly later to about 90–100 or so, and this now seems more likely.[44]

Similar questions surround the author's location. The Greek is of fairly high quality and filled with quotations and allusions to the Septuagint. A setting in Rome is a possibility, but rather unlikely. Because Acts makes quite a lot of the early days of the church in Antioch—where the disciples were first called "Christians" (Acts 11:26)[45]—many scholars have located the writing there. But the author shows far more direct awareness of local landmarks and events in the cities of the Aegean, especially Ephesus and Corinth. Given the author's attachment to Pauline tradition and strong sense of gentile mission, one of the cities of Paul, probably Ephesus, is preferable, but certainty is not possible. Ultimately, any conclusion about the authorship, date, or location is dependent on how one understands the genre and composition as well as the occasion and intention of the work.

A Two-Volume Narrative

Even though Luke and Acts are separated from one another in the New Testament canon and all extant manuscripts reflect this fact, scholars are now unanimous in the view that it was originally a single work. This view has given rise to the shorthand designation "Luke-Acts" to refer to its original, unitary form. Internal indicators also confirm the continuous quality of the narrative through the two volumes. They include linguistic and stylistic similarities, thematic continuities, and even parallel episodes or doublets occurring in the Gospel and Acts.[46] For example, the centurion Cornelius in Acts 10 resembles the unnamed centurion of Luke 7, and the two scenes constitute a kind of doublet on these Roman soldiers who are attracted first to Jesus and later to the Jesus movement. So also Jesus's first sermon at Nazareth in Luke 4 finds many verbal and thematic parallels in the story of Peter's Pentecost sermon in Acts 2.[47]

The most important single piece of evidence, however, is the presence in each volume of an authorial prologue with important interconnections:

Luke 1:1–4: Since many have undertaken to set down an orderly account of the events that have been fulfilled among us, just as they were handed on to us by *those who from the beginning were eyewitnesses and servants of the word, I too decided, after investigating everything carefully from the very first, to write an orderly account for you, <u>most excellent Theophilus,</u> so that you may know the truth concerning the things about which you have been instructed.*

Acts 1:1–2: In the first book, <u>O Theophilus,</u> I wrote about all that Jesus did and taught from the beginning until the day when he was taken up to heaven after giving instructions through the Holy Spirit to the apostles whom he had chosen.

The fact that both prologues address the work to a person named Theophilus and that Acts refers to a "first book" dealing with the deeds and teachings of Jesus make the conclusion of a unitary composition inescapable. Multivolume historical works of this sort were quite common in antiquity, and the type of prologue found in Luke-Acts is quite typical.

More Than a Gospel: The Genre of Luke-Acts

The nature of the Lukan prologue also says something about the literary level of the work, since it would typically indicate a work that was formally "published." Publication in this sense means that the work was intentionally produced for wider distribution and adhered to certain literary conventions. In this regard, the address to Theophilus again becomes important, since it was normal to dedicate such works to the patron who paid for the publication, meaning the costs of papyrus, ink, secretaries, and copyists and in many cases support for the author. For a work of any appreciable length, these costs could be substantial. The two-volume form of Luke-Acts is by far the longest work in the New Testament (by more than double) and one of the longest during the first two centuries of the Christian movement. Thus, there are much higher literary pretensions and expectations at work in this composition.

This literary self-consciousness brings us to the issue of the genre of Luke-Acts. As we shall discuss in the Epilogue, the Gospels are generally considered to be part of the ancient literary genre known broadly as "Lives." Although not governed by the same concerns as modern biography, these ancient "Lives" were devoted to the words and deeds of important figures, including philosophers, emperors, rhetoricians, and religious figures. An important parallel in Jewish tradition is Philo's two-volume *Life of Moses,* discussed in Chapter 3. Whereas the Gospel of Luke seems to fit well enough with the genre of "Lives," it goes well beyond the literary expectations of Mark.

Moreover, Acts clearly continues the story, but lacks the central figure to qualify as a "Life" in strict terms. Because it traces the rise of the early Christian movement for some thirty years or more, many features in Acts have been likened more to the genre of ancient "history."[48] Charles Talbert, an expert in ancient literature, has noted, however, that the two volumes correspond to a pattern in the "Lives" of Greek philosophers, where the life of the "founder" is followed by a description of his successors and their school.[49] In this way, Luke-Acts may still be called a "Life," but more within the philosophical tradition, and thus set more firmly in the broader Greco-Roman environment.

In recent scholarship, it has been noted that there are many features of the story and the style, especially in the lengthy travel narratives, that seem to fit better with the ancient genre of the "novel" or "romance." A greater degree of literary artistry may be seen in the fact that the travels of Paul, which dominate the latter half of Acts, are paralleled by the Lukan creation of a travel narrative (Luke 9:51–19:27) for Jesus. Thus, each of these ancient genres—"Lives," history, and romance—contributes certain features to the work. It must also be remembered that the Exodus tradition was taken by Philo as a similar kind of "journey" story around which to build his narrative of the *Life of Moses*. The Lukan travel narrative, in particular, seems to emulate the Moses-Exodus tradition by linking the story of Jesus (or *Jeshua*) to that of his biblical namesake, Moses's successor, Joshua.[50] There were already precedents for blending these genres in the divine-man tradition.[51] Of all the canonical Gospels, Luke comes the closest to the divine-man tradition in portraying Jesus, especially in the birth narrative (see Chapter 10). But it may go farther; the divine-man elements may be more of a tool—rather than the goal—for the Lukan author.

Modeling Jesus in Luke-Acts

From the beginning of the birth narrative, the portrayal of Jesus in Luke-Acts is noticeably different. He is more than a human chosen by God as messianic instrument and then exalted to heaven, as seen in Mark. Nor is he merely the apocalyptic sage or Sophia's "child" of Q. Though both of these images contribute directly to the construction of Luke-Acts, a new combination emerges. We might even say it moves in the opposite direction from the Jewish teacher of Torah developed by the Matthean author. Now in the Gospel of Luke, Jesus is given a more "divine nature" from the moment of conception, as shown in Mary's visit to Elizabeth (1:39–45; see Chapter 10). On the other hand, this notion, taken from the divine-man tradition, makes no explicit claim on divine preexistence, as would develop in later Christian tradition.[52] Rather, a new sense of divine guidance or compulsion, similar to that of Plato's Socrates or Philo's Moses, now dominates the story of Jesus (see Chapter 9).

These elements of Lukan design can be seen through the role of the Holy Spirit, who serves as a kind of divine stage director for much of the action in both Luke and Acts.[53] Jesus's own clear awareness of a divine compulsion driving his actions and his fate is regularly expressed through the distinctive Lukan phrasing "I must" and "It is necessary."[54] Thus, his messianic "anointing," signaled in the Lukan version of the baptism and rejection stories (Luke 3:21–22; 4:16–18), now asserts a new sense of identity and mission. Similarly, his attitude in approaching the Passion has far greater sense of resolve and awareness of what is taking place. He is a more serene and self-possessed character in the Lukan version. Instead of the fearful and "pained" figure of Mark, the Lukan Jesus goes to his death as in a "contest" (Luke 22:44), like a hero and martyr against human enemies and cosmic forces of evil.[55]

The Philosopher-King

It has also been suggested that the death of Jesus in the Gospel of Luke resembles the death of Socrates in certain respects. Socrates, it must be remembered, chose to die by forced suicide rather than desist from his calling as philosopher. He was tried and condemned by the Athenian council. Plato's *Apology of Socrates* recounts the trial, Socrates' eloquent defense speech, and his final counsel for his disciples on the eve of his departure. A portion of Socrates' defense is also paraphrased in Peter's defense before the Sanhedrin according to Acts 5:29.[56] This speech also shows a Lukan perspective on the death of Jesus:

> When they had brought them, they had them stand before the council. The high priest questioned them, saying, "We gave you strict orders not to teach in this name, yet here you have filled Jerusalem with your teaching and you are determined to bring this man's blood on us." But Peter and the apostles answered, <u>"We must obey God rather than any human authority.</u> The God of our ancestors raised up Jesus, whom you had killed by hanging him on a tree. God exalted him at his right hand as <u>Leader and Savior</u> that he might give repentance to Israel and forgiveness of sins. And we are witnesses to these things, and so is the Holy Spirit whom God has given to those who obey him." (Acts 5:27–32)

The first line of Peter's reply (as underlined above) has strong verbal similarities in Greek to the statement of Socrates: "but I shall obey God rather than you."[57]

Like the death of Socrates in later Greek thought, the death of Jesus is viewed now as a colossal act of ignorance by the perpetrators, a result of mass rage against an innocent man. The Lukan author consciously transforms the trials of Jesus so as to exonerate Pilate further than Mark (or Matthew). The Lukan trial before Pilate, for example, is more like a Roman court proceeding.[58] In a uniquely Lukan insertion, Pilate even tries to get rid of the whole case by sending Jesus to Herod Antipas (23:6–16; see Chapter 7 and Box 7.5). Eventually, Pilate's interrogation convinces him that Jesus is not guilty of capital crimes, and he tries repeatedly to have Jesus punished but released. In the end, Jesus is never flogged in Luke.

Of course, none of this matches the reports about Pilate from contemporary sources, nor was it typical for provincial governors to insist on formal legal proceedings in cases involving non-Romans, especially where sedition was involved.[59] These Lukan alterations result in exculpating Pilate and placing the blame more squarely on the Jewish religious authorities who whipped up the crowds.[60] This idea is then repeated in several of the speeches in Acts as an apologetic refrain:

> *Let all the house of Israel therefore know assuredly that God has made him both Lord and Christ, this Jesus whom **you** crucified, . . . whom **you** delivered up and denied in the presence of Pilate, **when he had decided to release him**. (Acts 2:36; 3:13)*[61]

Thus the Lukan staging of the trials and crucifixion creates a new drama, likely with an eye on its predominantly non-Jewish audience. Unfortunately, it also results in a much more negative portrayal of the Jewish leadership and contributes to the further growth of Christian anti-Judaism.[62]

Needless to say, promoting this perspective on Jesus's death was not directed at Jews, especially at the time of the Lukan writing. Instead, it was meant to portray Jesus's death in a way that Greeks and Romans could understand—as the unjustified death of a noble philosopher of the stature of Socrates. Now the condemned criminal becomes a martyr. In large measure, it functioned apologetically, by showing that the "Christians," as they are now called (Acts 11:26), are not following some sort of Jewish criminal or revolutionary. Philo had similarly combined the philosopher and divine-man traditions in portraying Moses in response to earlier Greek polemics that he had merely been the leader of a band of rebellious Egyptian slaves.[63]

The description of Jesus as "Leader and Savior" in Acts 5:27–32 (quoted above) is functioning in a similar way, as it uses a common Greek term (*archēgon*) referring to the "leader" or "founder" of a nation, but also the founder of a philosophical school.[64] The exact word was used by Philo in describing Abraham as progenitor of the Jews, while Moses was given their "governing," "rule," and "kingship."[65] In Philo's view, the combination of all these roles is what makes Moses the ultimate "philosopher-king"; as such he becomes a "living law" for his people.[66]

Similar ideas are expressed by contemporary Greek philosophers, such as Musonius Rufus, a Roman Stoic of the mid-first century CE:

> *In general it is of the greatest importance for the good king to be faultless and perfect in word and deed, if indeed he is to be a <u>living law,</u> as it seemed to the ancients, effecting good government and harmony, suppressing lawlessness and dissension, a true imitator of Zeus, and like him, father of his people. But how could one be such a king if he were not endowed with a superior nature, given the best possible education, and possessing all the virtues that befit a human? If then there is another "science" which guides human nature to virtue and teaches it both to practice and to associate with the good, then let it be compared to see whether it or Philosophy is better capable of producing a good king. . . . For my part, I believe that <u>the good king is immediately and necessarily a philosopher, and the philosopher a kingly person.</u>*[67]

Book two of Philo's *Life of Moses* opens with this same aphorism (as underlined), taken directly from Plato, in order to show that Moses possessed both faculties.[68] Later Philo calls Moses the perfect "lawgiver," "king," "priest," and "prophet," where the term "lawgiver" (*nomothetēs*) is equivalent to "founder" in the national sense.[69] Acts 3:15 and 5:31 continue this same theme in the Lukan presentation of Jesus as founder of a new philosophy with the disciples as his successors. The continuation of this theme in Acts is nowhere more visible than in Paul's Areopagus speech (17:22–31), when he presents this new "philosophy" of Jesus to the Athenians themselves.[70] The Lukan travel narrative, in particular, sets up this idea by highlighting the portrayal of Jesus as the "philosopher-king."

A "Cynic" Social Critic

A key shift, then, in the Lukan image of Jesus is from the apocalyptic sage of the Q tradition to more of a philosopher, in the Greek sense. This likening of Jesus to Socrates may also account for the Lukan slant on socioeconomic criticism, for Socrates by the first century had been co-opted by several schools of Greek philosophy other than Platonism. In fact, there was by then a prevalent view of Socrates as a "cynic" philosopher, similar to Diogenes the Dog.[71] It should also be remembered that Diogenes was likewise something of an outcast in Athens because of his acute social criticism.[72] There was even a collection of fictional letters penned in the name of Socrates as well as other Cynic figures that functioned as a kind of novelistic portrayal of these ancient philosophers for later emulation.[73]

Central to these broader "cynicizing" ideals was a criticism of wealth and luxury; its principal ethos was self-sufficiency and a removal from worldly distractions.[74] Only by divesting oneself of care for worldly goods is one able to focus properly on moral self-improvement. This view is not always taken as an actual divesting of possessions as such, but rather as being overly concerned with them. Consequently, a number of these cynic-style philosophers of the first century talked about proper attitudes toward and use of wealth, including proper treatment of the poor. Jesus's teachings on the poor, as seen in the Lukan Beatitudes, could also be taken in this direction as a way of explaining his views to a predominantly Greco-Roman audience.[75]

A good example comes in the travel narrative where the Lukan author gives three distinctive parables about the proper use of wealth. They are the rich fool (12:13–21), the unjust manager (16:1–13), and the rich man and Lazarus (16:19–31). The point of all three parables is that one's wealth must be used to help the poor and that money is ultimately a gift from God to share. The burden of wealth is taking care of one's dependents, meaning social dependents as well as family and kin. In addition, emphasis is given to the fact that many of Jesus's followers, notably the women, are people of means, who support Jesus and his disciples (8:1–3).[76]

For the poor and outcast, however, like the beggar Lazarus, Jesus offers no immediate political reversal of fortunes except in the world to come.

Rather than a revolutionary stance, this view of the proper use of wealth is in line with the teachings of Paul and contemporary Greek and Roman moral philosophers, such as Seneca or Musonius Rufus.[77] Musonius was known for his critique of luxury and wealth, similar to the Cynics'.[78] In particular, greed was understood as a fatal vice that perverted the proper use of one's possessions. We find the same warning about greed in Luke 12:13–34 by juxtaposing the parable of the rich fool as an example of greed with the Q sayings on anxiety over worldly goods.[79] As Ronald Hock has shown, the ideals behind the parables of the rich fool and the rich man and Lazarus find direct parallels in Greek novels and rhetorical handbooks. The latter often reflect stereotypical patterns of moral values drawn from philosophy, but rendered into stories about characters in daily life.[80] So too in the Lukan "novel" these unique parables allow Jesus to tell similar "character tales" and to project an underlying philosophical, and specifically cynic, approach to wealth, ethics, and proper treatment of one's social dependents.[81] As a result, the Jesus of Luke comes off looking and sounding rather like the Greek and Roman moral philosophers.

Lord of the Banquet

The image of the philosopher also allows the Lukan author to draw together other lines of Jesus's identity, especially as prophet, messiah, and teacher, through the filter of the divine-man tradition. It is nowhere clearer than in the recurrent theme of Jesus's dinner discourses. On the one hand, the dinner evokes apocalyptic notions of the eschatological banquet. On the other hand, the Greek tradition of the *symposium* as philosophical dinner conversation provided a commensurate model from Greco-Roman culture. As a genre, *symposium* literature, as it is called, also offers a narrative device for presenting the wisdom of the sages.[82] A good example is Plutarch's fictional *Dinner of the Seven Sages,* which was contemporaneous with the writing of Luke-Acts.[83] Plutarch's version of this story changes some of the characters and, most notably, adds women to the scene. Having women there is anachronistic. It would have been unthinkable in the earlier Greek tradition of the *symposium,* but was more commonplace by Roman times.

So here we may take special note of the place of women in the Lukan banquet scenes and more generally around Jesus. Now we see the other effect of the Lukan reworking of the back-to-back stories of the anointing woman and the wealthy woman supporters near the end of the Galilee sections (7:36–8:3). Both are set in this same social arena of dining and patronage. Having a woman as a thoughtful participant, as opposed to merely serving or performing other duties, reminds us immediately of the uniquely Lukan scene of Jesus at dinner with Mary and Martha (10:38–42). Thus the Lukan dinner scenes serve an important function in creating a philosophical climate for the story. At the same time they function to narrativize key ideas from the earlier Jesus tradition, especially Jesus's eating with "tax collectors and sinners." This motif, drawn originally from Q20 (Luke 7:35) now takes on new cultural resonances in the Lukan narrative, as the poor, outcasts, women, tax collectors, sinners, and even Gentiles are all welcomed to Jesus's banquet.[84]

David Moessner has aptly characterized these Lukan themes as portraying Jesus as "Lord of the Banquet."[85] On the one hand, it portrays Jesus's prophetic/messianic identity in light of Moses and the Exodus. On the other, it portrays Jesus as the philosopher-king. In particular, Moessner stresses the image of Jesus as the "journey guest" who accepts the hospitality of those welcoming him along the way.[86] Yet in these very contexts his dinner discourses serve to instruct those present about proper attitudes and expectations. In doing so, Jesus himself becomes patron of the poor and oppressed, as we saw in his treatment of the "sinful" woman who anoints his feet (7:36–50), the second of the dinner scenes in Luke (see Chapter 2). While Jesus is the guest of Simon, by his treatment of the woman he turns into her champion; in his discussion of forgiveness, he assumes the role of patron to both Simon and the woman.

Other familiar episodes from the Gospels also receive new dramatic elements. The Lukan author adds a subtle touch to the feeding of the five thousand: when Jesus saw the crowds who had gathered at Bethsaida, "He *welcomed* them, and spoke to them about the kingdom of God, and healed those who needed to be cured" (9:11). Then as the day drew to a close, he performed the feeding miracle (9:12–17). So we notice that, in this instance, Jesus himself plays the role of host and patron, who "welcomes" the guests and takes care of their needs.[87] Once again, the Lukan author has narrativized key elements from the message of Jesus to frame these symbolic stories. In general, the Lukan version of the miracles functions to show Jesus as a benevolent patron, philosopher, and social reformer, but with supernatural powers. He is a divine man.

This banquet motif finally comes to its climax in the Passion narrative itself, in both the Last Supper (Luke 22:14–38) and the two dinner scenes after Jesus's resurrection at Emmaus and in Jerusalem (24:28–35; 36–49). Neither Mark nor Matthew contains anything like them. The former establishes the commemorative meal for the ongoing fellowship of the community. The latter scenes symbolically show the "presence" of Jesus whenever the meal is celebrated, as is shown by their continuation in Acts.[88] The banquet now becomes a symbol of the new community in the kingdom. In this way, Jesus is both "Lord of the Banquet" and Prince/Messiah. For Luke's audience, he is thus the perfect philosopher-king, like Moses according to Philo.[89]

Eschatological Prophet and Divine Man

Lukan eschatology is framed by two sermons—the one that opens Jesus's ministry (Luke 4:16–30) and Peter's on the day of Pentecost (Acts 2:1–40). These two

BOX 13.4

The Epochal View of History in Luke–Acts

1. The Epoch of the Law and Prophets
(from Abraham to John the Baptist)

"The law and the prophets were in effect until John came;
since then the good news of the kingdom of God is proclaimed,
and everyone tries to enter it by force."
(Luke 16:16)

Ends with the arrest and death of John the Baptist (Luke 3:19–20).
Note placement of Lukan genealogy as interlude (Luke 3:23–38).

2. The Messianic Epoch of the Proclamation of the Kingdom
(period of Jesus's ministry and death)

"The Spirit of the Lord is upon me . . . to proclaim
the year of the Lord's favor."
(Luke 4:18–19)

The beginning of Jesus's ministry with "Sermon and Rejection at Nazareth"
(Luke 4:14–30). Ends with the ascension (Acts 1:9–11).

3. The Epoch of the Kingdom in the Church
(beginning from the Day of Pentecost)

"So when they had come together, they asked him, 'Lord, is this
the time when you will restore the kingdom to Israel?' He replied,
'It is not for you to know the times or periods that the Father has set
by his own authority. But you will receive power when the Holy
Spirit has come upon you; and you will be my witnesses in Jerusalem,
in all Judea and Samaria, and to the ends of the earth.'"
(Acts 1:6–8)

The arrival of the Spirit on Pentecost (Acts 2:1–16).
Peter's Pentecost sermon; the prophecy fulfilled (Acts 2:17–47).

REFERENCES: This basic scheme was first proposed by H. Conzelmann in *The Theology of St. Luke* (New York: Harper & Row, 1961), 16–17. It has been revised in more recent works, such as that of J. A. Fitzmyer, *The Gospel According to Luke*, 2 vols. Anchor Bible (New York: Doubleday, 1981, 1985), 2:181–92. More recently, D. Moessner, in *Lord of the Banquet: The Literary and Theological Significance of the Lukan Travel Narrative* (Minneapolis: Fortress, 1989), makes a convincing argument that this scheme must be seen in the light of older theological understandings of Israel's history, notably the so-called Deuteronomistic theology.

scenes are pregnant with theological significance for Lukan historiography, as they are made to revolve around themes of messianic end-times, the pouring out of the Spirit, and the fulfillment of prophecy. They serve to divide the narrative as well as the framework of eschatological time into three main ages or epochs (see Box 13.4). For this reason it has been called an "epochal view of history" as well as a "history of salvation."[90] Both characterizations accurately reflect the theological dimensions of the way history is reconceptualized around the figure of Jesus and current world events. It will prove to be one of the most important reinterpretations of eschatology for the subsequent development of Christian theology and self-understanding. More important, it shows the place of Jesus as messiah and as eschatological figure in a divinely ordered scheme of "history." His arrival and ministry, as messianic interlude, serve as the eschatological break from old age; his death and departure open the door for the arrival of the new kingdom. As those of prophet-king, messiah, and divine man, his actions and words provide the blueprint for the kingdom. For the Lukan author, all of these roles are summed up, now for the first time, in the one title, "Son of God."

In the final analysis, the picture of Jesus in Luke-Acts may be read or heard on two different levels—inside and outside. For the *outsider*, Jesus comes off as more of a philosopher and founder of a philosophical school in the Greek tradition of Socrates, Diogenes, or Pythagoras. As social critic and martyr, he undergoes a heroic death that attests to the truth of his insights and his cause. As divine man, he expounds a philosophy that offers divine guidance and mystical insights to the human condition and speaks to the whole world.

For the *insider*, Jesus may still be viewed as prophet/messiah in the apocalyptic tradition, where his teaching is meant, like Moses's, to turn people—now Jews and Gentiles alike—back to the God of Israel. As social critic, he promotes God's justice for all; as messianic martyr, he shows the demonic distortion of the world and the need for divine intervention. As divine man, he shows the plan of God in preparing the world for apocalyptic intervention by sending his anointed Messiah as powerful and benevolent patron of humanity, at just the right time and by guiding the action through the Holy Spirit.

Although the "outsider" reading clearly has an apologetic function, we should not naively assume that outsiders actually read Luke-Acts or were expected to. Rather, this kind of apologetic was meant to provide "insiders"—that is, predominantly gentile Christians—with an alternative expression of their own understanding that might inform their dealings with outsiders. In large measure the same function and intent lay behind Philo's re-creation of Moses in the *Life of Moses* in the image of a divine man. In doing so, however, it also translates the image of Jesus (like that of Moses) into a new set of categories and expectations, even for insiders. The Lukan Jesus—a more fully "Christianized" Jesus than we have seen so far—now takes center stage in the theater of Roman culture.

CHAPTER FOURTEEN

The Man from Heaven

The Gospels of John and Thomas

Jesus said, "I am the light which is above all of them; I am the All. The All came forth from me and the All reached me. Split wood, I am there; lift up the stone, and you will find me there." (Gospel of Thomas 77)

Again Jesus spoke to them, saying, "I am the light of the world. Whoever follows me will never walk in darkness but will have the light of life." (John 8:12)

But Thomas (who was called the Twin), one of the twelve, was not with them when Jesus came. So the other disciples told him, "We have seen the Lord." But he said to them, "Unless I see the mark of the nails in his hands, and put my finger in the mark of the nails and my hand in his side, I will not believe."

A week later his disciples were again in the house, and Thomas was with them. Although the doors were shut, Jesus came and stood among them and said, "Peace be with you." Then he said to Thomas, "Put your finger here and see my hands. Reach out your hand and put it in my side. Do not doubt but believe." Thomas answered him, "My Lord and my God!" Jesus said to him, "Have you believed because you have seen me? Blessed are those who have not seen and yet have come to believe." (John 20:24–29)

The Gospels of John and *Thomas* introduce a new character into the drama of Jesus. His name is Didymus Judas Thomas, or Thomas "the Twin." The name *Th'oma* means "twin" in Aramaic; *Didymus* is its Greek equivalent. His given name seems to have been Judas—a different Judas, of course. But which one?

The answers will vary. The Gospel of John leaves out this tidbit, perhaps to steer the audience in a different direction.[1] Based almost entirely on the story in John 20:24–29, in most later streams of Christian tradition he came to be known as "Doubting Thomas." In some early forms of Christianity, however, he was a far cry from this wavering, quavering skeptic. For some ancient Christians, Didymus Judas Thomas was the truest disciple of all, and the source of the true words of Jesus in the form of the *Gospel of Thomas*.

A disciple simply named "Thomas" is listed in all the Synoptics as one of the "twelve"; however, he is never mentioned otherwise in these earlier narratives (Mark 3:18; Matt 10:3; Luke 6:15; cf. Acts 1:13). Nor is his "full" name ever reported or commented on, if it was even known. By contrast, he appears three times in the Gospel of John with a speaking part (11:16; 14:5; 20:24–29). All of them are key comments that propel the narrative. In his last appearance (21:1–3), he is listed prominently after Peter and with only five others in the final dramatic appearance of Jesus. As we shall see, ultimately the "Doubting Thomas" moniker is a misunderstanding of his true role in the Johannine story.

Other new characters, such as Nicodemus and Lazarus, also appear for the first time in the Gospel of John and play a big role in the evolving Johannine drama. Even so, Thomas seems an unlikely candidate to take center stage. One has to wonder why. Some scholars, at least, would argue that the reason he plays a more central part, and a more curious character, in the Gospel of John is precisely because he was by then known from an alternative Christian tradition.[2] In fact, five other works of early Christian literature bear the name of this Thomas: the *Gospel of Thomas*, the *Acts of Thomas*, the *Book of Thomas the Contender*, the *Infancy Gospel of Thomas*, and an *Apocalypse of Thomas*. Of these the earliest by far is the *Gospel of Thomas*, and it most likely antedates the Gospel of John. In order to understand it, we shall first examine the peculiar development of the Johannine story, including its relation to the Synoptics. Then we shall return to look at the construction of the *Gospel of Thomas* and its relation to the Gospel of John. Finally, we shall consider the complex images of Jesus as "man from heaven" in the two.

The Gospel of John

Since the early Christian period, the rather stark differences between the Synoptics and John have been noted. Distinctive features of language and symbolism appear from the very first words of the Gospel:

> *In the beginning was the Word, and the Word was with God, and the Word was God. He was in the beginning with God. All things came into being through him, and without him not one thing came into being. What has come into being in him was life, and the life was the light of all people. The light shines in the*

darkness, and the darkness did not overcome it. . . . And the Word became flesh
and lived among us, and we have seen his glory, the glory as of a father's only son,
full of grace and truth. (1:1–5, 14)

Those features continue to the end, as reflected in the peculiar staging of the Last Supper and crucifixion scenes relative to Passover (as discussed in the Prologue). Such issues have caused puzzlement and consternation. More often, however, they have been rationalized, harmonized, or just ignored.

One traditional way of dealing with the problem arose at the end of the second century at the same time that the four-Gospel canon of the New Testament was becoming the norm. In this view, the Synoptics were assumed to give the proper "historical" outline of Jesus's life, while the Gospel of John provided other information and insights. As noted by Tertullian (ca. 197 CE), John has a chronology that is incompatible with that of the Synoptics and is more concerned with theology and symbolism.[3] About the same time, Clement of Alexandria (ca. 203 CE) seems to have coined the now-indelible label for John as the "spiritual Gospel."[4] Even this view is somewhat problematic, as some scholars would hold that the Gospel of John is perhaps more accurate than the Synoptics on some historical details in the life of Jesus.[5]

Framing the Johannine Narrative

There are several ways in which the Gospel of John creates a different outline for the life of Jesus (see Box 14.1). One comes in the rearrangement of key episodes. For example, the cleansing of the Temple episode occurs in each of the three Synoptics just after the triumphal entry into Jerusalem, that is, at the beginning of the last week of Jesus's life (cf. Matt 21; Mark 11; Luke 19). By contrast, in John's Gospel the cleansing occurs as one of the very first acts of Jesus career (2:13–22). This repositioning of the Temple cleansing also helps create the uniquely Johannine "three-year" ministry for Jesus by adding two extra Passovers (2:13; 6:4; 19:31; see Box 14.2). As a result, the cleansing occurs two full years before his death and has no direct connection to either the triumphal entry or his arrest.[6] The anointing occurs at Bethany (as in Mark 14 and Matt 26),[7] but six days before the Passover (John 12:1) and just *prior to* (rather than after) the triumphal entry. Other characteristic differences derive from the fact that the Johannine Last Supper (John 13) is not a Passover meal and contains no institution of the Lord's Supper (as discussed in the Prologue; see also Box 1.1).

Such shifts also result in changing the overall geography of Jesus's ministry in John. As we have seen, in all three Synoptics, Jesus's ministry begins exclusively in the Galilee, and he only goes to Jerusalem at the end. Specifically, he only enters Jerusalem for the first time in the last week of his life. The overall time frame of Jesus's ministry in the Synoptics is thus under one year.

BOX 14.1

The Gospel of John

DATE: Final, ca. 95–120 CE

AUTHOR: Unknown

ATTRIBUTION: John, son of Zebedee (the "beloved disciple")

LOCATION: Syria and/or Ephesus

AUDIENCE AND OCCASION: Written for an early gentile Christian community that has now become fully separate from Judaism, although some tensions are still high. It also is facing some challenges from other Christians who espouse a docetic view of Jesus. The Gospel gives a portrayal of Jesus to support the community's self-understanding and ongoing church life.

OUTLINE

I. Prologue (1:1–51)

    A. Prologue (1:1–14)

    B. Testimony of John the Baptist (1:19–34)

    C. Call of the first disciples (1:35–51)

II. The Ministry of Jesus: The Book of Signs and Discourses (2:1–12:50)

    A. Act 1: From Cana to Jerusalem to Cana (2:1–4:54)

        1. "First miracle" at Cana (2:1–12)

        2. To Jerusalem for Passover: cleansing of the Temple (2:13–25)

        3. Discourse with Nicodemus (3:1–15) and editorial summary (3:16–21)

        4. John the Baptist's "decrease" and editorial summary (3:22–36)

        5. To Samaria: discourse with Samaritan woman (4:1–45)

        6. To Cana: "second miracle" at Cana (4:46–54)

    B. Act 2: From Jerusalem to Galilee to Jerusalem (5:1–10:42)

        1. Miracles in Jerusalem at a Jewish festival (Hanukkah?; 5:1–30)

        2. Confrontation with Jewish leaders (5:31–47)

        3. Galilee (at Passover): feeding the five thousand and walking on water (6:1–21)

        4. Bread of Life discourse and confrontation with Jews (6:22–71)

        5. Jerusalem: feast of Succoth, controversy, and near arrest (7:1–52)

        6. Light of the World discourse and condemnation of Jews (8:12–59)

        7. Healing of the blind man: expulsion from synagogue (9:1–41)

        8. Good Shepherd and Door discourses (10:1–21)

        9. Hanukkah: Jesus rejected and near arrest (10:22–42)

    C. Act 3: Final signs and confrontations in Jerusalem (11:1–12:50)

        1. Bethany: raising of Lazarus and Resurrection discourse (11:1–44)

        2. The high priest's plot to kill Jesus; Jesus retires to Ephraim (11:45–54)

3. Return to Bethany as Passover approaches; anointing (11:55–12:8)

4. Plot to kill Jesus and Lazarus (12:9–11)

5. Triumphal entry and discourses in Temple (12:12–50)

III. Act 4: The Passion Narrative (13:1–20:31)

    A. Before Passover: the last supper, betrayal plot, and discourse (13:1–14:31)

    B. Discourses on the way to Gethsemane (15:1–17:26)

    C. The betrayal and arrest (18:1–11)

    D. Trial before high priest and Peter's three denials (18:12–27)

    E. Trial before Pilate and sentencing (18:28–19:16)

    F. The crucifixion, death, and burial (on the day leading up to Passover; 19:17–42)

    G. The empty tomb and appearances in Jerusalem (20:1–29)

    H. Summary (20:30–31)

IV. Epilogue: Final Appearance in the Galilee and Testimonial (21:1–25)

By contrast, the Gospel of John has Jesus going back and forth to Jerusalem throughout his ministry and specifically in conjunction with Jewish festivals. The first half of the Gospel (chaps. 2–10) can be seen as a drama in two acts. They are constructed as two parallel but inverted geographical triptychs: the first goes from *Cana to Jerusalem to Cana* (2:1–4:54); the second, from *Jerusalem to Galilee to Jerusalem* (5:1–10:42). In the first, it is the performance of two miracles at Cana that provides a framing device and narrative thread, while the middle is built on the cleansing of the Temple (2:13–25) and two key discourses of Jesus, with Nicodemus (3:1–15) and the Samaritan woman (4:1–42). His return to Cana (4:45), where he heals the son of a Roman official, also includes a note about his actions "at the festival"—meaning the Temple cleansing—to draw this act into a tight ring composition. The curtain comes down with a concluding summary: "Now this was the second sign that Jesus did after coming from Judea to Galilee" (4:54).

In the second triptych, Jewish festivals in Jerusalem provide the framing device, while controversies and polemic now punctuate the three sections. If the unnamed festival of 5:1 is Hanukkah (cf. 10:22), as seems likely, then the entire act also has a symmetrical structure.[8] It functionally covers a full year of Jesus's life and leaves him in or near Jerusalem until his death (beginning at John 7:1; see Box 14.2). The section 7:1–10:42 places Jesus in Jerusalem for a span of three months. This act closes with Jesus retiring beyond the Jordan because of growing opposition in Jerusalem. It sets the stage for the final confrontations (beginning at 11:1–44 with the raising of Lazarus) and Jesus's entry into Jerusalem (12:12).

The third act now opens with these final confrontations (chaps. 11–12) that lead up to the conspiracy to kill Jesus. The Passion narrative follows, then, as Act 4 (see Box 14.1). An emerging plot device now links these scenes with the previous triptych as anticipation of Jesus's attendance at the festival offers an opportunity to arrest him (cf. 11:56; 7:8–14; 7:37; 10:39). The section occupies another three to four months in Judea and another smaller geographical triptych as Jesus goes from Bethany (11:1–44) to Ephraim (11:54) and back to Bethany (12:1) just six days before Passover. Having retreated from Jerusalem in 10:40, Jesus now returns in 12:12 (the triumphal entry) to complete another ring composition. The Passion narrative proper commences at 13:1 with the Last Supper and another reference to the approaching Passover. As discussed in the Prologue, this final Passover commences on the evening *after* Jesus has been crucified (see 18:28; 19:31) and creates the uniquely Johannine dramatic effect of the Lamb of God symbolism, first introduced at 1:29.

That this three-year temporal scheme is a Johannine construction is further attested by three features of the narrative: (1) Jewish festivals other than Passover are never mentioned in the Synoptics; (2) the Johannine author has inserted a reference to Passover into the "synoptic"[9] feeding miracle (John 6:4); and (3)

BOX 14.2

Jewish Festivals and the "Calendar" of the Johannine Narrative

Year (in the narrative)	Season (months)	Festival Name	Placement (in the narrative)
Year 1	(unspecified)	—	(1:19–2:12)
Year 2	Spring (March/April)	Passover	2:13 [Jerusalem]
	Fall (September/October) or Winter (December)	"a festival" [probably either Rosh Hashanah (New Year) or Hanukkah]	5:1 [Jerusalem]
Year 3	Spring (March/April)	Passover	6:4 [Galilee/Decapolis]
	Fall (September/October)	Sukkoth (Booths)	7:2, 37 [Jerusalem]
	Winter (December)	Hanukkah	10:22 [Jerusalem]
Year 4	Spring (March/April)	Passover	18:28, 19:31 [Jerusalem] (day of crucifixion)

the action jumps abruptly to make the festival structure work. For example, at 5:1 we are apparently at the winter festival of Hanukkah; at 6:4 we jump to the spring festival of Passover; and at 7:1, to the fall festival of Sukkoth. These jumps leave the intervening periods—of roughly three and seven months, respectively—unaccounted for. Driven by the festivals as a structuring device, the Johannine narrative thus leaps over long stretches of time with few episodes to fill the space temporally. Instead, Jesus's discourses predominate, ostensibly each one delivered at a single—and thus isolated—moment. Yet Jesus's words stretch across the temporal frame. The festival scheme is primarily a way of staging symbolic vignettes voiced through Jesus's discourses rather than any real sense of a day-to-day narrative of Jesus's life. One wonders too if these large gaps might not be intended to hold open "space" within this rather disconnected narrative for some of the better known, but unrehearsed, episodes in the Synoptics. We shall return to this question in the next section.

The Gospel of John recounts a scant seven miracles of Jesus, fewest of any of the canonical Gospels by a significant margin. Of these, only two (the feeding of the five thousand and the walking on the water, 6:1–21) have clear synoptic parallels. The healing of the paralytic at the pool of Bethesda (5:2–9) is probably based on the miracle in Mark 2:1–12, but is explicitly reworked to place it in Jerusalem rather than Capernaum. More striking is the fact that Jesus never performs an exorcism in the Gospel of John, while miracles involving demons are among the most common in the Synoptics. Instead, the Gospel of John seems to use a unique enumeration of miracle stories not found in the synoptic tradition. Usually called the "signs source," these stories may reflect an early collection of miracles in which the stories had already been enumerated: the "first sign" (2:11), the "second sign" (4:54), and concluding with a summary (20:31–32; see Chapter 8). In their present form these miracle stories are unique to John and seem to offer allegorical symbolism, such as water and wine.[10] The enumeration of "first" and "second" miracles also creates the narrative framework for the first geographical section (or tryptich) of the Johannine story.

Finally, the Gospel of John uses a peculiar form of self-disclosure discourse in which Jesus unfolds key elements of his identity to his followers. Called the "I am" discourses, these speeches employ a pronouncement formula regularly used in hymns or aretalogies of gods and heroes in Greco-Roman tradition. They also have affinities for a later genre sometimes called the "gnostic revelation dialogue," in which Jesus imparts secret information to one or more of the disciples.[11] More specifically, it has been argued that a fragment of an otherwise unidentified Gospel, known simply as Egerton Papyrus 2, might have served as a "dialogue" source for the Gospel of John.[12]

In John, these "I am" discourses are also frequently paired with miracle stories in which Jesus's actions exemplify a particular theme or symbol. For example, the "I am the bread of life" discourse (6:25–58) follows immediately on the feeding of the five thousand (6:1–14); the "I am the light of the world" discourse (8:12–58) is followed immediately by the healing of a blind man (9:1–34); and the "I am the resurrection and the life" pronouncement (11:25–27) is contained within the raising of Lazarus story (11:1–44). Thus, these peculiarly Johannine miracles represent a symbolic narrativization of the themes expressed in the "I am" discourses.

Did the Gospel of John Know the Synoptics?

All these differences ultimately beg the question: Did the Gospel of John "know" the Synoptics? The traditional answer is no, even though the statement of Clement of Alexandria (ca. 200 CE), suggests that he did:

> However, John, last of all, being conscious that the corpus [of the facts] had been made clear in the [prior] Gospels, was encouraged by those who knew him, and being divinely moved by the Spirit, he composed a spiritual Gospel.[13]

As we see here, Clement is the one who first christened John the "spiritual Gospel," in large measure as a way of explaining the many differences between it and the Synoptics. Generally, in premodern Christian thought, John was viewed more as a supplement to the Synoptics. But with the rise of historical criticism, questions regarding possible sources and motivations for making such dramatic changes raised other concerns. Many of these earlier debates were also bound up with implicit assumptions about apostolic authorship. After all, if John was an eyewitness and "inspired," how could he knowingly change things, and why? It was in many ways easier to assume that John had other sources of oral tradition.[14]

On the other hand, if the Johannine author(s) did not know the Synoptics, then it leaves us with some glaring gaps in the story, not the least of which are the baptism of Jesus and the Lord's Supper tradition. It seems now that both are presupposed in the narrative. For example, the actual baptism of Jesus is never described even though Jesus comes to John the Baptist at the beginning of the story (1:29), much like in the Synoptics. In the Johannine version, this is the first of two cases in succeeding passages where John calls Jesus the "Lamb of God" (cf. 1:36). Then John the Baptist is made to say:

> "I saw the Spirit descending from heaven like a dove, and it remained on him. I myself did not know him, but the one who sent me to baptize with water said to me, 'He on whom you see the Spirit descend and remain is the one who baptizes with the Holy Spirit.' And I myself have seen and have testified that this is the Son of God." (1:32–34)

Here John the Baptist is made to describe the descent of the Spirit, which occurs just after Jesus's baptism in the Synoptics. This characterization serves to interpret it as a prophetic sign of Jesus's identity.[15] To put it another way, the Johannine author presupposes that the audience already knows the synoptic story of Jesus's baptism and uses it as the base for the testimonial of John the Baptist. The synoptic "voice from heaven" now comes through the words of John the Baptist. He is made to interpret the messianic language from Psalm 2:7 as identifying Jesus not just as God's "son," the messiah, using the old kingship language, but as "Son of God" in a new sense.

A similar case can be made regarding the eucharistic allusions in the feeding miracle (6:1–14) and the "Bread of Life" discourse (6:22–59) based on the synoptic versions of the Lord's Supper. John 7:42 can likewise be read as presupposing knowledge of a Bethlehem birth narrative to establish Jesus's Davidic lineage.[16] It seems, then, that the Gospel of John relies on stories from the synoptic tradition as well as a knowledge of those stories by the audience in order to make its theological point.

As a result, the trend in recent scholarship has been to rethink the issue of the relation of John to the Synoptics. Key evidence in this regard can be drawn from the fact that there are direct parallels of language and episodes between John and Mark and/or Luke (see Box 14.3). The study of the problem by Moody Smith puts it this way:

> *John knows and reflects the synoptic narratives, but they are hardly his sources in the usual sense. John is very different from Mark, or the Synoptics, because of his distinct theological purpose; his intention was by no means to harmonize his account with theirs. . . .*
>
> *One must say simply that what was true of the relationship of the so-called apocryphal gospels to the Synoptics, and to the canonical four, even in the mid-second century, would have been all the more true of the relationship of John to the Synoptics. . . . Somewhat the same sort of independence that is suggested by what we know of the apocryphal gospels is to be found in the Gospel of John. Neither John any more than the apocryphal gospels seem to be composed under some sort of canonical constraint, even though both attest knowledge of synoptic material, whether based on synoptic tradition or on one or more of the Synoptic Gospels themselves. This state of affairs is very important for our assessment of Johannine-Synoptic relationships.[17]*

I agree with Smith. The position taken here is that the Gospel of John both knew and depended on one or more of the Synoptics (probably Mark and Luke, at least) as well as other early Gospel materials, but it radically reshaped the narrative for dramatic effect in light of new social and theological contexts. As we argued in the Prologue, these changes were intentional and relied on the audience's knowledge of older Gospels in order for the dramatic artistry of the new story to carry through. At stake ultimately is a new image of Jesus that basically preserves and yet fundamentally alters those images in the earlier synoptic tradition. At the same time, the Gospel of John leaves space, narratively speaking, for the other stories to operate, but in so doing, it serves as a theological filter by which the older versions may be reinterpreted.

BOX 14.3

Does the Gospel of John Know the Synoptics?

A. Direct Verbal Parallels

1. John and Mark
(in each case the language noted is peculiar to Mark among Synoptics, but also found in John)

John 5:8–9	Mark 2:11–12	Healing lame: "take up your pallet and walk"
John 6:7	Mark 6:37	Feeding of 5000: "200 denarii of bread"
John 12:3	Mark 14:3	Anointing: "costly nard"
12:5	14:5	Anointing: "sold for 300 denarii and given to poor"
John 14:31	Mark 14:42	At end of the prayer: "let us go"
John 18:18	Mark 14:54	Peter at high priest's house: "warming at the fire"
John 18:39	Mark 15:9	Pilate's question on whom to release

2. John and Mark
(in each case the language is in Mark, but with parallels in the other Synoptics as noted)

John 12:25	Mark 8:35	"Those who love their life lose it, and those who hate their life in this world will keep it for eternal life" cf. Matt 16:25; Luke 9:24 see also: Matt 10:39; Luke 17:33 [a Q variant]
John 13:20	Mark 9:37	"whoever receives one whom I send receives me; and whoever receives me receives him who sent me" cf. Matt 18:5; 10:40; Luke 9:48; 10:16

3. John and Luke-Acts
(in each case the language noted is peculiar to Luke among Synoptics, but also found in John)

John 13:2, 26	Luke 22:3	"Judas Iscariot, son of Simon"
John 13:38	Luke 22:34	"The cock will not crow until . . ."
John 18:10	Luke 22:50	"Cutting off his right ear"
John 11:1–44	Luke 16:19–31	Lazarus (name, a dead person)
John 12:3	Luke 7:38	At anointing: "wipe his feet with her hair"

Author and Audience

That the author was the apostle John, son of Zebedee, has been the "official" attribution at least since the time of Irenaeus in the later second century.[18] Even so, there were doubts and debates through the third and fourth centuries, because the Gospel of John was so popular among so-called Gnostic Christians.[19] Other allusions to the text are rare in the second century prior to the 170s and 180s, and this fact further suggests a relatively late date of composition. For example, when

John 12:2ff	Luke 10:38–42	Mary and Martha at Bethany (names and serving dinner)
John 18:13, 24	Luke 3:2; Acts 4:6	Annas, the high priest (reverse with Caiaphas)
John 20:2–10	Luke 24:12	Peter goes to see the empty tomb: "stooping and looking in, he saw the linen clothes"

B. Knowledge of Synoptic Episodes Indicated or Presupposed

1. Parallel Episodes

John 2:12–22	Mark 11:15–19	Cleansing the Temple
John 4:46–54	Luke 7:1–10 [Q]	Healing of official's son: reporting the exact hour in which he was healed
John 5:2–18	Mark 2:1–12	Healing of paralytic: "take up your bed and walk" and controversy over healing on Sabbath
John 6:5–14	Mark 6:30–44	Feeding of 5000
John 6:16–21	Mark 6:45–52	Walking on water (missing from Luke)

2. Information Assumed but Not Given

John 1:6–8, 15	Role of John the Baptist as forerunner
John 1:29–34	Baptism of Jesus presumed, but not described; John mentions seeing the "spirit like a dove" sitting on Jesus (assumes that audience knows the story)
John 3:24	The imprisonment of John the Baptist (merely alludes to arrest and death, but does not recount the episode; assumes that audience knows the story)
John 7:42	Presumes birth in Bethlehem and Davidic lineage
John 13	Presumes institution of Lord's Supper, but not given (cf. eucharistic wording in the Feeding of 5000 and "Bread of Life" discourse)

3. Information Assumed but Reformulated

| John 4:2 (cf. 3:22, 26) | Jesus (or disciples) "baptizing in Judea" cf. Luke 7:18–23 |

Justin Martyr compiled his first effort at a Gospel harmony, that is, an interweaving of the Gospels, in the 140s to early 160s, he did not include the Gospel of John and apparently did not know of it. The Gospel of John was only incorporated into later harmonies, such as Tatian's *Diatessaron*, compiled in the 180s. As a result, a final stage of composition in the mid-second century cannot be ruled out, although it is probably a bit earlier.

Regarding the authorship, the problem is that the author is not named. Like all of the Gospels, the titles were added later as the books were being compiled into formal collections. In this case, a key to the authorship seems to be its intentional avoidance of discussing the figure of John, son of Zebedee, whose name never appears in the Gospel, even in general lists of the disciples.[20] Instead, an important, but somewhat enigmatic, figure known as the "beloved disciple" becomes prominent in the Passion narrative.[21] The first of these scenes is the Last Supper (13:23), as the disciple "whom Jesus loved" is described as "reclining *in* (or *on*) *the bosom of Jesus*."[22] Various suggestions have been made as to the identity of this character other than John, including Lazarus (11:1–44) and Nicodemus (3:1–15; 19:39), and recent popular fascination has centered on Mary Magdalene. Absolute certainty is thus impossible; however, it seems clear that the audience of the Gospel was supposed to know the identity of this figure, especially in view of the testimonial about *him*[23] in the closing verses of the Gospel (21:20–24). At the least, we can say that they thought of him as the source of "their" Gospel and, more than likely, as the founder of their community. On several occasions he is explicitly treated as an "eyewitness" to key events, at least as described in the Johannine narrative.[24] The weight of the evidence, therefore, points in favor of the "beloved disciple" being understood as the apostle John, son of Zebedee, as the later traditions also affirmed.[25]

Even so, the final testimonial to the role of the "beloved disciple" raises other issues. The passage comes in conjunction with Jesus's last appearance to the disciples after the resurrection (21:1–14). What follows (21:15–19) is a discourse between Jesus and Peter that serves as a recapitulation of Peter's three denials (18:15–17, 25–27), as Jesus now asks Peter three times, "Simon, do you love me?" Then at the end of this discourse, Jesus predicts Peter's death, as is clearly reflected in the narrator's editorial comment: "He [Jesus] said this to indicate the kind of death by which he [Peter] would glorify God" (21:19). What follows next is a similar testimony regarding the "beloved disciple" as authorial figure:

> Peter turned and saw the disciple whom Jesus loved following them; he was the one who had reclined next to Jesus at the supper and had said, "Lord, who is it that is going to betray you?" When Peter saw him, he said to Jesus, "Lord, what about him?" Jesus said to him, "If it is my will that he remain until I come, what is that to you? Follow me!" So the rumor spread in the community that this disciple would not die. Yet Jesus did not say to him that he would not die, but, "If it is my will that he remain until I come, what is that to you?"
>
> This is the disciple who is testifying to these things and has written them, and we know that his testimony is true. (21:20–24)

The narrator (or authorial voice) takes great pains here to make sure the audience knows who is being described by referring back to the story of the Last Supper at which this same disciple, "whom Jesus loved," reclined next to Jesus (13:23–25). Next, in another editorial comment similar to the one about Peter, the narrator explains that a "rumor spread in the community that *this disciple* would not die"

(21:23). The narrator then goes on to explain that the rumor was false, since it was based on a misunderstanding of what Jesus had meant. In other words, the author of the Gospel is having to account for the fact that the "beloved disciple" is now dead and some followers have found it disconcerting.

This editorial comment tells us several things about the authorship of the Gospel. First, it shows that the Gospel, as we now have it, was completed only after John's (or the "beloved disciple's") death. Several early legends held that John was the last of the original disciples to die, in about the year 95 CE.[26] The testimonial also shows that there were some Christians who thought John would not die before the return of Jesus, so the occasion of his death has caused chagrin that the author is trying to allay. Since the rumor is attributed to a saying of Jesus himself, it may well derive from a variation on the statement reported in Mark 9:1: "Truly I tell you, there are some standing here who will not taste death until they see that the kingdom of God has come with power." John's death raised once again a traditional apocalyptic expectation that the author(s) of the Gospel had to dispel. On the other hand, the testimonial finally says that this is indeed "John's" Gospel; however, it also adds an affirmation: "and *we* know his testimony is true" (21:24). Here we have evidence that others in the community, people who thought of themselves as disciples of the "beloved disciple," have carried on the process and completed the Gospel after his death.

Who, then, compiled John's Gospel? We do not really know. The most widely accepted theory is that what we now know as the Gospel of John is really the product of several distinct stages of transmission and editing, the earliest core of which was thought to be from John himself.[27] According to this theory, there were as many as five distinct stages of editing and composition, of which at least the last two or three occurred *after* the death of John. For example, it is usually suggested that John 20:30–31 represents an earlier ending of the Gospel as a culmination of the enumerated "signs" tradition:

> *Now Jesus did many other signs in the presence of his disciples, which are not written in this book. But these are written so that you may come to believe that Jesus is the Messiah, the Son of God, and that through believing you may have life in his name.*

In this view, then, all of chapter 21, containing the final appearance at the Sea of Galilee and the testimonials about Peter and the "beloved disciple," would have been added later.[28] What other portions of the Gospel or what other compositional features also belong to these last stages of reworking are less clear and regularly debated among scholars.[29]

For example, the incorporation of the feeding miracle (6:1–14) represents a "rough" editorial seam. The narrative jumps immediately from a speech of Jesus set in Jerusalem (5:19–47) to a setting in Galilee with an awkward transition: "After this Jesus went to the other side of the Sea of Galilee, also called the Sea of

Tiberias" (6:1). It suggests that either something has been deleted or the miracle episode has been inserted at a later stage. It is also significant that this passage incorporates one of the added Passover references (6:4). Hence, the temporal and geographical scheme built around the festivals likely derives from one of these later stages. On the other hand, so does the figure of the "beloved disciple." It has also been argued that the supposed "signs source" for the miracles does not represent a pre-Johannine tradition, but rather a distinctive tradition of the later Johannine school.[30]

If John, the son of Zebedee, died as late as ca. 95 CE,[31] it easily pushes the date of final composition into the mid-second century. Even if he died earlier, as some of the legends hold, this multiphase process of composition would have stretched well into the early second century. An early manuscript fragment of John 18 ($\mathfrak{p}^{52}$), once thought to come from ca. 125–150, was previously taken to deny such a late date; however, this manuscript may date as late as the early third century.[32] So a reasonable date for the *final* stages of composition is sometime between 110–120 CE, if not later.

As to the place of composition, several legends placed John in Ephesus at the end of his life, and this has been the traditional assumption.[33] Good arguments have also been made that the Gospel—or at least some of its layers—reflects the situation of a Christian community in Syria.[34] It is possible that the trajectory of this Gospel involves not only multiple layers of authorship, but also several changes in social location. This fact may help to account for the complex nature of the Johannine composition.

Anti-Jewish Polemics and the Situation of the Gospel

The uniquely Johannine "I am" discourses also reflect the changing social location. They serve as occasions for controversy, especially where the "Jews" react negatively to Jesus's self-disclosure. At the same time, each discourse reveals new aspects of Jesus's heavenly nature, as understood by the Johannine authors, and these two features are mutually reinforcing. The basic structure is this: Jesus announces his "descent from the Father" in conjunction with a basic metaphor or symbol; then the "Jews" react, and Jesus denounces them using some form of the same symbolism. Here is the pattern as reflected in two moments within the "Bread of Life" discourse, which plays on the symbolism of the manna from heaven in Exodus 16 (cf. John 6:31, 49).

> Jesus said to them, "*I am the bread of life.* Whoever comes to me will never be hungry, and whoever believes in me will never be thirsty. But I said to you that you have seen me and yet do not believe. Everything that the Father gives me will come to me, and anyone who comes to me I will never drive away; *for I have come down from heaven,* not to do my own will, but the will of him who

sent me. And this is the will of him who sent me, that I should lose nothing of all that he has given me, but raise it up on the last day. This is indeed the will of my Father, that all who see the Son and believe in him may have eternal life; and I will raise them up on the last day."

Then the Jews began to complain about him because he said, "<u>I am the bread that came down from heaven.</u>" They were saying, "Is not this Jesus, the son of Joseph, whose father and mother we know? How can he now say, 'I have come down from heaven'?" (6:35–42)

Your ancestors ate the manna in the wilderness, and they died. This is the bread that comes down from heaven, so that one may eat of it and not die. <u>I am the living bread that came down from heaven.</u> Whoever eats of this bread will live forever; and the bread that I will give for the life of the world is my flesh."

The Jews then disputed among themselves, saying, "How can this man give us his flesh to eat?" So Jesus said to them, "Very truly, I tell you, <u>unless you eat the flesh of the Son of Man and drink his blood, you have no life in you. Those who eat my flesh and drink my blood have eternal life,</u> and I will raise them up on the last day; for my flesh is true food and my blood is true drink. <u>Those who eat my flesh and drink my blood abide in me, and I in them.</u> Just as the living Father sent me, and I live because of the Father, so <u>whoever eats me</u> will live because of me. (6:49–57)

One will quickly recognize that the discourse plays on eucharistic metaphors from early Christian worship.[35] Its liturgical resonance also gives it confessional force for members of the Johannine community.

The "I am" discourses are, on the one hand, pivotal to the Johannine Gospel's Christology—Jesus as a heavenly figure—and, on the other, pivotal to its castigation of Jews. They function as boundary-defining mechanisms for the Johannine community. Increasingly these controversies become more heated as the Johannine Jesus denounces the Jews in harsher and harsher terms:

"I know that you are descendants of Abraham; yet you look for an opportunity to kill me, because there is no place in you for my word. I declare what I have seen in the Father's presence; as for you, you should do what you have heard from the Father. . . .

"You are indeed doing what your father does." They said to him, "We are not illegitimate children; we have one father, God himself." Jesus said to them, "If God were your Father, you would love me, for I came from God and now I am here. I did not come on my own, but he sent me. Why do you not understand what I say? It is because you cannot accept my word. <u>You are from your father the devil, and you choose to do your father's desires.</u>" (8:37–44)

This passage comes at the end of the "Light of the World" discourse and bases the confession as well as the denunciation in retrospect of the crucifixion. These

denunciations are symbolically very powerful, because they are paired with liturgical and confessional elements, and thus make the Johannine polemic some of
the most inflammatory anti-Jewish rhetoric in the early Christian tradition.

The Gospel of John thus represents a social situation of much greater separation
of the Christian community from its Jewish neighbors. The theme of rejection of
the message about Jesus has now been magnified into a total rejection of Jesus as
the one sent from heaven by God. The community's own confessional statements
about Jesus now function as strict boundary markers against Judaism per se. At
the same time, there are reflections of the ongoing tensions that must have led to
this harsh turn in the polemics of separation.

The miracle of the blind man (9:1–34) that follows the "Light of the World"
discourse exemplifies the dilemma. Jesus heals a man who had been blind from
birth, but the Pharisees—anachronistically portrayed as religious authorities who
oversee piety compliance—challenge the one who had been healed and his parents
in order to denigrate Jesus's power. Finally, they threaten anyone who persists in
confessing Jesus with expulsion from the synagogue (9:22). When the now sighted
man does so, they "cast him out" of the synagogue (9:34).

An anachronism for the days of Jesus, this dramatization of the miracle story
reflects the experience of some within the Johannine Christian community for
whom confession of Jesus had meant expulsion from the Jewish community.[36] Yet
in the social context of the author and audience this experience cannot have been
the norm any longer, as the distance from Judaism has grown. The story thus
serves as further rationale for the denunciation of Judaism because *it* had rejected
both Jesus and his followers. For the Johannine community, at least, the breach
with Judaism had become irreparable. The Johannine Christology—Jesus, the
man from heaven—is a nascent form of creedal confession that provides a correlative theological warrant for separateness.[37] On the other hand, some features
within the story seem to reflect growing tensions *within* Christian circles over the
image of Jesus as the "man from heaven."

The Gospel of Thomas

*These are the secret words which the living Jesus spoke, and Didymus Judas
Thomas wrote them down.*

And he said, "He who finds the meaning of these words will not taste death."

*Jesus said, "Let him who seeks not cease seeking until he finds, and when he
finds, he shall be troubled, and when he is troubled, he will marvel, and he will
rule over the All." (Gos. Thom., prologue, 1–2)*

The *Gospel of Thomas* is a collection of 114 sayings (or *logia*) of Jesus originally
composed in Greek. It is explicitly attributed to Didymus Judas Thomas using
the full form of the name.[38] Crucial to his identity in this tradition is his given

name Judas and the double affirmation of being a "twin." Although implicit rather than explicit in the *Gospel of Thomas,* he is identified with Jesus's brother Judas (or Jude).[39] In other words, he is taken to be the twin brother of Jesus himself.[40] Among its sayings are a large number from Q (many with Lukan colorations) as well as others that parallel Mark and unique material in Matthew and John.[41] It has been argued that at least part of the sayings tradition used by the *Gospel of Thomas* is independent of the synoptic tradition, even though its date of final composition may well be later[42] (see Box 14.4).

BOX 14.4
The Gospel of Thomas

DATE: Early layers: ca. 60–70 CE; later layers: late first or early second century

AUTHOR: Unknown

ATTRIBUTION: Didymus Judas Thomas

LOCATION: Syria

AUDIENCE AND OCCASION: An early source tradition that has been reworked for a new community situation. Stress on a docetic image of Jesus and asceticism. Thomas, "the twin," is symbolic of the esoteric teachings communicated in the text and for the relationship between the human community and the spiritual Jesus.

OUTLINE: The text in its present (later) form is made up of 114 sayings (*logia*) that do not have a clear sequential or thematic order. It is possible, however, to group them by key themes or topics that recur throughout. The numbers at the right refer to the standard numbering of the *logia*.

1. Secrecy	1, 2
2. Proper Understanding	3, 5, 6, 13, 15, 17, 19, 21, 56, 62, 108
3. Jesus (and Thomas)	Prologue, 10, 13, 15, 17, 18, 24, 28, 37, 38, 43, 59, 61, 62, 72, 77, 91, 108, 111, 113
4. Eating and Drinking	7, 11, 14, 27, 28, 60, 61, 63
5. Male and Female, the Body	21, 22, 37, 61, 87, 112, 114
6. Becoming One, Being Solitary	11, 22, 23, 48, 49, 61, 75, 79, 106
7. The Bridal Chamber	75, 104, 106
8. Discipleship, Election (vs. Materialism)	13, 18, 19, 23, 42, 49, 50, 55, 56, 64, 65, 75, 108, 111, 113
9. The Kingdom	3, 20, 22, 27, 46, 49, 54, 57, 76, 82, 96, 97, 98, 99, 107, 108, 113, 114

The dates suggested for the *Gospel of Thomas* range from as early as 60–70 to as late as ca. 180–200 CE. The work is not explicitly mentioned by other Christian writers until the end of the second century, when it was already considered "heretical."[43] The earliest extant fragments of the text are three Greek papyri dating to the beginning and middle of the third century CE. The full text was preserved only in a Coptic version of the later fourth century discovered in 1945 among the Nag Hammadi codices (II.2; see Box 14.5).[44] An early date has recently become popular in some scholarly circles, but caution is still warranted, in part because we cannot be sure that the Coptic text from Nag Hammadi represents the original form.[45] For example, there is at least one known difference in the order of the *logia* between the Greek and Coptic versions.[46] Another saying (12) seems to pit the authority of the apostle Thomas against that of James, the "other brother" of Jesus, who was closely associated with the early Jewish form of the Jesus movement in Jerusalem. This feature may well suggest an emergent Christian group growing up in some conflict with the Jerusalem church or the traditions associated with it. It is also likely that an earlier form of the text was later supplemented with elements from the canonical Gospels or other apocryphal Gospel materials.[47]

The original provenance of the work is usually thought to be in Roman Syria, and specifically Edessa in the Osrhoene region of upper Mesopotamia. Some layers of the Gospel of John may also come from this region of Syria, and the two texts show a number of verbal similarities (to be discussed below). For these reasons, therefore, it seems best to date the *Gospel of Thomas*, as we now know it, early in the second century. It is also in the early decades of the second century that we start to hear of debates among different groups of Christians over the kind of "docetic" Christology found in the *Gospel of Thomas* and other sources.[48] *Docetism* refers to a belief that Jesus was only a heavenly or divine figure who never physically became flesh and blood and, thus, who could not suffer and die. The Johannine tradition is, in part, a conscious refutation of this view (John 1:14; 1 John 4:1–3). To put it another way, the *Gospel of Thomas* grew up in this form sometime after the synoptic Gospels of Matthew and Luke were completed and just about the same time as (or slightly before) the Gospel of John. Thus, possible literary relationships among all these Gospels will need to be considered.

Audience and Trajectory

The theology of the *Gospel of Thomas* shows marked development to meet the needs of a new community situation. The eschatology is thoroughly spiritualized or "realized," and Jesus speaks as a heavenly figure—with the voice of Wisdom (Sophia)—giving instructions to those who are presently in the divine kingdom. These shifts are in some cases created by giving a slightly different emphasis or change of wording to some traditional sayings (see Chapter 9). They seem to be addressed to a particular community of believers with regard to membership and

BOX 14.5

Manuscripts of the *Gospel of Thomas*

Above: *Gospel of Thomas*, Codex II.2 from Nag Hammadi (Chenoboskion), Egypt. Coptic codex showing the last page and the subscription (title). Late fourth century CE. *Used by permission of the Institute for Antiquity and Christianity, Claremont, CA.*

Left: *Gospel of Thomas*, P. Oxy. 654, Greek manuscript on papyrus from Oxyrhynchus, Egypt, containing the opening and the first seven *logia*. Early third century CE. The right half of the page is missing. A sublinear bar at the left margin and a bold mark in the line signal the beginning of each new saying. From *The Oxyrhynchus Papyri*, ed. Grenfell and Hunt, vol. 4, Plate I. *Used by permission © Egypt Exploration Society, London.*

life within the community. Most striking is the fact that there is no reference to Jesus's death, burial, and resurrection. Instead, the figure of Jesus has docetic features that are symbolized in the idea of "twinship." The human believer is symbolized by Thomas, the twin, while "the living Jesus" (1) is an entirely spiritual image to be known and emulated through his words. He is the inner spiritual light (24).

A good example of the role of Thomas as both authorial namesake and exemplar of faith may be seen in saying 13:

> *Jesus said to his disciples, "Make a comparison and tell me whom I am like." Simon Peter said to him, "You are like a righteous angel." Matthew said to him, "You are like a wise man." Thomas said to him, "Master, my mouth will not be able to say what you are like." Jesus said to him, "I am not your master. Because you drank, you are drunk from the bubbling spring which I measured out." And he took him and went aside. He spoke to him three words. When Thomas returned to his companions, they asked him, "What did Jesus say to you?" Thomas said to them, "If I tell you even one of the words which he said to me, you will pick up stones; you will throw them at me. And fire will come from the stones and consume you."*

Clearly this saying is modeled after the confession at Caesarea Philippi in the synoptic tradition (Mark 8:27–33 and parallels). In fact, it might be argued that the responses here attributed to Peter and Matthew are meant to represent the image of Jesus in the Gospels of Luke (or Mark) and Matthew, respectively. At the very least, they point to views of other forms of Christianity, but here they are understood to be deficient. The reference to Matthew, however, seems like a more overt statement, because the figure of Matthew plays no significant role in the Gospels of Mark or Luke. In other words, it presupposes that the figure of Matthew has become more prominent, probably as a result of the Gospel attributed to him.[49] Significantly, it is only Thomas who responds correctly, and he is then given secret knowledge by Jesus in the form of "three words." What are the three words? Thomas does not tell his fellow disciples, but the audience is supposed to know. Though they remain opaque and ultimately uncertain, one possibility is that the three words are his name, "Didymus Judas Thomas." In other words, he is now the authoritative transmitter of Jesus's eternal wisdom and a model of understanding for others to follow.

For the followers of this tradition, the ritual of baptism, also likened to a "bridal chamber," serves as an entry into, not only emulation of Jesus through inner knowledge, but also a spiritual union with Jesus. The traditional baptismal symbol of disrobing now means a removal of the physical body (21, 37). In keeping with this ideal, the ethics of the text invoke an ideal of ascetic renunciation of material life in terms of possessions and sexuality (11, 22, 23, 30, 49, 75, 106), and gender symbols are often used to embody these ideals (22, 114). The final saying, 114, at first seems terribly misogynistic, because it states that "every woman who makes herself male will enter the kingdom of heaven."

There are two ways of taking this saying. In the light of saying 22, it may mean that females and males both need to be transformed or re-created—either asexually or androgynously—in part through ascetic practice in order to enter heaven.[50] In the *Acts of Thomas,* however, the heavenly spirit who anoints and saves is explicitly identified as female, as "holy mother," and she comes on believers in baptism.[51] She is in some measure the Sophia figure of the earlier Jewish wisdom tradition, but now set in relation to Jesus as savior. As a result, saying 114 may be taken as bridal-chamber symbolism; it means that all human believers must become "male spirits" in order to be united with the "heavenly mother." Saying 101 may also reflect this idea in a unique addition to the Q saying about hating father and mother; in it Jesus is made to say, ". . . but my true mother gave me life."[52]

Finally, the sayings in their present form are intentionally formulated to be esoteric, enigmatic, or mysterious. There is no discernible ordering principle and no indicators of the way they were intended to be used except for didactic purposes. Whether they were "performed" communally or recited antiphonally cannot be determined. They presuppose a more fully developed system of "Christian" thought of a type that we should not normally expect prior to the very end of the first century CE. They require interpretation or instruction in order for them to be used as a means of entry into the community. Thus, the text serves simultaneously as a community-defining *collection* of the holy words of Jesus and as a reflection on the image of Jesus as a heavenly figure. Ultimately, these two senses reinforce one another, at least for insiders.

Changing Traditions in *Thomas*

As has been noted, the *Gospel of Thomas* represents the type of sayings collection known from the Q tradition, but in a highly evolved form. There are forty-six passages that show parallels between the *Gospel of Thomas* and Q (see Box 12.1). At least in part, it seems to reflect an independent trajectory of these sayings that developed contemporaneously or in parallel with the synoptic tradition.[53] A good example is the great banquet parable (*Gos. Thom.* 64), which, like the version in Luke 14:13–24, seems to preserve a very early form of the parable. Nonetheless, the adaptations in the Thomasene version represent a different set of antimaterialistic concerns and a more urban setting than one finds in either of the synoptic versions of the same parable (see Chapter 9, and Box 9.3 for the text).

Other sayings in *Thomas* may reflect the distinctive tradition of the Gospel of Mark. Here is one example, where we can also compare the Greek and Coptic versions of the *Gospel of Thomas:*

Jesus said, "No prophet is accepted in his own hometown; no physician heals those who know him." (31, NHC II.2.39)

Jesus said, "A prophet is not acceptable in his own country, nor does a physician perform cures on those who know him." (31, P.Oxy. 1.31–36)

It has been argued that the Thomasene version of this saying, especially in the earlier Greek version given above (from P.Oxy. 1), reflects an older form of the aphorism that comes at the end of the Markan version of the rejection at Nazareth:

> *Then Jesus said to them, "Prophets are not without honor, except in their home-town, and among their own kin, and in their own house." And he could do no deed of power there, except that he laid his hands on a few sick people and cured them. And he was amazed at their unbelief. (Mark 6:4–6a)*

In this case, it appears that the Markan version has taken the final part of the saying and narrativized it into the ironic story of Jesus being unable to cure many people due to the unbelief of the Nazarenes.[54]

Or could it be the other way round? Has the *Gospel of Thomas* taken the Markan narrative and turned it into an isolated saying? Many of the parallels between *Thomas* and Mark suggest that the Thomasene version preserves the older form. Quite a number of these are in the genre of community rules and some have close parallels with Q material.[55] If so, it means that the *Gospel of Thomas* also has a version of sayings materials from both the Q and Markan trajectory, but they have been recast to fit the theological and social context of the *Thomas* community. On the other hand, the Greek text of saying 31, quoted above, uses wording almost identical to that in the Lukan version of the same saying: "And he said, "Truly I tell you, no *prophet is accepted in his hometown*" (4:24). The key change is the word "accepted" (or "favored"), which is a thematic word in the Lukan scene of the rejection at Nazareth, based on its presence in the quotation from Isaiah 61:2.[56] Since the Lukan version seems to be a variation on that of Mark (quoted above), there is a good chance, then, that the version of *Thomas* is based on that of Luke.

In a few cases, however, we need to be even more cautious. For example, *Gospel of Thomas* 63 seems to be the same as the uniquely Lukan parable of the rich fool (Luke 12:13–21), for which there is no evidence of a pre-Lukan version. Similarly, the Thomasene version of the "render unto Caesar" saying (found in Mark 12:14–17) has a peculiar opening. Here are both versions:

> *"Is it lawful to pay taxes to the emperor, or not?"... But knowing their hypoc-risy, he said to them, "Why are you putting me to the test? Bring me a denarius and let me see it." And they brought one. Then he said to them, "Whose head is this, and whose title?" They answered, "The emperor's." Jesus said to them,*

"Give to Caesar the things that are the Caesar's, and to God the things that are God's." (Mark 12:14–17)

*They showed Jesus a gold coin and said to him, "Caesar's men demand taxes from us." He said to them, "Give Caesar what belongs to Caesar, give God what belongs to God, and give me what is mine." (*Gos. Thom. *100, NHC II.2.49)*

In this case, it might be argued that the Thomasene version is primary, because of its lack of additional narrative to fit it into a literary frame.[57] On the other hand, the opening seems incongruous: Why would they show him a coin, and especially a *gold* coin, if they are complaining about having to pay taxes? The narrative setup does not fit the ostensible problem. On the other hand, a coin with the image of Caesar on it, as described in Mark also, must be presupposed as a narrative device in order to set up the wordplay in the final saying. The "gold coin" in the *Thomas* version is meant to encapsulate this narrative component. The point is that a gold coin immediately suggests a Roman imperial mint and thus an image of the emperor on the coin.[58]

As a basic *chreia* and as narrative device, it makes more sense for Jesus to ask to see a coin, as in the synoptic versions, rather than having the coin "shown" at the outset of the *chreia* for no apparent reason. Nor would common folks in Jesus's day be likely to possess gold coins on an ordinary basis. The denarius of the Markan story would likely be a more common bronze coin. The fact that it bears an imperial image is brought out through the narrative setup. Moreover, in the earlier synoptic tradition tax collectors could hardly be called "Caesar's men" (cf. Mark 2:14; Matt 9:9; Luke 5:27; Luke 19:2), because they were typically locals who worked for the provincial administration. But in this truncated version, they need to be called "Caesar's men" in order to set up Jesus's reply, which already hinged on the word "Caesar." Again, it is refracting elements of the narrative into the dialogue.

In this case, then, it may be argued that the Thomasene version presupposes a denarrativized form of the Markan (or synoptic) episode, where most of the extraneous material, including the narrative frame, has been removed (cf. Matt 11:15–22; Luke 20:20–26). The coin is an essential component and is retained, but in a rather awkward and artificial manner. Nor is this particular saying demonstrably from an early, pre-Markan tradition. Rather, it seems to come precisely from the Markan composition and reflects political tensions in the aftermath of the first Jewish revolt. In other words, in the Markan story, Jesus is portrayed as resisting revolutionary impulses against paying taxes. On this point, at least, the Markan Jesus is antirevolutionary, and the Matthean and especially the Lukan versions expand this idea.

The Thomasene version of this saying (100) may be taken as a further reworking into a more condensed form, but presupposing some of the underlying narrative setup found in the expanded Markan *chreia*. Neither version represents an early (i.e., pre-70) saying, but the version in *Thomas* must depend on the Markan (or synoptic) tradition. The Thomasene version is further shown to be a secondary adaptation by its addition of the final line in which Jesus says, "and give me what is mine." In effect, it is this last line that drives the Thomasene reworking.

It may be argued as well that saying 13 (discussed earlier) has gone through a similar process. It too depends on a Markan (synoptic) sayings unit, the confession at Caesarea Philippi, and even retains the basic structure: a question of Jesus about his assumed identity, a variety of answers from different disciples followed by the *best* answer from one disciple, and a concluding blessing (Matthew) or chastising (Mark and Matthew) of that disciple. Both the addition of Peter and Matthew as disciples who provide deficient answers and the final exchange between Thomas and the other disciples are recognizably Thomasene fingerprints on this basic structure. Consequently, *Gospel of Thomas* 13 also depends on a Markan/synoptic unit that has been reworked without a substantial narrative frame. It has become a small dialogue instead, like the Thomasene version of the "render unto Caesar" *chreia*.

Parallels Between *Thomas* and John

The kind of adaptation of earlier sayings materials seen here, whether from Q, Mark, or the other Synoptics, shows conscious reworking of existing traditions from several different sources in a new context. This same phenomenon can be seen when we look at the parallels between *Thomas* and John; they show similar adaptations of sayings and correlative theological interests in their presentation of Jesus. For example, John 6:67–71 shows another reworking of the "confession" of Peter, who now calls Jesus "the Holy One of God." Typically, the traditional view of these similarities has been that the *Gospel of Thomas* must be dependant on the Gospel of John, but this view has now been questioned by Helmut Koester and others.[59] Koester observes that the distinctive feature of the Gospel of John is that its narrative, while still a narrative, is largely focused on the dialogues of Jesus, and especially the "I-am" sayings. As we noted earlier, the narrative action of the Gospel of John is quite sporadic for the time frame that it purports to cover. Thus the way each of these later Gospels adapts and uses certain types of earlier sayings is worth noting.

Koester lists a number of close parallels of language between the two (see Box 14.6). A good example is the "I am the light" saying found in *Gospel of Thomas* 77 and in John 8:12 (quoted at the beginning of this chapter). Significantly, the Coptic formulation of the "I am" pronouncement is a direct translation of the Greek found in John 8:12 and the rest of the "I am" sayings. The basic saying may derive in part from the saying Q33, as reflected also in a second pair, *Thomas* 24b and John 12:35–36. All these variations may be set out in parallel as follows:

Q 33
Luke 11:33–36

No one after lighting a lamp puts it in a cellar, but on the lampstand so that those who enter may see the light.

Your eye is the lamp of your body. If your eye is healthy, your whole body is full of light; but if it is not healthy, your body is full of darkness. Therefore consider whether the light in you is not darkness.

If then your whole body is full of light, with no part of it in darkness, it will be as full of light as when a lamp gives you light with its rays."

Q 33
Matthew 5:15

No one after lighting a lamp puts it under the bushel basket, but on the lampstand, and it gives light to all in the house.

Matthew 6:22–23

The eye is the lamp of the body. So, if your eye is healthy, your whole body will be full of light; but if your eye is unhealthy, your whole body will be full of darkness.

If then the light in you is darkness, how great is the darkness!

John 8:12

Again Jesus spoke to them, saying, "I am the light of the world. Whoever follows me will never walk in darkness but will have the light of life."

Thomas 77

Jesus said, "I am the light which is above all of them; I am the All. The All came forth from me and the All reached me. Split wood, I am there; lift up the stone, and you will find me there."

John 12:35–36

Jesus said to them, "The light is with you for a little longer. Walk while you have the light, so that the darkness may not overtake you. If you walk in the darkness, you do not know where you are going. While you have the light, believe in the light, so that you may become children of light."

Thomas 24b

There is light within a man of light, and he (or it) lights the whole world. When he (or it) does not shine, there is darkness

---

The Thomasene and Johannine versions have developed the idea in a different way from the earlier source traditions preserved in the Synoptics. Both the Gospel of John and *Thomas* take it in the direction of the "true nature" of Jesus as heavenly light that enlightens humans to eternal life. Light and darkness are paired against life and death. In effect, these "light sayings" are a metaphor for their notion of salvation through some special knowledge or understanding about and from Jesus. The same idea is contained in the "bubbling spring" sayings, which

BOX 14.6
Parallels Between the Gospels of *Thomas* and John

Gospel of Thomas	Gospel of John	Themes
		Finding/Keeping the Word of Jesus
Logion 1	8:51	*"not taste/see death"*
111	8:52	*"not taste/see death"*
18b	6:63	
19c	6:68–69	
19b	8:31–32	
		The Bubbling Spring of Life
13	4:14	
108	7:37–38	
		The Light
24b	11:9–10; 12:35–36	*"light vs. darkness"*
77a	8:12; 3:31	*"I am the light"*
19a	8:58	*"before/above all"*
		Coming and Return
49	16:28	

have a natural resonance to baptismal imagery (cf. *Gos. Thom.* 13, 108; John 4:14; 7:37–38, respectively). In other words, the formulation of these key self-disclosure sayings in *Thomas* and John are much more similar to one another than they are to the earlier traditions.

At the same time, Koester notes that there are some differences of detail, especially in the sense that many of the sayings in *Thomas* have to do with the fate of the disciple in personally obtaining the light or the return to heavenly kingdom.[60] In that way, the *Thomas* tradition takes the meaning of salvation through Jesus as a process of self-discovery, in keeping with the "twinship" imagery. In contrast, the Johannine tradition makes the person of Jesus the source of salvation; he is now fully divine, but personally imparts salvation to humans. Koester argues that the Johannine tradition, in the form that we now know it, moves in the same direction as the *Thomas* tradition, but serves as a corrective to it.[61]

Gospel of Thomas	Gospel of John	Themes
50a	8:14b	
	1:9	
	13:3	
38b	13:33	
	7:34; 8:21	"seeking me"
24a	14:3	
69a	14:7	"knowing me / knowing the Father"
	8:19	
37a	14:22	"revealed to us"
		Farewell Sayings
49	16:28	
92a	16:23b–24	
92b	16:4b–5	
	cf. 16:12, 23a; 30	
		God as "the/my Father" and Death/Life
61	5:18	
	3:35; cf. 13:3	
11	11:26	
29	3:6	"flesh vs. spirit"

Compiled by L. M. White, based on H. Koester, *Ancient Christian Gospels: Their History and Development* (Philadelphia: Trinity Press International, 1990), 113–24.

This feature may be seen in a variety of ways in these parallel sayings, but one of the most poignant is the use of the word "the Father" or "my Father" for God. It occurs some thirty times in the *Gospel of Thomas* and over a hundred times in the Gospel of John. The unusual title "living Father" also occurs in both (*Gos. Thom.* 3; John 6:57). In *Thomas,* however, it is often a reference to the kingdom as the place of salvation for the disciple. In John, on the contrary, it almost always points to the unique relation between God and Jesus as "Son." Finally, whereas the *Gospel of Thomas* stresses finding the esoteric meaning of Jesus's words as a path to enlightenment, the Gospel of John makes it finding Jesus himself as the "living word" from God, harking back to the wisdom tradition and Philo. This is seen especially in two key discourses in John 8 and 16. The latter is part of Jesus's farewell discourse, usually seen as one of the latest additions to the Gospel of John; it recapitulates many of the earlier sayings.

The Man from Heaven

As we have now seen, both the Gospel of John and the *Gospel of Thomas* show direct awareness of the synoptic tradition and share a number of common tendencies with one another. Both are highly reshaped presentations that reflect a distinct theological trajectory regarding the image of Jesus. Both assume that Jesus was first and foremost a heavenly figure who speaks for God, like Sophia in the wisdom tradition or Philo's *Logos*. Though they show theological affinities based on this image, they ultimately stand in direct opposition to one another, most notably on the understanding of Jesus's humanity.

In the *Gospel of Thomas* Jesus speaks divine words whose inner secrets must be grasped by "true" followers. But the figure of Jesus is a *disembodied* voice, and its nonnarrative preservation of the sayings may well reflect—or "perform"—this new emphasis. If so, it is a reversion to a sayings collection not only in form. It would suggest that this particular form of presentation or performance was assumed to carry theological significance. By contrast, the Gospel of John makes Jesus the *embodied* "word" of God, and his divine words are displayed narratively in the distinctively symbolic combination of discourse and miracle.[62] The Jesus of John now "performs" God on the human stage, while the Jesus of *Thomas* looms mysteriously, like the wizard's voice in the palace of Oz.[63]

This brings us back to John 20 and the postresurrection scene in which Jesus and Thomas come face-to-face in the climax of the Gospel.[64] It is all the more telling for the outlook of the Gospel of John that Thomas, of all people, is now made the vehicle for seeing and touching the flesh of the risen Christ. Moreover, Thomas's earlier speaking parts point naively toward Jesus's death and resurrection (John 11:16; 14:5). It seems to be a conscious effort on the part of the Johannine author(s) to counteract the more extreme forms of docetic theology of the *Gospel of Thomas*.[65] If so, it raises serious questions about whether John 20 and the enumerated "signs" really belong to an earlier form of the Gospel. It also shows that the Johannine audience is now facing self-definition questions on two very distinct fronts. The "man from heaven" Christology had emerged as a remarkably successful tool in ratifying the separation from Judaism, but now some Christians have taken it too far. The older tradition of the Jesus movement—with its Jewish messiah and emphasis on the death and resurrection—is being reinterpreted and replaced.

In the final analysis, the Gospel of John appears to be a conscious effort to hold together two rather different traditions about Jesus. One is drawn from the Synoptics and views the death and resurrection of the human Jesus as the crucial event. The other is drawn from the docetic tradition of the "heavenly man" found also in the *Gospel of Thomas*. The older death and resurrection/exaltation tradition has now become the basis or model for a new scheme—Jesus's descent from and ascent to heaven. The Johannine Passion narrative is very much like that of the

Gospel of Mark.[66] The Johannine discourses are much more like the sayings tradition found in the *Gospel of Thomas*. Yet ultimately the Gospel of John narrativizes these sayings into a temporal and geographical framework that leads inexorably to the crucifixion and resurrection and the distinctively Johannine coloration of Jesus as the Lamb of God. Even the miracles of Jesus in John serve to reinforce the uniquely Johannine Christology: the man from heaven who comes to earth in human form as direct revelation of God.[67]

In sharp contrast to the Synoptics, however, Jesus does not "suffer," even in death. In fact, the word "suffer" never occurs in the Gospel of John.[68] Jesus is calm, serene, and fully in charge, and his death is merely a departure. Unlike the Gethsemane scene in Mark (14:33–36), the Johannine Jesus refuses to ask God to save him from death (12:27). Instead, he calls on God to "glorify" his "name," at which point a voice rings from heaven, emulating and yet recasting the transfiguration story (12:28). In John "glorification" has taken the place of "suffering." One ultimately wonders how human he really is. It is in this sense too that the Johannine use of the title "Son of God" takes on an entirely new meaning, what we now call an "incarnational Christology."

On the other side, the Gospel of John places considerable stress on *seeing* or *witnessing to* Jesus as the basis for belief. The recurrent theme of the "eyewitness" who stands behind the story is matched by references to looking and seeing in conjunction with the testimonies to Jesus's divine identity: "We have *seen* his glory, the glory as of a father's only son" (John 1:14). The Johannine narrative also creates very visual scenes through the combination of dramatic action and poignant symbols, as seen in both the "I am" discourses and the narrativization of the Lamb of God symbolism in staging the crucifixion (see Chapter 1).

This use of visual dramatization also stands in sharp contrast to the invisible Jesus in the *Gospel of Thomas*. It may finally say something about the point of the story of Thomas in John 20. The closing line has Jesus say to Thomas: "Have you believed because you have *seen* me? Blessed are those who have *not seen* and yet have come to believe" (20:29). This statement may suggest that there are two kinds of "seeing" at work in the Gospel of John. One is the visible form of Jesus, the *heavenly Logos made flesh* (1:14), as an antidocetic affirmation. The other is the heavenly Jesus, now departed to return to the Father, who may only be *seen* through the eye of faith, but who promises his presence nonetheless. Both are "performed" or enacted through the Gospel narrative. The Gospel of John thus creates a visual sense of the embodied Jesus for a new generation of believers.

CHAPTER FIFTEEN

⸺ ⸙ ⸺

Gospels and More Gospels

Peter said to Mary, "Sister, we know that the Savior loved you more than all other women. Tell us the words of the Savior that you remember, the things which you know that we don't because we have not heard them."

Mary responded, "I will teach you about what is hidden from you." And she began to speak these words to them. (Gospel of Mary 6:1–4)

Wisdom (Sophia), whom they call barren, is the mother of the angels, and the consort of Christ is Mary Magdalene. The [Lord loved Mary] more than all the disciples, and he kissed her. . . . The other [disciples saw]. . . . They said to him, "Why do you [love her] more than us? The Savior answered them, "Why do I not love you as I do her?" (Gospel of Philip 63:30–64.5)[1]

Gospels and more Gospels. With new characters and twisting plots, they often baffle modern readers. Sometimes they baffled early Christians too. Where did they come from? And why *so many*—and *so different*? How can they all be "true"? But it must be remembered that there were already questions and debates of this sort over Mark and Matthew by the early part of the second century, as reflected in the comments of Papias in trying to explain away their differences (quoted and discussed in the Prologue and Chapter 11). As we have seen in the previous chapter, the Gospel of John seems to have developed, at least in part, as a response to a similar problem and as an effort to hold diverging views of Jesus together. By the end of the second century, the proliferation of new Gospels would become its own problem, but by then there were even more.

Let's pause for a moment to take stock. As we have already seen, there were at least six to eight different Gospels or collections already known by the time the Gospel of John was completed about 120 CE or so. They include Mark and Q, Matthew and Luke, John and *Thomas,* and probably a few others, such as the untitled dialogue Gospel (Egerton 2)[2] and the source tradition behind the resurrection scene in the *Gospel of Peter*.[3] By 200 CE there were another twenty new Gospels. They include the *Protevangelium of James,* the *Infancy Gospel of Thomas,* the *Gospel of Mary,* the *Gospel of Judas,* the *Gospel of Philip,* and others. This partial list represents those that bear the name of an apostle or other close follower from the time of Jesus. Without worrying for the moment whether they were written by that person, what might this pattern of attribution suggest about issues of authority and theological diversity as we near the end of the second century (see Box 15.1)? As we reflect on this continuing process, we shall first look at some basic types of Gospels that emerge in the later centuries and then examine some of the tendencies, both literary and theological, that produced them.

Different Types of Gospels

In general we may divide the bulk of these later Gospel "books" into two main types of stories: *narratives* and *dialogues* (as reflected in Box 15.1). This distinction is somewhat arbitrary, of course, because the two naturally overlap at some points. Narratives about Jesus typically contain moments of dialogue, and dialogues often intersperse narrative transitions. For our purposes, the difference is rather one of degree or proportion.[4]

Narrative Gospels

What we may classify as *narrative Gospels* are characterized by a strong narrative structure that shapes the flow of Jesus's actions and allows his words—whether isolated sayings, complex pronouncements, or dialogues—to be set in some specific narrative context within the story. In general, this type of narrative corresponds to the synoptic tradition, even though, as we have seen, the Gospel of Matthew creates lengthy sermons of Jesus. At an early stage in the development, the Markan storyteller had consciously crafted an episodic narrative in order to link otherwise disconnected units of tradition, especially regarding the death of Jesus (see Chapters 7 and 11). It set the stage for one major stream of the Gospel tradition.

Sayings of Jesus circulated independently in the Q tradition; the later stages of the synoptic tradition carefully integrated these isolated sayings into narrative frameworks as a way of giving them new context and meaning. In this way too the Gospel of John should be classified as a narrative Gospel with synoptic features, even though it integrates the lengthy "I am" discourses. These self-disclosure discourses, in turn, may be based on an older, more dialogical source tradition.[5] As we showed in Chapter 14, it seems that the Gospel of John was intentionally trying to hold the narrative tradition of the Synoptics—with their emphasis on

BOX 15.1

Other Gospels

Narrative Gospels

Type / Title	Features	Date
Narrative Episodes		
P.Oxy. 840: *title unknown* (fragmentary) Greek	"Synoptic" expansion with anti-Semitic elements; based on the story of Jesus in the Temple (cf. Matt 23:27).	second or third century CE
Secret Gospel of Mark (fragmentary) Greek	"Synoptic" expansion, with Johannine elements (e.g., Lazarus); a possible effort to harmonize or conflate Mark and John	by 200 CE
Jewish-Christian Gospels		
Gospel of the Nazarenes (fragmentary, preserved in Eusebius, Jerome, and some late Latin excerpts) Syriac or Aramaic (perhaps from Greek)	In content and general scope closely related to Matthew, perhaps including the Matthean nativity and the Sermon on the Mount, but with some reworking of episodes and sayings.	mid-second century CE
Gospel of the Ebionites (fragmentary, preserved only in Epiphanius) Greek	An abridged version of Matthew with other materials drawn from Jewish-Christian sources, e.g., the *Kerygmata Petrou;* seems to lack a birth narrative.	mid-second century CE
Gospel of the Hebrews (fragmentary, preserved only in excerpts from Cyril of Jerusalem and Jerome) Greek and Latin	Account of Jesus given under the authority of his brother James, who is listed among the apostles, attends the Last Supper, and is the first one to whom Jesus appears after the resurrection (cf. 1 Cor 15:7); some verbal similarities to the Letter of James, but some traits similar to the Sophia tradition and the *Gospel of Thomas.* Represents a different form of Jewish-Christian text from the *Gospel of the Nazarenes* or the *Gospel of the Ebionites.*	mid-second century CE
Passion/Resurrection Stories		
Gospel of Peter (fragmentary) Greek *For discussion and text, see Appendix C*	Synoptic conflation (fragmentary) of Passion-resurrection narrative with anti-Semitic elements and recasting of Pilate and Herod; told as first-person account by Peter.	late second century CE

Type / Title	Features	Date
Epistula Apostolorum Coptic (from Greek), Ethiopic	Postresurrection dialogue of Jesus with apostles, prefaced by "letter of the apostles"; Johannine, antidocetic elements (Thomas touches Jesus).	late second-third century CE
The Letter of Pilate (from the Acts of Peter and Paul) Greek and Latin	A "letter" of Pilate to the emperor Claudius (*sic*, Tiberius) explaining how the execution of Jesus transpired and confirming the Matthean story about bribing the guards. Also some similarities to the treatment of Pilate in the *Gospel of Peter*.	by ca. 200 CE but only pre-served in late versions (fourth–seventh century)
Paradosis (Trial) of Pilate (or Acts of Pilate)	Later version of the *Letter of Pilate* (now to Tiberius), combined with an account of Pilate's trial in Rome, final confession of faith, and an added legend about an emissary to Judea who meets Veronica and returns to Rome with her "towel."	fourth century CE ?
The Acts of Pilate (Gospel of Nicodemus) Greek (also Latin, Coptic, Syriac, Armenian, and Arabic versions)	An account of Pilate's return to Rome and "confession" regarding the death of Jesus; blames Jews and depicts Pilate as a believer. Based on the type of tradition in the *Letter* and *Paradosis of Pilate*. The Gospel of Nicodemus is a later composite form of the text added in the Latin version and includes Christ's descent to hell.	after fourth century CE; with a later editorial addi-tion, after sixth-seventh century
Birth/Infancy Narratives		
Protevangelium (or Proto-Gospel) of James Greek (also Latin, Coptic, Syriac, Ethiopic, Armenian, Georgian, and Slavonic versions)	Expansion of Lukan birth narrative projected backward to the birth and life of Mary and carried forward into birth of Jesus, including the account of the midwife, Salome, and fabulous tales of their sojourn in Egypt; source for much of the later *Golden Legend*.	early layers date from late second century but with later additions
Infancy Gospel of Thomas Greek or Syriac (also later Latin, Slavonic, Arabic, Armenian, Ethiopic, and Georgian versions)	Some features shared with *Gospel of Thomas* (cf. *log.* 77); following a first-person prologue, stories of Jesus's miraculous powers as a young boy (before age 12)	second half of second century CE

Type / Title	Features	Date
Gospel of Pseudo-Matthew ("On the Origin of the Blessed Mary and the Childhood of the Savior") Latin	A late composite of several birth and infancy traditions: begins with Mary's earlier life (from *Protevangelium of James*), the birth of Jesus (with elements from Matthew and Luke, plus legendary accretions from *Protevangelium of James*), and ends with stories of the miraculous powers of the boy Jesus (from *Infancy Thomas*).	eighth–ninth century CE, based on earlier sources (third-fourth century)
Latin Infancy Gospel (Arundel Manuscript) Latin	A late composite tradition based largely on the *Gospel of Pseudo-Matthew* and its principal sources, but with an added birth scene based on an alternative tradition of a midwife from that in *Protevangelium of James*.	Early layers: second–fourth century; later edition: ninth century+
Arabic Infancy Gospel Arabic (from Syriac); some late Latin parallels. **Armenian Infancy Gospel** Armenian (from Syriac)	A late composite tradition similar to *Gospel of Pseudo-Matthew*, but without the earlier life of Mary. Based on *Protevangelium of James* and *Infancy Thomas*, with several stories reworked in novelistic fashion. *Arabic Infancy* probable source for some legends about Jesus in the Qu'ran. *Armenian Infancy* probably derived from the same Syriac tradition, but with some different elements.	seventh–ninth century
The Death of Joseph Coptic and Arabic	A late expansion on the *Protevangelium of James* told from Joseph's perspective and concluding with an account of his death and burial by his grown son James, while Jesus is a boy. The death and burial scenes have similarities to the story of Adam's death in the *Life of Adam and Eve*; some elements may reflect other Coptic traditions in the *Apocalypse of Elijah*.	After eighth or ninth century CE
Other Legends		
Jesus's Correspondence with King Abgar of Edessa Greek	A series of letters to and from Jesus as healer regarding the king's medical condition; Jesus says he cannot come visit, but promises to send an emissary, Thaddeus (Addai).	by early fourth century CE

Dialogue Gospels

Type / Title	Features	Date
Dialogues of Jesus		
P. Egerton 2: *title unknown* (fragmentary) Greek	"Johannine" style self-disclosure dialogues with Synoptic influences and anti-semitic elements.	early second century CE
Dialogue of the Savior Nag Hammadi Codex III.5 Coptic (from Greek)	"Johannine" or "Thomas" style sayings; later expansion of dialogues with cosmogonic myths	second century, preserved in Coptic version of late fourth century
Apocryphon of James Nag Hammadi Codex I.2 Coptic (from Greek)	Dialogues of Jesus with disciples (after resurrection), prefaced with a letter from James; some independent Synoptic elements and similarities to both John and Thomas; "gnostic" features and cover letter added later.	early/mid-second century, preserved in Coptic version of late fourth century
Gospel of the Savior (fragmentary) Coptic (from Greek)	Discourses of Jesus of Johannine type, with some apparent reference to the Last Supper or the arrest scene (from either John 14 or Matt 26) followed by a transfiguration scene (of Synoptic type) and then a crucifixion followed by a departure discourse (similar to John 20?). Some similarities in form to *Epistles of the Apostles,* but amount of narrative has been severely reduced.	late second century, preserved in Coptic version of fourth–seventh century CE
The Book of Thomas the Contender (or Athlete) Nag Hammadi Codex II.7 Coptic (from Greek)	A dialogue between Jesus and his twin brother Thomas prior to the ascension, resembling the opening of the *Gospel of Thomas,* but "transcribed" by Matthias, who was present. Primarily concerned with instructions on ascetic living. The latter part of the text may be from a separate work, a single monologue of Jesus addressed to a group of disciples in the form of a long series of "woes" and "blessings." A Book or "Gospel" of Matthias was also mentioned in the *Pistis Sophia,* as well as listed by Origen and Eusebius.	Late second–third century, preserved in Coptic version of late fourth century CE

Type / Title	Features	Date
Questions of Bartholomew Greek (also Latin and Slavonic)	A dialogue, or more precisely a series of questions and answers (*erotapokriseis*), between Jesus and Bartholomew in which he explains what happened during the crucifixion, specifically about his disappearance from the cross and descent into the underworld, and how the Temple veil was torn. In a second part, Bartholomew and Peter ask Mary to explain about how she bore Jesus. The latter presumes some form of tradition about Mary's early life (as in *Protevangelium of James*), while the former depends on a more fully developed tradition of Christ's descent to Hades (as preserved later in *Gospel of Nicodemus*). The last part of the text deals with Bartholomew's confrontation with Beliar (Satan) as a description of judgment.	Some layers may go back to the third century; known by late fourth century, but likely with later additions
The Gospel of the Egyptians (fragmentary, preserved in Clement of Alexandria, Hippolytus, and Epiphanius) Greek [NB: This is a different work from the Coptic text with the same title in Nag Hammadi Codex III.2, IV.2. The latter is not a "gospel" in any literary sense.]	Primarily a series of sayings attributed to Jesus dealing with marriage and sexuality. A woman named Salome is the chief interlocutor of Jesus, as in *Gospel of Thomas* 61 (cf. Mark 15:40; 16:1). Clement of Alexandria associates the work with the encratite (or ascetic) Christian school of Cassianus; similar ascetic sayings appear in 2 *Clement* 12.1-2 and *Gospel of Thomas* 22, 37. The work was apparently influential among Egyptian "gnostic" Christians.	late second century CE
"Gnostic" Gospels		
Gospel of Philip Nag Hammadi Codex II.3 Coptic (from Greek)	A Valentinian anthology of some 107 (?) excerpts from earlier works, similar in form to the *Excerpts of Theodotos* of Clement of Alexandria. Contains short discourses and other independent allegories and sayings with some similarities to those in *Gospel of Thomas* as well as the synoptic tradition.	late second or third century (?), preserved in Coptic version of late fourth century

Type / Title	Features	Date
Gospel of Truth Nag Hammadi Codex I.3, XII.2 Coptic (from Greek)	A sermon or meditation on Christian mystical gnosis and salvation, perhaps by Valentinus himself. A highly crafted literary and rhetorical work, not really a "gospel" in genre, although some of its sayings resemble those in Gospels of *Thomas* and John. It refers to "Jesus Christ" who "was nailed to a tree" (18.15, 24).	second century, preserved in Coptic version of late fourth century
Gospel of Mary **(Magdalene)** (fragmentary) *P.Ryl.* 463, *P.Oxy.* 3525, BG 8502.1 Greek and Coptic	A dialogue of the risen Jesus with the disciples, including Mary Magdalene, with similarities to the Nag Hammadi codices in form and date. The first part of the text is an exposition on sin as a cosmological defect. The second part has Mary comfort and instruct the disciples from secret teachings of Jesus and includes a confrontation with Peter (cf. *Gospel of Thomas* 114).	second century, preserved in third century ms. (Greek) and late fourth century version (Coptic)
Gospel of Judas (fragmentary) Codex Tchacos Coptic (from Greek)	A dialogue of Jesus and Judas regarding the role of Judas in the crucifixion, with similarities to the Nag Hammadi codices in form and date. Based in part on the portrayal of the misunderstanding disciples in Mark, but Judas is a demonic figure.	second century, preserved in Coptic version of late fourth century
Pistis Sophia (or Books of the Savior) Coptic (from Greek)	A late compilation of disparate "gnostic" lore about Sophia's fall and repentance, set, in part, as a dialogue of Jesus with the disciples some 11 years after his resurrection. Uses the *Odes of Solomon* and Matthew 10, now applied to the "gnostic" missionary.	third–fourth century CE

the Passion—together with the type of sayings tradition already known from the *Gospel of Thomas* and the Egerton 2 Gospel. Later forms of narrative stories, such as infancy and miracle gospels or elaborations of Passion stories, naturally fall into this category. Consequently, we may see that later narrative Gospels continue many of the tendencies of the synoptic trajectory.

Dialogue Gospels

What we may classify as *dialogue Gospels* are characterized by a weak narrative structure that gives little sense of narrative flow or episodic sequence. They focus, rather, on the words of Jesus or on the verbal interaction of the characters. Often they are set in some vague time during Jesus's ministry, especially around the Last Supper, or between his death and ascension. We may trace the developmental trajectory to an equally early stage in the Q tradition. It was in turn more fully developed in the *Gospel of Thomas* and in the early dialogue Gospels, such as Egerton 2, the *Dialogues of the Savior,* and the *Apocryphon of James.* Here too the Gospel of John was influential to the later development. Its *logos* theology and self-disclosure dialogues offer both a model and inspiration for expansions and interpretations.

The genre characteristic of much of the so-called Gnostic literature relies heavily on this form. Sometimes called the "Gnostic revelation dialogue," it lends itself to the creation of vivid revelatory scenes based in part on the model of older apocalyptic literature. At the same time, it takes on features of Greek philosophical discourse. One of the dynamics of this genre is the authority of the speaker and the attentiveness or compliance of the hearers. As we shall see, however, some of these later dialogue Gospels may well presume knowledge of a basic narrative tradition, as reflected in the canonical Gospels. They will nonetheless transform the story into this type of dialogical setting, often to pursue a new theological purpose. These basic genre distinctions will also help us to understand how or why certain patterns of storytelling might correlate with other literary and theological tendencies. In what follows, therefore, we shall explore these tendencies and look at some key examples.

What Led to the Proliferation of Gospels?

Many of the factors that led to the production of later Gospels arose naturally from popular sentiments and questions. Jesus was a carpenter (Mark 6:3) or at least the son of a carpenter (Matt 13:55), we are told. He had brothers—James, Joses, Simon, and Judas—and several sisters (Mark 6:3). One of them, James, became a leader of the Jesus movement in Jerusalem by the late 30s CE (Gal 1:19; 2:9).[6] Such tidbits of information offer tantalizing hints of a larger story. Yet we hear little more. Was James a follower of Jesus during his ministry? The canonical Gospels say nothing, but the Markan and Lukan narratives both leave a negative impression.[7] Yet the *Gospel of Thomas* has Jesus refer to this James (*log.* 12). Even more important, Paul's oral tradition explicitly mentions an appearance of the risen Jesus to "James and all the apostles" (1 Cor 15:7). At least one later text, called the *Gospel of the Hebrews,* says that James was among the disciples of Jesus, attended the Last Supper, and was the first person to whom Jesus appeared after the resurrection.[8] The Ebionites, a later stream of Jewish Christianity, revered James along with Peter as their patron apostles.[9] Another text, the *Apocryphon of James,* claims to be the "secret teachings of Jesus" in the form of a dialogue written down by James.[10] Both of these texts date to the middle part of the second century. Yet another text, the *Protevangelium of James,* which dates to the late second century, gives an account of the birth and early life of Mary (see Box 15.1).

In each case, there appears to be a fascination with the idea of finding out more about Jesus's life or his teachings from one of his own siblings. Thus, as with the earlier development of the synoptic tradition, we see disconnected nodes of tradition serving as the skeleton for creation of larger stories through which to explore new questions and new ideas about Jesus. In each new case, we see the historical figure of James being scripted into very different roles—Jewish Christian on the one side, Gnostic Christian on the other. Some, like the *Protevangelium of James,* were virtually canonical, while others were mostly viewed as "heretical," at least by the emerging orthodoxy at the end of the second century. Here we may look at three such tendencies and the different types of stories they produced.

Filling the Gaps

There are many gaps in the earliest Gospels: missing years of Jesus's life, information about his parents or family, enigmatic characters and "shady ladies." The continual retelling of the traditional stories naturally raises certain questions or begs for additional information. Later Gospels often tried to supplement the stories to fill in these gaps. One sign of popular imagination is that nameless characters get named, and fuller stories get built around them. For example, in later tradition the centurion at the cross not only receives a name, Longinus, but also becomes a saint for his "confession."[11] Even Pilate is later portrayed as a believer, as in the *Gospel of Peter.*[12] In another elaboration, we get the story of his apocryphal trial at Rome. In it, Pilate is made to deliver an impassioned account of what really happened to Jesus, and he manages even to convince the emperor Claudius (*sic*) that Jesus really was the Son of God after all.[13] Despite glaring anachronisms and other historical difficulties, such stories seek to smooth out narrative connections or cover over nagging questions.

Among the most popular of the apocryphal writings were the various infancy Gospels that dealt with the birth or early years of Jesus. Of course, one notable problem that had to be addressed arose from the substantial differences between the birth narratives in Matthew and Luke (see Chapter 10). Here we may take two key examples.

The Protevangelium of James

A good example is the *Protevangelium* (or *Proto-Gospel*) *of James*.[14] Its earliest layers date to the latter half of the second century, but it continued to be used and augmented over several more centuries. It became one of the most popular legends in medieval Christianity, in both East and West, and was considered virtually "canonical" through later elaborations, including the *Golden Legend*, and Marian devotion. The story is ostensibly told by James the brother of Jesus, who is now assumed to be a half brother to Jesus, Joseph's child by a previous marriage (*Prot. Jas.* 25.1). Joseph is an old widower with sons, while Mary is a twelve-year-old virgin living in the Temple (9.2). The story fills in three other key areas of the story: Mary's family background and birth, how she came to be betrothed to Joseph, and the details of Jesus's conception and birth.

The story of Mary's birth in the *Protevangelium of James* is rather clearly based on the Lukan birth narrative, but projected back onto Mary's parents, who are now given names—Joachim and Anna. They resemble Zechariah and Elizabeth, the parents of John the Baptist, in Luke. Both stories are modeled on the story of Anna (Hannah),[15] the mother of Samuel, which in turn had already been used as the base for the Lukan birth narrative. Accordingly, Joachim and Anna were old, but childless. The text extracts and paraphrases explicit lines from both 1 Samuel and Luke to create the new story.[16] Anna even utters an abbreviated version of the *Magnificat* at Mary's birth.[17] At age two Mary was taken to the Temple to live, like the young Samuel (1 Sam 1:27–28; 2:18–26). There she grew up as the darling among the priests until she was twelve (7.1–8.3). After Joseph was chosen miraculously to betroth her (9.1–2), the young Mary left the Temple, a parallel to Jesus's return at the same age in Luke 2:41–52; the story further emulates the Lukan narrative in ascribing to Mary the special birth and precocious childhood of the divine-man tradition.

Next, the betrothed Mary now begins to work along with other virgins on weaving a new veil for the Temple, the same veil that will be torn at Jesus's death.[18] This narrative device has the dramatic effect of simultaneously tying *her* birth into the Passion of Jesus *and* heightening her virginity as a theological issue. The story is consciously linked directly to the Lukan birth narrative, as it says that this was the time that "Zechariah became dumb," a reference to the annunciation of the birth of John the Baptist.[19] One day, while she was working at home, Mary went out to a spring to draw water, and there the angel first announced that she would have a child. This scene has no parallel in the Lukan narrative, but became a popular feature in later legend (see Box 15.2). On returning to the house, the angel appeared again, and we have the fuller Lukan annunciation scene followed by the visit to Elizabeth. Mary is now sixteen, we are told. When she returns after several months and Joseph discovers her to be pregnant, he fears being shamed and plans to put her away. Here we pick up the Matthean birth narrative, as Joseph is told in a dream all will be well.[20] It is augmented with another novel scene in which Joseph and Mary are taken to the Temple to be tested for adultery by drinking the "water of conviction" for her inappropriate pregnancy.[21] But they were both found to be pure.[22]

Next, the birth story proper is narrated, beginning with the Lukan census and their journey toward Bethlehem. Mary is described riding an ass, and they are accompanied by Joseph's son (presumably James himself); they stop as the time nears, and Jesus is born in a nearby cave. Joseph finds a midwife named Salome who helps with the delivery, using the words of Simeon in Luke 2; she then confirms gynecologically that Mary is still a virgin, using the same words of Thomas in John 20.[23] The story then ends with Mary and Joseph preparing to take Jesus to the Temple, as Herod's furor rises because the wise men have tricked him (following Matthew).[24] Herod's slaughter of the children (Matthew) now forces Elizabeth to flee with the infant John (Luke), as her husband Zechariah is murdered in the Temple by Herod's men (22.3–24.3). Simeon, the old priest of Luke 2, now takes over for Zechariah.[25] The text closes with the personal testimonial of James, who now becomes an "eyewitness" to all these events (25). Accordingly, the *subscriptio* of the text also calls it "The Birth of Mary, A Revelation of James."

The usual title of this work, *Protevangelium* or *Proto-Gospel,* refers to the fact that this story fills in information about Joseph and Mary's life *before* the actual Gospel or "story" of Jesus commences. In other words, it constitutes what we now commonly call a "prequel." It tells the backstory of an established character or series, like the later installments of the *Star Wars* trilogy or the *Batman* movies. Thus, it relies on the fact that the audience already knows the main story line and characters. At the same time, such fictional expansions provide new, explanatory information to help understand why "later" events transpire as they do. Nameless characters now get names, and their personalities are filled in to fit later perceptions.

In the *Protevangelium of James,* there are three main results. First, the contrasting features of the Matthean and Lukan birth narratives are interwoven narratively. This helps to harmonize them to some extent. Second, it explains why Mary was chosen to become the mother of Jesus and in the process why she should be elevated in later forms of Christian devotion. Third, it "solves" a nagging theological problem that rose in later Christian speculation: how Jesus could have brothers and sisters even though Mary had come to be viewed as remaining a virgin in perpetuity. Thus, filling in the gaps also has important theological motivations and ramifications.

The Infancy Gospel of Thomas

Other very popular legends grew up around the "missing years" of Jesus's early life. The earliest and most popular of these is called the *Infancy Gospel of Thomas,* or the *Gospel of Thomas the Israelite Philosopher.*[26] Only the Gospel of Luke gives

BOX 15.2
Illustrating the Gospel Drama

These carved ivory plaques served as covers for a Gospel book, meaning the four canonical Gospels bound together as a separate volume, dating to the fifth century CE. Five ivory panels make up each cover; they are arranged as a central triptych with a wide panel at top and bottom. The two central scenes with the "Lamb of God" (front) and "Jeweled Cross" (back) are silver gilt decorated with gemstones and set into the ivory panels. At the top corners are the symbols of the four Evangelists that had become standard by the fourth

On the front we see (1) the Lukan nativity in a manger (with addition of the ox and ass from Isa 60:3), and (2) the Matthean slaughter of the innocents. On the left are (3) the first annunciation to the virgin at a spring, (4) the three magi and the star (Matt), and (5) the baptism of Jesus. On the right are three Temple scenes: (6) Mary at the Temple, (7) Jesus at the Temple at age twelve (Luke), and (8) the triumphal entry. Scenes 3 and 6 are both from the life of Mary in the *Protevangelium of James*.

century: the winged man (Matthew) and the ox (Luke), on the front, with the lion (Mark) and the eagle (John), on the back. The figures at the bottom corners may be the same. Each cover shows an interweaving of scenes from the Synoptics, John, and apocryphal Gospels. The side panels may be read vertically as well as horizontally and suggest a unified thematic and symbolic composition. The iconography shows a number of similarities to imperial church decorations in Ravenna.

On the back we see (1) the Matthean adoration of the magi and (2) the Johannine wedding feast at Cana. On the left are three miracles: (3) the healing of two blind men (Matt), (4) the healing of the paralytic who carries his bed (Mark or John), and (5) the raising of Lazarus (John). On the right are (6) Christ enthroned on the orb of the world flanked by Peter and Paul, (7) the Last Supper, and (8) the widow's mite, with Jesus again seated on the orb (Mark and Luke). Tesoro del Duomo di Milano. Photos by Erich Lessing. *Used by permission, Art Resource, NY.*

any information about Jesus's life between his birth and the beginning of his adult career. It comes in a single story of Jesus visiting the Temple at age twelve, where he confounds the teachers with his wisdom (Luke 2:41–52). As we have seen, this particular episode is characteristic of the divine-man tradition (see Chapters 3, 10, and 13). In later popular imagination, however, such stories could hardly but raise questions about what Jesus was like as a boy. The *Infancy Gospel of Thomas* seeks to fill in this gap by telling stories about him growing up in Nazareth from age five. It ends by repeating the story of Jesus going to the Temple at age twelve.

The character of most of these stories fits well with the divine-man genre, as they portray Jesus as a precocious child with prodigious wisdom and magical powers. He is also a bit of a brat. The result is a series of charming episodes to display Jesus's powers as they grow and as he learns to control them and focus his energies on the task set before him. In that sense, this work too is very much a prequel in that it anticipates many themes that will arise in the later tradition about Jesus's messianic identity and role in salvation, all overlaid with divine-man qualities.

One of the more charming episodes occurs as Joseph, who is now identified as a carpenter who makes ploughs and yokes, is seen in his workshop with the boy Jesus looking on. When Joseph inadvertently cuts a beam too short, Jesus simply stretches it to match the other piece (*Inf. Gos. Thom.* 13). In another episode, the young Jesus accompanies his elder brother James to gather wood. When James is bitten by a snake, Jesus miraculously keeps him from dying (16). As in the *Protevangelium of James* we see elements that try to explain other issues in the traditional story.

Some of the episodes also suggest that there are deeper theological issues lying behind these seemingly folksy tales. In one, Jesus is playing on the upper story of a house with some young friends. When one of the other boys falls from the house and dies, Jesus brings him back to life (*Inf. Gos. Thom.* 9). This episode is probably based on the story of Paul and Eutychus in Acts 20:7–12. An added feature is that some bystanders blame Jesus for throwing the boy down, thus providing a tone of challenge and proof through the miracles of Jesus.

Such confrontational elements form a consistent theme in the text that shows up from the very first episode. In it, Jesus is playing at a stream near his house and making little pools out of the mud. He also makes some birds from the clay. When a "certain Jew" sees that Jesus is doing this on the Sabbath, he reports the breach of piety to Joseph. When Joseph comes to reprimand him, Jesus responds by clapping his hands. To Joseph's astonishment, the clay birds fly away (2.1–4). As charming as this may be, elements of increasing anti-Jewish polemic are apparent here. The rest of the episode makes it even more explicit:

> *The Jews were amazed when they saw this, and went away and told their elders what they had seen Jesus do. But the son of Annas the scribe was standing there*

with Joseph; and he took a willow branch and dispersed the water that Jesus had gathered together. When Jesus saw what he had done, he was enraged and said to him: "You irreverent and reckless Sodomite, what have these pools done to harm you? See, now you will likewise wither like a tree, and bear neither leaves, nor root, nor fruit!" And immediately the boy withered up completely; and Jesus left and went into Joseph's house. But the parents of the one who was withered took him away bewailing his youth. They brought him to Joseph and reproached him (saying): "What a child you have who does such things." (2.5–3.3)[27]

In addition to the obvious elements of anti-Jewish rhetoric, this story adds some telling features. The name Annas is, of course, prominent in the canonical Gospels; in Luke-Acts he is the high priest along with Caiaphas at the time of Jesus's execution (Luke 3:2; Acts 4:6).[28] The Gospel of John (18:13) identifies Annas as the father-in-law of Caiaphas, but adds that Jesus was tried before each of them in turn (18:24). In John, ironically it is Caiaphas who devises the plot to kill Jesus (11:49–50).

Thus, this story takes a theme from the canonical Gospels by having Jesus criticized for performing miracles on the Sabbath, but it then links it to a character involved in the crucifixion. The fanciful equation is created by making Annas a scribe, and thus some vague sort of religious official, some twenty-five years earlier, who would somehow rise to the office of high priest. Far-fetched as this may be, the story could be read in popular Christian imagination as if Annas was still holding a grudge against Jesus all those years later. Never mind that this future "priest" was apparently living in Nazareth instead of Jerusalem. Such historical blunders would be lost on the audience; realism has given way to creative invention. Thus, many of these episodes are intended to foreshadow themes and tensions that will play out in the adult career of Jesus as known from the canonical Gospels. They become increasingly anti-Jewish in rhetoric and tone. The stock of theological allusions is made complete in the very words that the child Jesus uses to curse the son of Annas, for they are similar to those uttered by the Markan Jesus in cursing the fig tree and, by extension, the Temple itself (Mark 11:12–14; Matt 21:18–19).

These two infancy Gospels continued to be popular in both eastern and western Christian traditions through the Middle Ages and continue to inform many elements of popular piety down to the present day. A later form of these traditions, known under the title the *Gospel of Pseudo-Matthew* (see Box 15.2), is an effort to weave the two together to build a composite story of Mary's life and Jesus's birth and early years. It was further expanded to include an account of the holy family's sojourn in Egypt, which included more miracles like those in the *Infancy Gospel of Thomas*. Most of these texts fall into the category of narrative Gospels and are modeled predominantly on Matthew and Luke.

Harmonizing Gospels

As we have seen, these infancy Gospels increasingly seek to harmonize the divergent birth traditions, beginning with the differences between Matthew and Luke. Early illustrations of the Gospel stories often placed scenes from one alongside those from another (see Box 15.2). Other new stories would seek to do the same with various components of the narrative found in the four canonical Gospels. These texts likewise tend to be narrative Gospels, sometimes focusing on one particular segment of the story and other times seeking to synthesize the entire narrative. They start by observing key differences among the Gospels and then try to resolve them by one or another combination of story elements.

The Secret Gospel of Mark

One example of this tendency is a document now called the *Secret Gospel of Mark*. It is known only from one brief quotation preserved in a letter ascribed to Clement of Alexandria (ca. 200 CE). The text of the letter was found copied by hand in Late Byzantine Greek onto the two final leaves (two pages and part of a third) of a seventeenth-century book contained in the library of the Greek Orthodox monastery of Mar Saba.[29] If the *Letter of Clement* is genuine, it would date the Gospel being described somewhat earlier in the second century.

The *Letter of Clement* describes two distinct documents known from Alexandrian Christian usage: first, an expanded version of the Gospel of Mark, supposedly penned by Mark himself after coming to Alexandria from Rome, where he had written the earlier version; second, a "pirated" copy of this early text that was supplemented with "heretical" teachings by the Carpocratians, a second-century "Gnostic" group from Alexandria.[30] Here is the central portion of the description by Clement:

> As for Mark, then, during Peter's stay in Rome he wrote an account of the Lord's doings, not however, declaring all of them, nor yet hinting at the secret ones, but selecting what he thought most useful for increasing the faith of those who were being instructed. But when Peter died a martyr, Mark came over to Alexandria, bringing both his own notes and those of Peter, from which he transferred to his former book [the Gospel] the things suitable to whatever makes for progress toward knowledge. Thus he composed a more spiritual Gospel for the use of those who were being perfected. Nevertheless, he did not divulge the things not to be uttered, nor did he write down the hierophantic teaching of the Lord, but to the stories already written he added yet others and, moreover, brought in certain sayings of which he knew the interpretation would, as a mystagogue, lead the hearers into the innermost sanctuary of truth hidden by seven veils. Thus, in sum, he prepared matters, neither grudgingly nor incautiously, in my opinion,

and dying, he left his composition to the church in Alexandria, where it even yet is most carefully guarded, being read only to those who are being initiated into the great mysteries.[31]

Clement of Alexandria was well aware of the many other Gospels. His writings, especially the *Stromateis* (or *Miscellanies*), are replete with references to them and often short quotations. Apparently he had a substantial library. Many of the traditions preserved in Eusebius derive from the work of Clement.

In order to evaluate this particular tradition, we must first notice that it incorporates a variation on the traditional account of how "Mark" got his Gospel from Peter, known from the *testimonia* of Papias and Clement, both preserved only in Eusebius. Using the Papias tradition, however, the Christian historian Eusebius of Caesarea had Mark going to Alexandria very early on after writing the Gospel in Rome.[32] Since these traditions would place the writing of the Gospel of Mark in Rome and somewhere between ca. 37 and 64 CE, they have little or no direct historical value. At most, they represent basically the same legend of Mark's later life in Alexandria known to Eusebius in the early fourth century CE.

More important is the next section of the *Letter of Clement* in which he instructs Theodore on which portions of the expanded *Secret Gospel* are "authentic," meaning not tampered with by the Carpocratians. The key passage is:

To you, therefore, I shall not hesitate to answer the questions you have asked, refuting the falsifications by the very words of the Gospel. For example, after "And they were in the road going up to Jerusalem" *[Mark 10:32a], and what follows, until* "After three days he shall arise" *[Mark 10:34b], it [the Secret Gospel] brings the following material word for word:*

"And they came into Bethany. And a certain woman whose brother had died was there. And coming, she prostrated herself before Jesus and says to him, 'Son of David, have mercy on me.' But the disciples rebuked her. And Jesus, being angered, went off with her into the garden where the tomb was, and straightway a great cry was heard from the tomb. And going near, Jesus rolled away the stone from the door of the tomb. And straightway, going in where the youth was, he stretched forth his hand and raised him, seizing his hand. But the youth, looking upon him, loved him and began to beseech him that he might be with him. And going out of the tomb they came into the house of the youth, for he was rich. After six days, Jesus told him what to do and in the evening the youth came to him, wearing a linen cloth over his naked body. And he remained with him that night, for Jesus taught him the mystery of the kingdom of God. And thence arising he returned to the other side of the Jordan."

After these words follows the text, "And James and John came to him" *[Mark 10:35a], and all that section. But* "naked man with naked man," *and the other things about which you wrote, are not found.*[33]

As noted in the quotation, the passages mentioned in the Gospel of Mark are the third Passion prediction (Mark 10:32–34) and the discussion of Jesus with the sons of Zebedee (Mark 10:35–45). According to the *Letter of Clement,* then, the additional episode was inserted into the *Secret Gospel* between these two passages. What we have here is a rather clear variation on the raising of Lazarus episode from the Gospel of John (11:1–44). Within it, however, are some characteristically "Markan" stylistic features, such as the use of "straightway" (meaning immediately). The end of the episode has Jesus retreat to the other side of the Jordan, similar to John 10:40 and 11:54, the framing narratives for the Lazarus story.

Virtually from the beginning, there have been debates over this discovery, made by Morton Smith in 1958.[34] It was compounded further when the actual manuscript later disappeared, although photographs of it still exist. There are three possible sets of issues regarding its authenticity and resulting implications for historical study. I rehearse these implications here because they are basic historical questions applicable to any of our ancient texts, including recent discoveries such as the *Gospel of Judas* (to be discussed in the next section).

1. *The letter of Clement to Theodore might be genuine.* If so, it means that *Secret Mark* was some form of early Gospel text purporting to go back to the author of the Gospel of Mark as an expansion done in Alexandria. An authentic letter of Clement has three possible historical implications:

   a. If the internal claim of authorship were true, then it would date *Secret Mark* to the late first century. It would thus be a very early witness to the development of the Gospel tradition and potentially a source text for some elements in the Gospel of John. If this were true, it would be one of the most important Gospels known.[35] *As noted above, this view is extremely doubtful.*

   b. On the other hand, if Clement's statement—that *Secret Mark* was later tampered with by "heretics"—were true, then it might cause us to guess that the entire text was a pseudepigraphical product of the Carpocratians (or some other group) from the latter half of the second century CE. In this view, Clement's distinction between the "authentic" *Secret Mark* and the "Carpocratian" additions would be moot. *This view is possible, but less likely.*

   c. It is more likely that *Secret Mark* known by Clement was itself a pseudepigraphical product of the later second century, prior to any Carpocratian "tampering." It seems to be based on Mark and John as written precursors and serves as an effort to harmonize them. If so, it would represent an important stage in the subsequent development of the canonical Gospels, parallel to any other "apocryphal" Gospel from the second century. *This view is possible.*

2. *The letter purporting to be from Clement might be relatively ancient but not by Clement himself.* Given Clement's reputation in the early Christian world, the letter might be an ancient forgery (or pseudepigraph). In this case, it would suggest that the *Secret Gospel* being described was also an ancient document, but its date of composition might be somewhat later, depending on when the spurious "Clement letter" was produced. If this were true, the *Secret Gospel* would still be of some importance for later developments in the Gospel tradition, but its importance would be directly correlative with its date of composition. Because the copy of the text is in a Late Byzantine hand, the original might date any time between the time of Clement and the sixteenth century; however, a date before the eleventh century would be more likely. *This view is also possible.*

3. *The entire document might be a modern forgery by Smith himself.* In this case, no part of the letter or the text has any value for study of the Gospel tradition or of early Christianity itself. *This view has been alleged and has strong proponents on both sides. It is possible, but in my view rather unlikely.*

For purposes of our present examination of the storytelling patterns in earliest Christianity, I will here assume option 1.c as the most likely possibility.[36] In other words, we may assume for the moment that *Letter of Clement* is genuine, but that the text quoted by Clement as "authentic" to *Secret Mark* is a second-century expansion on the Gospel of Mark in an effort to harmonize it with elements from the Gospel of John.

As noted earlier, there are a number of direct verbal similarities between Mark and John where Mark has a distinctive wording among the Synoptics (see Chapter 14 and Box 14.3). This fact, when combined with some enigmatic features of the Markan narrative, could have led the ancient readers to speculate on a possible relationship. The key connection seems to be the description of the "young man" who followed Jesus "wearing nothing but a *linen cloth*" to Gethsemane and then "ran away naked" (Mark 14:51). There are also hints of the rich young man story, whom Jesus loved (Mark 10:17–22, esp. 21). As most New Testament scholars have noted, this same enigmatic character is somehow connected dramatically and literarily in Mark to the "young man, dressed in a white robe" who was in the empty tomb when the women arrived (Mark 16:5). Who better to announce Jesus's resurrection than Lazarus, whom Jesus had raised from the dead with the symbolic statement "I am the resurrection and the life" (John 11:25)? The equation of the two characters would have the further implication of making Lazarus the "beloved disciple" of the Gospel of John.[37] Such a harmonization between the Markan and Johannine stories would serve to link the two Gospels and solve some of the literary disjunctures among the Gospels.

The Diatessaron

Such efforts at harmonization were commonplace from the middle of the second century as more of the Gospels came into wider use and their differences became known. One of the first was by Justin Martyr, a Christian philosopher and teacher at Rome from ca. 140–164 CE. Among his writings was an *Apology* for the Christians, in which he describes Christian worship. In it he says:

> And on the day that is called the Day of the Sun there is a meeting together in one place of all who dwell in cities or the country. As long as time permits the memoirs of the apostles or the writings of the prophets are read. When the reader has finished, the president gives exhortation in a discourse and invitation to imitate these good things. Then we all rise up in unison and offer prayers, and, as we said before, when we have finished praying bread is brought and wine with water.[38]

By the "memoirs of the apostles" Justin means the Gospels, but which Gospels? Analysis of the pattern of his quotations from the Gospels makes it rather clear that he means Matthew, Mark, and Luke. He apparently did not know or use the Gospel of John at all. Even more to the point, most of his explicit quotations often seem to reflect a conscious and systematic interweaving of parallel verses from the three Synoptics, with Matthew and Luke alternately taking precedence.[39] In the same way, Justin made extensive use of narrative sections of the Synoptics, in which he also integrated extensive quotations from the Jewish scriptures to augment or parallel those already used in the Gospels themselves.

Apparently, the preferred mode of reading the Gospels used in Justin's church was in this harmonized version rather than in the three independent versions. Writers both before and after Justin, including Clement of Alexandria, continued to use these harmonized quotations. There were also early Latin harmonies of this type, some of which were created prior to or in lieu of full translations of the Gospels into Latin. Until the late second century, however, there does not seem to be an effort to introduce the Gospel of John into the mix.

The first known effort to compile a harmony of the four Gospels, Matthew, Mark, Luke, John, comes from a student of Justin, Tatian the Syrian. He died ca. 185 CE. A philosopher in his own right, he also wrote extensively in Greek, including an *Oration to the Greeks,* but he is usually credited with the first efforts to create Christian literature in his native Syriac language. His harmony of the Gospels is called the *Diatessaron,* meaning "through the four." It was compiled sometime in the 170s and shows some awareness of one or more of the noncanonical Gospels, especially the early Jewish-Christian Gospels (see Box 15.1).[40] As late as the fifth and sixth centuries, the *Diatesseron* was still in wide use in the churches of the Syrian east.[41] It may well be that the work was composed originally in Syriac. If so, it would seem to be prior to the four Gospels being separately rendered into

Syriac. A fragment of an early Greek version also exists and at least leaves open the possibility that a Greek prototype, based on the existing Greek Gospels, served as a model. Tatian was probably drawing on Justin's harmony as a source.[42] The fuller form of the text is known only in Syriac and Arabic versions rendered from the Syriac.

THE GREEK *DIATESSARON*

Matt 27:56 only	[. . . and the mother of the sons of] Zebedee,[45]
Mark 15:40 only	and Salome,
Luke 23:49	and the women,
Editorial	*among those*
Luke 23:49; cf. Matt 27:55	who followed together with **him from the Galilee**,
Editorial, cf. Luke 23:49	*who saw him crucified.*
Editorial (a section heading?)	*Now it was the day of Preparation, as the Sabbath was dawning.*
Matt 27:57; cf. Mark 15:42	Now since it **was the evening**
Mark 15:42	of the (day of) Preparation, which is (the day) before the Sabbath,
Matt 27:57	there came *forward* a man,
Luke 23:50; cf. Mark 15:43	a member of the **Council,**
Luke 23:51b + *Editorial*	who was from *Erinmathaia,* a city *of Judea,*
Luke 23:50 only	by name Joseph, a good (and) righteous man,
John 19:38 only	being a disciple of Jesus, but secretly because of fear of the Judeans,
Mark 15:43	and he was
Luke 23:51c; cf. Mark 15:43	awaiting **the kingdom of God.**
Luke 23:51a only	This man had not consented with the plan [and . . .

Italics: Words supplied by the editor for grammar or flow
Bold: Words found in more than one of the Synoptics

Based on the preserved examples, it seems that Tatian's harmony used Matthew as its base text for the narrative, and the other Gospels were assimilated to it, sometimes on a line by line basis.[43] At times, the harmonization is laborious and detailed, working carefully to have each of the four Gospels represented in a particular episode.[44] In other cases, there seem to be larger blocks of material that are effectively summarized or abbreviated in the process of interweaving the variant forms. Some theological tendencies that appear include ascetic ideals and anti-Jewish sentiments. In order to see the effects we may examine the short passage known from the lone Greek manuscript, found at Dura-Europos in Roman Syria, shown on the previous page. It dates to before 256 CE. The preserved portion gives the account of Jesus's burial by Joseph of Arimathea and the women who witness it. The passage starts in the middle of a sentence naming the women and carefully tries to preserve the distinctive features of all four Gospels.

In the actual manuscript, this passage is of course written in continuous prose form. It is broken down here line by line and phrase by phrase, so that we can observe the precise use of wording from the individual Gospels. We can see that the text is extraordinarily careful about the wording and the grammar. Though this passage still seems very traditional in most respects, there are some notable changes. For one, the order of certain phrases or sentences has to be switched to make them fit grammatically or to give it a proper narrative flow.

Another change is occasioned by the compiler's attempt to keep all the distinctive features of each Gospel, specifically in the names of the women. In each of the Synoptics there are only three named women who visit the tomb:

Matthew 27:56 lists "Mary Magdalene, Mary the mother of James and Joseph, and the mother of the sons of Zebedee."

Mark 15:40 lists "Mary Magdalene, Mary the mother of James *the small* and Joses, and Salome."

Luke 24:10 lists "Mary Magdalene, Joanna, Mary the mother of James, and the other women."

Although the text is broken off, the sequence given in the Greek fragment of the *Diatessaron* most likely went: "Mary Magdalene, Joanna, Mary the mother of James *the small* and Joses, and the mother of the sons of Zebedee, and Salome, and the women among those who followed him from Galilee."[46] As a result of the compiler's activity, there are now five women named in the *Diatessaron* who witness the burial and who will come to visit the empty tomb.

Significantly, also discovered at Dura-Europos was a house converted for use as a Christian church building, still the earliest one known from archaeological evidence. The art of the Dura Christian building actually depicts the empty-tomb scene with these five women (see Box 15.3). Other paintings in the room

BOX 15.3
Art of the Dura-Europos Christian Building

Dura-Europos was a military garrison town on the eastern frontier of the Roman Empire. The Christian building was originally an ordinary house converted for use as a church building ca. 241 CE. One of the rooms was adapted for use as a baptistery and was decorated with scenes from the Christian Gospels, apparently following the harmony of the *Diatessaron*. The scene in the lower register shows five women approaching the tomb of Christ. A fragment of the *Diatessaron* was found not far from this building in debris used to build a fortification when the city was under attack by Sassanian armies. The city was destroyed and buried in 256 CE, leaving these remains frozen in time.

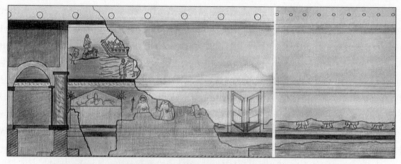

Top: A scale reconstruction of the paintings from the north and east walls of the Christian baptistery room. The baptismal font is at the left. The scenes include: *upper register:* healing of lame man who carries his bed (Mark 2:1–12; John 5:2–9) and Peter walking on water with Jesus (Matt); *lower register:* five women approach the tomb of Jesus (*Diatessaron*), which continues on to the east wall (at right). At left, *inside the font lunette:* The good shepherd (Luke 15:3–7; John 10:1–5). Drawing by L. M. White. *Bottom:* The Dura baptistery. Photo of the north wall and baptismal font. Photo from the Yale University Art Gallery. *HarperCollins Concise Atlas of the Bible.*

reflect a mixture of synoptic and Johannine scenes. It would seem, then, that the Christians of Dura used the *Diatessaron* as their main form of the Gospels. In the *Diatessaron,* other parts of the Gospels received equally significant changes. Even well-meaning efforts to hold the different Gospels together can thereby result in important changes at the narrative level. For later audiences, at least, even these changes sometimes proved a challenge. On the other hand, some form of inter-weaving of passages from various Gospels continues to be the typical way that the story of Jesus is told in most forms of Christianity down to the present day.

New Theological Explorations

In the infancy Gospels discussed above, we already see some modes of new theo-logical exploration through harmonization of diverse traditions and efforts to answer theological questions or extend certain theological implications. Other Gospels were even more intent on probing new theological ideas. In these cases dialogue settings provided a more direct way to do so by having Jesus himself or one of the disciples explain secret teachings. Like the dialogues of Plato, they serve to flesh out and interpret the teachings of the master—whether Socrates or Jesus—in the light of later, more systematic theological and philosophical ideas. This approach is already at work in the Gospels of *Thomas* and John, but it was more fully developed in the later dialogue Gospels, and especially in the so-called Gnostic Gospels. Two of these have received greater attention in recent years and will be discussed in detail. The rest are summarized in Box 15.1.

The Gospel of Mary Magdalene

The *Gospel of Mary* is a dialogue Gospel with apparent "gnostic" elements. In it Mary Magdalene stands forward as the "beloved disciple" of Jesus who reveals—from secret words given to her alone—his true teaching to the remainder of the disciples. This portrayal of Mary as Jesus's favorite is also found in several later works. Especially notable is the *Gospel of Philip,* also found in the Nag Hammadi codices (quoted at the beginning of this chapter), which is a collection of disparate sayings out of the same tradition. The *Gospel of Mary* dates to the late second cen-tury and is preserved in three principal manuscripts.[47] Two are fragmentary Greek papyri found at Oxyrhynchus and dating to the third century (*P.Ryl.* 463; *P.Oxy.* 3525). The third is somewhat more complete in a Coptic version akin to the Nag Hammadi codices and dating to the early fifth century.[48] The actual title "Gospel of Mary" appears as the *subscriptio* in two of these manuscripts.

The story breaks into three main parts. The first section, partially lost, is a dialogue between Jesus and the disciples. In it Jesus answers a question on the origins and nature of sin; instead of being a moral category, sin is a result of a cosmological disorder created by the mixing of matter and spirit.[49] At the end of this discourse Jesus departs with a commission for the disciples to go and preach, patterned perhaps after Matthew 28:18–20. The disciples are saddened by his departure, and Mary then starts to comfort them, saying:

> *Do not weep; do not be distressed; and let not your hearts be irresolute. For his grace will be with you all and will shelter you. Rather we should praise his greatness, for he has prepared us and made us true Humans.*[50]

At this point, the disciples begin to debate the meaning of Jesus's words.[51] Peter now asks Mary to reveal to them the secret words that Jesus had given to her (quoted at the beginning of this chapter).[52]

The revelation, the second section of the work, is in the form of a dialogue between Mary and Jesus, in which she asks him several questions. This idea may be based on *Gospel of Thomas* 21, where Mary asks Jesus, "Whom are your disciples like?" Other early Christian writers also referred to "gnostic" texts known as "Questions of Mary"; these otherwise lost texts may be referring to this same tradition.[53]

In the *Gospel of Mary,* her first question is about how visions are received. Jesus answers by explaining it in terms of the relation between soul, mind, and spirit, with the mind serving as the faculty of communication between soul and spirit.[54] Here the human soul is the principal object. After a gap in the text, her dialogue with Jesus resumes at their last exchange, as she now describes how the soul rises above the four material elements of the world into the realm of the spirit.[55] This release of the soul from its material bonds is understood as the process of spiritual salvation.

The third section of the text now opens with a dispute over Mary's words raised first by Andrew, who expresses doubts that Jesus had said such things. Peter then seconds Andrew's criticism and asks whether Jesus would speak to a woman about such things.[56] This scene may have resonances to the final saying in *Gospel of Thomas* 114, where Peter asks Jesus to make Mary leave them (see Chapter 14). Weeping, Mary now protests, saying she had neither made up these ideas nor lied. Then Levi rises to her defense. After commenting on Peter's bad temper, he expresses his trust in her and says, "Surely the Savior's knowledge of her is reliable. That is why he loved her more than us."[57] The text then ends with a final admonition from Levi in defense of Mary's teaching:

> *"Rather, we should be ashamed. We should clothe ourselves with the perfect Human, acquire it for ourselves as he commanded us, and announce the good news, not laying down any other rule or law that differs from what the Savior*

said [to Mary]." After [he had said these] things, they started going out [to] teach and to preach.[58]

This last section of the text, then, is meant to show tension between these "gnostic" groups and some form of institutional Christianity of the time.[59] The debate among the disciples over Jesus's words reflects debates among the various streams of Christianity. Other "gnostic" texts, such as *Pistis Sophia* and the Nag Hammadi *Gospel of the Egyptians,* seem to reflect this same tension. It may be that the first part of the text was originally a separate tradition, and the revelation of Mary and the conflict over it represent the amalgamation of these traditions. In any case, the text represents a current of esoteric theology on the nature of the soul and the process of spiritual salvation, given under the authority of Mary, as Jesus's beloved.

In one sense, the role of Mary Magdalene in this text, as in others that reflect similar traditions about her, constitute a kind of "filling the gaps" of their own. They are based in part on the unique place of Mary in the canonical Gospels, and especially Mark and Matthew, where she is the only one who sees the empty tomb. Even more important is the postresurrection encounter between Jesus and Mary in the Gospel of John (20:11–18). It gives tantalizing hints at a more intimate relationship between them that have long fueled other speculation. When combined with the tendency to amalgamate Mary with one or another of the nameless "loose" women known from earlier Gospels, such fanciful speculations are taken as clues to special knowledge.[60] These "gnostic" texts, however, tend to be extremely ascetic in rejecting all forms of materiality and human passion.

The *Gospel of Mary,* as with other texts from "gnostic" trajectories, provide a very firm sense of her role as the "intimate" of Jesus's divine persona, modeling her on the image of Sophia in earlier Jewish and Christian tradition. She now serves as the interpretive voice for the words of Jesus, in ways similar to Thomas in the *Gospel of Thomas.* At the same time, it pushes the theological speculation in new directions as gender symbolism, rather than twinship, is taken to embody mystical insights into the true "spiritual" nature of the divine realm and the pathway for human salvation.

The Gospel of Judas

Another "gnostic" dialogue is the *Gospel of Judas.* It too dates to the later second century and was mentioned by Irenaeus, writing in ca. 180 CE.[61] Until 1983, no actual manuscript of this work had been identified. Its overly sensational debut in a *National Geographic* "Easter special" has unfortunately suggested that it somehow revises our knowledge of the historical Judas and what really happened to Jesus.[62] Nothing could be farther from the truth. The *Gospel of Judas,* like the *Gospel of Mary,* is a later theological exploration predicated on using a character known from the canonical Gospels as an interpretive filter for a new way of understanding the teachings of Jesus or, more precisely, the theology about Jesus.

The manuscript containing the *Gospel of Judas* does not come from the Nag Hammadi codices, although it has affinities to them.[63] It is a Coptic manuscript (Codex Tchacos) of similar date and generally of the same type. Contained within the manuscript are other known "gnostic" texts from the same time.[64] It may well represent a different Christian "library" containing a mixed collection of canonical and apocryphal materials. Since the first publicity over the text, some of the claims over its radically "revisionist" picture of Judas have also been seriously reconsidered. Most important, rather than recasting Judas as Jesus's most faithful disciple and his confidant in preparing for the crucifixion (as proposed in the *National Geographic* account), recent analysis suggests an even more negative view of Judas than in the canonical tradition.[65] Yet, as we shall see, such a view would be entirely consistent with this type of "gnostic" theological speculation.

As we noted earlier (Chapter 7), the character of Judas changes in each successive account among the canonical Gospels. He goes from being a misguided revolutionary (Mark), to a disloyal friend (Matthew), to diabolical schemer (Luke), and finally to demonic antagonist (John). The play of each scene varies with the depiction to create the desired characterization and a suitable end. Significantly, Judas plays no role at all in the earliest oral tradition (from Paul) about Jesus's death, nor is he mentioned in the *Gospel of Thomas*. One feature of the evolving tradition about Jesus's death helped to raise further questions about Judas's role. The Synoptics stress the fact that Jesus must die, and Mark and Matthew, at least, show him to be filled with doubt, fear, and anxiety; on the cross he screams his sense of abandonment (Mark 14:34–42; Matt 26:38–46). In Luke, the sense of anguish is nearly gone (22:40–46), and the necessity of his death "by the definite foreknowledge and plan of God" is made emphatic (Luke 24:26, 46; Acts 2:23). By the time we get to the Gospel of John, however, Jesus knows fully what will happen to him and takes charge of the situation. He is serene and calm and seems not to suffer at all, even in the moment of death (18:4; 19:28–30). But if Jesus's death is a divinely ordained plan, and if he was fully aware and fully in charge of the events, what part did Judas really play? Was it really a "betrayal" after all? Or did he somehow help Jesus fulfill his mission? Could he resist the divine will? If not, how could Judas be faulted?

Such questions had apparently begun to arise by the time of the Gospel of John. Yet the Johannine tradition still stresses the death of Jesus. Docetic Christianity, including later gnostic streams, said that Jesus had not really suffered and died at all. According to Irenaeus, Basilides had claimed that the phantom Jesus escaped the cross and laughed at his would-be executioners as Simon of Cyrene died instead.[66] Such stories are clearly dependent on the Passion tradition found in the Synoptics, but they change the role of Judas. As we have seen, each narrative shift forces other dramatic accommodations.

The *Gospel of Judas* now offers an answer to this question from the perspective of a gnosticizing tradition. It opens with a dialogue between Jesus and the twelve disciples before and during the Passover (Last Supper). The disciples describe a nightmarish vision they have received and ask Jesus to explain its meaning. The dream is about the Temple and sacrificial animals, and Jesus interprets it allegorically to tell them that they must stop offering sacrifices. Although a portion of this section is missing, it seems to mean that they should stop thinking of his "death" as a sacrificial offering. Instead, they should try to deliver the souls of humanity as spiritual "first fruits" to God.[67]

Next Judas steps forward, but he stands apart from the twelve. He asks Jesus now to hear his vision. Laughing, Jesus replies, "Why do you compete [with them], O Thirteenth Demon?" (44.20–21). Judas now narrates his vision, describing how he saw the other disciples throwing stones at him and chasing him (44.24–26). After Jesus begins to interpret the dream and correct Judas for being led astray, Judas retorts, asking why Jesus has set him apart from their generations to be cursed (45.1–47.1). Jesus then begins to instruct him on the secret meaning of his dreams and his place in the divine drama. He begins to describe a gnostic view of the cosmic aeons and the powers that rule over each level (47.2–53.16). There follows a series of questions, including how spirits came into humans and whether they will die. After the exchange Jesus laughs at Judas, and the archons ("rulers") of the earthly realms, for thinking that they can contain his spirit and those of the elect (53.17–58.8).[68] Judas himself is one of the demonic archons rather than a human disciple. The text concludes with Judas having been shown his error, yet a captive to his own demonic fate, as he proceeds to bargain with the Temple priests to "betray" Jesus. In the end, we must imagine Jesus laughing. At this point we have reentered the synoptic narrative (roughly at Mark 14:10–11; Matt 26:14–16; Luke 22:3–6), and the text comes to an end (58.9–29).

As we see, this text assumes that the audience knows the basic story of Judas, perhaps in some composite form from the canonical tradition. Judas is already viewed as a hated figure, but "asks" why that should be so. He is thus a foil for the questions arising naturally in popular tradition by the latter half of the second century. Yet the answer is anything but a recapitulation of Judas, as might be expected if one were to focus simply on the "divine necessity" of Jesus's death. *Jesus Christ Superstar* will of course take it in this other direction. Instead, in the *Gospel of Judas* he is even more deluded and more demonic, because he belongs to the realm of worldly "rulers" who mistakenly think that they can in fact kill Jesus at all. In that sense, their mistake would seem to be a trap that allows the divine realm to release the human spirits that they have previously held captive.[69] At the same time, the other disciples have also had their misguided understanding corrected, as Jesus's "crucifixion" is not a sacrificial death either. In fact it is not a real death at all. Now as truly enlightened Gnostics, they are called upon to help deliver the human spirits back to God.

Harmony and Discord in the Gospel *Quire*[70]

Once again, we see how, by filling the gaps and creating new narratives or dialogues, the drama of Jesus can take on new colorations. In the final analysis each one of these expansions—whether later considered orthodox or not—relies on a knowledge of the earlier Gospels. By filling in gaps, harmonizing differences, and taking the story in new directions, they offer new filters for understanding the Gospel tradition. In effect, they create new dramas of Jesus. Yet, as we have seen, each earlier Gospel had essentially done the same thing.

There are thus three preliminary points to observe. First, the production of Gospel stories was not limited to those now in the Christian canon. As we have already seen, these early Gospels were a product of a dynamic, living process of storytelling within specific communities. The process continued without interruption as many others were produced for diverse types of Christian communities very much like the process that gave rise to Mark or John.

Second, these proliferating Gospels increasingly show awareness of one another, as we have already seen in the use of Mark in the writing of Matthew and Luke. There were also various lines of interaction in the composition of *Thomas* and John. Storytelling was thus a mechanism of creative interaction, of change and transformation, as well as a vehicle of faith.

Third, within this process of creating other new Gospels, there is little concern over "what really happened" to Jesus. This very modern notion was not part of ancient assumptions about storytelling or "history" (we shall return to this issue in the Epilogue). The competition and conflict seen among the Gospels—whether *among* the Synoptics, or *between* them and John or *Thomas,* or *between* all of these and later "apocryphal" Gospels—are really more about evolving beliefs and diverging faiths rather than alternative "histories." In that way too each new context and each new Gospel continues to produce a new image of Jesus. Even when there were conscious efforts to synthesize divergent traditions, as in the Gospel of John, it yielded a new drama. In the final analysis, the impulses and needs that produced the earliest Gospels continued unabated into the later centuries.

By way of conclusion, then, we may stop to reflect on the process by thinking about where the lines of authenticity should be drawn. Although I doubt that many will step forward to defend the rather extreme mythological schemes seen in some of these later Gnostic trajectories, it must still be said that some ancient Christians believed them as expressions of a true faith, even if they were not *true histories* as such. But then the Gospel of John did much the same with its recasting of the synoptic Passover/Last Supper narrative. What is the difference? Perhaps it comes down to the limits of diversity and disharmony.

What we tend to see in the evolving canonical form of the fourfold Gospel is that, for all their differences, they were still able to be held together, even if rather tenuously, by a basic narrative framework that included the ministry, miracles, teachings, and Passion of Jesus. The later battles of Christian history, first to form the canon of the New Testament and then to solve the subsequent trinitarian and Christological debates, may be seen at root to be a creative effort to work out the harmony between these very different, and sometimes discordant, stories. At the same time, we may become more aware that such a harmonized synthesis invariably obscures some of the distinctive features of earlier individual versions. There is, after all, insight and creativity to be seen in both. There is both encouragement and a warning in this realization. Scripting Jesus is now, and has always been, more about faith than about history. We will turn to this final issue in the Epilogue.

〰〰

Tales of Fancy, Acts of Faith

And early in the morning he came walking toward them on the sea. But when the disciples saw him walking on the sea, they were terrified, saying, "It is a ghost!" And they cried out in fear. But immediately Jesus spoke to them and said, "Take heart, it is I; do not be afraid." Peter answered him, "Lord, if it is you, command me to come to you on the water." He said, "Come." So Peter got out of the boat, started walking on the water, and came toward Jesus. But when he noticed the strong wind, he became frightened, and beginning to sink, he cried out, "Lord, save me!" Jesus immediately reached out his hand and caught him, saying to him, "You of little faith, why did you doubt?" When they got into the boat, the wind ceased. And those in the boat worshiped him, saying, "Truly you are the Son of God." (Matthew 14:25–33)

The Gospels are "faithful" stories about Jesus. By that I mean they were intended to inspire and instill faith in their audience. But as we have seen in the preceding chapters, the author of each Gospel does so by different means at the level of story. This fact is nowhere clearer than in the radically different birth narratives in the Gospels of Matthew and Luke (Chapter 10).

Oral traditions and basic story forms provided a stock of components—death and resurrection, miracles and sayings—for assembling each narrative, but the storytellers were perfectly free to alter older traditions or create new stories in order to articulate a message about Jesus. The Passion narrative grows and becomes more elaborate, with new episodes and insights. Miracles can take on new shape or be transformed into teaching stories. Isolated sayings can be moved around and combined in new ways to form longer discourses or sermons. Parables can be transformed into allegories to reflect new situations or stacked together to create new intertextual meanings. Through the medium of storytelling, traditions can be reshaped and rearranged—fused and blended, expanded or condensed, or omitted entirely. Each choice and variation inevitably yields a new narrative framework. As we saw in Act III, each Gospel is thus its own assemblage of components old and new, its own dramatization of Jesus's life and deeds—a new script. In the end, each script brings a new interpretation, a new image of Jesus.

The issue of faith or, more precisely, how they inculcate faith is paramount here. For example, the synoptic Gospels tend to address issues of faith by describing the different reactions of characters within the story, as we saw in the Markan motifs of secrecy and misunderstanding. A good example is the way that contrasting understandings of Jesus are juxtaposed in the double miracle of the woman with the hemorrhage and Jairus's daughter (Mark 5:21–43; see Chapter 9). In this way, characters in the story are meant to reflect matters of concern between the author and audience. Even so, the verb "to believe" only occurs thirty times in all three Synoptics combined; the derived noun "faith," only twenty-four times in all three. The majority of these occur in parallel passages drawn from Mark. The Gospel of John does some of this, but adds a new dimension as the author/narrator addresses the audience directly about belief:

> Now Jesus did many other signs in the presence of his disciples, which are not written in this book. But these are written **so that you may come to believe** that Jesus is the Messiah, the Son of God, and [so] **that through believing** you may have life in his name. (20:30–31)

The verb "believe" now becomes more of an issue, occurring ninety-eight times in John alone, while the noun "faith" does not occur at all. Even this linguistic trend shows basic differences in the portrayal of Jesus's words and thought.

A good example of the shaping and reshaping of these stories occurs in the Matthean adaptation of the second storm miracle, where Jesus walks on the water (Matt 14:22–33, quoted at the beginning of this chapter). It is one of the few miracles in the Gospel of Matthew that is actually longer than the corresponding story in Mark 6:45–52. In Mark, the emphasis is on the fear of the disciples and their lack of understanding:

> But when they saw him walking on the sea, they thought it was a ghost and cried out; for they all saw him and were terrified. But immediately he spoke to them and said, "Take heart, it is I; do not be afraid." Then he got into the boat with them and the wind ceased. And they were utterly astounded, for they did not understand about the loaves, but their hearts were hardened. (6:49–52)

The Markan ending is stark and enigmatic. The disciples do not quite get it. In the Markan drama their lack of understanding, even after they have seen Jesus calm a storm for a second time, becomes almost slapstick. But as the audience chuckles in amusement at the hapless disciples, they are simultaneously nodding assent to their own faith and understanding of the Markan message.

In sharp contrast, the Matthean author has added a new wrinkle to this same story by having Peter get out of the boat and walk on the water with Jesus. As his faith then wavers, Peter begins to sink, but Jesus saves him and warns him about doubt. At the end, when they get into the boat and the winds calm, the disciples all confess: "Truly you are the Son of God" (14:33). Thus, the Matthean author has added a new vignette to the basic miracle story that dramatically alters its character and meaning as a lesson about faith.

It also alters the picture of the disciples and their "faithful" understanding of Jesus. The phrase used of Peter, "you of little faith," however, is a distinctively Matthean fingerprint. In the Gospel of Matthew it becomes a repeated thematic device in addressing the disciples, as they progressively become more understanding and more faithful.[1] By changing the story, the Matthean author clearly seeks to dramatize faith for the audience, but in a different way to make a different point. Though we may rather easily catch the purpose of the Matthean alteration in the story, it does raise another question: Which one—Mark's or Matthew's—is more "historical"?

The uniquely Johannine miracle of healing a man born blind (9:1–41) shows a similar function, but with greater emphasis on the characters as examples. As Raymond Brown says, this closely knit story represents "Johannine dramatic skill at its best."[2] The miracle itself, although modeled on standard miracle form, is actually rather brief (9:6–8). The bulk of the story focuses on what transpired *after* the man was healed. It contrasts the blind man's belief in Jesus (9:13–17, 35–38) with the lack of belief of the Pharisees, who are portrayed anachronistically as synagogue officials (9:18–22). In a dramatic reversal, however, it is the blind man who ultimately teaches them about proper piety toward God (9:30–34). Brown calls this "one of the most cleverly written dialogues in the New Testament."[3] In turn, because of the man's steadfast belief in Jesus despite their threats, they finally cast him out of the synagogue (9:22, 34). At the end Jesus calls them "blind" (9:39–41), recouping the themes of blindness and light (and *enlightenment*) in a ring composition. So here again is a story meant to instill faith, but for whom?

In this case, however, we have a clearer clue what the author is up to; for the extreme nature of the opponents' response could hardly reflect the historical circumstances of Jesus's own day. The Pharisees had no such role as authorities in local synagogues at Jesus's time; they too were a minority sect. Nor were they some sort of "piety police," as depicted in John. These ideas are anachronistic, or worse. Instead, this Johannine story more accurately reflects the experience of later Christians, at a point in time when the growing tensions of separation from Judaism prompted "excommunications" on both sides.[4] The central play of the story, in which the blind man is expelled from the synagogue for confessing his belief in Jesus, emulates the tensions of this later period in Jewish-Christian relations.[5]

In other words, the Johannine author has retrojected an experience from a much later time into the life of Jesus by creating this fictional story, probably by elaborating on the healing of the blind stories from the other Gospels.

This internal reshaping of the story is then expanded thematically over several chapters of the Johannine narrative. As we noted in Chapter 14, the Johannine Gospel characteristically pairs such miracles with the "I am" discourses of Jesus. In this case, the "light of the world" discourse (8:12–20) mirrors and reinforces the miracle story. Its main theme is reprised at the beginning of the miracle story (9:5) and then brought full circle with the polemic about the Pharisee's blindness at the end (9:39–41). The discourse about Jesus as "light of the world" and the story of the blind man's "enlightenment" form an intertextual play about faith. The integral composition of these two stories is thus meant to serve as a commentary on later Christians' belief in Jesus and in the midst of growing anti-Jewish polemics. At the same time, it is deeply etched with themes from Christian baptismal symbolism and practice.[6]

This act of clever and creative storytelling, then, interweaves not only putative events and characters from the life of Jesus, but also circumstances and attitudes from the time of the author and audience. Nor is this a covert act or an exercise in deception. Rather, author and audience are consciously joined in a moment of suspended reality, as past and present—characters and audience—are blurred at the level of the story. Ultimately, the story is meant to shore up the faith of the audience, who are now Christians fully separate from Judaism, by arming them with a polemical edge against Jewish belief and practice. It is an overt act of sectarian self-definition for the Johannine community through dramatic storytelling.[7] History—at least as it relates to Jesus's own lifetime—recedes into the background.

What's Historical About Ancient "Lives"?

To be sure, Christian attitudes toward the Gospels (at least those in the canon) in later centuries tended to view them as factual "histories" of Jesus's life.[8] As early as the mid-second century CE, however, the radical differences among the Gospels were being noted, raising serious questions of believability and prompting the first efforts at harmonization.[9] Key concerns were raised about the historical reliability of the Gospels of Mark and John by the time of Clement of Alexandria (ca. 200 CE):

> *[Clement] said that among the Gospels, those containing the genealogies were written first, but that according to Mark had this dispensation: When Peter had publicly preached the word in Rome and by inspiration expounded the Gospel, those present, being many, encouraged Mark—as one who had followed him for a long time and remembered what had been said—to make a written account of what had been delivered orally. And having done so, he shared the Gospel with*

those who asked him. When it was disclosed to Peter imploringly, he neither forbid nor encouraged it. However, John, last of all, being conscious that the corpus [of the facts] had been made clear in the [prior] Gospels, was encouraged by those who knew him, and being divinely moved by the Spirit, he composed a **spiritual** *Gospel.*[10]

Apparently, this was Clement's way of accounting for the differences. The Markan Gospel was an "unauthorized biography," which Peter neither repudiated nor recommended. Notably, in contrast to the oral preaching of Peter and the composition of John, he does not call Mark "inspired." He says further that the Gospel of John made no pretense of being "historical," but was instead a "spiritual Gospel."

Yet such concerns were not present for the original author and audience of each Gospel, canonical and noncanonical alike. In part, this may be due to the fact that each of these Gospels was originally produced within a community of discourse for whom the stories already operated on another level of expectation, as we have earlier suggested for the Gospel of John (see the Prologue). The wider distribution of Gospels into new areas and the resultant problem of comparing their differences only came later, by a generation or two. We shall return to this point later.

Far more significant in understanding the original perception of the Gospels as stories is the literary and performative culture out of and for which they were produced. As has often been said, the ancient Gospels do not conform to modern notions of biography. Instead, they are closer to ancient "Lives," as a common literary type in the Greco-Roman world. As we saw earlier (Chapter 3) in the case of Philo's *Life of Moses* and Philostratus's *Life of Apollonius of Tyana*, such "Lives" tend to have novelistic elements as well as apologetic interests. These two examples, at least, clearly take the story in the direction of a divine-man representation of the hero. Suetonius and other imperial biographers did not hesitate to repeat the fabulous legends associated with the births and deaths of Julius Caesar and Octavian (Augustus). Suetonius recounts similar portents and legends for his subjects in his *Lives of the Poets* (ca. 120 CE), especially the more famous ones, such as Vergil. Consequently, divine-man traditions also influenced other types of "Lives."

Not all authors of "Lives" took this tack, however, choosing instead to use the genre as a moral paradigm or an intellectual compendium. Thus, the literary goal of the author further conditions the shape of the story. For example, *The Lives of the Eminent Philosophers,* by Diogenes Laertius (early third century CE), is far more concerned with the philosophical systems than with biographical details, except where such detail can be correlated with the philosophy.[11] In this work there are occasional efforts to sort out fact from fiction, as when the author attempts to distinguish genuine from spurious writings of the philosopher under discussion.[12]

Plutarch's *Parallel Lives,* written ca. 80–120 CE and thus contemporaneous with the writing of the Gospels, surveys forty-six lives in pairs, one Greek and one Roman—Solon and Publicola, Aristides and Cato the Elder, and so forth—so that the traits of one may be compared to the other.[13] Sometimes these comparisons are favorable; other times, critical. But it is also noteworthy that some are historical characters of relatively recent time, such as Cicero, Julius Caesar, Marc Antony, and Brutus, while others are legendary figures from Greek and Roman mythology, such as Theseus and Romulus. This arrangement thus presupposes an effort on the part of Plutarch to massage the characters to fit his program, even when he clearly had historical sources of information from which he could draw. His treatment of Alexander the Great is a good case in point, as Plutarch clearly incorporates elements of the legendary and romantic "Lives" of Alexander that predominated by the Roman period. Even with such differences of approach, Diogenes Laertius actually used Plutarch's *Parallel Lives* as one source. Sometimes Plutarch's moralizing sentiments creep into Diogenes' portrayals. Consequently, the problem of sources and how they are handled was no less acute for these Greek and Roman biographers than for the authors of the Gospels.

"Lives" as an Ancient Genre

The ancient biographical genre of "Lives" arose out of the genres of "history" and "memoir" in Greek tradition, beginning in the fifth century BCE. By contrast, there really was no independent biographical genre in Jewish literature, except where Greek influence was present.[14] For example, no comprehensive works on "the lives of the prophets" were composed except under Greek influence.[15] When we do get treatments of the careers of individual kings or prophets (such as David, Solomon, Samuel, Elijah, or Elisha), they are usually contained in larger national epics—such as the Deuteronomistic History—that are driven by thematic and theological concerns.[16] These narratives are sometimes called "sagas," and the treatment of individual characters is called "ideal [or idealized] biography."[17] Even then there are numerous legendary or fictional elements represented, as we saw in the miraculous traditions associated with Elijah and Elisha (Chapter 8).

Works associated with the name of an individual character in the Jewish tradition tend to be more novelistic in genre, as seen in the first six chapters of Daniel, Ruth, and Esther, all of which are rather late compositions from the Hellenistic period.[18] The creation of other fictional narratives may be seen in several Hellenistic Jewish romances, such as Tobit, Judith, and *Joseph and Aseneth,* all of which were composed in Greek.[19] The last purports to tell the story of Joseph's eventual marriage to an Egyptian wife. This fanciful tale carries the story well beyond the biblical legends; it serves ultimately as a theological apologetic for intermarriage and social interaction for a much later generation with a new set of cultural concerns.[20] These Greek writings were extremely influential in both Jewish and Christian tradition. The Jewish canon of scriptures was not codified in its present form until sometime in the first half of the second century CE, and only then were these Greek writings generally excluded.[21] In contrast, such Greek expansions continued to be used in Diaspora contexts for some time and were included in the early Christian canon up to and through the medieval period, in both the Latin and Greek Orthodox tradition.[22]

In studies of the development of the Greek biographical tradition, two principal streams are usually identified emerging from Aristotelian tradition. One stream (sometimes called the Peripatetic) is associated with Plutarch's *Parallel Lives*. The other stream (sometimes called the Alexandrian) is associated with Suetonius and Diogenes Laertius, who wrote *Lives of Illustrious Men* and *Eminent Philosophers*, respectively.[23] The former tends to be organized chronologically and manifest literary pretensions; the latter tends to be organized thematically and was more suitable to compendia of like types rather than just special individuals.[24]

These two types of "Lives" were recognized in ancient discussions of rhetoric and education. For example, in his *Institutes* 3.7.10–22, the Roman rhetorician Quintilian (ca. 70–90 CE) breaks the discussion of "Lives" into two groups, those deserving praise and those deserving denunciation.[25] Under praise he then describes two modes, which correspond to the two types discussed above:

> *Praise of character is always just [lit., true], but not in one way only is it given. It has sometimes proved more effective to trace a man's life and deeds in their chronological order, praising his natural gifts as a child, then his progress in school, and after this the whole course of his life, including words as well as deeds. At other times, however, it is well to divide our praise into the species of virtue—fortitude, justice, self-control, and the rest—and to assign to each of the virtues those deeds that were performed under its influence.*[26]

Likewise, under denunciation he adds the following:

> *The mind has as many vices as there are virtues, and these may be denounced, as virtue may be praised, in two different ways.*[27]

Here praise for a worthy life and denunciation for the opposite are set in terms of standard lists of virtues and vices. Quintilian then goes on to discuss the need for pleasing the audience, in some cases, and for conferring lasting disrepute, in others.[28] Such negative examples also form moral paradigms.

It is interesting to note also that the prime example Quintilian gives for such a "disreputable" life is Moses, "founder of the Jewish superstition."[29] In other words, Quintilian's "Life of Moses," if he had ever written one, would surely not portray him as a heroic leader and lawgiver.[30] Conversely, it is precisely this type of anti-Jewish polemic that prompted Philo and others to create their own, more positive portrayals of Moses. But both types—polemical and apologetic—give the story a spin to idealize the character in specific ways, whether good or bad. In contrast to modern notions of biography, the ancient genre was largely concerned with famous people as exemplary or representative *types;* almost all are thus more idealistic than realistic portrayals. Treatment of the unique, individual personality is rare.[31] The genre typically included background information on family and ethnic or tribal origins, plus signal episodes from the career and public life. All of these features tend to be drawn from standard story forms, as we saw earlier in Act II.

Realism and Idealism

The problem of idealism versus realism was certainly an issue for the ancient writers of the various subcategories of historical prose. It can be glimpsed in the rather different picture of Socrates that one gets from the ancient sources. For example, in Aristophanes' comedy *The Clouds,* written while Socrates was still alive, he is portrayed as a bombastic sophist, who only wants to teach youngsters how to become pseudo-intellectuals, like himself, in order to become rich and famous.[32] Of course a different picture emerges from Plato's *Dialogues* and the *Memorabilia* of Xenophon, both written in the generation or so after Socrates' death in 399 BCE. Both men knew Socrates personally and tried to retell his story in order to counteract his "defamation," as they saw it, when Socrates was condemned by the Athenian council. Plato was especially intent on removing the charge of "sophist" that had lingered from Aristophanes' parody. But the resulting "Lives" are noticeably different. Interestingly, Aristotle, who knew these works, classified the Socratic dialogues as a form of prose *mimesis* (or "mimes"), works that imitate reality, and thus as a category of fiction.[33]

In Xenophon there is less day-to-day detail of where, when, and to whom Socrates' teachings were delivered. What one finds are schematic renditions of his core ideas in rather simple, pedagogical form. The Socrates of Xenophon is a far more conventional moralist of the day. Plato's *Dialogues,* by contrast, are rather more dramatic and literary portrayals of the master with a great deal more philosophical refinement. In the later Platonic *Dialogues,* in particular, Socrates becomes little more than a mouthpiece for Plato's own maturing philosophical ideas. Even key moments of Socrates' verbal exchanges with his disciples change dramatically from one author to the next. In the final analysis, neither version is completely historical or "true." Both have apologetic intents, to reclaim Socrates' reputation and to further his ideas, at least as each author understood them and carried them forward.[34] To this day, the historical Socrates, or what is known as the "Socratic problem," remains something of a mystery. The Gospels operate in much the same way.

Dialogue and Invention

As Arnaldo Momigliano argues, apologetic speeches ostensibly delivered by a protagonist, such as Plato's *Apology of Socrates* or Isocrates' *Antidosis,* should also be understood as one of the prototypes of the ancient biographical genre.[35] In these cases, the putative words of the protagonist, whether historically accurate or not, are intended to establish a positive image. Conversely, the speeches of antagonists typically show their ignorance or malevolence. Thus, characterization, as we have already seen in the portrayal of the Pharisees in John 9 (and elsewhere in the Gospels), is an important mechanism for valorizing the plot and its outcome. Reality is another matter.[36]

In a famous passage, the Greek historian Thucydides defends the truthfulness of his "facts" in recounting the Peloponnesian War while simultaneously admitting that he himself had concocted many of the speeches he attributed to historical figures. A portion of his comment is worth quoting:

> As to the speeches that were made by different men [during the course of the war] . . . it has been difficult to recall with strict accuracy the words actually spoken, both for me as regards that which I myself heard, and for those who from various sources have brought me reports. Therefore, the speeches are given in the language in which, as it seemed to me, the several speakers would express . . . the sentiments most befitting the occasion.[37]

In other words, Thucydides admits to creating the speeches to make them fit the idealized situations he describes. But what does this statement suggest for later writers, such as Plutarch, who used Thucydides' speeches to compose "Lives" of any individual characters?

At the same time, Thucydides decries other chroniclers who "please the ear rather than telling the truth" by resorting to fabulous and incredible tales in the name of history.[38] Even the ancients were aware of the problem of using dreams to validate personal actions; inevitably, it seems, one only understands the "real" significance of the dream well after the fact, when the outcome has become clear.[39] But how did later outcomes reshape the memory of the dream? Or how would a later author know the real content of the dream any better than a speech? When does this practice constitute "history," and when is it self-serving apologetic? Why do author and audience give tacit acceptance to such patently fictitious rationalizations? One need only look at the "autobiography" of Josephus and others, to see the problem.[40] We shall return to Josephus a little later.

Such criticisms of other historians, however, became a conventional literary device in ancient history writing.[41] It may be seen in Seneca,[42] a contemporary of Paul, as well as in the preface of Herodian's *History of the Roman Empire*:

> Most of those engaged in compiling histories . . . show contempt for the truth and an excessive concern for vocabulary and style in their narratives, believing confidently that, even if they might mythologize to some extent, they would bear fruit from their hearers, while the accuracy of their records would not be criticized. And there are those who—either out of enmity and hatred toward tyranny or out of flattery for some emperor or city—bequeathed to benign and trivial deeds a sense of importance greater than truth deserves.[43]

Rather than promising an unvarnished historical exposé in any modern sense, Herodian's statement signals his conscious intent to provide an alternative *interpretation* of Rome's imperial history as seen from his vantage point in the early third century CE. His comments also reflect an awareness of the different biases from which other historians might have distorted history—some to decry tyranny; others to praise certain emperors or Rome itself. By the same token, Diogenes Laertius had his own agenda to promote, namely, to show that all philosophy was ultimately a Greek phenomenon and thereby the Greeks' contribution to world civilization.[44] Diogenes Laertius, Herodian, Cassius Dio, and Philostratus were, in fact, contemporaries, each with his own axe to grind in response to Roman imperial domination.

Truth and Fiction in Ancient Biography

To return to the biographical genre, then, we may note the self-consciousness with which Plutarch approaches the task of writing lives of figures from the distant and more mythical past. He opens his life of Theseus, whom he will pair with Romulus, as follows:

> *Just as among the geographers . . . , when even the most scientific (* historikos*)* *squeeze things eluding their knowledge onto the extreme edges of their charts,* *they add notes by way of explanation, saying* "**What lies beyond are waterless** **dunes full of wild beasts,**" *or* "**dark bog,**" *or* "**Scythian ice,**" *or* "**frozen** **sea,**" *so also in writing my Parallel Lives, now that I have passed beyond the* *period which is reachable by apparent reason and possible by narration of facts,* *I may well have to say concerning these earlier lives,* "**What lies beyond is full** **of wonders, inhabited by tragic poets and mythmakers; it has nothing of** **belief nor anything true.**" *But having produced my treatise on Lycurgus, the* *lawgiver, and Numa, the king, I thought it not unreasonable to go back farther* *to Romulus, since we are coming near his times in my narration, and I posed to* *myself the question . . .* "**Whom shall I pit against him? Who is up to the** **task?**" *It seemed to me that I must set against and compare the founder of fair* *and famed Athens to the father of invincible and glorious Rome. May I then* *subjugate Myth and take on a semblance of history for you, by purifying her [i.e.,* *Myth] with reason. But where she willfully refuses to become credible and turns* *away even a modicum of probability, I shall pray for kindly hearers—those that* *receive ancient tales in a gentle manner.*[45]

Two points are worth noting here. First, in contrast to the definition used by some modern scholars, Plutarch's comment clearly locates "Lives" somewhere between "myth" and "history." Second, facts, as he notes, are a rare commodity; credibility, in any absolute sense, is elusive at best. But it did not stop him from trying, and Plutarch's *Theseus* offers judgments on his deeds and character along the same lines of those for better-known historical figures.

A number of recent studies of Greek and Roman literature have now taken up these questions by probing the interrelationship between "truth" and "fiction" in ancient historical and biographical writings.[46] In this light, much of ancient historical prose, including memoirs and "Lives," was profoundly influenced by both epic poetry and novelistic or "romance" literature. The former stood prominently in the cultural background from the earlier Greek period; the latter increasingly became the popular medium of the later Roman period. The Gospels, and especially Luke-Acts, not to mention the plethora of apocryphal Gospels and Acts, have now regularly been compared to this novelistic medium. So how was ancient "fiction" conceived in relation to historical prose? Or to put it another way, what was the line of demarcation between "fiction" and "lies" in the minds of ancient storytellers and their audiences?

Contemporary Jewish "Lives"

Let's take two brief examples from contemporary Jewish tradition. The first is from the Jewish historian Josephus. It dates to the period during which the Gospels were being written. Joseph ben Mattathias was born in 37 CE, a Hasmonean descendant of a prominent Jerusalem family. He eventually commanded the Jewish revolutionary army in the Galilee at the beginning of the first revolt (66–67 CE). Josephus wrote his autobiographical "Life" with a strongly apologetic intent in light of his role in the war. Similarly, in his account *The Jewish War*, he describes his military exploits against the Romans in glowing terms. In one case he details his daring "naval" attack on a Roman garrison by commandeering a flotilla of local fishing boats to approach from the Sea of Galilee. In fact, it was all a ruse; the boats were empty. Yet he had thereby cleverly forced their city to surrender out of sheer terror.[47]

He also describes his realization that God had "called him"—through dreams, like a prophet—to help bring the war to an end. He only came to "realize" the import of these dreams when he was facing death in a cave after the defeat of his armies at Jotapata.[48] After all but one of his officers committed suicide, he went over to the Roman side, saying God had decreed that they should win the war. At that moment, he prayed to God, and he gives these exact words, or so he says:

> *Since it has been deemed by you to punish the tribe of the Judeans, whom you established, and fortune has crossed entirely to the Romans, and since you have chosen my very own soul to tell what is about to transpire, I, on the one hand, turn my hand to the Romans and go on living; on the other, I bear witness that I am no traitor. Rather, I go as your minister.*[49]

Through all of this Josephus was convinced that his survival was an act of divine intervention, because he had been chosen by God. He then recounts how he saw in a dream that the Roman general Vespasian, to whom he had surrendered, would become the next emperor, and how this revelation helped to endear him to the general.[50] He eventually wrote his *Jewish War, Antiquities,* and *Life* while living in Rome as a retainer of the Flavian imperial family. From them he took the name Flavius Josephus.

To suspect that his account of what transpired in the cave was a convenient, not to mention self-serving, fiction is perhaps obvious. Whether Josephus believed it or some of it might even be true is of little consequence. Along similar lines, both the Maccabean chronicles and rabbinic texts in the Mishnah and Talmud consciously employ fictional stories about the past, both distant and near, to convey important ideas.[51]

The second example dates to the time of Jesus himself. Philo's *Life of Moses* elaborates and transforms both biblical and extrabiblical traditions about Moses with a healthy dose of divine-man themes, and all for apologetic purposes. To put it another way, Philo intentionally recast the story of Moses in numerous ways, many of which are clearly fictional elaborations, in order to bolster belief on the part of other Jews and acceptance by non-Jews, both of whom had heard negative portrayals. The result is what we now would call a divine-man biography of Moses (as discussed in Chapter 3).

In this connection, it is useful to look more closely at the prologue to the second volume of Philo's *Life of Moses*. It has strong similarities in form and tone to the prologues of Luke and Acts. It also shows some of the thematic interests in Philo's recasting of the story. Here is how the second volume opens:

> *The former composition concerns, on the one hand, the birth of Moses and his upbringing, and yet, on the other, with his education and principles, which he conducted not only in a blameless manner but also in an exceedingly praiseworthy one. It also concerns the things accomplished in Egypt, and in the wanderings, both at the Red Sea and in the wilderness, which surpass the power of all words, and besides concerning the evils which he set right and the inheritance he apportioned to those who fought as soldiers. But what we now compose concerns the things deriving and following [from the first]. For it is said, and not off the mark, that thus only will cities advance toward the better, if their **kings practice philosophy or philosophers rule as kings**. But Moses will be found to have displayed, and more, to have combined in his single person, not only these two powers—the kingly and the philosophical—but also three others, one of which is concerned with law-giving, the second with the offices of the high priest, and the last with prophecy.[52]*

The first thing to note here is that, historically speaking, Moses was neither a king, a philosopher, nor the high priest of Israel.[53] Even the notion of "law-giving" here used by Philo reflects the Greek tradition of the founding of Athens as a way of depicting Moses's reception of the law on Sinai.

It is rather clear, then, that Philo is shaping the image of Moses in certain ways to speak to his Greek cultural context. Even the political maxim he cites, that "kings practice philosophy or philosophers rule as kings," is a nearly verbatim quotation of a rather famous saying of Socrates, at least as presented by Plato.[54] We observed the same saying earlier, as used by a first-century Stoic writer, Musonius Rufus, a contemporary of Paul (see Chapter 13). There we saw how Lukan themes in the portrayal of Jesus took a similar line. The point, once again, is that ancient "Lives" were not governed by modern notions of history. Even Philo, who was still largely following the biblical account of Moses's life from the book of Exodus, felt free to expand and reshape it to fit his apologetic goals and cultural context.

Homer: Fact or Fiction?

One way of probing ancient sensibilities regarding history and fiction is to think of the role of the Homeric epics in Greek and Roman culture. The *Iliad* and *Odyssey* have often been called the "Bible of the ancient world." But how or to what extent were they actually believed by the ancients? The answer, for the most part, is that few people questioned the basic historical "facts" surrounding the Trojan War and therefore the historicity of at least basic characters and episodes. In some measure, they were considered "divinely inspired" by the Muses themselves.[55] Their logic ran like this: "If such stories had been handed down by our cultural ancestors, they must be based on *something*."[56] Of course, the answer is very different now.[57]

Even so, by the Roman period much in Homer was interpreted allegorically, especially in philosophical circles, precisely because the mythological elements could no longer be considered "real" in any literal sense.[58] The process had already begun in classical Greece, as seen in Plato's *Timaeus*. Plato himself had said, "Hesiod and Homer and the other poets . . . composed false stories which they told people and are still telling them."[59] From the mid-first century CE comes the little-known work of L. Annaeus Cornutus, house pedagogue of Seneca's family and the teacher of the Roman poets Persius and Lucan. Entitled *An Excursus on the Traditions of Greek Theology*, his treatise is a tour de force allegorization of Greek myth through the lens of Stoic philosophy and physics.[60] In it, Zeus becomes the "Worldsoul," Hera is "air"; Hermes, the messenger, is the rational *logos* that pervades all of nature and infiltrates the human soul, while Athena is the intelligence of Zeus who acts as Providence. This tradition of allegorical interpretation directly influenced the reading of biblical stories by Philo and other Jewish allegorists as well as early Christian allegorists such as Clement of Alexandria and Origen.[61]

Even more to the point is Dio Chrysostom's *Oration* 11. Perhaps the most famous orator of the later first century CE, Dio was born ca. 40–50 CE at Prusa in the Roman province of Bithynia; his career as an orator began near the end of Nero's reign (ca. 68 CE). After experiencing fame under Titus (79–81) and then exile under Domitian (81–96), he was returned to his former status under Trajan (98–117).[62] His career thus spans the precise period during which the Gospels were being composed. Delivered between 71 and 80 CE at Roman Troas (Troy or Ilium), the *Trojan Oration*, as it is called, takes as its theme that Troy's present-day citizens ought to be roundly criticized for ever believing what Homer had recounted about their ancestors. Homer, he sets out to prove, was a liar and makes many false statements about the events of the Trojan War. Here is the opening section of his speech:

> *I am all but certain that it is difficult to teach the whole of humanity, but it is easy to deceive them. . . . Or how is it that falsehood should seem stronger than truth, if it did not win the victory through pleasure? But whereas, it is hard to teach [humans], as I said, reeducating them anew is far harder still, especially when they have been used to hearing lies for a long time. . . . Thus, even now I would not be amazed at you, men of Ilium, if you decided to consider Homer more faithful—despite his telling the most troublesome lies against you—than me, when I tell you the truth.[63]*

Now it has been plausibly argued that Dio was engaged in a farcical exercise of rhetorical hyperbole to show his powers of persuasion and that he never really intended to deny the total credibility of Homer or the Trojan War.[64] He is well known for using feigned criticism of his audience to make his point. On the other hand, Dio elsewhere raises questions of Homer's intentions, while still praising his style.[65] In the *Trojan Oration* he argues insightfully that the death of Patroclus was fictitious and modeled on what really happened to Achilles.[66] At the least, it shows that questions about the historicity of the Homeric epics were not beyond the pale.[67] Similar criticisms had also been raised of Hesiod, Herodotus, and others.[68]

Fiction and Verisimilitude

In discussing the notion of fiction in antiquity as it relates to the rise of novelistic literature, classics scholar David Konstan says:

> *If fiction is simply that which is not fact, then much of what is called history will come under the rubric of fiction. This is too broad: fiction is not the same as falsehood, which in turn may be subdivided into the two categories of lies and error, depending on whether the deception is intentional or not.[69]*

He then goes on to argue that fiction as a literary genre is different from myth or history in that it contains an implied contract between author and audience to enter the fictive world of the story. Here he cites the distinction drawn by Quintilian:

We have three types of narrative: **myth,** *which you get in tragedies and poets [i.e., epics], and which is removed not only from truth but the appearance of truth;* **fictitious story** *[Lat.* argumentum, *Gk.* plasma*], which comedies invent—false but verisimilitudinous; and* **history,** *in which there is an exposition of something that actually happened.*[70]

According to this definition, then, Homer is myth, and Thucydides is history. But the latter, as we have already seen, admits to creative elaboration in reconstructing the words and actions of certain individuals.[71] The comedies, novels, and other works are fiction. What makes them fiction is that they are not based on any real characters or, if the characters were real, not based on actual events, yet they seem "real" ("verisimilitudinous") nonetheless. This type of fiction may be seen in Plato's own experiment with the fictional story of Atlantis, which in its literary context was prompted by Socrates' urging that he describe the ideal state. Whether it is based on any kernel of historical reality is beside the point; its inherent "truth" resides in its expression of agreed-on values of the world inhabited by the author and audience, rather than the putative world of the Atlantians themselves.[72]

On this basis, then, it seems that ancient Greek and Roman culture operated with an implicit—and sometimes explicit—distinction between "fiction" and "lies."[73] For the ancients, fiction in any strict literary sense should be limited to stories of strange worlds, such as those seen in the Greek novels or the apocryphal Acts. By virtue of their verisimilitudinous correspondence with reality they nonetheless evoke truths. Such fictions did not intend to deceive but to inspire a better perception of reality, at least as the writers understood it.[74] It may well be that the genre of the novel emerged from the plots and spirit of New Comedy combined with the narrative prose of history and rhetorical style of Second Sophistic oratory.[75] It was also related to the development of the biographical genre.[76]

A good example comes from the extant fragments of speeches by Marcus Antonius Polemo, the city rhetorician of Smyrna in the early second century. Two of them are extended fictional "funeral speeches" for heroes of the battle of Marathon, which had taken place some six hundred years earlier (in 490 BCE).[77] The nature of the fiction is explicit: they are posed in the first person as if being delivered by the fathers who are looking at their sons' bodies after being returned to Athens. In this way the speech is full of verisimilitudinous detail of the battle and of the heroes' personal traits and exploits. But the fabulous is also present. In one, the young Greek hero Cynegirus was so valiant in battle that even after his arm was severed from his dead body, it continued to fight all by itself. In the other, the whole body of the hero Callimachus exhibited its true valor and loyalty to Athens by refusing to fall over even after he was killed; the young hero continued to stand tall even in death, like a guardian statue. These stories are thus a blend of oratory, history, humor, and biography, but they were clearly recognized by the audience to be entirely fictional. In their time the speeches of Polemo were famous as both entertainment and patriotic reminiscence of the glorious Greek past.

By the same token, both history and biography in antiquity carried many of these fictional aspects, insofar as they were based loosely on an event or character, even when the overall story line and its narrative details could be freely invented by the author. The difference was merely the degree of "fictiveness" at work in creating the story.[78] Such fictionalized narratives in this broader sense—what I have here called "tales of fancy"—also rely on the implicit contract between author and audience to convey a "truth" even though it is not in itself a true story. On the whole, then, most ancient histories and biographies created and maintained extended fictions around known events and persons in an effort to convey messages or meanings their authors believed to be true. Such works were intended to be both didactic and persuasive. Rhetoric and drama were apt tools to both ends.[79] The ancient authors were more interested in the lessons to be learned than the facts themselves.[80] Of necessity, author and audience had to accept the fictionality of the story being told, while recognizing and believing the underlying truths being expressed.

The Gospels as Ancient "Lives"

Although some scholars have questioned whether the Gospels properly belong to the ancient genre of "Lives," it is now widely accepted that they do.[81] The Gospels reflect the same problems of history and fiction discussed above. Those who have argued that they should be understood rather as extensions of the oral kerygma (or proclamation) about Jesus or as primarily liturgical expositions[82] do not account for the dramatic, rhetorical, and thematic elements that drive the Gospels as stories.[83] As we have seen, both suggestions have a legitimate part in shaping the Gospels as performance narratives. The Lukan version of the rejection at Nazareth is a good example, as it creates a new outlook for Jesus's ministry from its start (see Chapter 13). Equally important is the Matthean creation of five lengthy sermons, both as a way of restructuring the career of Jesus and as a way of creating a distinctively Jewish image of him.

Likewise, the Gospels were forged out of the storytelling cultures, both Jewish and Greco-Roman, in which they were born. Consequently, the one who steps into the ancient fictive world of the Gospels knowing little of their notions of history and fiction risks much. Claims of sameness to Greek and Roman histories and "Lives"—because the Gospels are "historical" rather than fictitious—are out of tune. Claims of difference from them—because the Gospels are uniquely "true"—ring hollow. In content, form, and function, the Gospels are ancient "Lives" and written with all the same literary and historiographical conventions.[84] That is not to say that nothing in them is historical or that everything was made up. Yet, in the end, they must still be read as dramatized and idealized narratives. Each had its own spin and message and its own image of Jesus.

That having been said, however, it remains to ask: How are they intended to convey their message and thereby to inculcate faith? The Gospels as stories are not merely confessional statements or creedal formulations. Anything but. To read them as straight-on statements to be repeated confessionally is to miss the point altogether. As we have seen, most of the early Gospels, including many of the noncanonical texts, operate by narrative indirection and dramatic irony. This is especially true of the Gospel of Mark, as we saw in Chapter 11. It gives a picture of a Jesus who conceals his identity and message from all but his closest disciples; but even when they are shown the secret, they fail to comprehend it. At each of these turns, however, the audience is expected to understand the message that characters within the story fail to grasp. The audience is thus called upon to enter the fictive world of the characters and react to them.

Nor is it the case, as is so often assumed, that the Gospels were written as missionary tracts whose primary audience was nonbelievers. Instead, the principal audience was the community of faith to which each one was addressed and for which it was produced. Even most apologetic literature, such as Philo's *Life of Moses,* was directed first at other insiders, in this case Jews, and then indirectly at outsiders, or more precisely at the prejudices of outsiders against Moses and Judaism. In that sense, the Gospels emerged organically from the storytelling medium and from older units of oral tradition. These components were already being combined in innovative ways within the dynamic context of an ongoing communal dialogue focused on the figure of Jesus as the object of faith while simultaneously facing new political, social, and religious challenges. The apologetic function is important, because it seeks to address ongoing questions arising within the community, where external forces have fueled the questions and raised, even minimally, issues of doubt. Hence, this apologetic function, whether explicit or implicit in structuring the story, shapes the way the story of Jesus was told. It sets key themes and parameters. It raises questions of authority and piety.

In both these respects the storytelling medium assumes at its base an ongoing dialogue within the community. This fundamental dynamic also means that the author and audience already shared a set of assumed beliefs as well as questions about the story of Jesus as operative within their community of discourse and worship.[85] I would also argue that what we now know as the written Gospels are merely the last versions of scripts that had been performed or heard many times before.[86] Coming from our modern world, where books and movies are hastily consumed and replaced, we often forget that ancient literature was "read"—that is, read aloud or performed—over and over again. Like other ancient "Lives," these stories were meant to be heard and to serve as a common ground for building communal identity and understanding.[87] In that sense, they are like dramatic plays in many ways, but plays that had been performed many times before.

For this reason, we may think of these *texts*—as we now know them—primarily as *scripts* of, or for, an oral performance. The audience knew what was coming and could recognize nuanced changes and adaptations. In other words, the clever rhetoric and inside jokes that the original audience knew and took for granted are usually opaque to outsiders. It is especially difficult for modern readers to reenter that ancient realm of discourse and to "know" what the ancient author *and* audience assumed, but the same was even true of other audiences in the ancient world. This fact may help to explain why the later Gospels—canonical as well as apocryphal—sometimes misunderstand and reinterpret elements in the earlier sources. Within their original settings, however, this process allowed for constant refinement and adaptation of the story.

In the end, I would liken it to any stage performance where performers rehearse and polish the same piece over and over again. Sometimes they may try a new twist or nuance in shaping a character or episode, or they may introduce a whole new vignette and rework the surrounding story to smooth it into the plotline. If it works, it stays; if it does not, it goes. With such dramatic experimentation the story becomes richer and more nuanced. Yet the audience will be able to catch the rhetorical ploys and allusions because they are part of the process. In each case, the audience's reaction and interaction is a catalyst, and each new performance allows for further modification. This is the same process we glimpsed earlier (Chapter 5) in the initial stages of development of the oral tradition as a performative and repetitive process. The interactive process of storytelling helps to forge the community of discourse. In turn, the communal discourse helps to forge the narrative world of the story. In this way too the Gospels, as tales of fancy, may nonetheless be acts of faith.

APPENDIX A

∽∾∽

The Geography of Jesus's World

The region of Judea underwent several important political changes during and after the time of Jesus.[1] According to the Gospels of Matthew (2:1; 2:19–23) and Luke (1:5, 26), Jesus was born before 4 BCE, while Herod the Great was still alive. According to the Gospel of Luke (3:1), he began his ministry about 26–28 CE, depending on how one calculates the "fifteenth year of the reign of Emperor Tiberius," while Pontius Pilate was governor of the Roman province of Judea.[2] By that time, Judea had undergone two changes in political administration that resulted in boundary modifications.

Map A.1 reflects the boundaries that would have existed during Jesus's lifetime. Prior to 4 BCE, the entire region was under the direct rule of Herod the Great as client-king of Judea. After Herod died in 4 BCE, his kingdom was divided among three of his sons: Archelaus in Judea proper, Antipas in Galilee, and Philip in Iturea and Trachonitis.[3] Antipas and Philip had long and relatively stable reigns, lasting until 37 and 34 CE, respectively, but Archelaus was deposed by Augustus in 6 CE. He was replaced by a Roman governor, and Judea became a Roman province for the first time. The regions of Antipas and Philip continued as client-kingdoms, or "tetrarchies." According to Josephus and other historical sources, the census under Quirinius (Luke 2:1) took place at this time (see Chapter 10 and Box 10.2). This situation continued to 41 CE.

The geographical divisions reflected in Map A.1 were the political reality during the entire adult life of Jesus.[4] After Jesus's death, however, the situation changed again, and would change several more times while the Gospels were being developed. After Philip died (34 CE) and Antipas was deposed (37 CE), a grandson of Herod the Great was sent to take over their two tetrarchies. His name was Herod Agrippa I, and he was sent by his friend, the emperor Gaius, better known as Caligula (37–41 CE; cf. Acts 12:1–4). In 41, Caligula named Agrippa ruler over a reunited "Kingdom of Judea"; however, Agrippa died suddenly in 44 CE. At that point in time, the entire Herodian kingdom became the Roman province of Judea.

Some years later (in 52 CE), the son of Agrippa, Herod Agrippa II, was named ruler of a new tetrarchy composed of Iturea and Trachonitis (Philip's territories), plus a portion of the Galilee. These two divisions, the province of Judea, ruled by a Roman governor, and Agrippa's tetrarchy, persisted down to the death of Agrippa II ca. 92–93 CE and are reflected in Acts 23–26. During the period of the first Jewish revolt (66–74 CE), however, the province and some of Agrippa's territory were placed under a Roman commanding general. After 74 the bulk of Agrippa's territory was restored.

Map A.2, therefore, reflects the political boundaries that would have been operative during the early period of the growth of the Jesus movement and during the time that letters of Paul (ca. 50–58 CE), the Q tradition (ca. 60–70), and the Gospel of Mark (ca. 70–75) were being written. The Gospel of Matthew (ca. 80–90/93) probably came near the end of this period or just after.

After the death of Agrippa II, his territories were reabsorbed into the Roman provincial structure. The areas to the west, including the Galilee and Bethsaida, were rejoined to Judea, while the areas to the east were annexed to the province of Syria. Eventually, the old Nabatean kingdom to the south and east was transformed into the province of Arabia in 106 CE. This was the political situation down to the time of the second Jewish revolt in 132 CE and is reflected in Map A.3. The Gospels of Luke (ca. 90–100), *Thomas* (ca. 90–110), and John (ca. 100–120) were all written during this period. For the implications within the Gospel narratives, see Appendix E below.

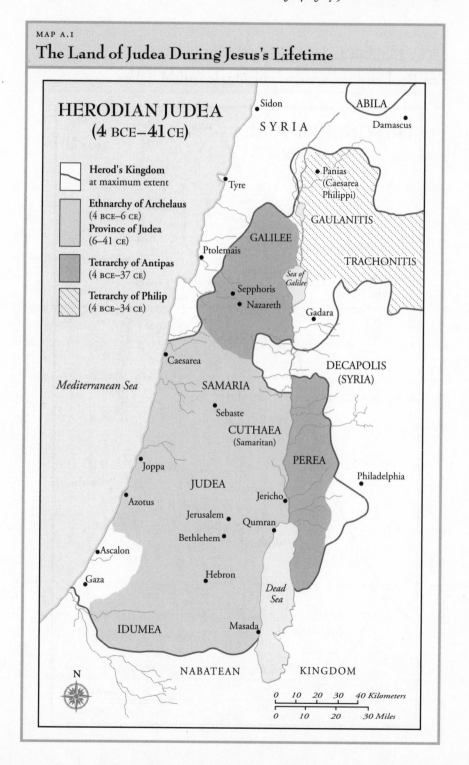

MAP A.I

The Land of Judea During Jesus's Lifetime

HERODIAN JUDEA
(4 BCE–41 CE)

Herod's Kingdom
at maximum extent

Ethnarchy of Archelaus
(4 BCE–6 CE)
Province of Judea
(6–41 CE)

Tetrarchy of Antipas
(4 BCE–37 CE)

Tetrarchy of Philip
(4 BCE–34 CE)

Sidon

ABILA

SYRIA

Damascus

Tyre

Panias
(Caesarea
Philippi)

GAULANITIS

GALILEE

TRACHONITIS

Ptolemais

Sea of
Galilee

Sepphoris

Nazareth

Gadara

Caesarea

DECAPOLIS
(SYRIA)

Mediterranean Sea

SAMARIA

Sebaste

CUTHAEA
(Samaritan)

PEREA

Joppa

Philadelphia

JUDEA

Azotus

Jericho

Jerusalem

Qumran

Bethlehem

Ascalon

Hebron

Gaza

Dead
Sea

IDUMEA

Masada

N

NABATEAN

KINGDOM

0   10   20   30   40 Kilometers

0   10   20   30 Miles

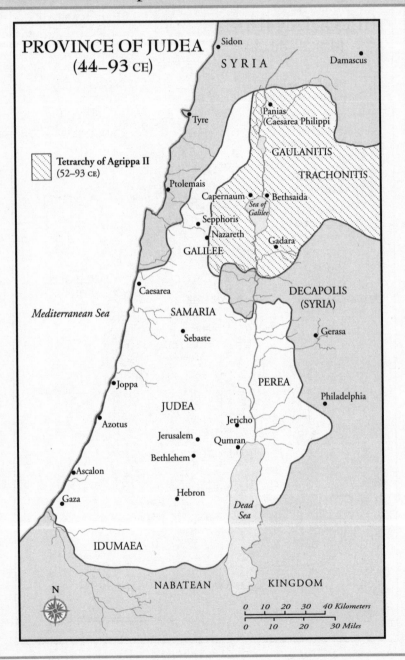

MAP A.2

The Land of Judea During the Time
of Paul and the Gospels of Mark and Matthew

PROVINCE OF JUDEA
(44–93 CE)

SYRIA

Sidon

Damascus

Tyre

Panias
(Caesarea Philippi)

GAULANITIS

TRACHONITIS

Tetrarchy of Agrippa II
(52–93 CE)

Ptolemais

Capernaum · Bethsaida
Sea of
Galilee

Sepphoris

Nazareth

Gadara

GALILEE

Caesarea

DECAPOLIS
(SYRIA)

Mediterranean Sea

SAMARIA

Sebaste

Gerasa

Joppa

PEREA

Philadelphia

JUDEA

Azotus

Jericho

Jerusalem

Qumran

Bethlehem

Ascalon

Gaza

Hebron

Dead
Sea

IDUMAEA

N

NABATEAN   KINGDOM

0   10   20   30   40 Kilometers

0   10   20   30 Miles

The Land of Judea During the Time
of the Gospels of Luke and John

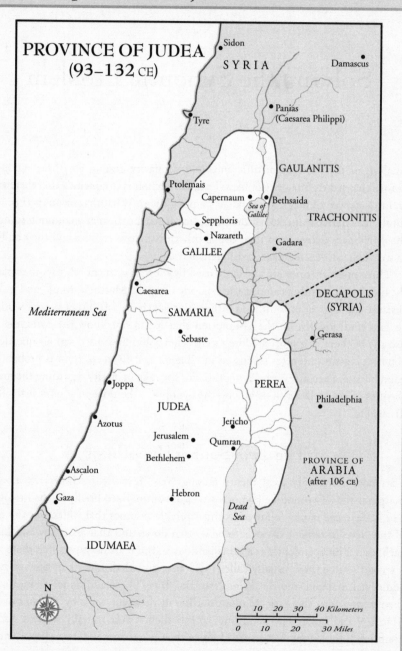

PROVINCE OF JUDEA
(93–132 CE)

Sidon

SYRIA

Damascus

Panias
(Caesarea Philippi)

Tyre

GAULANITIS

Ptolemais

Capernaum • Bethsaida

Sea of
Galilee

TRACHONITIS

Sepphoris

Nazareth

Gadara

GALILEE

Caesarea

DECAPOLIS
(SYRIA)

Mediterranean Sea

SAMARIA

Sebaste

Gerasa

Joppa

PEREA

JUDEA

Philadelphia

Azotus

Jericho

Jerusalem • Qumran

Bethlehem

PROVINCE OF
ARABIA
(after 106 CE)

Ascalon

Gaza

Hebron

*Dead
Sea*

IDUMAEA

N

0   10   20   30   40 Kilometers

0   10   20   30 Miles

Solving the Synoptic Problem

Analysis of the patterns of difference and similarity among the three synoptic Gospels has led the majority of New Testament scholars to conclude that there was an intricate web of literary dependency among them. What that means is this: the similarities derive from two of the Synoptics using the third as a common source; the differences derive from their use of other distinctive sources and their ability to weave the stories together in different ways.

Three main theories are currently used by New Testament scholars to explain the literary relationships among the synoptic Gospels: Matthew, Mark, and Luke. Because the Gospel of John is so different, it is usually left out of these theories, at least traditionally, on the assumption that it did not know the Synoptics or use any of them as a source. More recent scholarship has raised serious questions about this assumption (as discussed in Chapter 14). Even so, John is probably a good bit later than any of the Synoptics. For the sake of clarity regarding the main theories of interrelationships among the Synoptics, then, we may omit it for this discussion.

The Two-Source Hypothesis

The most commonly used theory among New Testament scholars by a wide margin is the "Two-Source Hypothesis." It is summarized briefly in the Prologue and is the basic model followed in this study. It assumes that Mark was the first of the New Testament Gospels to be written down and that Matthew and Luke each used it independently as a principal source. But it also assumes that there was a second source (now usually called "Q") that provided more than 250 verses of additional material, mostly sayings (see Box B.I). These additional sayings were then woven into the basic Markan outline in different ways by the authors of Matthew and Luke. The main lines of this theory were initially worked out by Heinrich Julius Holtzman in 1863.[1] Since then it has received considerably more

BOX B.I

The Two-Source Hypothesis

The majority opinion among biblical scholars; first proposed in 1863; stresses Markan priority.

Mark was written first, and Matthew and Luke both used it as a source. Matthew and Luke also used a second source, usually called "Q," as well as other unique materials.

```
                          Oral Tradition

            M        Mark            Q              L

                 Matthew                   Luke
```

---

sophisticated and nuanced treatment based on the nature of oral tradition and lines of transmission.[2]

Not all New Testament scholars have accepted the Two-Source Hypothesis, but those who do not are a small minority. Other theories have been proposed over the years, but none of them have much of a following among New Testament scholars.[3] The two main alternatives now cited are noteworthy for what they also suggest about the process of composition of the Gospels. Both of them are skeptical that a separate Q source ever existed or that it exercised such a profound influence. These two theories, discussed in turn, are the "Two-Gospel Hypothesis" and the "Farrer-Goulder Hypothesis."

The Two-Gospel Hypothesis

What is usually now called the Two-Gospel Hypothesis was first developed in the 1780s and popularized by Johann Griesbach. It is sometimes still called the "Griesbach Hypothesis."[4] Working from traditional assumptions about the chronological order of the canonical Gospels going back to St. Augustine, it proposes that Matthew was written first. Augustine had called "Mark" the abbreviator of Matthew. Thus the Two-Gospel Hypothesis argues that the Gospel of Matthew had a unique source for the teachings of Jesus (sometimes called "M"). It thus contained all of the Q materials as identified by the Two-Source Hypothesis. The Matthean narrative order (rather than the Markan) established the basic outline for the synoptic tradition, including the Passion narrative.

It further argues that Luke was based on Matthew, but made some major changes in the order and contents. Finally, Mark was composed as a blending of

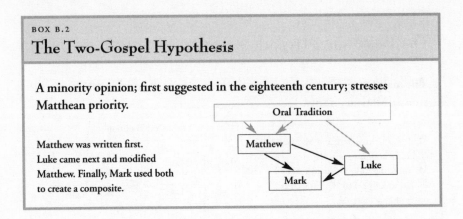

BOX B.2

The Two-Gospel Hypothesis

A minority opinion; first suggested in the eighteenth century; stresses Matthean priority.

Matthew was written first.
Luke came next and modified
Matthew. Finally, Mark used both
to create a composite.

the two, sometimes following Matthew and sometimes Luke.[5] This theory was revived largely in the 1970s and is followed by a small but very dedicated group of scholars.[6] What it does not explain is how or why the Markan author would so consistently delete the additional sayings material found in Matthew and in Luke, even to the point of providing no sermons of Jesus's at all (see Box B.2).

The Farrer-Goulder Hypothesis

The third hypothesis appears to be something of a compromise theory. It accepts the view that Mark was written first, but denies the existence of "Q." First propounded by J. H. Ropes in 1934 but then popularized by Austin Farrer (1952) and Michael Goulder (1974), it is now usually called the Farrer-Goulder Hypothesis. It explains the relationships by arguing that Matthew was based on Mark and added the Q material. Then Luke independently rewrote Mark but used Matthew as a second source, but only for its added Q material, which it then freely modified (see Box B.3). Though this theory has gained some adherents, they are still a small minority.[7] What it does not explain is how or why Luke would have deconstructed so much of the Matthean material, especially the sermons of Jesus, in order to revert to the Markan outline, while taking most of the same sayings material found in the Matthean sermons and redistributing it in the narrative.

Difficulties with the Alternative Hypotheses

One difficulty with each of these two alternative theories is the rather sharp differences in order and content between Matthew and Luke, seen especially in their respective birth narratives. In order to argue that Luke used Matthew as a direct source, as they both do, they must assume that the author of Luke was willing

BOX B.3

The Farrer-Goulder Hypothesis

A minority opinion; first suggested in 1934; supports Markan priority.

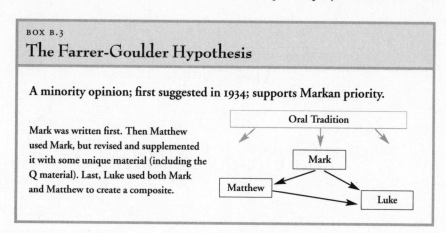

Mark was written first. Then Matthew used Mark, but revised and supplemented it with some unique material (including the Q material). Last, Luke used both Mark and Matthew to create a composite.

to make much more radical changes in the contents of its source Gospels than the Two-Source Hypothesis assumes. In other words, the Two-Source Hypothesis calls for a more benign view of the authorial process by having Matthew and Luke independently make changes and additions to Mark and the Q source.

In addition, there are a number of episodes found in all three Gospels that in Luke contain details found only in the Markan version but not in the Matthean. A good example is the miracle of the boy with the demon (Mark 9:14–29; cf. Luke 9:37–43; Matt 17:14–21). Similarly, in the case of Q materials, the Lukan version shows awareness of elements not found in Matthew. Another good example is the parable of the great banquet (Luke 14:15–24; cf. Matt 21:1–10). In particular, the pattern of the excuses of the invited guests is missing in Matthew, but present in Luke. Comparison of the version in the *Gospel of Thomas* suggests that these excuses are original to the parable. It appears, therefore, that the Lukan version of this material depends on something other than Matthew, which both of the alternative theories say is its source for the Q elements.[8] Finally, the feeding of the five thousand story occurs at Bethsaida in the Gospel of Luke (9:10–17), and this location can only come from Mark, as all references to Jesus visiting Bethsaida are missing from Matthew (see Chapter 13 and Appendix E). Consequently, neither the Two-Gospel Hypothesis nor the Farrer-Goulder Hypothesis adequately explains all of these literary relationships.

The Gospel of Peter

The *Gospel of Peter,* as we now know it, was discovered in a single, partial manuscript in a tomb in Akhmim, Egypt, in the late nineteenth century.[1] Based on burial artifacts, the tomb dates to the eighth–ninth centuries CE; this fact indicates that the particular manuscript is a later copy. The text was contained within a Greek codex with several documents, most copied by a single scribe.

Since then other fragments of the text have been confirmed among the papyri at Oxyrhynchus, one of the richest sources for early Christian papyri. This copy dates to the beginning of the third century CE. It comprises two fragments, originally discovered in 1972 and published as *P.Oxy.* 2949; they correspond at least partially with one extant portion of the Akhmim text (*Gos. Pet.* 2.3–5).[2] As a result, the *Gospel of Peter* may be dated to the later second century CE.

Further testimony of its existence by this time comes from references to a "Gospel put forward in the name of Peter" by the Christian writer Serapion, bishop of Antioch between 180 and 192 CE.[3] The comments of Serapion also suggest that it was circulating in Asia Minor (Turkey), while he had himself only come to know the text lately, in the context of debates over its authenticity as a writing of Peter. In its present form, the *Gospel of Peter* is clearly a product of the second century and depends on knowledge of the canonical Gospels.[4] In other words, it is not in and of itself the source text for Mark.

The Akhmim manuscript of the *Gospel of Peter* was contained in a larger codex of Christian texts that had probably been the personal property of the monk with whom it was buried. This particular copy is incomplete at both the beginning and the end. The fact that it is marked with decorative borders at both the beginning and the end indicates that such was also the state of the earlier manuscript from which it was reproduced. No complete text is preserved. As a result, we can only guess the full extent of the narrative.

The narrative picks up, apparently, near the end of the trial, just after Pilate had washed his hands, otherwise found only in Matthew 27:24.[5] It assumes that the sentence of death by crucifixion has already been handed down. The story proceeds through the plans for the burial, then the crucifixion proper (including the two criminals), the removal from the cross (even removing the nails from his hands), and the burial by Joseph in his own "garden" (*Gos. Pet.* 6.24; cf. John 19:41). Following a lament by the "Jews and the elders and the priests" over the "great evil they had done" (*Gos. Pet.* 7.25) comes the first indication that the story is actually being narrated in the first person: "But I mourned with my fellows, and being wounded in heart we hid ourselves . . ." (7.26). That the narrator is ostensibly Simon Peter himself is made clear by a similar first-person narrative at the end of the preserved portion of the text (14.60).

Next, we get the story of the Jews asking Pilate to place guards at the tomb, and the rest of the resurrection narrative is built around this story frame (8.28–11.49). Then comes the empty-tomb scene, which (as in Mark) has no direct connection to the guards episode (12.50–13.57). Finally, the text ends with what seems to be the beginning of an appearance (or appearances) to the *twelve* (!) disciples (14:58–60). It is here that the narrator is clearly mentioned: "But I, Simon Peter, and my brother Andrew, took our nets and went to the sea" (14.60).[6] The text then breaks off in what seems to be a list of the twelve disciples that resembles peculiarly Markan elements.[7] It would appear from this outline that the *Gospel of Peter* contained only a Passion narrative, at least as far as can be deduced from the preserved portions. Where the narrative would have commenced, however, cannot be ascertained.

Clearly many features of this text are later additions and anachronisms. It blames Herod for Jesus's death in collusion with the Jewish priests, and he seems to have the authority to order crucifixion. Among the canonical Gospels a Herodian ruler plays no role in the trials of Jesus, except in Luke as discussed in chapter 7. In the *Gospel of Peter,* by contrast, "Herod the King"[8] presides over the trials and orders Pilate to carry out the death sentence. Pilate is thus completely exonerated and ultimately confesses that Jesus must have been the "son of God" (11.43–46; see below). The anti-Jewish element has been intensified, as the elders and priests recognize their "evil" and lament, "Woe, because of our sins, the judgment and the end of Jerusalem is at hand" (7.25). The anti-Jewish element is strengthened by inclusion of the guards at the tomb, found otherwise only in Matthew (see above).

It has been argued that this particular version of the text was based on an earlier one that could antedate Mark. Here, however, scholars differ on which portions, if any, might represent this earlier tradition. Because it contains a version of the guards at the tomb not interrupted by the empty-tomb scene, as in Matthew, it has been argued that this component is from a pre-Matthean (and pre-Markan) text.[9] Others argue, instead, that the *Gospel of Peter* has reworked the Matthean narrative of the guards.[10] In fact, the story of the guards in *Gospel of Peter* is intercalated with a different scene concerning the tomb. In other words, it too has been reworked around the present narrative. So we need to examine it more closely.

Here is a translation of the scene of the guards at the tomb, ending at the point when the women come to the tomb and find it empty:

> [9.35] *Now in the night in which the Lord's Day dawned, when the soldiers were keeping guard, two by two in every watch, a loud voice rang out in heaven;* [36] *And they saw the heavens opened and two men full of great brightness came down from there and drew near the tomb.* [37] *But that stone which had been laid against the entrance to the tomb, having rolled by itself, moved a distance off to the side. And the tomb opened and both the young men entered.*
>
> [10.38] *When the soldiers [on watch] saw this, they awakened the centurion and the elders—for they were present also guarding [the tomb].* [39] *And while they were relating what they had seen, they then saw three men exit the tomb, two supported the one, and a cross followed them.* [40] *The heads of the two reached to heaven, but the one whom they supported with their hands stretched beyond the heavens.* [41] *And they heard a voice from the heavens which said, "Have you proclaimed to those who are asleep?"* [42] *And they heard an answer from the cross, "Yes."*
>
> [11.43] *Those men therefore took counsel with one another to go and report these things to Pilate.* [44] *And while they were still deliberating, the heavens again appeared opened and someone came down and entered the tomb.* [45] *When they had seen these things, those of the centurion's company hastened by night to Pilate, having left the tomb that they were guarding, and reported everything they had seen, agonizing greatly and saying, "Truly he was God's son."* [46] *Pilate answered and said, "I am clean from the blood of the son of God, for it was you who decided this thing."* [47] *Then all came to him, beseeching and exhorting him to command the centurion and the soldiers to say to no one what they had seen.* [48] *For they said, "It is better for us to be guilty of the greatest sin before God than to fall into the hands of the Jewish people and be stoned."* [49] *Pilate therefore commanded the centurion and the soldiers to say nothing.*
>
> [12.50] *Now at the dawning of the Lord's Day, Mary Magdalene . . . (*Gospel of Peter *9.35–12.50)*[11]

Clearly many features of this text bear the marks of later composition, such as having Roman guards express a sense of guilt "of the greatest sin before God" (11.48). The use of the term "Lord's Day" for Sunday is entirely anachronistic and reflects a later Christian cultural matrix. Some features of the story clearly reflect the Markan narrative. For example, when the women come to the tomb, they are coming to fulfill their "womanly" responsibilities by anointing the body, and they ask only who will roll away the stone for them (12.50–53). It seems clearly to be a secondary elaboration on Mark 16:1–2. Similarly, the women find a single "young man in brightly shining clothes" inside the tomb (13.55), very much as in Mark 16:5. The women finally leave the tomb frightened (13.57: cf. Mark 16:8).

Other features of the *Gospel of Peter* seem rather like expansions on Matthew. For example, the soldiers are now clearly Roman—a centurion named Petronius and his company (*Gos. Pet.* 8.31)—instead of the vague statement of Pilate in Matthew 27:65. The latter leaves some ambiguity because it may be translated either as a statement—"you have a guard of soldiers"—or as an imperative—"have (i.e., take) a guard of soldiers." In other words, the passage in Matthew leaves unclear whether the soldiers are their own (i.e., "Jewish") or Pilate's (i.e., "Roman"), respectively.[12] *Gospel of Peter* 10.38 clarifies this issue by making the soldiers clearly Roman but in the company of Jewish "elders," who are also guarding the tomb overnight. Here it should be noted that *Gospel of Peter* presents this as an editorial comment, likely meant to explicate Matthew 27:66: "So *they* went *with the guard* and made the tomb secure by sealing the stone."[13]

Other elements in the text, especially in the trial and mocking scenes, seem to reflect some distinctively Johannine wording, and ties to Lukan wording are discernible.[14] Some have used these commonalities to argue that it contains an early Passion narrative used by all the canonical Gospels, each one deriving some individual elements.[15] It is just as easy to argue the reverse, that *Gospel of Peter* is a conscious effort to weave elements of the canonical Gospels into a coherent narrative.[16] In my view the latter is correct, at least for most aspects of the narrative, and especially the guards at the tomb. It seems that these Matthean elements are intentionally being reconfigured to fit a Markan story line.

The actual opening of the tomb in the *Gospel of Peter* (10.38–42), however, is the most distinctive and striking scene in the story. It fits neither Mark, where nothing is reported, nor Matthew, where a single angel rolls the stone away and sits atop it to address the women as they are arriving. Instead, in *Gospel of Peter* 9.37, the stone rolls away by itself as two radiant men come down from heaven and enter the tomb. They then leave carrying a third man out with them, followed by the cross (10.39–40). Despite a strong verbal similarity, these "two men" must not be the same as the two men "in dazzling clothes" who appear in the Lukan empty-tomb scene (24:4).[17] The *Gospel of Peter* 11.44 then has a fourth "man" who descends from heaven afterward, and he is the "young man" whom the women find in the empty tomb (13.55), just as in Mark. Finally, there is the "third man" whom the first two carry out of the tomb. This "third man" is obviously Jesus, who is followed by the cross. A heavenly voice asks, "Have you proclaimed to *those who are asleep?*" (meaning the dead), and the cross (!) answers, "Yes" (10.41–42). The story of the guards resumes intermittently at 10.38 and 11.43, and ends at 11.45–49, when they report everything to Pilate.[18]

Oddly enough, this scene depicts—for the first time in any preserved literary form—the actual moment of the resurrection. The statement that Jesus's head "stretches beyond the heavens" must refer to his exaltation and ascension at that moment. For then the three men depart. Because it seems to contain a form of the "harrowing of hell" scene (cf. Matt 27:52–53), it has been assumed that this is an older form of the empty-tomb scene. This view may also be supported by the fact that the emergence of an apparently dead Jesus would be out of keeping with docetic tendencies alleged by Serapion of Antioch for the *Gospel of Peter*.[19] But it must be remembered that *Gospel of Peter* 12:50–13:57 also contains a separate empty-tomb scene with the women, very similar to that in Mark, while the story of the guards is kept functionally separate from the empty tomb (in sharp contrast to Matthew). Also, the resurrection/ascension scene does not preempt the appearance to the "twelve" that comes at the end of the preserved portion of the text.

So, is this a later effort to combine elements from Mark, Matthew, and John into a composite narrative? That is likely true in part. As such, it thus shows that the process of storytelling by reshaping and recombining elements had not disappeared in the second century, even after there were written Gospels.[20] Given the fact that it dismantles the Matthean guard story to keep it separate from the empty tomb, thus preserving a more Markan form, one should perhaps think of it as an effort to restore "Peter's" Gospel, in large measure by giving priority to Mark. Much of the *Gospel of Peter* in its present or final form can be accounted for on these terms.[21] But this leaves open the question whether there are *any* "pre-Markan" elements at all.

In this vein, some elements seem to exhibit features of an early form of the Passion tradition, notably an appearance to Peter and the "twelve disciples" (*Gos. Pet.* 14.59–60). This element is clearly there in the early Pauline tradition (as discussed above; see 1 Cor 15:5[22]), but is incompatible with the Markan narrative due to the role of the Judas character in the story. Consistent with this point is the fact that there is *apparently* no mention of Judas or a "betrayal" in the *Gospel of Peter*.[23] The "resurrection story" in the *Gospel of Peter* also bears striking similarities to the transfiguration scene in the Synoptics; the versions in Matthew and Luke are derived from Mark 9:2–8. It is also worth noting that another "Petrine" text, the *Apocalypse of Peter,* also contains a postresurrection appearance and ascension scene with unmistakable resemblance to the transfiguration.[24] (See Chapter 7.) Significantly, our main Greek manuscript of the *Apocalypse of Peter* was also found at Akhmim in the same eighth–ninth century codex as the *Gospel of Peter*. Both texts were copied by the same scribe.[25]

∞∞∞∞

A "Transcript" of Q

There is no independent text of Q. It only exists as embedded within the Gospels of Matthew and Luke, at least following the Two-Source Hypothesis, discussed in Appendix B. Yet it is very difficult for most ordinary readers, and even a few scholars, to get a sense of what is contained in Q. By definition, then, the content of Q is represented by those passages of Matthew and Luke that are nearly verbatim, or at least very similar verbally, but that have no corresponding passage in the Gospel of Mark. Even then, there are considerable debates over which one of the Gospels, Matthew or Luke, has the more original wording. Although many scholars favor Luke in this regard, especially for ordering the Q material, it varies from case to case. Many of the Matthean sayings are found to contain the more original forms, even if they have been repositioned. What follows then is a "transcript" based on the usual reconstructions of order and wording[1] (see also Box 12.1).

Q3–4
The Preaching of John

(Luke 3:7–9 / Matt 3:7–10 + Luke 3:16b–17 / Matt 3:11–12)

Q3 [. . . Now John the Baptizer came preaching][2] and said, [3.7]"You brood of vipers, who showed you to flee from the coming wrath? [8]Bear fruits worthy of repentance, and do not say to yourselves, 'We have Abraham as our father.' For I say to you that from these stones God is able to raise up children to Abraham. [9]But even now the ax is poised at the root of the trees; therefore, every tree that does not produce good fruit will be cast into the fire."

Q4   [And he said,] [16]"Whereas I baptize you in water [for repentance], there is one coming who is stronger than I am, whose sandals I am not fit to bear; he will baptize you in the holy spirit and in fire. [17]His winnowing fan is in his hand, and he will clear his threshing floor. He will gather the grain into his storehouse, but the chaff he will burn with unquenchable fire."

Q5–6
The Appearance and Testing of Jesus

(Luke 4:2–13 / Matt 4:2–11)

Q5   [Now Jesus came and . . .][3]

Q6   [4.2]Now when Jesus had fasted, [3]the Tester said to him, "If you are the son of God, speak to these stones that they should become bread." [4]But answering Jesus said, "It is written, *A person shall not live by bread alone* [Deut 8:3]."[4] [9]Next, the devil took him to the holy city and stood him upon the pinnacle of the temple, and said to him, "If you are the son of God, cast yourself down, [10]for it is written, *He has commanded his angels about you* [11]*and they will lift you up in their hands, lest you strike your foot against a stone*' [Ps 90:11–12]." [12]But answering, Jesus said to him, "Again it is written, *You shall not test the Lord your God*' [Deut 6:16]." [5]And the devil took him to a high mountain[5] and showed him the kingdoms of the cosmos and their glory[6] [6]and said to him, [7]"All these I shall give you, if you will bow before me." [8]But answering, Jesus said to him, "It is written, *You shall bow before the Lord your God, and him alone shall you worship*' [Deut 6:13; 5:9]." [13]And the devil departed and left him alone.

Q7–14
A Sermon

(Luke 6:20–49a / Matt 5:1–7:21 and varia)

Q7   . . . [6.17][coming down from the mountain . . .][7] [20]and opening his mouth he spoke to them saying,

Q8   "Blessed are the poor, because the kingdom of God is theirs. [21]Blessed are those who hunger, for they will be satisfied. Blessed are those who mourn, for they will be comforted. [23]Blessed are you when they rebuke and persecute you and speak evil against you on account of me; rejoice and be glad, for great is your reward in heaven; for so also they did to the prophets.[8]

Q9   [27]"And I say to you, Love your enemies, and pray for those that mistreat you. [29]To one who strikes you on the cheek, turn to him even the other; and to one who wishes to take you to court and take your tunic, give him even your cloak; [30]to one who begs from you, give; and to one who wishes to borrow from you, do not turn away.

Q10 [36]"Be merciful, then, just as your Father is merciful. [37]And judge not, that you may not be judged. [38]For the measure by which you measure, it will be measured to you.

Q11 [39]"But if a blind man leads a blind man, will not both fall into a pit? [40]A disciple is not above his teacher; it is enough for the disciple to be like his teacher.

Q12 [41]"Why do you see the speck that is in your brother's eye, but not notice the beam that is in your own eye? Or how can you say to your brother, 'Let me remove the speck that is in your eye,' when you yourself do not see the beam that is in your own eye? Hypocrite, first remove the beam from your own eye, and then you will see clearly to remove the speck that is in your brother's eye.

Q13 [44]"For each tree is known by its fruit. For figs are not gathered from thorns nor grapes from brambles. [43]For a healthy tree does not bear bad fruit, nor can a rotten tree bear good fruit. [45]For from that which overflows the heart the mouth speaks. The good man produces good out of his good store, and the evil man produces evil out of his evil store.

Q14 [46]"Why do you call me 'Lord, Lord,' and do not do what I say? [47]Everyone who comes to me and hears my words and practices them [48]is like a person who built his house upon a rock, and when torrents came against that house, they were not able to shatter it. [49]But he who hears my words and does not do them is like a person who built his house upon the ground. When the torrents came against it, it collapsed and its ruin was great."

Q15–34
John, Jesus, and Their Generation

(Luke 7:1–13:35 / Matt 8:5–13 and *varia*)

Q15 [7.1]When Jesus had finished these words in the hearing of the people, he entered Capernaum. [2]A centurion came and begged him saying, "Lord my slave is lying paralyzed at home and suffering greatly." [6]And he said, "I will come and heal him." But the centurion answered him, [7]"Lord, I am not worthy to have you come under my roof. Rather speak a word, and my slave will be healed. [8]For I too am a person under authority, with soldiers under me; and I say to one, 'Go,' and he goes; and to another, 'Come,' and he comes; and to my slave, 'Do this,' and he does it. [9]When Jesus heard this he marveled and said to those who followed him, "Truly, I tell you, I have not found such trust in Israel." [10]And to the centurion,

Jesus said, "Go, as you have trusted, so will it be done." And his slave was healed in that very hour.

Q16–20 About John and Their Generation

Q16 ¹⁸Now when John heard about [. . .], ¹⁹he sent two of his disciples to Jesus, saying, "Are you the Coming One, or should we expect another?" And answering, Jesus said to them, "Go and tell John what you see and hear: the blind recover their sight, the lame walk, lepers are cleansed, and the deaf hear, the dead are raised, and the poor are given good news.⁹ ²³And blessed is anyone who has not been offended by me."

Q17 ²⁴Now when they had departed, Jesus began to say to the crowd concerning John, "What did you go out to the wilderness to observe? A reed shaken by the wind? ²⁵But what did you go out to see? A person clothed in soft garments? Behold those in soft garments are in royal houses. ²⁶But what did you go out to see? A prophet? Yes, I tell you, and more than a prophet. ²⁷This is the one concerning whom it is written, *'Behold, I send my messenger (angel) before your face, who will prepare your way before you'* [Mal 3:1; Exod 23:30; Isa 40:3]. ²⁸Truly I tell you, among those born of women none is greater than John; yet the least in the kingdom of heaven is greater than he.

Q18 ¹⁶·¹⁶"From the days of [John] until now, the kingdom of God suffers violence and violent people try to seize it. [For the prophets prophesied until/about John.]¹⁰

Q20 ⁷·³¹"To whom shall I compare the people of this generation? ³²They are like children seated in the market places who call out to others and say, 'We played the flute for you and you did not dance; we sang a dirge, and you did not weep.' ³³For John came neither eating nor drinking, and you said, 'He has a demon.' ³⁴The Son of Man came eating and drinking, and you said, 'See, a glutton and a drunkard, a friend of tax collectors and sinners.' ³⁵Yet Wisdom (*Sophia*) is justified by all her children."

Q21–24 Discipleship and Mission Instructions

Q21 ⁹·⁵⁷And someone said to him, "Teacher, I will follow you wherever you go." ⁵⁸And Jesus said to him, "The foxes have dens and the birds of heaven nests, but the Son of Man has nowhere to lay his head." ⁵⁹But another said to him, "Lord, permit me first to depart and bury my father." ⁶⁰But Jesus said to him, "Follow me, and leave the dead to bury their own dead."

Q22 ¹⁰·²And to [those who followed him] he said, "The harvest indeed is plentiful, but the laborers few; therefore beg the master of the harvest that he send laborers into his harvest. ³Behold, I send you as lambs among wolves. ⁴Carry no purse, nor knapsack, nor sandals, and greet no one along the way. ⁵But into whatever house you enter, first say, 'Peace to this house.' ⁶And if there is a son of peace there, let your peace come upon him. But if not, let it return to you. ⁷Eat what is set before you, for the laborer is worthy of his reward. Do not move from house to house. ⁸And into whatever city you enter and they receive you, ⁹cure the sick in it and preach, saying to them, 'The kingdom of God has come upon you.' ¹⁰And whoever does not receive you, departing from that city ¹¹shake the dust from your feet. ¹²But I say to you that it will be more tolerable for the Sodomites on the day of judgment than for that city.

Q23 ¹³"Woe to you, Chorazin, woe to you, Bethsaida; for if the wonders that were done in you had been done in Tyre and Sidon, they would long ago have repented in sackcloth and ashes. ¹⁴But I say to you, it will be more tolerable for Tyre and Sidon on the day of judgment than for you. ¹⁵And you, Capernaum, will you exalt yourself in heaven? You will go down to Hades.

Q24 ¹⁶"The one welcomes you welcomes me, and the one welcomes me welcomes the one who sent me."

Q25–28 Prayers for the Disciples

Q25 ²¹In that hour Jesus said, "I praise you, Father, Lord of heaven and earth, because you hid these things from the wise and intelligent and revealed them to small children; yes, Father, because this has been your good pleasure. ²²All things were handed over to me by my Father, and no one knows the Son except the Father and no one knows the Father except the Son and the one to whom the Son wishes to reveal him."

Q26 ²³And he said, "Blessed are the eyes that see the things which you see; ²⁴for truly I say to you that many prophets and kings wanted to see the things which you see and did not see them, and to hear the things which you hear and did not hear them."

Q27 ¹¹·²"When you pray say, 'Father, may your name be sanctified; may your kingdom come; ³daily give us our bread sufficient for the day; ⁴and forgive us our debts as we also forgive our debtors; and do not lead us to the test.'

Q28 ⁹"Ask and it will be given to you, seek and you will find, knock and it will be opened to you. ¹⁰For everyone asking receives and one seeking finds and to one knocking it will be opened. ¹¹Or what father among you, whose son will ask him for bread, will give him a stone? ¹²Or if he will ask for a fish will give him a snake? ¹³Therefore if you who are evil know how to give good gifts to your children, so much more the Father of heaven will give good things to those asking him."

Q29–34 Signs and Controversies

Q29 ¹⁴And he cast out a demon that was mute; and after the demon was cast out the mute man spoke, and the crowds were amazed. ¹⁵But some said, "By Beelzebul the prince of demons he casts out demons." [17]Knowing their thoughts, he said to them: "Every kingdom divided against itself is destroyed and house falls against house. [18]And if Satan is divided against himself, how will his kingdom stand? [19]And if I cast out demons by Beelzebul, by whom do your sons cast them out? Therefore they will be your judges. [20]But if by the hand of God that I cast out demons, then the kingdom of God has come upon you. [23]One who is not for me is against me, and one not gathering with me scatters.

Q30 [24]"When the unclean spirit goes out of a person, it goes through dry places seeking rest and it does not find any. Then it says, 'I will return to the house from which I departed.' [25]And coming he finds it swept and beautified. [26]Then he goes and takes seven other spirits more evil than himself and entering he lives there; and the last state of that person is worse than the first."

Q31 [[27–28]][11]

Q32 [16]But others said to him, "Teacher, we want to see a sign from you." [29]But he answered and said to them: "An evil generation seeks a sign, and no sign will be given it except the sign of Jonah. [30]For as Jonah became a sign to the Ninevites, so will the Son of Man be to this generation. [31]The queen of the South will be raised in the judgment with this generation and she will condemn it, for she came from the ends of the earth to hear the wisdom of Solomon, and see, there is more than Solomon here. [32]The men of Nineveh will rise in the judgment with this genera- tion and they will condemn it, for they repented at the preaching of Jonah, and see, there is more than Jonah here.[12]

Q33 [33]"No one lights a lamp and puts it under a basket, but on the lampstand, and it gives light to all who enter. [34]The lamp of the body is the eye. If your eye is sincere, your whole body will be full of light; but if your eye is malicious, your whole body will be full of darkness. [35]If then the light in you is darkness, how great is the darkness!

Q34 [39]"Woe to you Pharisees, for you cleanse the outside of the cup and the dish, but the inside they are full of plunder and self indulgence. [40]Hypocrite, cleanse first the inside of the cup, [41]and its outside will also be clean. [42]Woe to you, Pharisees, for you tithe the mint and dill and cumin and leave aside the weightier things of the Law, judgment and love; these you ought to have done without ne- glecting the others. [43]Woe to you, Pharisees, for you love the first place in the feasts and the first seat in the synagogues and greetings in the market places. [44]Woe to you, Pharisees, for you are like unmarked graves and people walking over them do not know it. [46]Woe to you, Pharisees, for you bind heavy burdens and put them on the shoulders of people, but you yourselves do not wish to move them with your finger. [47]Woe to you, Pharisees, for you build the tombs of the prophets; and you say, 'If we had been in the days of our fathers, we would not have been their companions in the blood of the prophets.' [48]Therefore you witness to yourselves that you are the sons of those who killed the prophets and you fill up the measure of your fathers. [49]Therefore Sophia also said: 'I will send to them prophets and wise men, and some among them they will kill and persecute, ⁵⁰so that upon them will come the blood of all the prophets that has been shed on the earth, ⁵¹from the blood of Abel to the blood of Zechariah whom they killed between the altar and the house; amen I say to you, all these things will come upon this generation.' ⁵²Woe to you, Pharisees, for you close the kingdom of God before people; for you do not enter nor do you allow those entering to enter.

[³⁴"Jerusalem, Jerusalem, killing the prophets and stoning those sent to her, how often did I want to gather your children as a hen gatherings her chicks under her wings, and you did not want it. ³⁵See, your house is left to you. But I say to you, you will not see me again until the time comes when you say, 'Blessed is the Coming One in the name of the Lord.' "]¹³

Q35–42
On Anxiety, or the Fate of God's Messengers

(Luke 12:2–34 / Matt 10:26–23; 6:29–34 and *varia*)

Q35 [And he began to say to them,] ¹²·²"There is nothing covered which will not be revealed, and nothing hidden which will not be made known. ³What I say to you in the darkness speak in the light, and what you hear whispered proclaim from the housetops.

Q36 ⁴"And do not fear those who kill the body, but cannot kill the soul; ⁵but fear rather the one who can destroy both soul and body in Gehenna. ⁶Are not two sparrows sold for a pence? And not one of them will fall to the earth without God's knowledge. ⁷But the hairs of your head are also numbered. Do not fear: you are worth more than many sparrows.

Q37 ⁸"Everyone who will confess me before men, the Son of Man will also confess him before the angels; ⁹but whoever will deny me before me, the Son of Man will also deny him before the angels.

Q38 ¹⁰"And everyone who will say a word against the Son of Man, will be forgiven; but whoever will say a word against the Holy Spirit, will not be forgiven.

Q39 ¹¹"But when they bring you before rulers and authorities, do not worry about how or what you are to say; ¹²for it will be given to you in that hour what to say."

Q40 [¹²⁻¹³, ¹⁶⁻²¹]¹⁴

Q41 ²²"Therefore I say to you, 'Do not worry about your life what you will eat, nor about your body what you will wear. ²³Is not life more than food, and the body more than clothing? ²⁴Consider the ravens, they neither sow nor reap nor gather into barns and God feeds them. Are you not more important than the birds? ²⁵But who among you by worrying can add one cubit to his height? ²⁶And about clothing, why do you worry? ²⁷Consider the lilies, how they grow; they do not toil or weave; but I say to you that not even Solomon in all his glory was clothed like one of these. [28]But if God so clothes the grass which today is in the field and tomorrow is thrown into the oven, will not God much more clothe you, ones of little faith? [29]Do not worry saying, 'What are we to eat?' and 'What are we to drink?' and 'What are we to wear?' [30]For the Gentiles seek all these things; but your Father knows that you need all these things. [31]But seek first his kingdom, and all these things will be added to you.

Q42 [33]"Do not treasure for yourselves treasures on earth, where moth and decay destroy and where thieves dig through and steal; but treasure for yourselves treasures in heaven where neither moth nor decay destroys and where thieves do not dig through nor steal; [34]for where your treasure is there also will be your heart."

Q43–48
On Judgment

(Luke 12:35–59 / Matt 22:11–14; 25:1–13; 24:42–51; 10:34–36; 16:2–3; 5:25–26 and *varia*)

Q43 [12.35-37]"Let your belts be fastened and your lamps be lit, and be like those who are awaiting their master to come from the marriage feast, so that when he comes and knocks, they may open the door immediately. Blessed are those servants whom the master finds awake when he comes.

Q44 [39]"But know this that if the householder knew at what watch the thief would come he would not allow his house to be dug into. [40]You also must be ready; for the Son of Man is coming at an hour you do not expect.

Q45 [42b]"Who therefore is the faithful and wise servant whom the Lord set over his household to give them the measure of grain at the right time? [43]Blessed is that servant whom his Lord when he comes will find so doing. [44]Amen I say to you that he will set him over all his possessions. [45]But if that servant says in his heart, 'My Lord is delayed,' and begins to beat the men servants and the women servants, and eats and drinks with drunkards, [46]the Lord of that servant will come on a day he does not expect and at an hour he does not know, and he will cut him in two and put his lot with the faithless.

Q46 [51]"Do you think that I came to cast peace on earth? I came not to cast peace but a sword. [52]And a person's enemies will be those of the person's household. [53]For I came to divide a son against his father and a daughter against her mother and a daughter-in-law against her mother-in-law."

Q47 [54-56][And he said,] "When you see cloud in the evening, you say, 'Good, for the sky is red,' and in the morning, you say, 'Today it will rain, for the sky is dark.'

Q48 ⁵⁸"Be reconciled with your adversary while you go with him on the way, lest the adversary hand you over to the judge and the judge to the guard and the guard will throw you into prison. ⁵⁹Truly, I say to you, you will not leave there until you have paid back the last penny."

Q49
Parables of Growth

(Luke 13:18–21 / Matt 13:31–33)

Q49 ¹³·¹⁸And he said: "What is the kingdom of God like and to what shall I compare it? ¹⁹It is like a mustard seed which a man took and cast into his garden, and it grew and became a tree and the birds of heaven nested in its branches." ²⁰And again he said: "To what shall I liken the kingdom of God? ²¹It is like leaven which a woman took and buried in three measures of flour until it leavened the whole."

Q50–57
The Two Ways

(Luke 13:24–14:35 / Matt 7:13–23; 8:11–12; 20:16; 22:1–10; 23:6–12, 37–39; 10:37–39; 5:13)

Q50 ¹³·²⁴"Strive to enter through the narrow door; for, I say to you, many will seek to enter and will not be able. ²⁵And the door will be closed. And you will say, 'Lord, open it for us.' And I will say to you, 'I do not know you.' ²⁶And you will say, 'Lord, did we not prophesy in your name, and did we not cast out demons in your name, and did we not do miracles in your name?' ²⁷And I will say to you, 'I do not know you; depart from me all you who practice injustice.'

Q51 ²⁹"Many will come from the east and the west and recline at table ²⁸ᵇwith Abraham and Isaac and Jacob in the kingdom of God. ²⁸ᶜBut the sons of the kingdom will be cast out into the outer darkness. ²⁸ᵃThere will be weeping and gnashing of teeth; ³⁰for the last will be first and the first will be last.

Q52 ³⁴"O Jerusalem, Jerusalem. You who kill the prophets and stone those sent to you. How often did I want to gather your children as a hen gathering her chicks under her wings, and you refused. ³⁵Behold, your house is forsaken. But I say to you, you will not see me until the time comes when you say, 'Blessed is the One Coming in the name of the Lord.'¹⁵

Q54 ¹⁴·¹¹"Everyone who exalts himself will be humbled and everyone who humbles himself will be exalted. [cf. 18:14b]

Q55 ¹⁶"A man made a feast and invited many. ¹⁷And he sent his servant to say to those invited, 'Come, for all is now ready.' ¹⁸And they all began to make excuses. The first said to him, 'I bought a field and I need to go and inspect it. I ask you to excuse me.' ¹⁹And another said, 'I bought five yoke of oxen and I am going to examine them. I ask you to excuse me.' ²⁰And another said, 'I have married a wife and therefore cannot come.' ²¹And the servant came and reported all they had said. Then the master became angry and said to his servant, 'Go out into the roads and as many as you find gather into the feast.' ²³And the servant went out into the roads and gathered all he found, and the house was filled. ²⁴For I tell you, none of those who were invited shall taste the banquet.

Q56 ²⁶"Whoever does not hate his father and mother cannot be my disciple; whoever does not hate his son and daughter cannot be my disciple; ²⁷whoever does not take up his cross and follow after me cannot be my disciple. ³³Whoever finds his life will lose it, but whoever loses his life will find it.

Q57 ³⁴"Salt is good; but if the salt loses its taste, how can it be restored? ³⁵It is fit neither for the soil nor the manure pile; they throw it away."

Q58–64
Miscellaneous Sayings

(Luke 15:4–10; 16:13–18; 17:1b–6b / Matt 18:12–14; 6:24; 11:12–13; 5:18, 32; 18:6–22; 17:19–20)

Q58 ¹⁵·⁴"What man among you having a hundred sheep and having lost one of them will not leave the ninety-nine on the mountains and go and seek the lost one? ⁵And if he finds it, amen I say to you, he rejoices over it more than over the ninety-nine who were not lost. ⁷Thus there will be joy in heaven over one who is found."

Q59 [⁸⁻¹⁰]¹⁶

Q60 ¹⁶·¹³"No one can serve two masters; for he will either hate the one and love the other, or he will cling to the one and despise the other; you cannot serve God and mammon.

Q61 ¹⁶"The prophets prophesied until/about John; from then the kingdom of God suffers violence and violent people seize it.¹⁷ ¹⁷But it is easier for heaven and earth to pass away than for a stroke to be dropped from the Law. ¹⁸Everyone who divorces his wife and marries another commits adultery, and the one who marries a divorced woman commits adultery.

Q62 ¹⁷·¹ᵇ"It is necessary that offenses come, but woe to the person through whom they come; ²it were better for him if a great millstone were placed around his neck and he be cast into the sea.

Q63 [3]"If your brother sins against you, admonish him; and if he repents, forgive him; [4]and if he sins against you seven times and seven times repents, you will forgive him.

Q64 [6]"If you have faith like a mustard seed, you would say to this mulberry tree, 'Be uprooted and planted in the sea,' and it would obey you."

Q65–68
Eschatological Sayings

(Luke 17:20–37; 19:12–26; 22:28–30 / Matt 24:23–42; 25:14–30; 19:27–29)

Q65 [[17.20–21]][18]

Q66 [17.23]"And if they say to you, 'Behold, he is in the desert,' do not go out; or 'Behold, he is in the innermost rooms,' do not believe it. [24]For as the lightning goes out from the east and shines to the west, so will be the day of the Son of Man. [26]For as were the days of Noah, so will be the day of the Son of Man. [27]For as they were eating and drinking, marrying and being given in marriage, until the day Noah went into the ark, and the flood came and took them all; ([28]likewise, as it was in the days of Lot—they ate and drank, they bought and sold, they planted and built, [29]but on the day when Lot left Sodom, fire and sulphur rained down from heaven and destroyed them all);[19] [30]so also will be the day of the Son of Man. [34]Two men will be in the field, one is taken and the other is left; [35]two women will be grinding at the mill, one is taken and the other is left. [37]Wherever the corpse is, there the vultures will be gathered together."

Q67 [19.12]And he said to them, "It is like a man going on a journey, who called his servants [13]and gave them money: to one he gave five talents, to another two, and to another one, and he left on a journey. And the one who received five talents went and earned another five; likewise the one who received two earned another two. But the one who received one went out and dug in the earth and hid his Lord's money. [15]And the Lord of those servants came and called them. [16]And the one who received five talents came and said, 'Lord, you gave me five talents; see, I earned another five talents.' [17]And he said to him, 'Well done, good servant, you have been faithful over a few things, I will set you over many.' [18]And the one who received two talents came and said, 'Lord, you gave me two talents; see, I earned another two talents.' [19]And he said to him, 'Well done, good servant, you have been faithful over a few things, I will set you over many.' [20a]And the one who received one talent came and said, [20b]'And fearing I went out and hid your talent in the earth; see, you have your money. [21]Lord, I know you, that you are a hard man, harvesting where you did not sow and gathering from where you did not scatter.'

[22]And he said to him, 'Evil servant, you knew, did you, that I am a hard man, harvesting where I did not sow and gathering from where I did not scatter? [23]It was necessary for you to hand over my money to the bankers, and when I returned I would have recovered it with interest. [24]Take the talent from him and give it to the one who has ten talents. [26]For to everyone who has, more will be given; and from the one who has not, even what he has will be taken from him.' "

Q68 [22.28]"You who have followed me [30]will sit on thrones in the kingdom of God judging the twelve tribes of Israel."

Q69 [15.11/28][Now, he told them a parable.][20] [28]"What do you think? A man had two sons; he went to the first and said, 'Son, go and work in the vineyard today.' [29]He answered, 'I do not want to'; but later he changed his mind and went. [30]The father went to the second and said the same; and he answered, 'I go, sir'; but he did not go. [31]Which of the two did the will of his father?" They said, "The first." Jesus said to them, "Truly I tell you, the tax collectors and the prostitutes are going into the kingdom of God ahead of you. [[32]For John came to you in the way of righteousness and you did not believe him, but the tax collectors and the prostitutes believed him; and even after you saw it, you did not change your minds and believe him.]"

Mapping the Narrative World of Luke

The Gospel of Luke has a distinctive geographical framework in depicting the Galilean ministry of Jesus. One key feature is its location of the feeding of the five thousand and the confession of Peter (Luke 9:10–17, 18–22). They are consecutive episodes, both set in Bethsaida. In sharp contrast, the Gospels of Mark and Matthew place the same two episodes farther apart and in different locations: the feeding of the five thousand somewhere near Capernaum; the confession at Caesarea Philippi, approximately twenty-five miles to the north of Bethsaida, on the southern slopes of Mt. Hermon. The two episodes are separated from one another by several chapters: the feeding of the five thousand is at Mark 6:32–44 and Matthew 14:13–21, while the confession is at Mark 8:27–33 and Matthew 16:13–23. What does this change of location suggest about the narrative world of the Lukan story?

Bethsaida

Bethsaida-Julias (probably modern et-Tell, Israel) is located where the upper stream of the Jordan River enters the Sea of Galilee on its north end.[1] The village was refounded in 30 CE as a city with fortifications by Herod's son Philip, tetrarch of Gaulanitis 4 BCE–34 CE. Its local Aramaic name was Bethsaida, but Philip renamed it Julias in honor of Augustus's wife, Livia Julia, mother of the emperor Tiberius.[2] On his death in 34 CE, Philip was buried there. Philip's territories, including Bethsaida, were later ceded to Herod Agrippa II (52–93 CE).[3] On the east side of the Sea of Galilee, Agrippa's kingdom included the Decapolis cities of Hippos and Gadara.[4] The rest of the Decapolis cities to the south, including Scythopolis (Beth Shan) on the west side of the Jordan (near Nain), were annexed to the province of Syria (see Map A.2 above). Early in the first Jewish revolt, Bethsaida, still under Agrippa's control, was the site of a battle. Josephus commanded the Jewish insurgents against Agrippa's armies.[5]

After 93 CE a portion of this region, including Bethsaida itself, was joined to the Galilee in the reorganized province of Judea (the lighter area on Map E.1; see also Map A.3 above). The rest of Agrippa's territories to the east of the Sea of Galilee, including Hippos and Gadara, were attached to the Decapolis and annexed to the province of Syria (the darker area on the map). As the Lukan treatment of Bethsaida as part of the Galilee shows, these were the political boundaries of the region at the time that the Gospel of Luke was written.[6] The Gospel of John (12:21) also calls Bethsaida a city of the Galilee.[7]

MAP E.1

Galilee and Neighboring Regions as Depicted in Luke

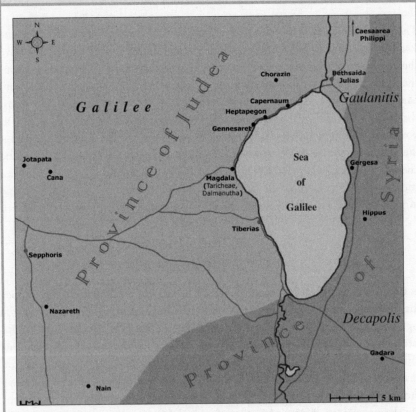

Political boundaries are those after the death of Herod Agrippa II in 93 CE. The lighter color shows the Galilee, annexed to the province of Judea and includes a portion of Gaulantis to the east of the upper Jordan River. The darker color shows the remaining parts of Gaulanitis and Decapolis, which were annexed to the province of Syria.

The Feeding of the Five Thousand

The exact location of the feeding of the five thousand is not given in Mark (or Matthew). The traditional site associated with this miracle and the Sermon on the Mount is Heptapegon, meaning "Seven Springs" in Greek (modern Tabgah, Israel), on the west side of the Sea of Galilee just south of Capernaum. A succession of Christian churches built there beginning in the fourth century commemorate the event, as do early pilgrimage traditions dating to the end of the same century.[8] The Markan narrative, however, clearly places the feeding of the five thousand in a "wilderness" or "uninhabited region," where Jesus and the disciples traveled by boat (Mark 6:31–32). The fact that the crowds "follow" and catch up with them by land has been taken to mean it was near their previous location, *apparently* on the Galilean side (Mark 6:6), as Jesus then sent his disciples to surrounding villages; their return (in Mark 6:30) is the occasion for the feeding of the five thousand.

The Matthean version of the story helps create the perception that it was to the south of Capernaum and clearly on the Galilean side of the Sea of Galilee, because the Matthean author separates the mission of the Twelve (Matt 9:35–10:5) from the feeding of the five thousand (14:13–21). The traditional location is most likely based upon this reworked Matthean narrative, as shown also by its association with the Sermon on the Mount, which has Jesus based in Capernaum during this portion of his ministry (cf. Matt 12:1). By contrast, the feeding of the five thousand in the Gospel of John (6:1–14) is explicitly set on the "other side" of the Sea of Galilee, clearly meaning the side opposite Capernaum, as shown in John 6:16–21 (the Johannine version of the walking on the water miracle). Even so, the language of "other side" is not very precise.

The "Other Side"

In the Gospel of Mark Jesus and the disciples frequently travel to the "other side" of the Sea of Galilee. In Markan usage, "other side" generally means anything to the east and northeast from Capernaum and reflects the territories of Philip or the Decapolis. For example, the Markan section leading up to the blind man at Bethsaida story (8:22–26) has the following travel sequence: they travel to the region of Tyre (7:24) and return "by way of Sidon towards the Sea of Galilee, in the region of the Decapolis" (7:31), leaving them on the east or north side of the Sea, where the feeding of the four thousand takes place (8:1–9). Then they cross by boat to Dalmanutha (traditionally the same as Magdala/Tarichaea farther to the south) on the Galilee side (8:10), and then cross back to the "other side" (8:13–21), after which they arrive at Bethsaida (8:22).

The only time the term "other side" is used in the Lukan narrative is when they cross to the country of the Gerasenes; on their way Jesus stills the storm

(8:22). The following scene in Luke explicitly adds explanatory information about this region: "which is opposite Galilee" (8:26). The regional designation "country of the Gerasenes" comes from the Markan version of this miracle as taken over directly by the Lukan author. By contrast, the Gospel of Matthew gives the location as "country of the Gadarenes" (8:28). The problem is that Gerasa (Jerash) is considerably farther to the south and not contiguous to the Sea of Galilee. The Matthean change is more feasible, but would place the location at the very bottom end of the Sea of Galilee, near Gadara in the Decapolis, and thus an exceedingly long crossing from the area of Capernaum. In some manuscripts of the Gospels, both names are changed to variations of "Gergesenes." It is usually assumed now that this is the more likely intent of the Markan story, since the village of Gergesa lay directly across from Capernaum on the east shore of the Sea of Galilee. It was part of the Gaulanitis, in the tetrarchy of Philip and later Agrippa II.

The Feeding of the Four Thousand

One notable difference between the Gospel of Luke and those of Mark and Matthew is that the Lukan narrative makes no mention of a second miracle of feeding the multitudes. It has been traditional to assume that the feeding of the four thousand took place at Bethsaida even though the precise location is not mentioned by the Gospels of Mark or Matthew (15:29–31). The confusion is created by a false assumption about the Lukan version of the feeding of the five thousand, because it explicitly names Bethsaida as the location. Because this location is at odds with that in Mark and Matthew, the supposition arose that Luke had effectively combined the two feeding miracles into one, using the location of the second. This explanation does not work, however, for two reasons: first, because no other elements of the feeding of the four thousand occur in the Lukan version of the feeding of the five thousand, and, second, because there is no reference to Bethsaida in the other accounts of the feeding of the four thousand. The Gospel of Mark explicitly locates the episode in the Decapolis (7:31), but Bethsaida was never part of the Decapolis.

Geography and the
Narrative World of the Gospels

What this also shows is that the Markan author considers Bethsaida the "other side," from the Galilee, at least from Capernaum. Until 93 CE it was part of Gaulanitis. Traveling across to Bethsaida represents one of Jesus's standard "crossing routes" in the Gospel of Mark, but never in Matthew. In fact no episodes in the Gospel of Matthew are set at Bethsaida, and the city is only mentioned once in a saying taken from Q (Q23; Matt 11:21; Luke 10:13). The Gospel of Mark has

Jesus and the disciples cross by boat to Bethsaida immediately after the feeding of the five thousand (6:45) and again when they are en route to Caesarea Philippi (8:13–22). In the Markan narrative all of these stories are set outside the Galilee.

In contrast, the Lukan author clearly takes Bethsaida to be in the Galilee proper, which it was by the time that the Gospel of Luke was written. In keeping with this change, the phrase "other side" is never used by the Lukan author in referring to Bethsaida. The Q tradition also associates it with the Galilee, and specifically with the cities of Chorazin and Capernaum (cf. Q23; Luke 10:13). John 12:21 calls it "Bethsaida of the Galilee," where it is identified as the home of the disciples Philip, Andrew, and Peter (cf. John 1:44). On the other hand, in Mark 1:29–31 the house of Simon and Andrew is at Capernaum (cf. 1:21). Although Caesarea Philippi had also been in the tetrarchy of Philip and later given to Agrippa II, at some point—either just after the first revolt or on the death of Agrippa II in 93 CE—it was ceded to the province of Syria. This fact too may have some bearing on the change in the Lukan narrative. The geography of the narrative in the individual Gospels says something about the political situation at the time in which each one was written.

A final example of the role of geography in the narrative is the story of Jesus raising the son of the widow of Nain, which only occurs in the Gospel of Luke (7:11–17). The miracle is modeled after those of Elijah and Elisha from the Jewish scriptures (1 Kgs 17:8–9; 2 Kgs 4:8–37; 5:14). Earlier in the Gospel of Luke, Jesus is presented as referring precisely to Elijah's raising of a widow's son "at Zarephath in Sidon" as ministering to Gentiles (4:25–27). What may be at work here is that the village of Nain, which is not mentioned in any of the other Gospels, lay in the Jezreel Valley near the borders of the Decapolis city of Scythopolis (Beth Shan). This region was part of Syria, both earlier and at the time that the Gospel of Luke was written. Though there was some Jewish population at Scythopolis, the region was mixed. Thus, the Lukan story of the widow of Nain, in addition to emulating the story of Elijah, may also be linked geographically to this mixed gentile-Jewish area as a way of symbolizing Jesus's openness to Gentiles. In this way too the two stories set at Nain and Bethsaida each reflect Jesus going to the edges of the Galilee as a foreshadowing of what will come later in the geographical shift of the Lukan story, first in the Lukan travel narrative (9:51–19:27) and then in the travel narratives of Acts. Thus, geographical details may play an important role in creating the particular narrative world within each Gospel story.

NOTES

Preface

1. L. M. White, *From Jesus to Christianity* (San Francisco: HarperSanFrancisco, 2004).

Prologue: Scripting Jesus

1. The three versions are given "synoptically" in P. Bertram and B. W. Kliman, eds., *The Three-Text Hamlet: Parallel Texts of the First and Second Quartos and the First Folio* (New York: AMS Press, 1991), 122–23. I want to thank my friend Dr. James H. Dee, a scholar of the Homeric text tradition, for suggesting this comparison. It came out of our ongoing conversations about matters of mutual interest and curiosity.

2. So H. Jenkins, editor of the "Arden Hamlet," the version used for Kenneth Branagh's 1996 (1997) film version. See R. Rosenbaum, "Shakespeare in Rewrite," *New Yorker*, May 12, 2002, 68–77; and H. Jenkins, ed., *Hamlet*, Arden Edition (London: Methuen, 1982).

3. W. Shakespeare, *Hamlet*, ed. G. R. Hibbard (Oxford: Clarendon, 1987), 22–23; cf. *Hamlet*, ed. M. Hattaway (Basingstoke: Macmillan, 1987), 16.

4. Rosenbaum, "Shakespeare in Rewrite," 70.

5. Directed by John Madden (1999).

6. Albert Schweitzer gave it this title in his 1906 book, *The Quest of the Historical Jesus: From Reimarus to Wrede*. It was first published in German in 1906 under the original title, *Von Reimarus zu Wrede* [*From Reimarus to Wrede*]; "Quest of the Historical Jesus" was actually the German subtitle. The first English translation appeared in 1910, edited by F. C. Burkitt and translated by W. Montgomery (repr., New York: Macmillan, 1961).

7. Josephus *Antiquities* 17.168–92.

8. We shall deal with the problem of the census under Quirinius mentioned in Luke 2:1–4 and its dates when we deal with the birth narratives. For discussion, see also L. M. White, *From Jesus to Christianity* (San Francisco: HarperSanFrancisco, 2004), 32–35.

9. The earliest of these is that of Papias, bishop of Hierapolis, ca. 130 CE, as preserved in Eusebius *Church History* 3.39.14–15, discussed below.

10. See Gal 2:1–14 and discussion in White, *From Jesus to Christianity*, 231–32, 393 (discussing Eusebius *Church History* 2.24).

11. For the sense of "generation" as used here in reference to the developmental stages of the early Jesus movement, see White, *From Jesus to Christianity*, 4–5.

12. L. T. Johnson, *The Real Jesus: The Misguided Quest for the Historical Jesus and the Truth of the Traditional Gospels* (San Francisco: HarperSanFrancisco, 1996), 110 (his emphasis).

13. I have consulted with a legal expert, Brook Brown, partner in a prestigious law firm in Austin, who reports that it "is up to the court to determine whether to admit hearsay evidence, and it can do so only where the law recognizes an exception" in order to permit hearsay testimony. The legal consideration is this: such "exceptions" are instances where there exists "circumstantial guarantees of trustworthiness" that substitute for "the ideal testimonial conditions of oath, presence at trial, and cross-examination." Quoted from O. G. Wellborn, "Hearsay," in *Texas Rules of Evidence Handbook* (*Houston Law Review* 1983: 479), citing J. Wigmore, *Evidence in Trials at Common Law*, rev. ed. (Boston, 1974), Sec. 1420 (p. 203, fn. 1), and T. Starkie, *A Practical Treatise of the Law and Evidence*, 8th American ed. (Philadelphia, 1960), 44–65. See also S. Goode, O. G. Wellborn, and M. Sharlot, *Guide to the Texas Rules of Evidence*, 3rd ed. (St. Paul: Thomson Reuters, West, 2002).

14. Wellborn also says that "human belief evidence," even of a firsthand nature, is susceptible to certain defects, which the law tries to minimize through the requirement of an oath, the physical presence of the witness before the trier of fact, and cross-examination. He further describes these defects as follows: "First, a belief may be erroneous because it results from a false impression of objective reality—a defect of perception—a lamentably common product of our imperfect physical and psychological faculties. Second, even a true perception may yield a false belief at a later time because of tricks of human memory: the unconscious scrambling and regrouping of elements drawn from disparate experiences, and from fantasies. Third, even an accurate memory of one person may mislead when used as evidence by another, if it is accidentally communicated imperfectly. However carefully focused, our instruments of communication, both verbal and non-verbal, may be clouded by ambiguity and its counterpart, misinterpretation. Finally, a valid memory may be falsified intentionally. . . . The modern Anglo-American trial at common law represents one attempt to provide controlled conditions designed to minimize or expose defects in human belief evidence" ("Hearsay," 478). Again my thanks to Brook Brown for an enlightening exchange on rules of evidence.

15. Eusebius *Church History* 3.39.15.

16. The Synoptics do not clearly state that the triumphal entry into Jerusalem occurred on Sunday prior to Jesus's death (Mark 11:1–10). The practice of celebrating the event on "Palm Sunday," as the beginning of Holy Week, is not attested before the fourth century CE. In contrast, the Gospel of John gives a more explicit temporal reference by stating that the anointing at Bethany occurred "six days before the Passover" (12:1) while the triumphal entry occurred "the next day" (12:12). Depending on how one reckons the "six days" prior to Passover, the triumphal entry might be placed on the prior Sunday or, more likely, the Monday according to the Johannine sequence. In either case, it is noteworthy that the order of these two events in the Gospel of John is markedly different than that in Mark and Matthew, both of whom place the anointing several days *after* the triumphal entry (Mark 14:3–9; Matt 26:6–13) and just before the Last Supper. In the Gospel of Luke, however, the anointing has been moved back to an earlier point in the narrative (7:36–50).

17. It is noteworthy that the Greek word used in all four texts is *paraskeuē* ("preparation"). In modern Greek, the same word is used for Friday as a day of the week and reflects the long-standing tradition of this calendar in Greek Orthodox Christianity.

18. Matt 26:17 omits the latter part of the sentence, "when the Passover lamb is sacrificed."

19. As early as ca. 200 CE, so Tertullian *Against Marcion* 4.2. For the specific nature of the differences in the chronology of the Last Supper as a Passover meal, see also J. Jeremias, *The Eucharistic Words of Jesus*, 3rd ed. (London: SCM, 1966), 15–36; R. E. Brown, *The Gospel According to John*, 2 vols., Anchor Bible 29 (Garden City, NY: Doubleday, 1966–70), 2:555–57; *The Death of the Messiah*, 2 vols. (Garden City, NY: Doubleday, 1994), 2:1350–78.

20. See Jeremias, *Eucharistic Words*, 36–41; Brown, *Death of the Messiah*, 2:1375–76.

21. These are surveyed by Jeremias, *Eucharistic Words*, 20–26; Brown, *Death of the Messiah*, 2:1361–69.

22. Jeremias emphatically follows the Synoptics in asserting that the Last Supper was a Passover meal (*Eucharistic Words*, 41–54); Brown thinks it was probably not, though he refrains from being too emphatic on the historicity of John (*Death of the Messiah*, 2:1372–73).

23. Brown, *Gospel According to John*, 2:910–11.

24. More literally the Greek reads: "A bone *from it* shall not be broken." The quotation is not exact and no single verse in the Hebrew scriptures corresponds precisely to that given in John 19:36. It seems to be based on the Greek translation of the Septuagint (LXX), in which the same statement also occurs in Exod 12:12. In Greek the possessive "his" and "its" are the same. The variant formulation in Num 9:12 is: "*They* shall not break a bone of it." The verb supplied in John 19:36 seems to come instead from Ps 34:20 (33:21, LXX), which refers collectively to the suffering righteous ones: "[God] keeps all their bones; not one of them [lit., from among them] *will be broken*."

Chapter One: Acting the Part: Messiah

1. Directed by Richard Lester (1966).

2. See P. Zanker, *The Power of Images in the Age of Augustus* (Ann Arbor: University of Michigan Press, 1988), 96–97, 231.

3. K. Galinsky, *Augustan Culture* (Princeton: Princeton University Press, 1996), 251.

4. *My Darling Clementine* (John Ford, 1946; with Henry Fonda and Victor Mature); *Gunfight at the OK Corral* (John Sturges, 1957; with Burt Lancaster and Kirk Douglas); *Tombstone* (George Cosmatos, 1993; with Kurt Russell and Val Kilmer); and *Wyatt Earp* (Lawrence Kasdan, 1994; with Kevin Costner and Dennis Quaid).

5. Kurosawa's *Shichinin no Samurai* (1954) was dubbed into English and released in the United States as *The Seven Samurai* (1956); it reappeared as *The Magnificent Seven* (John Sturges) in 1960.

6. That the allusion was unmistakable is demonstrated further by the fact that a number of manuscripts of the Western text of the Lukan baptism scene (3:22) "complete" the quotation by adding the pregnant line that follows: "today have I begotten you." Similarly a number of early Christian commentators, including Justin, Clement of Alexandria, and Augustine, as well as the *Gospel of the Ebionites* (the Ebionites were a Jewish-Christian sect) do the same. For the *Gospel of the Ebionites*, see Chapter 15.

7. "Second Isaiah" (Isa 40–55) comes from around the time of the Persian conquest of Babylon (539 BCE); the actual author is not known, but was associated with the name of Isaiah in later tradition. Significantly, much of this material was later read as directly referring to Jesus. For discussion and further references, see R. J. Clifford, "Isaiah, Book of (Second Isaiah)," in D. N. Freedman, ed., *Anchor Bible Dictionary*, 6 vols. (New York: Doubleday, 1992), 3:490–501.

8. See Paul D. Hanson, *The Dawn of Apocalyptic: The Historical and Sociological Roots of Jewish Apocalyptic Eschatology* (Philadelphia: Fortress, 1979), 32–45.

9. The historical setting of 2 Kgs 16; 18:13–20:19 may be compared to that in Isa 7:1–8:18; 36:1–39:8, respectively. For an overview of the historical issues in the composition of Isaiah, see C. Seitz, W. Millar, and R. J. Clifford, "Isaiah, Book of," *Anchor Bible Dictionary* 3:472–507.

10. See B. Anderson, "The Apocalyptic Rendering of the Isaiah Tradition," in J. Neusner, P. Borgen, E. Frerichs, and R. Horsley, eds., *The Social World of Formative Christianity and Judaism* (Philadelphia: Fortress, 1988), 17–38.

11. See L. M. White, *From Jesus to Christianity* (San Francisco: HarperSanFrancisco, 2004), 71–72, 384–85.

12. On the history and background, see G. W. E. Nickelsburg, *Jewish Literature Between the Bible and the Mishnah* (Philadelphia: Fortress, 1981), 46–54; M. E. Stone, *Scriptures, Sects, and Visions: A Profile of Judaism from Ezra to the Jewish Revolts* (Philadelphia: Fortress, 1980), 37–56. See also M. Barker, *The Lost Prophet: The Book of Enoch and Its Influence on Christianity* (Nashville: Abingdon, 1988).

13. See 2 Pet 2:4; Jude 6; Heb 4:13; 12:2–3; Rev 19:20; 20:3.

14. N. Perrin, *The New Testament: An Introduction* (New York: Harcourt Brace, 1974), 65.

15. The notion of the "end of the world" is a very late version of this idea that results from subsequent stages of Christian reinterpretation when combined with Stoic ideas.

16. The serpent or dragon is variously called Leviathan or Rahab in the Hebrew versions of the myth; see Pss 74:12–17; 89:8–12; Isa 27:1; 51:9–11; Job 26:7–13; 41:1–34. Leviathan is from Ugaritic Litan (or less properly Lotan), the sea dragon in the myth of Baal and Anat. In later apocalyptic texts the name is taken over for the

"satan" figure or his henchmen; see *2 Bar.* 29:4; *Odes Sol.* 22:5. In *1 En.* 6:7–10, 24 these dragons dominate the oceans during the reign of evil, but will be served up as food for the righteous at the eschatological triumph. The seven-headed beast of Rev 13 and 17 is similarly derived from Leviathan through apocalyptic. See R. A. Oden, "Cosmogony/Cosmology," *Anchor Bible Dictionary*, 1:1163–66; J. Day, "Dragon and Sea, God's Conflict with," *Anchor Bible Dictionary*, 2:228–31, and "Leviathan," *Anchor Bible Dictionary*, 4:295–96.

17. For a useful discussion of how this language is translated through sociological categories for group formation, see J. Gager, "The End of Time and the Rise of Community," in *Kingdom and Community: The Social World of the Early Christians* (Englewood Cliffs, NJ: Prentice Hall, 1975), 19–36.

18. The term *messiah* ("anointed") only occurs in Dan 9:25–26 and refers to past kingly figures who had already been deposed, probably Zerubbabel and Onias III, respectively.

19. Such a view of history is also seen in the anonymous work called the *Book of Biblical Antiquities*, which dates from the later part of first century CE and was wrongly attributed to Philo of Alexandria (about whom we will say more later in Chapter 3). *Biblical Antiquities* is a work of wholesale reinterpretation of biblical events and chronology from Adam to Saul, with a strong sense of God's ultimate deliverance following the Deuteronomic theme of Judges; however, the work has no mention of any kind of messianic figure. It is possible that its portrayal of good and evil leaders in Israel's past is a reaction to the failed messianic hopes of the first Jewish revolt (66–74) against the Roman Empire. See Nickelsburg, *Jewish Literature Between the Bible and the Mishnah*, 265–68; F. J. Murphy, *Pseudo-Philo: Rewriting the Bible* (New York: Oxford University Press, 1993), 9–25, 260–80.

20. The Hasmonean dynasty, sometimes called the Second Hebrew Commonwealth, arose from the lineage of Judas the Maccabee, after the Maccabean revolt (167–164 BCE). It ruled Judah as a monarchy, 152–43 BCE, until replaced by the monarchy of Herod the Great in 40 BCE. See E. J. Bickerman, *From Ezra to the Last of the Maccabees* (New York: Schocken, 1967); L. M. White, "Herod and the Jewish Experience of Augustan Rule," in K. Galinsky, ed., *Cambridge Companion to the Age of Augustus* (Cambridge: Cambridge University Press, 2005), 361–87.

21. See Nickelsburg, *Jewish Literature Between the Bible and the Mishnah*, 203–12. This document was included in some Greek versions of the Hebrew scriptures and so would have been read as authentically by Solomon himself.

22. There are, of course, other interpretations of how and by whom these scrolls were produced and deposited in the caves. For discussions of the various theories, see Geza Vermes, *The Dead Sea Scrolls: Qumran in Perspective* (London: Collins, 1977), 116–30.

23. On the history of the community, see Vermes, *Dead Sea Scrolls*, 136–56.

24. Quotations from the Dead Sea Scrolls are from Geza Vermes, *The Dead Sea Scrolls in English*, 2nd ed. (New York: Penguin, 1975).

25. See Geza Vermes, *Jesus the Jew: A Historian's Reading of the Gospels* (Minneapolis: Augsburg Fortress, 1981), 160–90.

26. See n. 18, above.

27. On the origins of the title and its application in the Gospels, see A. Y. Collins, "The Origins of the Designation of Jesus as 'Son of Man,'" *Harvard Theological Review* 80 (1987): 391–407; D. R. A. Hare, *The Son of Man Tradition* (Minneapolis: Fortress, 1990); D. Burkett, *The Son of Man Debate: A History and Evaluation* (Cambridge: Cambridge University Press, 1999).

28. Notably, the references to the suffering of the "Son of Man" are more self-referential, while the eschatological expectations are all couched as "third party."

29. The main examples come from very fragmentary references in the Dead Sea Scrolls, whose messianic expectations have already been discussed. See now A. Y. Collins and J. Collins, *King and Messiah as Son of God: Divine, Human, and Angelic Messianic Figures in Biblical and Related Literature* (Grand Rapids, MI: Eerdmans, 2008).

30. On the historical background and editorial development of 4 Ezra, see Nickelsburg, *Jewish Literature Between the Bible and the Mishnah*, 287–94; T. A. Bergren, "Christian Influence on the Transmission History of 4, 5, and 6 Ezra," in J. C. VanderKam and W. Adler, eds., *The Jewish Apocalyptic Heritage in Early Christianity* (Minneapolis: Fortress, 1996), 102–27.

Chapter Two: Logos and Wisdom's Child

1. The comment is missing from the equivalent passage in the Lukan Passion narrative, between Luke 23:47 and 48.

2. *The Great Muppet Caper* (Jim Henson, 1981) offers a charming example of literary self-consciousness in dramatic production. Without prompting, Lady Holiday (Diana Rigg) has just explained her entire family history to Miss Piggy, a new employee whom she does know at all. In describing the problems of her shiftless brother, she thus provides the backstory for the movie's plot. When she finishes, Miss Piggy (Frank Oz) blurts out, "Why are you telling me all this?" To which Lady Holiday replies nonchalantly, "It's plot exposition. It has to go somewhere."

3. This passage has generated considerable speculation about the woman and her "sins," especially since Jesus sends her away with the precise phrase in Greek usually translated, "Your faith has made you well" (cf. Luke 8:48). Here, however, it is usually translated, "Your faith has saved you." This phrasing was preserved in the Latin Bible and was noted by Augustine (*Sermon* 49.6), who suggested that her sin was the "disease" or "demon" of prostitution. See also the next note.

4. Besides the change of location and position within the narrative, there are other key changes. First, in Mark and Matthew, the host is Simon, a leper presumably healed by Jesus. Simon remains a positive character; the criticism of Jesus comes from another guest. Second, in Mark and Matthew the criticism of her action has nothing to do with her being a "sinner," but rather that the oil should have been sold in order to care for the poor. We shall discuss the dramatic significance of this scene as it appears in the Gospel of Mark in Chapter 11.

5. On the basis of the immediately following passage in Luke 8:2, where Mary Magdalene is identified as a woman whom Jesus had healed of "seven demons," the tendency was to conflate the story of Mary Magdalene with the story of the other unnamed women. That a "Mary" was this unnamed woman is provided by the Gospel

of John, which makes her Mary of Bethany, the sister of Martha and Lazarus (12:1–8). But it must be noted that Mary of Bethany is clearly not the same as Mary Magdalene (or Mary of Magdala) in the Gospel of John (19:25; 20:1). In the Gospel of Luke Mary and Martha do not live in Bethany (cf. 10:38–42), but this Mary is different both from the anointing woman and Mary Magdalene (8:2; 24:10). The process of harmonization also drew in various stories of unnamed women found in completely independent episodes from other Gospels. The most notable conflation is that with the woman caught in adultery from John 7:53–8:12, which is now recognized as a very problematic passage even within the Johannine tradition. By the medieval period, therefore, it had become common to identify the anointing woman of Luke 7:36–50 as a prostitute with the name Mary Magdalene.

6. It is significant, therefore, that in a passage unique to the Gospel of Luke (10:17–18), Jesus seems to make a reference to the story of the fall of the angels derived from *1 Enoch*. Thus, in Luke, as in other Jewish traditions of the time, apocalyptic and the wisdom tradition are intertwined. Another part of the early Enochic tradition was a treatise on astronomical features called the "Book of the Heavenly Luminaries" (*1 En.* 72–82), given as a tour of the heavenly realm conducted by the archangel Uriel. In general on the relation between the wisdom tradition and apocalyptic, see J. Z. Smith, "Wisdom and Apocalyptic," in P. Hanson, ed., *Visionaries and Their Apocalypses* (Philadelphia: Fortress, 1983), 101–20; J. Blenkinsopp, *Wisdom and Law in the Old Testament: The Ordering of Life in Israel and Early Judaism* (New York: Oxford University Press, 1983), 151–58.

7. It is generally agreed, however, that this portion of Genesis comes from later stages of the editorial process (P), most probably in the period after the Babylonian exile. In other words, even this scene, which establishes the paradigm of the paternal blessing as a form for the passing down of proverbial wisdom, comes from the period of Babylonian and Persian rule.

8. The same period is likely for the composition of Qoheleth (Ecclesiastes). See M. Hengel, *Judaism and Hellenism*, 2 vols. (Philadelphia: Fortress, 1974), 1:107–74, esp. 115–30, 153–56.

9. This was a very widely known ethical motif in Greek philosophical tradition and is best represented by the version told by Xenophon in *Memorabilia* (2.1.21–34). The tale of the young Herakles is attributed to Prodicus, a contemporary of Socrates and, like him, a sophist and sage. Xenophon himself was a contemporary (ca. 430–354 BCE), who was among the group of Greek mercenaries accompanying the Persian prince Cyrus the younger on his eastern campaign, which began in 401 and ended in 399 BCE, the same year in which Socrates died. Thus Xenophon is an example of both the Greek philosophical side of this tradition and its intersection with a syncretistic Persian tradition.

10. In the medieval Latin Bible Sirach was given the title Ecclesiasticus (not to be confused with Ecclesiastes, or Qoheleth, in the Hebrew scriptures). See G. W. E. Nickelsburg, *Jewish Literature Between the Bible and the Mishnah* (Philadelphia: Fortress, 1981), 55–65. Fragments of the work in Hebrew found at Qumran and Masada are thought by some to represent the original version. The work seems to have circulated widely in its Greek form. See also Hengel, *Judaism and Hellenism*, 1:131–50.

11. It should be remembered that Alexandria is where the Hebrew scriptures were first translated into Greek in what would become the standard form of the scriptures for most Jewish and Christian readers of the early Roman period. This version was called the Septuagint (abbreviated LXX) from the tradition of the seventy (or seventy-two) elders who made the translation at the behest of Ptolemy II Philadelphus (285–246 BCE). In reality, however, this legend only refers to the first translation of the Torah proper (i.e., the Pentateuch, or first five books of the Hebrew scriptures). The actual process of translation of the remaining books occurred over several centuries. Moreover, the list of writings included in the LXX was longer than that now in the Jewish and Protestant Bibles. In fact, it included both Sirach and the Wisdom of Solomon as scripture.

12. See also the discussion of the Jewish philosopher Philo of Alexandria later in the chapter.

13. In the translations of passages from Sirach and Wisdom of Solomon, I use the Greek term "Sophia" wherever it occurs in the text, instead of rendering it "Wisdom" with the NRSV, in order to highlight the use of the Greek terminology and capture more of the tone of the personification.

14. On aretalogy, see Chapter 4.

15. This idea is similar to that associated with the Shekinah (the "abiding" or "presence" of the Lord) in later rabbinic thought, and it should be noted that this term is likewise feminine. In later kabbalistic mysticism, the feminine dimensions of the divine are also preserved, especially in conjunction with the *sephiroth*, or attributes of the divine king/throne. There too she is called either Hochma or Shekinah.

16. See Nickelsburg, *Jewish Literature Between the Bible and the Mishnah*, 175–85.

17. Wis 13–15 is a polemic against idolatry similar in argument to that found in Paul (Rom 1:18–27). Cf. also Paul's description of the role of the Holy Spirit (Rom 8) with the way wisdom is described; also the so-called Christ hymn of Col 1:15–20.

18. The same Greek word, *monogenes*, is used in John 3:16 (usually translated "only" or "only begotten") in reference to Jesus as God's son. As we shall see below, the Johannine Logos theology has roots in the wisdom tradition as well.

19. In rabbinic literature, Torah is sometimes depicted as the daughter of God, and thus also as both bride and mother of the sage. In the wisdom tradition, the Sinai event in which Moses received the Torah could also be depicted as a wedding (so Prov 7:4; Sir 15:2). Cf. also Philo *On Preliminary Studies*.

20. Hengel (*Judaism and Hellenism*, 1:162–64) argues that this equation was already at work in the personification of Wisdom in Prov 8 and thus assigns a rather late date to the composition of the latter. He links this development to the work of the earliest of the Jewish philosophers, Aristobulus (ca. 170 BCE), who attempted a reconciliation between the ideas of Moses and Plato.

21. Note the use of the term *monogenes* (translated "unique") in Wis 7:22, compared to John 3:16, translated "only" (RSV, NRSV). Other translations of John 3:16 place more symbolic weight on the term by rendering it as "only begotten" (KJV) or "one and only" (NIV). Likewise note the use of the term "image" (Gk. *eikon*) in Wis 7:26, compared with Col 1:15, but also see the discussion of Philo below.

22. See J. M. Robinson, "*Logoi Sophon:* On the *Gattung* of Q," in J. M. Robinson and H. Koester, *Trajectories Through Early Christianity* (Philadelphia: Fortress, 1971), 71–113.

23. See V. Tcherikover, *Hellenistic Civilization and the Jews*, 2nd ed. (New York: Jewish Publication Society, 1959); M. Hengel, *Jews, Greeks, and Barbarians* (Philadelphia: Fortress, 1980).

24. On Philo's family, life, and works, see the excellent introductions E. R. Goodenough, *An Introduction to Philo Judaeus*, 2nd ed. (Oxford: Oxford University Press, 1962); and Samuel Sandmel, *Philo of Alexandria:*

An Introduction (New York: Oxford University Press, 1979). See also Wayne A. Meeks, *The Moral World of the First Christians* (Philadelphia: Westminster, 1986), 81–85. The complete works of Philo are available in the Loeb Classical Library.

25. See Josephus *Antiquities* 20.102.
26. Philo *On the Creation of the World* 3.
27. Philo *Life of Moses* 1.48.
28. Philo *On Abraham* 68.
29. Philo *On the Migration of Abraham.*
30. Philo *On the Creation* 22.
31. This interpretation underlies much of Philo's thought, but it is most clearly seen in two writings, his *Allegorical Interpretation of Genesis* 2–3 and his *Questions and Answers on Genesis.*
32. The word *anthrōpos* in Greek is often translated "man," but is better translated as "human" since it does not on its own connote gender.
33. Philo *Allegorical Interpretation of Genesis* 1.31.
34. See also Meeks, *Moral World of the First Christians,* 84.

Chapter Three: Divine Man

1. I give here a more literal translation from the Greek to capture the sense of the statement.
2. For similar expressions in the other Gospels, cf. Mark 4:41; Matt 8:27; Luke 8:25.
3. See H. C. Kee, *Miracle in the Early Christian World* (New Haven: Yale University Press, 1983), esp. 1–73; *Medicine, Miracle, and Magic in New Testament Times* (Cambridge: Cambridge University Press, 1986).
4. A useful summary of this worldview is given in L. H. Martin, *Hellenistic Religions: An Introduction* (New York: Oxford University Press, 1987), 3–15, 35–57.
5. Discussed also in Martin, *Hellenistic Religions,* 16–34.
6. Cf. Matt 2:1–12, where *magi* play a very positive role in the Matthean birth narrative, with Acts 8:9–13, the story of Simon *magus.* Notice that in the former the term applies to the more specifically Persian practitioners; the latter passage concerns a more general form of magic.
7. For example, it should be remembered that Socrates was usually described by his later followers as having been accompanied by a "genius" (from Lat., whence we get the term "genie"), but the Greek term from which this came was actually *daimon.* Socrates, the wise sage, was guided by a good demon. The terms did not have their immediate good/evil associations in the Greek magical tradition. Indeed, one of the common divine epithets found in inscriptions is "To the Good Demon."
8. L. Bieler, *Theios Aner: Das Bild des "göttlichen Menschen" in Spätantike und Frühchristentum,* 2 vols. (Vienna, 1935), 1:20.
9. Plutarch *Life of Alexander* 2.1–5
10. Plutarch *Life of Alexander* 30.5.
11. Suetonius *Lives of the Caesars: The Deified Augustus* 2.94.1–7. Note that this is the same author who gives the account of Augustus's apotheosis to heaven (see Chapter 4).
12. Julia Domna's family were hereditary priests of the sun god Elagbalus (*Sol Invictus Elagbalus*), tutelary deity of Emesa. Her father was high priest of Emesa, as was her grandnephew, who took the name Elagbalus when he became emperor in 218.
13. Severus Alexander was actually the grandson of Julia Domna's sister, Julia Mamea. Born in 209, he was first adopted by his cousin, the emperor Marcus Aurelius Antoninus Elagbalus (218–222), who in turn had earlier been adopted by Caracalla. Elagbalus had been assassinated in 222; therefore, Severus Alexander claimed the epithet "son of the deified Antoninus (Caracalla)."
14. Cf. *Historia Augusta, Alexander* 29.2. The work is not altogether reliable as a historical source.
15. Philostratus *The Life of Apollonius of Tyana* 1.3. The complete text may be found in Loeb Classical Library edition, trans. F. C. Conybeare, 2 vols. (Cambridge, MA: Harvard University Press, 1948–50). The text is full of anachronisms, such as references to the territories annexed by Septimius Severus (Ctesiphon) as being already Roman at the time Apollonius was alive. See the discussion in Kee, *Miracle in the Early Christian World,* 256–65.
16. See Philostratus *Life of Apollonius* 1.2. A detractor named Euphrates, a philosopher and sophist, appears frequently in the letters of Apollonius. These letters were also used by Philostratus, but they may be pseudepigraphic productions (cf. the Loeb edition, 2:408–81). In one letter (16), Apollonius replies to the putative charge of Euphrates that, since he follows Pythagoras, he is not really a philosopher, but a magician. A four-volume attack on Apollonius by a certain Moiragenes is mentioned by Philostratus (*Life of Apollonius* 1.3) and by Origen, a Christian writing ca. 240s CE (*Against Celsus* 6.41). Neither the work nor its author is otherwise known. Celsus was a pagan detractor who wrote ca. 185 CE. Origen's point in the reference is to criticize Celsus's unwillingness to admit that even philosophers are sometime attracted to (or duped by) magic, while Celsus was quick to criticize the Christians for being ignorant and superstitious because of some of their beliefs. In this vein, Origen cites the account of Apollonius's life to show that Moiragenes had shown him as a charlatan and magician and that two known philosophers (one an Epicurean) were taken in by him. Cf. the contemporaneous case of *Alexander, the False Prophet* (by Lucian) discussed below.
17. See Philostratus *Life of Apollonius* 1.1; there Pythagoras himself is also presented with some of the attributes of a divine man, especially that he had direct visitations from Apollo and that he died and came back to life. Notice that the slightly later *Life of Pythagoras* as told by Iamblichus (third century CE) was also a divine-man portrayal, probably based on such earlier versions. In reality, however, the philosophy of Apollonius seems to be much more eclectic. According to Philostratus, Pythagoras was especially devoted to the worship of Proteus, so these two lines are connected.
18. See Philostratus *Life of Apollonius* 1.3, 7, 32; 4.16; 6.11; 8.7. Cf. the description of John the Baptist in Luke 7:31–35, discussed in Chapter 2.
19. See esp. D. L. Tiede, *The Charismatic Figure as Miracle Worker* (Missoula, MT: Society of Biblical Literature, 1972); E. Koskenniemi, *Apollonios von Tyana in der neutestamentlichen Exegese* (Tübingen: Mohr, 1994); D. S. du Toit, *Theios Anthropos* (Tübingen: Mohr, 1997); A. Pilgaard, "The Hellenistic *Theios Aner*—A Model for Early

Christian Christology," in P. Borgen and S. Giverson, eds., *The New Testament and Hellenistic Judaism* (Aarhus: Aarhus University Press, 1996), 101–22. All four are efforts to claim that the category of "divine man" did not really exist in the time of Jesus or the Gospels. On the contrary view, see nn. 20–21 to follow.

20. D. Zeller, "The *Theia Physis* of Hippocrates and Other 'Divine Men,'" in J. T. Fitzgerald, T. H. Olbricht, and L. M. White, eds., *Early Christianity and Classical Culture* (Leiden and Atlanta: Society of Biblical Literature, 2003), 54–55.

21. The recent debates are summarized in Zeller, "The *Theia Physis* of Hippocrates and Other 'Divine Men,'" 49–69. Zeller offers new and compelling evidence that both "divine man" and "divine nature" were used of certain individuals both before and after the time of Jesus and the Gospels.

22. G. Anderson, *Sage, Saint, and Sophist: Holy Men and Their Associates in the Early Roman Empire* (London: Routledge, 1994), 28–33.

23. See Josephus *Against Apion* 1.279; cf. *Antiquities* 3.180. See also the discussion of Moses in Zeller, "The *Theia Physis* of Hippocrates and Other 'Divine Men,'" 57–58.

24. See R. Jewett and J. S. Lawrence, *Captain America and the Crusade Against Evil* (Grand Rapids, MI: Eerdmans, 2003).

25. Philo *Life of Moses* 2.188, esp. in regard to his oracular and prophetic powers.

26. Josephus *Antiquities* 4.329; Philo *Life of Moses* 1.57. See J. Gager, *Moses in Greco-Roman Paganism* (Nashville: Abingdon, 1972), 140–43.

27. See D. Georgi, *The Opponents of Paul in Second Corinthians* (Philadelphia: Fortress, 1986), 250–58.

28. See Gager, *Moses in Greco-Roman Paganism*. Among others, the legends were known to Apuleius, the author of *The Golden Ass* (see above), and he used them in defending himself against charges of practicing harmful magic.

29. As seen in Celsus's polemic (so Origen *Against Celsus* 1.23, 26; 5.41–43). See Gager, *Moses in Greco-Roman Paganism*, 95, 134.

30. Philo *Life of Moses* 1.18–21, 25–26.

31. This tradition comes from the Jewish historian Artapanus (first century BCE), as preserved in Eusebius *Preparation of the Gospel* 9.27.1–4. He argues that the Greeks later divinized Moses for his gifts to their culture, and so they called him Hermes, the messenger and interpreter of the gods. The "proof" offered for this claim is that Moses was rightly recognized as the recipient and *interpreter* of God's eternal law, delivered on Sinai. The Greek word "interpreter" (*hermeneutes*) is homonymous with Hermes. In Stoicism, Hermes was also equated with the divine Logos that pervades all nature. This notion may suggest another point of connection to Philo's thought (as discussed in Chapter 2).

32. Philo *Life of Moses* 2.70; cf. Exod 34:33–34.

33. Philo *Life of Moses* 2.288.

34. The text is available in the Loeb Classical Library edition of the works of Lucian, trans. A. M. Harmon (Cambridge, MA: Harvard University Press, 1925), 4:173–254.

35. So Lucian *Alexander* 59. This particularly disgusting manner of death was virtually a commonplace itself and is regularly used of any number of characters who are portrayed as enemies. In the case of Alexander, it is only fitting that it should have been his leg, since he had wantonly displayed his thigh wrapped in some sort of golden girdle as part of religious ceremonies. One is led to infer that the disease began in his groin, again befitting his sexual excesses. The miserable death is a sign of divine wrath and just retribution. Cf. the account of the death of Herod Agrippa I in Acts 12:21–23.

Chapter Four: Savior

1. The abbreviated version of the ascension scene at the end of the Gospel of Luke (24:50–53), the companion work to Acts, says only "and was carried up into heaven" (24:51). It should be noted, however, that the Greek term used here (*anapherein*) does not occur in the Acts account or elsewhere in the New Testament with this meaning. A number of early manuscripts of the Gospel of Luke omit this phrase; see E. J. Epp, "The Ascension in the Textual Tradition of Luke-Acts," in E. J. Epp and G. D. Fee, eds., *New Testament Textual Criticism: Its Significance for Exegesis* (Oxford: Clarendon, 1981), 131–45. It has also been argued that the entire ascension scene was added to the Gospel of Luke at some later time, thus leaving the account in Acts 1:9–11 as the primary Lukan version; see A. N. Wilder, "Variant Traditions of the Resurrection in Acts," *Journal of Biblical Literature* 62 (1943): 307–318; H. Conzelmann, *The Theology of St. Luke* (New York: Harper, 1961), 93–94; *Acts of the Apostles: A Commentary* (Philadelphia: Fortress, 1987), 4.

2. Note 1 Thess 1:9–10; Phil 2:8–11, two of the earliest units of Christian oral tradition, found encapsulated in letters of Paul dated to the early and mid-50s CE, respectively. They will be discussed in Chapter 6 below.

3. Justin Martyr *Apology* 1.21–22 (my translation).

4. Celsus's attack on Christianity, entitled *The True Word*, is now lost, but we know the substance of his argument from a Christian counterattack, *Against Celsus*, by Origen (ca. 246). Indeed, Origen quotes nearly three-fourths of Celsus's work in his refutation. The quotation is Origen's paraphrase or summary of Celsus's key points distilled from the refutation in *Against Celsus* 3.22–43, in D. R. Cartlidge and D. L. Dungan, eds., *Documents for the Study of the Gospels*, 2nd ed. (Minneapolis: Fortress, 1994), 9. It is clear that Celsus is citing the same examples used by Justin in *Apology* 1.21 (quoted above), and it is often suggested that Celsus was responding directly to Justin's work.

5. This is the depiction suggested by the Gospel of Luke. See Chapter 13.

6. The legend of the phoenix is used explicitly in the *First Letter to the Corinthians* (also called *1 Clement*) of Clement of Rome (ca. 96–120 CE), 24–25, and it would become one of the most common themes in later Christian art.

7. This is the reconstruction of Celsus's text in R. Joseph Hoffmann, *Celsus: On the True Doctrine* (New York: Oxford University Press, 1987), 77–78. The sections of Celsus are quoted by Origen in *Against Celsus* 4.13–19.

8. This view is called *docetism* and is especially associated with later Gnostic Christianity; it will be discussed in Chapters 14 and 15. See also L. M. White, *From Jesus to Christianity* (San Francisco: HarperSanFrancisco, 2004), 314–18, 348–49.

9. This view is called *adoptionism;* it remained the norm within Jewish Christianity for centuries; the Jewish Christian Gospels will be discussed in Chapter 15.

10. A close synonym, *apathanatisis* (meaning "to make immortal" or "to deify"), is often used in its place. This is the term (in verb form) used by Justin Martyr in the passage quoted above.

11. Both are funerary reliefs preserved in Rome, dating to ca. 136 and 160 CE, respectively.

12. Justin actually lived in Rome ca. 140–64 CE, during the reign of Antoninus Pius (138–60), to whom he ostensibly addressed his *First Apology.*

13. The actual Latin word here is *consecratus,* the typical equivalent for the Greek *apotheosis.*

14. Suetonius *Lives of the Caesars: The Deified Julius* 88.

15. Suetonius *Lives of the Caesars: The Deified Augustus* 100.4.

16. Dio Cassius *Roman History* 69.11.2.

17. Justin Martyr *Apology* 1.29.

18. For a fuller discussion of this tradition in ancient Israel, see Chapter 1.

19. Suetonius *Lives of the Caesars: The Deified Augustus* 2.94.1–7, quoted in Chapter 3.

20. From an inscription in pseudo-Egyptian hieroglyphics dedicated by Hadrian at Rome.

21. Cartlidge and Dungan, *Documents for the Study of the Gospels,* 6.

22. Josephus *Jewish War* 1.414–5; *Antiquities* 16.124–38.

23. The inscription is *OGIS* 458.30–64, as translated in N. Lewis and M. Reinhold, *Roman Civilization: A Sourcebook* (New York: Harper & Row, 1955, 1966), 2.64 (adapted and italics added).

24. *I. Olympia* 53, quoted in S. Price, *Rituals and Power: The Roman Imperial Cult in Asia Minor* (Cambridge: Cambridge University Press, 1984), 55.

25. Cf. the language of Paul in Rom 13.1–7.

26. For discussion of the situation and tension between these two works, see White, *From Jesus to Christianity,* chap. 11.

27. This view was expressed in antiquity by Suetonius and is the basis of the modern novel *I Claudius,* by Robert Graves, which was later produced as a twelve-part BBC miniseries (1976, directed by Herbert Wise).

28. Both are reported in Suetonius *Nero* 33. Cassius Dio (*Roman History* 60.35) reports the second as having become proverbial in Greek after originating with Nero.

29. Suetonius *Nero* 9.

30. Suetonius *Claudius* 45.

31. The work has been attributed to Seneca since ancient times, but the authorship is not entirely certain.

32. The word "pumpkinification" here comes from older studies that used the English (U.K.) word "pumpkin" to translate the Greek. It does not mean the same as what Americans think of with this term, i.e., a specific species of the gourd/squash family. Especially in light of the actual crops of the ancient Mediterranean, we should more properly render Seneca's made-up word as "gourdification" (or perhaps "gourding away") or, as here, "zucchinification," but the insult is the same.

33. An allusion to the legendary "Labors of Hercules."

34. The term may be seen in reference to the Ptolemaic pantheon (cited above at n. 21) and in reference to Augustus (cited above at n. 23).

35. Cf. the wording in Luke 8:48: "Your faith has *made you well* (*sesoken*)," where the reference is clearly to healing from disease, to that in Luke 7:50: "Your faith has *saved* you (*sesoken*)," the case of the sinful woman who anoints Jesus. See also the discussion of this passage in Chapter 2.

36. This is the sense in which Paul uses it in Phil 4.12; it may be translated literally: "In any and all circumstances *I have become an initiate* (or *I have been initiated*) in facing plenty and hunger, abundance and want."

37. Homer *Hymn to Demeter* 235.

38. Homer *Hymn to Demeter* 240.

39. The name comes from a famous poet or hymnodist, Orpheus, who was closely associated with this particular form of Dionysiac myth. Orpheus himself was later accorded a divine status by some and was especially associated with the afterlife, as a kind of guide to the underworld.

40. This version of the myth of Dionysus relates how the infant Dionysus, son of Zeus, was captured and devoured by evil Titans. Enraged, Zeus then destroyed the Titans with his thunderbolt and scattered their ashes over the earth. Dionysus, however, was "saved" when his heart was rescued from the Titans and implanted in Zeus's thigh, whence a "new" Dionysus was born. Meanwhile, the ashes of the Titans, which contained the old Dionysus they had devoured, became the seeds of the human race. This myth thereby explains two key concepts in later Greek religious thought: first, why humans possess both good and evil traits, and, second, why there is a divine spark in the human soul that seeks immortality. Orphism was also associated with the notion of a judgment in the afterlife for one's behavior while on earth.

41. As reflected in the wall paintings of the Temple of Isis at Pompeii. Io was a priestess of Hera seduced by Zeus. When Hera found out, she punished Io by turning her into a white cow who wanders haplessly around the world, similar to Lucius in *The Golden Ass.* Io finally reaches Egypt, where she is transformed again by Zeus. In the later revisions of this myth, it is Isis who transforms her and with whom she is then identified. It is an easy mythic interplay, because Isis also had acquired bovine symbols (notably the horns typical of her Egyptian iconography) from her association with Hathor.

Chapter Five: Orality, Memory, and Performance

1. We shall deal with the issues of dating the Gospel of Mark in more detail in Chapter 11.

2. The text is the NRSV, as quoted at the beginning of this chapter, but here I have supplied the bracketed phrases to reflect the actual context within the letter. See also 1 Cor 14:3–5, 13–15.

3. The following discussion is based on A. Y. Collins, "Psalms, Philippians 2:6–11, and the Origins of Christology," *Biblical Interpretation* 11 (2002): 362–63. Collins likens the setting of the hymn in Paul to the practice described by Philo.

4. Philo *On the Contemplative Life* 80 (my translation).

5. Philo *On the Contemplative Life* 75–79, quoting from 76.

6. Philo *On the Contemplative Life* 81–82.

7. Ezekiel the Tragedian dates to the mid-second century BCE. See P. W. van der Horst, "Ezekiel the Tragedian," in D. N. Freedman, ed., *Anchor Bible Dictionary*, 6 vols. (New York: Doubleday, 1992), 2:709; J. H. Charlesworth, ed., *The Old Testament Pseudepigrapha*, 2 vols. (Garden City, NY: Doubleday, 1985), 2:803–30.

8. Tertullian *Apology* 39.17–18 (my translation; italics added).

9. D. E. Aune, *Prophecy in Early Christianity and the Ancient Mediterranean World* (Grand Rapids, MI: Eerdmans, 1983), 339–46; see also M. E. Boring, "Prophecy (Early Christian)," *Anchor Bible Dictionary*, 5:495–502.

10. Aune, *Prophecy in Early Christianity*, 296–99; for the text, see Charlesworth, *Old Testament Pseudepigrapha*, 725–71.

11. See esp. the last ode (*Odes Sol.* 42:2–20).

12. By definition, Q is composed of those units of nearly identical material found in Matthew and Luke that are not contained in Mark. See Chapter 12 and Appendix D.

13. B. Mack, *The Lost Gospel: Q and Christian Origins* (San Francisco: HarperSanFrancisco, 1993); J. D. Crossan, *The Historical Jesus: The Life of a Mediterranean Jewish Peasant* (San Francisco: HarperSanFrancisco, 1991).

14. L. T. Johnson, *The Real Jesus: The Misguided Quest for the Historical Jesus and the Truth of the Traditional Gospels* (San Francisco: HarperSanFrancisco, 1996).

15. The extensive scholarship on Q is too large and complex to summarize here. The pioneering work of James M. Robinson on the genre of Q as "wisdom sayings" led to the influential studies of John Kloppenborg, who has been one of the most vocal proponents that Q was (or at least had become) a written source sometime prior to its use by the Gospels of Matthew and Luke. See J. M. Robinson, "*Logoi Sophon:* On the *Gattung* of Q," in J. M. Robinson and H. Koester, *Trajectories Through Early Christianity* (Philadelphia: Fortress, 1971), 71–113; J. S. Kloppenborg, *The Formation of Q: Trajectories in Ancient Wisdom Collections* (Philadelphia: Fortress, 1987); *Excavating Q: The History and Setting of the Sayings Gospel* (Minneapolis: Fortress, 2000). The most vocal critic of this view has been Richard Horsley, who denies more strenuously than others that Q was ever written down. See his "Introduction" and his essay "Performance and Tradition: The Covenant Speech in Q," in R. Horsley, ed., *Oral Performance, Popular Tradition, and Hidden Transcript in Q*, Semeia 60 (Atlanta: Society of Biblical Literature, 2006).

16. For this aspect, see esp. W. Kelber, "The Verbal Art in Q and *Thomas:* A Question of Epistemology," in Horsley, *Oral Performance, Popular Tradition, and Hidden Transcript in Q*, 25–42; *The Oral and Written Gospel* (Philadelphia: Fortress, 1983); "Sayings Collections and Sayings Gospel: A Study of Clustering Management of Knowledge," *Language and Communication* 9 (1989): 213–24.

17. R. A. Horsley and J. A. Draper, *Whoever Hears You Hears Me: Prophets, Performance, and Tradition in Q* (Edinburgh: Clark, 1999), 153.

18. In addition to the studies by Horsley listed in the preceding notes, see J. A. Draper, ed., *Orality Literacy, and Colonialism in Antiquity*, Semeia 47 (Atlanta: Society of Biblical Literature, 2004). For evaluation of these debates, see the response by V. Robbins, "Oral Performance in Q: Epistemology, Political Conflict, and Contextual Register," in Horsley, *Oral Performance, Popular Tradition, and Hidden Transcript in Q*, 109–22; and the review of the same volume by J. Verheyden in *Review of Biblical Literature* 10 (2007).

19. R. Thomas, *Literacy and Orality in Ancient Greece* (Cambridge: Cambridge University Press, 1992), 1. One need only scan the list of items among the "gift tags" catalogued by Martial in bk. 14 of his *Epigrams* (later first century CE); numerous classical works as well as writing implements are mentioned.

20. See H. Y. Gamble, *Books and Readers in the Early Church* (New Haven: Yale University Press, 1995).

21. H. G. Snyder, *Teachers and Texts in the Ancient World: Philosophers, Jews, and Christians* (London: Routledge, 2000); L. V. Rutgers, P. W. van der Horst, H. W. Havelaar, and L. Teugels, *The Use of Sacred Books in the Ancient World* (Leuven: Peeters, 1998).

22. E. Fantham, *Roman Literary Culture: From Cicero to Apuleius* (Baltimore: Johns Hopkins University Press, 1996); D. Armstrong, J. Fish, P. A. Johnston, and M. B. Skinner, *Vergil, Philodemus, and the Augustans* (Austin: University of Texas Press, 2004); B. Gold, *Literary and Artistic Patronage in Ancient Rome* (Austin: University of Texas Press, 1982); and J. Griffin, *Latin Poets and Roman Life* (London: Duckworth, 1985).

23. See Pliny *Epistles* 3.21; 5.3; 8.21; 9.40; Matthew Roller, "Pliny's Catullus: The Politics of Literary Appropriation," *Transactions of the American Philological Association* (1998): 265–304.

24. P. Wiseman, "Caesar and Oral Performance," in K. Welch and A. Powell, eds., *Julius Caesar as Artful Reporter* (London: Classical Press, 1998); Andrew Riggsby, *Caesar in Gaul and Rome: War in Words* (Austin: University of Texas Press, 2006).

25. Quintilian 10.6.1, which discusses the habits of speaking and writing. See J. P. Small, *Wax Tablets of the Mind: Cognitive Studies of Memory and Literacy in Classical Antiquity* (London: Routledge, 1997), 182–85.

26. A good example may be seen in the opening lines of Dio Chrysostom's *Oration* 38, which has an incomplete sentence that must have been "finished" with a physical gesture rather than words. See the note in the Loeb Classical Library edition of Dio's orations, H. L. Crosby, *Dio Chrysostom IV* (Cambridge, MA: Harvard University Press, 1946), 50–51.

27. Pliny *Epistles* 9.36.

28. Eusebius *Church History* 6.23.1–2.

29. See Thomas, *Literacy and Orality*, 15–28.

30. W. V. Harris, *Ancient Literacy* (Cambridge, MA: Harvard University Press, 1989), 13. Harris's book has been one of the major revisionist studies of the phenomenon of ancient literacy.

31. Harris, *Ancient Literacy*, 248–284.

32. Meir Bar-Ilan, "Illiteracy in the Land of Israel in the First Century CE," in S. Fishbane and S. Schoenfeld, eds., *Essays in the Social Scientific Study of Judaism and Jewish Society* (Hoboken, NJ: Ktav, 1992), 46–61. The more optimistic estimate comes from the perspective of later rabbinic sources, which tend to stress the "education" of the rabbis as cultural norm. See S. Safrai, "Education and the Study of Torah," in S. Safrai and M. Stern, eds., *The Jewish People in the First Century*, 2 vols. (Philadelphia: Fortress/Van Gorcum, 1987), 946–49.

33. Thomas, *Literacy and Orality*, 10.

34. *P.Oxy.* 2673. For the text and discussion, see L. M. White, *The Social Origins of Christian Architecture*, 2 vols., Harvard Theological Studies 42 (Valley Forge, PA: Trinity, 1996–97), 2:166–70. The subscription of the

text, in Greek, says explicitly: "I, Aurelius Ammonius [the 'reader'], swore the oath [regarding the property], as said above. I, Aurelius Serenus, write on his behalf, because he does not know letters."

35. The terminology of "illiteracy" as found in the papyri is discussed by H. C. Youtie in two important articles: "Hypographeus: The Social Impact of Illiteracy in Graeco-Roman Egypt," *Zeitschrift für Papyrologie und Epigraphik* 17 (1975): 201–21; "Because They Do Not Know Letters," 19 (1975): 101–8.

36. See esp. M. Beard, "Ancient Literacy and the Function of the Written Word in Roman Religion," K. Hopkins, "Conquest by Book," and A. E. Hanson, "Ancient Illiteracy," in J. H. Humphrey, ed., *Literacy in the Roman World,* JRA Supplements 3 (Ann Arbor, MI: Journal of Roman Archaeology, 1991).

37. Thomas, *Literacy and Orality,* 11.

38. For discussion of the situation of Romans, see L. M. White, *From Jesus to Christianity* (San Francisco: HarperSanFrancisco, 2004), 209–14.

39. *Corpus Inscriptionum Latinarum* 6.32323.

40. *Corpus Inscriptionum Latinarum* 13.1668; cf. Tacitus *Annals* 11.24.

41. Because it has become commonplace now to think of "Homer" not as a single author, we here use it as a scholarly shorthand. It can refer either to the fictional author or the work that circulated under this name.

42. For two who have tried to incorporate it more fully, see Ellen B. Aitken, *Jesus' Death in Early Christian Memory: The Poetics of the Passion* (Göttingen: Vandenhoeck & Ruprecht, 2004); and Antoinette C. Wire, *Holy Lives, Holy Deaths: A Close Hearing of Early Jewish Storytellers* (Atlanta: Society of Biblical Literature, 2002).

43. Thomas, *Literacy and Orality,* 29.

44. Thomas, *Literacy and Orality,* 29. The most extensive recent work out of the Parry-Lord model is G. Nagy, *Homeric Questions* (Austin: University of Texas Press, 1996); *Poetry as Performance: Homer and Beyond* (Cambridge: Cambridge University Press, 1996); and *Homeric Responses* (Austin: University of Texas Press, 2003).

45. For a brief discussion of the key features of their theory as well as some subsequent refinements, see Thomas, *Literacy and Orality,* 31–44.

46. See Nagy, "An Evolutionary Model for the Making of Homeric Poetry," in *Homeric Questions,* 40–43.

47. E. Cook, *The Odyssey in Athens: Myths of Cultural Origins* (Ithaca, NY: Cornell University Press, 1995).

48. M. West, *Studies in the Text and Transmission of the Iliad* (Munich: Saur, 2001) 3, citing A. Parry, "Have We Homer's *Iliad*?" *Yale Classical Studies* 20 (1966): 177–216.

49. Some of the recent work in this vein includes: R. H. Finnegan, *Oral Poetry: Its Nature, Significance, and Social Context* (Cambridge: Cambridge University Press, 1977); K. Dickson, *Nestor: Poetic Memory in Greek Epic* (New York: Garland, 1995); E. J. Bakker, *Poetry in Speech: Orality and Homeric Discourse* (Ithaca, NY: Cornell University Press, 1997).

50. I wish to express gratitude to my former student Gene McMurray, who made this very compelling observation in a senior honors thesis at the University of Texas on the subject of oral tradition and oral performance in Q and the Gospels.

51. Creating variation through oral performance also occurred in antiquity, especially in Greek drama. See D. L. Page, *Actors' Interpolations in Greek Tragedy* (Oxford: Clarendon, 1934).

52. B. Gentili, *Poetry and Its Public in Ancient Greece: From Homer to the Fifth Century* (Baltimore: Johns Hopkins University Press, 1988), xii. This way of approaching oral performance goes beyond older notions of "speech-act" theory, as described by R. P. Martin (*The Language of Heroes: Speech and Performance in the Iliad* [Ithaca, NY: Cornell University Press, 1989]) and others.

53. The point that oral storytelling still operates by literary convention in its development of characters and plots is well made in N. Worman, *The Cast of Character: Style in Greek Literature* (Austin: University of Texas Press, 2002).

54. Thomas, *Literacy and Orality,* 36.

55. Nagy, *Homeric Questions,* 17.

56. Nagy, *Homeric Questions,* 30.

57. Nagy, *Homeric Questions,* 34–35.

58. J. D. G. Dunn, *Jesus Remembered, Christianity in the Making,* vol. 1 (Grand Rapids, MI: Eerdmans, 2003). The comments given here follow the basic lines of my own paper "Remembering as Performance," as an invited response to a critique of Dunn by the late Daryl Schmidt, "Remembering Jesus: Assessing the Oral Evidence," Plenary Address at the Southwest Regional Meeting of the Society of Biblical Literature, Ft. Worth, TX, March 5–6, 2005.

59. Dunn, *Jesus Remembered,* 210. Dunn here follows the work of K. E. Bailey ("Informed Controlled Oral Tradition and the Synoptic Gospels," *Asia Journal of Theology* 5 [1991]: 34–54), which draws extensively on personal experience in contemporary Middle Eastern villages rather than on historical work on orality in the ancient world. Bailey's theory was also used in N. T. Wright, *Jesus and the Victory of God* (Minneapolis: Fortress, 1996), 136. Schmidt (see preceding note) offered a very serious criticism of Bailey's model as taken over by Dunn. See also below.

60. Dunn, *Jesus Remembered,* 223 (emphasis added).

61. Dunn, *Jesus Remembered,* 238.

62. From Dunn's earlier essay "Jesus in Oral Memory: The Initial Stages of the Jesus Tradition," now incorporated in *Jesus Remembered,* 118–19. I owe this observation to Schmidt.

63. See White, *From Jesus to Christianity,* 118–42, for an effort to locate this oral tradition phase in an appropriate historical and social context.

64. See n. 59, above.

65. Bailey's work was published in two articles that did not circulate widely: "Informal Controlled Oral Tradition and the Synoptic Gospels," *Asia Journal of Theology* 5 (1991): 34–54; "Middle Eastern Oral Traditions and the Synoptic Gospels," *Expository Times* 106 (1994–95): 63–67.

66. See the extensive review of Bailey's work by T. J. Weeden, "Kenneth Bailey's Theory of Oral Tradition: A Theory Contested by Its Evidence," *Journal for the Study of the Historical Jesus* 7 (2009): 3–443. A crux of Weeden's critique is that Bailey claims these village "storytelling" sessions (called *haflat samar* in Arabic) were consciously intended to "preserve" the stories. Weeden shows that no notion of "preservation" occurs in the actual Arabic term (*samar*) used to describe them (38–42).

67. Bailey, "Informal Controlled Oral Tradition," 48–49; Weeden, "Kenneth Bailey's Theory," 29–32. It should be noticed that Bailey's accounts of these stories are rather brief. Weeden has taken the trouble to research the sources used by Bailey to provide greater detail and nuance.

68. Bailey, "Informal Controlled Oral Tradition," 46–47; Weeden, "Kenneth Bailey's Theory," 12–21.

69. Bailey, "Informal Controlled Oral Tradition," 47–48; Weeden, "Kenneth Bailey's Theory," 26–29.

70. J. D. G. Dunn, "Kenneth Bailey's Theory of Oral Tradition: Critiquing Theodore Weeden's Critique," *Journal for the Study of the Historical Jesus* 7 (2009): 44–62.

71. See J. Fentress and C. Wickham, *Social Memory* (Oxford: Blackwell, 1992); J. Assmann, *Das kulturelle Gedächtnis: Schrift, Erinnerung und politische Identität in frühen Hochkulturen* (Munich: Beck, 1992); P. Burke, "History as Social Memory," in T. Butler, ed. *Memory: History, Culture, and the Mind* (Oxford: Blackwell, 1989), 97–113; J. Le Goff, *History and Memory* (New York: Columbia University Press, 1992).

72. A. M. Gowing, *Empire and Memory: The Representation of the Roman Republic in Imperial Culture* (Cambridge: Cambridge University Press, 2005), 7.

73. Gowing, *Empire and Memory*, 10 (emphasis his).

74. The pioneering work on the subject of "constructed memory" is that of M. Halbwachs on sites associated with the Gospels: *La topographie légendaire des Évangiles en Terre Sainte: Étude de mémoire collective* (Paris: Presses universitaires de France, 1941). See also the collection of his work edited by Lewis Coser, *On Collective Memory* (Chicago: University of Chicago Press, 1992).

75. S. Alcock, *Archaeologies of the Greek Past: Landscape, Monuments, and Memories* (Cambridge: Cambridge University Press, 2002), 1–36.

76. *Oxford English Dictionary*, s.v. "monument."

77. She here refers to the work of Halbwachs; see n. 74, above.

78. Alcock, *Archaeologies of the Greek Past*, 23–32, with additional bibliography cited there on both examples.

79. B. Gerhardsson, *Memory and Manuscript: Oral Tradition and Written Transmission in Rabbinic Judaism and Early Christianity* (Lund: Gleerup, 1961), 42. See also his *Tradition and Transmission in Early Christianity* (Lund: Gleerup, 1964). These two works were republished together (Grand Rapids, MI: Eerdmans, 1998). See also *The Origins of the Gospel Traditions* (Philadelphia: Fortress, 1979). Much of his earlier work was collected together into a new publication entitled *The Reliability of the Gospel Tradition* (Peabody, MA: Hendrickson, 2001).

80. Gerhardsson, *Memory and Manuscript*, 63.

81. Gerhardsson, *Memory and Manuscript*, 27.

82. Gerhardsson, *The Origins of the Gospel Tradition*, 17–24. These features include: terse condensation (to create memorable units); rhetorical devices (poetical or didactic, e.g., mnemonics, symmetry, parallelism, key words); repetition patterns (doublets or triplets of similar action); recitation patterns (musical, chantlike quality); and writing (partial or whole units).

83. Dunn, *Jesus Remembered*, 198. See esp. J. Neusner, *The Rabbinic Traditions About the Pharisees Before 70* (Leiden: Brill, 1971); *From Politics to Piety: The Emergence of Pharisaic Judaism*, 2nd ed. (New York: Ktav, 1979). In a preface to the 1998 reprint of Gerhardsson's *Memory and Manuscript*, xxv–xlvi, Neusner withdrew some of the more negative aspects of his earlier criticism. It is worth noting, however, that Neusner still insists that the rabbinic traditions be thought of as "paradigmatic" rather than "historical thinking" in a strict sense.

84. C. Milikowsky, "Midrash as Fiction and Midrash as History: What Did the Rabbis Mean?" in J. A. Brant, C. W. Hedrick, and C. Shea, eds., *Ancient Fiction: The Matrix of Early Christian and Jewish Narrative*, Symposium 32 (Atlanta: Society of Biblical Literature, 2005), 115–27.

85. N. A. Dahl, "*Anamnesis:* Memory and Commemoration in Early Christianity," in *Jesus in the Memory of the Early Church* (Minneapolis: Augsburg, 1976), 11–29. In contrast to Gerhardsson, Dahl sees the same tendencies in rabbinic tradition.

86. On the historical issues surrounding the Exodus narrative, see K. A. Kitchen, "Exodus, The," in D. N. Freedman, ed., *Anchor Bible Dictionary*, 6 vols. (New York: Doubleday, 1992), 2:700–708. For a more negative assessment of the problems, see I. Finkelstein, "Patriarchs, Exodus, Conquest: Fact or Fiction," and A. Mazar, "Patriarchs, Exodus, Conquest Narratives in Light of Archaeology," in I. Finkelstein and A. Mazar, *The Quest for the Historical Israel: Debating Archaeology and the History of Early Israel*, ed. B. Schmidt (Atlanta: Society of Biblical Literature, 2007), 41–55, 57–71.

87. G. Porton, "Haggadah," *Anchor Bible Dictionary*, 3:19–20.

88. Both this and the following quotation are from the definition of "master stories" in M. Goldberg, *Jews and Christians, Getting Our Stories Straight: The Exodus and the Passion-Resurrection* (Nashville: Abingdon, 1985), 13 (italics his).

89. See also Kelber, *The Oral and Written Gospel*, 71; J. Vansina, *Oral Tradition as History* (Madison: University of Wisconsin Press, 1985), 94. (Both also cited by Weeden in his review of Bailey; see n. 59, above.)

90. R. Bauckham, *James: Wisdom of James, Disciple of Jesus the Sage* (London: Routledge, 1999).

91. Whereas scripture quotations from the LXX are marked formulaically (e.g., Jas 2:11; 2:23; 4:5, 6), only four aphorisms in the work are actually marked in the text by the vague introductory formula "you know" (Jas 1:3; 3:11; 4:4; 5:20), but none are explicitly credited to Jesus himself.

92. Bauckham, *James*, 91.

93. J. Kloppenborg, "The Reception of Jesus Traditions in James," in J. Schlosser, ed., *The Catholic Epistles and the Tradition* (Leuven: Leuven University Press, 2004), 93–141.

94. Kloppenborg, "The Reception of Jesus Traditions in James," 116–17.

95. Kloppenborg, "The Reception of Jesus Traditions in James," 117, n. 71, citing Theon *Progymnasmata* (Hock-O'Neil, *Chreia*, 1:94–95; Kennedy, *Progymnasmata*, 19).

96. Kloppenborg, "The Reception of Jesus Traditions in James," 117, and notes cited there, including epigraphic and papyrus examples of copybooks.

97. Kloppenborg, "The Reception of Jesus Traditions in James," 118.

98. Kloppenborg, "The Reception of Jesus Traditions in James," 141.

99. H. Koester, "Written Gospels or Oral Traditions?" *Journal of Biblical Literature* 113 (1994): 293–97.

100. D. Moody Smith, *John Among the Gospels: The Relationship in Twentieth-Century Research* (Minneapolis: Fortress, 1992), 192.

Chapter Six: Heralding the Crucifixion

1. The Greek verb *kērussein,* from which *kerygma* comes, is usually translated "to herald or proclaim," but sometimes, less correctly, "to preach." The related noun *kērux* was the standard title for the "herald" of a city, who was charged with making official public announcements.

2. C. H. Dodd (*The Apostolic Preaching and Its Developments* [London: Hodder & Stoughton, 1936]) was the first to propose that it arose from early Christian preaching about Jesus; however, his once popular view that Peter's sermon in Acts 10:34–43 was the historical source for a basic outline of all the Gospels has now been generally rejected in more recent scholarship.

3. The phrase was first coined in 1892 by M. Kähler, in *The So-Called Historical Jesus and the Historic, Biblical Christ* (German ed., 1892; Philadelphia: Fortress, 1964), 80, n. 11.

4. See Victor Paul Furnish, *Jesus According to Paul* (Cambridge: Cambridge University Press, 1993), 19–39.

5. Of all of these only the Last Supper tradition (1 Cor 11:23–26) is cited by Paul as a statement of Jesus, and it remains the closest in wording, though it is still not exact. It will be discussed later in this chapter. Of the other sayings, Paul specifically cites "the Lord" as his source for statements only in 1 Cor 7:10–11 (cf. Mark 10:11–12) and 1 Cor 9:14 (cf. Luke 10:7); however, neither passage is identical to that found in the Gospels. If "Lord" is indeed a reference to Jesus (rather than to God), it is also interesting that he feels free to expand them in certain ways or to editorialize (as in 1 Cor 7:10, where he insists that a divorced woman remain single). Several other passages have been suggested as "echoes" of Jesus's sayings found in the Gospels. These include Rom 12:14, 17; 1 Cor 4:17 (cf. Matt 5:44; Luke 6:28); Rom 13:7 (cf. Mark 12:17 and parallels); Rom 14:4, 10, 13 (cf. Matt 7:1; Luke 6:37); 1 Cor 13:2 (cf. Mark 11:22; Matt 17:20; 21:21). For discussion, see Furnish, *Jesus According to Paul,* 40–65; see also David Dungan, *The Sayings of Jesus in the Churches of Paul* (Philadelphia: Fortress, 1971).

6. H. Koester, *Ancient Christian Gospels: Their History and Development* (Philadelphia: Trinity Press International, 1990), 3–7.

7. The Latin word *crucifigere* (from which we get "crucifixion") is more precise in that it combines the word *figere,* meaning "to fix or affix" (by means of pins or spikes), and *crux* "cross." The Greek word *stauros* actually means an upright pale or stake. The verb *stauroō* could mean either "to build a stockade fence (using pales)" or "to impale a corpse." By the Roman period, however, these Greek words were commonly used to translate the more technical Latin terms.

8. See L. M. White, *From Jesus to Christianity* (San Francisco: HarperSanFrancisco, 2004), 176–85. See also J. Jeremias, *The Eucharistic Words of Jesus* (London: SCM, 1966), 101–5; A. M. Hunter, *Paul and His Predecessors,* rev. ed. (Philadelphia: Westminster, 1961), 15–20; 117–18.

9. M. Dibelius, *From Tradition to Gospel* (London: Nicholson and Watson, 1934), 21; cf. the rabbinic tractate *Pirke Aboth* 1.1.

10. The word "handed on" in Greek is a verb form of the word "tradition" (*paradosis*).

11. For the chronology of Paul's career, see White, *From Jesus to Christianity,* 150–53.

12. See M. de Jonge, *Christology in Context: The Earliest Christian Response to Jesus* (Philadelphia: Westminster, 1988), 36.

13. For this word, a cognate of *kerygma,* see n. 1.

14. The phrase "in accordance with the scriptures" found in 1 Cor 15:3–4 does not occur elsewhere in Paul. The phrase "as it is written" occurs some nineteen times in Paul; cf., e.g., Rom 1:17; 3:4; 10:15; 11:26; 1 Cor 1:31; 2:9. In numerous other cases he uses the simpler formulation "it is written."

15. See Mark 8:31; 9:30; 10:34; Matt 27:63. Cf. the further Matthean elaboration in Matt 12:40, which yields "three days and three nights" based on a metaphoric reading of the Jonah story (cf. Jon 1:17).

16. This is a literal translation from the LXX; cf. the English rendering of the verbatim text in the NRSV of Acts 2:27. Another allusion to the passage is found in Acts 13:37. The numbering of the Psalms differs between the Hebrew version and the LXX. The numbering in English Bibles follows that of the Hebrew. The number in brackets is the LXX's. The difference in the numbering comes from the fact that Ps 9 was split into two parts (Pss 9 and 10) in the Masoretic text (Hebrew), which was followed by the English; while the LXX (Greek) version kept them together, which was followed by the Vulgate (Latin). As a result, in modern Hebrew and English versions of the Psalms, the numbering is one higher than in the LXX and Vulgate from Ps 10 to 150. In the LXX and Vulgate, there is also a Ps 151, which does not appear in the Masoretic or English text.

17. Here note that the words "perishable" (*phthora* and *phtharton*) and "imperishable" (*aphtharsia* and *aphtharos*) that occur frequently in this passage (e.g., in 15:42–43; 52–53) are actually cognates of the word *diaphthora* in Ps 15:10 (LXX). See next note.

18. The Greek word here translated "corruption" (*diaphthora*) generally connotes decay, and thus may result from a notion that after three days a dead body would begin to decompose. The Hebrew of Ps 16[15]:10, however, literally reads "you do not forsake my soul to Sheol." The Latin follows the Greek, rendering the word as *corruptionem.*

19. My translation from the Greek in both passages.

20. See B. M. Metzger, "A Suggestion Concerning the Meaning of 1 Cor. XV.4b," *Journal of Theological Studies* 8 (1957): 122; N. T. Wright, *The Resurrection of the Son of God* (Minneapolis: Fortress, 2003), 639; K. Komaranitsky, "Ps 16:10, The Origin of the Christian 'Third Day' Belief" (an unpublished paper, courtesy of the author). One also wonders if the "harrowing of hell" passage added by the Gospel of Matthew (27:52–53) might also suggest a use of this same scripture in conjunction with the death and resurrection. See also L. W. Hurtado, *Lord Jesus Christ: Devotion to Jesus in Earliest Christianity* (Grand Rapids, MI: Eerdmans, 2003), 628–35.

21. The Greek is not identical in this case. The closest formulation is in Isa 53:5, where the LXX reads, "He was abused on account of (*dia*) our sins." The rendering in 1 Cor 15:3 (with the preposition *hyper,* "on behalf of") may already reflect an earlier conflation of terms.

22. As shown above in the case of Ps 16[15]:19. In the case of Isa 53:4–6, it is worth noting that the LXX renders several different words with the Greek word for "sin" (*hamartia*), thus making it more central to the passage in the Greek version. One of these cases in the Hebrew (in v. 4) refers instead to illness or physical infirmities. So it would appear even here that the appropriation depends on the Greek.

23. On the early Aramaic substratum of the Jesus movement, see White, *From Jesus to Christianity,* 122–25. That Paul was familiar with an Aramaic oral tradition is confirmed by his use of *marana tha* (1 Cor 16:22) and *abba* (Gal 4:6; Rom 8:15). See also n. 37, below.

24. Some scholars have argued that the Pentecost miracle of the tongues (Acts 2:1–4) is a later variation of the appearance to the five hundred, but if this were the case, it shows a rather radical change in the story.

25. Cf. Matt 28:16 (eleven) ; Luke 24:13–32 (only two); 24:33 (eleven); Acts 1:26; 2:5 (eleven); John 20:19–25 (only ten); 20:26–29 (eleven); 21:1–3 (only seven).

26. Matt 27:3–10; Acts 1:15–26. See Chapter 7.

27. Although James is not mentioned by name in the early chapters of Acts, Acts 1:14 does mention that the mother of Jesus and his brothers were with the disciples in Jerusalem after Jesus's ascension and presumably part of the group that experienced the events at Pentecost. It is possible, therefore, that the author of Luke-Acts shows some awareness of this Pauline passage, but an actual appearance to James the brother of Jesus is never mentioned in the canonical Gospels. Cf. *Gospel of the Hebrews* on pp. 376 and 383.

28. For this practice, cf. 1 Cor 14:26 and see discussion on pp. 125–127.

29. The same verb is used in the tradition summary formula, where it is used in the more rudimentary sense of "to deliver or hand on."

30. Cf. Mark 14:16; Matt 26:19; Luke 22:13.

31. Mark 14:10–11, 18, 20–21; Matt 26:15–16, 21, 23–24; Luke 22:5–6, 21–22; John 13:2, 21 (cf. John 6:71). On the proper translation, see also R. E. Brown, *The Death of the Messiah*, 2 vols. (New York: Doubleday, 1994), 1:211–13; 2:1399.

32. See W. Klassen, *Judas: Friend or Betrayer of Jesus?* (Minneapolis: Fortress, 1996), 35; "Judas Iscariot," in D. N. Freedman, ed., *Anchor Bible Dictionary*, 6 vols. (New York: Doubleday, 1992), 3:1091–96; and Brown, *Death of the Messiah*, 2:1394–1418.

33. In the case of Athens and Rome, this has sometimes been more than just an imaginary enterprise. See S. Alcock, *Archaeologies of the Greek Past: Landscape, Monuments, and Memories* (Cambridge: Cambridge University Press, 2002), also discussed in Chapter 5, p 101, and nn 75, 78. In the case of Athens, Alcock (3–5) discusses the example of the "stripping of the Acropolis" in the nineteenth century, citing the work of R. A. McNeal, "Archaeology and the Destruction of the Later Athenian Acropolis," *Antiquity* 65: 49–63. In the case of Rome, consider the role of archaeological "restoration" in the Mussolini era.

34. Neither the institution of the commemorative meal nor the words of Jesus occur in the Last Supper scene in the Gospel of John (13:1–35).

35. In Hebrew the word is *berekah*. On the Jewish meal blessings, see P. Bradshaw, *The Search for the Origins of Christian Worship* (New York: Oxford University Press, 1992), 24–26; however, as rabbinic scholars have noted, the Jewish blessings reflected in the Mishnah were not formalized until the second century. See B. Bokser, "Ma'al and Blessings over Food: Rabbinic Transformation of Cultic Terminology and Alternative Modes of Piety," *Journal of Biblical Literature* 100 (1981): 557–84. It is also worth noting that Philo makes the similar substitution of *eucharistein* ("to give thanks") for the blessing formula (*berekah* or *eulogein*).

36. J. Jeremias, *The Eucharistic Words of Jesus* (London: SCM, 1966), 109, 113; H.-J. Klauck, "Lord's Supper," *Anchor Bible Dictionary*, 4:365.

37. *m. Ber.* 6:1–3. See Bradshaw, *Search for the Origins of Christian Worship*, 24–25.

38. Bradshaw, *Search for the Origins of Christian Worship*, 25; see also his *Eucharistic Origins* (New York: Oxford University Press, 2004), 9. In later rabbinic Judaism, the *hodayot* were said at the end of the meal in a three-part prayer of blessing, thanksgiving, and petition. Typically, the thanksgiving was for life (as in *Jub.* 22:6–9) or, later, for God's gifts to Israel, including the Torah and covenant (as in *m. Ber.* 6:8).

39. It is worth noting that, although not directly connected to eucharistic language or ritual, on one occasion (2 Cor 1:3) Paul also substitutes "blessed" (*eulogētos*) for "give thanks" in his formulaic structures of letter writing—what is usually called the "thanksgiving" section found typically at the beginning of each letter.

40. It should be noted that the word for "give thanks" is used for the cup in both Mark and Matthew. We should also observe that the two feeding miracles, widely viewed as prefiguring the language of the Last Supper, use "bless" in one instance and "give thanks" in the other (see Mark 6:41; Matt 14:19; and Mark 8:6; Matt 15:36, respectively). Moreover, only Mark and Matthew contain both versions of the feeding miracle. The Lukan version of the feeding of the five thousand uses "bless," following Mark (9:15), but the Johannine version of the same miracle uses "give thanks" (6:11). Finally, the recapitulation of the Last Supper scene in the road to Emmaus story, which only occurs in Luke, says Jesus "took bread, and *blessed* and broke it, and gave it to them" (24:30).

41. This same scene in the Gospel of Luke has been moved much earlier to Luke 7:36–50. See the discussion in Chapter 2.

42. The word "remembrance" (or "memorial"; Mark 14:9; Matt 26:13) is *mnemosunon*, whereas 1 Cor 11:24 has *anamnesis*. Acts 10:4 uses the same word for "memorial" (of virtuous actions before God) as found in Mark and Matthew.

43. V. E. Robbins, "Last Meal: Preparation, Betrayal, and Absence," in W. E. Kelber, ed., *The Passion in Mark: Studies in Mark 14–16* (Philadelphia: Fortress, 1976), 21–40, esp. 36; K. E. Corley, *Private Women, Public Meals: Social Conflict in the Synoptic Tradition* (Peabody, MA: Hendrickson, 1993), 102–6; *Women and the Historical Jesus* (Santa Rosa, CA: Polebridge, 2002), 137; cf. E. Schüssler Fiorenza, *In Memory of Her: A Feminist Theological Reconstruction of Christian Origins* (New York: Crossroad, 1983), 152–54.

44. B. Mack, *A Myth of Innocence: Mark and Christian Origins* (Philadelphia: Augsburg Fortress, 1988), 311–12.

45. G. Feeley-Harnik, *The Lord's Table: The Meaning of Food in Early Judaism and Christianity* (Washington, DC: Smithsonian Institution Press, 1994), 112–27.

46. See B. M. Metzger, *A Textual Commentary on the Greek New Testament* (New York: [United Bible Societies], 1983), 174–76.

47. For other suggestions on how two distinct traditions may have been transmitted, see the discussion in Bradshaw, *Eucharistic Origins*, 6–10.

48. Klauck, "Lord's Supper," 4:365.

49. 1 Cor 11:25; the Greek may be translated more literally as "after he had eaten supper/dinner" and clearly refers to an evening meal. The version in Luke follows Paul in this addition (22:20). See Box 6.2. The view taken here is different from that of Jeremias, who argues that the phrase was original to the original Passover form of Jesus's meal (*Eucharistic Words of Jesus*, 115–22). Yet in that context the cup ought to come first. In the context of

Paul's discussion regarding abuses of the Lord's Supper in Corinth, this addition would suit his argument that the whole meal becomes a sacred moment of community solidarity. It also is closer to a traditional Greek banquet. See also W. A. Meeks, *The First Urban Christians*, 2nd ed. (New Haven: Yale University Press, 2000), 157–62; D. E. Smith, *From Symposium to Eucharist: The Banquet in the Early Christian World* (Minneapolis: Fortress, 2003), 188.

50. This distinction is the basis for the requirement of having seen Jesus before "he was taken up from us" in selecting a replacement for Judas according to Acts 1:21–26. The phrasing "was taken up" (from Gk. *analambanein*) is one of the standard terms used in Acts for the ascension (so 1:2). See n. 52, below.

51. See also Acts 22:6–21; 26:4–23. All three accounts have a vision/voice from heaven, although other details differ substantially.

52. See 1 Cor 15:25–28, where the reference is to his exaltation to heaven, based on Ps 110:1. The term for Jesus being "raised from the dead" in Paul is *egeirein*, as in the oral tradition unit in 1 Cor 15:4. The word "resurrection" (Greek *anastasis/anistanai*) is also used in the genuine letters of Paul, typically in reference to the Jewish belief in a general resurrection of the dead (Rom 1:4; 1 Cor 15:12, 21; Phil 3:10), but occasionally in reference to the resurrection of Jesus (1 Thess 4:14). More frequently Paul uses the verb *egeirein* to refer to the raising of Jesus from the dead. For example, in 1 Cor 15:12–19 the general "resurrection of the dead" (*anastasis*) is juxtaposed to Jesus's being "raised from the dead" (*egeirein*). However, in the light of 1 Thess 4:14, this distinction should not be pressed for Paul. On the other hand, Luke-Acts uses the same two terms (*anistinai* and *egerein*), but makes them interchangeable (see Luke 24:7: "raised up [*anastēnai*] on the third day"). In contrast, Luke-Acts wants to keep the terms for resurrection distinct from those for the ascension. It uses three distinct words for the event of the ascension—"taken up" (*analambanein*, Acts 1:2; Luke 9:51), "lifted up" (*epairein*, Acts 1:9), and "carried up" (*anapherein*, Luke 24:51)—but none of them is the same as those used for the resurrection (Luke 9:22; 24:34). Significantly, none of the three terms for the ascension used in Acts is used by Paul in conjunction with the exaltation of Jesus to heaven.

53. W. A. Meeks, "The Social Context of Pauline Theology," *Interpretation* 36 (1982): 274; E. J. Epp, "The Ascension in the Textual Tradition of Luke-Acts," in E. J. Epp and G. D. Fee, eds., *New Testament Textual Criticism: Its Significance for Exegesis, Essays in Honor of Bruce M. Metzger* (Oxford: Clarendon, 1981), 131–32.

54. For the date, background, and circumstances of the letter, see White, *From Jesus to Christianity*, 173–76.

55. The translation is that of the NRSV, but I have laid it out so that its verbal structure is clearer.

56. See de Jonge, *Christology in Context*, 34–35.

57. Cf. 1 Cor 15:28, which also uses "son" in reference to this heavenly exaltation, with everything subject to him (cf. Phil 2:9–10, discussed below, pp. 120–121). See also Hurtado, *Lord Jesus Christ*, 101–8.

58. See de Jonge, *Christology in Context*, 49.

59. The exalting and returning of Christ is also the referent of Paul's description of him as "heavenly man" in 1 Cor 15:47–49.

60. For discussion, see Abraham J. Malherbe, *The Letters to the Thessalonians*, Anchor Bible 32B (New York: Doubleday, 2000), 118–22, 129–33.

61. My translation and arrangement in order to keep as close as possible to the Greek.

62. R. P. Martin, *Carmen Christi: Philippians ii.5–11 in Recent Interpretation and in the Setting of Early Christian Worship* (London: Cambridge University Press, 1967), 24–41. See also R. P. Martin and B. J. Dodd, eds., *Where Christology Began: Essays on Philippians 2* (Louisville: Westminster John Knox, 1998), 20–24.

63. See Hurtado, *Lord Jesus Christ*, 115, n. 87.

64. In Greek the phrase is *kyriakon deipnon*, in which the first word is an adjective derived from *kyrios* ("lord"). Hence the more common translation using a possessive ("Lord's") is perhaps better rendered "Lordly."

65. Cf. 1 Cor 12:3. See de Jonge, *Christology in Context*, 46–47.

66. R. H. Fuller, *The Foundations of New Testament Christology* (New York: Scribner, 1965), 204. A number of the elements of the Philippians hymn can be read against the backdrop of Isa 53, which was widely used in the early Jesus tradition to refer to his suffering and death. It has also been suggested that the Pauline statement "died for our sins" in 1 Cor 15:3 also alludes to Isa 53:4–6, as discussed above.

67. Martin, *Carmen Christi*, 94–95.

68. Martin, *Carmen Christi*, 302–5.

69. So also Fuller, *Foundations of New Testament Christology*, 182–86.

70. Here we should note that Paul refers to this event as the pivotal moment of his "call" or "conversion" in Gal 1:15–16: "When God . . . was pleased to reveal his Son to me." See White, *From Jesus to Christianity*, 154–58.

71. For the use of Ps 110 as a source text already in Pauline formulations, see 1 Cor 15:27; Rom 8:34. For a continuation in later Pauline tradition, cf. Acts 2:34–35; Eph 1:20; Col 3:1. See D. M. Hay, *Glory at the Right Hand: Psalm 110 in Early Christianity* (Nashville: Abingdon, 1973).

72. On the use of this apocalyptic phrase in worship and in Paul, see G. Bornkamm, *Early Christian Experience* (New York: Harper & Row, 1969), 169–79; Hurtado, *Lord Jesus Christ*, 110. On its roots in early Aramaic speaking communities of the Jesus movement, see White, *From Jesus to Christianity*, 122–25.

Chapter Seven: Marking the Passion

1. NRSV, with boldface added to represent quotations from the LXX, to be discussed below. The first comes from Ps 146[145]:6, although the same doxological address is found elsewhere; the second is Ps 2:1–2. A more literal translation of the LXX version of the latter is given in the text at n. 6, below.

2. R. E. Brown, *Death of the Messiah*, 2 vols. (Garden City, NY: Doubleday, 1994), 1:760–61.

3. We have not yet addressed the question of precisely who the Gospel authors were or how many people might have been involved. It is typical these days, for example, to refer to the Gospel of John as a "community product," suggesting multiple authors and group interaction in the final product. (So R. E. Brown, *The Community of the Beloved Disciple* [New York: Paulist, 1979]; cf. J. Painter, *The Quest for the Messiah: The History, Literature, and Theology of the Johannine Community*, 2nd ed. [Nashville: Abingdon, 1993].) My view is that all of the Gospels have similar patterns of compositional activity involving multiple stages of authorial activity and audience inter-

468 *Notes to pages 125–135*

actions, rather than the traditional view of a single author working more or less in isolation. We shall discuss this issue further in Act III.

4. Cf. Luke 23:25; Mark 15:15; Matt 27:26. For a chart illustrating the different trial sequences in the Gospels, see Box 7.5. On Roman trial procedure, see A. N. Sherwin-White, *Roman Law and Roman Society in the New Testament* (Oxford: Clarendon, 1963), 24–47. Sherwin-White allows that the Lukan trial is more typically Roman than the ones in Mark and Matthew, even though there are other glaring problems with the time frame of the story in Luke. Here, again, the Johannine trial before Pilate is even more extremely elaborated to stress the flogging and public presentation of Jesus. At the same time, it should be remembered that the historical Pilate was known for ordering the execution of Jews even without a trial (Philo *Embassy to Gaius* 302; *Against Flaccus* 105). This prerogative was under the *imperium* of the procurator of Judea, as specified when it was made a province in 6 CE (Josephus *Jewish War* 2.117–18).

5. See L. M. White, *From Jesus to Christianity* (San Francisco: HarperSanFrancisco, 2004), 247–358.

6. This more literal translation from the Greek text of the LXX shows how the passage was read in conjunction with the story of the trial before Antipas.

7. With only minor grammatical modification of the opening words, to make them fit the syntax of the Lukan introductory phrase, they are nearly identical to LXX version of Ps 146[145]:6, with a close parallel in Neh 9:6; cf. Isa 37:16; 2 Kgs 19:15; Exod 20:11.

8. We shall return to this issue in Chapter 10 in dealing with the birth narratives. In contrast to the Gospel of Matthew, where the narrator delivers the prophecy-fulfillment interpretation as commentary on the narrative, in the Gospel of Luke the characters themselves frequently quote or paraphrase the scriptures to evoke the same interpretive conclusions for readers. In other words, in the Lukan version, the "prophetic" interpretations are typically woven into the narrative as dialogue.

9. Brown, *Death of the Messiah*, 1:778–86. Brown argues that it might be based on some historical kernel relating to Antipas's antipathy toward Jesus. Apart from the Markan statement (6:14) that Antipas thought Jesus was somehow John the Baptist come back to life, such an "antipathy" is not otherwise documented in any ancient source, including Josephus. Yet he admits that it has been narrativized by the Lukan author in this present form. It also runs counter to the portrayal of Herod's awareness of Jesus as reflected in Mark 6:4–16. Lukan thematic interests are further indicated by the fact that Acts also shows Paul being tried both by the Roman governor Festus and the later Herodian king Agrippa II (25:23–26:32).

10. Cf. Mark 15:32; Matt 27:44; Luke 23:39–43. See Brown, *Death of the Messiah*, 2:968–71. See also n. 23, below.

11. E.g., the comments of Antipas (Luke 23:14–15) and the centurion at the cross (23:47).

12. W. Klassen, *Judas: Friend or Betrayer of Jesus?* (Minneapolis: Fortress, 1996), 205–7. Other scholars have proposed that this was the real motivation of Judas, assuming that the story is indeed historical.

13. W. Klassen, "Judas Iscariot," in D. N. Freedman, ed., *Anchor Bible Dictionary*, 6 vols. (New York: Doubleday, 1992), 3:1093.

14. It should be noted also that the Gospel of Matthew adds some dialogue of Jesus and Judas at the actual arrest scene. After Judas addresses Jesus as "Rabbi," Jesus replies, "Friend, do what you are here to do" (26:49–50). The use of the word "friend" in this context is intended to suggest an awareness on Jesus's part of being wronged, but also a note of potential reconciliation. In that way it already anticipates in some ways Judas's sense of remorse and suicide. See also Klassen, "Judas Iscariot," 3:1093. On the theme of "friendship and reconciliation," see J. T. Fitzgerald, "Anger, Reconciliation, and Friendship in Matthew 5:21–26," in D. B. Capes, A. DeConick, H. K. Bond, and T. A. Miller, eds., *Israel's God and Rebecca's Children: Christology and Community in Early Judaism and Christianity* (Waco: Baylor University Press, 2007), 359–69.

15. Matt 27:2 flows perfectly into 27:11. Cf. the same sequence in Mark 15:1–2:2.

16. Zech 11:12–13 ("thirty shekels of silver . . . this lordly price"); Jer 18:2–3 ("the potter's house"); 32:9–10 ("bought the field").

17. These are Ps 68:25 and 108:8 in the LXX. The first of these is used as an allusion in Matt 23:38 in reference to the destruction of Jerusalem (cf. Jer 22:5).

18. Cf. Acts 5:1–11 (the greediness and death of Ananias and Sapphira); 12:20–23 (the arrogance and death of Herod Agrippa I).

19. Brown, *Death of the Messiah*, 2:1396.

20. The Gospel of Matthew, for example, elicits Zech 11:12–13; Jer 18:2–3; 32:6–15 (see p. 130 and n. 16 above). In contrast, the Gospel of John alludes to Ps 41:9 (the one who "ate of my bread"); Isa 57:4; Prov 24:22 ("son of perdition," LXX). All of these constitute secondary "theological explanations" by the different Gospel authors; so Brown, *Death of the Messiah*, 2:1402.

21. Brown (*Death of the Messiah*, 2:1402) suggests that it all springs from the allusion in Mark 14:18–21, which in turn is based on an allusion to Ps 41:9: "Even my bosom friend in whom I trusted, who ate of my bread, has lifted the heel against me." See n. 20, above.

22. Rom 6:6; 1 Cor 1:17, 18, 23; 2:2, 8; 2 Cor 13:4; Gal 2:20; 3:1; 5:24; 6:1, 12; Phil 2:8; 3:18.

23. Mark 15:24–25; Matt 27:35; Luke 23:33; John 19:23. See Brown, *Death of the Messiah*, 2:945.

24. See M. Hengel, *Crucifixion* (Philadelphia: Fortress, 1978); Brown, *Death of the Messiah*, 2:945–52. A good example is the comment of Plutarch (Athens, late first century CE); in the treatise *On the Divine Retribution* he states that vice imprints punishment on each person in the same way that "each of those being punished as criminals bears his cross on his body" (*Moralia* 554B, my translation). The only question is whether Plutarch's statement is meant to be metaphorical rather than literal (marks on the body), but it still seems to show a knowledge of the practice of having the condemned carry his own instrument of execution at least regularly enough to elicit such an axiom.

25. Cf. Mark 15:21; Matt 27:32; Luke 22:26; John 19:17.

26. Brown, *Death of the Messiah*, 2:989.

27. The Hebrew version of this verse is usually translated: "My hands and feet have shriveled" (NRSV).

28. Here too there is a change, as the statement is rendered into a mixture of Aramaic and Hebrew in Mark, but altered slightly in Matt 27:46. The statement is deleted in both Luke and John probably to remove the sense of desperation; see Brown, *Death of the Messiah*, 2:1047–51, 1077–78.

29. For discussion, see Brown, *Death of the Messiah*, 2:953–55; for the latter scene, see also the discussion in the Prologue.

30. See Brown, *Death of the Messiah*, 2:968–71. It is often overlooked that the term "bandits" (Gk. *lēstēs*) as found in Mark 15:27 and Matt 27:38 is also used in the Temple cleansing scene in the phrase "den of robbers/bandits" (Mark 11:17; Matt 21:13; Luke 19:46, drawing from Isa 56:7; Jer 7:11). The same term is used by Josephus for the "brigands" or "revolutionaries" who helped provoke the first revolt against Rome (*Jewish War* 2.253–54; 4.504). The word in both Mark and later Gospels is probably meant to connote this "revolutionary" element, as seen in the arrest scene in Mark 14:48 and in John 18:40 when Barabbas is labeled with this term instead of the more conventional word for "revolutionary" in Mark 15:7. That Jesus was executed on such a charge of fomenting revolution, as suggested by the inscription, is very likely historical, which may well explain why the Lukan author was so intent on stating Jesus's innocence, even to the point of having one of the "bandits" say so in direct discourse with Jesus (23:41). See n. 8, above.

31. See Brown, *Death of the Messiah*, 2:960–68.

32. See John 19:14, 17–20; Brown, *Death of the Messiah*, 2:958–60, 964–67.

33. Brown (*Death of the Messiah*, 2:1292, 1299–1307) thinks that the Gospel of Matthew—not the *Gospel of Peter*—is the source of this additional material. For the issue of historicity in the guard story, see Brown, *Death of the Messiah*, 2:1310–13. We shall return to the *Gospel of Peter* as a possible source for the Passion narrative in the concluding section of this chapter.

34. Brown, *Death of the Messiah*, 2:1311.

35. The Gospel of Luke has a very different slant at this point, as discussed below. The Gospel of John has appearances of Jesus to the disciples both in Jerusalem and in the Galilee.

36. This last scene with Peter going to the tomb may be the Lukan equivalent to the special appearance to Peter mentioned in 1 Cor 15:5; however, Jesus does not actually appear to him in this scene. The Gospel of John has both Peter and the "beloved disciple" go to the tomb (20:3–8).

37. The "Longer Ending" of Mark (16:9–20) is the one found in some of the ancient manuscripts; however, several alternative versions of it are known from others. All are rather clearly later additions. Some of the most important ancient manuscripts of the Gospels, however, end at Mark 16:8, with the departure of the frightened women from the tomb. Numerous proposals have been made to suggest that some part of the original ending was lost, but there are also good literary grounds for seeing 16:8 as the actual ending. We shall discuss this issue in Chapter 11.

38. D. P. Senior, *The Passion Narrative According to Matthew* (Leuven: Leuven University Press, 1975).

39. Another clue that this challenge was also leveled against the Markan version or its predecessors is seen in the Lukan addition of having Peter immediately run to see the empty tomb for himself (24:12). In the Gospel of John it is both Peter and John who go to see the tomb (20:3–10), and it likewise provides an editorial gloss on the first reactions among the disciples: "for as yet they did not understand the scripture, that he must rise from the dead" (20:9).

40. Brown (*Death of the Messiah*, 2:1280) poses a similar issue; however, he is perhaps too willing to accept the legend regarding the site of the Church of the Holy Sepulchre at face value. Though it is just as likely, and probably more so, than any other "favorite" spot (such as the so-called Garden Tomb), there is no evidence for early veneration of the site prior to the early fourth century. See Brown, *Death of the Messiah*, 2:1281–83; R. Smith, "On the Tomb of Jesus," *Biblical Archaeologist* 30 (1967): 74–90.

41. In general, see E. M. Meyers, *Jewish Ossuaries: Reburial and Rebirth* (Rome: Biblical Institute Press, 1971); E. M. Meyers and J. F. Strange, *Archaeology, the Rabbis, and Early Christianity* (Nashville: Abingdon, 1981), 92–109; L. Y. Rahmani, "Ancient Jewish Funerary Customs and Tombs," *Biblical Archaeologist* 45 (1982): 43–52, 109–19.

42. R. Hachlili, *Ancient Jewish Art and Archaeology in the Land of Israel* (Leiden: Brill, 1988), 89–119; also summarized in R. Hachlili, "Burials, Ancient Jewish," *Anchor Bible Dictionary*, 1:789–94. The so-called James ossuary, once touted as that of Jesus's brother, was proven to be hoax. Though the ossuary itself was indeed ancient, the inscription mentioning the name of James was shown to be modern.

43. Two Greek terms are typically used of tombs in the New Testament—*taphos/taphē* (meaning "tomb" or "grave") and *mnēmeion/mnēma* (meaning "tomb" or "memorial"). Even though *mnēmeion* would more logically refer to the long-term burial, both words are used of the tomb of Jesus in the Gospels. The Gospel of Matthew uses both in the same passage (27:60–61). Generally, the terms are used interchangeably, perhaps because the practice of reburial as described here was not commonplace in the Greco-Roman world and seems to have been limited even in Jewish practice to the period from the late first century BCE to the early second century CE. Rooms, chambers, or crypts, whether for single or multiple burials, were common throughout the Greco-Roman world and might be constructed as above-ground edifices, or located in caves or below-ground tunnels (or "catacombs"). Consequently, it is not possible to use the Greek words to refer exclusively to the "first" or "second" type of burial place.

44. See B. Mack, *A Myth of Innocence: Mark and Christian Origins* (Philadelphia: Augsburg Fortress, 1988), 311.

45. D. Juel, *Messiah and Temple: The Trial of Jesus in the Gospel of Mark* (Missoula, MT: Scholars Press, 1977).

46. G. W. E. Nickelsburg, "Passion Narrative," *Anchor Bible Dictionary*, 5:172.

47. All these stories (and texts) come from the period between the return from Babylonian exile and the early second century CE.

48. 2 Maccabees is one of two main chronicles of the Maccabean revolt. Written in Greek during the early to middle part of the first century BCE, it has strong anti-Hasmonean elements, even though Judas and other heroes of the revolt—including these martyrs—are portrayed favorably. See G. W. E. Nickelsburg, *Jewish Literature Between the Bible and the Mishnah* (Philadelphia: Fortress, 1981), 118–21.

49. 4 Maccabees was written in Greek sometime between the late first century BCE and the late first century CE. The tone suggests that it comes from an area under Roman rule, and a date in the 40s CE has been proposed. It seems to come from a Diaspora context where Jews were experiencing persecution and philosophical debate. A location in Antioch has been proposed, and it is worth noting that Antioch has also been proposed for the composition of the Gospels of Mark and Matthew. It was also revived in the period of the second Jewish revolt, and some rabbinic versions of the "seven sons" story place their martyrdom in the time of Hadrian (117–38 CE). See Nickelsburg, *Jewish Literature Between the Bible and the Mishnah*, 223–27.

50. For discussion of Wisdom of Solomon, see Chapter 2. It is usually dated to the early part of the first century CE and probably stems from a Greek-speaking Diaspora context. See also G. W. E. Nickelsburg, "The Genre and Function of the Markan Passion Narrative," *Harvard Theological Review* 73 (1980): 154–84.

51. See the discussion of 1 Cor 5:7 in Chapter 6. For the use of *paschein* ("to suffer"), see Mark 8:31 (in the first prediction of the Passion).

52. See Brown, *Death of the Messiah*, 2:1492–1517, for a list of major New Testament scholars and their views on this matter.

53. A connection is also made plausible because the Gospel of Mark is associated by early legends with Peter (e.g., Eusebius *Church History* 3.39.15). See the discussion in Chapter 11. Another "Petrine" text that has sometimes been mentioned in this regard is the *Apocalypse of Peter*, which will be discussed in Appendix C. Even though the latter was widely considered "apostolic" and included in early canon lists, it has been shown to be a later expansion and is thus not a viable candidate as an authentic work of Peter. On the other hand, it may well support a notion of continuing Petrine oral traditions.

54. Although not the first to suggest it, Rudolf Bultmann (*The History of the Synoptic Tradition* [German ed., 1921; New York: Harper & Row, 1963], 259) popularized the idea. Among others, see R. Fuller, *The Formation of the Resurrection Narratives* (New York: Macmillan, 1971), 87; N. Perrin, *The Resurrection According to Matthew, Mark, and Luke* (Philadelphia: Fortress, 1977), 24–25; C. E. Carlston, "Transfiguration and Resurrection," *Journal of Biblical Literature* 80 (1961): 233–40; M. E. Thrall, "Elijah and Moses in Mark's Account of the Transfiguration," *New Testament Studies* 16 (1970): 305–17.

55. See R. Stein, "Is the Transfiguration (Mark 9:2–8) a Misplaced Resurrection Account?" *Journal of Biblical Literature* 95 (1976): 79–96; E. Schweizer, *The Good News According to Mark* (Richmond, VA: John Knox, 1970), 180. However, the statement of E. Boring (*Mark: A Commentary* [Louisville: Westminster John Knox, 2006]) that this discussion "has rightly been virtually abandoned" (260) is vastly overstated. At the very least, it refers only to the older theories of "misplacement." Boring does not mention the *Gospel of Peter* in this connection and argues elsewhere (12) that the Markan author did not use any other Gospels, canonical or noncanonical, as sources.

56. C. S. Mann, *Mark*, Anchor Bible 27 (Garden City, NY: Doubleday, 1986), 355–62. Mann makes no mention of the *Gospel of Peter*, but suggests instead that the transfiguration, based on an early oral tradition, constitutes an insertion into Mark (362).

57. G. W. E. Nickelsburg, "Enoch, Levi, and Peter: Recipients of Revelation in Upper Galilee," *Journal of Biblical Literature* 100 (1981): 575–600; A. Y. Collins, "Apotheosis and Resurrection," in P. Borgen and S. Giverson, eds., *The New Testament and Hellenistic Judaism* (Aarhus: Aarhus University Press, 1995), 96–100; *Mark: A Commentary*, Hermeneia (Minneapolis: Fortress, 2007), 415. Collins (*Mark*, 415, n. 8), although generally negative toward the older theories of the transfiguration, cites with approval the unpublished paper of B. Nongbri, "Mark 9:2–8: Transfiguring the Resurrection" (2001), which further discusses the relationship of the transfiguration to the *Gospel of Peter*'s resurrection scene. I am grateful to Dr. Nongbri for providing me with a copy of this paper.

58. Cf. Mark 16:7; Matt 27:7; also Mark 14:28; Matt 28:16.

59. "After three days" (the resurrection): cf. Mark 8:31; 9:31; 10:34; "after two days" (the Last Supper): cf. 14:1. Thrall makes much of this point as a resurrection detail ("Elijah and Moses in Mark's Account of the Transfiguration," 311).

60. My translation. See Appendix C and Chapter 15 for fuller text and discussion.

61. F. Watson, "The Social Function of Mark's Secrecy Theme," *Journal for the Study of the New Testament* 24 (1985): 55. Among the synoptic transfiguration scenes, the pronouncement of the heavenly voice in 2 Pet 1:17 is closest to that in Matt 17:5, but it remains clear that the transfiguration scene is the referent and that the import of "receiving honor and glory" is his exaltation to heaven. See also R. J. Miller, "Is There Independent Attestation for the Transfiguration in 2 Peter?" *New Testament Studies* 41 (1996): 625.

62. The Johannine version makes it "two angels in white," while the Lukan ascension scene alters the wording only slightly to "two men in white robes."

63. See 2 Kgs 2:9–12 for the story of Elijah's ascent to heaven via a fiery chariot and a whirlwind.

64. Much of the later expectation is based on Mal 3:1 and esp. 4:5 (= MT 3:23; LXX 3:22), as alluded to in Mark 9:11–12 (immediately after the transfiguration scene) and other references in Mark (see below). For Elijah in apocalyptic thought, see the *Apocalypse of Elijah* (in J. H. Charlesworth, ed., *The Old Testament Pseudepigrapha*, 2 vols. [Garden City, NY: Doubleday, 1985], 1:721–53), although some parts of this work are later Christian additions. See D. Frankfurter, *Elijah in Upper Egypt: The Apocalypse of Elijah and Egyptian Christianity* (Minneapolis: Fortress, 1993).

65. Philo *Life of Moses* 2.288 (my translation). The following passage (291) refers to his ascension to heaven as "when he was being *taken up*" (using *analambanein*; cf. Acts 1:2; Luke 9:51, discussed in Chapter 6, nn. 50, 52, above) and "so that he might steer his course flying off into heaven." See also Chapter 3.

66. This ending is preserved only in the Ethiopic version; the Greek version breaks off just before this point. I give here the translation of H. Deunsing in E. Hennecke and W. Schneemelcher, eds., *New Testament Apocrypha* (Philadelphia: Westminster, 1963–65), 2:682. Passages in italics represent language probably drawn from the canonical Gospels and Acts.

67. This is the same word used four times in 1 Cor 15:5–8. See Chapter 6.

68. This wording and order is significant in Mark, but will later be changed to "Moses and Elijah" in both Matt 17:3 and Luke 9:30.

69. The final reference to Elijah in Mark 15:35–36 (at the crucifixion) also reflects this theme of misunderstanding. See below.

70. This links further to the opinion of "King Herod" (6:14), who killed John the Baptist (6:17–29), but note also "the yeast of Herod" in 8:15, which anticipates the mention of John in the "confession" scene only six verses later.

71. As seen in *Gos. Pet.* 14.59.

72. See A. Y. Collins, *The Beginning of the Gospel: Probings of Mark in Context* (Minneapolis: Fortress, 1992), 146.

73. The wordplay is set up in the Greek of Mark 15:36 with the word *kathairein* ("to take down"). The standard words used for the ascension are *epairein* (Acts 1:9) and *analambanein* (Acts 1:2), both of which may be translated "to lift up" or "to take up." See also nn. 50, 52, above).

Chapter Eight: Casting Spells

1. Cf. Mark 11:20–25; Matt 21:10–17; Luke 19:45–46. The shift of the Temple cleansing to John 2, which also occurs at Passover, is one of the key changes in the Gospel of John that creates the "three-year" ministry of Jesus; cf. John 6:4, which refers to another Passover between John 2 and the one at which Jesus dies (13:1; 19:31). See also the Prologue and Box 1.1.

2. P. J. Achtemeier, "Miracles (NT)," in D. N. Freedman, ed., *Anchor Bible Dictionary,* 6 vols. (New York: Doubleday, 1992), 4:368; R. T. Fortna, "Signs/Semeia Source," *Anchor Bible Dictionary,* 6:18–22; R. T. Fortna, *The Gospel of Signs* (London: Cambridge University Press, 1970).

3. The verbs "take," "bless (or give thanks)," "break," and "give" describe the central miraculous moment in both cases (see Mark 6:41; 8:6). Of course, these are the same verbs—and in the same order—used in the Last Supper scene. This rather obvious eucharistic symbolism has long been noticed in reflecting on Markan storytelling technique.

4. See n. 7, below.

5. P. J. Achtemeier, "Toward the Isolation of Pre-Markan Miracle Catenae," *Journal of Biblical Literature* 89 (1970): 265–91.

6. This comment is missing entirely from the Matthean version of this same miracle (14:22–33). The summary statement referring to the two feeding miracles in Mark 8:19–21, noted above, thus represents the third time that the Markan author draws the audience's attention to the miracles and the disciples' failure to understand. By contrast, the Matthean version of this last scene (16:5–12) ends with the disciples now fully understanding Jesus's point, but it is a different point than in Mark.

7. Achtemeier considered the healing of the blind man (Mark 8:22–26) part of this formal sequence, but he placed it opposite the exorcism in Mark 5:1–20. I include it in this position for sake of completeness, even though it is outside of the second miracle sequence. There is another possibility, however, due to the fact that both of the miracles in 5:21–43 (a healing and a resuscitation) bear some similarities to the Syrophoenician woman story (an exorcism). Similarly, the healing of the deaf-mute (7:31–37) shares some features with the raising of Jairus's daughter (5:21–24, 35–43). Thus, one or more of these episodes may be receiving additional editorial manipulation by the Markan author. It can be seen most clearly in the Markan shaping of the double miracle of 5:21–43, which will be discussed further below.

8. It has also been suggested that the Gospel of Luke knew a different version of the Gospel of Mark in which this whole section, Mark 6:45–8:26, was missing; however, this view is contradicted by the fact that the Lukan Gospel retains parts of this section, but in different positions. Hence, it looks like more of a conscious decision on the part of the Lukan author. For example, the raising of the widow's son at Nain may well represent a reworking of the story of the Syrophoenician woman episode, but it has been moved to a different position in the Gospel and made to resemble a story from the Elisha tradition. See the discussion below.

9. We shall return to this question in Chapter 14 and suggest that the Johannine author did indeed use one or more of the Synoptics as a source.

10. Whether this suggests that the author of John knew both of the Markan source collections depends on how we assess the relationship between John and the Synoptics. Since only Mark and Matthew contain both of them in the same order, it might well suggest that the author(s) of John knew the Gospel of Mark. See H. Koester, *Ancient Christian Gospels: Their History and Development* (Philadelphia: Trinity Press International, 1990), 286–87, and further discussion in Chapter 14.

11. In the three synoptic Gospels there are a total of thirty-two individual miracle stories, *not* counting the parallels where the same basic story occurs in either two or all three Gospels (e.g., the Gadarene/Gerasene demoniac: Matt 8.28–34; Mark 5.1–20; Luke 8.26–39). Of these, eleven occur in all three Synoptics, while eight more occur in two out of the three.

12. See G. H. Twelftree, *Jesus the Exorcist* (Tübingen: Mohr, 1993); Twelftree argues that the historical Jesus had a self-consciousness of being an exorcist.

13. There are eleven different exorcism episodes in the three Synoptics; this number does not include the parallels but does include summary statements with reference to exorcism. The nine in Mark are: 1:23–28 (f); 1:29–31 (s); 1:39 (s); 3:7–12 (s); 5:1–20 (f); 6:1–6 (s); 7:24–30 (f); 9:14–29 (f); and 9:38–41 (s), where *s* designates a "summary" or allusion to an exorcism and *f* designates a "full" exorcism story (as discussed below).

14. F. Graf, "Prayer in Magic and Religious Ritual," in C. Faraone and D. Obbink, eds. *Magika Hiera: Ancient Greek Magic and Religion* (New York: Oxford University Press, 1991) 188–213.

15. Cf. Jesus's cursing of the fig tree (Mark 11:12–14, 20–25; Matt 21:18–22).

16. See F. Graf, *Magic in the Ancient World* (Cambridge, MA: Harvard University Press, 1997), 56–60, 65–88; H. C. Kee, *Miracle in the Early Christian World* (New Haven: Yale University Press, 1983), 1–41.

17. For the phenomenon and language, see Graf, *Magic in the Ancient World,* 118–34. See also J. Gager, *Curse Tablets and Binding Spells from the Ancient World* (New York: Oxford University Press, 1992), for terminology and examples in pagan, Jewish, and Christian tradition. For the usage in relation to Matthew, see R. H. Hiers, "'Binding' and 'Loosing': The Matthean Authorizations," *Journal of Biblical Literature* 104 (1985): 233–50; D. C. Duling, "Binding and Loosing: Matthew 16:19; 18:18; and John 20:23," *Forum* 3/4 (1987): 3–31.

18. Elijah and Elisha lived in the mid- to later ninth century BCE. Although based on earlier sources, 1 and 2 Kings were written in their present form no earlier than the sixth century BCE, probably near the end of the Babylonian exile (586–539 BCE) or somewhat later. A postexilic date for the entire Deuteronomistic History (Joshua–2 Kings) is now favored by many scholars; see S. W. Holloway, "Kings, Book of 1–2," *Anchor Bible Dictionary,* 4:70–73.

19. Josephus *Jewish War* 4.459–64 (my translation; italics added).

20. H. Kee (*Aretalogies, Hellenistic "Lives," and the Sources of Mark* [Berkeley, CA: Center for Hermeneutical Studies, 1975], 14) prefers the term "wonder stories."

21. The Greek and Latin equivalents, respectively, for these terms are: "marvels" (*terata, prodigia* or *portenta*); "powers" (*dunameis, potestates* or *virtus*); "signs" (*sēmeia, portenta* or *signa*). In the Gospel of John the term "sign" (*sēmeia*) is used almost exclusively, while the other Gospels use a more varied array of these terms in describing the miracles of Jesus.

22. J. L. Bailey and L. D. Vander Broek, *Literary Forms in the New Testament: A Handbook* (Louisville: Westminster John Knox, 1992), 137–44; G. Theissen, *The Miracle Stories of the Early Christian Tradition* (Philadelphia: Fortress, 1983); H. D. Betz, "The Early Christian Miracle Story: Some Observations on the Form-Critical Problem," *Semeia* 11 (1978): 69–81; A. C. Wire, "The Structure of the Gospel Miracle Stories and Their Tellers," *Semeia* 11 (1978): 83–113.

23. Pausanias *Description of Greece* 6.26.1–2 (my translation).

24. See R. MacMullen, *Paganism in the Roman Empire* (New Haven: Yale University Press, 1981), 18–34.

25. In general on the phenomenon of demon possession in the New Testament world, see E. Sorensen, *Possession and Exorcism in the New Testament and Early Christianity* (Tübingen: Mohr Siebeck, 2002).

26. Cf. Lucian *The Lover of Lies* 16.

27. Apuleius *Florida* 19.

28. Philostratus *Life of Apollonius* 4.45; my translation, with italics added to reflect some of the formal components of the miracle to be discussed in the next section.

29. This is a simplified outline of the overall genre, rather than an outline of a specific story. Cf. Bailey and Vander Broek, *Literary Forms in the New Testament*, 139–41.

30. The speech impediment may also be meant to show that it was a long-term condition.

31. Though both Matthew and Luke retain some allusions to this idea, they all occur in passages parallel to Markan ones. The "secrecy" motif, as it is sometimes called, is far less pronounced in Matthew and even less so in Luke. This Markan literary device will be discussed more thoroughly in Chapter 11.

32. From the Jerusalem Talmud, as translated in D. R. Cartlidge and D. L. Dungan, *Documents for the Study of the Gospels*, 2nd ed. (Minneapolis: Fortress, 1994), 159. The paragraph divisions and numbers have been added. Rabbi Tanchuma lived about 350 CE.

33. The Lukan version of this story (8:22–25) is almost identical to Mark, while the inserted Q saying appears in an entirely different narrative context (9:57–60).

34. Cf. Luke 9:39; Mark 9:18 (convulsions and foaming at the mouth); the same symptoms are repeated in Luke 9:42 and Mark 9:20. Cf. Matt 17:16; Mark 9:22 (casting him into the fire and water).

Chapter Nine: Spinning Parables

1. J. Jeremias, *The Parables of Jesus* (New York: Scribner, 1955), 12, n. 11, 71–72, 89.

2. K. L. Schmidt, *Der Rahmen der Geschichte Jesu* (Berlin: Trowitzsch, 1919), 44, 152.

3. Using H. C. Kee's classification of the Q material in *Jesus in History*, 3rd ed. (Fort Worth: Harcourt Brace, 1996), 81–83. The block is generally reflected in the Lukan order of material in chaps. 12–15. Although the Gospel of Matthew distributes these same units more widely throughout the story, several smaller clusters of sayings, including parables, retain the same relative order as found in the Lukan parallels. In the *Gospel of Thomas*, parables regularly occur in pairs.

4. Even the lone reference to a miracle in the Q tradition, the healing of the centurion's slave (Matt 8:5–13; Luke 7:1–10), largely reduces the miracle to serve as the setup for Jesus's conversation with the centurion about faith. The actual healing is never described. The miracle-story form discussed in the previous chapter is absent or at least reduced only to the description of the encounter. In the Gospel of Matthew the discussion between Jesus and the centurion is then supplemented by several additional sayings (8:11–12); however, they derive from independent units of Q tradition that are found elsewhere in Luke (12:28–30).

5. The point of the metaphor is made explicit in Isa 5:7–10. It opens with an explanation of the allegory: "For the vineyard of the Lord of hosts is the house of Israel, and the people of Judah are his pleasant planting; he expected justice, but saw bloodshed; righteousness, but heard a cry!" (5:7)

6. Cf. Ezek 11:16–17; 20:3, 5, 27; 37:12, 19, 21; Isa 32:9; 42:23; 51:4; Jer 13:15.

7. Prophets and prophecy were not unique to Israelite and Jewish tradition. They were a widespread phenomenon in ancient Near Eastern cultures as well as in Persian, Greek, and Roman traditions. The unique development of Jewish prophetic tradition, especially in relation to the Babylonian exile, gave rise to the kinds of ideas and expectations that later flowered as apocalyptic. See J. C. VanderKam, *From Revelation to Canon: Studies in the Hebrew Bible and Second Temple Literature* (Leiden: Brill, 2002), 240–75.

8. Coined by H. H. Rowley, *The Relevance of Apocalyptic* (London: Lutterworth, 1944), 13; see also D. S. Russell, *The Method and Message of Jewish Apocalyptic* (Philadelphia: Westminster, 1964), 94.

9. J. J. Collins, *The Apocalyptic Imagination: An Introduction to Jewish Apocalyptic Literature*, 2nd ed. (Grand Rapids, MI: Eerdmans, 1998), 1–42.

10. The sage is also a common figure in Jewish tradition. Like "prophet," therefore, it allows for easy lines of influence and transition between Jewish and Greco-Roman cultures.

11. Elijah and Jeremiah both suffered imprisonment or exile for their teaching (1 Kgs 17; Jer 37:11–38:6). According to apocryphal tradition Isaiah was martyred (*Martyrdom and Ascension of Isaiah*, also alluded to in Heb 11:32–38, esp. v. 37). Socrates was condemned by the Athenian council and forced to commit suicide (Plato *Apology of Socrates*). Diogenes was treated as a pariah and thus earned his nickname, "the Dog" (*kyōn*), which then became the name of his school, the Cynics (*kynikos*, "doglike").

12. Josephus *Antiquities* 18.11–25. See L. M. White, *From Jesus to Christianity* (San Francisco: HarperSanFrancisco, 2004), 75–84.

13. On the image and role of the sage in Second Temple Judaism, see J. Blenkinsopp, *Sage, Priest, Prophet: Religious and Intellectual Leadership in Ancient Israel* (Louisville: Westminster John Knox, 1995), 9–64.

14. Plato *Apology of Socrates* 29DE, my translation. In this passage, the word "God" in all three instances translates the Greek *ho theos*, i.e., the noun plus the definite article. In Greek usage this is a typical way of referring to a particular god, who has usually already been identified. But it is also used as an abstraction for the divine, especially in Plato, where it often has monistic implications.

15. See J. C. Thom, *The Pythagorean Golden Verses* (Leiden: Brill, 1995). For example, the maxim, "In everything, moderation (or due measure) is the best," is attributed to Pythagoras, according to Thom (97).

16. This is the Latin equivalent of the Greek *autos ephē*. Closely associated with the words of Pythagoras, it became a kind of mystical teaching sometimes couched in number symbolism.

17. M. Dibelius, *From Tradition to Gospel*, 2nd ed. (New York: Scribner, 1965); R. Bultmann, *The History of the Synoptic Tradition*, 2nd ed. (New York: Harper & Row, 1963); H. Koester, *Ancient Christian Gospels: Their History and Development* (Philadelphia: Trinity Press International, 1990).

18. E. V. McKnight, *What Is Form Criticism?* (Philadelphia: Fortress, 1969); N. Perrin, *What Is Redaction Criticism?* (Philadelphia: Fortress, 1969). The original German terms *Formgeschichte* and *Redaktionsgeschichte* actually mean "form history" and "redaction history," referring to the historical process of preservation and transmission of each basic type of sayings unit.

19. Within such studies, miracles were generally given much less attention than the teachings of Jesus, in part because after the Enlightenment they were often dismissed on historical or scientific grounds. The ancient authors and audiences of the Gospels did not operate with this kind of rational skepticism.

20. C. H. Dodd, *The Parables of the Kingdom* (London: Nisbet, 1935); N. Perrin, *Rediscovering the Teaching of Jesus* (New York: Harper & Row, 1976); B. B. Scott, *Re-Imagine the World: An Introduction to the Parables of Jesus* (Santa Rosa, CA: Polebridge, 2001).

21. V. K. Robbins, "Form Criticism (NT)," in D. N. Freedman, ed., *Anchor Bible Dictionary*, 6 vols. (New York: Doubleday, 1992), 2:841–44.

22. M. A. Powell, *What Is Narrative Criticism?* (Minneapolis: Fortress, 1990); N. Petersen, *Literary Criticism for New Testament Critics* (Philadelphia: Fortress, 1978); S. D. Moore, *Literary Criticism and the Gospels: The Theoretical Challenge* (New Haven: Yale University Press, 1989); J. C. Anderson and S. D. Moore, *Mark and Method: New Approaches in Biblical Studies* (Minneapolis: Fortress, 1992).

23. Different systems of classification have been employed by New Testament scholars since the time of Rudolf Bultmann (*The History of the Synoptic Tradition* [German ed., 1921; New York: Harper & Row, 1963], 1–7). This catalogue represents a simplified version. See also McKnight, *What Is Form Criticism?* 17–33.

24. J. L. Bailey and L. D. Vander Broek, *Literary Forms in the New Testament: A Handbook* (Louisville: Westminster John Knox, 1992), 98–99.

25. Ahikar is a shadowy sage figure from the Babylonian and Persian traditions, from whom an extensive proverbial collection is preserved in Arabic. The same figure is mentioned in the Jewish apocryphal book of Tobit. For the collection of sayings of Ahikar, see J. H. Charlesworth, ed., *Old Testament Pseudepigrapha*, 2 vols. (Garden City, NY: Doubleday, 1985), 2:479–508.

26. The phrase occurs a total of twenty-five times in Proverbs, either in the singular or plural.

27. The admonitory opening "my child (son)" occurs nineteen times, beginning in 2:1 and running throughout the work.

28. See also n. 25, above.

29. See J. T. Sanders, *Ben Sira and Demotic Wisdom* (Chico, CA: Scholars Press, 1983).

30. See Xenophon *Memorabilia* 2.1.21–34. This tradition was also the basis for an extended allegory on the two roads, in which both virtue and vice are described as women, in the *Tabula of Cebes*, a philosophical moral tractate from the first century CE. For discussion, see J. T. Fitzgerald and L. M. White, *The Tabula of Cebes: Text, Translation, and Commentary* (Chico, CA: Scholars Press, 1983), 14–16.

31. Both date to the second century BCE. The *Epistle of Aristeas* is an anonymous work that recounts the legendary origins of the LXX. In the passage regarding the rule, the source is said to be "the teaching of Wisdom."

32. R. Goldenberg, "Hillel the Elder," *Anchor Bible Dictionary*, 3:201–2. Many teachings of Hillel are preserved in rabbinic literature and especially in *Pirke Aboth* (or "Sayings of the Fathers"), which likewise is based on the proverbial wisdom tradition and form. See R. T. Herford, ed., *Pirke Aboth. The Ethics of the Talmud: Sayings of the Fathers* (New York: Schocken, 1962).

33. Soncino edition.

34. These may be found in *m. 'Abot* 2:10 (Eleazar) and *'Abot R. Nat.* xxvi.f27a (Akiba). The latter is clearly modeled on the Hillel episode.

35. R. F. Collins, "Golden Rule," *Anchor Bible Dictionary*, 2:1070–71. The article also discusses parallels among the early Greek philosophers.

36. In addition to the "whole Torah" phrase, the use of the word "neighbor" suggests that this was consciously based on the formulation of Lev 19:18: "You shall love your neighbor as yourself," which is the basis of the "second" commandment.

37. Musonius Rufus, Fragment 18B (my translation). For the works of Musonius, see C. E. Lutz, *Musonius Rufus, The Roman Socrates* (New Haven: Yale University Press, 1960); this passage is on p. 119 (ll. 15–18).

38. Clement of Alexandria *The Paedagogue* 2.1.5.

39. On a lighter note, I once found the same saying in a fortune cookie at a Chinese restaurant in New Haven, which means that it is implicitly attributed to Confucius.

40. Thucydides *History of the Peloponnesian War* 2.97.4; cf. Xenophon *Cyropaideia* 8.2.7. The phrase in Thucydides (*lambanein mallon ē didonai*) uses exactly the same words as in Acts, but inverts the word order slightly.

41. Plutarch *Moralia* 173d (*Sayings of Kings and Commanders*).

42. For the formal category of "blessings" or beatitudes, see the next section. The construction of this added saying may also be dependant on the peculiar Lukan rendering of the "measure for measure saying" (6:38). See also *1 Clement* 13.1–2, where this saying is incorporated into a listing of Jesus's teachings.

43. See J. Z. Smith, "Wisdom and Apocalyptic," *Map Is Not Territory* (Leiden: Brill, 1978), 67–87; and the collection of essays on the question by B. G. Wright and L. M. Wills, eds., *Conflicted Boundaries in Wisdom and Apocalypticism* (Atlanta: Society of Biblical Literature, 2005), esp. the first two articles, by G. W. E. Nickelsburg and S. J. Tanzer.

44. Cf. Luke 6:43–46, which has some of the same elements in a different, and less pointed, order; and it is placed in the frame of a separate saying about the treasure of one's heart (cf. Matt 12:34–35). Hence, both sayings come from the Q tradition, but they have been combined and reshaped in different ways in Matthew and Luke.

45. D. E. Aune, *Prophecy in Early Christianity and Ancient Mediterranean World* (Grand Rapids, MI: Eerdmans, 1983), 166; see also Bailey and Vander Broek, *Literary Forms in the New Testament*, 123–24.

46. Bultmann, *History of the Synoptic Tradition,* 166–79; McKnight, *What Is Form Criticism?* 51–56.

47. The terminology comes from E. Käsemann, "Sentences of Holy Law in the New Testament," in *New Testament Questions of Today* (London: SCM, 1969), 66–81; see also Bailey and Vander Broek, *Literary Forms in the New Testament,* 124–25; and Aune, *Prophecy in Early Christianity,* 166–68. Aune prefers the term "pronouncements of sacral law."

48. This phrase (with *amen*) is more frequent in Matthew (thirty-two times, twenty of which are in material unique to Matthew) than either Mark (nineteen total) or Luke (twenty-six times, fourteen of which are unique to Luke). It is found twelve times in Q material. The double phrase *amen, amen* (translated "truly, truly" or "very truly") is used some twenty-nine times in John. See Aune, *Prophecy in Early Christianity,* 164.

49. As argued by J. Jeremias (*The Prayers of Jesus* [Philadelphia: Fortress, 1978]) and others, but refuted by many others. See Aune, *Prophecy in Early Christianity,* 165, 393, nn. 111–15.

50. Aune, *Prophecy in Early Christianity,* 164–65, 169.

51. V. K. Robbins, "The Chreia," in D. E. Aune, ed., *Greco-Roman Literature and the New Testament* (Atlanta: Scholars Press, 1988), 3.

52. R. F. Hock and E. N. O'Neil, *The Chreia in Ancient Rhetoric,* vol. 1., *The Progymnasmata* (Atlanta: Scholars Press, 1986), 26.

53. Robbins, "The Chreia," 1–24; Hock and O'Neil, *The Chreia in Ancient Rhetoric,* 1:1–47, esp. 23–26.

54. See below, n. 62.

55. "Pronouncement story" is the older term used in Gospel studies prior to the recent work on *chreiai.* In some cases, scholars have gone too far in trying to define typologies based almost exclusively on the Gospels, whereas now the *chreia* is seen as a more basic form. See Bailey and Vander Broek, *Literary Forms in the New Testament,* 114–22.

56. Diogenes was born ca. 410–403 BCE in Sinope, on the Black Sea, later home of the early Christian "heretic" Marcion. After 362 his family was exiled, and he spent the rest of his life in Athens and Corinth. He died in ca. 324–321 and was buried at Corinth in the eastern suburb called the Craneum. The main ancient source for his life and thought is Diogenes Laertius (early third century CE) *Lives of the Philosophers* 6.70–73, but *chreiai* recording his sayings were widely preserved in many ancient sources, especially the rhetorical handbooks known as *progymnasmata* (or "preliminary exercises"). On the *progymnasmata,* see R. F. Hock and E. N. O'Neil, *The Chreia in Ancient Rhetoric,* vol. 2, *Classroom Exercises* (Atlanta: Scholars Press, 2002).

57. Hock and O'Neil, *The Chreia in Ancient Rhetoric,* 1:85 (no. 22). This and the next example come from the treatise of Aelius Theon of Alexandria, *On the Chreia.* The full text is found in Hock and O'Neil, 1:82–107.

58. Hock and O'Neil, *The Chreia in Ancient Rhetoric,* 1:85 (no. 23).

59. Hock and O'Neil, *The Chreia in Ancient Rhetoric,* 1:89 (no. 25). This is Aelius Theon's example of an "action *chreia,*" which does not require a saying. In his definition of *chreia,* Aelius Theon says that it might also be just an action on the part of the sage with no explicit saying; in this case the action is itself demonstrative of his thought or opinion in the matter (Hock and O'Neil, *The Chreia in Ancient Rhetoric,* 1:83). This type of *chreia* does not occur in the Gospels, although a number of sayings do rely on an action of Jesus in response to the situation in order to help make the point of the spoken component that follows. Examples include Mark 9:36–37; Mark 12:13–17, to be discussed further below.

60. Diogenes Laertius 6.73.

61. Hock and O'Neil, *The Chreia in Ancient Rhetoric,* 1:91 (no. 48), from Aelius Theon.

62. Hock and O'Neil, *The Chreia in Ancient Rhetoric,* 1:289 (no. 25 var.), from the Vatican Grammarian, *On Chreiai.*

63. Hock and O'Neil, *The Chreia in Ancient Rhetoric,* 1:175 (no. 26), from Hermogenes of Tarsus, *On the Chreia.*

64. Hock and O'Neil, *The Chreia in Ancient Rhetoric,* 1:175 (no. 26 var.), from Hermogenes of Tarsus, *On the Chreia,* showing variations by mixing an action and a saying.

65. Hock and O'Neil, *The Chreia in Ancient Rhetoric,* 2:159, from Libanius, *Progymnasmata.*

66. Aelius Theon, *On the Chreia* (Hock and O'Neil, *The Chreia in Ancient Rhetoric,* 1:101–7).

67. Hock and O'Neil, *The Chreia in Ancient Rhetoric,* 1:101–3.

68. See Hock and O'Neil, *The Chreia in Ancient Rhetoric,* 2:1–49.

69. The technical distinction between simile (which makes the comparison explicit using "X is like Y") and metaphor (which leaves the comparison implicit by saying "X is Y") should be observed; however, in simpler forms, they are often used interchangeably. More precise discussion of the more complex forms, parable and allegory, will be given below.

70. As noted above, the parable that Nathan confronted David with (2 Sam 12:1–10) is unique in the tradition of the Hebrew prophets. See Bailey and Vander Broek, *Literary Forms in the New Testament,* 106.

71. Cf. Judg 14:10–18; Mic 2:4; Ezek 17:1–24. The last uses the Hebrew terms *chida* ("riddle") and *mashal* interchangeably. The word *mashal* is usually translated "proverb" in these texts, as in Ezek 12:23; 16:44, but sometimes as "allegory." Although there are allegorical elements in Ezek 17, it is not a fully developed allegory in the sense to be discussed here.

72. The title of the book of Proverbs in Hebrew is *mishlei,* also from *mashal.*

73. C. Westermann, *The Parables of Jesus in the Light of the Old Testament* (Minneapolis: Fortress, 1990), 9.

74. Bailey and Vander Broek, *Literary Forms in the New Testament,* 106; D. Stern, "Jesus's Parables from the Perspective of the Rabbinic Literature: The Example of the Wicked Husbandmen," in C. Thoma and M. Wyschogrod, eds., *Parable and Story in Judaism and Christianity* (New York: Paulist, 1989), 42–80.

75. As reflected in the definition of the parable by C. H. Dodd: "The parable is a metaphor or simile drawn from nature or common life, arresting the hearer by its vividness or strangeness, and leaving the mind in sufficient doubt about its precise application to tease it into active thought" (*The Parables of the Kingdom,* 3rd ed. [New York: Scribner, 1936], 16; rev. ed. [New York: Scribner, 1961], 5). J. D. Crossan (*In Parables,* 75–78) also stresses the paradoxical nature of many of the parables in the Gospels that he takes to be more authentic to the teaching of Jesus; see Bailey and Vander Broek, *Literary Forms in the New Testament,* 111–12.

76. Bailey and Vander Broek, *Literary Forms in the New Testament,* 106.

77. The King James and English Revised Versions translated it as "parable." The Latin Vulgate translated it as "proverbial" (*proverbium*). The Greek word generally carries the sense of "proverb" or "adage," but the root word does connote comparison.

78. This is the definition of parable given by B. B. Scott in *Hear Then the Parable* (Minneapolis: Fortress, 1989), 8; cf. Bailey and Vander Broek, *Literary Forms in the New Testament*, 106.

79. Following Bultmann (*History of the Synoptic Tradition*, 166–74) and Dodd (*Parables of the Kingdom* [1936], 18; [1961], 7), many scholars reserve the word "similitude" for this simpler kind of parable; cf. Bailey and Vander Broek, *Literary Forms in the New Testament*, 107. I prefer to keep all the "true parables" in a single category, to be differentiated only by complexity on a case-by-case basis, so that an allegory in the Gospels is given its proper place in the taxonomy.

80. A more literal translation of v. 15 is: "Or is your eye evil because I am good?" (as in the KJV and ERV). The word translated "generous" in the NRSV (and "generosity" in RSV) is the Greek *agathos*, which literally means "good," but has a wide range of connotations. Based on Greek usage, in this context it might mean either "well off" (i.e., "aristocratic or wealthy"), "virtuous," or "beneficent." The sense of "wealth" is perhaps supported by the "evil eye" comment and creates an intertextual allusion to the rich young man in the previous passage. On the other hand, the sense of "beneficence" is suggested by the opening of the previous passage, when the rich young man asks, "What good thing (*agathon*) must I do to inherit eternal life?" The word *agathon* does not appear at this point in either the Markan or Lukan parallels to this story. Consequently, it is a Matthean modification, which in turn creates an intertextual link to the following story of the laborers. Moreover, because the householder (Gk. *oikodespotēs*, 20:1) is later called "Lord of the vineyard" (20:8), a traditional metaphor for God and Israel, the beneficence of God seems to be implied.

81. Note that the two sayings that flank the parable (Matt 19:30; 20:16) are phrased inversely: the first is "first-last," while the second is "last-first." Within the parable, then, the last hired are paid first, and the first hired are paid last.

82. Jeremias, *The Parables of Jesus*, 70, 88; Dodd, *Parables of the Kingdom* (1936), 13–19; (1961), 3–7; Bultmann, *History of the Synoptic Tradition*, 197–201; McKnight, *What Is Form Criticism?* 31; Bailey and Vander Broek, *Literary Forms in the New Testament*, 110–11.

83. Augustine *Quaestiones Evangeliorum* 2.19, slightly abridged, in Dodd, *Parables of the Kingdom* (1936), 11–12; (1961), 1–2.

84. This is not meant to be a definition of allegory as such, but it is a characteristic of the use of allegory within the synoptic Gospels. In general, however, allegory is often used as a medium of cultural reinterpretation of older traditions. See D. Dawson, *Allegorical Readers and Cultural Revision in Ancient Alexandria* (Berkeley: University of California Press, 1992).

85. The Matthean author has also added a small passage in 13:16–17, in between the passage on the reason for parables (Matt 13:10–15; Mark 4:10–12) and the interpretation of the parable of the sower (Matt 13:18–23; Mark 4:13–20).

86. A small portion of this passage appears in Matt 13:12 instead.

87. Cf. the added passage in Matt 13:16–17.

88. Mark 4:26 uses the Greek word *sporos* for "seed," while Matt 13:24 uses *sperma*. But both Greek words derive from the same root and are used interchangeably. The Matthean change in wording is somewhat more literarily crafted, because it opts for an alliterative phrasing using the cognate verb and noun, thus: *anthrōpō speiranti kalon sperma* ("to a man sowing good seed").

89. The Greek word *therismos* ("harvest") has been substituted in the Markan quotation of Joel 3:13 (LXX) for a different Greek word (*trygētos*) meaning "grape harvest." The word used in Mark is more suitable to the situation of seed and a grain harvest, as the parable requires; however, the Matthean version further emphasizes that this is about "grain" and a "grain harvest" with "harvesters" (*therismos* and *theristai*).

90. The six passages are Matt 8:12; 13:42; 13:50; 22:13; 24:51; 25:30. The last two come at the end of the apocalyptic discourse, and both are allegories.

91. For a discussion of the Q trajectory and its social location, with specific comments on this parable, see the discussion in White, *From Jesus to Christianity*, 133–42. U. Luz (*Matthew: A Commentary*, Hermeneia [Minneapolis: Fortress, 2005], 3:47) does not follow most scholars in thinking that the Matthean version goes back to the Q tradition. I will argue, on the contrary, that both parts of the Matthean version derive from two distinct parables in the Q tradition.

92. Jeremias, *The Parables of Jesus*, 37. See also D. E. Smith, *From Symposium to Eucharist: The Banquet in the Early Christian World* (Minneapolis: Fortress, 2003), 253–72; D. P. Moessner, *Lord of the Banquet: The Literary and Theological Significance of the Lukan Travel Narrative* (Minneapolis: Fortress, 1989). We shall return to this issue in Chapter 13.

93. The metaphor includes such themes as the bridegroom, the eschatological or messianic banquet, and wedding feasts. See D. E. Smith, "Messianic Banquet," *Anchor Bible Dictionary*, 4:788–91.

94. The so-called *Messianic Rule* from Qumran (1QSa) is an appendix to the *Rule of the Community* (1QS). The key passage is 1QSa 2.11–22. See P. Bilde, "The Common Meal in the Qumran-Essene Communities," in I. Nielsen and H. S. Nielsen, eds., *Meals in a Social Context* (Aarhus: Aarhus University Press, 1998), 145–66, esp. 153.

95. The theme of the destruction of Jerusalem already seems to be present both in Mark in the parable of the wicked tenants (12:1–12) and in Q (listed here); however, the Gospel of Matthew seems to be expanding on this theme and giving it further weight as part of a polemic against opponents to the Matthean community.

96. Also discussed in Jeremias, *The Parables of Jesus*, 37–38, 131–32.

97. Cf. Sir 5:8.

98. A quotation from Wis 9:8.

99. Soncino edition.

100. See also Jeremias, *Parables of Jesus*, 132.

101. I am convinced that there are a few such "shadow" passages that probably derive from Q, but they are not usually identified as such because the parallels are not as close as most of the recognized Q passages. In each case

we find similar themes, but either the Matthean or Lukan version has altered the passage so dramatically that the base version is obscured. In the case of the ten bridesmaids, I am proposing that the two Matthean versions are more dramatically altered and the Lukan parallel is closer to the Q original. Another example is the parable of the two sons in Matthew (21:28–32) compared with the parable of the lost or prodigal son (and his brother) in Luke (15:11–32). In this case, the Lukan version has been more dramatically changed, while the Matthean version seems to be closer to the original form, presumably from Q. We shall return to this point in Chapter 12.

102. This "delayed" arrival of the eschaton is another theme in the Gospel of Matthew.

Chapter Ten: Plotting the Nativity

1. Ironically, it may be argued that such awareness of birth stories has developed in Western (Christian) culture because of the place of the Gospel birth narratives and attendant rituals associated with the Advent and Christmas season.

2. With the exception of apocryphal Gospels, notably the *Protevangelium of James* and a medieval Latin text known as the *Arundel Manuscript,* virtually nothing is said about the medical details of the birth of Jesus in the earliest Gospels. These two texts add a midwife to the story. In the case of the *Arundel Manuscript,* however, its putative use of the medical details has a clear apologetic program in supporting the emerging doctrine of Mary's perpetual virginity. See D. R. Cartlidge and D. L. Dungan, *Documents for the Study of the Gospels,* 2nd ed. (Minneapolis: Fortress, 1994), 96–98 (selections). On the medical background, most of which is sadly overlooked in relation to the Gospels, see esp. L. Dean-Jones, *Women's Bodies in Classical Greek Science* (Oxford: Oxford University Press, 1994). One of the principal ancient sources is Soranus of Ephesus, *Gynaecology* (Baltimore: Johns Hopkins University Press, 1956), a handbook for midwives written in the second century CE. See also A. E. Hanson, "Conception, Gestation, and the Origin of Female Nature in the *Corpus Hippocraticum,*" *Helios* 19 (1992): 31–71; J. Blaney, "Theories of Conception in the Ancient Roman World," in B. Rawson, ed., *The Family in Ancient Rome* (London: Croom Helm, 1986), 230–36; V. French, "Midwives and Maternity Care in the Graeco-Roman World," in M. B. Skinner, ed., *Rescuing Creusa: New Methodological Approaches to Women in Antiquity* (Lubbock: Texas Tech University Press, 1987), 69–84. Also on New Testament topics, see H. J. Cadbury, "The Ancient Physiological Notions Underlying John I 13 and Hebrews XI 11," *The Expositor* 9.2 (1924): 430–39; P. W. van der Horst, "Sarah's Seminal Emission: Hebrews 11:11 in the Light of Ancient Embryology," in D. L. Balch, E. Ferguson, and W. A. Meeks, eds., *Greeks, Romans, and Christians* (Minneapolis: Fortress, 1990), 287–302.

3. I have added the word "who" in brackets to clarify the parallel structure of the Greek grammar.

4. R. E. Brown, K. P. Donfried, J. A. Fitzmyer, and J. Reumann, eds., *Mary in the New Testament* (Philadelphia: Fortress, 1978), 36–39. The parallelism of the two phrases (i.e., descending from David and being declared as Son of God by the resurrection) is the main rationale for suggesting pre-Pauline roots; however, both phrases are affirmations of Jesus's messianic identity.

5. In the Greek, the word "Gospel" (*euangelion*) does not precede the phrase "concerning his son" in verse 3. The correct wording is "the Gospel of God . . . concerning his son, who . . ."

6. Brown et al., *Mary in the New Testament,* 42.

7. Brown et al., *Mary in the New Testament,* 43.

8. That is, at the time that Galatians and Romans were written, sometime in the late 50s. On the dates and situation of writing, see L. M. White, *From Jesus to Christianity* (San Francisco: HarperSanFrancisco, 2004), 197–214.

9. *Crèche* (French) literally means "crib" in the sense of stable or manger. Only in North American usage does it come to mean the "manger scene" of the Christmas season. In the United Kingdom and elsewhere it typically means a nursery or daycare center.

10. Specifically on the magi in later Christian tradition, see R. E. Brown, *The Birth of the Messiah* (Garden City, NY: Doubleday, 1977), 197–200.

11. This popular American Christmas song was originally composed as "Carol of the Drum" in 1941 by Katherine K. Davis. It was first recorded under this title in 1957. It was re-arranged and recorded under the title "The Little Drummer Boy" in 1958, which is the form now most widely known. It is a good example of how the storytelling imagination works. It creatively pivots from what seems to be a modern context, something like a crowd going to see a crèche, to the ostensible moment of Jesus's birth. Historical and fictional elements blend, as the little drummer boy joins the characters in the crèche; the ox and the ass "keep time," and baby Jesus smiles. No one today would ever think of claiming that any of it is "real" or historical, as though crowds of people were there to see the holy family in the stable. On a certain level, we are prepared to tolerate or even appreciate it as a pious fiction. Popular imagination allows for such a fiction as a reflection of how later generations of believers perceive the significance of the birth through their own experience and cultural filters. In all probability, some of the early legends about the birth were treated the same way. But after many centuries, such perceptions may change as the historical disjuncture fades into the distant past. Who knows; perhaps in a few more centuries crèches will also include a little drummer boy next to the magi and shepherds.

12. Justin Martyr *Dialogue with Trypho* 78. The Hebrew of Isa 33:16 may be translated as follows: "They will live on the heights; their refuge will be the fortresses of rocks; their food will be supplied, their water assured" (NRSV).

13. The word *kyrios* in Greek (as found in the LXX of Isa 1:3) can be translated "Lord" in reference to the divine, or as "lord/master" (or just "sir") in reference to humans. The Hebrew of Isa 1:3 has *bōalai,* which more properly yields the sense of "lord/master."

14. Mary riding the donkey to Bethlehem is already present in the *Prot. Jas.* 16.4–10. This is how she is commonly depicted in later Christian iconography. The ox and ass both appear in the birth narrative in an apocryphal Gospel now called the *Gospel of Pseudo-Matthew* (eighth–ninth century) and in *The Golden Legend.* For the former, see M. R. James, *The Apocryphal New Testament* (Oxford: Clarendon, 1975), 70–79; Cartlidge and Dungan, *Documents for the Study of the Gospels,* 91–95 (selections); for the latter, see W. G. Ryan, *The Golden Legend: Readings on the Saints by Jacobus De Voragine* (Princeton: Princeton University Press, 1993).

15. See Brown, *Birth of the Messiah*, 170–73. We shall return to this point later in this chapter.

16. In Orthodox churches the baptism is now called Theophany (or the Lesser Epiphany) and also celebrated on January 19–20. It includes a blessing of the waters as a principal ritual.

17. O. Cullmann, "The Origins of Christmas," in *The Early Church: Studies in Early Christian History and Thought* (Philadelphia: SCM, 1966), 17–36. March 25 eventually became the Feast of the Annunciation as well as the feast day for Mary.

18. It is reflected in the Roman calendar of 354. See M. R. Salzman, *On Roman Time: The Codex Calendar of 354 and the Rhythms of Urban Life in Late Antiquity* (Berkeley: University of California Press, 1990).

19. J. A. Fitzmyer, *The Gospel According to Luke*, 2 vols., Anchor Bible 28 (Garden City, NY: Doubleday, 1981–85), 1:309–11.

20. One popular misconception used to account for the differences in the two genealogies (discussed below) is that the Matthean version is through Joseph while the Lukan is really through Mary. Yet both stress Davidic lineage, whereas the Lukan account of Mary's kinship with the Levite Elizabeth makes this impossible. In fact, the Mary of Luke is not of Davidic descent. The names in the Lukan genealogy also make it clear that it is Joseph's lineage that establishes Jesus's Davidic descent.

21. Based on the appearance of several key women in the Matthean genealogy, the role of Mary is more central to the Matthean construction of Jesus's Davidic lineage. See Brown, *Birth of the Messiah*, 73–74. Though this distinctive feature of the Matthean genealogy is primarily concerned with the virginal conception as a divine intervention, a further implication is that Mary, like Joseph, may be thought of as instrumental to Jesus's Davidic lineage. *Prot. Jas.* 10.4 explicitly identifies Mary as of the lineage of David.

22. See Brown, *Birth of the Messiah*, 86–90; 503–4. See also n. 19, above.

23. Brown, *Birth of the Messiah*, 189.

24. Brown, *Birth of the Messiah*, 514–15.

25. Here we may notice that the order specifies male children in and around Bethlehem age two years or younger (Matt 2:16). The fact that he would need to cover children up to two years has been taken to indicate that time line of the Matthean narrative is somewhat protracted; however, the two years actually derives from the Moses tradition. See nn. 42–43, below.

26. Based on the levitical laws (Lev 12:1–8) concerning the period of "purification" after giving birth, as mentioned in Luke 2:22, it should be forty days (thirty-three days after the circumcision) for a male child; however, the Lukan narrative is (intentionally) vague on the amount of time by mentioning only the circumcision on the eighth day. As Brown notes, the Lukan author seems to have confused two different Jewish birth rituals in order to create an appropriate setting for the scene in the Temple that follows (*Birth of the Messiah*, 447–49). One is the presentation (or "redemption") of the firstborn male (Exod 13:11–16); the other, the levitical purification noted above. The latter did not require a trip to the Temple and was typically performed at home. See also Fitzmyer, *Gospel According to Luke*, 1:424.

27. Brown, *Birth of the Messiah*, 176.

28. Brown, *Birth of the Messiah*, 123, 129.

29. The Greek of Matt 1:25 literally reads "and he did not *know* her until she gave birth to a son." The use of the word "to know" with the sense of having sexual relations already had a long history in the Jewish scriptures.

30. Italics added to show the sequence. Brown, *Birth of the Messiah*, 514–15.

31. Josephus *Antiquities* 18.26: "In the 37th year after Caesar's defeat of Antony at Actium." The Battle of Actium occurred in 31 BCE and made it possible for Octavian to assume the title Caesar Augustus as first emperor of Rome in 29 BCE.

32. Josephus *Antiquities* 17.355; 18.1–4; 26 (quoted in Box 10.2); cf. *Jewish War* 2.117–18.

33. Josephus *Jewish War* 2.117–18. The rebellion led by Judas is also mentioned in the passage about Quirinius and Coponius in *Antiquities* 18.1–4.

34. Brown, *Birth of the Messiah*, 551.

35. On the division of Herod's kingdom among his three surviving sons, see White, *From Jesus to Christianity*, 26 (fig. 2.2), 30–32.

36. In the Gospels, Antipas is just called Herod, and this fact has often led readers to confuse him and his father. For the death of John, see Mark 6:17–29; Matt 14:3–12; cf. Luke 3:19–20. Josephus (*Antiquities* 18.116–18) confirms the fact that Herod Antipas was responsible, but gives a different picture of how it occurred. Most notably, the account in Mark (followed by Matthew) shows confusion regarding the prior marriage of Herodias. The trial of Jesus before Herod Antipas is mentioned only in Luke 23:6–16, and also appears to be a Lukan creation. For discussion, see Chapter 7.

37. Brown, *Birth of the Messiah*, 549.

38. On the problems of the dating, see B. Reicke, *The New Testament Era* (Philadelphia: Fortress, 1968), 106, 136; Brown, *Birth of the Messiah*, 547–56; J. Fitzmyer, *Gospel According to Luke*, 1:399–405; D. Potter, "Quirinius," in D. N. Freedman, ed., *Anchor Bible Dictionary*, 6 vols. (New York: Doubleday, 1992), 5:588–89; and additional bibliography cited in Box 10.2.

39. See White, *From Jesus to Christianity*, 31–34.

40. Brown, *Birth of the Messiah*, 555.

41. The Greek of the passage clearly speaks of "boys" (*paidas*) rather than the generic "children," as it is often translated.

42. Brown, *Birth of the Messiah*, 225–26.

43. Brown, *Birth of the Messiah*, 227. The other case alluded to in this quotation is the story of the magi in Matthew, as discussed by Brown in *Birth of the Messiah*, 188–190.

44. Brown, *Birth of the Messiah*, 227–29.

45. See U. Luz, *Matthew: A Commentary*, Hermeneia (Minneapolis: Fortress, 2005), 1:118–20.

46. The quotation is based on a very loose form of Isa 11:1, as it transforms the Hebrew word "root" (*nezer*) into "Nazorean" (*nozri*) to make it fit.

47. As suggested earlier, the Pauline reference is more about Jesus's messianic identity. On historical questions regarding Jesus's Davidic lineage, see Brown, *Birth of the Messiah*, 505–12.

48. A number of scholars have argued that Jesus was actually born in Nazareth, and even Brown gives a nod to the historical possibility (*Birth of the Messiah*, 513–16). See also J. P. Meier, *A Marginal Jew: Rethinking the Historical Jesus*, 3 vols. (New York: Doubleday, 1991–2002), 1:214–19.

49. Brown (*Birth of the Messiah*, 107) draws the same basic conclusion.

50. Cf. Gen 5:1; 6:9; 10:1; 11:10; 11:27. The Matthean wording is identical to that of Gen 5:1, LXX.

51. This scheme generally follows that of Brown (*Birth of the Messiah*, 50–52), but with some modifications. He treats Matt 2:1–12 as one scene, whereas I subdivide it into two (A.2 and A.3). The import of this division will be discussed further below. Because Brown's *Birth of the Messiah* is such an exhaustive work, it has dominated the scholarly discussion over the past generation. As a result, it is frequently necessary in this study to reflect on his conclusions regarding individual issues before we can offer new alternatives.

52. This is my own formulation of the scheme. The "who" and "where" organization of the birth narrative was first proposed by K. Stendahl, "*Quis et Unde?* An Analysis of Mt 1–2," in W. Eltester, ed., *Judentum, Urchristentum, Kirche*, Festschrift für J. Jeremias (Berlin: Töpelmann, 1964), 94–105. Stendahl applied it to the two chapters respectively, i.e., chapter 1 deals with "who" and chapter 2 deals with "where." The scheme was modified by Brown to yield four elements: "who, how, where, and whence" (*Birth of the Messiah*, 52–54). But these terms are more artificial than in Stendahl's scheme, since each of the last two might easily be termed "whence," referring to where Jesus came from. In my view, the "where" component is equally important in each act as one of the "prophetic" signs of Jesus's identity.

53. Brown, *Birth of the Messiah*, 109–16, Table VII. For other scholars, see the notes in Brown.

54. Brown, *Birth of the Messiah*, 117.

55. Brown, *Birth of the Messiah*, 118.

56. Brown, *Birth of the Messiah*, 111 (his italics).

57. Brown, *Birth of the Messiah*, 111. The terms are his although paraphrased from his actual statement: "partially and approximately the content of the narrative that Matthew drew on."

58. On the similar structure and phrasing, see Brown, *Birth of the Messiah*, 107–8, Table VI.

59. See Brown, *Birth of the Messiah*, 143–53.

60. See esp. K. Stendahl, *The School of St. Matthew and Its Use of the Old Testament*, 2nd ed. (Philadelphia: Fortress, 1968).

61. See Brown, *Birth of the Messiah*, 168–70.

62. This is a literal translation of the LXX text of the passage. In each case I have italicized the words that are identical in Greek to the Matthean passage.

63. So also Brown, *Birth of the Messiah*, 170–73, 188–89. Astronomical phenomena were in fact commonly taken as portents in antiquity, but the story need not be based on any specific event. It should also be remembered that Julius Caesar's apotheosis was said to be visualized as a new star in the heavens. See Chapter 4.

64. See also the discussion in Brown, *Birth of the Messiah*, 190–96, for a similar argument. Brown, however, argues that the magi and star motif came from a separate "pre-Matthean" tradition that was joined by the Matthean author with the dream tradition discussed above. I cannot agree. It seems, instead, to be an entirely Matthean construction and in my view serves as the crux of the entire Matthean birth narrative.

65. See the discussion of Ps 2 in Chapter 1. Other instances of the "scepter/rod," using the same word, as a Davidic royal symbol occur in Isa 11:4; Gen 49:10; Ps 45:6–7; 2 Sam 7:14. In Ps 74:2 (where it is sometimes translated "tribe") it is used of Mt. Zion (and the Temple) as symbol of God's rule.

66. There are two key changes in the Greek: first, the word "scepter" becomes "man" (using the Greek word *anthrōpos*); second, the word "rise up" goes from active to passive ("be raised up").

67. This is also how the LXX renders Num 24:7, an earlier section of Balaam's blessing of Israel; it is altered to read: "A man shall come forth from his [Jacob's] seed and he shall rule over many nations."

68. Bar Kochba was the leader of the second Jewish revolt against Rome (132–35 CE). His real name was Simon bar Cosibah, and he claimed to be a descendant of David. His messianic name "Bar Kochba" comes from the Hebrew word for "star" (*kokab*) in Num 24:17. His name (or title) thus means "Son of the Star" and symbolizes the apocalyptic return of the Davidic kingdom to Israel. According to rabbinic legend, this title was given to him by Rabbi Akiba (*y. Ta'an.* 68d). For discussion, see White, *From Jesus to Christianity*, 361–65 and other bibliography cited there.

69. Cf. the phrasing in Pss 2:7, 45:1–2; Isa 11:1–4; 61:1–3; Joel 2:28–29. See the discussion of the *T. Jud.* passage in Chapter 1.

70. See 1 Thess 4:14; Mark 8:31; 9:9; see also Chapter 6, n. 52. In the Gospel of Matthew, however, the word typically used is *egerein*.

71. Philo *Life of Moses* 1.267–94, which retells the entire story of Num 22–24, but with heavy colorings of Greek tradition. The explicit references noted above occur in 1.277 and 278.

72. Brown argues that the Joseph-Moses and Joseph-Jesus parallel is a principal motif in the Matthean construction of the narrative (*Birth of the Messiah*, 228–29).

73. Philo explicitly calls Moses the ideal prophet, king, lawgiver, and high priest of the Jews (*Life of Moses* 1.334; 2.3–6, 66, 187–88), even though there was no kingship in Israel until centuries later. Although Moses was of the tribe of Levi, he was never considered the high priest; that lot fell to his brother, Aaron, from whom the Zadokite (or high-priestly) line traditionally descends.

74. Although some scholars have found less direct connection between the themes of the birth narrative and the rest of the Gospel of Matthew, Brown argues that there is greater continuity (*Birth of the Messiah*, 48–50). I agree and offer this reading of the symbols at work as further support. We shall return to these elements in Chapter 12.

75. Here I am taking a rather different line on the overall shape of the Lukan birth narrative. Brown (*Birth of the Messiah*) limits his discussion to Luke 1–2 only; however, taking the narrative through to the genealogy is warranted on the literary level, even though it extends the birth narrative to include the "arrival" of both John and Jesus as adult characters. In that sense the "extended birth narrative" of the Gospel of Luke covers birth and early life, including the entire career of John the Baptist as the last of the prophets, the one who announces the arrival of the messiah.

76. So also Brown, *Birth of the Messiah*, 246–47.

77. Even if Mary was a mere teenager when Jesus was born (prior to 4 BCE), by the time that Luke was written, she would have been in her late nineties at the earliest, and that only if one posits a rather early date for the writing of Luke-Acts, ca. 80 CE. If one assumes a later date of composition ca. 90 or even 100 CE, as many scholars would now suggest, she would have been well over a hundred years of age. We shall return to the dating of Luke-Acts in Chapter 13.

78. Brown, *Birth of the Messiah,* 252.

79. Brown argues that the entire episode of Jesus in the Temple at age twelve (2:41–51) was added at the second stage and that the presentation of the infant Jesus at the Temple was significantly expanded as well (2:28–33; *Birth of the Messiah,* 251–52).

80. *Birth of the Messiah,* 252, n. 49; cf. 244, n. 30. See also Fitzmyer, *Gospel According to Luke,* 309, 357–60.

81. In Box 10.1, I have outlined them the same way, but using a different numbering system to show the double narrative (marked A for John and B for Jesus) and the points of intersection where the two stories converge (marked C).

82. See also Brown, *Birth of the Messiah,* 316–19.

83. See P. S. Minear, "Luke's Use of the Birth Stories," in L. E. Keck and J. L. Martyn, eds., *Studies in Luke-Acts* (Nashville: Abingdon, 1966), 112–15.

84. See Brown's discussion of the LXX texts used in the angelic announcements, *Birth of the Messiah,* 272–78, 310–16. More generally on the extensive use and influence of the LXX in Luke, see Fitzmyer, *Gospel According to Luke,* 113–25.

85. In the Greek, the name of Anna's father (*Phanouēl,* 2:36) can hardly help but evoke the name *Samouēl* in the LXX.

86. See n. 75, above, and Brown, *Birth of the Messiah,* 251–52, 339–41.

87. See Fitzmyer, *Gospel According to Luke,* 357–59.

88. Brown, *Birth of the Messiah,* 306.

89. Brown, *Birth of the Messiah,* 304–306.

90. P. S. Minear, "Luke's Use of the Birth Stories," 112–15.

91. Fitzmyer classifies this as a biographical apothegm, i.e., a kind of *chreia,* in which the saying of Jesus is the key point, set up by the action (*Gospel According to Luke,* 436–37). See the discussion of *chreiai* in Chapter 9. Some would argue that it comes from a pre-Lukan "infancy gospel," but I think it unlikely. It is instead a natural extension of the birth narrative to show the precociousness and wisdom of the special child, as signaled in the two summary statements that frame the episode (2:40; 2:52).

92. M. P. Bonz, *The Past as Legacy: Luke-Acts and Ancient Epic* (Minneapolis: Fortress, 2000).

93. Notice how the beginning of Jesus's ministry is set off by the direction of the Spirit in the temptation story (4:1), in his first ministry in Galilee (4:14), and then in his first sermon in Nazareth (4:18). With the last consider also Luke 4:43 and the following note.

94. In Greek these are really the same phrase, and they are characteristic of the Lukan prose, in reference to the Passion tradition in particular. Cf. Luke 4:43; 22:(7,) 37; 24:26, 44; Acts 1:16, 21; 3:21. See Fitzmyer, *Gospel According to Luke,* 180 (in general), 443 (for Luke 2:52).

Chapter Eleven: *The Misunderstood Messiah: The Gospel of Mark*

1. We shall discuss the ending of the Gospel of Mark later in this chapter. The earliest manuscripts have it end at 16:8, when the women leave the empty tomb. As we noted in Chapter 7, the Markan author omits any direct reference to Jesus's appearances to the disciples after the resurrection.

2. Also discussed in Chapter 10. In the case of the Gospel of Matthew, the passage reflecting their view that he is insane is simply deleted. Cf. Mark 3:19–21; Matt 12:22–24.

3. On the characterization of the disciples, see C. C. Black, *The Disciples According to Mark: Markan Redaction in Current Debate* (Sheffield: Sheffield Academic Press, 1989).

4. This is the view of F. C. Burkitt, in *The Gospel and Its Transmission* (Edinburgh: Clark, 1907). For a brief overview of this early period of Markan research, see M. D. Hooker, "Mark, Gospel of," in J. H. Hayes, ed., *Dictionary of Biblical Interpretation* (Nashville: Abingdon, 1999), 2:125–26.

5. The phrase was coined first in 1892 by M. Kähler in *The So-Called Historical Jesus and the Historic Biblical Christ* (German ed., 1892; Philadelphia: Fortress, 1964), 80, n. 11. Kähler's statement was really about all the canonical Gospels, but it has been taken as especially apt to the Gospel of Mark.

6. Wilhelm Wrede, *Das Messiasgeheimnis in den Evangelien: Zugleich ein Beitrag zum Verständnis des Markusevangeliums* (Göttingen, 1901; repr., 1969); Eng. trans.: *The Messianic Secret* (Cambridge: Clarke, 1971), 125–29. It should also be remembered that Wrede's work, and the beginning of Schweitzer's own study, stood as the end point of Albert Schweitzer's 1906 survey of previous scholarship on the historical Jesus: *The Quest of the Historical Jesus: A Critical Study of the Progress from Reimarus to Wrede* (London: Black, 1910), 330–97. Notably Schweitzer's original German title was reversed: *Von Reimarus zu Wrede: Eine Geschichte der Leben-Jesu-Forschung* (Tübingen: Mohr, 1906).

7. For a survey of these stages in scholarship on Mark, see J. C. Anderson and S. D. Moore, "The Lives of Mark," in *Mark and Method: New Approaches in Biblical Studies* (Minneapolis: Fortress, 1992), 1–22, esp. 2–12. For discussion of the secrecy motif in Wrede and later scholarship, see C. M. Tuckett, *The Messianic Secret* (Philadelphia: Fortress, 1983).

8. See Anderson and Moore, "The Lives of Mark," 12–19; E. S. Malbon, "Narrative Criticism: How Does the Story Mean?" in Anderson and Moore, eds., *Mark and Method,* 23–49; D. Rhoads, J. Dewey, and D. Michie, *Mark as Story: An Introduction to the Narrative of a Gospel,* 2nd ed. (Minneapolis: Fortress, 1999).

9. W. Shiner, *Proclaiming the Gospel: First-Century Performance of Mark* (Harrisburg, PA: Trinity Press International, 2003); C. Bryan, *A Preface to Mark: Notes on the Gospel in Its Literary and Cultural Settings* (New York: Oxford University Press, 1993), 123–54; J. Dewey, "Oral Methods of Structuring Narrative in Mark," *Interpretation* 43 (1989): 32–44.

10. Eusebius *Church History* 3.39.15–16 (my translation). The portion in single quotes seems to represent what Papias records of the words of John of Ephesus on Mark; the remainder is apparently Papias's further comments on the statement attributed to John; however, some parts may be edited by Eusebius. Here we see that even the "testimony" of Papias already shows an awareness that the order of Mark is different from that in other Gospels.

11. Eusebius *Church History* 2.15–17, 24. See L. M. White, *From Jesus to Christianity* (San Francisco: Harper-SanFrancisco, 2004), 393.

12. On this chronology, see White, *From Jesus to Christianity*, 145–53, 169–71.

13. Cf. Mark 15:16 (use of the technical Latin term *praetorium*); 7:3–4, 11–12 (where Jewish customs and terminology are explained). The Gospel always translates Aramaic terms into Greek; so 5:43; 7:11, 34; 15:34.

14. A composition in Rome is mentioned both in the Papias legend (quoted above) and in the comments of Clement of Alexandria, quoted in the Epilogue.

15. See White, *From Jesus to Christianity*, 223 (Fig. 9.2).

16. Josephus *Jewish War* 7.23–42.

17. In fact, any of the other cities of Syria, such as Berytus or Tyre, might be considered possible. T. J. Weeden has also argued for Caesarea Philippi (*Mark: Traditions in Conflict* [Philadelphia: Fortress, 1971]).

18. The later Christian writer Clement of Alexandria (ca. 200 CE) discusses another version of Mark, known as the *Secret Gospel of Mark*, and says that Mark brought it from Rome to Alexandria. See M. W. Meyer, "Mark, Secret Gospel of," in D. N. Freedman, ed., *Anchor Bible Dictionary*, 6 vols. (New York: Doubleday, 1992), 4:558–59. It will be discussed in Chapter 15 below.

19. For the course of the war and other Jewish responses to it, see White, *From Jesus to Christianity*, 217–31.

20. Josephus *Jewish War* 2.293–308.

21. Josephus *Jewish War* 4.182–83; for the further atrocities of the Zealots, meaning the followers of John of Gischala, against the Jewish population, even to the point of killing the Temple priests, see *Jewish War* 4.305–13. For John's plundering of the Temple in May–June of 70, see *Jewish War* 6.562–66.

22. Josephus *Jewish War* 6.93–95.

23. Josephus *Jewish War* 6.254–66; for the accompanying atrocities and Josephus's account of supernatural portents that signaled the ultimate loss of the Temple as divine symbol, see *Jewish War* 6.271–309. For the Roman ritual of sacrificing to the military standards within the Temple court, followed by execution of the remaining priests, see *Jewish War* 6.316–22.

24. For the various theories regarding the referent, see A. Y. Collins, *Mark: A Commentary*, Hermeneia (Minneapolis: Fortress, 2007), 608–12.

25. I am not persuaded by the arguments of Collins and others that the further warning, "then those in Judea must flee to the mountains," should be taken as evidence that the "desecration" must be some earlier event that necessitates a date of composition of the Gospel prior to the actual destruction of the Temple. Rather, the point is rhetorical. Jesus is made to predict the events; therefore, if the audience had understood what he was saying, they would have fled the city at the beginning. It is rhetorical hyperbole. The "desolating sacrilege" covers the entire process from 66 to 70 CE, but seen for its full significance only in retrospect.

26. In contrast to the later Gospels, it is primarily the chief priests who view Jesus as a serious threat and seek to kill him, specifically after the cleansing of the Temple (Mark 11:18, 27; cf. 14:1–2, 10, 43, 55; 15:11). See D. Juel, *Messiah and Temple in the Gospel of Mark: The Trial of Jesus in the Gospel of Mark* (Missoula, MT: Scholars Press, 1977).

27. Discussed in Chapter 8 and Box 11.2. See P. J. Achtemeier, "Toward the Isolation of Pre-Markan Miracle Catenae," *Journal of Biblical Literature* 89 (1970): 265–91.

28. On the geographical framework, see esp. E. S. Malbon, *Narrative Space and Mythic Meaning in Mark* (San Francisco: Harper & Row, 1986; Sheffield: Sheffield Academic Press, 1991).

29. See J. R. Edwards, "Markan Sandwiches: The Significance of Interpolations Within the Markan Narrative," *Novum Testamentum* 31 (1989): 193–216.

30. Four of the oldest, most reliable manuscripts omit everything after v. 8, ending at "for they were afraid." They represent three main streams of textual transmission: the Alexandrian Greek (Codex Sinaiticus, Codex Vaticanus), the Old Syriac (Codex Sinaiticus Syriacus), and the Old Latin. Its omission is even attested in a letter of Jerome regarding his edition of the later Latin Vulgate (*Epistle* 120.3). There are actually several different versions of these added verses found in the later manuscript tradition.

(1) In one version (called the "Shorter Ending") there is an addition at the end of v. 8 that reads:

> And all that had been commanded them they told briefly to those around Peter. And afterward Jesus himself sent out through them, from east to west, the sacred and imperishable proclamation of eternal salvation.

(2) The more common "Longer Ending" (vv. 9–20) is likewise attested only in later manuscripts, and in many cases even then is marked with scribal notes saying that it was missing from the older manuscripts. Because these verses were contained in both the Vulgate and the King James, it became standard in all later English versions to include them, even after the manuscript evidence became known. Since the late nineteenth century, however, it has been typical in scholarly editions to mark these verses with some notation indicating the variant manuscript evidence. This practice has carried over into critical English versions beginning with the Revised Standard (1948, 1952).

(3) A variant version of the "Longer Ending" that includes the "Shorter Ending" occurs in some manuscripts.

(4) There is also an additional variant (called the "Freer Logion") on the "Longer Ending" found in a few manuscripts; it adds another lengthy section between vv. 14 and 15, as follows:

> And those men began to excuse themselves, saying, "This age of lawlessness and unbelief is under Satan, who does not allow the truth and power of God to prevail over [put an end to] the unclean things of the [evil] spirits [alternate: who does not allow what lies under the unclean spirits to comprehend the truth and power (or true power) of God]. Therefore, reveal your righteousness now." Thus, these men spoke to Christ. And Christ began to address them, "The span of years of Satan's power has been fulfilled, but other such things draw near. And on behalf of those having sinned, I was delivered unto death, in order that they may inherit the spiritual and incorruptible glory of righteousness which is in heaven."

For discussion of the manuscript evidence see B. M. Metzger, *A Textual Commentary on the Greek New Testament*, 2nd ed. (New York: United Bible Society, 1994), 122–26; B. M. Metzger and B. D. Ehrman, *The Text of the New Testament*, 4th ed. (New York: Oxford University Press, 2005), 322–27; Collins, *Mark*, 802–18.

31. For the growing consensus, see Collins, *Mark*, 797–801.

32. For this older view, that v. 8 is the end of the manuscript *as known*, but the further ending was somehow truncated or lost, see Metzger, *Textual Commentary*, 126; Metzger and Ehrman, *Text of the New Testament*, 325–26; and Collins, *Mark*, 797–99. In light of ancient manuscript production and use, it is less likely that the end of a text would be lost in this manner, especially in the case of scrolls. The end of the scroll was closest to the center and thus least susceptible to damage, even in the case of fire. This fact has been amply demonstrated by the carbonized papyrus scrolls found at Herculaneum (destroyed in the eruption of Mt. Vesuvius in 79 CE). Furthermore, because all the manuscript evidence for the Gospel of Mark shows a break at the same point, after 16:8, it means that the argument for a "lost ending" or a "lost last page" faces another logical conundrum. It must presuppose that the loss occurred to one (and only one) manuscript, potentially even the original (or "autograph"), which then became the sole source (or "exemplar") for all derived forms of the text. And all of this must have occurred before the text of Mark began to be circulated along with other Gospels, which we know commenced in the second century CE. Otherwise, given the nature of ancient methods in scribal production of copies, one would not expect the "last page" or "last column" to occur at precisely the same point. Consequently, the theories of a lost ending become far less likely.

33. See D. Juel, *A Master of Surprise: Mark Interpreted* (Minneapolis: Fortress, 1994), 107–21; F. Kermode, *The Genesis of Secrecy: On the Interpretation of Narrative* (Cambridge: Cambridge University Press, 1979), 125–45.

34. Like the exorcism of the Gerasene demoniac, which precedes it, this miracle has some features that are intentionally odd. In the case of the demoniac, it is the fact that the demon at first tries to exorcize Jesus by using magical language: "I adjure (conjure) you by God" (5:7). In this case, it is the fact that the woman is healed instantly when she touches Jesus's cloak. Jesus only notices when he feels the power drain from his body, and only then does he turn and address her. The normal sequence of having the miracle worker address the problem directly has been intentionally altered. Such changes would have been immediately noticeable to the audience, and they help set up the dramatic elements of how the characters in the story react to Jesus.

35. See n. 29, above.

36. Two other miracles may be noted with similar allegorical function. One is the boy with the demon (9:14–29); the other is the healing of the blind man Bartimaeus (10:46–52). Other than the cursing of the fig tree (11:12–25), these are the last two miracles in the Gospel of Mark. See Box 11.3. The story of Bartimaeus occurs immediately after James and John ask Jesus for seats of honor in his "kingdom" (10:35–45), which in turn comes immediately after the third prediction of the Passion (10:32–34). Consequently, the theme of blindness appears to continue the allegorical sense of the blind man of Bethsaida. The exorcism of the boy with the demon comes immediately after the transfiguration, when Jesus and the three disciples rejoin the rest. In Mark this complex miracle actually includes two stages: first the exorcism proper and then a resuscitation of the boy, who has apparently died. At the end, the other disciples ask Jesus why they could not cast out the demon, to which Jesus replies enigmatically, "This kind can come out only through prayer" (9:29). The play of the Markan version, with its struggle with demons followed by death and resuscitation, seems to be an allusion to the death of Jesus or perhaps his prayer in Gethsemane. In any case, some allusion to Jesus's death is made clear by the following passage, the second prediction of the Passion (9:30–32).

37. P. D. Duff, "The March of the Divine Warrior and the Advent of the Greco-Roman King: Mark's Account of Jesus's Entry into Jerusalem," *Journal of Biblical Literature* 111 (1992): 55–71.

38. Cf. Ps 80:8. I give here the translation of the RSV, because it gives a more literal rendering of the actual terms. Even so, it is without question here that the word "man" (Heb. *enosh*) means *human* without respect to gender. In Hebrew the term "son of man" is *ben-adam*, where "adam" is another word for a human as well as the "name" of the first human. In Gen 2:7 it is taken as a wordplay on the fact that the *adam* is created from the "dust" (*adamah*) of the ground.

39. See *1 En.* 46–53, discussed in Collins, *Mark*, 59. A balanced treatment of the development in Judaism and reappropriations in early Christianity is that of W. Horbury, *Messianism Among Jews and Christians* (London: Clark, 2003), 125–56.

40. Cf. *1 En.* 37–71; 11QMelch (the *Melchizedek* text from Qumran). See A. Y. Collins, "The Origin of the Designation of Jesus as 'Son of Man,'" *Harvard Theological Review* 80 (1987): 391–407; D. Burkett, *The Son of Man Debate: A History and Evaluation* (Cambridge: Cambridge University Press, 1999). These studies show that despite suggestions that the title often just means "human," in these cases it does have eschatological meaning in keeping with Jewish apocalyptic tradition. See also D. R. A. Hare, *The Son of Man Tradition* (Minneapolis: Fortress, 1990).

41. Rudolf Bultmann, followed by others, thus assumed that the historical Jesus never referred to himself by the title "Son of Man" and that the self-referential usage found in Mark is a reflection of later views in the development of the tradition. For the history of this scholarly debate, see Hare, *Son of God Tradition*, 4–10; Collins, "The Origins of the Designation of Jesus as 'Son of Man,'" 406–7; and Burkett, *Son of Man Debate*, 37–43.

42. See N. Perrin, "Mark XIV.62: The End Product of a Christian Pesher Tradition?" in *A Modern Pilgrimage in New Testament Christology* (Philadelphia: Fortress, 1974), 10–22.

43. Here I am taking a slightly different view from that of N. Perrin ("Towards an Interpretation of the Gospel of Mark" in H. D. Betz, *Christology and a Modern Pilgrimage: A Discussion with Norman Perrin* [Claremont, CA: New Testament Colloquium, 1971], 1–78), who sees the title "Son of Man" as the most important and revolutionary contribution of Mark's Christology. In my view, that is, instead, the way "Son of God" is used to condition and explain "Son of Man."

44. See Collins, *Mark*, 148–150. See also J. D. Levenson, *The Death and Resurrection of the Beloved Son: Transformations of Child Sacrifice in Judaism and Christianity* (New Haven: Yale University Press, 1993), 30–31, who argues that the "beloved" language is a direct allusion to the sacrifice of Isaac in the LXX version of Gen 22:2. It may well be that both uses were in the minds of the Markan author and audience in scripting this story.

45. For the boy with the demon as an allegorical allusion to the death of Jesus, see n. 33, above.

46. See also Collins, *Mark*, 69–70.

47. I give here a translation of the Greek version from the LXX. In the Greek, both instances of the word "Lord" are the same. In the Hebrew, however, they are different; the first is the Tetragrammaton; the second, the word *adonai* ("lord" or "master"). This difference is clearly reflected in the English translation from the Hebrew as rendered in the NRSV.

48. See D. M. Hay, *Glory at the Right Hand: Psalm 110 in Early Christianity* (Nashville: Abingdon, 1973).

49. As Hay also suggests (*Glory at the Right Hand*, 109). The point is that it plays on the ambiguity of the earlier Jewish usage.

50. It is important to notice that there is nothing in this Pauline usage that hints at using Ps 110 in reference to any preexistent heavenly status for Jesus. That idea will only come much later, specifically in Hebrews. The latter is also based on the Greek of Ps 110(109), but with a new emphasis on vv. 3–4. See White, *From Jesus to Christianity*, 320–23.

51. Cf. the sequence in 1 Thess 1:9–10.

52. The other two are the hemorrhaging woman (5:25–34) and the Syrophoenician woman (7:24–30).

53. This narrative thread may also account for how she later came to be associated with Mary Magdalene, who appears for the first time in Mark only in the crucifixion and resurrection scenes.

54. Collins also argues that this scene was not part of the pre-Markan passion tradition (*Mark*, 643).

55. See K. E. Corley, *Private Women, Public Meals: Social Conflict in the Synoptic Tradition* (Peabody, MA: Hendrickson, 1993), 102–7; J. Dewey, *Disciples of the Way: Mark on Discipleship* (Cincinnati, OH: United Methodist Church, 1976), 133; cf. E. Schüssler Fiorenza, *In Memory of Her: A Feminist Theological Reconstruction of Christian Origins* (New York: Crossroad, 1983), xiii–xv.

56. See the "Letter of Pilate to Herod" in the apocryphal *Acts of Pilate* (in M. R. James, *Apocryphal New Testament* [Oxford: Clarendon, 1975], 155); cf. Collins, *Mark*, 771.

57. The views are surveyed in Collins, *Mark*, 768–770, who argues in favor of a serious form of irony in line with the martyrdom tradition.

58. This is the view of E. S. Johnson, in "Is Mark 15:39 the Key to Mark's Christology?" *Journal for the Study of the New Testament* 31 (1987): 3–22; see also Juel, *Master of Surprise*, 74.

Chapter Twelve: The Righteous Teacher of Torah: The Gospel of Matthew

1. See L. M. White, *From Jesus to Christianity* (San Francisco: HarperSanFrancisco, 2004), 128–42. H. T. Fleddermann argues for a later date than most other scholars, i.e., just after the war but prior to the Gospel of Mark (*Q: A Reconstruction and Commentary* [Leuven: Peeters, 2005], 167, 182–83).

2. Fleddermann argues that there are no *chreiai* in the strict sense in Q; however, he is using a more limited definition than other scholars (*Q*, 96–97). For a different view on Q, see J. G. Williams, "Parable and Chreia: From Q to Narrative Gospel," *Semeia* 43 (1988): 85–114; V. K. Robbins, "The Chreia," in D. E. Aune, ed., *Greco-Roman Literature and the New Testament* (Atlanta: Scholars Press, 1988), 1–23.

3. See R. A. Piper, "Matthew 7:7–11 par. Luke 11:9–13: Evidence of Design and Argument in the Collection of Jesus's Sayings," in J. S. Kloppenborg, ed., *The Shape of Q: Signal Essays on the Sayings Gospel* (Minneapolis: Fortress, 1994), 131–37.

4. See J. S. Kloppenborg, *Q Parallels: Synopsis, Critical Notes, and Concordance* (Sonoma, CA: Polebridge, 1988), xxxi–xxxiii.

5. See Chapter 2. Cf. Wis 6:12–23; 10:15–11:1; Sir 4:11; 24:23–29.

6. See Kloppenborg, *The Shape of Q*, 51–58 (the influential essay on genre by J. M. Robinson), 138–155 (Kloppenborg on instructional features). See also J. M. Robinson, *"Logoi Sophon:* On the *Gattung* of Q," in J. M. Robinson and H. Koester, *Trajectories Through Early Christianity* (Philadelphia: Fortress, 1971), 71–113, now reprinted in J. M. Robinson, *The Sayings Gospel Q: Collected Essays,* ed. C. Heil and J. Verheyden (Leuven: Peeters, 2005), 37–74.

7. This is the view of J. D. Crossan, *The Historical Jesus: The Life of a Mediterranean Jewish Peasant* (San Francisco: HarperSanFrancisco, 1991), 227–28; and B. L. Mack, *The Lost Gospel: The Book of Q and Christian Origins* (San Francisco: HarperSanFrancisco, 1993), 29–39.

8. This is the view of J. Kloppenborg, *The Formation of Q* (Philadelphia: Fortress, 1987), 92–98; see also F. G. Downing, *Doing Things with Words in the First Christian Century* (Edinburgh: Clark, 2000), 87–94.

9. There is no basis for such a claim in treating the Jewish wisdom tradition. For discussion, see Chapters 2 and 9 and works cited there.

10. H. Koester, "The Sayings of Q and Their Image of Jesus," in *From Jesus to the Gospels: Interpreting the New Testament in Its Context* (Minneapolis: Fortress, 2007), 251–63. See also C. Tuckett, "On the Stratification of Q," in J. S. Kloppenborg and L. E. Vaage, eds., *Early Christianity, Q, and Jesus,* Semeia 55 (Atlanta: Scholars Press, 1991), 213–22; H. A. Attridge, "Reflections on Research into Q," in Kloppenborg and Vaage, eds., *Early Christianity, Q, and Jesus,* 223–34.

11. Fleddermann, *Q: A Reconstruction and Commentary,* 169–80; A. D. Jacobson, "The Literary Unity of Q," in Kloppenborg, *The Shape of Q,* 98–115.

12. Q16–20 contains a series of other sayings comparing or linking Jesus and John. See also the discussion of Q7–14 below and Q69 in Appendix D.

13. J. Kloppenborg, *Excavating Q: The History and Setting of the Sayings Gospel* (Minneapolis: Fortress, 2000), 214–61.

14. Kloppenborg, *Excavating Q,* 196–213.

15. Fleddermann argues that Q originated among gentile followers (*A Reconstruction and Commentary,* 164); however, most scholars disagree. The view taken here is that it originated within Jewish contexts, but where increasing tension with other Jews and growing contact with Gentiles is causing the followers of Jesus to broaden their horizons. See also White, *From Jesus to Christianity,* 133–42.

16. Kloppenborg ("The Formation of Q and Antique Instruction Genres," in *The Shape of Q* (148–50), lists the following Q units in this connection: Q 7–14, which contain the original elements of the "Sermon on the Mount/Plain" (Luke 6:20b–49); Q21–26 (Luke 9:57–62; 10:2–16, 21–24); Q35–39 (Luke 12:2–12); Q41–42, 44

(Luke 12:22b–34, 39–40). See also D. Zeller, "Redactional Process and Changing Settings in the Q-Material," in Kloppenborg, *The Shape of Q*, 116–30.

17. A striking omission in Luke-Acts is the lack of any reference to these cells of the Jesus sect in the Galilee.

18. The italicized portion represents a separate Q saying. See the discussion below.

19. In sharp contrast, the Lukan version has been modified to emphasize the centurion's piety and his esteem among the Jewish leaders (7:3–6). It is used to illustrate the Lukan theme that the mission to the Gentiles had begun with Jesus's own ministry.

20. So also Fleddermann, *Q, A Reconstruction and Commentary*, 347–53, 881. The Johannine miracle of the royal official's son (4:46–54) is probably based on this same story. A question remains whether it comes directly from Q (as argued by some scholars) or whether the Gospel of John is dependant on the synoptic version (so Fleddermann). As we shall see in a later chapter, the Johannine tradition does seem to depend on direct knowledge of at least some streams of the synoptic tradition.

21. The other is Q29 (Luke 11:14), an exorcism; it too is condensed and serves primarily as the setup for a dialogue and saying of Jesus (11:15–23).

22. See H. J. Held, "Matthew as Interpreter of the Miracle Stories," in G. Bornkamm, G. Barth, and H. J. Held, *Tradition and Interpretation in Matthew* (Philadelphia: Westminster, 1963), 165–295.

23. It is replicated six times in Matthew: 8:12; 13:42; 13:50; 22:13; 24:51; 25:30. See the discussion of the Matthean reshaping of parables in Chapter 9.

24. On the sectarian elements in Q, see White, *From Jesus to Christianity*, 125–42.

25. Two of these passages are the summary statements of the Gospel of Mark, as discussed in Chapter 11.

26. The Gospel of Luke also alters this narrative connection, but in an entirely different way than Matthew.

27. As a result, the comparable portions in the Matthean version of this miracle constitutes only 37.2 percent of the Markan version in terms of word count in Greek.

28. This miracle is one of the few in Matthew that is not drastically abbreviated from its Markan source. Instead, the Matthean author has made only minor condensation in wording plus an overall expansion by the addition of the Peter vignette, missing from Mark. The entire miracle is missing from the Gospel of Luke.

29. The translation here is my own in order to render it more literally and show the similarities to the other occurrences. In Greek the first six words of the formula, equivalent to "And when he had finished . . . Jesus . . ." in English, are identical in all five cases.

30. The main exception occurs in the section of controversy stories in Matt 11:2–12:50, which is a combination of Q units with a series of controversy episodes drawn from Mark 2–3.

31. On the "covenant renewal sermon" in Q, see J. Kloppenborg, "City and Wasteland: Narrative World and the Beginning of the Saying Gospel [Q]," in D. E. Smith, ed., *How Gospels Begin*, Semeia 52 (Atlanta: Scholars Press, 1991), 145–60; J. A. Draper, "Jesus' Covenantal Discourse on the Plain (Luke 6:12–7:17) as Oral Performance," in R. Horsley, ed., *Oral Performance, Popular Tradition, and Hidden Transcript in Q* (Atlanta: Society of Biblical Literature, 2006), 71–98; R. A. Horsley, "The Covenant Renewal Discourse: Q6:20–49," in R. Horsley and J. Draper, *Whoever Hears You Hears Me: Prophets, Performance, and Tradition in Q* (Edinburgh: Clark, 1999), 195–227.

32. The Matthean sermon is 1,968 Greek words in total, of which roughly 879 are unique to Matthew.

33. The Greek (*dikaiosunē*) typically translates the Hebrew word *tsedekah*, which can mean acts of piety (such as sacrifice or observance of Torah) or charity. "Charity" is the usual meaning of the term in the rabbinic sources when referring to human action (e.g., *m. 'Abot* 5.13). Of course, the same term also figures prominently in Pauline thought, where it likewise stems from his own Pharisaic background. See E. P. Sanders, *Paul and Palestinian Judaism* (Philadelphia: Fortress, 1977), 198–205.

34. It may be suggested that the first section anticipates the Mission Discourse of Matt 10, the second section anticipates the woes against the Pharisees in Matt 23, and the third section anticipates the sermon on discipline in Matt 18 and the section on judgment in Matt 25.

35. The Markan parallel from the apocalyptic discourse is Mark 13:9–13. Significantly, the Matthean author has moved a portion of the Markan passage (13:9–12) into the Mission Discourse (as Matt 10:17–21). Thus, the two sermons in Matthew are directly linked by this imagery.

36. Irenaeus *Against Heresies* 3.1.1; cf. Papias (in Eusebius *Church History* 3.39.16, quoted below).

37. Cf. the testimonies of Irenaeus *Against Heresies* 1.26.2 (late second century) and Epiphanius *Panarion* 28.5.1–3 (late fourth century).

38. Preserved in Eusebius *Church History* 3.39.16. This is the passage immediately following Papias's comment regarding the tradition of Mark (discussed in Chapter 11). Cf. the statement of Irenaeus quoted above. Irenaeus may be dependent on the Papias legend.

39. Based in part on the statement attributed to Papias, the idea of a "Hebrew Matthew" was once considered a possibility, and several medieval manuscripts in Hebrew were taken to support this view. It has now been shown, however, that the oldest of these Hebrew texts is a late translation of the Greek Matthew into Hebrew with various theological and polemical alterations. For a description and bibliography, see G. Howard, "Matthew, Hebrew version of," in D. N. Freedman, ed., *Anchor Bible Dictionary*, 6 vols. (New York: Doubleday, 1992), 4:642–43.

40. U. Luz, *Studies in Matthew* (Grand Rapids, MI: Eerdmans, 2005), 43–47.

41. Luz, *Studies in Matthew*, 39–53.

42. It is unlikely, however, that the Q tradition was transmitted solely through the Matthean community. At least two other trajectories of usage can be seen in the Gospels of Luke and Thomas, respectively. We shall discuss both in the following chapters.

43. Cf. the lists of disciples: Matt 10:2–4; Mark 3:16–19; Luke 6:15. For discussion of the problem, see D. C. Duling, "Matthew [Disciple]," *Anchor Bible Dictionary*, 4:618–22.

44. For these arguments based on a location in Antioch, see J. P. Meier, "Matthew, Gospel of," *Anchor Bible Dictionary*, 4:623–26. Over against this view, see W. R. Schoedel, "Ignatius and the Reception of the Gospel of Matthew in Antioch," in D. L. Balch, ed., *Social History of the Matthean Community* (Minneapolis: Fortress, 1991), 129–77.

45. E. M. Meyers and J. F. Strange, *Archaeology, the Rabbis, and Early Christianity* (Nashville: Abingdon, 1981), 31–47; D. R. Edwards and C. T. McCollough, *Archaeology and the Galilee* (Atlanta: Scholars Press, 1997);

S. Freyne, *Galilee, Jesus, and the Gospels* (Philadelphia: Fortress, 1988); "Galilee, Hellenistic-Roman," *Anchor Bible Dictionary*, 2:895–98;

46. This is the view now taken by D. Harrington, *The Gospel of Matthew* (Collegeville, MN: Liturgical Press, 1991); J. A. Overman, *Matthew's Gospel and Formative Judaism: The Social World of the Matthean Community* (Minneapolis: Fortress, 1990), 158–60; *Church and Community in Crisis: The Gospel According to Matthew* (Valley Forge, PA: Trinity Press International, 1996), 16–19; A. J. Saldarini, *Matthew's Christian-Jewish Community* (Chicago: University of Chicago Press, 1994). See also A. Segal, "Matthew's Jewish Voice," in Balch, ed., *Social History of the Matthean Community*, 3–37; and L. M. White, "Crisis Management and Boundary Maintenance: The Social Location of the Matthean Community," in Balch, ed., *Social History of the Matthean Community*, 211–47.

47. Luz, *Studies in Matthew*, 250–56; White, "Crisis Management and Boundary Maintenance," 238–42.

48. In my article "Crisis Management and Boundary Maintenance," I argue for a setting in the Upper Galilee, but near or just after the end of the reign of Herod Agrippa II, the last living Herodian ruler, who died ca. 90–93 CE. At this time there was a significant reapportionment of his territory, and the uppermost portions of the Galilee were reassigned to the province of Syria, later renamed Phoenicia. Such regional changes might have had a profound effect on both Jewish identity and relations between Jews and non-Jews in the region.

49. See K. Stendahl, *The School of St. Matthew and Its Use of the Old Testament*, 2nd ed. (Philadelphia: Fortress, 1968); Luz, *Studies in Matthew*, 83–114; J. D. Kingsbury, *Matthew: Structure, Christology, Kingdom* (Philadelphia: Fortress, 1975).

50. Whereas in Mark this phrase means "the synagogue of a particular locality," in Matthew it takes on a new and expanded force. The source passage is Mark 1:39 (parallel to Matt 4:23; Luke 4:44), but cf. Matt 9:35; 10:17; 12:9; 13:54, where the word "their" is added in each case.

51. The Matthean construction of the opening *chreia* for this sermon is discussed in Chapter 12.

52. So Luz, *Studies in Matthew*, 93–95. Luz stresses the idea that the Matthean author's use of this term is still very close to that found in Mark. On the other hand, by virtue of its open declaration by Peter, it has lost the immediacy of concern over its meaning as reflected in Mark. This view stands in sharp contrast to that of J. D. Kingsbury, who argues that it has been elevated over the Markan use (*Matthew: Structure, Christology, Kingdom*, 42–83). On the other side, see also G. Stanton, *A Gospel for a New People: Studies in Matthew* (Louisville: Westminster John Knox, 1993), 170; D. Verseput, "The Role and Meaning of the 'Son of God' Title in the Gospel of Matthew," *New Testament Studies* 33 (1987): 532–56.

53. Stanton, *Gospel for a New People*, 170–85.

54. *Yeshua* is the Aramaic form of Joshua; in Greek it is rendered as *Iēsous* (Jesus), as in the New Testament.

55. Although the use of the title is already seen in the Gospel of Mark, the emphasis given here is developed in a unique way by the Gospel of Matthew.

56. The title "Son of Man" appears in the following Q sayings (with their Matthean versions): Q20 (11:16–19); 21 (8:18–22); 38 (12:31–32); 44 (24:42–44); 66 (24:23–28, 37–42). See Box 12.1 and Appendix D.

57. See also Luz, *Studies in Matthew*, 97–114. This view stands in sharp contrast to that of Kingsbury; see n. 52, above.

Chapter Thirteen: The Martyred Sage: The Gospel of Luke

1. Caesarea Philippi lies approximately twenty-six miles to the north of Bethsaida Julias, at the upper edge of the Herodian territories also inherited by Philip and Agrippa II. See Chapter 11 for discussion of its importance in the Markan narrative. On the location, see also Appendix E.

2. See Appendix E. See also nn. 5–8, below.

3. The exact location of the feeding of the five thousand is not given in Mark (or Matthew). See Appendix E and n. 6, below.

4. It should be remembered that several of these scenes are the miracle "doublets" from the Gospel of Mark. These doublets also function as an important Markan thematic device in conjunction with the secrecy/misunderstanding motif. See Chapter 11 and Box 11.2. Joseph Fitzmyer argues that removing the doublets is an intentional feature of the Lukan author's literary taste. See J. Fitzmyer, *The Gospel According to Luke*, 2 vols., Anchor Bible 28 (Garden City, NY: Doubleday, 1981–85), 1:82, 762. As we see from this discussion, the Galilee emphasis of Luke 4:14–9:50 provides another impetus; it will then be matched by the Jerusalem motif in the latter part of the Gospel and throughout the book of Acts. Another result of this omission is the way it affects the portrayal of the disciples. All of these features will be discussed in the last section of this chapter.

5. Two of the deleted Markan episodes also had Jesus and the disciples traveling to Bethsaida. First, Mark 6:45 (the walking on water) apparently has them sailing from the west side of the Sea of Galilee to Bethsaida. Next, Mark 8:22 opens the healing of the blind man story with them arriving at Bethsaida, after returning by boat from the west side of the Sea of Galilee at Dalmanutha (8:13–21).

6. See also Appendix E. Although not widely recognized, this Lukan change clearly shows that the author was drawing directly on Mark as his source, since both of the preceding references to Bethsaida were removed in the Matthean version. The Matthean parallel to Mark 6:45 is at Matt 14:22, and the omission of "Bethsaida" results in having them go a different direction. The Matthean author deletes the entire episode of the blind man at Bethsaida. In fact, the only reference to Bethsaida in the Gospel of Matthew occurs at Matt 11:21 (= Luke 10:13, Q23). No Matthean episode is ever set at Bethsaida. Consequently, the Lukan reference to Bethsaida can only have come from the Markan version of the episode (the walking on water) that immediately follows the feeding of the five thousand, but the walking on water episode itself (which presupposes a boat crossing) was then intentionally deleted by the Lukan author in order to keep them in Galilee. Similarly, the Lukan author has also removed the boat crossing of Mark 8:13–21 and the blind man at Bethsaida, which follows (8:22–26). Even so, this Bethsaida episode, although deleted, provides the geographical marker by which the Lukan author can now place the confession immediately after the feeding of the five thousand. Finally, as Fitzmyer shows, the Lukan version of the feeding of the five thousand cannot be explained as a blending of the Markan and Matthean versions; nor is it a result of blending the two Markan feeding miracles, the second of which has been deleted in Luke. See Fitzmyer, *Gospel According to Luke*, 1:762–63.

7. See Appendix E. The Lukan author clearly takes Bethsaida to be in the Galilee proper, which it was by the time that the Gospel of Luke was written. The Q tradition also associates Bethsaida with the Galilee, and specifically with the cities of Chorazin and Capernaum (cf. Luke 10:13 = Q23). This fact may offer an additional perspective on the date and development of this Q saying, because Bethsaida was not part of the Galilee at any point during Jesus's lifetime. Caesarea Philippi had also been in the tetrarchy of Philip and later given to Agrippa II, but at some point—either just after the first revolt or on the death of Agrippa II in 93 CE—it was ceded to the province of Syria. This political placement seems to be the situation at the time of the Gospel of Luke, and possibly also of the Gospel of Matthew.

8. Three other structural changes are at work here. First, the Lukan author has inverted the preceding episodes in Mark, where Jesus heals multitudes (Mark 3:7–12) and then goes up on a mountain to "call" the twelve disciples (Mark 3:13–19a). The Lukan order has him go up the mountain first (6:12–16) and then come down with the newly chosen disciples to a "level place" (6:17–19). The "sermon" takes place here. Second, the Lukan author removes the section from Mark 3:19b–30 and repositions it in the travel narrative section at Luke 11:14–23, where it will be combined with a different set of Q materials. Third, Mark 3:31–35 will be repositioned to later in the Galilee section at Luke 8:19–21.

9. For the Q "sermon," see Chapter 12 and Appendix D. For the Matthean restructuring, see Chapter 12 and Box 12.4.

10. They are based on Q16, 17, and 20, and will be discussed further below. These sayings are elaborated by a uniquely Lukan discourse (7:27–30) and then culminate with the poignant statement about John and himself: "Nevertheless, Wisdom is vindicated by all her children" (7:35) drawn from Q20. For discussion of this passage, see Chapter 12.

11. The scene is taken from its original placement in the Markan Passion narrative (14:2–9).

12. For discussion of this sequence of episodes, see also Chapter 2. The Lukan comment is drawn from the statement in Mark 15:41; cf. Luke 23:49.

13. The Lukan author here deletes the story about the death of John the Baptist (Mark 6:17–29). It has been repositioned and severely abbreviated at Luke 3:19–20, just prior to the story of Jesus's baptism.

14. It has often been called "Luke's special section," but here I follow D. P. Moessner, *Lord of the Banquet: The Literary and Theological Significance of the Lukan Travel Narrative* (Minneapolis: Fortress, 1989).

15. It is sometimes described as running from Luke 9:51 to 18:14, because it is composed almost entirely of Q and uniquely Lukan material, whereas 18:15–19:27 returns to the basic Markan outline as Jesus and the disciples approach Jericho.

16. Within the travel narrative, the Lukan author has deleted the opening passage from Mark 10:1–12, in which Jesus leaves Galilee for Judea and discusses divorce. The immediately following passages in Mark (10:13–16; 17–31) occur at Luke 18:15–17, 18–30, when the Markan sequence resumes. The two preceding passages in Mark (9:42–47, 48–50) have both been abbreviated and repositioned in the travel narrative at Luke 17:1–2 and 14:34–35, respectively. Also the discourse between Jesus and the sons of Zebedee (Mark 10:35–45) has been removed from this sequence and reworked into the setting for the Last Supper (at Luke 22:24–27). Consequently, the overall Lukan reworking of the travel narrative effectively covers the span from Jesus's departure for Jerusalem (Luke 9:51 = Mark 10:1) to his arrival at Jerusalem (Luke 19:28 = Mark 11:1). See Box 13.2. For a similar view of the Lukan narrative structure, see C. H. Talbert (*Literary Patterns, Theological Themes, and the Genre of Luke-Acts* [Missoula, MT: Scholars Press, 1974], 51) and Moessner (*Lord of the Banquet*), who end the travel narrative at 19:46 and 19:44, respectively. That is, they both carry it through the triumphal entry and into the first Jerusalem episode(s).

17. Among the few Markan episodes found in this section is the so-called Beelzebul controversy (Luke 11:14–23); however, it has been dramatically repositioned from its original Markan setting in the Galilee section (Mark 3:22–27). Another is the great commandment episode found in Luke 10:25–28. It has been repositioned from Mark 12:28–31; Matt 22:34–40, which falls in the Jerusalem section, just prior to the Passion narrative.

18. The other uniquely Lukan parables in this section include the following: the friend at midnight (Luke 11:5–9); the slave's wages (12:47–48; 17:7–10); a fig tree parable (13:6–9); a parable on humility (14:7–14); the lost coin (15:8–10); the unjust manager (16:1–13); the unjust judge (18:1–8); and the Pharisee and the tax collector (18:9–14).

19. See also J. Fitzmyer, *Gospel According to Luke*, 1:527; L. M. White, "The Pentecost Event: Lukan Redaction and Themes in Acts 2," *Forum* 3 (2000): 75–103.

20. The Lukan author adds Jesus teaching in synagogues in 4:15, so that the first three episodes in the Galilee section are all set up this way; cf. 4:16; 4:31. The last of these is the parallel to Mark 1:21 (Jesus in the synagogue at Capernaum), and this passage may have allowed for the Lukan framing device, because the Markan rejection story (Mark 6:1) opens with very similar wording.

21. Fitzmyer, *Gospel According to Luke*, 1:532.

22. See L. I. Levine, *The Ancient Synagogue: The First Thousand Years* (New Haven: Yale University Press, 2000), 135–43. As Levine points out, Luke-Acts (in two stories, this one and Acts 13:14–15) is the *only* ancient source to suggest this practice of reading from the Prophets during the pre-70 period. The more usual practice in this period would have been a regular reading only from the Torah. Readings from the Prophets were introduced into the synagogue service, but only much later, in the rabbinic period.

23. My translation.

24. White, "The Pentecost Event," 94.

25. The omitted portions of the LXX of Isa 61:1–2 are as follows: (v. 1) "to heal the brokenhearted," immediately following "to the poor"; (v. 2): "and a day of recompense to comfort all those who mourn," immediately following "year of the Lord's favor." There are several notable differences between the Greek text of the LXX and the Hebrew original. The latter is reflected in the NRSV of Isa 61:1–2.

26. Cf. Isa 66:1–24. On the later sections of Isaiah, see P. D. Hanson, *The Dawn of Apocalyptic,* rev. ed. (Philadelphia: Fortress, 1979), 32–208; for the later interpretations of Isaiah in apocalyptic Judaism and early Christianity, see B. W. Anderson, "The Apocalyptic Rendering of the Isaiah Tradition," in J. Neusner, P. Borgen, E. S. Frerichs, and R. Horsley, eds., *The Social World of Formative Christianity and Judaism* (Philadelphia: Fortress, 1988), 17–38.

27. For the place of these ideas in Paul's thought, see L. M. White, *From Jesus to Christianity* (San Francisco: HarperSanFrancisco, 2004), 209–18; "The Pentecost Event," 93.

28. The same passage is used by Paul in reference to his own calling and mission. See Gal 1:15 and discussion in White, *From Jesus to Christianity*, 156–59.

29. See Chapter 12 for discussion of the Q and Matthean forms of this story. See also Appendix D.

30. The two stories are found in 1 Kgs 17:8–24 and 2 Kgs 4:8–37. In the first case, the story of Elijah's raising of a widow's son is set at Zarephath, near Sidon, a clearly non-Israelite area. In the second case, the woman is a "Shunammite" from near the borders of northern Israel. Though wealthy, she is somewhat marginal because she has no children. Elisha then performs two miracles, the first to make it possible for her to bear a son and the second to raise the child from death.

31. Even though the widow at Nain is not explicitly called a Gentile, the location, near the gentile regions of the Decapolis, may be an additional geographical clue to the story's symbolic function This is probably the Lukan replacement for the Markan episode of the Syrophoenician woman (Mark 7:24–30). For the location, see Appendix E.

32. The Matthean parallel (11:2–3) is relatively later and adds the detail that John was already in prison. In other words, the relative position of Luke 7:18–35 is just prior to the parables, and thus equivalent to Mark 3:19–35, all of which has been removed from this section of Luke. By comparison the arrest and death of John occurs at Mark 6:17–29 in the Beyond Galilee section, which is comparable to Luke 9:9.

33. Clearly the depiction of the relationship between John and Jesus in the Q tradition is somewhat at odds with that in the Lukan birth narrative. It may be that the Lukan author has intentionally tried to smooth out these differences by creating this sequence, which then follows directly from the integrated structure of the birth narrative, with its series of prophetic encounters between John and Jesus. The last of these, the baptism, is also the first node in this Lukan reformulation of the Q tradition. See Chapter 10.

34. See R. Tannehill, *The Narrative Unity of Luke-Acts*, 2 vols. (Minneapolis: Fortress, 1986, 1990), 1:108–25.

35. The second "sermon" in Matthew. The comparable verses for this Q material are Matt 9:37–38; 10:7–16; 10:40.

36. The woes against Galilean cities (Luke 10:13–15), which derive from Q23, now look back to his earlier ministry in the Galilee with a sense of rejection. They serve as warnings to the Judean villagers that Jesus will visit during his journey to Jerusalem. If they do not welcome him and his disciples, it will be better for gentile cities, like Tyre and Sidon, at the judgment.

37. The great commandment episode is one of the few Markan units in "Luke's special section" (9:51–18:14). See Box 13.2 and pp. 31–32.

38. See Chapter 9, n. 101 (p. 476) and Appendix D, n. 20. On the place of Samaritans in the emergent Jesus movement according to Luke-Acts, see also Acts 8:4–25.

39. A person named Luke is mentioned only once (Phlm 24) in the genuine letters of Paul, and there without further description. It is now widely recognized that the Philemon letter (like Philippians) was not written from Rome, but Ephesus. (See White, *From Jesus to Christianity*, 185–97.) He is called "Luke the physician" only in Col 4:14, one of the debated letters of Paul, probably written in the 90s CE. He is also mentioned in 2 Tim 4:11, written in the mid-second century CE. Consequently, neither Colossians nor 2 Timothy offers concrete historical information about the Luke mentioned by Paul in Philemon. Later, however, this "Luke the physician" was identified as the author of both the Gospel and Acts in the early list of the New Testament known as the *Muratorian Canon*.

40. According to the more fully developed form of the legend, as found in the apocryphal *Acts of Paul* 11.1 (late second century), Luke returned from a mission to Gaul to meet Paul and Titus in Rome, and he remained with him until Paul's execution. On the *Acts of Paul*, see also White, *From Jesus to Christianity*, 400–403.

41. See Acts 16:10–17; 20:5–15; 21:8–18; 27:1–16.

42. See White, *From Jesus to Christianity*, 147–51.

43. See White, *From Jesus to Christianity*, 247–55; L. T. Johnson, "Luke-Acts, Book of," in D. N. Freedman, ed., *Anchor Bible Dictionary*, 6 vols. (New York: Doubleday, 1992), 4:403–20.

44. For this later dating, see H. Conzelmann, "Luke's Place in the Development of Early Christianity," in L. E. Keck and J. L. Martyn, eds., *Studies in Luke-Acts* (Nashville: Abingdon, 1966), 298–316; W. G. Kümmel, *Introduction to the New Testament* (Nashville: Abingdon, 1965), 186. Conzelmann argues for a range of 90–110. A few scholars now would also place it perhaps as late as ca. 140, but this view has not won a wide following. The geographical lines of the story in the Gospel of Luke also support a date close to 100 CE; see Appendix E.

45. See White, *From Jesus to Christianity*, 121–22.

46. Tannehill, *The Narrative Unity of Luke-Acts*, 2:138–41.

47. White, "The Pentecost Event," 91–102.

48. In particular, the speeches in Acts; see M. L. Soards, *The Speeches in Acts: Their Content, Context, and Concerns* (Louisville: Westminster John Knox, 1994), 134–43. The speeches will be discussed further in the last section of this chapter.

49. Talbert, *Literary Patterns, Theological Themes*, 125–36.

50. So Moessner, *Lord of the Banquet*, 259–84. Actually, in the LXX, the biblical hero Joshua is likewise called Jesus, because the name Jesus is the ordinary Greek vocalization of the Aramaic *Yeshua*, which in turn is equivalent to the Hebrew *Joshua*.

51. A travel narrative (to India) plays a similar role in the *Life of Apollonius of Tyana* (see Chapter 3). The later apocryphal *Acts* also make extensive use of these novelistic elements, including fanciful journeys to far-off lands.

52. As discussed above in Chapter 3, the divine-man tradition does not typically claim that these figures are gods in any strict sense, at least as understood in the Greco-Roman world. Certainly, that is not what Philo is suggesting for Moses. Even so, it is clear that Philo's Moses has a special "divine nature" that makes it possible for him to serve on behalf of God and to be taken to be with God at the end of his earthly life. We will only start to see such ideas in the later Gospels, especially John and the so-called Gnostic Gospels.

53. Notice how the beginning of Jesus's ministry is set off by the direction of the Spirit in the temptation story (4:1), in his first ministry in Galilee (4:14), and then in his first sermon in Nazareth (4:18). With the last, consider also Luke 4:43 and the next note.

54. In Greek these are really the same phrase, and they are characteristic of the Lukan prose, in reference to the Passion tradition in particular. Cf. Luke 4:43; 22:(7,) 37; 24:26, 44; Acts 1:16, 21; 3:21. See Fitzmyer, *Gospel According to Luke*, 1:180 (in general) and 1:443 (on Luke 2:52).

55. The Lukan author adds a new component to the scene of Jesus's prayer in the garden prior to his arrest (22:40–46). The two-verse addition (vv. 43–44) has him visited by an angel to give him added strength and resolve. Then it calls it his *agonia* in Greek, often translated "agony" or "anguish." This precise term is used only once in the entire New Testament, here in Luke 22:44. Among the philosophers, it was a common term for the moral contest with vice and the victory over evil. Rather than portraying Jesus as "agonizing" and fearful in our sense, it shows the opposite. On the apocalyptic dimensions of this battle, see S. Garrett, *The Demise of the Devil: Magic and the Demonic in Luke's Story* (Minneapolis: Fortress, 1989).

56. On the speeches in Acts as Lukan constructions, see M. L. Soards, *The Speeches in Acts: Their Content, Context, and Concerns* (Louisville: Westminster John Knox, 1994), 182–208; E. Schweizer, "Concerning the Speeches in Acts," in L. E. Keck and J. L. Martyn, eds., *Studies in Luke-Acts* (Nashville: Abingdon, 1966), 208–16. On the relationship between the speeches and narrative themes in Luke-Acts, see the discussion of the Lukan trial before Herod Antipas in Chapter 10. See also R. Tannehill, *The Narrative Unity of Luke-Acts*, 2 vols. (Minneapolis: Fortress, 1986, 1990), 2:32–42.

57. Plato *Apology of Socrates* 29D, quoted in full and discussed in Chapter 9.

58. On the Lukan trial, see A. N. Sherwin-White, *Roman Society and Roman Law in the New Testament* (Oxford: Clarendon, 1963), 24–47.

59. For the contemporary reports of Pilate's judicial savagery, see Philo *Embassy to Gaius* 302; he mentions Pilate's "venality, his violence, his thefts, his assaults, his abusive behavior, his frequent executions of prisoners without trial, and his endless savagery." Cf. Josephus *Jewish War* 2.169–77, which shows Pilate ready to slaughter Jews without provocation. Josephus says also that he in fact killed a group of Samaritans and that this episode was the reason for his eventual recall to Rome (*Antiquities* 18:85–89).

60. Following Mark, it is the "chief priests, scribes, and elders" who try to trick Jesus into making treasonous statements (Luke 20:20; 23:2). Even the Pharisees who had received criticism earlier in the Lukan Gospel now disappear from the Passion narrative as opponents of Jesus. See M. Smith, "The Pharisees in the Gospels," and J. A. Ziesler, "Luke and the Pharisees," in J. Neusner, *From Politics to Piety: The Emergence of Pharisaic Judaism*, 2nd ed. (New York Ktav, 1979), 155–72.

61. Cf. Acts 3:14–15; 4:27; 7:52; 10:39. Cf. D. L. Tiede, *Prophecy and History in Luke-Acts* (Philadelphia: Fortress, 1980), 103–117.

62. J. Gager, *The Origins of Anti-Semitism* (New York: Oxford University Press, 1983), 149–51; J. B. Tyson, *Images of Judaism in Luke-Acts* (Columbia: University of South Carolina Press,, 1992).

63. Note Josephus's refutation (*Against Apion* 75–90; 227–50) of this type of charge against Moses, attributed to the Hellenistic Egyptian historian Manetho. Cf. Philo *Life of Moses* 1.2–7, which stresses that Moses was a Chaldean by race, rather than an Egyptian; it is probably responding to the same idea. J. Gager, *Moses in Greco-Roman Paganism* (Nashville: Abingdon, 1972), 113–33.

64. The same term can sometimes be translated "author" in the sense of the progenitor of an idea or an effect. Thus, Acts 3:15 uses this same term to refer to Jesus as "the *Author* of life, whom God raised from the dead." Cf. Isocrates 3.28 (in reference to Teucer, founder of a "race," meaning a nationality); Aristotle *Metaphysics* 983B.20 (in reference to Thales, as founder of a school, or natural philosophy itself).

65. See Philo *Life of Moses* 1.7 (Abraham); 1.148. The terms used in the latter passage are *hegemōn, archē,* and *basileia.*

66. Philo *Life of Moses* 2.2, 4.

67. Musonius Rufus, Fragment 8, "That Kings Should Study Philosophy," in C. E. Lutz, ed., *Musonius Rufus: The Roman Socrates,* Yale Classical Studies 10 (New Haven: Yale University Press, 1947), 65.

68. Philo *Life of Moses* 2.2. It is quoted in full in the epilogue.

69. See Philo *Life of Moses* 1.2; 2.3–6, 202; cf. Plato *Republic* 429C.

70. See D. L. Balch, "The Areopagus Speech: An Appeal to the Stoic Historian Posidonius Against Later Stoics and Epicureans," in D. L. Balch, E. Ferguson, and W. A. Meeks, eds., *Greeks, Romans, and Christians: Essays in Honor of A. J. Malherbe* (Minneapolis: Fortress, 1990), 52–79; H. Conzelmann, "The Address of Paul on the Areopagus," in Keck and Martyn, eds., *Studies in Luke-Acts,* 217–30. Both articles stress the Lukan theme that the "philosophy" of Jesus is the dawning of a new truth, in contrast to Stoic views that human society had tended to degenerate.

71. A. J. Malherbe, *The Cynic Epistles* (Missoula, MT: Scholars Press, 1977), 27–29. See also R. Hoistad, *Cynic Hero, Cynic King: Studies in the Cynic Conception of Man* (Uppsala: Blackwell, 1948).

72. For a comparison of the appropriation of "hero" traditions, and specifically Cynic and Stoic use of the legends of Herakles, see D. E. Aune, "Heracles and Christ: Heracles Imagery in the Christology of Early Christianity," in Balch, Ferguson, and Meeks, eds., *Greeks, Romans, and Christians,* 3–19; cf. A. J. Malherbe, "Herakles," *Reallexikon für Antike und Christentum* 108/109 (1988): 559–83. For a use of Herakles imagery in later catacomb art, parallel to depictions of Jesus as magician, see Chapter 8 and Box 8.3.

73. Malherbe, *Cynic Epistles,* 28. For the collection see Malherbe, *Cynic Epistles,* 219–307. There are thirty-five letters attributed to members of the Socratic circle, of which the first seven are attributed to Socrates himself.

74. A. J. Malherbe, "Self-Definition Among the Cynics," in *Paul and the Popular Philosophers* (Minneapolis: Fortress, 1989), 11–24.

75. So note the themes in Luke 6:20–26 (the Beatitudes and woes) and 16:1–13 (the unjust manager, to be discussed below). For a later Christian effort to interpret Jesus's teachings in this way, see the oration of Clement of Alexandria (ca. 200 CE), *Who Is the Rich Man That Shall Be Saved?* See L. M. White, "Moral Pathology: Passions, Progress, and Protreptic in Clement of Alexandria," in J. T. Fitzgerald, ed., *The Passions in Greco-Roman Thought* (London: Routledge, 2008), 284–321.

76. This motif is carried over directly into Acts through similar stories about followers who support Paul or the other apostles out of their means: cf. Acts 4:32–37; 9:36–42; 16:11–15; 18:1–4.

77. A. J. Malherbe, "'Gentle as a Nurse': The Cynic Background to 1 Thessalonians 2," in *Paul and the Popular Philosophers,* 35–48.

78. See Lutz, ed., *Musonius Rufus,* 27–30.

79. A. J. Malherbe, "The Christianization of a Topos," *Novum Testamentum* 38 (1986): 123–35.

80. R. F. Hock, "Why New Testament Scholars Should Read Ancient Novels," in R. F. Hock, J. B. Chance, and J. Perkins, eds., *Ancient Fiction and Early Christian Narrative* (Atlanta: Scholars Press, 1998), 121–38.

81. A number of the Lukan parables are modeled after the Roman social ideal of household patronage. For a look at the moral encoding of these "householder" parables in Luke, see L. M. White, "Scaling the Strong Man's Court (Luke 11:21)" *Forum* 3 (1987): 3–28. "Character tales" as I use it here reflects a standard genre of moral exposition called *ethopoiia*, which might be translated more literally as "character-ization," i.e., descriptions of character by conventions of behavior and action. See R. F. Hock, "The Parable of the Foolish Rich Man (Luke 12:16–20) and Graeco-Roman Conventions of Thought and Behavior," in J. T. Fitzgerald, T. H. Olbricht, and L. M. White, eds., *Early Christianity and Classical Culture: Comparative Studies in Honor of A. J. Malherbe* (Leiden and Atlanta: Society of Biblical Literature, 2003), 181–96; "Lazarus and Micyllus: Greco-Roman Backgrounds to Luke 16:19–31," *Journal of Biblical Literature* 106 (1987): 447–63.

82. In general on the *symposium* tradition and its relation to Luke-Acts, see D. E. Smith, *From Symposium to Eucharist: The Banquet in the Early Christian World* (Minneapolis: Fortress, 2003), 47–66, 253–72; "Table Fellowship as a Literary Motif in the Gospel of Luke," *Journal of Biblical Literature* 106 (1987): 613–38. See also R. P. Martin, "The Seven Sages as Performers of Wisdom," in C. Dougherty and L. Kurke, eds., *Cultural Poetics in Ancient Greece: Cult, Performance, Politics* (Cambridge: Cambridge University Press, 1993), 108–28.

83. Plutarch was an Athenian philosopher and priest of Delphi; he flourished from ca. 70 to ca. 114 CE. His *Dinner of the Seven Sages* was modeled after similar stories of Plato (*Protagoras* and *Symposium*) and Xenophon (*Symposium*). The story is set well before the time of Socrates, when several renowned sages from early Greek history supposedly come together for a dinner and conversation. It is entirely fictional in that some of these figures did not live at the same time. Plutarch even adds some new characters, such as Aesop and the women Cleobulina and Melissa, to the standard mix of Thales, Bias, Pittacus, Solon, Chilon, Cleobulus, and Anacharsis. Other versions included Periander, Peisistratus, or others. The number seven became fixed with various substitutions. For discussion, see J. Mossman, "Plutarch's *Dinner of the Seven Sages* and Its Place in *Symposium* Literature," in J. Mossman, ed., *Plutarch and His Intellectual World* (London: Classical Press of Wales, 1997), 119–40. Among his other works, Plutarch also wrote an extensive account of his own *symposia* in conversation with other notables of the day; it is usually called the *Table Talk*.

84. The dinner scenes in Luke occur in 5:27–32; 7:36–50; 9:52–56; 10:38–42; 11:37–52; 14:1–24; 19:5–10; 22:14–38 (the Last Supper); 24:28–35 (the Emmaus story); 24:36–49 (the appearance to the disciples in Jerusalem). The theme is continued in Acts, as the opening of the Pentecost story (2:1) has them still gathering in the same "upper room" where they had held the Last Supper (cf. 1:12–14). The dinner gatherings are repeated in Acts 2:42–46; 5:42; 20:7–12.

85. D. P. Moessner, *Lord of the Banquet: The Literary and Theological Significance of the Lukan Travel Narrative* (Minneapolis: Fortress, 1989).

86. Moessner, *Lord of the Banquet,* 173–81.

87. The word "welcome" in the Greek is a technical term for the offering of hospitality. H. Moxnes sees this to be emblematic of Jesus's depiction of the hospitality of the kingdom (*The Economy of the Kingdom: Social Conflict and Economic Relations in Luke's Gospel* [Philadelphia: Fortress, 1988], 127–37); cf. Smith, *From Symposium to Eucharist,* 267–272.

88. Moessner, *Lord of the Banquet,* 176–85. See also A. A. Just, *The Ongoing Feast: Table Fellowship and Eschatology at Emmaus* (Collegeville, MN: Liturgical Press, 1983), 219–62.

89. The figure of Moses is prominent in the Lukan exposition as shown by Moessner, *Lord of the Banquet,* 279–84; Tannehill, *Narrative Unity of Luke-Acts,* 2:33.

90. This line of interpretation was first proposed by H. Conzelmann, *The Theology of St. Luke* (New York: Harper, 1961), 16–17, but has been modified in more recent work. See references in Box 13.4.

Chapter Fourteen: The Man from Heaven: The Gospels of John and Thomas

1. He is referred to as "Thomas, who is called 'the Twin'" on three occasions in the Gospel of John (11:6; 20:24; 21:2), but the name Judas is never mentioned. In the Gospel of Thomas, he is explicitly called by all three names, Didymus Judas Thomas.

2. E. Pagels, *Beyond Belief: The Secret Gospel of Thomas* (New York: Random House, 2005), 50–75; cf. H. Koester, *Ancient Christian Gospels: Their History and Development* (Philadelphia: Trinity Press International, 1990), 263.

3. Tertullian *Against Marcion* 4.2.

4. As credited in Eusebius *Ecclesiastical History* 6.14.7, quoted below on pp. 352 and 408 (in full).

5. R. E. Brown, *The Gospel According to John,* 2 vols., Anchor Bible 29 (Garden City, NY: Doubleday, 1966–70), 1:xlii.

6. The Temple cleansing is the occasion or cause for the "conspiracy" to kill Jesus in Mark 11:18 and Luke 19:47.

7. But cf. Luke 7:36–50, where it occurs much earlier in Jesus's ministry, while he was still in the Galilee.

8. Since John 2:13 and 6:4 are explicitly set at the spring festival of Passover, the unnamed "festival" of 5:1 is most likely the winter festival of Hanukkah, at the latest. It creates symmetry in this triptych as it ends with another Hanukkah at 10:22. The final three months of Jesus's life are then spent in Judea and lead up to the crucifixion at the next Passover (18:28; 19:31). The "festival" of John 5:1 could also be one of the fall cycle (Rosh Hashanah, Yom Kippur, or Sukkoth), although it seems less likely that any one of these major festivals would go unnamed. The parallelism of 5:1 and 10:22 as bracketing devices thus favor it being Hanukkah. Hence, the second triptych covers at least one full year, and perhaps as much as a year and a quarter.

9. The feeding of the five thousand (John 6:1–14) is clearly the same story as that in the Synoptics as reflected in the peculiar refrain about "two hundred denarii" worth of bread; see esp. Mark 6:30–44; Luke 9:10–17. Yet there is no reference to Passover in any of the synoptic versions of this story. The Passover reference in John 6:4 looks strange and artificial, especially since Jesus does not go to Jerusalem on this occasion. The reason for the insertion is twofold: to create the three-year cycle and to link the feeding miracle and the following Bread of Life discourse with eucharistic symbols drawn from the synoptic version of the Last Supper. On the location, see Appendix E.

10. The second of these, however, has some similarities to the healing of the centurion's servant derived from Q (Luke 7:1–10; Matt 8:5–13) as well as the raising of Jairus's daughter (Mark 5:21–43).

11. As reflected in the *Gospel of Thomas,* but even more directly in the *Dialogue of the Savior* and the *Book of Thomas the Contender* along with other texts from Nag Hammadi. The *Gospel of Judas* also falls into this category. They will be discussed in the next chapter.

12. Koester, *Ancient Christian Gospels,* 215.

13. From Eusebius *Church History* 6.14.5–7 (my translation). The full passage from Clement is quoted and discussed in the Epilogue.

14. For a general history of the problem, see D. M. Smith, *John Among the Gospels: The Relationship in Twentieth-Century Research* (Minneapolis: Fortress, 1992), 1–42; Brown, *Gospel According to John,* 1:xlv–xlvii. Brown argues for independence: Smith concludes the opposite.

15. Cf. Mark 1:9–11; Matt 3:13–17; Luke 3:21–22. In the Markan version, it seems that only Jesus saw the Spirit/dove and heard the voice.

16. Cf. John 4:44–45, when Jesus returns to Cana. The editorial comment, "for Jesus himself had testified that a prophet has no honor in the prophet's own country" here seems out of place in light of the following verse in which the Galileans who had witnessed him in Jerusalem "welcomed him." The original synoptic version of this statement occurs in conjunction with Jesus's rejection at Nazareth (Mark 6:4); however, in John it seems to be a reference to his treatment in Judea.

17. Smith, *John Among the Gospels,* 188, 192.

18. Irenaeus *Against Heresies* 3.1.2; Eusebius *Ecclesiastical History* 3.39.6; 5.8.4. See also E. Pagels, *The Johannine Gospel in Gnostic Exegesis* (Missoula, MT: Scholars Press, 1972).

19. A fact already noted in Irenaeus *Against Heresies,* 3.2.12. Cf. Origen's *Commentary on John,* which was directed as a counter to an earlier commentary by a Gnostic interpreter named Heracleon (ca. 170 CE).

20. There is only one oblique reference to "the sons of Zebedee" in John 21:2. If one assumes a knowledge of the synoptic lists of the disciples or stories such as that in Mark 10:35–40, then this clearly points to John. Even so, John as a character is never mentioned by name.

21. The other references to the "beloved disciple" are 13:23; 19:26–27; 20:1–8; 21:7; 21:20–24. The last of these refers directly to the passage in 13:23 and will thus become important. We shall return to it below. In two other passages (18:15–16; 19:35) an unnamed disciple may well be the same as the "beloved disciple" based upon the testimonial formula in 21:24. Some scholars take a different view, and certainty is not possible. See n. 23, below.

22. This is a more literal translation of the Greek and means that he was lying with his back "up against the chest" of Jesus. The NRSV reads: "was lying close to the breast of Jesus"; however, the traditional mode of reclining at dinner makes clear the posture that is being described. Cf. the wording of John 21:20, in reference to the same scene: "who reclined *upon his [Jesus's]* chest at the supper" (my translation). See D. E. Smith, *From Symposium to Eucharist: The Banquet in the Early Christian World* (Minneapolis: Fortress, 2003), 14–18.

23. All the articles, pronouns, and adjectives used in John 21 to refer to this character are masculine singular in the Greek.

24. See John 18:15–17 (at the high priest's court); 19:26, 35 (at the cross); 20:3–9 (at the empty tomb); 21:24 (general).

25. See Brown, *Gospel According to John,* 1:xcii–cii

26. This tradition was also related to the date and authorship of Revelation. See L. M. White, *From Jesus to Christianity* (San Francisco: HarperSanFrancisco, 2004), 279–90, 399–400, 414–19.

27. This is the widely accepted view of R. E. Brown (*The Community of the Beloved Disciple* [New York: Paulist, 1979], 93–144; *Gospel According to John,* 1:xxxiv–xxxix). See also R. A. Culpepper, *The Johannine School* (Missoula, MT: Scholars Press, 1975).

28. See Koester, *Ancient Christian Gospels,* 246–53. This final episode also has similarities to the ending of the *Gospel of Peter,* discussed in Chapter 7 and Appendix C.

29. One of these other passages is John 6:51–59.

30. U. Schnelle, *Antidocetic Christology in the Gospel of John* (Minneapolis: Fortress, 1992), 150–63.

31. Mark 10:35–40 has been taken by some to indicate that both of the sons of Zebedee had died before or during the first revolt, as Acts 12:1–4 confirms for James. Some early martyrologies confirm this view for John too.

32. Some have argued that $\wp^{52}$ (John Rylands Papyrus 457) can be dated as early as 125 thus making a date for the Gospel as late as 120 seemingly impossible; however, the merits of this dating for $\wp^{52}$ are very questionable on papyrological grounds. See B. Nongbri, "The Use and Abuse of $\wp^{52}$: Papyrological Pitfalls in the Dating of the Fourth Gospel," *Harvard Theological Review* 98 (2005) 23–48.

33. Brown, *Gospel According to John,* ciiii. The situation of 2 and 3 John reflect this tradition. See White, *From Jesus to Christianity,* 411–414. For the later legends see Irenaeus *Against Heresies* 2.22.3; 3.1.2; 3.4; Justin Martyr *Dialogue with Trypho* 81.4; Clement of Alexandria *Who is the Rich Man?* 42; Eusebius *Church History* 3.18.1; 23.3–4; 39.3–4; 4.18.6–8; 5.8.4; 18.14; 20.6. An apocryphal *Acts of John* that circulated in Asia Minor in the latter half of the second century also placed John in Ephesus. See White, *From Jesus to Christianity,* 399.

34. This is the view of Koester (*Ancient Christian Gospels,* 245) and locates the composition of the Gospel of John in closer proximity to that of the *Gospel of Thomas.*

35. The discourse also presupposes a recognition of eucharistic ritual patterns in the feeding miracle, based on the use of key terms: "take," "give thanks," "give out" (6:11). It has also been suggested that the Markan version of the feeding of the five thousand already assumes the symbolism of the manna of Exod 16. If so, it further supports the view that the Gospel of John knew the earlier synoptic tradition and expanded upon some of its subtle themes, narrativizing them to make them more overt.

36. See J. L. Martyn, *History and Theology in the Fourth Gospel* (New York: Harper & Row, 1968), 10–41.

37. W. A. Meeks, "The Man from Heaven in Johannine Sectarianism," *Journal of Biblical Literature* 91 (1972): 44–72.

38. Other than in the Coptic text of *Gos. Thom.* 1, the full name Didymus Judas Thomas only occurs in a Syriac manuscript of the Gospel of John (at 14:22) and in the Greek version of the Syriac *Acts of Thomas* in the opening lines and in chap. 1. In the Greek papyrus fragment (*P.Oxy.* 1), his name is apparently given as "Judas who is also called Thomas," but there is a lacuna in the next line.

39. See Mark 6:3; Matt 13:55, both of which list Jesus's brothers as "James and Joses/Joseph and Simon and Judas." The Letter of Jude in the New Testament is also attributed to this brother.

40. Only in the Syrian Thomas literature, and especially in the *Acts of Thomas*, is the equation made more explicit that this Judas is the "twin brother" of Jesus himself. In the *Book of Thomas the Contender* (Nag Hammadi Codex II.7) Jesus refers to him as "my twin and true companion." For the later literature associated with the Thomas tradition, see White, *From Jesus to Christianity*, 389–93.

41. A total of sixty-eight sayings have some affinity for one of the canonical Gospels, including John. For a complete catalogue of these relationships, see Koester, *Ancient Christian Gospels*, 86–128.

42. Koester, *Ancient Christian Gospels*, 85.

43. Hippolytus *Against all Heresies* 5.7.20. That is, unless the "Doubting Thomas" scene in John is taken as an explicit reference. The frequent references to docetism occurring in the early to mid-second century CE (see n. 45, below) may well be based on a tradition very much like the *Gospel of Thomas*, but there are other candidates as well. Consequently, they cannot be used to provide a terminal date before which it must have been written.

44. See White, *From Jesus to Christianity*, 395–98.

45. R. Valantasis (*The Gospel of Thomas* [London: Routledge, 1997], 12–17) and B. Layton (*The Gnostic Scriptures* [Garden City, NY: Doubleday, 1987], 377–79) both argue for a date ca. 100–110 CE. S. Patterson (*The Gospel of Thomas and Jesus* [Sonoma, CA: Polebridge, 1993], 113–18) argues for a date in the mid-first century CE. H. Koester (*Introduction to the New Testament*, 2nd ed., 2 vols. [New York: De Gruyter, 2000], 1:157) accepts a first-century date for the earliest layers of the text only, but argues for later reworking in the form of the text now known. U-K. Plisch (*The Gospel of Thomas: Original Text with Commentary* [Stuttgart: Deutsche Bibelgesellschaft, 2008]) says it contains both presynoptic and postsynoptic elements and could date as late as the 130s in this form. The latest date suggested is ca. 180–200, in part limited by the fact that Hippolytus, writing in the early third century, knows the work (see n. 43, above). Using this date, N. Perrin (*Thomas and Tatian: The Relationship Between the Gospel of Thomas and the Diatessaron* [Atlanta: Society of Biblical Literature, 2002]) argues that the *Gospel of Thomas* was originally composed in Syriac and was based on the Syriac *Diatessaron* (a four-gospel harmony) of Tatian, which dates to ca. 180. This very late dating and its literary assumptions has not found other proponents. The *Diatessaron* might have been composed first in Greek and will be discussed further in the next chapter.

46. The last line of 77 ("Split wood and I am there. Lift up the stone and you will find me there.") is contained, with the two phrases reversed, in 30 in the Greek version of *P.Oxy.* 1. Unfortunately, not enough of the Greek version is preserved in the three separate fragments presently known in order to make a full assessment of this problem.

47. H. Koester, "Gospels and Gospel Traditions in the Second Century," in *From Jesus to the Gospels* (Minneapolis: Fortress, 2007), 26–27. Cf. Plisch, *The Gospel of Thomas*, 16.

48. As in Ignatius of Antioch *To the Smyrneans* 5.2 and *To the Trallians* 10.1; 1 John 4:1–2; 2 John 7, all dating from ca. 115 to the 130s. See White, *From Jesus to Christianity*, 314–18, 348–49. See also Schnelle, *Antidocetic Christology in the Gospel of John*, 60–70.

49. The figure of Matthew only shows up as a real actor in the Gospel of Matthew. See Chapter 12. One must conclude, therefore, that this *logion* in the *Gospel of Thomas* betrays some knowledge of the Gospel of Matthew or the kind of Christianity associated with it. In the second century and after, the Gospel of Matthew came to be associated especially with Jewish Christianity (with its "adoptionist" Christology), even though it was also used alongside the other Synoptics among other Christian groups. See White, *From Jesus to Christianity*, 404–6.

50. So Valantasis, *Gospel of Thomas*, 195.

51. *Acts of Thomas* 27 and 50, both hymns used in conjunction with liturgical rituals.

52. Q56; cf. Luke 14:26–27 (17:33); Matt 10:37–39.

53. Koester, *Ancient Christian Gospels*, 95.

54. So Koester, *Ancient Christian Gospels*, 111.

55. Koester, *Ancient Christian Gospels*, 107–12.

56. The quotation from Isa 61:2 as found in Luke 4:19 ends with the phrase, "to proclaim the year of the Lord's *favor*." The word "favor" is the same Greek word (*dektos*) as here rendered "accepted." In the Lukan story the point of the rejection would seem to be a wordplay: Jesus is not "accepted" in his hometown when he comes to proclaim the "accepted" year of the Lord, i.e., an eschatological symbol.

57. So Koester, *Ancient Christian Gospels*, 112.

58. The assumption of the story must be this: local coinage, much of which was in bronze, might not have any imperial images on it, whereas gold coinage was more likely to be from imperial mints and thus contain an image of the emperor.

59. The traditional view is stated by Brown (*Gospel According to John*, 1:lxx). The revisionist view is that of Koester (*Ancient Christian Gospels*, 113–24), but see also now Plisch (*Gospel of Thomas*, 16).

60. Koester, *Ancient Christian Gospels*, 118–19.

61. Koester, *Ancient Christian Gospels*, 123–24, 260–64.

62. There is a play on the term *logos* ("word") in John, since it can mean "reason," a "spoken word," "a word (in the grammatical sense)," a single "saying," a "story," or "a speech or discourse." It must be remembered too that Philo had used the same term as a synonym for Sophia, as the designation for the "heavenly man" created in the image of God. See Chapter 2.

63. *The Wizard of Oz*, directed by Victor Fleming (Warner Bros., 1939).

64. The question of the relationship between the Gospel and 1 John is discussed in White, *From Jesus to Christianity*, 314–17. The statement "whom we have *touched with our hands*" in 1 John 1:1 may be a reflection on the story in John 20:24–29. It may also be the "source" for the story; see the next note.

65. This is the view of Schnelle (*Antidocetic Christology in the Gospel of John*, 139–44), who also argues that the Gospel in its final form is subsequent to 1 John (53–63). On this view, the date of the Gospel of John would move later still, since 1 John already contained a denunciation of docetism (1 John 4:1–3).

66. Koester, *Ancient Christian Gospels*, 253–55.

67. Schnelle, *Antidocetic Christology in the Gospel of John*, 164–75.

68. In the synoptic Gospels, Jesus predicts his "suffering and death" on several occasions (Mark 8:31; Matt 16:21; Luke 9:22; Matt 17:12; Mark 9:12; Luke 17:25; Luke 22:15), and Luke-Acts stresses "his suffering" as the main reference to the crucifixion event in retrospect (Luke 24:26, 46; Acts 1:3; 3:18; 9:16; 17:3). In all these cases the Greek word used is a form of the verb *paschein,* meaning "to suffer." This word never occurs in the Gospel of John.

Chapter Fifteen: Gospels and More Gospels

1. The *Gospel of Mary* is quoted from K. L. King, *The Gospel of Mary of Magdala: Jesus and the First Woman Apostle* (Santa Rosa, CA: Polebridge, 2003), 14 (BG 8502.2/10.1–10). The *Gospel of Philip* is quoted from J. M. Robinson, ed., *The Nag Hammadi Library,* 3rd rev. ed. (San Francisco: HarperSanFrancisco, 1990), 148 (NHC II.3).

2. P.Egerton 2. For the text, see E. Hennecke and W. Schneemelcher, eds., *The New Testament Apocrypha,* 2 vols. (Philadelphia: Westminster, 1963–65), 1:94–96; for further discussion, see H. Koester, *Ancient Christian Gospels: Their History and Development* (Philadelphia: Trinity Press International, 1990), 205–16.

3. Sometimes called "The Cross Gospel"; see Chapter 7 and Appendix C.

4. For the problem of genre and definition, see Koester, *Ancient Christian Gospels,* 43–48, 173.

5. Koester, *Ancient Christian Gospels,* 205–15.

6. Cf. Acts 15 and Josephus *Antiquities* 20.200. For discussion, see L. M. White, *From Jesus to Christianity* (San Francisco: HarperSanFrancisco, 2004), 133, 229–31.

7. See Mark 3:21, 31–35. In Acts 1:14 the mother and brothers of Jesus appear to be among the disciples immediately after Jesus's ascension; however, James is not explicitly mentioned by name until later in Acts 12:17; 15:13; 21:18.

8. For text and introduction, see Hennecke and Schneemelcher, eds., *New Testament Apocrypha,* 1:158–65.

9. For the Ebionites and their literature, see White, *From Jesus to Christianity,* 404–6; the *Gospel of the Hebrews* is usually associated with this same group, although there is another text known as the *Gospel of the Ebionites* that has direct literary connections to other known works of the Ebionites, such as the *Kerygmata Petrou* ("Preachings of Peter") and the so-called *Pseudo-Clementine* literature. See also Box 15.1 for synopsis.

10. For text and discussions, see Robinson, ed., *The Nag Hammadi Library,* 29–37; Koester, *Ancient Christian Gospels,* 187–200; R. Cameron, *Sayings Traditions in the Apocryphon of James* (Philadelphia: Fortress, 1984).

11. Mark 15:39; Matt 27:54; Luke 23:47. For the later tradition, see the *Acts of Pilate* (Box 15.1). See also Chapter 11.

12. For the text and discussion of the *Gospel of Peter,* see Chapter 7 and Appendix C.

13. As is often the case in these later legends, we see glaring anachronisms. Tiberius (14–37 CE) was the emperor during Pilate's tenure as governor of Judea (26–36 CE). Claudius did not become emperor until 41 CE. See the *Letter of Pilate, Trial of Pilate,* and *Acts of Pilate* in Box 15.1. There are some similarities to the treatment of Pilate in the *Gospel of Peter.* See the previous note.

14. For text and discussion, see Hennecke and Schneemelcher, eds., *New Testament Apocrypha,* 1:370–388; Koester, *Ancient Christian Gospels,* 308–14; R. F. Hock, *The Infancy Gospels of James and Thomas* (Santa Rosa, CA: Polebridge, 1995), 2–81.

15. In Greek the two names are identical. Of course, Anna is also the name of the old prophetess who blesses Jesus in the Temple in Luke 2:38.

16. Both of them pray for a miracle, and Anna promises to give the child to the Lord, "whether male or female"; *Prot. Jas.* 1.1–4.1; cf. 1 Sam 1:22.

17. *Prot. Jas.* 5.2; cf. Luke 1:46; 1 Sam 2:1.

18. *Prot. Jas.* 10.1; cf. Mark 15:38; Matt 27:51.

19. *Prot. Jas.* 10.2; Luke 1:20–22.

20. *Prot. Jas.* 13–14; Matt 1:19–24.

21. The premise is entirely fictional; there is no historical evidence that such a procedure was used in cases of betrothed couples.

22. *Prot. Jas.* 15–16; cf. Num 5:11–31.

23. *Prot. Jas.* 19–20; cf. Luke 2:30–32; John 20:25. For a character named Salome who is with Mary Magdalene at the empty tomb, see Mark 15:40; 16:1. Salome also shows up in *Gos. Thom.* 61 and the *Gospel of the Egyptians,* in both cases as an interlocutor of Jesus.

24. *Prot. Jas.* 21.1–22.1; cf. Matt 2:8–12.

25. *Prot. Jas.* 24.4; cf. Luke 2:25–26.

26. Prior to the discovery of the Nag Hammadi codices, it was common to refer to this work as the *Gospel of Thomas.* We now use the fuller title to distinguish it from the sayings or Coptic *Gospel of Thomas* (discussed in Chapter 14), especially as our knowledge of the Thomas tradition has grown. For the text and discussion, see Hennecke and Schneemelcher, eds., *New Testament Apocrypha,* 1:388–400; Koester, *Ancient Christian Gospels,* 311–14; Hock, *Infancy Gospels of James and Thomas,* 84–146.

27. My translation.

28. Matt 26:57 names only Caiaphas. Josephus (*Antiquities* 18.35, 95) does not confirm this relationship explicitly, but describes the high-priesthood of Caiaphas as 25–35 CE.

29. For the discovery of the text, its reconstruction, and translation, see M. Smith, *Clement of Alexandria and a Secret Gospel of Mark* (Cambridge, MA: Harvard University Press, 1973); *The Secret Gospel: The Discovery and Interpretation of the Secret Gospel According to Mark* (New York: Harper & Row, 1973).

30. For Carpocrates, see Irenaeus *Against Heresies* 1.25; Clement of Alexandria *Stromateis* 3.2; Hippolytus *Refutation of All Heresies* 7.20.

31. Folio 1^R, line 16–Folio 1^V, line 3. The translation is that of Smith, *Clement of Alexandria and the Secret Gospel,* 446. These statements attributed to Clement need to be compared with those of Clement in Eusebius *Church History* 6.14.5–6 (quoted in the Epilogue).

32. For discussion of the Papias tradition and the evidence from Eusebius relative to the date and authorship of Mark, see Chapter 11. For Clement, see the Epilogue.

33. *The Secret Gospel of Mark,* Folio 1^V, line 21–Folio 2^R, line 14. The translation is that of Smith, *Clement of Alexandria and the Secret Gospel,* 447, with some alteration, indicated in brackets. I have added the verse references for the passages quoted from the Gospel of Mark.

34. Q. Quesnell, "The Mar Saba Clementine: A Question of Evidence," *Catholic Biblical Quarterly* 37 (1975): 48–67; M. Smith, "On the Authenticity of the Mar Saba Letter of Clement," *Catholic Biblical Quarterly* 38 (1976): 196–99; Q. Quesnell, "A Reply to Morton Smith," *Catholic Biblical Quarterly* 38 (1976): 200–203; S. C. Carlson, *The Gospel Hoax: Morton Smith's Invention of Secret Mark* (Waco: Baylor University Press. 2005); S. G. Brown, "Reply to Steven Carlson," *Expository Times* 117 (2006): 144–49; S. G. Brown, "Factualizing the Folklore: Stephen Carlson's Case Against Morton Smith," *Harvard Theological Review* 99 (2006); S. G. Brown, "The Question of Motive in the Case Against Morton Smith," *Journal of Biblical Literature* 125 (2006): 351–83.

35. A variant of this argument has been proposed by M. W. Meyer ("The Youth in the Secret Gospel of Mark," in R. Cameron, ed., *The Apocryphal Jesus and Christian Origins,* Semeia 49 [Atlanta: Scholars Press, 1990], 129–54). Meyer offers the possibility that *Secret Mark* might even be the pre-Markan version from which the Gospel of Mark and the Gospel of John were drawn. J. D. Crossan (*Four Other Gospels: Shadows on the Contours of Canon* [Minneapolis: Winston, 1985], 91–121) takes basically the same view.

36. The only significant change I would argue in assuming option 2 instead is that the date of the writing would be later and largely indeterminate. As a result, the document would become less and less valuable for our understanding of early apocryphal traditions, although it would be relevant for understanding the theological climate of whatever era produced it.

37. A possibility that has been suggested for the Gospel of John quite apart from anything to do with the *Secret Gospel of Mark.*

38. Justin Martyr *Apology* 1.67.

39. See Koester, *Ancient Christian Gospels,* 360–402.

40. W. L. Petersen, "Tatian's Diatessaron," in Koester, *Ancient Christian Gospels,* 403–30.

41. Petersen, "Tatian's Diatessaron," 428.

42. Peterson, "Tatian's Diatessaron," 428.

43. For an extended example in English (drawn from the Arabic version), see H. C. Kee, *Jesus in History: An Approach to the Study of the Gospels,* 3rd ed. (Fort Worth: Harcourt Brace, 1996), 266–75.

44. See Petersen, "Tatian's Diatessaron," 419–27.

45. The Greek text is taken from C. B. Welles, J. O. Fink, and F. Gilliam, *The Parchments and Papyri,* Final Report V.1: *The Excavations at Dura-Europos* (New Haven: Yale University Press, 1959), 73–74. The arrangement, translation, and reference notations provided here are my own.

46. The Arabic version lists four, excluding Joanna.

47. For text and discussion, see King, *The Gospel of Mary of Magdala;* Robinson, ed., *Nag Hammadi Library,* 523–27; Hennecke and Schneemelcher, eds., *New Testament Apocrypha,* 1:340–45.

48. The Coptic text is from the *Papyrus Berolinensis* (or Berlin Papyrus) 8502, better known as the Berlin Gnostic Codex, or BG 8502. The *Gospel of Mary* is the first text in the codex and is missing the first six pages and several others from the middle of the text. It was discovered in 1896 in Egypt and was not part of the Nag Hammadi horde discovered in 1945. On study, however, it became clear that this codex was similar to the manuscripts from Nag Hammadi in both form and content. Of the four texts contained in BG 8502, two are found among the Nag Hammadi codices. As a result, it is usually considered part of the Nag Hammadi "library" in the broader sense. They are the *Apocryphon of John* (BG 8502.2), which has three other copies at Nag Hammadi (NHC II.1, III.1, IV.1). The other is the *Sophia of Jesus Christ* (BG 8502.3), which is identical to the text *Eugnostos the Blessed* (NHC III.3, V.1). The last text in the codex (BG 8502.4) is the *Act of Peter.* For the discovery and publication history, see King, *Gospel of Mary of Magdala.*

49. Robinson, ed., *Nag Hammadi Library,* 523.

50. *Gos. Mary* 5.8 (BG 8502.2/9.14–20). The two references correspond to the numbering of the text in King's edition and the page and line numbers in the Berlin Papyrus, used also in the *Nag Hammadi Library* edition.

51. *Gos. Mary* 5.9–10 (BG 8502.2/9.23–24).

52. *Gos. Mary* 6.1–4 (BG 8502.2/10.1–10).

53. See Hennecke and Schneemelcher, eds., *New Testament Apocrypha,* 338–39.

54. *Gos. Mary* 7 (BG 8502.2/10.10–23).

55. *Gos. Mary* 9 (BG 8502.2/15.15–17.7).

56. *Gos. Mary* 10.1–4 (BG 8502.2/17.8–22).

57. *Gos. Mary* 10.10 (BG 8502.2/18.13–15).

58. *Gos. Mary* 10.11–14 (BG 8502.2/18.15–19.4).

59. Robinson, ed., *Nag Hammadi Library,* 523; King, *Gospel of Mary of Magdala,* 83–90.

60. The name Mary Magdalene indicates that she should come from the town of Magdala on the west side of the Sea of Galilee. The only description of Mary Magdalene that provides any background comes in Luke 8:2–3, where she is described as one of the women of means who provided for Jesus and the disciples; in particular, she was said to have been cured of "seven demons." The "anointing woman" of Mark 14:3–9; Matt 26:6–13; Luke 7:36–50 is not called a "sinner" except in Luke 7:39, and her name is never given. In Mark and Matthew she is in Bethany; in Luke she is in the Galilee. John 12:1–8 explicitly identifies the anointing woman as Mary of Bethany, the sister of Martha and Lazarus; no comment is made about her moral condition, nor is she called Magdalene. Finally, the "woman caught in adultery" (John 7:53–8:11) is not named. Moreover, this particular episode is not reflected in the earliest manuscripts of the Gospel of John. In later tradition, all these women would be amalgamated into the character of Mary Magdalene.

61. Irenaeus *Against Heresies* 1.28.9.

62. The program aired in April 2006. For the history of the text and its treatment by the *National Geographic* producers, see J. M. Robinson, *The Secrets of Judas: The Story of the Misunderstood Disciple and His Lost Gospel* (San Francisco: HarperSanFrancisco, 2006), 1–119.

63. See n. 48, above.

64. The manuscript contained two texts also known from the Nag Hammadi codices, the *Letter of Peter to Philip* (NHC VIII.2) and *Allogenes* (NHC XI.3).

65. The discussion follows the critique and reconstruction of A. D. DeConick, in *The Thirteenth Apostle: What the Gospel of Judas Really Says* (New York: Continuum, 2007).

66. Irenaeus *Against Heresies* 1.24.4

67. *Gos. Jud.* 39.6–44.14 (the text is numbered according to the page and line numbers of Codex Tchacos). Quotations are from the translation of DeConick, *The Thirteenth Apostle*, 66–91.

68. A portion of this section is missing.

69. Sometimes called the "fishhook" theory of the atonement, this early view had proponents in some orthodox circles, including St. Augustine and Gregory the Great.

70. "Quire" is an Elizabethan form of the word "choir"; both forms are pronounced the same. From the same root (French *cahier*, from Old French *quaer[n]* for Lat. *quaternum*), a "quire" is also the technical term for a portion of a bound codex book. It is formed by folding a stack of folio-sized sheets of paper in half to form a series of pages, which could then be written on front and back. Several quires might be sewn together to form a larger codex. With but a few exceptions, the earliest surviving Gospel manuscripts are from this type of bound codex. See H. Y. Gamble, *Books and Readers in the Early Church* (New Haven: Yale University Press, 1995).

Epilogue: Tales of Fancy, Acts of Faith

1. It may derive from a single Q saying, but it has been expanded in Matthew. The Q material is found in Matt 6:30; Luke 12:28 (from the "lilies of the field" saying). This saying contains the only occurrence of the peculiar term "little faith" (Gk. *oligopistos*) in Luke, but the Gospel of Matthew repeats it four other times, and the parallel passages in Mark and Luke show that it is clearly a Matthean addition in each instance; see Matt 8:26; 14:31; 16:8; 17:20. Consequently, it appears that the Matthean author has picked up a minor feature of one Q saying and used it as a thematic device by inserting it into several other episodes. On this tendency in Matthew, see Chapter 14.

2. R. E. Brown, *The Gospel According to John*, 2 vols., Anchor Bible 29 (Garden City, NY: Doubleday, 1966–70), 1:376.

3. Brown, *Gospel According to John*, 1:377.

4. See L. M. White, *From Jesus to Christianity* (San Francisco: HarperSanFrancisco, 2004), 312–14; Brown, *Gospel According to John*, 1:380.

5. See White, *From Jesus to Christianity*, 313–14. For an extended analysis of the dramatic representation of this story as a Johannine production, see J. L. Martyn, *History and Theology in the Fourth Gospel* (New York: Harper & Row, 1968), 3–41.

6. Brown, *Gospel According to John*, 1:lxxviii, 380–81.

7. See W. A. Meeks, "The Man from Heaven in Johannine Sectarianism," *Journal of Biblical Literature* 91 (1972): 44–72; White, *From Jesus to Christianity*, 312–14.

8. The discussion began in the middle of the second century, prompted in large measure by external criticisms of Christian belief and by growing awareness of "other" Gospels and competing theological claims. See G. Bowersock, *Fiction as History: Nero to Julian* (Berkeley: University of California Press, 1994), 2–5; R. M. Grant, *The Earliest Lives of Jesus* (New York: Harper, 1961), 14–22; J. H. Koester, "Gospels and Gospel Traditions in the Second Century," in *From Jesus to the Gospels* (Minneapolis: Fortress, 2007), 24–38.

9. T. Baarda, "*Diaphonia* and *Symphonia*: Factors in the Harmonization of the Gospels, Especially in the Diatessaron of Tatian," in W. L. Peterson, ed., *Gospel Traditions in the Second Century* (Notre Dame, IN: University of Notre Dame Press, 1989), 133–56.

10. From Eusebius *Church History* 6.14.5–7 (my translation).

11. As we noted in Chapter 9 with the use of *chreiai* in preserving and expanding the traditions attributed to Diogenes the Cynic.

12. So for the putative writings of Diogenes the Cynic, see Diogenes Laertius 6.80–81.

13. Actually, only thirty-eight of them are paired.

14. D. E. Aune, "Greco-Roman Biography," in D. E. Aune, ed., *Greco-Roman Literature and the New Testament* (Atlanta: Scholars Press, 1988), 107.

15. A work under the title "Lives of the Prophets" (*Vitae Prophetarum*) was produced in Greek in the first century CE. See Aune, "Greco-Roman Biography," 107, n. 1; J. H. Charlesworth, ed., *The Old Testament Pseudepigrapha*, 2 vols. (Garden City, NY: Doubleday, 1985), 2:379–99.

16. The Deuteronomistic History comprises Joshua–2 Kings in the Hebrew Bible and is closely associated with the composition of the book of Deuteronomy in the Torah. For the extent, themes, and dates of composition, see S. L. McKenzie, "Deuteronomistic History," in D. N. Freedman, ed., *Anchor Bible Dictionary*, 6 vols. (New York: Doubleday, 1992), 2:160–68.

17. D. E. Aune, *The New Testament in Its Literary Environment* (Philadelphia: Westminster, 1987), 37–38.

18. See T. L. Holm, "Daniel 1–6: A Biblical Story Collection," in J. Brant, C. W. Hedrick, and C. Shea, eds., *Ancient Fiction: The Matrix of Early Christian and Jewish Narrative*, Symposium 32 (Atlanta: Society of Biblical Literature, 2005), 149–66.

19. Aune, *New Testament in Its Literary Environment*, 37; L. M. Wills, *The Jewish Novel in the Ancient World* (Ithaca, NY: Cornell University Press, 1995). Wills also discusses Daniel and the Greek additions to Daniel (Susanna, Bel and the Dragon) among these Hellenistic Jewish novels.

20. R. S. Kraemer, *When Aseneth Met Joseph* (New York: Oxford University Press, 1998); Kraemer also addresses the question of whether this work is a Jewish or Christian composition.

21. On this process and the issue of dates, see the discussion in White, *From Jesus to Christianity*, 295–96, 441–56, with additional bibliography cited there.

22. These are the books now typically called the Apocrypha. They were removed from the Protestant canon only after the Reformation.

23. A. Momigliano, *The Development of Greek Biography*, rev. ed. (Cambridge, MA: Harvard University Press, 1993), 65–100.

24. Aune, "Greco-Roman Biography," 108.
25. Aune, "Greco-Roman Biography," 108.
26. Quintilian *Institutes* 3.7.15.
27. Quintilian *Institutes* 3.7.21.
28. Quintilian *Institutes* 3.7.16; 3.7.22.
29. Quintilian *Institutes* 3.7.21.
30. See J. Gager, *Moses in Greco-Roman Paganism* (Nashville: Abingdon, 1972), 80.
31. Aune, "Greco-Roman Biography, 109–10.
32. *The Clouds* was first performed at the Dionysia in 423 BCE, but did not win the prize. Aristophanes later revised part of the work, and the surviving manuscripts reflect some of this revised version.
33. Aristotle *Poetics* 1447b.5–10.
34. The preceding summary is based on C. W. Votaw, *The Gospels and Contemporary Biographies in the Greco-Roman World* (Philadelphia: Fortress, 1970), 30–62. He gives an extensive comparison of the methods and goals of both Plato and Xenophon, including various efforts by Socrates scholars to deal with the "problem." He then uses this comparison to discuss the Gospels as ancient "Lives" of the same sort.
35. A. Momigliano, "Ancient Biography and the Study of Religion," in *On Pagans, Jews, and Christians* (Middletown, CT: Wesleyan University Press, 1987), 167.
36. Aristotle describes the overly wicked characterization of Menelaus in Euripides' *Orestes*, thus making his character less plausible and "unreal" (*Poetics* 1454a.25–30).
37. Thucydides *History of the Peloponnesian War* 1.22.1, trans. C. F. Smith, Loeb Classical Library (Cambridge, MA: Harvard University Press, 1919).
38. Thucydides *History of the Peloponnesian War* 1.21.1.
39. Momigliano, "Ancient Biography," 169.
40. On Josephus, see pp. 415–16. Momigliano ("Ancient Biography," 169–73) also discusses the autobiographical accounts of Lucian and Apuleius as examples of this problem. More generally on the problems of dreams in historical prose, see Bowersock, *Fiction as History*, 77–98. See also J. B. Chance, "Divine Prognostications and the Movement of Story: An Intertextual Exploration of Xenophon's *Ephesian Tale* and the Acts of the Apostles," in R. F. Hock, J. B. Chance, and J. Perkins, eds., *Ancient Fiction and Early Christian Narrative* (Atlanta: Scholars Press, 1998), 219–34.
41. See T. P. Wiseman, "Lying Historians: Seven Types of Mendacity," in C. Gill and T. P. Wiseman, eds., *Lies and Fiction in the Ancient World* (Austin: University of Texas Press, 1993), 122–46.
42. See Seneca's *Natural Questions* 7.16 compared with his *Apocolocyntosis* (or "Gourdification") *of the Divine Claudius* (discussed in Chapter 4). Both are discussed in Wiseman, "Lying Historians," 122–23.
43. Herodian *History of the Roman Empire* 1.1.1–2 (my translation).
44. Momigliano, "Ancient Biography," 171.
45. Plutarch *Theseus* 1.1–3 (my translation).
46. The scholarly literature on this subject is now quite extensive, and I shall attempt to survey some of the key discussions in the following paragraphs.
47. Josephus *Jewish War* 2.632–37.
48. Josephus *Jewish War* 3.340–408; also discussed in White, *From Jesus to Christianity*, 227–31.
49. Josephus *Jewish War* 3.354.
50. This tale is also told of Rabbi Johanan ben Zakkai of his escape from the siege of Jerusalem, but there the general is erroneously named as Vespasian (instead of Titus). This version, which comes from rather late rabbinic and talmudic texts, is likely dependent on Josephus. See G. G. Porton, "Yohannan ben Zakkai," *Anchor Bible Dictionary*, 6.1025.
51. See also the preceding note; S. R. Johnson, "Third Maccabees: Historical Fictions and the Shaping of Jewish Identity in the Hellenistic Period," and C. Milikowsky, "Midrash as Fiction and Midrash as History: What Did the Rabbis Mean?" in Brant, Hedrick, and Shea, eds., *Ancient Fiction: The Matrix of Early Christian and Jewish Narrative*, 185–198, 117–128. On pronouncement stories (*chreiai*) as a biographical form in rabbinic tradition and the issue of fictional treatments there, see P. S. Alexander, "Midrash and the Gospels" and "Rabbinic Biography and the Biography of Jesus: A Survey of the Evidence," in C. M. Tuckett, ed., *Synoptic Studies: The Ampleforth Conferences* (Sheffield: JSOT Press, 1984), 1–18, 19–50.
52. Philo *Life of Moses* 2.1.1–3 (my translation).
53. According to Exod 28:1–3, it was Moses's brother, Aaron, who served as the high priest; Exod 6:25 (cf. 28:1, 40–43), all the priestly families descended from Aaron's line. Cf. Num 18:1–32.
54. Plato *Republic* 5.473D. The words in italics in the Philo quotation are identical to those in Plato, but in inverted order.
55. E. L. Bowie, "Lies, Fiction, and Slander in Early Greek Poetry," in Gill and Wiseman, eds., *Lies and Fiction in the Ancient World*, 10–14.
56. See G. Schmeling, "The Spectrum of Narrative: The Authority of the Author," in Hock, Chance, and Perkins, eds., *Ancient Fiction and Early Christian Narrative*, 25.
57. For a summary of problems in dating the Trojan War, if there was one, as based on the archaeology, see S. Hood, "The Bronze Age Context of Homer," in J. B. Carter and S. P. Morris, eds., *The Ages of Homer* (Austin: University of Texas Press, 1995), 25–32.
58. P. Veyne, *Did the Greeks Believe Their Myths? An Essay on Constitutive Imagination* (Chicago: University of Chicago Press, 1988). For the reception of Homer in the Second Sophistic period, see L. Y. Kim, *Homer Between History and Fiction in Imperial Greek Literature* (Cambridge: Cambridge University Press, forthcoming).
59. Plato *Republic* 377d4–6; cf. 414b8–c. These views of Plato are discussed by C. Gill, in "Plato on Falsehood—Not Fiction," in Gill and Wiseman, eds., *Lies and Fiction in the Ancient World*, 38–87.
60. See G. L. Most, "Cornutus and Stoic Allegoresis: A Preliminary Report," *Aufsteig und Niedergang der Römishen Welt* 2.36.3:2014–65. An English translation and commentary is now in preparation by D. Armstrong and L. M. White.
61. One good example is the interpretation of Moses's name from Musaios (the hymnodist of Orpheus) as the founder of Greek philosophy and as a misunderstanding of Hermes (as the *hermeneutic logos*). Attributed to

the Jewish apologist Artapanus, this story is recorded in Eusebius *Preparation of the Gospel* 9.27.1–4 and Josephus *Antiquities* 2.10.238–53. In general on this type of allegorization, see also Chapter 3; D. Dawson, *Allegorical Readers and Cultural Revision in Ancient Alexandria* (Berkeley: University of California Press, 1992).

62. For his career and relations with Rome and the emperors, see C. P. Jones, *The Roman World of Dio Chrysostom* (Cambridge, MA: Harvard University Press, 1978); specifically for the chronology of his works, see 133–40. On the *Trojan Oration* and Dio's treatment of Homer, see Kim, *Homer Between History and Fiction*.

63. Dio Chrysostom *Oration* 11.1–2, 4 (my translation).

64. Also discussed in Grant, *Earliest Lives of Jesus*, 44–45.

65. Cf. *Oration* 53 (*On Homer*) and *Oration* 57 (*On Homer's Portrayal of Nestor*).

66. Dio *Oration* 11.37–38. On the hero cults associated with the Trojan War continuing well into the Roman period, with further production of mythic texts, see Flavius Philostratus, *On Heroes*, ed. J. K. B. Maclean and E. B. Aitken (Atlanta: Society of Biblical Literature, 2001/2002).

67. Cf. (Ps.)Heraclitus, *Homeric Problems*, ed. D. S. Russell and D. Konstan (Atlanta: Society of Biblical Literature, 2005).

68. So Plutarch *On the Malice of Herodotus* and Favorinus *Corinthian Oration* (= Dio *Oration* 37.7).

69. D. Konstan, "The Invention of Fiction," in Hock, Chance, and Perkins, eds., *Ancient Fiction and Early Christian Narrative*, 4.

70. Quintilian *Institutes* 2.4.2, quoted in D. C. Feeney, "Towards an Account of the Ancient World's Concepts of Fictive Belief," in Gill and Wiseman, eds., *Lies and Fiction in the Ancient World*, 232. I have added the italics and expanded the editorial comments [in brackets] for the sake of clarity.

71. Thucydides *History of the Peloponnesian War* 1.22.1, quoted earlier in the Epilogue.

72. Gill, "Plato on Falsehood—Not Fiction," 63–71.

73. See J. R. Morgan, "Make-Believe and Make Believe: The Fictionality of the Greek Novels," in Gill and Wiseman, eds., *Lies and Fiction in the Ancient World*, 187–93. On 192 he quotes a passage from Augustine's *Soliloquies* (2.9.26) that articulates the distinction in these terms.

74. Morgan, "Make-Believe and Make Believe," 225–29. This is also the point of the catchy title of his article.

75. On the influence of the Second Sophistic, see B. P. Reardon, "The Second Sophistic and the Novel," in *Approaches to the Second Sophistic* (University Park, PA: Penn State University Press, 1974), 23–29.

76. T. Hägg, *The Novel in Antiquity* (Berkeley: University of California Press, 1983), 109–24.

77. For the text and introduction, see W. W. Reeder, *The Severed Hand and the Upright Corpse: The Declamations of Marcus Antonius Polemo* (Atlanta: Scholars Press, 1996).

78. Feeney, "Towards an Account of the Ancient World's Concepts of Fictive Belief," 233.

79. R. W. Cape, "Persuasive History: Roman Rhetoric and Historiography," in W. J. Dominik, ed., *Roman Eloquence: Rhetoric in Society and Literature* (London: Routledge, 1997), 212–28.

80. Schmeling, "The Spectrum of Narrative," 27.

81. S. Byrskog, *Story as History—History as Story: The Gospel Tradition in the Context of Ancient Oral History* (Leiden: Brill, 2002), 45.

82. For those who have argued thus, see Aune, *The New Testament in Its Literary Environment*, 44–45.

83. See Aune, *The New Testament in Its Literary Environment*, 23–37; for the history of this debate in Gospels scholarship see R. A. Burridge, *What Are the Gospels? A Comparison with Greco-Roman Biography*, 2nd ed. (Grand Rapids, MI: Eerdmans, 2004), 53–101.

84. Aune, *The New Testament in Its Literary Environment*, 47–57; for detailed formalistic comparisons, see Burridge, *What Are the Gospels?*

85. In this regard I am following the theoretical lines of narrative criticism currently at work in New Testament studies; however, I would still stress the historical setting of author and audience as a condition for understanding the text as text. J. D. Kingsbury describes it as a kind of ideal or "imaginary reader" for whom the text always comes across completely; see *Matthew as Story*, 2nd ed. (Philadelphia: Fortress, 1988), 38. According to M. A. Powell, following Kingsbury, "To read in this way it is necessary to know everything that the text assumes the reader knows and to 'forget' everything that the text does not assume the reader knows"; see *What Is Narrative Criticism?* (Minneapolis: Fortress, 1990), 20. See also N. R. Peterson, *Literary Criticism for New Testament Critics* (Philadelphia: Fortress, 1978). Of course, in our view the "implied reader" is really an "implied hearer." It is precisely at this point, then, that the historical situation and cultural background of author, audience, and story become most important.

86. Here I would also agree with Powell (*What is Narrative Criticism?* 20) and others that the "implied reader" is not likely a "first-time reader." In my view, rather, the audience (i.e., the hearers/readers) was an active participant in an ongoing communal dialogue through the medium of performative storytelling.

87. This view is growing in study of the Gospels and of Mark, in particular; see W. Shiner, *Proclaiming the Gospel: First Century Performance of Mark* (Harrisburg, PA: Trinity Press International, 2003). See also C. Bryan, *A Preface to Mark: Notes on the Gospel in Its Literary and Cultural Setting* (New York: Oxford University Press, 1993), 123–54; J. Dewey, "Oral Methods of Structuring Narrative in Mark," *Interpretation* 43 (1989): 32–44. Both Bryan and Dewey are reacting to older theories of orality that stressed primarily oral sources rather than an oral product, so W. Kelber, *The Oral and Written Gospel: The Hermeneutics of Speaking and Writing in the Synoptic Tradition, Mark, Paul, and Q* (Philadelphia: Fortress, 1983), 44–80.

Appendix A: The Geography of Jesus's World

1. For a fuller discussion of the historical background, see L. M. White, *From Jesus to Christianity* (San Francisco: HarperSanFrancisco, 2004), 22–39, 102–4.

2. Tiberius was co-regent with the emperor Augustus, his adopted father, from 11 (or 12) to 14 CE and then emperor from 14 to 37. Pontius Pilate served as governor of the province of Judea from 26 to 36 CE. Hence, a date between 26 and 28/9 is indicated, during which time the death of Jesus occurred. For discussion of the problems

and possibilities, see J. Fitzmyer, *Gospel According to Luke*, 2 vols., Anchor Bible 28 (Garden City, NY: Doubleday, 1981–85), 1:455–56.

3. Also mentioned in Matt 2:22; Luke 3:1.

4. This is the situation reflected in the trials of Jesus according to Luke 23:1–12. See the discussion in Chapter 7.

Appendix B: Solving the Synoptic Problem

1. See M-É. Boismard, "Two-Source Hypothesis," in D. N. Freedman, ed., *Anchor Bible Dictionary*, 6 vols. (New York: Doubleday, 1992), 6:679–82; C. M. Tuckett, "Synoptic Problem," *Anchor Bible Dictionary*, 6:263–70; B. Reicke and D. B. Peabody, "Synoptic Problem," in J. H. Hayes, ed., *Dictionary of Biblical Interpretation* (Nashville: Abingdon, 1999), 2:517–24. See also C. M. Tuckett, ed., *Synoptic Studies: The Ampleforth Conferences* (Sheffield: JSOT Press, 1984).

2. For a substantive treatment of recent views, see H. Koester, *Ancient Christian Gospels* (Philadelphia: Trinity Press International, 1990), 128–73. Among newer theories, see D. E. Burkett, *Rethinking the Gospel Sources: From Proto-Mark to Mark* (Edinburgh: Clark International, 2004). Burkett argues that there were earlier forms of Mark (called "Proto-Mark" A and B) that were used as the source for what we now call the Gospel of Mark; Matthew (A) and Luke (B) each used one of these earlier forms, along with Q, as its principal source. Several other variations of this type of thesis have also been proposed, including one that argues that the Gospels of Matthew and Luke used a *later* form of Mark (a postcanonical or "deutero-Mark") plus Q.

3. For other older as well as newer theories, see Reicke and Peabody, "Synoptic Problem."

4. It is not clear that Griesbach actually invented this hypothesis independently, and it is sometimes called the "Owen-Griesbach Hypothesis." See Reicke and Peabody, "Synoptic Problem," 518. On Griesbach himself, see C. Berger, "Griesbach, Johann Jakob (1745–1812)," in Hayes, ed., *Dictionary of Biblical Interpretation*, 1:468–69.

5. See D. L. Dungan, "Two-Gospel Hypothesis," *Anchor Bible Dictionary*, 2:671–679.

6. For proponents, see W. R. Farmer, *The Synoptic Problem: A Critical Analysis,* 2nd ed. (Dillsboro, Western North Carolina Press, 1977); T. R. W. Longstaff, *Evidence of Conflation in Mark? A Study of the Synoptic Problem* (Missoula, MT: Scholars Press, 1977); A. J. McNicol, D. L. Dungan, and D. B. Peabody, *Beyond the Q Impasse: Luke's Use of Matthew* (Valley Forge, PA: Trinity Press International, 1996). For a review, see C. M. Tuckett, *The Revival of the Griesbach Hypothesis: An Analysis and Appraisal* (Cambridge: Cambridge University Press, 1983).

7. For proponents, see E. P. Sanders and M. Davies, *Studying the Synoptic Gospels* (London: SCM, 1989); M. Goodacre, *The Synoptic Problem: A Way Through the Maze* (New York: Sheffield Academic Press, 2001); *The Case Against Q: Studies in Markan Priority and the Synoptic Problem* (Harrisburg, PA: Trinity Press international, 2002); M. Goodacre and N. Perrin, *Questioning Q: A Multidimensional Critique* (Downers Grove, IL: InterVarsity, 2004).

8. See the discussion of this parable in Chapter 12 and Box 12.3.

Appendix C: The Gospel of Peter

1. For the history of the discovery and publication of the manuscript, see H. Koester, *Ancient Christian Gospels: Their History and Development* (Philadelphia: Trinity Press International, 1980), 216–18; R. E. Brown, *Death of the Messiah*, 2 vols. (Garden City, NY: Doubleday, 1994), 2:1317–21 (including a translation of the text). A translation (with introduction) is also available in E. Hennecke and W. Schneemelcher, eds., *New Testament Apocrypha*, 2 vols. (Philadelphia: Westminster, 1963–65), 1:179–87; D. R. Cartlidge and D. L. Dungan, eds., *Documents for the Study of the Gospels*, 2nd ed. (Minneapolis: Fortress, 1994), 76–79; R. Cameron, *The Other Gospels* (Philadelphia: Westminster, 1982), 76–82.

2. Other fragments thought to belong to the *Gospel of Peter* have been discovered (P.Oxy. 1224, 4009), but have not been matched with any portion of the Akhmim manuscript.

3. Eusebius *Church History* 5.22.1 (for the dates of Serapion); 6.12.2–6 (for his comments on the *Gospel of Peter*).

4. Koester, *Ancient Christian Gospels*, 217; Brown, *Death of the Messiah*, 2:1306.

5. The first extant passage refers to the fact that neither Herod nor the other Jews "washed their hands," presumably refusing to emulate Pilate's action; Pilate then rises (as though to leave; *Gos. Pet.* 1.1).

6. This is probably an allusion to the postresurrection appearance in John 21:3–8. The reference to "the sea" would seem to necessitate a Galilean setting (as in John 21 as well as Matt 28; cf. Mark 16:7) for this final portion of *Gospel of Peter;* however, no change of location is indicated in the surviving portion of the narrative. *Gos. Pet.* 7.26 says only that Peter and the disciples were "hiding."

7. It lists Levi son of Alphaeus, a tax collector; cf. Mark 2:13–14; 3:13–19; Matt 9:9–13; 10:2–4.

8. *Gos. Pet.* 1.2. This presumably means Herod Antipas, son of Herod the Great, and tetrarch of the Galilee 4 BCE–37 CE, who shows up in connection with the trials and death of Jesus only in the Gospel of Luke, as discussed above. On the other hand, the text is sufficiently vague, and the characterization of Herod is particularly negative, so that it almost appears to be an anachronistic use of the Matthean characterization of Herod the Great.

9. This is the view of J. D. Crossan, *The Cross That Spoke: The Origins of the Passion Narrative* (San Francisco: Harper & Row, 1988), 352–55; see also Koester, *Ancient Christian Gospels*, 234–37 (Koester's view of the text as a whole is somewhat less extreme than Crossan's).

10. Brown, *Death of the Messiah*, 2:1305–10.

11. The translation is that of C. Maurer in Hennecke and Schneemelcher, eds., *New Testament Apocrypha*, 1:185–86, adapted by the author in comparison with the Greek and the translation in Brown, *Death of the Messiah*, 1320.

12. As noted in the footnotes to the NRSV and other translations. Cf. Brown (*Death of the Messiah*, 2.1295–96), who discusses the merits of both ways of understanding the statement. Brown favors reading it as Roman

soldiers, in part on the basis of the interpretation of the *Gospel of Peter.* The other major argument in favor is that the guards are concerned that the "theft" story will come back to Pilate (Matt 28:14). The major argument in favor of it being a Jewish guard is that, after the resurrection, they report first to the chief priests (Matt 28:11).

13. By clarifying that there were also some of the Jewish "elders" at the tomb helping guard it overnight, the *Gospel of Peter* solves both issues in the Matthean passage. Yet this very fact lends additional weight to the argument that it is an expansion on Matthew rather than the source for Matthew. As Brown (*Death of the Messiah,* 2:1395, n. 23) also notes, there are other such efforts to explain the passage in Matthew in later manuscripts of the Gospels.

14. Cf. *Gos. Pet.* 3.7 (the "judgment seat") and John 19:13; *Gos. Pet.* 3.9 (striking Jesus) and John 18:22; 19:3; *Gos. Pet.* 12.50 ("for fear of the Jews") and John 20:19; although some of this has been argued as a pre-Johannine version. So Koester, *Ancient Christian Gospels,* 225–26.

15. This is the view first suggested by H. Koester ("Apocryphal and Canonical Gospels," *Harvard Theological Review* 73 (1980): 105–130, reprinted in *From Jesus to the Gospels: Interpreting the New Testament in Its Context* [Minneapolis: Fortress, 2007], 1–23, esp. 20–23). The idea was carried farther by J. D. Crossan in *Four Other Gospels: Shadows on the Contours of Canon* ([Minneapolis: Winston, 1985], 125–82) and in *The Cross that Spoke.* The fullest treatment of the argument in favor, but with criticisms of Crossan, is that of Koester who concludes that "the *Gospel of Peter,* as a whole, is not dependent upon any of the canonical gospels" (*Ancient Christian Gospels,* 240), but contains elements of a pre-Markan Passion source (237–38).

16. This is the position taken by Brown (*Death of the Messiah,* 2:1325–49, esp. 1332) following his more detailed critique of Crossan in "The *Gospel of Peter* and Canonical Gospel Priority," *New Testament Studies* 33 (1987): 321–43.

17. It must also be remembered that "two men" are also present at the ascension scene in Acts 1:9–11. We shall return to this point below.

18. Notice that in Matt 28:11–15 they report to the chief priests instead.

19. The comment of Serapion alleged that the *Gospel of Peter,* though "apostolic" in origin, had been corrupted by "docetic" teachings, meaning that it held a view of Christ in which he was never a flesh-and-blood human. The docetic elements noted in the letter of Serapion are not much in evidence in the preserved portion of the text, but may be reflected in the fact that Jesus is said to "feel no pain" while hanging on the cross (4.10) and that at the moment of his death he was "taken up," rather than just "he died" (5.19).

20. This is one of the important observations of Koester's work. See also his "Written Gospels or Oral Traditions?" *Journal of Biblical Literature* 113 (1994): 293–97; "The Text of the Synoptic Gospels in the Second Century," in W. L. Petersen, ed., *Gospel Traditions in the Second Century: Recensions, Text, and Transmission* (Notre Dame, IN: University of Notre Dame Press, 1989), 19–37.

21. Brown, *Death of the Messiah,* 2:1332.

22. The reference to an appearance to Peter in Luke 24:34 undoubtedly comes from the reference in 1 Cor 15:5.

23. I say "apparently" because we obviously do not possess the entire text. The preserved text opens during the last stage of the trial scenes and thus after Jesus's arrest. On the other hand, that Judas was not singled out is a discrete possibility, because the final appearance scene refers to the "twelve" still as a group (*Gos. Pet.* 14.59).

24. *Apoc. Pet.* 16b–17. The opening is likewise set "on a mountain," but is clearly meant to resemble the setting on the Mount of Olives of the apocalyptic discourse in Mark 13:1; Matt 24:1 as well as that of the ascension scene in Acts 1:9–11.

25. This text also dates to the middle part of the second century CE, probably after 135. It was often considered canonical in the early centuries. For date, setting, and content see L. M. White, *From Jesus to Christianity* (San Francisco: HarperSanFrancisco, 2004), 411–13. For the text and fuller introduction. see Hennecke and Schneemelcher, eds., *New Testament Apocrypha,* 2:663–83.

Appendix D: A "Transcript" of Q

1. The following reconstruction of the text of Q generally follows the Greek text of H. T. Fleddermann (*Q: A Reconstruction and Commentary* [Leuven: Peeters, 2005], 874–913) with some modifications by the author. It follows the numerical and thematic order of J. Kloppenborg (*Q Parallels* [Sonoma, CA: Polebridge, 1988] xxxi–xxxiii), as reflected in Box 12.1. The organization and translation provided here is that of the author. In keeping with current scholarly convention, the verse references in the transcription are based on the enumeration of the passages in the Lukan version.

2. The opening passages (Q1–2), which likely introduced the preaching of John the Baptist, are presumably lost. So Kloppenborg, *Q Parallels,* xxxi; however, Fleddermann (*Q: A Reconstruction and Commentary,* 210–11) argues that there is no such introductory summary.

3. The opening of this section (Q5), which describes the first appearance of Jesus, is apparently lost. A baptism at the hands of John seems unlikely, because Q16 (Luke 7:18–19) only later has John *hear* about Jesus's works. Thus the opening probably assumes some sort of prophetic calling or pronouncement, perhaps modeled on Isa 42:6–7 or 61:1 (as in Q16 = Luke 7:22–23; cf. Luke 4:18), followed immediately by a scene of testing the messiah. Cf. Mark 1:9–13. On the other hand, some scholars argue that the "Temptations" unit (Q6) does not belong to Q at all. See Kloppenborg, *Q Parallels,* 20.

4. The wording of these quotations derives from the LXX and further indicates a Greek-speaking context for the transmission of Q.

5. The Matthean order of the temptations, reflected here, is most likely the original; the Lukan rearrangement reflects its Jerusalem motif. See the discussion of Luke-Acts in Chapter 13.

6. This formulation ("kingdoms of the cosmos and their glory") is the Matthean wording. It may well refer to the planetary spheres rather than earthly kingdoms, as in Luke, which inserts the same distinctive word (*oikoumene*) found in Luke 2:1 in reference to the Augustan empire.

7. An opening setting is lost and remains uncertain. Matt 5:1–2 locates it on a mountain, whereas Luke 6:17 locates it on a seaside plain, after he had come down from a mountain (6:12). Both texts mention his disciples.

Consequently, some narrative frame concerning the disciples may be supposed. Both the Matthean and Lukan authors have reformulated the setting to address the crowds of people. See Kloppenborg, *Q Parallels*, 22.

8. This saying would appear to be a combination of two otherwise independent but similar units. The first should read something like this: "Blessed are you when they rebuke and persecute you; for so also they did to (or persecuted) the prophets." The second one should read: "Rejoice and be glad, when they [reject you/cast you out and] speak evil against you on account of me; for great is your reward in heaven." The two sayings have been woven together in an earlier stage of shaping the Q tradition.

9. An allusion to Isa 42:6–7; 61:1–2; it probably serves as a reprise of the "prophetic calling" scene that opens Q5. See n. 3, above

10. The opening temporal construction may or may not be a reference to John; it could refer to the "days of the prophets." Many scholars treat the final saying as a secondary insertion even though some common wording appears in Matthew and Luke; however, the Lukan version is at 16:16 (= Q61); therefore, it perhaps does not belong here. On the other hand, if the Lukan version is considered a secondary relocation and reformulation, then the wording should probably be something more like: "For all the prophets prophesied about John," as an adumbration of the sentiment in Q17.27. In that case, we might also prefer to move the saying after v. 27 and before v. 28. Luke 7:29–30, which some have labeled Q19, has so few commonalities with its putative parallel (Matt 21:31–32) as to make its authenticity questionable. See Kloppenborg, *Q Parallels*, 56–58.

11. Q31, which lacks a Matthean parallel, is doubtful even though there is a parallel in *Gos. Thom.* 79. See Kloppenborg, *Q Parallels*, 96; cf. Fleddermann, *Q: A Reconstruction and Commentary*, 192, 889.

12. The Matthean order (12:41–42) reverses the order of the final verses in the Lukan version (11:31–32), given here. Some scholars favor the Matthean order. See Kloppenborg, *Q Parallels*, 100.

13. Q34b is found in this position in Matthew, but as Q52 in Luke, as below. Though clearly part of the Q tradition, scholars are divided over which is the original placement. See Kloppenborg, *Q Parallels*, 158.

14. Q40, which lacks a Matthean parallel, is doubtful, even though there are parallels in *Gos. Thom.* 72, 63, respectively. See Kloppenborg, *Q Parallels*, 128.

15. See n. 13, above, at Q34b.

16. Q59, the parable of the lost coin, is doubtful due to the fact that there is no parallel in Matthew (or *Gos. Thom.*), although some scholars argue for its inclusion based on the strong verbal similarities to Q58 in Luke 15:3–7.

17. See Q18 and n. 8, above.

18. Q65, which has no Matthean parallel, is debated, even though it has a parallel in *Gos. Thom.* 3. See Kloppenborg, *Q Parallels*, 188.

19. Verses 28–29 are debated because there is no Matthean parallel; however, thematic use of the Sodom story suggests that these verses may belong to the original. See Kloppenborg, *Q Parallels*, 192–94; see also discussion in Chapter 12.

20. I add this passage on the assumption that the Lukan parable of the prodigal son is an extensive reworking of an older parable about two sons in something like this form. Following convention, I give here the initial numbering from the placement of the Lukan parable (15:11–32), but the verse numbers used in the text are from the Matthean parallel (21:28–32), which seems to provide the more original form of the parable from the Q tradition. The final portion of the passage (vv. 31b–32) is perhaps a Matthean elaboration; however, the repetition of the word "change one's mind" (vv. 29, 32) suggests that it might be original. The end of the passage is also reminiscent of the comments about John and himself in Q20. The placement of this unit in the usual sequence of Q is difficult to guess. The Matthean placement would put it near the end, as suggested here. The Lukan placement is clearly secondary, but could possibly go in the section on judgment (Q43–48).

Appendix E: Mapping the Narrative World of Luke

1. On the site, see R. Arav, "Bethsaida," in E. Meyers, ed., *Oxford Encyclopedia of Archaeology of the Ancient Near East* (New York: Oxford University Press, 1997), 1:302–5; B. Pixner, "Searching for the New Testament Site of Bethsaida," *Biblical Archaeologist* 48 (1985): 207–16.

2. The renaming of the city as Julias probably occurred after Jesus's death.

3. Josephus *Jewish War* 2.168; 3.35–40, 57; *Antiquities* 18.28.

4. These two cities were formerly "free cities" of the Decapolis, but they had been granted to Herod by Augustus in 20 BCE. They remained in Philip's tetrarchy of Gaulanitis and from there succeeded to Agrippa II. They were finally rejoined to the Decapolis on Agrippa's death in 93 CE and were annexed to Syria.

5. Josephus *Life* 71–73.

6. In general on the Lukan treatment of the Galilean region, see S. Freyne, *Galilee, Jesus, and the Gospels: Literary Approaches and Historical Investigations* (Philadelphia: Fortress, 1988), 90–115. As Freyne notes (90) there is some confusion in Luke whether Jesus is operating in Galilee or in Judea in the early phase of his career (which we have called the "Galilee section" in Chapter 13); however, it must be remembered that by the time Luke-Acts was written, the Galilee had been attached to the province of Judea and so was part of Judea.

7. Contrary to older assumptions, there were not two cities named Bethsaida in the region, one in Philip's tetrarch and the other in the Galilee. The confusion comes from the shift of political boundaries after the death of Herod Agrippa II, and specifically the conflicting references to Bethsaida as part of the Galilee or Gaulanitis.

8. See B. Pixner, "The Miracle Church at Tabgah on the Sea of Galilee," *Biblical Archaeologist* 48 (1985): 196–206.

ANCIENT WRITINGS INDEX

Other Ancient Writings

SUBJECT INDEX